ASSOCIATION FOOTBALL IN VICTORIAN ENGLAND

A History of the Game from 1863 to 1900

Philip Gibbons

UPFRONT PUBLISHING
LEICESTERSHIRE

ASSOCIATION FOOTBALL IN VICTORIAN ENGLAND:
A History of the Game from 1863 to 1900
Copyright © Philip Gibbons 2001

ISBN 1 84426 035 6

First Published 2001 by
MINERVA PRESS

Second Edition 2002 by
UPFRONT PUBLISHING
Leicestershire

ASSOCIATION FOOTBALL IN VICTORIAN ENGLAND

A History of the Game from 1863 to 1900

Pictured on the front cover – top left clockwise:

W N Cobbold, Tinsley Lindley, Steve Bloomer, Charlie Athersmith, Fred Spiksley, James Crabtree, William McGregor, Charles Alcock, Arthur Kinnaird, Howard Spencer and Frank Forman.

Pictured on the back cover:

Cigarette cards of the FA Cup-winning teams of Aston Villa, Sheffield United and Bury.

A £10 reward offered for the return of the FA Cup stolen from the shop window of W Shillcock of Newtown, Birmingham, following Aston Villa's FA Cup Final victory of 1895.

The Royal Engineers FA Cup-winning team of 1875.

Acknowledgements

The author would like to thank the Royal Engineers Library, W Winter of Derby, Eric Doig and especially Tony Mathews for their kind permission to reproduce the photographs in this book. Every effort has been made to contact the source or copyright holder of each photograph.

There remain few people in England who witnessed a professional football game during the nineteenth century, so little first-hand knowledge is available about the level of skill or attitudes towards the Association game during the Victorian period, except for the myths grown out of distant memories. However, we can be certain that the life of a professional footballer was hard and short-lived, with few opportunities of earning more than a living wage, while the gentlemen players of the south, on the other hand, tended to play the game as a form of exercise, as their careers were pursued outside the Association game.

Contents

Chapter I

THE FOOTBALL ASSOCIATION IS FORMED – 1863 TO 1871

THE FREEMASONS' TAVERN
CHARLES ALCOCK AND ARTHUR KINNAIRD EXCHANGE IDEAS
THE 'CAMBRIDGE RULES' ARE DEVISED
A CHALLENGE CUP IS SUGGESTED
ENGLAND MEET SCOTLAND AT THE KENNINGTON OVAL

From the Public Schools to Beyond

The game of football has been popular in England for many years. Initially, it was played under rules varying from those of the modern game, which emerged on 26 October 1863 when representatives of eleven London-based clubs held a meeting at the Freemasons' Tavern in Holborn to discuss the possibility of forming the English Football Association.

Prior to 1863, organised football tended to be played in public schools, where vigorous games were part of daily life in the belief that a healthy body would breed a healthy mind. However, each school usually played to its own rules, which included handling the ball. Charterhouse School allowed players to use only their feet and had as many as twenty a side participating. Rugby School allowed handling, as long as players remained stationary, while Eton had their Wall Game, which was a mixture of running, kicking and handling, with dribbling seen as an individual skill. The varying rules of the game meant that the public schools were unable to compete against each other. This need for a set of rules and regulations for the majority to abide by led a group of students from Cambridge University to convene a meeting to discuss the introduction of a set of rules that would be acceptable to the majority of schools and universities. A decision was made by the students that, under the 'Cambridge Rules', a player could stop the ball with his hands. However, it would not be permissible for that player to run while holding the ball. While teams tended to play their games only loosely to the Cambridge Rules, the new rule structure, at least, saw the game emerge outside the public school system.

As the public schoolboys took their places in society in the context of the spreading Industrial Revolution, a new breed of gentlemen was born who now had the time to pursue the sporting interests they had enjoyed at school, especially Association Football, which was now acceptable within the middle and upper classes of Victorian society. It was during this period of the late

1850s and early 1860s that the Old Etonians, Old Carthusians and other Old Boys' teams were formed, and a team as far north as the Sheffield Club was playing to rules similar to those of Cambridge University as early as 1855.

The Brothers Alcock

During the mid-1850s, J F and C W Alcock, who had recently left Harrow School, decided to form a football team of Old Harrovians called the Forest Club. They played their games on a pitch on the edge of Epping Forest near Snaresbrook under the Cambridge Rules. However, owing to a shortage of players, the team was disbanded, only to be reformed in 1864 as the Wanderers.

Charles Alcock would eventually be acknowledged as one of the founding fathers of the Association game. He created the FA competition and prompted the first international game between England and Scotland. While serving the English Football Association as secretary for a quarter of a century, Alcock became chairman of Surrey Cricket Club and organised the first test match in England against Australia.

An Important Meeting in Holborn

While the Cambridge Rules were generally accepted by the majority, many teams changed the rules to suit the wishes of visiting teams rather than lose the fixture, which led many to believe that the time was right to form a Football Association with one set of rules applying to all. A meeting was held at the Freemasons' Tavern, Great Queen's Street, Holborn, with the intention of forming the English Football Association. The following gentlemen were present: J F Alcock and A W Mackenzie of the Forest Club, Arthur Pember (N N Kilburn), E C Morley and P D Gregory of the Barnes Club, E Wawn (War Office), H T Steward (Crusaders), G W Shillingford (Perceval House, Blackheath), F Day (Crystal Palace), F W Moore and F Campbell (Blackheath), W J Mackintosh (Kensington School), H Bell (Surbiton) and W Gordon (Blackheath School). Mr B F Hartshorne of Charterhouse School, attended the meeting as an observer rather than a possible representative of the Association. However, there were no representatives from Cambridge University, which had instigated the first set of rules.

By late 1863, the new rules were generally agreed upon, but not without arguments from various teams that eventually led to the formation of the Rugby Union in 1871. It would be nearly twenty years before the whole of England played to one accepted set of rules. The early years of the Football Association were generally difficult, as games continued to be played on a friendly basis with varying rules.

In 1866, a game was arranged between London and Sheffield, and the London team, captained by Charles Alcock, won with ease. However, the

Sheffield team were a little annoyed that, upon contacting the Football Association three years earlier, they had received little encouragement and were seriously considering establishing their own Football Association. Eventually, this led to Mr C W Bough of the Sheffield Club accepting a position on the Football Association Committee to oversee the needs of clubs in the north of England rather than those in the capital city.

With the game now establishing such a stronghold in the Sheffield area, it swiftly spread to Nottingham. There remained great rivalry on the cricket field, which led to Nottingham versus Sheffield Association games, thus encouraging more teams from surrounding areas to travel farther afield to fulfil fixtures.

Meanwhile, rules were changing on a regular basis. Handling was completely abolished, while a tape was placed across the goalposts as in the Cambridge Rules. Goal kicks came into force in 1869, corner kicks in 1872, umpires in 1874, cross bars in 1882, while eleven-a-side games were instigated in 1870, as was the addition of a goalkeeper. Prior to the addition of the goalkeeper, the player nearest to the goal was responsible for punching the ball out of harm's way.

Charles Alcock Sets the Ball Rolling

Upon becoming secretary of the Football Association in 1870, Charles Alcock felt that the progress of the Association game had been a little slow, owing to the lack of competitive matches. Teams continued to play friendly games with very little at stake, which resulted in Alcock contacting the *Sportsman* newspaper to announce that there would be a game between England and Scotland, to take place at the Kennington Oval on 5 March 1870.

The Scottish team were all London-based and the game ended in a one-all draw. However, Alcock was greatly encouraged by the interest shown in the game, which led him to write to the *Glasgow Herald* inviting nominations for a Scottish team to play a return game on 19 November, again at the Oval.

Robert Smith, a Queens Park player who was based in the capital city, was nominated to organise the proceedings on behalf of the Scots, who once again fielded a London-based team, with the following players selected:

J Kirkpatrick (Civil Service), A F Kinnaird (Old Etonians), G E Crawford (Harrow School), H W Primrose (Civil Service), C E Nepean (University College, Oxford), Quinton Hogg (Wanderers), G F Congreve (Old Rugbeians), Robert Smith (Queens Park), G G Kennedy (Wanderers), J F Inglis (Charterhouse), A K Smith (Oxford University), W H Gladstone (Old Etonians).

England won by one goal to nil against a Scottish team that tended to have Scottish connections rather than birthright. However, many of the 'Scotsmen' would find fame in other fields. William Gladstone, for instance, the son of the

British Prime Minister, became a member of parliament for both Chester and Whitby. Quinton Hogg would be partially responsible for the growth of the Polytechnic movement in England and became the grandfather of a future Lord Chancellor. Arnold Kirke-Smith would spend many years of his life as the vicar of Boxforth, following his ordainment in 1875. However, Kirke-Smith was to enjoy a couple of successful years on the playing fields of England, which would see him captain Oxford University in the 1873 FA Cup Final, as well as captaining the English national side on two occasions against the Scots, thus earning the distinction of representing both England and Scotland at the Association game. The Right Honourable Arthur Fitzgerald Kinnaird (later Lord Kinnaird) was perhaps the most notable member of the Scottish team who, together with Charles Alcock, would be acknowledged as one of the founding fathers of the Association game.

A F Kinnaird, who was the son of the tenth Baron Kinnaird of Perthshire, had finished at Eton and gone up to Trinity College, Cambridge, where he met Charles Alcock, with whom he discussed the possibility of arranging an international game between England and Scotland. Ultimately, this led to his election onto the Football Association Committee, where he would remain for the rest of his life.

There were further England–Scotland games during the following months that resulted in a one-all draw in February 1871, a 2–1 victory to England in November 1871, as well as a 1–0 English win in February 1872. Regular intercity games saw the continuing growth of competitive fixtures, which led Charles Alcock to recall his schooldays at Harrow where a football knockout competition had been played.

On 20 July 1871, Charles Alcock, together with the Football Association Committee, which included Captain Francis Marindin of the Royal Engineers, A Stair (Treasurer) and M P Betts, passed a resolution that all clubs belonging to the Association would compete for a Challenge Cup on a knockout basis. Charles Alcock firmly believed that the Football Association Challenge Cup would accelerate the growth of football in England, as well as involve teams from all corners of the land in competing for the trophy.

Chapter II

THE GROWTH OF FOOTBALL IN THE MIDLANDS

FROM DERBY JUNCTION TO WEDNESBURY STROLLERS
ASTON VILLA, SMALL HEATH, WOLVERHAMPTON WANDERERS, WEST
BROMWICH ALBION, NOTTS COUNTY, NOTTINGHAM FOREST, DERBY COUNTY
AND STOKE SEE THE LIGHT OF DAY

The Black Country Leads the Way

During the mid-1870s, the growth of the Association game had been swift, especially in the Midlands. However, it had flourished in the Derby, Nottingham and Black County areas long before it had obtained a footing in the Birmingham area.

In the summer of 1875, Mr John Carson, a member of the Queens Park Club, and John Campbell-Orr, a former student of St Andrews University, arrived in Birmingham to fulfil business appointments that eventually led them to form a team known as Birmingham Clerks FC, which then changed its name to the Calthorpe Club. It was to become the most powerful club in the city.

Teams in the outlying areas of Birmingham were much stronger, especially in Wednesbury, where Wednesbury Strollers were already playing the likes of Nottingham Forest and the Sheffield Club.

Wednesbury Old Athletic were the acknowledged champions of the Midlands, while Elwells were a works team who were known as fine exponents of the passing game. Stafford Road Works were the finest team in Wolverhampton. They were captained by Charles Crump, later to become the President of the Birmingham Football Association. However, it was generally felt that there were more skilful teams in the Walsall area than in the rest of the Midlands. Walsall Town and Walsall Town Swifts were the finest teams in the area, with the Swifts a democratic club, while the Town were usually represented by young men of good social position.

In West Bromwich, the local club was captained by George Salter. The Dartmouth and Sandwell clubs had flourished long before West Bromwich Albion came into existence. Albrighton, Belbroughton, Shifnal and Hagley were other clubs formed in the surrounding areas of the Black Country.

It was now apparent that the seeds of the Association game had been sown in the Birmingham area with the Calthorpe Club, Aston Villa, St George's,

Excelsior and Small Heath playing to a reasonable standard. However, owing to financial pressures, the Calthorpe, St George's and Excelsior clubs would soon fade away, while the likes of Small Heath and Aston Villa would go from strength to strength.

ASTON VILLA

Aston Villa were formed in 1874, by a group of young men connected with the Villa Cross Wesleyan Chapel Cricket Team, who felt the need to pursue physical exercise during the winter months.

Improvement was slow because of the lack of competitive games. However, upon the arrival of George Ramsay, a young Scot, who had been invited to join the club, the Villa side greatly improved. Ramsay, who offered encouragement to the players, thus created a disciplined and well-run team.

When out on a morning stroll one day, Ramsay came upon a field in Wellington Road, Perry Barr, which soon became the venue for Villa's home fixtures as they began a quarter of a century of success, well served by Mr Ramsay, with the help of Archie Hunter, a fellow Scot.

Archie Hunter had arrived in Birmingham in 1878 to seek employment as well as to pursue a football career with the Calthorpe Club. However, unable to find the club, a workmate suggested he contact Aston Villa, who were captained by George Ramsay. Hunter, who liked what he saw, immediately joined Villa, where he would remain for the rest of his days, eventually succeeding Ramsay as club captain. Hunter, a born leader with a strong personality, would lead the Villa team to their first FA Cup success in 1887. However, he was denied a Scottish cap by the Scottish FA's refusal to recognise players who earned their living in England. Like many Victorian footballers, Archie Hunter was to die young. However, he secured his place in history as one of the finest footballers of Victorian times.

As well as Archie Hunter, Villa had signed Eli Davis and Howard Vaughton from Wednesbury Strollers, which would soon see them monopolise the Midlands Championship.

SMALL HEATH ALLIANCE

Small Heath Alliance (later Birmingham City) were founded a few months after Aston Villa, again by a group of young men wishing to pursue a winter sport.

During 1875, members of the Holy Trinity Cricket Club formed the Small Heath Football Club with W Edmunds, Will, Tom and George Edden, together with Tom and Frank James as the pioneers of the club. They played their early football against local sides on waste ground in Arthur Street, Small Heath, prior to moving to a ground in Ladypool Lane, Sparkbrook.

In 1877, the Small Heath side moved yet again to a ground in Muntz Street, where they would remain unbeaten for twenty-two games, which included excellent wins against Walsall Swifts and Aston Villa. As the decade came to an end, the Small Heath team were drawn against the powerful Wednesbury Old Athletic side in the Birmingham Cup. The Wednesbury team paid Small Heath the sum of five pounds to switch venues. However, the change in venues made little difference to the Small Heath side, as they won with ease, thus confirming their growing reputation as one of the most improved teams in the Midlands.

WOLVERHAMPRON WANDERERS

Wolverhampton Wanderers were formed in 1877 by John Baynton and John Brodie, who were connected with St Luke's School, Blakenhall. Upon joining forces with a team known as the Wanderers, the Wolverhampton side played their early games in a field near to the home of Sir Alfred Hickman. However, it was not until 1883 that the club played their first important game against the Stafford Road Railway Works, who were regarded as the most powerful club in Wolverhampton.

The works team were captained by Charles Crump, while J Whitehead on the wing had regularly been included in the Birmingham FA representative side. Twice they had reached the final of the Birmingham Cup, only to lose to Wednesbury Old Athletic, which reaffirmed the difficult task that lay ahead for the Wanderers. However, the Wanderers, surprisingly, won by five goals to one, to the delight of their growing band of supporters. Upon moving to a new ground near Dudley Road, the Wanderers were once again drawn against the Stafford Road Railway Works in a local cup tie, where they found themselves two goals down at the halfway stage. However, the Wanderers rallied in the second half to score four times without reply, thus confirming their position as the finest team in the area. Wanderers won their first cup in 1884 by defeating Hadley in the final of the Wrekin Trophy by fifteen goals to nil, which preceded a 4–0 victory against Long Eaton Rangers in the FA Cup. Despite this, they were well beaten by Wednesbury Old Athletic in the following round, halting their progress in the national competition.

WEST BROMWICH ALBION

West Bromwich Albion were formed in 1879 by a group of young cricketers known as the West Bromwich Strollers, who played their engagements at Dartmouth Park. Upon changing their name to West Bromwich Albion, the young men tended to play local games against the likes of Smethwick Trinity and Handsworth Grove, prior to seeking fixtures outside the district. This led them to enter the Birmingham Cup for the 1881–82 season. To coincide with this progressive step forward, the West Bromwich side moved to a permanent ground in Walsall Street, where they enjoyed an excellent cup run, which included victories against the Calthorpe Club and Elwell's prior to losing to Wednesbury Old Athletic in the semi-finals.

In 1882, Albion moved to the Four Acres ground where the Dartmouth Cricket Club rented them a pitch, which brought instant success, including a

26–0 victory against Coseley in the early rounds of the Birmingham Cup and an excellent victory against Stoke in the final of the Staffordshire Cup. Albion would enjoy many cup fighting exploits that were borne out of a fine team spirit, as the majority of their side were local players, including Harry Bell, a hard-working fullback, together with his brother George on the wing, Harry Green and Ezra Horton as splendid defenders, and Tom Green and Jem Bayliss as regular goal scorers for the club.

NOTTS COUNTY

As previously noted, the Association game was played in the Nottingham area long before it took a hold in Birmingham and the surrounding towns. However, when the game spread from the Yorkshire area, the great rivalry between the Yorkshire and Nottinghamshire cricketers spread to the football field.

Notts County were founded in 1862 by a group of young men who had played their early matches on The Park, prior to moving to The Meadows in late 1863. Blake Baillon captained the side during this period, while players included Richard Daft, Major Hack and George Parr, one of the finest cricketers in the land. However, County would show little progress until 1867, which coincided with the arrival of E H Greenhalgh, a future England international, who would greatly improve results, due mainly to his great influence and leadership.

During the early 1870s, the Nottingham side had become so enterprising as to play the mighty Queens Park team in Glasgow, which resulted in a 6–0 defeat. Nevertheless, County showed that lessons had been learned a few months later by holding the Glasgow side to a one-all draw in Nottingham.

County began to enjoy a reputation as one of the more skilful teams in the north, which attracted the finest players in the area, including brothers Harry and Arthur Cursham, who would both play for England. During the early 1880s, however, owing to a lack of interest, there was talk of the club going out of existence. This was soon forgotten as the club decided to play at a higher level as well as to sign players with greater experience.

The 1882–83 season saw the Nottingham side reach the semi-finals of the FA Cup with a team consisting of seven future or current international players. However, they were a little unfortunate to meet the Old Etonians at their finest, eventually losing the game by the odd goal in three. The following season saw County remain unbeaten at their Trent Bridge Ground, while once again reaching the semi-finals of the FA Cup, where they were drawn against Blackburn Rovers at the Aston Lower Grounds, Birmingham. County were again unfortunate, as they suffered a 1–0 reverse against the Lancashire side.

NOTTINGHAM FOREST

Neighbours Nottingham Forest, while living in the shadow of County, enjoyed much success during their early years following their formation in

1865 by a group of young men who played a form of hockey on the Forest recreation ground.

Amongst the original founder members were Charles Daft (the brother of Richard, of the County), W R Lymbery, W Brown, J G Richardson and R P Hawkesley. Their first important game was played at the Old Racecourse in the Forest against their old rivals County. This saw Forest win by the only 'touch down' of the game, the rules being more aligned with rugby than the Association game.

As the rules of the game began taking form, the Forest Club joined the Sheffield FA, which saw them become one of the first provincial teams in England to play the combination or passing game. The 1878–79 season saw them enter for the FA Cup for the first time where they were drawn against Notts County in the opening round. Forest won by three goals to one to proceed to the second round where they defeated the Sheffield Club (2–0). Further victories against the Old Harrovians and Oxford University saw them reach the semi-finals, where they were drawn against the Old Etonians for a place in the final (a situation Notts County would find themselves in four years later). However, Forest were a little unfortunate to lose to the eventual FA Cup winners, by the odd goal in three.

Forest, like County, were now acknowledged as one of the stronger provincial sides, which led to Sands, Luntley, Goodyer and Widdowson winning international honours with England.

The 1879–80 season saw a further semi-final appearance, with a 6–0 victory against Blackburn Rovers, the highlight of their cup run. However, the Nottingham side once again suffered a defeat in the semi-final, with a 1–0 reverse against Oxford University.

Then followed a number of seasons in which Forest hardly won a cup tie before they secured a semi-final place during the 1884–85 campaign. This had included an excellent win against the Old Etonians, to earn them the semi-final against the mighty Queens Park team from Glasgow. The tie ended in a one-all draw. In the replay at Merchiston Park, Edinburgh, the Glasgow side won by three goals to one in the only English FA Cup semi-final to be played north of the border.

Forest eventually achieved FA success towards the end of the century. They gave much to the English game during these early years, with Sam Widdowson responsible for the introduction of the shin guard in 1874, while 1878 saw the first whistle being used in a friendly game between Sheffield and Norfolk at the Forest ground.

DERBY COUNTY

Derby County were founded much later than the majority of teams in the East Midlands. The Derby area had long been identified with a type of football played at Ashbourne, on Shrove Tuesday, which consisted of two groups of men from local parishes kicking and carrying a ball from one end of the street to another with hardly a goal ever scored. Prior to the formation of Derby County in 1884, the Derby Midlands and Derby Junction Clubs were acknowledged as the finest in the area, while the County were associated with Derbyshire County Cricket Team, with many of their players assisting Derby County during the winter months.

Arthur Wilson, W M Jervis and William Morley were the early pioneers of the Derby side. Their first official game took place against Great Lever from the Bolton area of Lancashire, for whom John Goodall, who would later render great service with Derby, led the attack. Included in the Derby team against Great Lever were Benjamin Spilsbury, George Bakewell and Haydn Morley, who, together with Derbyshire County Cricketers Frank Sugg and William Storer, formed a side to be reckoned with. Though Derby were considered to be an excellent team, success would be a long time arriving, which would coincide with the arrival of Steve Bloomer, a pale-faced and slightly built young man, who would score prolifically for both Derby and the English national team, thus earning the reputation as the finest goal scorer of the Victorian era.

STOKE

The Stoke Club was formed as early as 1863 by a group of Old Carthusians who had played the game when handling was permitted. It took a further ten years before serious football was played by the Stoke Club, owing mainly to the enthusiasm of Tom Slaney. Without the efforts of Slaney as captain and club secretary, the Stoke Club may well have joined Cobridge, their main rivals, into footballing history. However, Stoke made excellent progress during this early period in their history, which included a 26–0 victory against the local Mow Cop team in a Staffordshire Cup Tie.

In 1884, with the legalisation of professionalism imminent, Harry Lockett took over as Stoke's club secretary, eventually leading them into the Football League, where he would double up as the League's first secretary.

Stoke signed many fine players during the late 1880s and early 1890s, including Rowley, Clare, Underwood and Schofield, who would all progress to the English national team. However, the Stoke Club tended to struggle during the 1890s as the game became more competitive and financially bound.

Non-Survivors of the Victorian Era

There were a number of Midlands teams who failed to survive the Victorian period, while producing many excellent players. These included Mitchell's St George's, which produced John Devey and Dennis Hodgetts, who would both play for Aston Villa and England. Birmingham Excelsior included England international, George Tait, in their line-up, Walsall Swifts regularly fielded international fullback, Alfred Jones, while England winger, George Holden, played for Wednesbury Old Athletic. However, Saltley College produced more players than any other club in the area. Tom Slaney and E Johnson signed for Stoke; George Copley, Tom Bryon and C S Johnstone joined Aston Villa; John Adams moved to Walsall, while John Brodie signed for Wolverhampton Wanderers.

Chapter III

THE GROWTH OF FOOTBALL IN THE NORTH

SHEFFIELD AND ACROSS THE PENNINES
THE PIONEERING SHEFFIELD CLUB
DARWEN – A CREDIT TO LANCASHIRE
SHEFFIELD UNITED, WEDNESDAY, EVERTON, BLACKBURN ROVERS, BOLTON
WANDERERS, DARWEN, PRESTON NORTH END, ACCRINGTON AND BURNLEY
ARE FOUNDED

The Pioneers of Sheffield

Football flourished in the Sheffield area as early as 1857, with the Sheffield Club acknowledged as the oldest club in the world. For years, the Sheffield Club stood alone as pioneers as the Wednesday were not formed until 1867, while Sheffield United would not see the light of day until 1889.

Sheffield's main rivals during the early days included Lockwood Brothers Works Team, Pye Bank, Broomhall, Heeley, Park Grange and Providence. However, the Sheffield side were so far ahead of their time that they would travel to play representative matches against London and Nottingham long before many of the Midlands and Lancashire teams were in existence.

The Sheffield Club produced many excellent players, including W H Stacey, H Muscroft, T Bishop, Daff Davy, Peter Andrews, Alf Liddell and T H Sorby, a future England international. They entered for the FA Cup on many occasions, only to fail against the Old Boys' teams from the south. Nevertheless, they had created an appreciation of football in the area, which would be continued by the Sheffield Wednesday and United teams into the following century. With the arrival of the professional player, the Sheffield Club could no longer have the pick of the better local players that had been their right during previous seasons, but the club had more than played their part in the growth of the Association game in the Yorkshire area.

WEDNESDAY

Wednesday, as previously noted, were formed in 1867, when members of the Wednesday Cricket Club, which had been in existence for nearly fifty years, decided to form a football section so that players would have a sporting interest the whole year round rather than just in the summer months.

The formation of the club took place at the Adelphi public house, on the corner of Arundel Street, on 4 September 1867, where Ben Chatterton, a local businessman, was elected president, F S Chambers vice-president, John Marsh secretary and captain, with John Pashley, who originally proposed the formation, completing the committee. Wednesday's first official fixture was played on the final day of 1867 against a local village side. It was a further ten years before the Wednesday became a force in football. This coincided with the arrival of J J Lang, Charles Clegg, William Clegg and William Mosforth, who all played their part in changing Wednesday from a reasonable local side to one capable of beating all comers.

J J Lang had arrived from Scotland with the promise of employment. Both Charles and William Clegg had played for the English national side while with the Sheffield Club. William Mosforth's skilful wing play would lead to international honours with England.

From 1877 until 1888, Wednesday won the Sheffield Challenge Cup on six occasions, and won the Wharncliffe Charity Cup five times during the same period. Their greatest success was in the FA Cup, with ten quarter-final appearances from 1882 to 1896. This resulted in two final appearances, one of which ended in a 6–1 defeat against Blackburn Rovers, and in the other they secured a deserved victory in 1896 with a 2–1 victory against Wolverhampton Wanderers.

SHEFFIELD UNITED

Sheffield United's late arrival on the football scene meant that much had to be learned in a very short time if they were to compete favourably against teams already playing in the newly formed Football League.

United were originally formed by the Sheffield United Cricket Club and shared their Bramall Lane ground during the winter months. They soon enjoyed success, due mainly to the efforts of J B Wostinholm, Charles Stokes and Harry Stones. Within months, United had turned professional, which saw the arrival of former England players, Jack Hudson and William Mosforth from Wednesday, as well as bespectacled goalkeeper Charles Howlett from Gainsborough Trinity. United were soon elected to the newly formed Second Division of the Football League, from where they secured immediate promotion to the First, as their growing reputation deserved.

Lancashire Catches On

Football continued to flourish across the Pennines, especially in the Liverpool area, where Bootle and St Domingo's were the dominant teams. However, until the late 1870s, Rugby Union tended to be the most popular sport in the area.

EVERTON

Everton were founded during November 1879 when the St Domingo's Club held a meeting at the Queen's Head Hotel, Village Street. A decision was made to change the club's name to that of the district, Everton, with their home games to be played in Stanley Park.

Following a 6–0 victory against St Peter's in their opening game at Stanley Park, the Everton team produced an excellent run of results, which saw them admitted into the newly formed Lancashire Football Association in 1880. Unhappily, Everton suffered an 8–1 defeat in a Lancashire Cup tie against Great Lever, thus confirming that they had a little way to travel on their journey to success.

Everton greatly improved following the arrival of Jack McGill and Dan Doyle from north of the border, which resulted in them winning the Liverpool Cup during the 1883–84 season. Upon moving to an enclosed ground in Priory Road in the Anfield district of Liverpool, the owner, a Mr Cruitt, decided to evict the club, owing to its often excitable supporters, which saw them move to a field in Anfield Road. While Everton enjoyed continued success on the field, John Houlding, a former president of the club and later Lord Mayor of Liverpool, felt that the ground rent should be raised in view of their success. However, the Everton committee totally rejected the suggestion. A further move resulted, to a ground in Goodison Road. Mr Houlding made every effort to retain the name of Everton, but with the majority of their players moving to the new ground, he was forced to change the name to Liverpool Football Club. Liverpool, like Everton, enjoyed much success during the final decade of the century.

BLACKBURN ROVERS

Blackburn Rovers were formed in 1875 by John Lewis and Arthur Constantine, two former public school boys, who convened a meeting at the St Leger Hotel, Blackburn, with the intention of forming a football club. Many of the young men who attended the meeting were from wealthy middle-class families and included the Greenwood brothers (Thomas, Doctor and Harry), Arthur Thomas (the brother of an alderman), J T Sycelmore (a master at the local grammar school) and A L Birch, a son of the vicar of Blackburn.

Following a couple of seasons of playing friendly games against local teams, the Blackburn side decided to enter for the 1879–80 FA Cup competition, where they suffered a 6–0 defeat at Nottingham Forest in the third round. However, the following season saw Rovers sign three Scotsmen, which coincided with an upturn in fortunes, certainly in the FA Cup competition.

Hugh McIntyre had previously played for both Partick Thistle and Glasgow Rangers. Jimmy Douglas had arrived from Renfrew. Fergie Suter completed the trio of Scotsmen, following his transfer from Darwen, having previously played for Glasgow Rangers.

The 1881–82 season saw Rovers move to a ground in Leamington Street, as well as signing local players Jimmy Brown and brothers Fred and John Hargreaves, who would all gain international honours with England. The season ended with a 1–0 defeat against the Old Etonians in the final of the FA

Cup. However, the disappointed Blackburn side made amends by defeating Accrington by three goals to nil in the final of the Lancashire Cup.

Rovers again won the Lancashire Cup during the 1882–83 season, while they were overshadowed in the FA Cup by local rivals Blackburn Olympic, who defeated the Old Etonians by two goals to one in the final, thus ending the southern domination of the trophy. Olympic's FA Cup exploits would be more than matched by the Rovers, who won the FA Cup in five of the following eight seasons as Olympic faded into football history.

BOLTON WANDERERS

Bolton Wanderers had officially seen the light of day on 28 August 1877. They had spent the three previous seasons as Christchurch Football Club, which had been formed by Thomas Ogden and his fellow schoolmasters in July 1874, with Ogden nominated as team captain, Tom Rawsthorne as club secretary, while J F Wright, the local vicar, was elected as club president. Christchurch tended to play the game under local rules, rather than the Cambridge Rules, against local sides on various grounds, prior to renting a field in Pikes Lane, which coincided with the change of name to Bolton Wanderers.

During 1878, the Wanderers invited Peter Parkinson, a local mill manager, to become an honorary member of the club, which greatly improved matters on and off the pitch. However, they had a little way to go to match the skills of Eagley, Halliwell and Great Lever, who were the leading teams in the area. Bolton moved to a field farther down Pikes Lane in 1881, where a grandstand was erected to shelter the spectators from the harsh weather conditions. This was followed by the arrival of Devlin (Arbroath) and Struthers (Glasgow Rangers) from north of the border, while the following season saw the Wanderers enter the FA Cup competition for the first time, where they suffered a defeat in the early rounds.

As the 1880s continued, Bolton were involved in a number of arguments concerning players receiving payments, which saw the likes of James Trainer, later of Preston North End, receiving fifty shillings per week when the paying of players was strictly illegal. With the appointment of Mr J J Bentley, one of the most respected administrators in the game, as well as the forthcoming legalisation of professional football, all was soon resolved.

The 1885–86 season saw Bolton win the Lancashire Cup, Bolton Charity Cup and Derby Charity Cup in their most successful season to date, which ended with the resignations of Peter Parkinson and J J Bentley following an angry general meeting. The Wanderers ended the season in turmoil, but the Lancashire side managed to persuade Mr Bentley to return to the club for the 1887–88 season to add stability to the rocky organisation. This step seemed to have worked, when Bolton were invited to join the newly formed Football League for the following season.

DARWEN

Darwen, a town not unlike the Coke town described by Charles Dickens in his novel *Hard Times*, were formed in 1875 for the benefit of the young men in the town, who toiled long hours in the cotton mills and coalmines and who were desperately in need of a sporting outlet rather than spending their spare time in drinking houses. The Darwen team shared their ground at Barley Bank with a team of local cricketers, where they would play friendly games against other teams in the area. Against all advice, the Darwen Club entered for the 1878–79 FA Cup competition, much to the astonishment of their supporters.

Darwen were drawn against the Birch Club of Manchester in the first round. Fortuitously, the Birch Club were scratched from the competition, which secured Darwen a second round tie against Eagley, one of the leading sides in the Bolton area. Owing to the late arrival of Dr J Gledhill, an inside forward in the Darwen side, the team played most of the game with ten men, though this made little difference to the result as Darwen ran out 4–1 winners, with Jimmy Love scoring a hat-trick, to earn a third round tie against the Remnants. Following a 3–2 victory against the Remnants, Darwen found themselves in the quarter-finals of the competition, where they were drawn against the mighty Old Etonians at the Kennington Oval, a situation beyond their wildest dreams.

The Old Etonians had a number of great players in their team who had appeared in previous FA Cup Finals as well as on the international stage. Darwen, on the other hand, had players who had never ventured outside of Lancashire. However, the northern side were well captained by J Knowles, with Jimmy Love an excellent goal scorer, while Fergie Suter, one of the finest defenders in Lancashire, appeared at fullback, where he was partnered by Brindle, who would soon make an appearance in the English national team. Love and Suter had previously played for the Partick club, which had visited the Lancashire area on a playing tour, with the two men deciding to remain in Darwen upon receiving offers of employment. It had been suggested that Love and Suter were in fact receiving payments from the club, who totally denied the allegations.

With the Old Etonian fixture forthcoming, FA Cup fever hit the town, which resulted in a fund being set up so that Darwen were able to travel to the Oval in style for the most important game in their short history. The Lancashire side selecting the following team:

J Duxbury

F Suter   W Brindle

W H Moorhouse   J Knowles   T Marshall

J Love   J Gledhill   W Kirkham   T Bury   R Kirkham

The Old Etonians chose the following players:

Major F Marindin

J C Wheldon H H Calvert

A F Kinnaird E Christian J B Chevallier

H B Sedgwick A G Bonsor H C Goodhart H Whitfield R D Anderson

On a snowy February afternoon, the Old Boys, having won the toss, decided to kick with the wind, which brought early success when Whitfield scored past the advancing Duxbury in the Darwen goal. Christian scored a second goal following excellent play by Bonsor. However, the situation worsened as the tie continued, as Goodhart netted a hat-trick for the Old Boys to secure a 5–0 lead, to seemingly put the result beyond doubt. Then followed a scrambled Darwen goal through the Old Etonian goalposts, while a Wheldon own goal, together with a Jimmy Love header, reduced the arrears to a two-goal margin.

Darwen then scored a fourth goal, which was initially disallowed. However, following protests from the visitors, the goal was allowed, while the Darwen comeback was completed during the final minutes of the game as Jimmy Love levelled the scores to five goals all. As the excitement came to an end, the tiring Old Etonian team declined Darwen's offer to play a period of extra time. The Old Boys generously acknowledged the wonderful effort made by all of the visiting team, who had been a credit to their town.

A replay was necessary, again at the Oval, with Darwen's thoughts on how to raise sufficient funds to finance a second trip to the capital city. However, they had little need to worry, as Charles Huntington, a local JP, promised to pay a third of any expenses incurred by the Darwen team. The Football Association generously donated ten pounds, while the ever sportsman-like Old Etonian team sent a five pound donation.

Following a period of extra time, the replay ended in a two-all draw, with Clarke and Whitfield on target for the Old Boys, with R Kirkham and Bury replying for the visitors. Sadly, when the tired Darwen team returned to London for a third game, they suffered a 6–2 defeat, and the Old Etonians went on to win the FA Cup.

Two years later, Darwen went one better to reach the semi-finals of the FA Cup, where they suffered a 4–1 defeat against the Old Carthusians, and they failed by a single vote to gain selection to the newly formed Football League in 1888.

Fergie Suter moved on to greater things with Blackburn Rovers, while his friend Jimmy Love suffered an early death during the bombardment of Alexandria in 1882.

PRESTON NORTH END

Preston North End, as with many sides in the Lancashire area, had begun life as a rugby-playing team prior to moving to the Association game towards the end of the 1870s. The 1880–81 season saw the Preston club move permanently to the Association Rules, which soon brought an embarrassing 16–0 defeat against Blackburn Rovers, however. The following season saw a great improvement on and off the field of play, due mainly to the involvement of William Sudell, who had joined the club as a sixteen-year-old in 1867. Sudell threw himself into the Preston club, determined to make them the finest team in England. He recruited players from the Edinburgh area, who received payments for playing for the Lancashire side, and offered employment in the cotton mills around the town. Jimmy and Nicholas Ross were Sudell's first major signings, with Nick an excellent tactician, and of the same mind as Sudell, while his brother, Jimmy, would become a prolific goal scorer for Preston.

Further signings from local teams in the Lancashire area included Bob Howarth, Robert Holmes, John Goodall and Fred Dewhurst, who would all gain international honours with England. Sudell continued in his determination to run a team of disciplined players, who would give all their energies to Preston with the incentive of financial payments.

Preston were drawn against Upton Park in the 1883–84 FA Cup competition, and then immediately expelled, following accusations that their players were receiving payments. However, William Sudell remained undeterred as he continued the fight to legalise professionalism, of which he would be the main instigator during 1885.

By 1886, Preston were the most feared team in England. Excellent victories against the leading Scottish sides, such as Queens Park (6–0) and Renton (7–0), confirmed their superiority, which inevitably led to an invitation to join the newly formed Football League, in which Mr Sudell would serve as its first treasurer.

Preston won two League Championships and finished as runners-up on three occasions during their first five seasons in the Football League, and reached the final of the FA Cup on two occasions, one of which ended in defeat against West Bromwich Albion (2–1), while the following season saw a 3–0 victory against Wolverhampton Wanderers. This earned the Preston team the distinction of winning both the League championship and the FA Cup during the same season.

William Sudell had made few friends in his meteoric rise to power, and his fall from grace evoked little sympathy as he received a three-year term of imprisonment for embezzling funds from his employer to finance his beloved Preston team. However, William Sudell must surely be given credit for enhancing the professional game in England during the 1880s.

ACCRINGTON FC

The Accrington club came into being in 1876 when the local cricket team decided to form a football section, playing a mixture of both rugby and Association Rules. However, it was in the summer of 1878, following a meeting at the Black Horse, Abbey Street, that the team decided to play strictly to the Association Rules.

Colonel John Hargreaves, a member of a wealthy local family, was appointed president of the club, J Cunliffe the treasurer, with William Eaton the club secretary. Dennis Talbot, Jim Yates, Dick Horne, Joe Hartley, Lightfoot, Heald and William Whittaker were the remaining committee members. Accrington's first official game ended in a 1–1 draw against Church Rovers, while the season saw them win fourteen of twenty-six fixtures, which included defeats against Darwen and Blackburn Rovers. However, the club greatly improved during the following season, as they entered for the Lancashire FA Cup. This resulted in defeat in the early rounds of the competition.

The 1880–81 season saw Accrington win twenty-one of their twenty-eight fixtures, which included a 6–4 success against the Park Road team in the final of the Lancashire Cup, following the ejection of both Blackburn Rovers and Darwen from the competition. The following season saw Blackburn secure the trophy at the expense of Accrington.

Accrington's success continued during the 1882–83 season, which coincided with the arrival of George Haworth, a skilful centre half who would serve the club for many years, as well as appearing in the English national side. Haworth briefly played for Blackburn Rovers, for whom he appeared in the 1885 FA Cup Final prior to returning to the Accrington club. Following three seasons of reasonable success, Accrington's progress came to a halt during the 1883–84 season when, following a heavy defeat by Blackburn Rovers, a trial was given to James Beresford of the Church Club, who scored twice on his Accrington debut. However, the Darwen club registered a complaint that Beresford had received payment for his single appearance. It was agreed that Beresford had, in fact, received a sum of money following his trial game. The Accrington club insisted, though, that the money had been paid by an individual unconnected with the Lancashire side.

The outcome of the enquiry found Accrington in breach of the rules, which resulted in a ban from playing other members of the English FA. The majority of Lancashire clubs thought the punishment a little harsh, and the English FA relented by reducing the ban from the FA Cup competition for the duration of the season.

Controversy continued during the 1884–85 season when, following an FA Cup victory against Southport, the Accrington side were once again ejected from the competition for fielding unregistered players. They eventually, however, received a little luck by winning the 1888 Lancashire Cup competition, albeit in unusual circumstances.

Accrington were due to play Preston North End in the final at Blackburn where, according to Preston, the local crowd would be a little too hostile towards them. The FA insisted that the game should take place. However, with

Preston failing to arrive for the final, the Accrington players took to the field and steered the ball between the goalposts to claim the trophy.

Despite many arguments for their exclusion, the Accrington Club were invited to become one of the twelve founder members of the Football League, which, on reflection, was certainly justified as they ended the campaign in seventh place. They also won the Lancashire Cup for the third time. However, Accrington's star began to fade during the final decade of the century. They suffered the indignation of relegation to the newly formed Second Division at the close of the 1892–93 season.

Relegation to the Second Division meant travelling as far away as London and Newcastle to fulfil League fixtures, thus incurring great expense. This would have left the club in financial ruins. Taking all of the possible problems into consideration, the Accrington Club decided to resign from the Football League with the intention of joining the less competitive Lancashire League. All clubs require a little good fortune, of which Accrington had very little. However, this was the price the smaller clubs paid for living in the shadow of the Blackburn Rovers and Preston North Ends of the world, who regularly enjoyed success at the expense of Accrington and their like.

BURNLEY FOOTBALL CLUB

Burnley Football Club first saw the light of day on 18 May 1882 when members of the Burnley Rovers Rugby Club met at the Bull Hotel to discuss the possibility of forming an Association Football team. Mr C J Massey was elected as club president, Mr Baron as treasurer, while Mr G C Waddington was elected secretary of the newly formed club.

Burnley's first game ended in a 4–0 defeat against Burnley Wanderers, which was hardly a surprise as the majority of the team had played the Rugby Union game during the previous season. However, Burnley continued to improve, with creditable performances against local sides such as Read, Great Harwood, Clitheroe and Kirkham, though with humiliating defeats against Astley Bridge (8–0) and Blackburn Rovers (10–0). This reaffirmed the belief that Burnley had a little way to go if they were to compete favourably against the leading sides in Lancashire.

The Lancashire side's regular team during this period saw Chase in goal, together with Hargreaves, Birley, Waddington, Cross and Marsland in defence, while Eastwood, Crabtree, French, Slater and Brown formed the attack.

James Crabtree eventually enjoyed a successful career with Aston Villa, with whom he won many honours, including a number of international caps for the English national team.

On 17 February 1883, the Burnley club moved to a ground at Turf Moor where their first visitors were Rawtenstall, who inflicted a 6–3 defeat on them. However, they ended their first season with an excellent 2–1 victory against Burnley Ramblers in the final of the Hospital Cup. During the summer of 1883, the Lancashire side began to sign players from north of the border. The process saw the arrival of Daniel Friel from the Vale of Leven Club, while further Scottish signings included Bryce, Harper, Gair, Beattie and McNee, who were all subject to financial inducements by the club.

Burnley were aware that to offer financial inducements was strictly illegal, which left them with no other alternative than to resign from the English FA. However, the FA Committee subsequently banned all their members from playing against teams who were not members of their Association, thus leaving Burnley with cancelled fixtures against the likes of Darwen and Blackburn Rovers.

With the legalisation of professionalism in 1885, the Burnley club were able to field their Scottish players, which saw an immediate improvement on the field of play. They lost just thirteen of fifty-eight fixtures during the season and enhanced their growing reputation as a difficult team to beat, a reputation that would lead to an invitation to be one of the twelve founder members of the newly formed Football League.

The South Drags its Feet

In the south of England, the game continued to be controlled by the leading amateurs of the day, and the growth rate of the professional clubs was much slower than of those in the north and Midlands.

Tottenham Hotspur had been formed as early as 1882, playing their games on Tottenham Marshes prior to moving to nearby Northumberland Park. In 1893, when the clubs were strictly amateur, the Tottenham side were fined by the London FA for purchasing a new pair of football boots for one of their new signings. However, within two years, Tottenham would become a professional club, which would lead to great success at the turn of the century.

Woolwich Arsenal were founded in 1886 by a group of young men employed at a company with the same name. Originally, they had been known as Dial Square, while their amateur status would be retained until the turn of the century. However, like their counterparts Tottenham Hotspur, their success would be of another century.

Chapter IV

THE WANDERERS' FA CUP DOUBLE – 1872 AND 1873

1872
WANDERERS WIN THE FA CUP
THE INAUGURAL ENGLAND–SCOTLAND GAME ENDS GOALLESS
1873
WANDERERS RETAIN THE FA CUP
ENGLAND 4 – SCOTLAND 2
KENYON-SLANEY SCORES A BRACE OF GOALS

The FA Cup Competition Commences

On 16 October 1871, Mr Alcock's proposal for teams to compete for a Challenge Cup was accepted by representatives of the Royal Engineers, Barnes, Wanderers, Lausanne, Upton Park, Hampstead Heathens, Crystal Palace, Windsor Home Park, Harrow Chequers, Clapham Rovers and the Civil Service clubs, with a further resolution that all clubs should contribute to a silver trophy, at a cost of twenty pounds, which would be played for annually. Queens Park of Glasgow, who were unable to attend the meeting, contributed one guinea towards the trophy, in recognition of the friendships made with Charles Alcock and Arthur Kinnaird during the England–Scotland international games.

Fifteen teams entered for the first FA Cup competition. Donington Grammar School, Hitchin, Wanderers, Reigate Priory, the Royal Engineers, Queens Park, Barnes, Civil Service, Crystal Palace, Hampstead Heathens, Great Marlow, Upton Park, Maidenhead, Clapham Rovers and Harrow Chequers competed for a place in the second round. However, after Harrow Chequers, Reigate Priory and Donington Grammar School were scratched from the competition, the numbers were down to a dozen. It may be assumed that the Nottingham and Sheffield clubs decided against entering for the competition as all cup ties were played in London, which meant an expensive trip to the capital city, an expense well beyond the finances of the working-class men in the north.

Five teams remained at the semi-final stages of the competition with the Wanderers, Crystal Palace, Hampstead Heathens, the Royal Engineers and Queens Park competing for a place in the final. The number was reduced to four following a 2–0 victory by the Royal Engineers against Hampstead Heathens.

In the semi-finals, the Royal Engineers had little difficulty in accounting for Crystal Palace by three goals to nil, while the Wanderers and Queens Park played to a goalless draw at the Kennington Oval. However, the Glasgow team were unable to return to London for the replay, which meant that the Wanderers, captained by Charles Alcock, faced the Royal Engineers, captained by Francis Marindin, in the first final of the FA Cup.

Marindin and Alcock, who had worked tirelessly in their efforts to instigate the FA Cup competition through their vigorous work on the FA Committee, would now face each other in the final.

Wanderers' FA Cup Victory

The Royal Engineers were favourites to win the trophy, following their relatively easy passage to the final, while the Wanderers had won one game and drawn two on their way to the final. A crowd in excess of 2,000 arrived at the Oval to witness the first FA Cup Final, with the Wanderers selecting the following team:

R De C Welch

C W Alcock   M P Betts

A G Bonsor   E E Bowen   W P Crake

T C Hooman   E Lubbock   A C Thompson   R W S Vidal   C H Wollaston

The Royal Engineers selected the following players:

Captain Merriman

Captain Marindin   Lt Addison

Lt Bogle   Lt Cotter   Lt Cresswell

Lt Goodwyn   Lt Mitchell   Lt Muirhead   Lt Renny-Tailyour   Lt Rich

A Stair, the assistant secretary of the Football Association, was appointed match referee. During the early stages of the final, Cresswell of the Royal Engineers sustained a broken collar bone, which saw him spend the remainder of the match as a passenger on the wing. In spite of the unfortunate injury, the game turned out to be an all-out attacking affair with Vidal and Hooman displaying excellent dribbling skills for the Wanderers, while Rich and Renny-Tailyour strove to outrun the Wanderers' defence.

Following a period of sustained pressure by the Wanderers, Charles Alcock converted a cross past the advancing Merriman in the Engineers' goal, which was immediately disallowed.

However, Wanderers soon gained the lead from a well-directed shot from M P Betts. Wanderers then exerted further pressure on the Engineers' defence, with only a post and Merriman denying them a second goal. The Engineers were expected to rally towards the final stages of the game, owing to their superior stamina. However, time ran out for the army side as the Wanderers held on to win the FA Cup.

The Wanderers and Royal Engineers were generally regarded as two of the finest teams in England during the 1870s. The Engineers suffered only three defeats in eighty-six games from 1871 to 1875, while the Wanderers won the FA Cup on five occasions during the decade.

An England Team Travel North of the Border

Following further links with the Queens Park Club during the 1872 FA Cup competition, Arthur Kinnaird and Charles Alcock were determined to send an English national team north of the border to compete against the strongest Scottish side available. As the Scottish Football Association was yet to be formed, the responsibility of selecting the Scottish side fell upon Robert Parker of the Queens Park Club, who arranged the game for 30 November 1872, to take place at the west of Scotland cricket club, Partick.

Scotland selected the following players, for what became accepted as the first official international fixture against England:

R Gardner

W Ker   J Taylor

J Thompson   J Smith   R Smith

R Leckie   A Rhind   W W McKinnon   J B Weir   D N Wotherspoon

With the exception of W Ker (Granville), the remaining members of the team were representatives of the Queens Park Club. However, James and Robert Smith, who had recently moved to London on business, were now playing for the South Norwood Club.

England selected the following eleven:

W J Maynard (1st Surrey Rifles)

E H Greenhalgh (Notts)   R De C Welch (Wanderers)

R Barker (Herts Rangers) J C Clegg (Sheffield)   F B Chappell-Maddison (OU)

J Brockbank (CU) A K Smith (OU)   C J Ottaway (OU) C J Chenery (Crystal Palace)   C J Morice (Barnes)

While the England selectors included Greenhalgh and Clegg from the industrial north, the majority of the side were from the universities and London-based teams, with Arnold Kirke-Smith, Frederick Chappell-Maddison and Cuthbert Ottaway representatives of Oxford University. Kirke-Smith had previously represented Scotland in the London-based international games, Chappell-Maddison would appear in three FA Cup Finals with Oxford

University and the Wanderers, while Ottaway was generally regarded as the finest sportsman to have ever studied at Oxford. As well as appearing in three FA Cup Finals, Ottaway played county cricket for both Kent and Middlesex, and gained Blues at Oxford in cricket, rackets, real tennis and athletics, prior to being called to the Bar in 1876. However, within two years Cuthbert Ottaway met a sudden death at the age of twenty-eight. Reginald de Courtney Welch was surprisingly the only representative from the successful Wanderers club, with whom he would win two FA Cup winners' medals, while Surrey cricketer Charles Chenery, would play for England on three occasions.

Of the remaining members of the England team, W J Maynard made a further appearance in 1876, while Barker, Brockbank and Morice were making their only appearance for the country of their birth.

A crowd in excess of 4,000 gathered to witness the first historic international game, which ended in a disappointing goalless draw, with England the more talented side. However, the visitors were unable to break down the Scottish defence, which relied upon the passing game, as well as on an excellent team spirit.

England Win the Return Game Against Scotland

The inaugural international game between England and Scotland had proved a great success. As well as forging stronger links between the English FA and the Queens Park Club, it led Charles Alcock to arrange a return game at the Kennington Oval on 8 March 1873. England made a number of changes in their line-up, with Greenhalgh and Chenery the only players retained from the visit to Glasgow. England selected a side with a Wanderers' influence. It saw the inclusion of R W S Vidal, A G Bonsor, Hubert Heron and William Kenyon-Slaney.

Robert Walpole Sealy Vidal, who had gained a rugby Blue at Oxford, appeared in the first three FA Cup Finals with Oxford University and the Wanderers, with whom he enjoyed the reputation of 'Prince of the dribblers'. However, his football career was short, following his ordainment in 1877. William Kenyon-Slaney, who scored two goals in his only England appearance, enjoyed a successful political career as the member of parliament for Newport, Shropshire. Alexander Bonsor, who scored in the first of his two England games, appeared in four FA Cup Finals with the Wanderers and Old Etonians.

Hubert Heron was a regular member of the England side for a number of years and enjoyed much FA Cup success with the Wanderers, while Pelham Von Donop, a stalwart of the Royal Engineers team, made the first of two England appearances in defence, prior to pursuing a career with the railways.

William Clegg (Sheffield) followed his brother Charles into the England team, where he made two appearances, six years apart. Their political and football services to the city of Sheffield saw both Clegg brothers receive knighthoods in their later years.

Kenyon-Slaney Scores Twice

The return game with the Scots attracted in excess of 3,000 spectators, who witnessed a 4–2 victory by the English, with Kenyon-Slaney (2), Bonsor and Chenery netting for the home side. Renny-Tailyour and Gibbs replied for the visitors. Renny-Tailyour, an accomplished sportsman, appeared in three FA Cup Finals for the Royal Engineers and represented Scotland at Rugby Union, thus becoming the only Scot to play for the country at both codes.

During the week following the international game, a Nottingham select eleven held the visiting London team to a goalless draw, which was an excellent result for the East Midlands team, as the visitors included internationals Charles Chenery, Arthur Kinnaird and Hubert Heron in their line-up.

The Wanderers Defend the FA Cup

As holders of the FA Cup, the Wanderers were exempt from the 1873 competition until the final, where they could be challenged for the right to win the trophy. Maidenhead, Windsor Home Park and Oxford University came through the second round stage of the competition at the expense of 1st Surrey Rifles, South Norwood and Clapham Rovers, while Queens Park and the Royal Engineers received byes into the third round, where Maidenhead defeated Windsor Home Park by one goal to nil, with Oxford University beating a strong Royal Engineers team by a similar score. However, Queens Park again received a bye, which left three teams remaining in the competition to challenge the Wanderers for the coveted trophy.

Oxford University then defeated Maidenhead by four goals to nil to secure a tie against Queens Park for a place in the final. However, owing to insufficient funds, the Scottish team were unable to travel to London, which resulted in them scratching from the competition, thus allowing the University side the opportunity of challenging the Wanderers for the FA Cup at the Amateur Athletic Ground, Lillie Bridge, a ground chosen by the Wanderers as holders of the trophy.

The final took place on 29 March, the day of the Oxford and Cambridge boat race, which meant that an early start was imperative to allow spectators the opportunity to view the great boating spectacle.

Wanderers selected the following team for the 1873 FA Cup Final in their bid to retain the trophy:

E E Bowen

C M Thompson   R De C Welch

A F Kinnaird (captain)   L S Howell   C H Wollaston

J R Sturgis   Rev. H H Stewart   W S Kenyon-Slaney R K Kingsford   A G Bonsor

Oxford University selected the following players:

A Kirke-Smith

A J Leach   C C Mackarness

F H Birley   R W S Vidal   C J Ottaway

W B Paton   F B Chappell-Maddison   C J Longman   H B Dixon   W E Sumner

A Stair was once again the official match referee.

Oxford made the running during the early stages of the final, with Howell and Thompson performing admirably in the Wanderers' defence to keep the University forwards at bay. However, following thirty minutes of constant pressure by the students, the cup holders secured an undeserved lead when Arthur Kinnaird ran on to a weak back pass by an Oxford defender to place the ball between the goalposts. Ends were then changed, which saw both teams play with a renewed vigour, with Sturgis and Kinnaird making a number of skilful runs for the Wanderers, while Kirke-Smith and Sumner were equally skilful for Oxford.

As the game progressed into the latter stages, the University side became a little desperate in their pursuit of an equalising goal, which led them to dispense with their goalkeeper in the hope of strengthening their attack. However, their tactics backfired when Charles Wollaston scored a second goal for the Wanderers to secure a second successive FA Cup Final victory. Ample time remained for their supporters to view the Varsity boat race.

Chapter V

OXFORD UNIVERSITY WIN THE FA CUP – 1874

SCOTLAND'S REVENGE VICTORY
THE QUEENS PARK CLUB – A GREAT INFLUENCE

Queens Park – A Great Influence

Some of the men who had, more than most, been responsible for the development of Association Football in England have already been mentioned, with Charles Alcock, Arthur Kinnaird and Francis Marindin amongst such men. There was little doubt, however, that the Queens Park Club of Glasgow had played a part in that development. Founded in 1867, the Queens Park team were undefeated until 1876, when they lost to the Wanderers. They were generally regarded as equal to the majority of the leading English sides of the day, as two English FA Cup Final appearances during the mid-1880s confirmed.

Queens Park became the prime movers during 1873 in forming the Scottish Football Association. They also won the Scottish FA Cup in the 1874–76, 1880–82, 1884, 1886, 1890 and 1893 seasons. However, following the formation of the Scottish League in the 1890–91 season, the Glasgow side refused to join until the turn of the century.

The Wanderers Suffer Their First FA Cup Defeat

While teams tended to play friendly games during the 1870s, interest in the FA Cup competition had increased by 1874, with twenty-eight teams pursuing the trophy. These included the Sheffield Club and Cambridge University. However, Cambridge were soon eliminated from the competition following a 4–1 defeat at Clapham Rovers in the second round.

Seven teams remained at the quarter-final stage, with Clapham Rovers drawn to play against the Sheffield Club. Maidenhead met the Royal Engineers, Oxford University received a difficult tie against the Wanderers, while the Swifts received a bye into the semi-finals. Clapham Rovers progressed to the semi-finals by defeating the Sheffield Club by the odd goal in three. The Royal Engineers secured a 7–0 victory against Maidenhead, while the shock of the round saw Oxford University defeat the Wanderers by one goal to nil, thus avenging their 1873 FA Cup Final defeat. Oxford University then secured a second successive final appearance following a 1–0 success against Clapham Rovers. The Royal Engineers defeated the Swifts by two goals to nil to take their place in the final, planned for the Kennington Oval on 14 March.

England Suffer a Narrow Defeat in Glasgow

A week prior to the FA Cup Final, the England national team travelled to Glasgow for the third international game against the Scots with a side showing many changes from the 1873 encounter. Hubert Heron (Wanderers) and Charles Chenery (Crystal Palace) were the only players to retain their places from the victory at the Oval. However, the England team continued to field a side with a Wanderers' influence with the inclusion of Robert Kingsford, Alfred Stratford and Charles Wollaston, as well as Hubert Heron and Reginald de Courtney Welch.

Kingsford and Stratford, who were both accomplished county cricketers, were making their only appearances for England, while Wollaston appeared twice more for his country, as well as playing in five FA Cup-winning sides for the Wanderers. Cuthbert Ottaway, the Oxford University captain, returned to the side in the light of his forthcoming FA Cup Final appearance, while his Oxford team-mate, Francis Birley, made the first of two appearances in an England shirt. Birley, a county cricketer with both Lancashire and Surrey, appeared in four FA Cup Finals, of which three were won prior to pursuing a career as a barrister.

Odd man out of the England line-up was James Hawley-Edwards (Shropshire Wanderers), who was playing his one England game up front. Hawley-Edwards also appeared for the Welsh national team against Scotland in 1876 prior to serving the Welsh Football Association as treasurer for a number of years.

In a most competitive game, the Scots managed a 2–1 victory to avenge the 1873 defeat at the Oval, with Robert Kingsford scoring England's consolation goal.

Oxford University Win the FA Cup

A crowd in excess of 2,000 arrived at the Oval to view the 1874 FA Cup Final, with Oxford University selecting the following players:

C B Nepean

R H Benson   C C Mackarness

F H Birley   F T Green   Rev. A Johnson

F B Chappell-Maddison C J Ottaway (capt.) F J Patton W S Rawson R W S Vidal

The Royal Engineers selected the following eleven:

Captain Merriman

Major Marindin (captain)   Addison

Blackburn   Digby   Olliver

Onslow   Rawson   Renny-Tailyour   Von Donop   Wood

A Stair was match referee for the third successive final.

Both the Oxford and Royal Engineers teams contained players with previous FA Cup Final experience. Birley, Vidal, Chappel-Maddison, Mackarness and Ottaway had appeared for the University side in the 1873 final, while Merriman, Addison, Marindin and Renny-Tailyour had been members of the losing Royal Engineers team in 1872.

Upon winning the toss, the University side decided to kick with a gale force wind behind them, which caused immediate problems for the Engineers' defenders, as Ottaway and Vidal made numerous runs down the wings.

The inevitable first goal arrived following a scrimmage in the Engineers' goalmouth, when Mackarness steered the ball between the posts to secure a one-goal lead for the University, who were well on top at this stage of the proceedings. However, with the changing of ends, the Royal Engineers were confident of securing an equalising goal, with the assistance of the strong wind at their backs. Oxford held firm for the remainder of the first half, to protect their one-goal lead, and they continued to dominate the game during the second half, which led to a further goal when Ottaway, aided by Chappell-Maddison and Vidal, dribbled their way towards the Engineers' goal, where Patton was waiting to slide the ball between the posts.

Renny-Tailyour hit the University goalpost towards the end of the game, which was too little too late, as Oxford held on to their two-goal advantage to win the FA Cup. While it had been a below-par performance by the Royal Engineers, success was not too far away for the military men.

Chapter VI

THE WANDERERS CONTINUE TO DOMINATE
THE FA CUP COMPETITION – 1875 TO 1878

1875
THIRD TIME LUCKY FOR THE ROYAL ENGINEERS
ENGLAND AND SCOTLAND SHARE THE SPOILS
1876
WANDERERS' THIRD FA CUP FINAL VICTORY
ENGLAND ARE WELL BEATEN
1877
WANDERERS RETAIN THE FA CUP
ENGLAND'S FIRST DEFEAT ON HOME SOIL
1878
WANDERERS' THIRD SUCCESSIVE FA CUP WIN
A HUMILIATING DEFEAT FOR ENGLAND
THE DEMISE OF THE WANDERERS

A Third Final Appearance for the Engineers

Wanderers were in excellent form during the early stages of the 1875 FA competition, which began with a 16–0 victory against Farningham, followed by a 4–0 success against Barnes. Clapham Rovers, Maidenhead, Woodford Wells and the Royal Engineers progressed to the last eight at the expense of the Pilgrims, Reigate Priory, Southall and Cambridge University. Oxford University and Shropshire Wanderers received walkovers, while the Old Etonians received a bye into the quarter-finals. Shropshire Wanderers then inflicted a 2–0 defeat on Woodford Wells in the quarter-finals, the Royal Engineers defeated Clapham Rovers by the odd goal in five, and Oxford University narrowly defeated the Wanderers by two goals to one. The Royal Engineers were a little fortunate to reach the semi-final stage, following a 1–0 victory against Maidenhead.

The Royal Engineers were then drawn against Oxford University in the semi-finals, where they managed a 1–0 victory in a replayed tie to secure their third FA Cup Final appearance in four seasons. Their opponents were the Old Etonians, who had narrowly defeated Shropshire Wanderers by the only goal of the game to secure the first of six FA Cup Final appearances in nine seasons.

Scotland and England Share the Spoils

The traditional annual game against Scotland took place at the Oval a week prior to the FA Cup Final, with England selecting Hubert Heron, Charles Alcock and Charles Wollaston from the Wanderers, together with William Carr, the tall Sheffield goalkeeper. There were recalls for Birley (Oxford University), Von Donop (Royal Engineers) and Bonsor, now of the Old Etonians.

Edward Haygarth (Swifts), an accomplished county cricketer, made his England debut at right fullback, while Geaves (Clapham Rovers) played his first England game at outside left.

Scotland performed heroically at the Oval to secure a two-all draw, with Alcock and Wollaston on target for the home team.

A Drawn FA Cup Final

The final of the 1875 FA Cup competition once again coincided with the University boat race, with the Royal Engineers selecting the following players:

Merriman

Sim   Onslow

Ruck   Von Donop   Wood

Rawson   Stafford   Renny-Tailyour   Wingfield-Stratford   Mein

The Old Etonians selected the following team:

Farmer

Kinnaird   Strong

Kenyon-Slaney   Benson   Patton

Ottaway   Bonsor   Thompson   E Lubbock   Wilson

Charles Alcock officiated as match referee.

Upon winning the toss, the Old Etonians decided to kick with the strong wind at their backs, which resulted in them spending long periods in the Engineers' half, eventually leading to the opening goal by Bonsor following a pass from Ottaway. However, with the changing of ends, it was now the turn of the Royal Engineers to exert pressure on the Etonian goal, resulting in the equalising goal from the ever busy Renny-Tailyour. Midway through the second period of play, Cuthbert Ottaway sustained a twisted ankle, which resulted in the Old Boys playing the remainder of the game with ten players. However, despite playing a man short, as well as a period of extra time, the Old Etonians held on for a replay.

Success for the Military Men

The Royal Engineers fielded an unchanged team for the replay, while the Old Etonians were forced to make four changes through injury. Drummond-Moray, Hammond, A Lubbock and Farrer replaced Kenyon-Slaney, Ottaway, Benson and Thompson.

With the Old Boys fielding such a weakened team, the Engineers took advantage of the situation. They dominated the proceedings, which led to a 2–0 victory for the army side, with Stafford and Renny-Tailyour scoring the all-important goals.

Edgar Lubbock and Arthur Kinnaird had been the pick of the players for the Old Boys, who had once again finished the game with ten men following an injury to Bonsor. However, the Royal Engineers had well deserved what would be their only FA Cup Final success.

Major Francis Marindin, who had moulded the Royal Engineers team into a great one, had missed the final owing to an overseas posting. However, he appeared in ten FA Cup Finals during his career – eight as a referee and twice as a player.

The Old Etonians Return to the Oval

The 1876 season saw many high-scoring games in the second round of the FA Cup competition, with the Old Etonians, Oxford University and Cambridge University securing eight-goal victories against Maidenhead, Hertfordshire Rangers and Reigate Priory, while Clapham Rovers scored a dozen goals without reply against Leyton.

Wanderers proceeded to the quarter-finals with a 3–0 success against Crystal Palace; Swifts enjoyed a 5–0 victory against South Norwood; while the Royal Engineers, who recorded a 15–0 victory against Wycombe in the first round, received a walkover into the last eight, together with the Sheffield Club.

Oxford University were then drawn against Cambridge University for a place in the semi-finals, with Oxford winning the tie by four goals to nil. Old Etonians secured a 1–0 victory against Clapham Rovers, while the Wanderers defeated the Sheffield Club by two goals to nil, and both proceeded to the semi-finals.

The Royal Engineers were expected to complete the semi-final line-up. However, they were outplayed by the Swifts Club, who recorded a surprising 3–1 success against the FA Cup holders. At the semi-final stage of the competition, the Swifts were a little unfortunate to suffer a 2–1 defeat against the Wanderers, while the Old Etonians scored the game's only goal against Oxford University, to secure a second successive FA Cup Final appearance, which would once again take place at the Oval on 11 March.

England Are Well Beaten

A week prior to the FA Cup Final, the England team travelled to Glasgow for the international game against Scotland, with Hubert Heron (Wanderers) the only player retained from the previous year's encounter. During the 1870s, the England side tended to be chosen on availability rather than skill alone. W J Maynard (1st Surrey Rifles) earned a recall for his second and final England game, while there were single appearances for Ernest Bambridge (Swifts), Frederick Heron (Wanderers), Frederick Green (Wanderers) and W S Buchanan (Clapham Rovers).

Ernest Bambridge was the first of three brothers to play for England, while Frederick Heron was the brother of Hubert.

Arthur Cursham, the skilful Notts County winger, who later played cricket for both Nottinghamshire and Derbyshire, was the most notable newcomer in the England line-up, where he would make six appearances. His career was cut short upon contacting a bout of yellow fever, which eventually led to an early death at the age of thirty-one.

England struggled throughout the game, which saw the home side run out winners by three goals to nil.

The Wanderers Triumph in a Cup Final Replay

A crowd in excess of 3,000 gathered at the Oval for the 1876 FA Cup Final, with the Wanderers selecting the following team:

W D Greig

A Stratford   Lindsay

F B Chappell-Maddison   F H Birley (captain)   C H Wollaston

J Hawley-Edwards J Kenrick   T Hughes   Hubert Heron   Frederick Heron

The Old Etonians selected the following players:

Quinton Hogg

J E Weldon   E Lyttleton

A C Thompson   A F Kinnaird   C Meysey

W S Kenyon-Slaney   A Lyttleton   J R Sturgis   A G Bonsor   H P Allene

Upon winning the toss, the Wanderers decided to kick with the wind behind them, which resulted in constant pressure on the Old Boys' defence, with only the excellent goalkeeping of Hogg keeping the Wanderers' forwards at bay. Following thirty-five minutes of play, however, Charles Wollaston advanced into the Etonian goal area, crossed to Hawley-Edwards, who secured a half-time lead for the Wanderers.

With the advantage of the blustery wind during the second half, the Old Boys soon secured an equalising goal when Bonsor converted a Kenyon-Slaney cross, but with the changing of ends, the Etonians were once again forced to defend their goal, which they managed owing to excellent displays by Thompson and Edgar Lyttleton, and the game ended in a one-all draw.

The Wanderers Win with Ease

A slightly higher attendance was recorded at the Oval for the replay. The Wanderers fielded an unchanged side, while the Old Etonians once again fielded a weaker team, with F H Wilson, M G Farrer, J H Stronge and Edgar Lubbock replacing the unavailable Hogg, Weldon, Meysey and Thompson.

All was even during the first half-hour's play, prior to Wollaston scoring for the Wanderers following excellent work by Hubert Heron. Hughes added a second goal, and the Wanderers ended the first half two goals to the good.

Hughes netted his second and Wanderers' third goal early in the second half, which then saw them relax, thus allowing the Old Etonians to take control of the game. However, the Old Boys failed to take advantage of the situation and the Wanderers ran out 3–0 winners to win the trophy for the third occasion in five seasons.

Alcock and Kinnaird Offer Encouragement

While clubs continued to play friendly games against other local sides during 1876, few teams ventured outside of their county, that is, with the exception of the Sheffield and Queens Park clubs. However, it must be mentioned that both Charles Alcock and Arthur Kinnaird greatly encouraged all comers to participate in the FA competition upon its instigation in 1872.

Oxford and Cambridge Reach the Semi-Finals

The one surprising result during the early stages of the 1877 FA Cup competition was the Old Etonians suffering a defeat at the first hurdle. However, the Wanderers, the Royal Engineers, Sheffield and Oxford University were still in the competition at the third round stage.

Cambridge University progressed to the quarter-finals with a 4–0 victory against Rochester, Upton Park managed a 1–0 win against Great Marlow, while the Royal Engineers defeated the Sheffield Club by a similar score.

Wanderers secured a quarter-final place with a 3–0 success against the Pilgrims, while Oxford University received a walkover as the Queens Park Club were unable to travel from Scotland. Five teams contested the quarter-finals, with Cambridge University drawn against the Royal Engineers, Oxford University due to play against Upton Park, and the Wanderers receiving a bye into the semi-finals.

Both Oxford and Cambridge managed one-nil victories in the quarter-finals, with Oxford the fortunate team to receive a bye into the final. Cambridge suffered a 1–0 defeat against the Wanderers to end their hopes of an all varsity FA Cup Final. However, matches between the Oxford and Cambridge universities continued to grip the nation well into the following century. Oxford University now met the Wanderers in the 1877 FA Cup Final at the Oval on 24 March in a repeat of the 1873 Final.

England Suffer Their First Defeat on Home Soil

Three weeks prior to the FA Cup Final, the English national team entertained Scotland at the Oval, with Arthur Cursham and Beaumont Jarrett the only survivors from the previous season's fixture.

Beaumont Jarrett, who would be ordained in 1878, was appearing in the second of three England games, while there were single England appearances for both Cecil Wingfield-Stratford (Royal Engineers) and Alfred Lyttleton (Old Etonians), who was generally regarded as one of the finest sportsmen of the day. Lyttleton had gained Blues at cricket, rackets, real tennis and athletics, though his greatest successes were on the cricket field, where he played for Worcestershire, Middlesex and England prior to his election as president of the MCC. He also became a successful member of parliament. Charles Wollaston (Wanderers) once again returned to the England team for his third international appearance, while William Mosforth, the skilful Wednesday winger, made the first of many England appearances. However, the team changes made little difference to England's performance as Scotland won by three goals to one, with Alfred Lyttleton scoring a consolation goal for the home side.

The Wanderers Retain the FA Cup

As the day of the 1877 FA Cup Final arrived, the Wanderers were favourites to win the trophy for a fourth time, while Oxford University were determined to erase the 2–0 defeat against the Wanderers in the 1873 Final.

Oxford University selected the following team for their third FA Cup Final appearance:

E Allington

J Bain   O R Donnell

J H Savery   A H Todd   E W Waddington

P Fernandez   A F Hills   H S Otter   E H Parry (captain)   W S Rawson

The Wanderers selected the following players:

A F Kinnaird

A H Stratford   W Lindsay

F T Green   F H Birley (captain)   C H Wollaston

Hubert Heron   T B Hughes   H Wace   C A Denton   J Kenrick

Oxford controlled the early play, with Bain and Fernandez making many excellent runs down the wings, well supported by Otter and Todd, which resulted in a controversial goal. Arthur Kinnaird held a long shot by Waddington, only to step back between the posts with the ball in his hands. Despite an appeal to the referee, the goal was allowed as the first half came to an end. The University side was one goal to the good.

Wanderers came more into the game during the early stages of the second half as Hughes, Heron and Wollaston ran at the Oxford defence in pursuit of an equalising goal, which eventually materialised when Kenrick slotted the ball between the varsity goalposts following an accurate cross by Hubert Heron. As the final whistle sounded, the much fitter Wanderers side dominated the period of extra time, which led to Lindsay scoring what turned out to be the winning goal to secure a fourth FA Cup Final success for the Wanderers.

Charles Alcock's Prophetic Words

With the quickening development of the Industrial Revolution, railways had become the normal means of travel between towns and cities, which meant that football teams and their supporters could travel to any town in England with few problems, other than financial ones.

Charles Alcock greeted the continuing growth of the Association game with what would turn out to be prophetic words:

> What was ten or fifteen years ago the recreation of a few has now become the pursuit of thousands. An athletic exercise carried on under a strict system and in many cases by an enforced term of training, almost magnified into a profession.

Alcock, who had been mainly responsible for the inauguration of both the FA Cup competition and the international games between England and Scotland, now perceived that the game was growing to huge proportions. However, for the time being, the Old Boys' dominance of the game remained, as the London-based amateur sides continued to supply the majority of the players to the England team, as well as dominate the FA Cup competition.

A Repeat of the First FA Cup Final

At the third round stage of the 1878 FA Cup competition, the Wanderers, Royal Engineers, Oxford University and Cambridge University were predictably amongst the teams pursuing a place in the quarter-finals.

The Wanderers proceeded to the quarter-finals following a 4–1 victory against Barnes. Oxford University narrowly defeated Clapham Rovers by the odd goal in five, while Upton Park secured a 3–0 win against the Remnants.

Cambridge University suffered a surprising 2–0 reverse against the Old Harrovians. Royal Engineers defeated the Druids by eight goals to nil, and the

Sheffield Club received a bye into the quarter-finals, which numbered six teams.

Old Harrovians continued their winning ways in the quarter-finals, with a 3–1 victory against Upton Park. The Wanderers scored three times against the Sheffield Club, without reply, while the Royal Engineers completed the semi-final line-up, with a 4–2 success against Oxford University.

With three teams remaining in the competition, the Wanderers, as reigning FA Cup holders, received a bye into the final. They would meet the Royal Engineers, who had managed a narrow 2–1 victory against the Old Harrovians to ensure a repeat of the first FA Cup Final.

The Scots Run England Ragged

The 1878 international game took place in Glasgow on 2 March, with the visitors making a number of changes in a bid to halt the run of Scottish successes.

William Mosforth, Hubert Heron, Arthur Cursham and Beaumont Jarrett were the only members of the team with previous international experience, while Edgar Lyttleton (Old Etonians), John Wylie (Wanderers), Conrad Warner (Upton Park) and Percy Fairclough (Old Foresters) were included for their only England appearances.

Henry Wace (Wanderers), who had gained Blues at Cambridge for both Rugby and Association Football, played the first of three England games at inside right. John Hunter (Sheffield) made the first of seven England appearances, while the most notable newcomer in the team was N C Bailey (Clapham Rovers), playing the first of nineteen games in an England shirt, over a ten-year period, prior to serving on the FA Committee.

England had fielded a side they thought capable of defeating the Scots. However, the home side had other ideas, as they scored seven times past Conrad Warner in the English goal, with Wylie and Cursham replying for the visitors, who returned home with a humiliating 7–2 defeat. It was apparent that England would have to change their style of play if they were to compete against the Scottish passing game, which was far more productive than the English style, which saw dribbling as the most essential part of the game.

A Fifth FA Cup Final Success for the Wanderers

The 1878 FA Cup Final took place at the Oval on 23 March, with the Wanderers selecting the following team:

J Kirkpatrick

A Stratford   W Lindsay

A F Kinnaird (captain)   F T Green   C H Wollaston

H Heron   J G Wylie   H Wace   C A Denton   J Kenrick

The Royal Engineers fielded the following eleven:

L B Friend

H H Barnett   F Bond

J H Cowan   C E Haynes   F C Heath

R S Hedley (capt.)   M Lindsay   C B Mayne   W G Morris O E Ruck

While the majority of the Wanderers team had enjoyed previous FA Cup Final and international experience, Ruck remained the only member of the Royal Engineers' 1875 FA Cup-winning side. Wanderers dominated the early play, with Kinnaird and Wace creating problems for the Engineers' defence, which resulted in a goal within minutes of the kick-off when Kenrick converted an excellent pass from Henry Wace. However, the army side soon settled down to their combination game, as they sought an equalising goal.

Midway through the first half, Kirkpatrick, the Wanderers' goalkeeper, sustained a broken arm, which ultimately led to the Engineers levelling the scores through inside forward Morris as the cup holders were re-arranging their defensive line-up to compensate for the loss of their custodian.

The Wanderers then began to concentrate on their wing play, hoping to unsettle the Engineers' defence, with Denton and Kenrick on the left, while Heron and Wollaston concentrated on the right flank. However, their second goal arrived from an unexpected source when Arthur Kinnaird scored direct from a free kick to secure a half-time lead for the Wanderers. Following the half-time break, the Engineers began the second half in fine spirits as they attacked the Wanderers' defence in pursuit of an equaliser. They thought it had been secured when Hedley steered the ball between the Wanderers' posts, but it was disallowed owing to an off-side decision. Midway through the half, the Wanderers secured a third goal against the run of play when Kenrick converted an excellent cross from Hubert Heron to score his second goal of the game.

As the game reached its final quarter, the Engineers continued in their efforts to reduce the arrears, with Ruck and Hedley exerting pressure on the Wanderers' defence. However, their efforts proved fruitless, as the cup holders held on to win their fifth FA Cup Final by three goals to one. Without the likes of Merriman, Marindin, Renny-Tailyour and Von Donop, the Royal Engineers were hardly the force of days gone by, as other teams copied and perfected the art of the passing game.

The Wanderers' Demise

Following their third successive FA Cup Final victory, the Wanderers were invited by the Football Association Committee to retain the trophy, however, the offer was refused by the cup holders, who returned the cup to the Football Association headquarters.

Old Boys' teams became a little more successful during the latter stages of the 1870s, as players with clubs like the Wanderers tended to play for their old school rather than club sides, which eventually led to the demise of the Wanderers.

The 1879 season saw the Wanderers drawn against the Old Etonians in the first round of the FA Cup, which resulted in a 7–2 victory for the Old Boys, while the following season saw the Wanderers once again defeated by the Old Etonians, as the five times FA Cup winners' reign came to an end.

Unable to field a side for the 1880 FA Cup competition, the Wanderers withdrew, never to play football again.

Association Football owes much to the pioneering Wanderers team, who had been the finest side in England during the 1870s, with a team that boasted many international players like R W S Vidal, the finest dribbler of the ball of his time, Charles Alcock, the founding father of the Association game and Arthur Kinnaird, who eventually appeared in nine FA Cup Finals (three with the Wanderers and six with the Old Etonians). Kenrick, Lindsay, Stratford and Hubert Heron had appeared in all three of the 1876, 1877 and 1878 Cup-winning sides, while Charles Wollaston had played in all five of the Wanderers' Cup-winning teams. The Wanderers were not prepared to exist as a second-rate team, hence their decision to disband. While they would be lost in the history of the Association game, the Wanderers had certainly made their mark.

Chapter VII

THE OLD ETONIANS AND CLAPHAM ROVERS WIN THE FA CUP – 1878 TO 1880

1878–79

THE OLD ETONIANS WIN THE FA CUP IN THEIR THIRD FINAL APPEARANCE

ENGLAND WIN A NINE-GOAL THRILLER AGAINST THE SCOTS

A NARROW VICTORY AGAINST THE WELSH

1879–80

CLAPHAM ROVERS SECURE THE FA CUP

SCOTLAND WIN A HIGH-SCORING ENCOUNTER

A FORTUNATE WIN AT WREXHAM

THE GROWTH OF THE NORTHERN CLUBS

Clapham Rovers Secure a Place in the Final

With the increase in teams applying for entry into the 1879 FA Cup competition, the early rounds commenced during the latter months of 1878 in an effort to complete the early stages of the competition for what had become the most coveted football trophy in England. Though the FA Cup would continue to be dominated by the Old Boys' clubs during the 1878–79 season, the spirited clubs of the industrial north had begun to show that they, too, had an important part to play in the growth of the Association game.

The early rounds of the competition saw the Old Etonians defeat the Wanderers; Oxford University accounted for the Royal Engineers by four goals to nil; Darwen secured an excellent 4–1 victory against Eagley; Remnants defeated Pilgrims by six goals to two; while Clapham Rovers inflicted a 10–1 defeat on Forest School, all to progress to the third round. These were joined by Minerva, Nottingham Forest, Old Harrovians, Barnes, Swifts and Cambridge University.

All five of the third round ties were keenly fought with Darwen, Oxford University and Clapham Rovers securing quarter-final places, following odd-goal victories against Remnants, Barnes and Cambridge University. Nottingham Forest defeated Old Harrovians by two goals to nil. Old Etonians enjoyed a 5–2 success against Minerva, and the Swifts received a bye to complete the quarter-final line-up.

Six teams were involved in the quarter-finals, which saw Clapham Rovers secure an 8–1 victory against the Swifts. Nottingham Forest managed a 2–1 win against Oxford University, while the third quarter-final tie between

Darwen and the Old Etonians proved to be the most exciting game in the history of the FA Cup competition.

The tie took place at the Oval where Darwen were 5–1 down with twenty minutes remaining. However, the Lancashire side fought back magnificently to level the scores to secure a replay at the Oval, which once again ended all square.

Now exhausted by a third trip to the capital city, the Darwen side suffered a 6–2 defeat in the second replay. They had shown such an excess of effort and spirit, however, that other teams in the north might be encouraged to challenge the domination of the Old Boys' teams in the south. Of the three teams remaining in the competition, Clapham Rovers were the fortunate side to receive a bye into the final, where they were joined by the Old Etonians, who had secured a 2–1 victory against Nottingham Forest, with the final again taking place at the Oval on 29 March.

The Welsh National Team Visit the Oval

January 18, 1879 saw the visit of the Welsh national team to the Oval for their first encounter against the English national side.

The Welsh were not a particularly strong team, having suffered a 9–0 defeat against Scotland during the previous season. However, the Association game had been growing steadily in North Wales for a number of years with teams from Bangor, Bala, Corwen and Chirk visiting English clubs. This led to Mr G A Clay-Thomas, a Welshman living in London, to organise international fixtures against Ireland, Scotland and England.

England included N C Bailey (Clapham Rovers), Arthur Cursham (Notts County), Henry Wace (Wanderers) and William Mosforth (Wednesday) from the team that had suffered a humiliating 7–2 defeat in Glasgow, while William Clegg (Sheffield) and L Bury (Old Etonians) were recalled for their second and final England appearances.

Five players were given their international debuts, including Rupert Anderson and Herbert Whitfield from the Old Etonians, who both made only single appearances for their country.

Anderson, usually a forward player, played in goal against the Welsh, while Whitfield, a Cambridge Blue at athletics and real tennis, as well as a county cricketer with Sussex, played in his only England game. Thomas Sorby (Sheffield), like Whitfield, enjoyed a goal-scoring debut, while Claude Wilson and Edward Parry of Oxford University completed the England line-up. Parry represented England on three occasions, while Wilson played twice for his country, prior to suffering a tragic death weeks before his twenty-third birthday. England were surprised by the level of skill shown by the Welsh team. However, they managed to win by two goals to one, with Sorby and Whitfield scoring the all-important goals.

A Narrow Victory for the Old Etonians

The extended 1878–79 season saw the FA Cup Final take place at the Oval on 29 March, with the England versus Scotland game during the following week. Clapham Rovers fielded the following eleven in their first FA Cup Final appearance:

R H Birkett

R A Ogilvie (captain)   E Field

N C Bailey   J F Prinsep   F L Rawson

A J Stanley   S W Scott   H S Bevington   E F Growse   C Keith-Falconer

The Old Etonians selected the following team:

J P Hawtrey

E Christian   L Bury

A F Kinnaird (captain)   E Lubbock   C J Clerke

N Pares   H C Goodhart   H Whitfield   J B Chevallier   H Beaufoy

Charles Alcock was the official match referee.

Clapham dominated the early stages of the final, with N C Bailey making two excellent attempts on the Etonian goal, while Herbert Whitfield made a fine run at the Clapham fullbacks with little assistance from his forwards, who were well held by Bailey and Prinsep at the heart of the Rovers' defence.

As the game continued to be dominated by both defences, the first half ended goalless. A much needed goal arrived midway through the second half when, following an excellent run by Goodhart, Clerke scored what was to be the only goal of the game to secure the FA Cup for the Old Etonians in arguably the poorest FA Cup Final to date.

Whitfield had been the most skilful player on view, while Bailey and Prinsep had performed soundly in the Rovers' defence. However, more important to the Old Etonians was their first FA Cup success in their third final appearance.

Vale of Leven's Hat-trick of Scottish Cup Victories

North of the border, where the Queens Park Club had reigned supreme, Vale of Leven had recently won the Scottish FA Cup for the third successive year. However, the 1879 victory had been marred by the failure of Glasgow Rangers to turn up for the replay following a disallowed goal in the previous final.

Queens Park soon returned to former glories, unlike the Wanderers and Royal Engineers, whose great days were behind them.

England Win a Thrilling Game

A week after the FA Cup Final, the Scottish national team arrived at the Oval, seeking a fourth successive victory against the English, who included Birkett, Prinsep, Sparkes and Bailey from the successful Clapham Rovers club.

Reginald Birkett had previously represented England at Rugby. James Prinsep's career lay in military service rather than sport. Francis Sparkes made two further appearances for his country, while Norman Bailey enjoyed a long and distinguished international career with England. Bailey, Henry Wace and William Mosforth were the only players retained from the victory against Wales, while E C (Charles) Bambridge (Swifts), Harold Morse (Notts Rangers), Edward Christian (Old Etonians), Arnold Hills (Oxford University) and Arthur Goodyer (Nottingham Forest) were all given their England debuts. However, with the exception of Bambridge, one of the finest dribblers of the ball in the land, who would eventually play eighteen games for England, in which he would score on eleven occasions, the remaining members of the team were all making their only international appearances.

In the most exciting England and Scotland game to date, the scores were level at four goals all with five minutes remaining, when the Scots scored what they believed to be the winning goal. However, the referee disallowed the goal owing to an off-side decision. The English forwards raced upfield to score the winning goal to secure their first victory against the Scots since 1873, with E C Bambridge (2), Bailey, Goodyer and Mosforth scoring for the home side.

Clapham Rovers Return to the Oval

As the decade headed towards its close, a larger number of teams from the Lancashire and Midlands areas of England began to enter the FA Cup competition. The likes of Blackburn Rovers and Aston Villa reached the third round of the 1879–80 competition. However, Blackburn were well beaten at Nottingham Forest by six goals to nil, while Villa scratched from the competition upon hearing that they had been drawn against three times finalists Oxford University for a place in the fourth round. Clapham Rovers progressed to the fourth round with a 7–0 victory against Pilgrims; the Old Etonians accounted for the Wanderers by three goals to one; Royal Engineers secured a 2–0 success against Old Harrovians; and Hendon, Greyfriars, Sheffield, West End and Maidenhead received byes.

Clapham Rovers' FA Cup success continued in the fourth round with a 2–0 home win against Hendon. Old Etonians had little difficulty in defeating West End by five goals to one, while Nottingham Forest progressed to the quarter-finals when the Sheffield Club refused to play a period of extra time following a 2–2 draw, which resulted in disqualification for the Yorkshire side.

Oxford University and the Royal Engineers completed the quarter-final line-up with narrow 1–0 victories against Maidenhead and Greyfriars.

Five of the most skilful sides in England remained in the competition at the quarter-final stage. Nottingham Forest received a bye into the semi-finals, while Clapham Rovers avenged their 1879 FA Cup Final defeat with a 1–0 win against the Old Etonians to progress to the semi-finals where they were joined by Oxford University, who had secured a 1–0 victory against the Royal Engineers in a replayed tie. With three teams remaining in the competition, the Clapham Rovers side received a bye into the final for the second successive year, where they met Oxford University, who had secured a 1–0 victory against Nottingham Forest. The final was due to take place at the Oval on 10 April.

The Scots Win by the Odd Goal in Nine

The 1880 international matches took place within a couple of days of each other with the Scottish game in Glasgow on 13 March, while the Welsh fixture took place at Wrexham on 15 March, with Thomas Brindle (Darwen), Edwin Luntley (Nottingham Forest), Francis Sparkes (Clapham Rovers), John Hunter (Wednesday) and William Mosforth (Wednesday) appearing in both games. Mosforth, Sparkes, Bailey and E C Bambridge were retained by the England selectors from the 1879 victory against the Scots, while Charles Wollaston (Wanderers) returned to the side for his final England appearance.

Harry Swepstone (Pilgrims) made the first of six appearances in goal, while Segar Bastard (Upton Park), who had officiated at the 1878 FA Cup Final, and Sam Widdowson (Notts County), generally acknowledged as the inventor of the shin guard, completed the England line-up for their single international appearances.

As in the previous season, the game with Scotland turned out to be a most exciting encounter, in which the Scots narrowly won by five goals to four, with Bambridge (2), Sparkes and Mosforth on target for the visitors.

England's Narrow Victory in Wrexham

Two days after the defeat in Glasgow, the England side travelled to Wrexham for their first international game on Welsh soil with Luntley, Brindle, Sparkes, Hunter and Mosforth retaining their places from the visit to Glasgow, while the remaining members of the England side were all making their international debuts. John Sands (Nottingham Forest) made his only England appearance in goal, while Thomas Marshall (Darwen) and Edward Johnson (Stoke) were included for the first of their two England games.

Fred Hargreaves (Blackburn Rovers) became the first Rovers player to wear an England shirt, while Harry Cursham (Notts County), the younger brother of Arthur, made the first of eight England appearances, in which he scored on five occasions.

Clement Mitchell (Upton Park), an accomplished county cricketer with

Kent, who would score five goals in as many games, completed the England line-up.

As in the previous season, the Welsh team were hardly a walkover, as the England side returned home with a narrow 3–2 victory, with Sparkes (2) and Brindle scoring the English goals.

Clapham's FA Cup Success

A crowd in excess of 6,000 arrived at the Oval to watch the 1880 FA Cup Final between Clapham Rovers, the losing finalists in 1879, and Oxford University, who were making their fourth and last FA Cup Final appearance. Clapham Rovers selected the following eleven:

R H Birkett

R A Ogilvie (captain) E Field

V Weston N C Bailey A J Stanley

H Brougham F J Sparkes F Barry E A Ram C Lloyd-Jones

Oxford University selected the following players:

P C Parr

C W Wilson C J S King

F A Phillips B Rogers G B Childs

F D Crowdy J B Lubbock R T Heygate (captain) J Eyre E H Hill

Major Francis Marindin was the appointed match referee.

Five members of the Clapham team had appeared in the 1879 final, while Oxford, on the other hand, were not as strong as in previous seasons, which made Clapham marginal favourites to win the cup.

Oxford had the better of the early exchanges, which saw Phillips narrowly miss the Rovers' goalpost, following an excellent run by Hill. However, Clapham soon responded as Sparkes and Lloyd-Jones went round the University defence, resulting in Ram hitting a post with a fine shot. With the first half ending goalless, the University side had the advantage of a gusty wind behind them during the second period of play, which resulted in three quick corners, ably dealt with by the Rovers' defence, much to the annoyance of the tiring Oxford defence, who had been constantly tormented by Francis Sparkes. However, with the prospect of extra time imminent, Sparkes made a clever run down the wing, crossed to the waiting Lloyd-Jones who had the simple task of slotting the ball between the Oxford goalposts to secure a one-goal lead for Clapham. Oxford had little time to recover as the final whistle sounded, with Rovers earning a well-deserved victory in a most entertaining final. However, like Oxford, this was their last appearance in an FA Cup Final.

The Growth Continues in the North

Throughout the 1870s, the Wanderers, Royal Engineers, Oxford University, Old Etonians and a few other Old Boys' teams had dominated the FA Cup competition, while the English national team consisted mainly of players from the Old Boys' clubs. With the arrival of the 1880s, however, the amateur teams in the south of England became less successful as clubs from the industrial north began to compete on level terms. Clubs from the north of England tended to draw upon working men, who were usually fitter and more skilful than the gentlemen in the south, who regarded the Association game purely as a form of exercise, while the players from the industrial towns saw it as a way out of their daily drudgery in the coal mines or cotton mills.

The late 1870s had seen a steady drift of players from Scotland joining the clubs in the north of England, with the offer of reasonably paid employment, as the paying of players was strictly against the Association Rules. However, there had been various accusations that the Darwen Club had offered James Love and Fergie Suter financial inducements to sign for the Lancashire side. While not denying that their employment in Darwen was far better paid than their previous jobs in Glasgow, Love and Suter insisted that they played for Darwen on an amateur basis.

Lancashire teams such as Bolton Wanderers were regularly seeking competition against the more skilful sides, which resulted in friendly games against Blackburn Rovers, Preston North End and Blackburn Olympic, as well as prestigious fixtures against teams north of the Border, such as Third Lanark, Dumbarton, Hibernian and Vale of Leven, while Blackburn Rovers, who were arguably the most ambitious club in Lancashire, had an even more comprehensive list of fixtures, despite not entering the FA Cup competition until the 1879–80 season.

Darwen, Bolton Wanderers and Blackburn Rovers were a few years ahead in their development compared with the likes of Preston North End, Everton, Accrington and Burnley, who were all making progress, albeit at a local level, while Midlands sides such as Nottingham Forest, Notts County and Aston Villa fulfilled fixtures on parallel with the more progressive northern clubs. Derby County, Wolverhampton Wanderers, West Bromwich Albion and Stoke were continuing their transition from local football to the national stage. However, lack of finances was the main problem facing the provincial teams, a situation that remained well into the 1880s.

Chapter VIII

THE OLD BOYS ENJOY FURTHER SUCCESS IN THE FA CUP – 1880 TO 1882

1880–81
OLD CARTHUSIANS WIN THE FA CUP
ENGLAND SUFFER EMBARRASSING HOME DEFEATS AGAINST WALES AND SCOTLAND
1881–82
OLD ETONIANS' SECOND FA CUP VICTORY
VILLA'S VAUGHTON AND BROWN SCORE NINE GOALS BETWEEN THEM, AGAINST THE LUCKLESS IRISH
SCOTLAND AND WALES INFLICT FIVE GOAL DEFEATS ON ENGLAND
CHARLES CLEGG'S CONCERNS
MR JACKSON'S EXCELLENT IDEA

The Year of the Charterhouse Boys

The 1880–81 FA Cup competition saw more teams from outside of the capital city reach the latter stages of the tournament. The Wednesday inflicted a 2–0 defeat on Turton, while the ever improving Aston Villa secured a 3–1 victory against Notts County to progress to the fourth round.

Glasgow Rangers suffered a 6–0 defeat against the Royal Engineers, Romford enjoyed a 2–0 success against Reading Abbey, while the Old Etonians scored three goals without reply against Hertfordshire Rangers.

Cup holders Clapham Rovers narrowly defeated the Swifts by the odd goal in three, while Darwen, Great Marlow, Grey Friars, Old Carthusians, Stafford Road Works and Upton Park received byes into the fourth round.

Old Carthusians produced the surprise of the fourth round with a 2–1 victory against the Royal Engineers. Romford and Stafford Road Works progressed to the quarter-finals following odd-goal wins against Great Marlow and Aston Villa, while Clapham Rovers managed a 5–4 success against Upton Park.

Old Etonians defeated Grey Friars by four goals to nil to secure a place in the final half a dozen teams where they were joined by Darwen, who had accounted for the Wednesday by five goals to one. Darwen's excellent FA Cup run continued in the quarter-finals with a 15–0 victory against the luckless Romford team.

Old Carthusians recorded a relatively easy 4–1 success against Clapham Rovers, while the Old Etonians completed the semi-final line-up with a 2–1 success against Stafford Road Works. With three teams remaining at the semi-final stage of the competition, the Old Etonians received a bye into the final, where they were joined by the Old Carthusians, who had little difficulty in defeating Darwen by four goals to one to reach their only FA Cup Final. This would take place at the Oval on 9 April.

An Excellent Win for the Welsh

The 1881 international games saw the Welsh national side visit Blackburn on 26 February, while the Scotland game took place at the Oval on 12 March.

England selected an inexperienced team against Wales with A L (Arthur) Bambridge (Swifts), the third of three brothers to play for his country, making his debut, while John Hargreaves (Blackburn Rovers) joined his brother Fred for the first of two international appearances. John Hunter and William Mosforth (Wednesday) were retained from the previous season's victory in Wrexham, while Tom Marshall (Darwen) played his final game in defence in an England side that included single appearances for Harvey (Wednesbury Strollers) and George Tait (Birmingham Excelsior).

John Hawtrey (Old Etonians) and 'Tot' Rostron (Darwen) made the first of their two England appearances, while Jimmy Brown (Blackburn Rovers) completed the England line-up for the first of five international games in which he scored on three occasions. England were a little overconfident against the Welsh who recorded their first victory on English soil with a 1–0 success. However, worse was to follow a couple of weeks later when Scotland visited the Oval.

England Are Humiliated

England retained Hawtrey, Rostron, Hunter and John Hargreaves after the Welsh defeat for the visit of the Scottish national side, while there were recalls for N C Bailey (Clapham Rovers), E C Bambridge (Swifts) and Clement Mitchell (Upton Park).

Claude Wilson (Oxford University) and Edgar Field (Clapham Rovers) made their final England appearances, while George Holden (Wednesbury Old Athletic) and Reginald Macauley (Old Etonians) completed the England team. Holden, a skilful outside right, made four appearances for his country, while Macauley, soon to be the Amateur Athletic Association's long jump champion, would play one game in an England shirt. England suffered a further humiliating defeat against the Scots, who returned home with a 6–1 victory, with E C Bambridge scoring the home side's consolation goal.

An Old Carthusian FA Cup Victory

The 1881 FA Cup Final saw the Old Etonians appear in their fourth final, while the Old Carthusians were making their first and only appearance in the final of the competition.

Old Etonians selected the following eleven:

J P Rawlinson

C W Foley   T H French

A F Kinnaird (captain)   B Farrer   R H Macauley

H E Goodhart   H Whitfield   P C Novelli   W J Anderson   J B T Chevallier

The Old Carthusians fielded the following players:

L F Gillett

E G Colvin   W H Norris

J F Prinsep   J Vincent   W R Page

E G Wynyard   J A Todd   E H Parry (captain)   L M Richards   W E Hensell

Old Etonians were a side full of previous FA Cup Final experience, with Arthur Kinnaird appearing in his seventh final, while the Old Carthusians were a team of little FA Cup experience, who were expected to taste defeat. However, the Old Charterhouse Boys totally dominated the first period of play, which saw them end the half one goal to the good when Richards converted a Prinsep corner between the Old Etonian goalposts.

Little changed during the second half as the Carthusians continued to dominate the proceedings, which saw Parry have a goal disallowed, owing to an off-side decision. However, Parry soon scored a further goal to secure a two-goal lead for the Carthusians. As the game entered the closing minutes, the Old Charterhouse Boys went further ahead when Todd scrambled the ball between the Etonian posts to ensure the Carthusians of a 3–0 victory. They had won the FA Cup for the only occasion.

Carthusians had handed out footballing lessons to Darwen, Clapham Rovers and the Royal Engineers on their way to the final. However, while they would continue to enter the FA Cup competition for many years to come, their future success lay in the FA Amateur Cup competition during the 1890s.

The Scottish Invasion Continues

North of the border, the Queens Park Club had defeated Dumbarton in the final of the Scottish FA Cup, while Walsall Swifts had scored the only goal of the game against Aston Villa in the final of the Birmingham Cup.

Meanwhile, in response to a number of newspaper advertisements, Scottish players continued their journey south, seeking employment in the industrial towns of Darwen, Preston and Blackburn, as well as pursuing their footballing careers, which usually offered financial inducements. The offer of payments eventually led to the Lancashire FA banning all players from north of the border.

Blackburn Rovers Reach the Final of the FA Cup

The early rounds of the 1881–82 FA Cup competition produced few surprises. Blackburn Rovers defeated Bolton Wanderers by six goals to two; Aston Villa secured a 4–1 success against Nottingham Forest; while Notts County inflicted a 5–3 defeat on Wednesbury Strollers in a tie that included two disputed goals. Following complaints from the Strollers, the game was ordered to be replayed, resulting in an 11–1 victory for the Nottingham side, with England winger Harry Cursham scoring nine of the goals. Aston Villa then managed to beat Notts County at the third attempt in the third round, only to suffer a 4–2 reverse at Wednesbury Old Alliance in round four. Upton Park and Blackburn Rovers progressed to the quarter-final stages of the competition with five-goal victories against Tottenham and Darwen.

Old Foresters defeated the Royal Engineers by the odd goal in three; Old Etonians secured a 6–3 win against Maidenhead; the Wednesday enjoyed a 3–1 success against Heeley; while Great Marlow received a walkover against Reading into the quarter-finals.

Wednesday's excellent FA Cup run continued in the quarter-finals with a 6–0 home win against Upton Park, with Cawley (3), Mosforth (2) and Rhodes on target, while Great Marlow managed a 1–0 victory against Old Foresters in a replayed tie.

Blackburn Rovers secured a 3–1 win against Wednesbury Old Alliance, while the Old Etonians completed the semi-final line-up by virtue of a bye.

Four teams remained in the competition at the semi-final stage with Blackburn Rovers drawn against Wednesday. Great Marlow were due to play the Old Etonians, who were seeking their third FA Cup Final appearance in four seasons. Rovers easily defeated the Wednesday by five goals to one, following a goalless draw, while the Old Etonians inflicted a 5–0 defeat on Great Marlow to take their place in the final at the Kennington Oval on 25 March.

The England Team Visit Belfast

The 1882 international games saw England play Ireland for the first time in Belfast on 18 February with the selectors including more players from the north and Midlands than in previous seasons. Howard Vaughton and Arthur Brown of Aston Villa made their first appearances in the attack, while the unusually named Doctor Greenwood joined his Blackburn Rovers team-mates, Jimmy Brown and Fred Hargreaves, in the England line-up. Harry Cursham (Notts County) and E C Bambridge (Swifts) were recalled by the selectors, while Robert King (Oxford University), Horace Barnet (Royal Engineers) and John Rawlinson (Old Etonians) were included for their only England appearances. Robert King would become the rector of Leigh-on-Sea, Horace Barnet retired as a colonel, following a long and distinguished army career, while John Rawlinson became a noted barrister prior to pursuing a parliamentary career. Alfred Dobson (Notts County) completed the England line-up for the first of four international appearances and was soon to be followed into the England side by his brother, Charles. Ireland were totally dominated by the visitors, who scored thirteen goals without reply with the Aston Villa pair of Vaughton and Brown scoring nine of the goals between them. Vaughton, who had joined Villa from Wednesbury Strollers just eighteen months earlier, scored five of the goals against the luckless Irish, while Brown scored four, with Jimmy Brown (2), Harry Cursham and E C Bambridge scoring the remaining England goals.

England Are No Match for the Scots

England visited Glasgow on 11 March for the annual fixture against the Scots with Howard Vaughton, Arthur Brown, E C Bambridge, D H Greenwood and Harry Cursham retaining their places from the excellent victory in Belfast. John Hunter (Wednesday), William Mosforth (Wednesday), Edward Parry (Old Carthusians) and N C Bailey (Clapham Rovers) were recalled to the side as England sought to avenge the previous season's defeat at the Oval. Harry Swepstone (Pilgrims) played his second England game in goal, while Alfred Jones (Walsall Town Swifts) made the first of three international appearances at fullback. The England changes were to no avail as Scotland won by five goals to one, with Howard Vaughton scoring the visitors' consolation goal.

England Concede Five Goals at Wrexham

England made one change in their team for the Welsh game at Wrexham on 13 March, with Percival Parr (Oxford University) replacing D H Greenwood for his only England appearance, with the visitors expecting a reasonably comfortable victory. The Welsh side fought magnificently to secure a 5–3 win, with Mosforth, Parry and Harry Cursham on target for England. While the England team had been as skilful as both the Welsh and Scottish teams, they tended to play as individuals, unlike the Welsh and Scots, who favoured the passing game in the style of the great Queens Park and Royal Engineers sides.

A Narrow Victory for the Old Boys

The 1882 FA Cup Final again took place at the Oval, with the Old Etonians selecting the following team:

J F P Rawlinson

T H French   P J de Paravicini

A F Kinnaird (captain)   C W Foley   P C Novelli

A T Dunn   R H Macauley   H C Goodhart   J B T Chevallier   W J Anderson

Blackburn Rovers selected the following eleven:

R Howarth

H McIntyre   F Suter

Fred Hargreaves (captain)   H Sharples   John Hargreaves

G Avery   J Brown   T Strachan   J Douglas   J Duckworth

Charles Clegg was appointed match referee.

Blackburn, who were the first provincial team to appear in an FA Cup Final, were without England defender D H Greenwood owing to injury. However, they were able to field a capable side, which included England internationals Fred Hargreaves, John Hargreaves and Jimmy Brown as well as Fergie Suter, who had recently signed from the Darwen Club. The Old Etonians, on the other hand, were able to field nine players with previous FA Cup Final experience. Upon winning the toss, the Old Boys decided to kick with the wind at their backs. This saw them dominate the early stages of the final with Dunn, Novelli and Macauley creating problems for the Rovers' defence, where McIntyre and Suter performed heroically. However, following an excellent through ball by Dunn, Macauley steered the ball between the Blackburn goalposts to secure a well-deserved half-time lead for the Etonians. Rovers winger, Avery, then suffered a serious leg injury, which made him a passenger for the remainder of the game. Yet the injury seemed to spur Blackburn into form as Duckworth, Douglas and John Hargreaves made valiant attempts to secure the equalising goal. Their efforts were ably dealt with by French and Foley in the Old Boys' defence.

Towards the end of the game, Rovers had a couple of chances to level the scores, which were easily dealt with by Rawlinson in the Etonian goal, while the game reached its conclusion with the Old Boys one goal to the good, to win the FA Cup for the second occasion.

The Old Etonians were the last 'All Amateur' side to win the FA Cup, as well as the last team south of Birmingham to win it during the nineteenth century. However, they appeared in their sixth final in 1883, where they met another team from Blackburn. For Blackburn Rovers, on the other hand, it was the start of a ten-year period in which they appeared in six FA Cup Finals.

Charles Clegg's Concerns

It had become more apparent during the 1881–82 season that the number of Scottish players signing for Lancashire clubs had increased, which resulted in the likes of Blackburn Rovers, Bolton Wanderers, Preston North End and Darwen fielding as many Scotsmen in their team as Englishmen, owing mainly to the offer of unofficial payments.

A concerned Charles Clegg felt that paying wages to players placed power into the hands of betting men, thus encouraging wide-scale gambling. This eventually resulted in the Football Association Committee introducing a rule barring the paying of players, other than for expenses or lost time at work. Clubs found guilty of paying players were to be excluded from the FA Cup competition and subsequently banned by the FA. Of further concern to Mr Clegg were the now regular defeats at international level, which led to Mr N L (Pa) Jackson, the assistant secretary of the FA, to arrange a meeting for 26 October to resolve the problem.

'Pa' Jackson's Corinthian Idea

Mr Jackson, who believed that the regular defeats were due to lack of under-standing rather than skill, suggested that the Corinthian Football Club be formed with the finest players in England gathered together to develop a team spirit equal to that of the Scots. As a club, the Corinthians were not allowed to enter the FA Cup competition, and only public school and university players were allowed membership, as the club was to run on a strictly amateur basis. Mr Jackson's idea of forming the 'Corinthian' team eventually saw nine of their players represent England against the Scots during the 1885–86 season, while the entire England team consisted of players with 'Corinthian' connections in a 5–1 victory against Wales in 1894.

Time and again during the Victorian period, the Corinthians showed that they were as skilful as any team in the land, as victories against Preston North End and Blackburn Rovers when they were reigning FA Cup holders confirmed. However, while they were barred from entering into the FA Cup competition, the Corinthians supplied in excess of seventy players for the England team during the nineteenth century. This included A M and P M Walters, R E Foster, E C Bambridge, Tinsley Lindley, W N Cobbold and Gilbert O Smith. 'Pa' Jackson's excellent idea served England well in their 'hour of need', while the name 'Corinthian' forever evoked the highest ideals in sport.

A Change in the FA Rules

On 6 December 1882, Major Francis Marindin chaired a meeting of the English FA, attended by members of the Irish, Welsh and Scottish Football Associations, to discuss a number of changes in the Rules of the Association game, which resulted in a joint decision to fit a crossbar to the goalposts rather than rely on a piece of tape, while a standard-sized ball was suggested to be used by all teams who were members of the various Football Associations. One-handed throw-ins were now banned, while the two-handed throw-in, used by teams north of the border, was now the accepted method under the FA Rules.

The Question of Professionalism

Once again the question of professionalism arose. The FA was well aware of its existence and they sought a solution to the problem of the game becoming a money-making business. Charles Alcock, Francis Marindin and Arthur Kinnaird now saw their original ideas questioned as teams from the north and Midlands sought to control their own destinies.

The rules set up by the Football Association were very much under scrutiny as teams from the north would go to any lengths to be successful, even if it meant paying financial inducements to players.

Chapter IX

TWO TEAMS FROM BLACKBURN WIN THE FA CUP – 1882 TO 1884

1882–83
THE OLYMPIC DO BLACKBURN PROUD
A CLEMENT MITCHELL HAT TRICK AGAINST THE WELSH
ENGLAND SCORE SEVEN AGAINST IRELAND
SCOTLAND SECURE VICTORY BY THE ODD GOAL IN FIVE
1883–84
THE FA CUP REMAINS IN BLACKBURN
HARRY CURSHAM SCORES A HAT-TRICK IN BELFAST IN HIS FINAL ENGLAND
APPEARANCE
A SINGLE GOAL DEFEAT IN GLASGOW
BROMLEY-DAVENPORT SCORES TWICE AGAINST WALES
WILLIAM SUDELL MAKES HIS MOVE AGAINST THE FA COMMITTEE

Blackburn Olympic Secure a Place in the Final

The 1882–83 season saw eighty-four teams from all corners of the United Kingdom enter the FA Cup competition. During the early rounds, teams tended to be drawn against each other on a local basis, all pursuing the dream of reaching the latter stages when they could be drawn against the Old Boys' teams in the south of England. Bolton Wanderers enjoyed an excellent start to the competition with a 6–1 victory against Bootle in the first round, with William Struthers, a recent signing from Glasgow Rangers, scoring five of the Bolton goals. Struthers scored two further goals in a 3–1 success against Liverpool Ramblers in round two. However, Wanderers' interest in the competition ended in the third round where they suffered a defeat against the Druids following two drawn games.

Aston Villa's FA Cup run began with four goal home wins against Walsall Swifts and Wednesbury Old Athletic in the opening two rounds, and their winning streak continued with a 3–1 success against Aston Unity in the third round.

Eagley reached the fourth round following victories against local teams, prior to suffering a 2–1 defeat against the Druids for a place in the quarter-finals. Blackburn Olympic inflicted a 2–0 defeat on the Church Club, while Aston Villa narrowly defeated Walsall Town by the odd goal in three to proceed to the quarter-finals.

Old Carthusians defeated a weakened Royal Engineers team by six goals to two. Notts County secured a 4–1 win against the Wednesday, Hendon and the Old Etonians progressed to the last eight at the expense of Great Marlow and the Swifts, and Clapham Rovers received a bye into the quarter-finals.

All four quarter-final ties produced outstanding games. Blackburn Olympic defeated the Druids by four goals to nil, Old Etonians secured a 4–1 victory against Hendon, and the Old Carthusians managed to win a close encounter against Clapham Rovers by five goals to three. However, the most memorable tie of the round saw Aston Villa play Notts County at the Castle Ground, Nottingham.

County raced into a three-goal lead with Harry Cursham scoring a hat-trick, but Villa clawed their way back into the game to level the scores. However, William Gunn regained the lead for the Nottingham side in the final quarter of the game, which left Villa with little option than to concentrate on an all-out attack, hoping to secure the equalising goal.

With two minutes remaining, a Villa player hit a goal-bound shot, which seemed to be fisted out by Harry Cursham, who denied touching the ball, in what would be known as the 'long arm' incident.

Villa's protests were in vain as County joined Blackburn Olympic, Old Carthusians and the Old Etonians in the semi-finals of the FA Cup. Blackburn Olympic surprised many in the semi-finals by inflicting a 4–0 defeat on the Old Carthusians, while the Old Etonians managed a narrow 2–1 victory against Notts County to secure their third successive FA Cup Final appearance, which would take place at the Oval on the final day of March.

Wales Are Well Beaten

The 1883 international games took place during the latter stages of the FA Cup competition and began with the visit of the Welsh national side to the Oval on 3 February. The England selectors chose an attacking side in the hope of avenging the 1881 and 1882 defeats against Wales.

Arthur Cursham (Notts County) joined his brother Harry in the England team. Clement Mitchell (Upton Park) was recalled for his third appearance for his country, while E C and A L Bambridge (Swifts) were chosen together for the first time.

Scottish-born defender, Stuart Macrae (Notts County), played the first of five England games. Bruce Russell (Royal Engineers) made a single appearance, while Henry Goodhart and Percy de Paravicini of the Old Etonians appeared in all three of the 1883 international fixtures. De Paravicini, a speedy two-footed defender, had earned a Blue at Cambridge and played county cricket for Middlesex, while Goodhart eventually became the Professor of Humanities at Edinburgh University.

N C Bailey (Clapham Rovers) retained his place in the England defence together with Harry Swepstone, the Pilgrims' goalkeeper, who had conceded fifteen goals in his three previous England appearances.

England finally found their form against the Welsh as a hat-trick by Clement Mitchell, together with further goals from Arthur Cursham and E C Bambridge, secured a 5–0 victory.

A Much Improved Irish Performance

England's game against Ireland took place in Liverpool on 24 February, with the visitors seeking to improve on their thirteen-goal defeat of the previous season. Harry Swepstone, Stuart Macrae, Henry Goodhart, Harry Cursham and Percy de Paravicini were retained from the victory against Wales, while the remaining members of the team were all being given their England debuts.

Olly Whateley (Aston Villa) made the first of two appearances as a just reward for his excellent performances in Villa's FA Cup run. Jack Hudson (Wednesday) played his only England game, while Henry Moore (Notts County), who was as good at cricket as he was at football, played the first of two international games.

Francis Pawson (Cambridge University), later to become the vicar of Ecclesfield, made one further appearance for England. Arthur Dunn (Old Etonians) played for England on four occasions, while William Neville Cobbold, who had played for Cambridge University and the Old Carthusians, was the most notable newcomer to the England side. W N Cobbold, an excellent all-round sportsman, who was considered by many to be the finest player in the land, scored on seven occasions in nine England appearances. England were once again far too skilful for the Irish, as Cobbold (2), Dunn (2), Whateley (2) and Pawson scored in a 7–0 victory.

Scotland Win by the Odd Goal in Five

The 1883 international game against Scotland took place in Sheffield on 10 March, with England hoping to improve on their dismal record of just two victories in eleven games against the Scots. Few changes were made by the England selectors from the victory against Ireland as Swepstone, de Paravicini, Macrae, Cobbold, Goodhart, Whateley and Harry Cursham retained their places, while Alfred Jones (Walsall Swifts), N C Bailey (Clapham Rovers), Clement Mitchell (Upton Park) and Arthur Cursham (Notts County) added further experience to the side. While England coped with the Scottish passing game, the visitors held on to a 3–2 win, with Mitchell and Cobbold on target for the English, who now felt that they were capable of defeating the Scots.

Blackburn Olympic's Finest Moment

A crowd in excess of 8,000 arrived at the Oval on the last day of March to watch the 1883 FA Cup Final, with Blackburn Olympic selecting the following eleven:

T Hacking

S A Warburton (captain)   J T Ward

W Astley   J Hunter   T G Gibson

T Dewhurst   A Mathews   J Yates   W Crossley   G Wilson

The Old Etonians selected the following players:

J F P Rawlinson

P J de Paravicini   T H French

A F Kinnaird (captain)   C W Foley   A T B Dunn

H W Bainbridge   J B T Chevallier   W J Andserson   H C Goodhart   R H Macauley

Charles Crump of the Birmingham FA was elected match referee.

Old Etonians were appearing in their third successive FA Cup Final. Kinnaird, Chevallier, Goodhart, French, Foley, Rawlinson and Macauley had appeared in all three, while Arthur Kinnaird was playing in his ninth final, in a game that the Old Etonians were favourites to win. Blackburn Olympic, on the other hand, had been formed only five years earlier when the Black Star and James Street football teams had joined forces as opposition to the Blackburn Rovers team.

Due mainly to the efforts of John Edmondson, the Olympic soon evolved into one of the finest sides in Lancashire, while Jack Hunter, an astute coach and tactician, taught the Olympic players the art of the passing game. Hunter, who organised many exhibition matches, had taken his team to Blackpool for a few days' relaxation prior to the final, which had been unheard of up until then.

There was little to choose between the teams during the early stages of the final, as de Paravicini and Kinnaird thwarted the Olympic attacks, while Hacking and Warburton kept the Old Boys' forwards at bay. However, the stalemate was broken following thirty minutes of play when Chevallier and Macauley began an attack and passed to Goodhart, who shot the ball between the Olympic goalposts to secure a half-time lead for the Old Boys.

Olympic came more into the game during the second half in their pursuit of an equalising goal, with their extra training now bearing fruit. Though the Old Etonians had begun to tire, the Old Boys were far from finished as Dunn and Bainbridge attacked the Blackburn goal, which resulted in Arthur Kinnaird having a goal disallowed following an infringement of the rules. Inevitably, the Olympic equaliser arrived midway through the half when winger Mathews dribbled around the Etonian defence to score an excellent individual goal. This coincided with Arthur Dunn retiring from the field of play following a heavy tackle by an Olympic defender, leaving the tiring Old Boys' team one player short with the prospect of extra time imminent. All remained equal during the first period of extra time. Following two minutes' play in the second half of extra time, Dewhurst ran at the Etonian defence, centred the ball to Crossley, who volleyed the ball through the Old Boys' goalposts to secure a 2–1 victory.

Upon receiving the FA Cup from Major Marindin, Blackburn Olympic had become the first team north of the capital city to have won the trophy, heralding the end of the southern domination of the competition. The FA Cup remained in the north and Midlands throughout the remaining years of the Victorian period. However, the amateur players from the south continued to play an important part at international level well into the following century.

The Pendulum Swings North

With the football pendulum now swinging from the south to the north, what was once the pastime of the gentlemen players in the south was becoming a serious financial business for the clubs in the north and Midlands. They now pursued success a little more vigorously, as their supporters demanded the finest players for their teams.

Successful clubs attracted more spectators, which generated extra revenue, thus enabling clubs to sign better players hoping to emulate the success of the likes of Darwen, Blackburn Rovers and Blackburn Olympic.

It had now become apparent that professionalism would be a progressive step in the growth of the Association game, with the working men of the north, who were without the private incomes of the amateur players in the south, believing that professionalism should be legalised to sustain the growth of the game. However, for the time being, the paying of players continued to be against the Rules of the Football Association Committee.

Provincial Teams Enhance Their Reputations

As the 1882–83 season came to a close, a number of provincial teams had enhanced their reputations. Aston Villa won both the Lord Mayor's Charity Cup and the Birmingham Cup. Small Heath defeated Wednesbury Old Athletic by four goals to one in the final of the Walsall Cup. West Bromwich Albion beat Stoke in the final of the Staffordshire Cup, while Blackburn Rovers, who had suffered a defeat against Darwen in the FA Cup competition, gained ample revenge by defeating Darwen in the final of the Lancashire Cup.

Accrington Suffer the Consequences

The 1883–84 season proved a little unsettling as the paying of players became an open secret, with the Football Association seeming to do little to enforce the rules concerning professionalism. A number of teams continued to object to playing FA Cup ties against professional clubs, while others felt that the introduction of professionalism would greatly improve the standard of football.

The early part of the season saw the likes of Bolton Wanderers, Preston North End, Aston Villa, Notts County and West Bromwich Albion travelling farther afield to fulfil friendly fixtures, which included trips north of the border to play the leading Scottish sides. However, success in the FA Cup competition remained the priority of the majority of clubs.

Wolverhampton Wanderers and West Bromwich Albion entered into the FA Cup competition for the first time during the 1883–84 season, with Wolves suffering a second round defeat against Wednesbury Old Athletic following a 4–1 success against Long Eaton Rangers in the first round. Albion suffered an early defeat at Wednesbury Town.

Bolton Wanderers secured victories against Bolton Olympic (9–0), Bolton Association (3–0) and Irwell Springs (8–1) to reach the fourth round, with Steel and Struthers scoring eleven of the goals between them. The Queens Park Club of Glasgow, who had entered the English FA Cup competition for the first time in five seasons, reached the fourth round stage with ease. This progress included a 15–0 success against Manchester Athletic Club in the second round.

Accrington, who had begun the season with a heavy defeat at Blackburn Rovers, improved in the following game with a 5–1 victory against Rossendale, with centre forward James Beresford scoring twice. Beresford, who usually played for the Church Club, had been given a trial by Accrington in the hope of solving their goal-scoring problems. However, following Beresford's return to the Church Club, directors of the Darwen Club accused both Accrington and the Church Club of paying Beresford, which resulted in Darwen reporting their allegations to the Football Association headquarters in London. Accrington's season continued with a second round FA Cup victory against Blackburn Park Road, but this was shortly followed by a request from the FA to answer the allegations that they had offered payments to James Beresford. The outcome of the enquiry saw the FA censure the Church Club for playing Beresford when they were aware that he also appeared for Staveley. However, no proof could be found that they had paid him to play, while Accrington finally admitted that a gentleman unconnected with the club had offered Beresford a sum of money in the hope that he would play for Accrington on a regular basis. Events proved that club secretary, Mr C F Critchley, and treasurer, John Grimshaw, were aware of the payment to Beresford, which left the FA with no other alternative than to disqualify Accrington from the FA Cup competition and to ban them from playing against other members of the English FA. However, following the resignations of both Critchley and Grimshaw, a number of clubs in Lancashire voiced the opinion that Accrington had been harshly dealt with, while the possibilities of forming a breakaway Football Association were discussed. Much to the joy of the Accrington club, the FA had second thoughts, which saw the Lancashire side reinstated to the English FA, while retaining their disqualification from the 1883–84 FA Cup competition. Meanwhile, the FA Cup had reached the fourth round stage, with sixteen teams competing for a place in the quarter-finals.

A Lancashire–Glasgow FA Cup Final

Blackburn Olympic continued their defence of the FA Cup with a 9–1 victory against Old Wykehamists in the fourth round. Their neighbours, Blackburn Rovers, secured a 5–0 home success against Staveley, while the Swifts and Northwich Victoria progressed to the quarter-finals following narrow victories against Old Foresters and Brentwood.

Notts County managed to beat Bolton Wanderers by the odd goal in three, following a two-all draw. Queens Park showed their intent by defeating Aston Villa by six goals to one, while Old Westminsters had little difficulty in securing a 5–1 success against Wednesbury Town.

The final tie of the round saw Upton Park and Preston North End play a one-all draw. However, Upton Park refused to travel to Preston for the replay, protesting to the FA that the Lancashire side had included a number of professional players in their team. As expected, the FA upheld the allegations, which resulted in Preston being dismissed from the FA Cup competition, much to the annoyance of William Sudell, who, rather than deny that his players had been offered financial inducements, suggested that the paying of players would attract more skilful players to the game. Predictably, Mr Sudell's comments fell on deaf ears as Upton Park were awarded the game to progress to the last eight. Great Lever, with six Scotsmen in their team and Burnley with seven, joined Accrington and Preston in their ban, while Walsall Town and Birmingham St George's in the Midlands received punishment for paying players for more than expenses.

The ongoing arguments were quieted in time for the FA Cup quarter-finals. Upton Park, who had secured a quarter-final place at the expense of Preston, then suffered a 3–0 defeat at Blackburn Rovers. Queens Park defeated Old Westminsters by the only goal of the game, while Notts County were a little fortunate to secure a one-nil victory against Swifts, following a one-all draw. However, Blackburn Olympic continued to dominate the competition with a 9–1 success against Northwich Victoria to take their place in the semi-finals.

Blackburn Rovers and Blackburn Olympic managed to avoid each other in the semi-finals, which left the town dreaming of an all Blackburn final. However, they were to be disappointed, as Olympic suffered a 4–1 defeat against Queens Park, while Rovers narrowly secured a 1–0 victory against Notts County to reach their second FA Cup Final. This was set at the Oval for 29 March.

England Tame the Irish

During the latter stages of the 1883–84 FA Cup competition, England played their annual fixtures against Ireland, Scotland and Wales beginning on 25 February when England selected an attacking side against Ireland in Belfast.

A L (Arthur) and E C (Charles) Bambridge were included in the attack, together with George Holden (Wednesbury Old Athletic) and Arthur Dunn (Old Etonians). Notts County were well represented by Alfred Dobson, Stuart Macrae and Harry Cursham.

Edward Johnson (Stoke) and N C Bailey (Clapham Rovers) were recalled to the defence, while William Rose, the Wolverhampton Wanderers' goal-keeper, and Joe Beverley of Blackburn Rovers were given their international debuts. As expected, England won with ease, as Harry Cursham scored a hat-trick in his final England appearance, and there were further goals from Edward Johnson (2), E C Bambridge (2) and A L Bambridge in a resounding 8–1 victory.

A Narrow Defeat in Glasgow

England made four changes in their team for the visit to Glasgow on 15 March, which saw the return of Howard Vaughton (Aston Villa), following his six goals in his three previous England appearances, while there were international debuts for William Gunn (Notts County), Charles Plumpton Wilson (Cambridge University) and William Bromley-Davenport (Old Etonians), who would all appear twice for their country. Wilson had played Rugby Union to an international level. William Gunn achieved greater fame as an international cricketer, as well as helping Nottinghamshire to secure six County Championships. Bromley-Davenport (later General Sir William) later became member of parliament for Macclesfield.

Following a 5–0 success against Ireland, the Scots were confident of stretching their winning run against England to five games, which they managed through a late goal from Dr Smith of the Mauchline Club. However, the visitors had at least deserved a share of the spoils.

England Win in Wrexham

Two days after the defeat in Glasgow, the England side travelled to Wrexham where they had previously suffered a 5–3 reverse against the Welsh. The England selectors made just one change. James Forrest (Blackburn Rovers) replaced Stuart Macrae (Notts County) for the first of eleven appearances in an England shirt. The Welsh had few answers to the skilful England forwards, as goals by Bromley-Davenport (2), Bailey and Gunn secured a 4–0 success for the English.

The FA Cup Remains in Blackburn

The 1884 FA Cup Final took place during the final week of March, with Blackburn Rovers selecting the following players:

75

H Arthur

J Beverley   F Suter

J Forrest   H McIntyre (captain)   J Lofthouse

J Douglas   John Hargreaves   J Brown   J Sowerbutts   J Inglis

Queens Park selected the following eleven:

G Gillespie

J MacDonald   W Arnott

C Campbell (captain)   J J Gow   W Anderson

J Watt   W Harrower   Dr J Smith   R M Christie   D Allan

Major Francis Marindin was the appointed match referee.

Queens Park dominated the early stages of the final, as their skilful passing game continued to baffle the Rovers' defence and eventually led to the opening goal of the game when Christie converted an Arnott cross. However, Rovers soon came more into the game, forcing Gillespie to make two fine saves, with team captain McIntyre leading by example with a number of excellent passes to his forward players.

Following a period of loose play by the Queens Park defence, James Forrest delivered an excellent pass to Jimmy Brown, who rounded two defenders, prior to crossing the ball into the Queens Park goalmouth. Gillespie rushed out of his goal, completely missing the ball, thus allowing Sowerbutts all the time in the world to score the equalising goal.

Then followed a period of even play, as the game entered the final minutes of the half. With the half-time whistle imminent, James Lofthouse returned a half-cleared ball into the Queens Park goalmouth, where James Forrest slotted the ball home to secure a half-time lead for the Lancashire side.

Blackburn continued to attack the Queens Park goal during the second period of play with Gillespie performing heroically between the posts. Jimmy Brown missed an easy chance to put the game beyond the Scots. However, Queens Park eventually came back into the game as Smith forced two excellent saves out of Herbie Arthur in the Rovers' goal.

Towards the end of the final, Major Marindin disallowed a couple of goals, which may well have changed the course of the game. However, both sets of players accepted the referee's decision and the game ended without further goals with Blackburn the victors by two goals to one.

In an exciting final, the fitter Rovers side had deservedly won the FA Cup with excellent displays by Brown, Beverley, McIntyre and Forrest, while Gillespie, Arnott, Christie and Anderson had performed admirably for the Scots. Both teams enjoyed greater success during the Victorian period, with Queens Park dominating the Scottish FA Cup competition and Rovers winning the English FA Cup on five occasions during an eight-year period.

Aston Villa Retain Two Local Trophies

As the 1883–84 season drew to a close, local cup finals became the main priority of the provincial teams with Birmingham St George's defeating West Bromwich Albion in the final of the Staffordshire Cup and Wolverhampton Wanderers registering an 11–1 victory against Hadley in the final of the Wrekin Trophy. Everton won the Liverpool Football Association Cup, while Aston Villa retained both the Birmingham Lord Mayor's Charity Cup and the Birmingham Association Cup.

The Ongoing Debate Against Professionalism

The debate on professionalism continued throughout 1884, much to the annoyance of the majority of the Football Association Committee, who felt that they would lose control of the game if the paying of players became legal. Charles Alcock argued that the professional player would enhance the Association game rather than destroy it. Mr Alcock had been the lone voice on the FA Committee to acknowledge the arrival of the professional player. However, the remaining members of the committee decided to introduce further rules to deter the growth of professionalism, which included banning all but Englishmen playing in the FA Cup competition, thus discouraging English clubs from importing players from north of the border.

Meanwhile, the Scottish Football Association were holding regular meetings to discuss the problems of professionalism, as well as their members moving south to join English clubs. This resulted in the Heart of Midlothian club receiving a ban by the Scottish FA, while two members of their team, namely McNee and Maxwell, were suspended for two years for accepting financial inducements to play for the club.

William Sudell, who was a little disappointed by the English and Scottish FAs' decision to outlaw the professional player, then chaired a series of meetings to discuss the proposal of forming the British Football Association, which would include the majority of the clubs in Lancashire, as well as the likes of Aston Villa and West Bromwich Albion. Mr Sudell's proposal for a breakaway Football Association certainly supplied food for thought for the members of the FA Committee.

Chapter X

BLACKBURN ROVERS RETAIN THE FA CUP – 1884–85

1884–85

BLACKBURN ROVERS RETAIN THE FA CUP IN A REPEAT FINAL AGAINST QUEENS
PARK

ENGLAND REMAIN UNBEATEN WITH DRAWS AGAINST SCOTLAND AND WALES

A M AND P M WALTERS MAKE THEIR ENGLAND DEBUTS

PROFESSIONALISM IS LEGALISED

A Repeat FA Cup Final

During the early rounds of the 1884–85 FA Cup competition, clubs tended to field weakened teams in their efforts to avoid the wrath of the Football Association, who had introduced further rules to discourage professionalism. However, there remained great interest in the competition as clubs sought the most coveted football trophy in the land. Accrington, who had been disqualified from the FA Cup during the previous season, managed to secure a 3–0 victory against Southport in the first round, despite leaving out a number of players who may well have been described as professional. Nevertheless, they were soon disqualified from the competition for fielding an unregistered player.

Inevitably, the decision caused local outrage as well as much animosity towards the FA, which led the *Accrington Gazette* to comment, 'If only local players could represent their clubs, it would mean poorer football for the spectators, who would not be willing to support a second rate team.' Bolton Wanderers had experienced similar problems to Accrington during the early stages of the FA Cup, which led them, together with their opponents, Preston Zingari, to withdraw from the competition to avoid punishment from the FA. Meanwhile, Blackburn Rovers and West Bromwich Albion had enjoyed reasonably comfortable passages into the fourth round, with Rovers securing an excellent victory against Blackburn Olympic in an earlier round, while Loach (2) and Bayliss were on target for Albion in a 3–0 success against Aston Villa at the local stage of the competition.

Three Old Boys' teams remained in the cup at the fourth round stage, which saw the Old Etonians inflict a 5–2 defeat on Middlesbrough, Old Carthusians score three times without reply against Grimsby Town, and the Old Wykehamists, who had suffered a 9–1 defeat against Blackburn Olympic at the same stage during the previous season, suffer a further embarrassing defeat against Queens Park by seven goals to nil. Darwen lost 3–0 to the Church Club, while Lower Darwen completed a miserable day for the town with a 1–0 reverse at Chatham. However, it had been a much better day for Nottingham, with County beating Walsall Swifts by four goals to one, while Sam Widdowson scored the only goal of the game as Forest secured a 1–0 home win against the Swifts.

Blackburn Rovers had little difficulty in accounting for Romford by eight goals to nil, while West Bromwich Albion turned up to play against the Druids, who failed to arrive at the stipulated time, which led the referee to award the game to Albion. However, when the Druids eventually arrived at the ground, Albion insisted upon playing the tie, and Loach scored the only goal of the game to secure a 1–0 win for the Black Country side.

With nine teams remaining in the competition, all but Chatham and the Old Carthusians received byes into the quarter-finals. These were eventually eight when the Old Boys inflicted a 3–0 defeat on the army side. Of the eight quarter-finalists, three teams had previously won the FA Cup, three sides had reached the semi-final stage, while West Bromwich Albion and the Church Club were quite inexperienced on the national stage. However, both performed splendidly in the quarter-finals, with Albion suffering a 2–0 defeat against Cup holders, Blackburn Rovers, while Church were narrowly beaten by the Old Carthusians by one goal to nil.

Notts County, who had suffered odd-goal defeats at the semi-final stage in each of the two previous seasons, were again out of luck following a 2–1 reverse against Queens Park in a replayed tie. Danks and Lindley were on target for Nottingham Forest, in a 2–0 success against the Old Etonians, to complete the semi-final line-up.

Blackburn Rovers had little difficulty in securing their third final appearance in four seasons with a 5–0 victory against the Old Carthusians, while the Queens Park–Nottingham Forest tie ended in a one-all draw. However, in the replay at Merchiston Park, Edinburgh, the Scots won by three goals to nil in what would be the only English FA Cup semi-final to be played north of the border. For the second year running, Blackburn Rovers and Queens Park contested the final of the English FA Cup.

The Meridian Brothers Make a Winning Debut

All three of the 1885 international games took place on English soil, with the opening game against Ireland in Manchester. The selectors chose Herbie Arthur, Joseph Lofthouse, Jimmy Brown and James Forrest from the successful Blackburn Rovers team. Goalkeeper Arthur and Lofthouse were making the first of seven international appearances, with Arthur never on the losing side, while E C Bambridge and N C Bailey joined the Blackburn quartet in all three of the 1885 England games.

The remaining members of the England team were all players with Corinthian connections. W N Cobbold was playing his third England game, Francis Pawson, lately of Cambridge University, made his second and final appearance for his country, while centre forward Benjamin Spilsbury, who had played for Derby County upon leaving university, played the first of three England games. However, the most notable newcomers in the England side were fullbacks A M and P M Walters, the Old Charterhouse boys with the Meridian initials.

Arthur Melmoth Walters and Percy Melmoth Walters were generally regarded as the finest fullbacks in England for a number of years, which was due mainly to their own defensive system based on the combination game used by the Royal Engineers during the early 1870s. The Walters brothers' England careers lasted from 1885 until 1890, with A M making nine appearances, while P M played thirteen international games. However, following the death of their brother, H M Walters, during a football game in 1890, the Walters brothers retired from international football in deference to their parents' wishes.

England beat the Irish with ease, albeit not as convincingly as in previous seasons, with Bambridge, Brown, Spilsbury and Lofthouse on target, in a 4–0 victory.

A Drawn Game with the Welsh

England made five changes in their team for the game against Wales at Blackburn on 14 March, with Henry Moore (Notts County) and James Ward (Blackburn Olympic) replacing the Walters brothers, who were unavailable, while Clement Mitchell (Upton Park) replaced W N Cobbold for his fifth international appearance.

John Dixon (Notts County), like Henry Moore, a county cricketer with Nottinghamshire, made his one England appearance at inside left, while Kenny Davenport became the first Bolton Wanderers player to represent England. However, he waited a further five seasons for his second England game. Wales managed to return home with a one-all draw, with Clement Mitchell scoring for the disappointing England side.

A Welcome Draw Against Scotland

A week following the draw at Blackburn, the Scottish national side arrived at the Oval for the final international game of the season. A M and P M Walters returned to the England side, together with W N Cobbold, while Andrew Amos (Old Carthusians), who was ordained in 1887, and Thomas Danks (Nottingham Forest) were given their England debuts.

As in the Welsh game, England managed a one-all draw with E C Bambridge on target to end the run of five successive defeats against the Scots.

Blackburn Rovers Retain the FA Cup

In a repeat of the 1884 FA Cup Final, Blackburn Rovers met Queens Park at the Oval on 4 April, with Rovers selecting the following eleven:

Arthur

Turner   Suter

Haworth   McIntyre   Forrest

Sowerbutts   Lofthouse   Douglas   Brown (captain)   Fecitt

Queens Park selected the following team:

Gillespie

Arnott   Macleod

Campbell (captain)   MacDonald   Hamilton

Anderson   Sellar   Gray   McWhannel   Allan

Major Francis Marindin once again refereed the final.

With the exception of Fecitt, Turner and Haworth, Blackburn were unchanged from the side that had won the trophy during the previous season, while Gillespie, Arnott, MacDonald, Campbell, Anderson and Allan had appeared in the Queens Park line-up in the 1884 final.

A crowd in excess of 12,000 arrived at the Oval during the Easter holidays to see Rovers take the early initiative, with Brown and Sowerbutts forcing excellent saves out of Gillespie in the Queens Park goal. However, the Scottish side soon came more into the game with fine play by Hamilton and Allan, which was firmly dealt with by Suter and McIntyre in the Rovers' defence. Halfway through the opening period of play, the ever alert Jimmy Brown rounded fullback Arnott prior to shooting against the Queens Park goalposts, which saw the ball rebound to the waiting James Forrest, who had the simple task of guiding the ball between the posts to secure a one-goal lead for Blackburn. As the half-time whistle approached, Arnott crossed the ball into the Rovers' goal area, which seemed to cross the goal line. However, Major Marindin awarded a foul to the Lancashire side, insisting that a Queens Park player had handled the ball. So the half ended with Blackburn one goal to the good.

Rovers continued to attack the Queens Park goal during the second period of play, resulting in a further goal by Jimmy Brown following excellent work by Forrest and Fecitt. This seemed to put the result beyond doubt. However, Queens Park tried desperately to reduce the arrears during the final quarter of the game as shots from Gray, Sellar and Anderson forced excellent saves out of Herbie Arthur in the Blackburn goal. Queens Park's efforts were to no avail as the final whistle sounded with Rovers the victors by two goals to nil. The Scottish team were a little unhappy that the Lancashire side had fielded players whose amateur status was questionable. Yet there was now little doubt that the professional player was here to stay.

Professionalism Is Accepted

As the 1884–85 season came to a close, the question of professionalism remained the most important issue throughout the land as the game had been deeply imbued with amateurism following the formation of the English Football Association in 1863 by a group of gentlemen associated with the Old Boys' clubs.

England had become a divided country, which meant that the decision on professionalism could no longer be avoided. The FA called a special meeting on 20 July to discuss this outstanding issue. Eventually, following the meeting at the Anderton's Hotel, the FA Committee, through Dr E S Morley, decided to legalise professionalism, with stringent rules.

1. Professional players would be allowed to compete in FA Cup, County Cup and inter-Association matches, providing they were born in the area in which they played, or resided within six miles of their club's ground for a period of two years.
2. Professional players could not play for more than one club during a season, unless obtaining special permission, while they would not be allowed to serve on any association committee, or represent any club at a meeting of the Football Association.
3. Professional players were to be registered annually in a book kept by the Football Association. They could not appear for a club unless they had been officially registered.

Charles Alcock, who had previously acknowledged that professionalism would play an important part in the growth of the Association game, hoped that through his leadership the decision to accept professionalism would be acceptable to all. However, William and Charles Clegg of the Sheffield Association felt that football would become a money-making sport, while Pierce-Dix of the Sheffield Club, who had refereed the 1881 FA Cup Final, argued that 'professionalism in football was an evil, and as such, should be repressed'.

With the legalising of the professional player, there remained a clear line between the amateurs and the professionals, with the amateurs continuing to run the game, while the professional players had become employees, who could now be controlled by those with financial means with little opportunity to argue their point. However, while a number of amateur teams continued to compete favourably against the professional clubs, the growth of clubs such as Aston Villa, Preston North End and Blackburn Rovers saw many of the leading amateur sides revert to playing the occasional friendly fixture. While professionalism was legalised in England in time for the 1885–86 season, the Scottish FA continued to outlaw professionals, which led to sixty-eight players receiving bans from playing any game on Scottish soil. The Scots went a step further by asking the English FA to ban James Forrest from their national team as they regarded him as a professional player. However, while the English FA were sympathetic towards the Scots, they were men of their word and would not be dictated to by the men of the Scottish FA.

Other Associations in England were a little slow in adjusting to professionalism. However, with the Association game booming, the changeover gained momentum and gave the likes of William Sudell of Preston North End the freedom to create a team capable of beating any in the land. In the Birmingham area, William McGregor worked tirelessly to assist Aston Villa in their changeover to professionalism. William McGregor had arrived in Birmingham from Perthshire during the late 1870s to open a draper's shop in the Newtown area, just a mile away from the Villa ground. Having a keen interest in the Association game, Mr McGregor was immediately impressed by Villa's strong Scottish connection, which resulted in him accepting an invitation to join the Villa Committee, following discussions with secretary George Ramsay and team captain, Archie Hunter. While not an early supporter of professionalism, Mr McGregor, like Charles Alcock before him, realised that professionalism had become an inevitable part in the growth of the Association game.

Many were surprised that the kindly God-fearing gentleman was an advocate of professionalism. However, Mr McGregor, who had always been interested in the welfare of his fellow man, believed that by encouraging the citizens of Birmingham to play and watch football matches it would keep men off the streets and away from local drinking houses, thus promoting local pride and loyalty.

Chapter XI

BLACKBURN ROVERS COMPLETE AN FA CUP HAT-TRICK – 1885–86

1885–86
BLACKBURN'S FA CUP HAT TRICK
BENJAMIN SPILSBURY SCORES FOUR AGAINST IRELAND
ENGLAND REMAIN UNBEATEN
THE PROBLEMS OF THE PROFESSIONAL CLUBS
ROYALTY MAKES A VISIT TO A PROFESSIONAL FOOTBALL GAME

Professionalism Creates Problems in the FA Cup

Success in the FA Cup competition remained the dream of the majority of teams as the 1885–86 season commenced. However, the recently instigated rules on professionalism would produce many farcical results, as clubs were unable to field their strongest sides.

The first round produced many high-scoring games, including a 15–0 victory for Notts County against Thornhill United, while Burnley, who were making their first appearance in the FA Cup, suffered an 11–1 defeat against Darwen Old Wanderers. Burnley were forced to field their reserve side, owing to the number of Scots in their first eleven, which led them to withdraw from the Lancashire Cup competition because of the same restrictions on their Scottish players.

As the FA Cup competition progressed, there were further repercussions when Bolton Wanderers drew with Rawtenstall in a second round tie. Rawtenstall were then expelled from the competition for failing to adhere to the rules of professionalism, leaving Bolton with a third round game against Preston North End. However, following a 3–2 defeat against Preston, it was discovered that Bolton had fielded Jack Powell, who had taken a job in Ruabon without informing the club committee, while Preston had fielded a couple of Scottish players, resulting in both teams receiving FA Cup bans.

With the FA Cup competition becoming more farcical, owing mainly to the professional clubs fielding their reserve sides, minor teams such as Staveley, Brentwood, South Shore, Church, Redcar, Davenham and Middlesbrough were able to progress to the fifth round. Meanwhile West Bromwich Albion made their way into the fifth round following excellent victories against Wednesbury Old Athletic and Wolverhampton Wanderers.

Small Heath Alliance had secured wins against the experienced Derby

County and Darwen teams to join the last sixteen teams remaining in the competition, while the Old Boys' clubs were represented by the Old Carthusians and Old Westminsters.

Blackburn Rovers then inflicted a 7–1 defeat on Staveley in the fifth round, and South Shore, Redcar and Small Heath Alliance progressed to the quarter-finals at the expense of Notts County, Middlesbrough and Davenham. Old Westminsters and Brentwood received walkovers. West Bromwich Albion defeated the Old Carthusians by the only goal of the game, while the Swifts completed the quarter-final line-up, with a 6–2 victory against the Church Club.

Brentwood were a little unfortunate to be drawn away at Blackburn Rovers in the quarter-finals, where they suffered a 3–1 defeat; Swifts secured a 2–1 home success against South Shore; Small Heath scored twice without reply against Redcar; and a Jem Bayliss hat-trick helped West Bromwich Albion to a 6–0 home victory against Old Westminsters.

Albion were then drawn against Small Heath Alliance in the semi-finals, to take place at the Aston Lower Grounds, the home of Aston Villa, while the Swifts and Blackburn Rovers were due to play their semi-final tie at the County Ground, Derby.

Rovers were expected to beat the Swifts with ease, but the amateur side matched the cup holders in every department and the Lancashire side managed only a 2–1 victory, with Strachan scoring a late goal to secure a third successive FA Cup Final appearance for Blackburn. West Bromwich Albion were far too experienced for the Small Heath side, as centre forward Loach scored a hat-trick to secure their first final appearance. This was to take place at the Oval on 3 April. Small Heath's share of the gate money had amounted to four pounds and five shillings, with each player receiving half-a-crown match fee, one shilling and six pence for a meal, as well as one shilling for the cab fare. However, for West Bromwich Albion the rewards were greater – an appearance in the final of the FA Cup competition.

Benjamin Spilsbury Scores Four Against Ireland

The 1886 international games saw a greater Corinthian influence than in previous seasons. England selected eight new caps for the game against Ireland in Belfast on 13 March, which saw Charles Dobson (Notts County), John Leighton (Corinthians), George Shutt (Stoke) and Thelwell Pike (Corinthians) make single appearances for their country.

Charles Dobson had followed his brother Alfred into the England team. Pike was an accomplished county cricketer with Worcestershire, while Shutt became a referee at the end of his playing career. Richard Baugh (Wolverhampton Wanderers) made the first of two England appearances at fullback, and Ralph Squire (Corinthians) appeared in all three of the 1886 international games. The most notable newcomers in the England line-up were Fred Dewhurst (Preston North End) and Tinsley Lindley, a Corinthian, who had occasionally played for Nottingham Forest.

Lindley, an excellent cricketer, who had learned his football at Cambridge University while studying law, scored fifteen goals in thirteen England appearances, while Dewhurst, a schoolmaster by profession, scored eleven goals in nine England games. Wolverhampton Wanderers' goalkeeper, William Rose, returned for his fourth England game, Benjamin Spilsbury (Derby County) made his second appearance, and P M Walters completed the England line-up. England totally dominated the Irish to record a 6–1 victory, with four goals by Benjamin Spilsbury, together with further goals from Tinsley Lindley and Fred Dewhurst.

A Well-Earned Success in Wrexham

England selected a stronger side for the Welsh game, in Wrexham on 29 March, with Herbert Arthur (Blackburn Rovers), N C Bailey (Clapham Rovers), Andrew Amos (Old Carthusians) and James Forrest (Blackburn Rovers) returning in defence, while P M Walters, Squire, Dewhurst and Lindley retained their places from the victory in Belfast.

Corinthians W N Cobbold and E C Bambridge returned up front, while George Brann (Swifts) made the first of three international appearances at inside right. Wales once again showed that they were as skilful as the English. However, the visitors held on to a 3–1 victory, with Lindley, Dewhurst and Bambridge on target.

Lindley Secures a Point in Glasgow

Two days after the win in Wrexham, the England team travelled to Glasgow for the all-important game against the Scots. There were two changes in their line up, with A M Walters replacing Andrew Amos in defence, while Benjamin Spilsbury returned in the attack, at the expense of Fred Dewhurst. An excellent display by the England defence earned a one-all draw, with Tinsley Lindley scoring for the visitors, who stretched their unbeaten run to seven games.

Blackburn Hold On for a Draw

On the Saturday following the England–Scotland game, the 1886 FA Cup Final took place at the Oval between Blackburn Rovers and West Bromwich Albion, with Rovers selecting the following eleven:

				Arthur				
			Turner		Suter			
		Heyes		Forrest		McIntyre		
	Douglas	Strachan		Sowerbutts		Fecitt		Brown (captain)

Albion selected the following players:

Roberts

H Green   H Bell

Horton   Perry   Timmins

Woodhall   T Green   Bayliss (captain)   Loach   G Bell

Major Francis Marindin refereed his third successive final.

Nine of the Blackburn team had appeared in the 1885 final, seven were appearing in their third successive final, while McIntyre, Suter, Brown and Douglas were playing in their fourth final in five seasons. Albion, on the other hand, were a team of little experience on the national stage, which was worsened when the inexperienced Charles Perry received a late call-up into the team when centre half Fred Bunn failed a fitness test. Perry eventually captained the club and appeared in the English national side. However, at this stage of his career, he had played no more than a handful of games for the West Bromwich side.

With the kick-off delayed until four o'clock, due to the Varsity boat race, Albion decided to kick with the wind upon winning the toss. Loach and Bayliss exerted early pressure on the Blackburn defence who were struggling to adapt to the adverse weather conditions. However, goalkeeper Arthur managed to thwart the Albion forwards at every opportunity and the first half ended goalless.

Albion continued to dominate proceedings during the second period of play against the unusually pedestrian Rovers' defence, which saw them miss a number of chances in front of goal when it seemed easy to score. Fecitt, in a rare Blackburn attack, seemed to place the ball between the Albion goalposts to secure a one-goal lead for the Rovers. Their joy was short-lived as Major Marindin insisted that the ball had gone wide of the post.

As the final whistle sounded, Rovers declined Albion's offer of a period of extra time, which meant that a replay was ordered for the following Saturday at the Racecourse Ground, Derby.

Blackburn's Hat-trick of FA Cup Victories

Blackburn made one change for the replay with Nat Walton replacing Heyes up front, while Albion remained unchanged for a game that the West Bromwich side should have won at the Oval. Albion continued where they had left off at the Oval during the early stages of the replay as they attacked the Rovers' goal, where Herbert Arthur once again performed magnificently. Further erratic shooting by the Albion forwards saw the scores remain equal. However, Rovers came more into the game as the first half progressed, with Fecitt, Brown and Sowerbutts displaying their excellent dribbling skills that had been missing at the Oval. These eventually led to Sowerbutts securing a one-goal lead for the Rovers, who finished the first half well on top.

Blackburn's domination continued during the second half, which inevitably brought a second goal for the cup holders when Jimmy Brown collected the ball in his own goal area, rounded two Albion players, ran the length of the field, to place the ball past the advancing Roberts to score arguably the finest FA Cup Final goal to date.

Albion were by now demoralised, with only goalkeeper Bob Roberts preventing the Blackburn forwards from scoring further goals. The final whistle sounded with Rovers the winners by two goals to nil. However, the result may well have been different if Albion had taken their chances in the first game at the Oval.

Blackburn Rovers had now joined the Wanderers in achieving three successive FA Cup Final victories, with further success ahead, while Albion would enjoy the reputation as one of the finest FA Cup fighting sides during the Victorian period.

The Traumatic Season Ends

As the traumatic 1885–86 season drew to a close, a number of clubs continued to question the strict code of rules and regulations laid down by the Football Association, which were mostly unacceptable to the majority of teams.

Bolton Wanderers, who had been disqualified from the FA Cup competition earlier in the season, went on to enjoy their most successful season to date by winning both the Bolton and Derbyshire Charity Cups, as well as the prestigious Lancashire Cup. Aston Villa had a poor season by their own standards, though they retained the Birmingham Lord Mayor's Charity Cup. West Bromwich Albion, on the other hand, gained a little consolation for their FA Cup Final defeat by winning both the Birmingham and Staffordshire Cups, while in Scotland, Arbroath inflicted a 36–0 defeat on Bon Accord in a Scottish FA Cup tie, with John Petrie scoring thirteen of the Arbroath goals.

Royalty Visit Lancashire

Meanwhile, in Lancashire, the Burnley club, who were a match for any team when able to field their Scottish players, had received a visit from Prince Albert, the son of Queen Victoria, who had arrived in town to open the New Victoria Hospital, which had been built through the generous donations of the local people. Association football had played its part in raising money for the hospital through events like the Hospital Charity Cup, with local teams competing for the trophy and the proceeds going towards the hospital. Burnley arranged a charity game against Bolton Wanderers, attended by Prince Albert as the guest of honour.

A crowd in excess of 9,000 arrived at Turf Moor to witness the first occasion when a member of the British royal family attended a football game between two professional clubs, thus unwittingly endorsing that professional football had become an acceptable way to earn a living.

Chapter XII

ASTON VILLA TRIUMPH IN AN ALL MIDLANDS FA CUP FINAL – 1886–87

ASTON VILLA TRIUMPH IN AN ALL MIDLANDS FA CUP FINAL
TINSLEY LINDLEY SCORES A HAT-TRICK AGAINST IRELAND
LINDLEY AND COBBOLD SCORE TWO GOALS APIECE AGAINST THE WELSH
ENGLAND FAIL TO REGISTER A VICTORY AGAINST THE SCOTS FOR THE EIGHTH
SUCCESSIVE SEASON
BAILEY, BAMBRIDGE AND COBBOLD RETIRE FROM INTERNATIONAL FOOTBALL

An FA Cup Competition Open to All Comers

Following the legalisation of professionalism, the need to generate money to pay players' wages became the main priority of the professional clubs and they sought to play games of a serious nature, rather than the friendly fixtures of previous seasons that tended to be cancelled at a moment's notice for no particular reason. Hence, there was a large number of entrants for the 1886–87 FA Cup competition, which included the likes of Cliftonville from Ireland, Chirk from Wales, as well as Renton, Partick Thistle and Glasgow Rangers from north of the border.

Cliftonville suffered a defeat during the early stages of the cup; Renton secured an excellent victory against Blackburn Rovers, the reigning FA Cup holders; and Chirk, Partick Thistle and Glasgow Rangers all proceeded to the fifth round stage of the competition. Bolton Wanderers secured wins against South Shore and Third Lanark during the early rounds, prior to suffering a third round defeat against Darwen by the odd goal in seven. Aston Villa and West Bromwich Albion enjoyed excellent cup runs into the last sixteen. Villa included England internationals Olly Whateley, Arthur Brown and Howard Vaughton in their line-up, as well as inspirational captain, Archie Hunter, while future internationals Albert Allen and Dennis Hodgetts were building their reputations as prolific goal scorers for the Villa team.

Hodgetts, Brown and Hunter all scored hat-tricks as Villa secured a 13–0 success against Wednesbury Old Athletic in the first round, while all three were again on target in a second round win against Derby Midlands (6–1) to set up a third round tie against Wolverhampton Wanderers. Wanderers had suffered a 5–1 defeat against Villa just a few weeks earlier. However, the Wolverhampton side, who had inflicted a 14–0 defeat on Crosswells Brewery in an earlier cup tie, were confident of earning a favourable result against the Villa team.

The game turned out to be the longest FA Cup tie to date, with four ties taking place between 11 December and 29 January. It began with a two-all draw at Perry Barr, followed by successive draws at Dudley Road, until finally Villa secured a 2–0 win at Perry Barr on the final Saturday of January to continue their success in the competition.

West Bromwich Albion began their FA Cup campaign with a 6–0 success against Burton Wanderers, followed by a 2–1 win against Derby Junction in the second round, prior to receiving a bye in the third round. A last-minute goal by Tom Green, in a close encounter with Mitchell's St George's, saw Albion into the fifth round. Preston North End had enjoyed a comfortable passage into the last sixteen, that is, with the exception of a cup tie at Hampden Park, Glasgow, against the Queens Park Club, which involved serious crowd scenes, resulting in Preston making a swift exit from the Glasgow area.

The Lancashire side, with their team of Scotsmen, were seen as the main instigators of the drift towards professionalism, while their aggressive approach against the Queens Park team resulted in a 3–0 victory that angered the home side who had rarely encountered such aggressive play. With the final whistle imminent, Jimmy Ross had fouled Harrower, the Queens Park centre forward, which resulted in the latter leaving the field of play to receive treatment, much to the annoyance of the Scottish supporters, who surged on to the pitch to vent their anger on Ross. However, Ross and his team-mates managed to evade the unhappy crowd to return home unscathed.

As a result of the angry crowd scenes at Hampden Park, Scottish teams decided to boycott the English FA Cup for the following season.

Of the sixteen teams remaining in the 1886–87 FA Cup competition, the Old Boys' Clubs were represented by the Old Westminsters, Old Foresters and Old Carthusians, Chirk represented Welsh interest, while Glasgow Rangers and Partick Thistle kept the Scottish hopes alive.

Horncastle and Lincoln City hailed from the east of England, Leek and Great Marlow were provincial sides, while Lockwood Brothers were a factory team from the north of England. However, it was generally expected that the eventual FA Cup winners would be either Aston Villa, Darwen, Notts County, Preston North End or West Bromwich Albion, the five professional teams remaining in the competition.

All five of the professional teams qualified for the quarter-final stages, with Darwen inflicting a 3–1 defeat on Chirk, Preston accounting for the Old Foresters by three goals to nil, and Brown scoring an excellent hat-trick for Aston Villa in a 5–0 success against Horncastle. Notts County secured a 5–2 win against Great Marlow, while West Bromwich Albion defeated Lockwood Brothers by the only goal of the game. However, following a number of protests from Lockwood Brothers' officials, the game was ordered to be replayed on a neutral ground, which Albion managed to win by the odd goal in three to proceed to the quarter-finals where they were joined by the Old Westminsters and Old Carthusians, who had registered narrow victories against Partick Thistle (1–0) and Leek (2–0).

Glasgow Rangers completed the quarter-final line-up with a 3–0 success against Lincoln City, while their excellent FA Cup run continued in the quarter-finals with a 5–1 victory against the Old Westminsters.

West Bromwich Albion joined Rangers in the semi-finals with a 4–1 win against Notts County; Preston North End managed a 2–1 success against the Old Carthusians; and Villa seemed certain of a semi-final place when goals by Dawson, Hunter and Hodgetts secured a 3–0 half-time lead against the visiting Darwen team. However, the Lancashire side, never a team to concede defeat, fought magnificently during the second half to reduce the arrears to a single goal as Villa held on for a 3–2 victory. Villa were then drawn to play at Crewe in the semi-finals against Glasgow Rangers, while West Bromwich Albion were due to meet Preston North End at Trent Bridge, Nottingham.

Albion, who had suffered a defeat against Blackburn in the previous season's final, soon found themselves a goal down against Preston, prior to Tom Pearson securing an equalising goal shortly before half-time. Pearson was once again on target early in the second half as Albion secured the lead. Then followed an all-out attacking policy by the Lancashire side in their pursuit of an equalising goal, which unfortunately led to a third goal by Albion when William Paddock slotted the ball between the Preston goalposts, albeit against the run of play, to secure Albion a second successive visit to the Oval.

Villa faced a difficult task against a Glasgow Rangers side full of Scottish international players. However, it turned out to be Villa's day, as two goals by Archie Hunter, together with a further goal by Brown, secured a 3–1 victory to earn them their first appearance in an FA Cup Final scheduled for the Oval on 2 April.

A Tinsley Lindley Hat-trick

The 1887 international matches began at Sheffield on 5 February with England selecting an attacking side for the visit by Ireland that included Fred Dewhurst, Tinsley Lindley, W N Cobbold and E C Bambridge up front. These all appeared in all three of the season's international games.

Herbert Arthur and James Forrest of Blackburn Rovers were retained by the England selectors. James Sayer and Edward Brayshaw of the Wednesday made their only appearances for their country, while Charlie Mason (Wolverhampton Wanderers), Bob Howarth (Preston North End) and George Haworth (Accrington) gained their first caps for England, with Mason making three appearances. Haworth would appear on five occasions, while Howarth, who would be part of the great Preston team of the late 1880s, eventually joined Everton, with whom he gained further international caps.

Ireland were again no match for the England team, who scored seven goals without reply, with Lindley (3), Dewhurst (2) and Cobbold (2) on target for the home side. England had scored forty-five goals and conceded two in six international games against the Irish.

Herbie Arthur's Final International Appearance

England made four changes in their line-up for the visit of the Welsh national team to the Oval on 26 February, with A M and P M Walters returning to the side at the expense of Bob Howarth and Charlie Mason, while Joseph Lofthouse (Blackburn Rovers) and N C Bailey (Clapham Rovers) replaced James Sayer and Edward Brayshaw.

Tinsley Lindley and W N Cobbold retained their excellent goal-scoring form against the Welsh with two goals apiece in a 4–0 victory in Herbert Arthur's seventh and final England appearance, none of which had ended in defeat for the Blackburn Rovers' custodian.

Farewell to E C Bambridge, N C Bailey and W N Cobbold

The England–Scotland game took place at Blackburn on 19 March. The selectors made just one change after the victory against Wales, with Bob Roberts of West Bromwich Albion replacing Herbie Arthur between the posts for the first of three England appearances, which was a just reward for his part in helping his club to two successive FA Cup Final appearances. While England's performance was equal to the Scots', the visitors managed to return home with a 3–2 success, with Dewhurst and Lindley on target for the home side, who had now failed to register a victory against Scotland for the eighth successive season.

For three of the England side, the defeat against the Scots marked the end of their international careers, which had begun when the likes of the Wanderers, Royal Engineers and Old Etonians had dominated the Association game. N C Bailey (Clapham Rovers), who had made his England debut in 1878, appeared in his nineteenth and final England game against the Scots, while E C Bambridge (Swifts), whose career had run almost parallel with Bailey's, decided to retire from international football following eighteen appearances in which he scored twelve goals, including two on his debut in 1879, when Scotland had last suffered a defeat against the English.

W N Cobbold, the third retiring Corinthian, who had scored seven goals in nine England games, had been generally regarded as the finest forward of the early 1880s, with the reputation as an excellent dribbler of the ball, able to shoot with either foot, while his determination to succeed had encouraged all those around him. Like E C Bambridge and N C Bailey, W N Cobbold had served his country well.

A New Name on the FA Cup

During the first fifteen years of the history of the FA Cup competition, eight different clubs had won the much coveted trophy, which became nine following the 1887 final between Aston Villa and West Bromwich Albion. Albion selected the following eleven for their second successive final appearance:

Roberts

H Green   Aldridge

Horton   Perry   Timmins

Woodhall   T Green   Bayliss   Paddock   Pearson

Aston Villa selected the following players:

Warner

Coulton   Simmonds

Yates   Dawson   Burton

Davis   Albert Brown   Hunter   Vaughton   Hodgetts

Major Francis Marindin once more officiated as match referee.

Villa had enjoyed an excellent season in which few games were lost and scored nearly 130 goals with Davis, Hunter, Brown and Hodgetts scoring the majority of them. Albion, who included eight members of their 1886 Cup Final side in their line-up, had defeated the likes of Darwen, Blackburn Rovers, Bolton Wanderers and Preston North End during a most successful season.

A crowd in excess of 15,000 arrived at the Oval to see Albion kick with the wind at their backs upon winning the toss, which inevitably saw them dominate the early play. Green, Bayliss and Paddock attacked the Villa defence. However, Coulton and Simmonds performed magnificently for Villa as the West Bromwich side failed to open the scoring. As the half-time whistle sounded, a dejected Albion team left the field of play, knowing full well that they should have finished the half with a healthy lead, especially with the advantage of the wind.

Albion seemed to lose heart during the second period of play as Villa began to dominate the game, which eventually led to Dennis Hodgetts scoring the opening goal with the Albion defence appealing for off-side. However, the West Bromwich side's appeals were in vain as Major Marindin allowed the goal to stand. Villa's continued domination led to a second goal by Archie Hunter two minutes from time when he latched on to a weak back pass to slide the ball past the advancing Bob Roberts and to secure a two-goal lead, which they held until the game reached its conclusion.

As Archie Hunter, the triumphant Villa captain, collected the FA Cup, the disappointed Albion players walked from the field of play following their second successive FA Cup Final defeat. However, the West Bromwich side soon returned to the Oval for a third FA Cup Final appearance.

Albion's Success at a Local Level

Albion were once again successful at a local level, with a 4–0 victory against Walsall Swifts in the final of the Staffordshire Cup, which was followed by a surprise defeat against Long Eaton Rangers in the final of the Birmingham Cup. Their near neighbours, Wolverhampton Wanderers, who had fought four keenly contested FA Cup ties against Aston Villa, secured the Birmingham Charity Cup.

Midlands teams enjoyed much success in the FA Cup competition during the remaining years of the Victorian period. West Bromwich Albion, Wolverhampton Wanderers, Nottingham Forest and Notts County emulated Aston Villa by winning the trophy, with Albion, Villa and Wolves appearing in a dozen finals between them by the century's end.

Football in the North-East

Association football had flourished in the north-east of England during the late 1870s and early 1880s with the likes of Sunderland, Middlesbrough, Newcastle West End, Sunderland Albion and Middlesbrough Ironopolis achieving a certain amount of success in the FA Cup competition. However, success on a national level did not come until the final decade of the century, following Sunderland's election to the recently formed Football League.

Meanwhile, in Lancashire, Blackburn Rovers were rebuilding the team that had achieved three successive FA Cup Final victories, while William Sudell continued to build a Preston North End side that would become physically and tactically superior to the majority of teams in England.

Chapter XIII

MR MCGREGOR'S LEAGUE SYSTEM IS APPROVED – 1887–88

THIRD TIME LUCKY FOR WEST BROMWICH ALBION
ENGLAND SCORE FIVE AGAINST WALES, SCOTLAND AND IRELAND
FRED DEWHURST AND TINSLEY LINDLEY SCORE IN ALL THREE ENGLAND GAMES
ALBERT ALLEN SCORES A HAT-TRICK IN HIS ONLY INTERNATIONAL APPEARANCE

Albion's Excellent Start to the Season

The 1887–88 season saw teams playing their usual friendly fixtures as well as local cup ties. However, the local games tended to lack the competitiveness of the FA Cup competition. West Bromwich Albion, who were a little disappointed following two successive FA Cup Final defeats, were now more determined to succeed and their season began with excellent victories against Stoke, Wednesday and Notts County, as well as a win against Small Heath in the Birmingham Cup. A 12–2 success against Burton Wanderers saw them make progress in the Staffordshire Cup, with Woodhall and Bayliss scoring hat-tricks together with a brace of goals from outside right Billy Bassett. Bassett had been considered too small to have pursued a career as a professional footballer. However, when Tom Green decided to leave Albion for Aston Villa, Bassett proved an instant success, resulting in more than 400 games for the West Bromwich side, as well as appearing in the English national team on sixteen occasions.

Prior to a first round FA Cup tie against Wednesbury Old Athletic, Albion were involved in an exciting friendly game with Blackburn Rovers, which saw the Black Country side race into a 5–0 lead during the opening half-hour's play, with Askin scoring three of the Albion goals. As half-time approached, the West Bromwich team allowed Rovers to pull back a couple of goals, and they ended the half 5–2 ahead.

Blackburn then dominated the second period of play. They scored four goals to secure a 6–5 advantage, but Albion soon levelled the scores. However, Rovers finished the game as victors, with the winning goal arriving during the final minute of play.

Albion soon returned to winning ways with a 7–1 victory in the FA Cup tie against Wednesbury Old Athletic, with Bayliss, Pearson and Wilson all scoring twice to secure a second round tie against Mitchell's St George's. This they won by one goal to nil, with Jem Bayliss scoring the only goal of the game.

Following a 2–0 success against Wolverhampton Wanderers in the third round, Albion received a bye in round four, while a 4–1 home win against Stoke in the fifth round saw the West Bromwich team proceed to the quarter-finals, with Woodhall and Bayliss once again amongst the scorers.

Meanwhile, Aston Villa had enjoyed a relatively easy passage into the last sixteen, with victories against Oldbury Town and Small Heath, as well as a fourth round bye, which then saw them drawn against Preston North End for a place in the quarter-finals.

Preston, who had registered a 26–0 victory against Hyde in the first round, prior to securing further victories against Halliwell and Everton, were then unwittingly involved in the most farcical FA Cup situation to date.

An FA Cup Farce in Lancashire

Everton had suffered a 1–0 defeat against Bolton Wanderers in the first round of the FA Cup, with Bob Roberts scoring the only goal of the game. However, Everton then claimed that Bolton forward, Robert Struthers, had been ineligible to play, which resulted in the FA ordering a replay. Following two drawn replayed ties, the Liverpool side won the fourth game by the odd goal in three. However, the tie was unfinished as far as Bolton were concerned, who complained to the FA that Everton had fielded two professional players, who were actually registered as amateurs. Following a further investigation by the FA, Everton were suspended for one month, while Bolton were reinstated in the second round of the competition where they played against Preston, who had previously defeated Everton at the same stage. However, the farce soon came to an end, as Preston inflicted a 9–1 defeat on the Bolton team to continue their march into the latter rounds of the cup.

A Lack of Crowd Control at Perry Barr

Further controversy of a different nature took place in the fifth round tie between Aston Villa and Preston at Perry Barr in front of 16,000 spectators who were tightly packed into all parts of the ground. During the game, the crowd continually spilled on to the field of play, which resulted in the arrival of mounted police and soldiers to keep order. However, with the crowd situation worsening, the two teams decided to treat the game as a friendly, with Preston leading by three goals to one.

The Football Association had other ideas, insisting that the game was an FA Cup tie and should be treated as such, and Preston were declared the winners to proceed to the quarter-finals.

Old Carthusians' Fifth Quarter-Final Appearance

The Old Carthusians and Old Foresters remained in the competition at the fifth round stage, thus confirming that the Old Boys' clubs were as capable as the professional teams. However, the Old Foresters suffered a 4–0 reverse at Middlesbrough, while the Old Carthusians secured a 2–0 home success against Bootle to progress to the quarter-finals.

Derby Junction had surprised many by reaching the fifth round stage of the competition, where they defeated Chirk by one goal to nil to take their place in the last eight, while their neighbours, Derby County, had opened their FA Cup run with a 2–1 first round success against Staveley, prior to securing a 6–0 victory against Ecclesfield in the second round, with Benjamin Spilsbury scoring a hat-trick. Spilsbury then scored a further hat-trick in a 6–2 win against Owlerton in the third round, prior to receiving a fourth round bye. However, their excellent FA Cup run came to an end in the fifth round with a 1–0 reverse at Crewe.

Nottingham Forest, who had held the mighty Queens Park team to a draw in the 1885 semi-finals, suffered a 4–2 defeat against the re-emerging Wednesday side, while Blackburn Rovers completed the quarter-final line-up with a 3–0 victory at Darwen.

West Bromwich Albion were then drawn against the Old Carthusians in the quarter-finals, a most difficult task for the Old Boys, who suffered a 4–2 defeat. Wilson (2), Woodhall and Pearson were on target to secure a third successive semi-final appearance for the West Bromwich side. The days of success in the FA Cup competition for the Old Carthusians had drawn to an end. However, they enjoyed further success during the 1890s following the inauguration of the FA Amateur Cup competition.

Derby Junction, once a force in Midlands football, gained their finest victory to date by defeating Blackburn Rovers by the odd goal in three to secure their only FA Cup semi-final appearance, while Crewe earned a place in the last four with a 2–0 victory at Middlesbrough, where they were joined by Preston North End who had enjoyed a 3–1 success against the Wednesday.

The semi-final ties were one-sided affairs, with Bayliss, Woodhall and Wilson scoring for West Bromwich Albion in a 3–0 victory against Derby Junction at the Stoke ground, while Preston inflicted a 4–0 defeat on Crewe at the Anfield Road Ground, Liverpool, to appear in their first FA Cup Final, due to take place at the Oval on 24 March.

Wales Are Soundly Beaten

The 1888 international games began at Crewe on 4 February, where England awarded seven new caps in a weakened side that included Bob Howarth (Preston North End) and Charlie Mason (Wolverhampton Wanderers) to replace the Walters brothers at fullback. Fred Dewhurst and Tinsley Lindley were the only players remaining from the previous England game. Frank Saunders (Swifts) made a single England appearance at right half back, Charles Holden-White, the Corinthian captain, played the first of two England games at left half back, while George Woodhall, soon to make his third successive FA Cup Final appearance for West Bromwich Albion, made the first of two appearances on the right wing. Harry Allen (Wolverhampton Wanderers), whose career was tragically cut short, made the first of five England appearances at centre half. Dennis Hodgetts (Aston Villa) would never be on the losing side in six England games, while William Moon, the Old Westminsters' goalkeeper, represented the country of his birth on seven occasions. However, the most significant newcomer in the England team was John Goodall (Preston North End), who gained the first of fourteen caps, in which he would score on a dozen occasions.

Goodall, whose international career continued following a transfer to Derby County, enjoyed the reputation as the pioneer of scientific play and played in the mould of the great amateur players of the 1870s. A great thinker of the Association game, John Goodall spent many seasons with Derby County, together with his brother Archie, who appeared for the Irish national team on ten occasions.

England performed splendidly against the Welsh, with Dewhurst (2), Lindley, Woodhall and Goodall on target in a 5–1 victory.

England's Finest Victory Against the Scots

England made just two changes for the all-important Scotland game in Glasgow on 17 March, with P M Walters returning in place of Charlie Mason, while George Haworth (Accrington) replaced Frank Saunders at half back.

In a brilliant display of attacking football, the England team returned home 5–0 winners, with Dewhurst (2), Lindley, Goodall and Hodgetts on target to secure England's finest victory against the Scots, as well as their first success on Scottish soil. However, the Scottish FA argued that the strain of losing their better players to English clubs had seriously affected their national team.

Third Time Lucky for Albion

A crowd of nearly 20,000 arrived at the Oval on 24 March to watch the 1888 FA Cup Final. Both Albion and Preston fielded full-strength sides, with Albion selecting the following eleven:

Roberts

Aldridge   H Green

Horton   Perry   Timmins

Woodhall   Bassett   Bayliss   Wilson   Pearson

Preston chose the following players:

Dr R Mills-Roberts

Howarth   Holmes

Nick Ross   Russell   Gordon

Jimmy Ross   John Goodall   Dewhurst   Drummond   Graham

Major Francis Marindin again officiated as match referee.

Albion included seven players who had appeared in their two previous FA Cup Finals. However, Preston were slight favourites to win the cup for the first time.

Having won the toss, Nick Ross, the Preston captain, decided to play with the sun on their backs, which resulted in difficulties for the Albion defence as the Preston forwards mounted early attacks. However, excellent defending by Perry and Aldridge, together with fine goalkeeping by Bob Roberts, kept the Preston forwards at bay.

Fred Dewhurst and John Goodall had a number of chances to score the game's opening goal, but were again thwarted by Bob Roberts when it seemed easy to score. Against the run of play, Billy Bassett dribbled the ball down the Preston left flank, prior to crossing to Jem Bayliss, who secured a one-goal lead for the West Bromwich side. As the game headed towards half-time, Jimmy Ross and Fred Dewhurst forced excellent saves out of Bob Roberts, and Albion ended the half one goal to the good.

Little changed during the second period of play as Preston sought the equalising goal, which eventually arrived after ten minutes of play when Preston's efforts were rewarded with a goal by Fred Dewhurst. The Lancashire side now began to play their finest football of the game as they continued to put pressure on the Albion fullbacks. However, with Aldridge and Green outstanding, they were unable to secure a second goal.

Up to the halfway stage of the second half, Albion's occasional attacks were efficiently dealt with by Nick Ross and Bob Howarth. As the half progressed, the Midlands side came more into the game. Bassett and Woodhall took on the Preston defence, while at the other end of the field, John Goodall saw a shot rebound from the Albion upright to safety. As the game reached the final stages, Albion looked the fresher side. The Preston defence had begun to tire, with only Nick Ross preventing the West Bromwich side from scoring a second goal as Bassett tormented their defence. However, with a little more than ten minutes remaining, Albion took the lead when a centre from Bassett found Woodhall, who turned sharply to steer the ball between the Preston goalposts. Preston rallied in pursuit of an equaliser, but to no avail, as the final whistle sounded with Albion the victors by two goals to one in one of the most competitively fought FA Cup Finals to date. Albion enjoyed their Cup Final victory, but the Preston team would enjoy greater success during the following season.

A Successful Visit to Belfast

A week after the FA Cup Final, the England team travelled to Belfast for the annual game against Ireland, with the visitors retaining Harry Allen, P M Walters, Fred Dewhurst, Tinsley Lindley and Dennis Hodgetts from the victory against Scotland, while Bob Roberts (West Bromwich Albion) earned a recall following his excellent performance in the FA Cup Final, together with his Albion team-mates, Alfred Aldridge and Billy Bassett.

Aldridge gained a second England cap after his transfer to Walsall Town Swifts, while Bassett became a regular member of the England team. Robert Holmes (Preston North End), later to become a referee, played the first of seven England games at fullback, while Charles Shelton (Notts County) and Albert Allen (Aston Villa) made single England appearances. Allen, who had been a member of the Villa side for less than a year, had struck up an excellent understanding with Dennis Hodgetts to help make the Midlands team one of the finest in the land. His career was cut short, though, by his early death at thirty-two years of age. However, Allen scored a hat-trick in his only England appearance, as the visitors returned home with a 5–1 victory, with Fred Dewhurst and Tinsley Lindley completing the scoring.

Villa and Albion's Successful Season

West Bromwich Albion's most successful season to date had seen Bayliss and Woodhall score in excess of thirty goals apiece, while Bassett, Pearson and Wilson all reached the twenty mark, out of an Albion total of 160. Horton, Perry, Bassett, Bayliss, Wilson and Pearson also represented the Birmingham FA eleven against a London eleven at the Oval. Roberts, Green, Aldridge and Timmins were selected for the Birmingham District team against Nottingham, while Roberts, Aldridge, Woodhall and Bassett were awarded international caps by the England selectors.

In fifty-one games during the season, the West Bromwich side suffered just six defeats as they contested three Cup Finals. However, in concentrating on their FA Cup run, Albion were defeated by Wolverhampton Wanderers in the final of the Staffordshire Cup and lost to Aston Villa in the final of the Birmingham Cup. Aston Villa, like Albion, had lost few games during the 1887–88 season, which included winning both the Birmingham Cup and the Lord Mayor's Charity Cup, thus confirming their reputation as one of the finest teams in the Midlands.

An Indifferent Season for Lancashire Teams

In the Lancashire area, Bolton Wanderers' season had lasted until May, when they had secured the Bolton Charity Cup. It was the end of an indifferent campaign that had included excellent victories against Wolverhampton Wanderers, Notts County and Stoke, as well as comprehensive defeats against

Blackburn Rovers, Preston North End and West Bromwich Albion. While Bolton were hardly the finest team in the Lancashire area, they became one of six clubs in the county to receive invitations to join the Football League upon its formation.

Burnley had enjoyed a greatly improved season which had resulted in nineteen defeats in fifty-nine games. However, the success of teams tended to be judged on goals scored rather than results, and the Burnley side had scored 136, while conceding eighty-six.

A tour of the south of England saw Burnley defeat Cambridge University, as well as secure a draw against the great Corinthian team. However, the highlight of the season was club captain Keenan being selected as a reserve for the England team for the international game against Wales.

Blackburn Rovers were continuing to rebuild their team, as many of the players from the 1884, 1885 and 1886 Cup-winning sides had left the club, or were nearing the end of their careers. Further FA Cup success lay a few years ahead, and Rovers remained one of the most skilful teams in Lancashire, as their 1887–88 FA Cup run had confirmed.

Preston North End were without doubt the finest team in Lancashire. They had lost the 1888 FA Cup Final to West Bromwich Albion when it should have been won, but defeats had been few as William Sudell continued his task of making Preston the finest team in England, which soon became a reality.

William McGregor's Concern

Towards the end of the 1887–88 season, William McGregor, a committee member of Aston Villa, as well as a member of the Birmingham FA, sent a circular to five of the leading professional clubs in England expressing his concern at what he saw as a crisis in the Association game. Mr McGregor, who had been a leading light in the Midlands when arguing for the legalisation of professionalism, felt that football was in a poor state, suggesting that a league system should be developed to keep the competition going rather than the friendly games of little importance. Fixtures were often cancelled on a Friday evening or Saturday morning for no particular reason, thus depriving thousands of spectators of their Saturday afternoon sport, while the lack of income brought about by these cancelled games forced clubs into bankruptcy, unable to pay players their wages.

The circular, sent on 2 March 1888, read as follows:

Every year, it is becoming more and more difficult for football clubs of any standing to meet their friendly engagements and even to arrange friendly matches. The consequence is, that at the last moment, through Cup Tie interferences, clubs are compelled to take on teams who will not attract the public.

I beg to tender the following suggestion as a means of getting over the difficulty, that ten or twelve of the most prominent clubs in England combine, to arrange home and away fixtures each season, the said fixtures to be arranged at a friendly conference about the same time as the international conference.

This combination might be known as the 'Association Football Union' and could be managed by a representative from each club.

Of course, this is in no way to interfere with the national Association, even the suggested matches might be played under Cup Tie Rules, however, this is a detail.

My object in writing to you at present, is merely to draw your attention to the subject and to suggest a friendly conference, to discuss the matter fully.

I would take it as a favour if you would kindly think the matter over and make whatever suggestion you may deem necessary.

I am writing to the following: Blackburn Rovers, Bolton Wanderers, Preston North End, West Bromwich Albion and Aston Villa, and should like to hear what other clubs you would suggest.

I am yours very truly,

William McGregor

PS How would Friday March 23rd 1888 suit for the friendly conference, at the Anderton's Hotel, London?

Great interest was shown in Mr McGregor's idea, especially by Mr J J Bentley of Bolton Wanderers, who suggested that the new league should consist of Preston North End, Bolton Wanderers, West Bromwich Albion, Aston Villa, Blackburn Rovers, Accrington, Burnley, Wolverhampton Wanderers, Halliwell, Notts County, Mitchell's St George's, Old Carthusians and Stoke, while Mr Tom Mitchell, the secretary of Blackburn Rovers, suggested that both Accrington and Burnley be invited to the initial meeting.

Mr McGregor then sent a second circular to Stoke, Wolverhampton Wanderers, Accrington, Burnley, Preston North End, Notts County, Blackburn Rovers, Bolton Wanderers, Aston Villa and West Bromwich Albion to confirm the meeting at the Anderton's Hotel to take place on the eve of the 1888 FA Cup Final.

The League System Is Approved

Following a second meeting, a decision was made to establish a league system. Mr McGregor had suggested it be called the 'Association Football Union'. However, it was felt that the Rugby Union would be a little unhappy with the title, which eventually resulted in the decision to name it the 'Football League'.

Mr Harry Lockett of the Stoke Club was appointed secretary of the newly formed League, while a further meeting was arranged for 17 April at the Manchester Royal Hotel to elect officers and draw up the rules.

At the Manchester meeting, it was decided that Preston North End, Bolton Wanderers, Accrington, Everton, Blackburn Rovers, Burnley, Aston Villa, West Bromwich Albion, Notts County, Wolverhampton Wanderers, Derby County and Stoke would be the founding twelve members of the Football League, with six clubs from Lancashire and six from the Midlands. This was hardly a surprise, as professional football did not exist south of Birmingham.

Mr McGregor Is Aware of the FA's Needs

A number of clubs, including Bootle, Wednesday, Darwen and Nottingham Forest, had made applications to join the newly formed League. However, while there was little doubt that these clubs were as skilful as the majority of the twelve founding members of the League, Mr McGregor felt that only twenty-two Saturdays were available during the season and a larger membership would result in teams struggling to fulfil their League fixtures.

As Mr McGregor took his place as president of the League, it was decided to play the opening League games on 8 September 1888. However, Mr McGregor was aware of the importance of not falling out with the Football Association in London. He felt that, together, they would see the game grow into a healthier state than it had been for a while. He believed the League competition to be one of skill and consistency, while the FA Cup would be won by the team playing the most spirited football over a few games.

Chapter XIV

PRESTON ACHIEVE THE FA CUP AND LEAGUE DOUBLE – 1888–89

THE LEAGUE TAKES PRECEDENCE
PRESTON WIN THE LEAGUE AND FA CUP
A FOUR-GOAL VICTORY AGAINST WALES
JACK YATES SCORES A DEBUT HAT-TRICK AGAINST IRELAND
SCOTLAND AVENGE THE DEFEAT IN GLASGOW
THE FOOTBALL LEAGUE PROVES A SUCCESS

The Football League Takes Precedence

While friendly fixtures continued to be played during the 1888–89 season, they no longer held the importance they had had in previous seasons as members of the newly formed Football League would often send their reserve eleven to fulfil a fixture.

A healthy League position, as well as an extended run in the FA Cup competition, had now become the main priority of the leading professional clubs, who needed to attract as many paying spectators as possible.

On 8 September 1888, the recently formed Football League played its opening fixtures, with all twelve founder members eager for success.

PRESTON NORTH END

Preston North End played their first League game at the Deepdale Ground, where 6,000 spectators saw them defeat Burnley by five goals to two, with Fred Dewhurst scoring their first goal in the League. Preston continued their winning run until they unexpectedly dropped a point in a two-all draw at Accrington. However, by the halfway stage of the campaign, they were well ahead in the race for the League title.

Fred Dewhurst and his England team-mate, John Goodall, were prolific goal scorers throughout the season, as was Jimmy Ross, the clever Scottish winger, who went on to score ninety-one goals in 130 League appearances in six seasons with the Lancashire side.

Jimmy's brother, Nick, who had, together with William Sudell, worked hard to build Preston into one of the finest teams in England, had surprisingly moved to Everton. However, he soon returned to Preston, where he would make ninety-six League appearances prior to contracting tuberculosis, which resulted in his death in 1894, at the age of thirty-one.

Preston's success had seen Holmes, Dewhurst, Goodall and Howarth appear in the English national team, while goalkeeper James Trainer had earned Welsh caps. However, the heart of the team contained a Scottish influence in Jack Gordon, Geordie Drummond, David Russell and the Ross brothers.

Russell enjoyed the reputation as one of the finest tacklers in England; Drummond made 139 League appearances in his ten seasons with the club; while Jack Gordon, an excellent crosser of the ball, played 125 League games for Preston, making many goals for Jimmy Ross, Fred Dewhurst and John Goodall.

Preston's success continued throughout the second half of the season, which saw them crowned as League champions as early as January 1889, with five games still remaining. The League programme eventually ended with Preston leading the table by a margin of eleven points, with eighteen wins and four draws from twenty-two games played, while scoring seventy-four goals and conceding fifteen.

Jack Gordon ended the first League campaign with ten goals, Fred Dewhurst scored twelve, while Jimmy Ross found the net on eighteen occasions. However, John Goodall, soon to leave the club for Derby County, finished the season as the leading League scorer, with twenty-one goals. William Sudell's dream of making Preston into the finest team in England had now been realised. All that remained was success in the English FA Cup.

ASTON VILLA

Aston Villa's opening League game took place at Dudley Road against Wolverhampton Wanderers where a crowd in excess of 2,500 witnessed a one-all draw. Tom Green scored Villa's first League goal, while the Wanderers' goal was scored by Villa defender Gersham Cox, who had the misfortune of kicking the ball through his own goalposts. Cox, who had joined Villa from the Birmingham Excelsior Club in 1887, gave the Midlands side six years of excellent service, in which he made nearly one hundred League appearances at fullback.

Then followed successive home wins against Stoke (5–1), Everton (2–1) and Notts County (9–1), with Albert Allen, Tom Green and Archie Hunter scoring the majority of the goals, as Villa secured second place in the League. Archie Hunter, who had spent nine seasons with Villa prior to the formation of the League, made less than forty League appearances before suffering a heart attack in a League game at Everton on 4 January 1890, which led him to retire from the game he loved and a premature death, at thirty-five years of age.

Villa suffered their first League defeat at Everton (2–0) during the opening week of October. However, the Midlands side soon returned to winning ways with a 6–1 success against Blackburn Rovers at Perry Barr, with Allen (2), Brown, Green, Hunter and Archie Goodall on target. Archie Goodall had joined Villa for the opening months of the season, which resulted in him scoring seven goals in fourteen appearances, prior to joining his brother John at Derby County.

A further victory at Bolton Wanderers (3–2) saw Allen, Hodgetts and Hunter score for the visitors, while Allen and Hodgetts were again on target the following week in a narrow 4–3 home win against Accrington, with Albert Brown scoring twice. Albert, the brother of England international Arthur, had replaced his brother in the Villa team when Arthur was forced to retire, following a bout of ill-health.

Albert Allen then scored his ninth League goal of the campaign in a one-all draw at Stoke, while Tom Green scored in a similar result at Preston, which was the only point that the Lancashire side conceded at home all season. However, a 5–1 reverse at Blackburn at the halfway stage of the campaign soon brought the Villa side down to earth.

Successive victories at home to Wolves (2–1) and at Notts County (4–2) saw Archie Goodall score a brace of goals in both games. This was followed by a one-all draw at Accrington, while the year ended with further home wins against Burnley (4–2) and Derby County (4–2), with Goodall, Green and Allen scoring in both victories.

Villa, who had suffered just two defeats in sixteen League games, were now in a position to challenge Preston for the League championship. However, they won only two of their remaining six League games, which eventually saw them settle for the runners-up position.

During the opening week of the new year, the Villa team arrived at Burnley with a couple of players short, who had missed their train owing to the appalling weather conditions. While the Lancashire side rightly took advantage of the situation by winning by four goals to nil, the Midlands side soon returned to form as Tom Green scored twice in a 6–2 home success against Bolton Wanderers, while Hodgetts and Allen were on target in a 2–0 home win against West Bromwich Albion. In the return game at West Bromwich, the Villa side managed a three-all draw, with Allen (2) and Green scoring for the visitors. However, there followed successive defeats at home to Preston (2–0) and away at Derby County (5–2) that saw Villa end their first League campaign as runners-up to Preston.

Villa had suffered just five defeats during the season, with Gersham Cox and Albert Brown appearing in all twenty-two League games in which sixty-one goals were scored and forty-three conceded. Archie Goodall, Albert Brown, Dennis Hodgetts and Archie Hunter ended the season with seven League goals apiece. Tom Green scored on thirteen occasions, while Albert Allen led the scoring with eighteen goals in twenty-one League appearances.

As one of the twelve founder members of the Football League, Villa were exempt from the qualifying rounds of the FA Cup competition. They secured a narrow 3–2 home win against Witton for a place in the last sixteen, with Green, Hunter and Allen scoring. Thus earning a second round home tie against Derby County, Archie Hunter (2), Dennis Hodgetts (2) and Albert Brown were then on target in a 5–3 success against Derby to secure a quarter-final tie at Blackburn Rovers. However, the Villa team were no match for the Blackburn side, who humiliated the visitors by eight goals to one, with John Southworth scoring four. Despite their disappointing exit from the FA Cup competition, the Villa side had enjoyed an excellent season, which had seen them retain both the Birmingham Cup and the Lord Mayor's Charity Cup, as well as share the West Bromwich Charity Cup with Albion and their second place League finish had enhanced their growing reputation.

WOLVERHAMPTON WANDERERS

Wolverhampton Wanderers' opening League game had resulted in a one-all home draw with Aston Villa, with Villa fullback Gersham Cox deflecting the ball past his own goalkeeper, to score the Wanderers' first goal in the League. Their excellent home form continued throughout the season with four goal victories against Accrington, Burnley, Stoke, Derby County and Everton, as well as wins against Bolton Wanderers, Notts County and West Bromwich Albion. Their one blemish on home soil during the season was a 4–0 defeat against Preston North End. Wanderers' indifferent away record saw them regularly trailing behind Preston and Villa. However, while away wins were recorded at Burnley, Everton, Stoke and West Bromwich Albion, the Black Country side suffered defeats at Villa, Preston, Bolton, Notts County and Derby County, which resulted in a creditable third place League finish.

In twenty-two League games, the Wanderers had won twelve, lost six and drawn four, while scoring fifty goals and conceding thirty-seven. Cooper and Knight scored seven League goals apiece; John Brodie scored eleven goals in fourteen appearances; while Harry Wood led the scoring, with sixteen goals in seventeen League games.

Wolves' excellent defensive record had resulted in half backs Alfred Fletcher, Arthur Lowder and Harry Allen representing England in the 1889 international games, while John Brodie had made a goal-scoring debut against Ireland.

Fullback Richard Baugh and winger Harry Wood soon joined their Wanderers team-mates in the England team, while W C Rose earned a recall in goal, as Wolves continued their policy of fielding mainly locally born players.

In finishing the season in third position, the Wanderers were just one point adrift from Aston Villa, who had recently defeated them in the final of the Birmingham Cup. However, Wolves had enjoyed an excellent FA Cup run during the season, which had begun with a 4–3 victory against the Old Carthusians.

BLACKBURN ROVERS

Blackburn Rovers' past achievements were glittering when compared against other teams in the Football League. However, while not as powerful as their

FA Cup-winning sides of the mid-1880s, Rovers had certainly earned the right to their newly acquired League status. Many of the players from their Cup-winning teams were nearing the end of their careers, including England goalkeeper Herbert Arthur, who sustained a serious knee injury during the season that put paid to his career. England international fullback, Joe Beverley, made eight League appearances before announcing his retirement from the game. Fergie Suter, who had played a major part in the club's rise to prominence during the previous eight seasons, as well as appearing in all three of Rovers' FA Cup Final victories, played in just one League game for Blackburn, while Jimmy Douglas, like Suter a three-times FA Cup winner, played in all but one of the 1888–89 League games prior to making the occasional appearance during the following three seasons. Suter and Douglas were victims of the Scottish policy of not selecting players from English clubs, thus preventing both players from representing the country of their birth, an honour they richly deserved.

England international Jimmy Brown, who had captained Rovers during their FA Cup triumphs, had officially retired in 1886, only to return to play in their opening League campaign, while Harry Fecitt had returned to the club from Accrington to bolster the attack.

Newcomers in the Blackburn team included future England internationals Nat Walton, William Townley and John Southworth, while John Forbes had arrived from north of the border, following two Scottish FA Cup Final appearances with Vale of Leven. All gave many years of excellent service to the Lancashire side, with Walton and Forbes making in excess of one hundred League appearances. John Southworth, who had signed from Blackburn Olympic during the previous season, scored ninety-seven goals in 108 League appearances in five seasons with the club prior to moving to Everton, where his prolific goal scoring continued. However, a serious leg injury forced Southworth into an early retirement, thus allowing him to pursue a musical career. Arguably the finest goal scorer in the Football League during the early years, Southworth scored in all three of his international appearances for England. William Townley, who like Southworth had arrived from the Blackburn Olympic Club, played a leading part in Rovers' re-emergence during the early 1890s, which would see him score thirty-seven goals in ninety-seven League games during a seven-year period. However, the most important member of the Blackburn line-up was England defender James Forrest, whose career stretched from the FA Cup-winning teams of the mid-1880s to the mid-1890s.

Blackburn enjoyed an excellent start to the season, which saw just one defeat in their opening eleven games, beginning with a thrilling five-all home draw with Accrington. Accrington secured an early lead when Kirkham charged Herbie Arthur over his own goal line, but Rovers soon drew level when John Southworth converted a cross from Harry Fecitt to secure Blackburn's first goal in the League.

Rovers then took the lead when Beresford headed home a Billy Townley free kick, which was followed shortly after by an Accrington equaliser when England international, Joseph Lofthouse, soon to return to Blackburn, passed the ball to Holden, who slid the ball past the advancing Herbie Arthur in the Rovers' goal. Accrington scored twice more during the first half to secure a 4–2 advantage. Billy Townley then scored twice, to once again level the scores, while James Southworth, the brother of John, had the misfortune to steer the ball past his own goalkeeper to put Accrington 5–4 ahead, with a little over ten minutes remaining. However, as the game neared its conclusion, Harry Fecitt scrambled the ball over the Accrington goal line to level the scores at five goals all.

Rovers were again at home the following week where they registered an excellent 6–2 victory against West Bromwich Albion, with Walton (2), Fecitt (2), John Southworth and Townley on target. This preceded successive draws at Wolves (2–2) and Notts County (3–3). Rovers' unbeaten run came to an end away at Aston Villa, where they suffered a 6–1 defeat.

Following a two-all home draw with Wolves, Blackburn ended the year with five straight wins that began at home to Stoke, with Walton (2), Townley, Fecitt and John Southworth scoring in a 5–2 success and continued at Burnley, where Southworth (3), Fecitt (2), Beresford and Forrest netted, in a 7–1 victory. Nat Walton and Almond were then amongst the goals in a 3–0 home win against Everton, which was followed by a 5–1 home success against Villa, with a hat-trick from Southworth, together with a couple of goals from Harry Fecitt. Harry Fecitt then scored his tenth and John Southworth his twelfth League goals of the season in a 2–0 victory at Derby County, which saw the Lancashire side move up to third place in the League table.

However, as wintry conditions arrived, Rovers had difficulty in maintaining their high position in the League. Early December saw Rovers suffer a 2–1 reverse at Stoke, which preceded a four-all home draw with Bolton Wanderers, with Townley scoring twice. John Southworth was again on target in a 5–2 home success against Notts County, but as the year reached its end, Blackburn suffered successive away defeats at West Bromwich Albion (2–1) and Preston North End (1–0). New Year began with a 2–2 draw in the return game with Preston, with Walton and Fecitt on target, which preceded a 2–0 victory against Accrington, with John Southworth scoring his usual goal. Then Walton and Southworth found the net in a 3–2 reverse at Bolton.

Blackburn then earned a one-all draw at Accrington in a first round FA Cup tie. Rovers won the replay with ease, with Haresnape (2), Walton, Townley and Barton scoring in a 5–0 victory to secure a home tie against Villa in the third round, having received a walkover against the Swifts in round two.

Prior to the replay against Accrington, Rovers had defeated Burnley by four goals to two in a League encounter at Ewood Park, which was followed by a brilliant display in the cup tie against Aston Villa, with Haresnape scoring a hat-trick, together with four goals by John Southworth, to register an 8–1 victory, thus securing a semi-final tie against Wolverhampton Wanderers at the Alexandra Ground, Crewe. Rovers were confident of beating the Wolverhampton side, who were a little inexperienced on the FA Cup front. However, following a one-all draw, Wolves won the replay by three goals to one to secure their first FA Cup Final appearance.

On their return to League action, Blackburn suffered a 3–1 reverse at Everton, though the season ended with a 3–0 home win against Derby County, leaving Rovers in fourth place in the League table, which may well have been higher if their early season form had been maintained. Nevertheless, they had enjoyed a most productive campaign, with James Southworth, Douglas, Almond, Forrest, Walton, Townley and John Southworth missing only the occasional game. Townley ended the season with eight League goals; Nat Walton scored ten goals; Harry Fecitt found the net on a dozen occasions; and John Southworth led the scoring with seventeen League goals.

BOLTON WANDERERS

Bolton Wanderers opened their first League campaign with a visit from Derby County, who arrived thirty minutes late, which had been quite normal up to the formation of the League. However, Bolton had few complaints as they raced into a three-goal lead with Kenny Davenport (2) and James Brogan on target for the home side. Unhappily, the Bolton defence crumbled in the second half as Derby scored six goals without reply to register a 6–3 victory.

A week later, Burnley visited the Wanderers, who once again raced into a three-goal lead through Brogan, Davenport and Cooper. However, the Bolton defence once again relaxed, allowing Burnley to return home with a 4–3 success. Bolton's run of defeats continued with a 3–1 reverse at Preston followed by a 6–0 home win against Everton, with Davenport, Milne and Tyrer all scoring twice. However defeats at Burnley (4–1), Everton (2–1) and Wolves (3–2), together with home reverses against Aston Villa (3–2), West Bromwich Albion (2–1) and Preston (5–2) saw the Bolton side struggling in the League, with the only wins at West Bromwich Albion (5–1) and at home to Stoke (2–1) keeping them away from the foot of the League table as the second half of the season began.

Wanderers were not exempt from the preliminary rounds of the FA Cup competition, which usually coincided with League fixtures, leaving Bolton with little alternative than to field their reserve side in FA Cup ties. However, following a walkover against the Hurst club, the Bolton side progressed to the following round where they secured a 9–0 success against West Manchester, with James Turner scoring a hat-trick. Turner, who had joined Bolton from Black Lane Rovers in 1888, eventually made three appearances for the English national side, the first as a Bolton player, followed by a second England cap as a

Stoke player, and a final England game as a member of the Derby County team.

Bolton's FA Cup run eventually came to an end with a 4–0 defeat at Linfield, on the same day that the first eleven suffered a defeat in a League encounter with West Bromwich Albion. Early December saw a return to form for the Wanderers, which coincided with the return of Welsh international fullback David Jones following a leg injury. Jones, who had helped Oswestry win the Shropshire Cup and assisted Chirk to win the Welsh FA Cup, had arrived at Bolton at the beginning of 1888. Following a transfer to Manchester City towards the end of the century, with whom he won a Second Division championship medal, Jones suffered an early death upon contracting tetanus.

A four-all draw at Blackburn marked the beginning of Bolton's improved form, with James Brogan scoring twice. Davie Weir scored the first League hat-trick by a Bolton player in a 4–1 home success against Accrington, which preceded further victories at Derby County (3–2) and at home to Wolverhampton Wanderers (2–1). The only blemish on Bolton's record during the final stages of the campaign was a 6–2 reverse at Aston Villa.

James Brogan then scored his ninth League goal of the season in a two-all draw at Stoke, which was followed by a 3–2 home victory against Blackburn Rovers, with Davie Weir scoring twice. Brogan then netted a brace of goals in a 4–0 success at Notts County.

There followed a Kenny Davenport hat-trick in a 7–3 home success in the return game with Notts County, while the season ended with a 3–2 win at Accrington, with Brogan and Davenport once again amongst the goals. Bolton ended their first League campaign in fifth place, with ten wins, two draws and ten defeats, while scoring sixty-three goals and conceding fifty-nine.

Brogan, Davenport, Milne, Roberts and Davie Weir had appeared in all twenty-two League games for Bolton, while Weir had ended the campaign with ten League goals, Kenny Davenport had found the net on eleven occasions, while James Brogan had led the scoring with thirteen League goals. Brogan, who had been a member of the Bolton side since 1884 following his arrival from the Heart of Midlothian Club, had scored five goals in a 10–1 victory against Sunderland, which earned him a place in the Lancashire County team, while he continued to serve the Wanderers until 1891. With the exception of Blackburn Rovers and Preston North End, Bolton's forwards had scored more goals than the remaining teams in the League, which gave them much encouragement for the season ahead.

WEST BROMWICH ALBION

West Bromwich Albion's opening League campaign began with a 2–0 victory at Stoke where Joe Wilson and George Woodhall found the net, which was followed by a 2–1 success at Derby County, with Tom Pearson and Billy Bassett on target. A humiliating 6–2 defeat at Blackburn ended their excellent start to the season. Then followed successive home wins against Burnley and

Derby County, as the West Bromwich side moved up to second place in the League table behind Preston North End, who soon confirmed their superiority over Albion by inflicting a 3–0 defeat on the Black Country side, with two of the goals arriving in the final ten minutes of play.

Albion soon returned to winning ways as Pearson scored twice in a 4–2 victory against Notts County, which was followed by a drawn game with Accrington, as well as defeats against Bolton Wanderers and Burnley. The halfway stage of the season arrived with a victory against Bolton Wanderers by the odd goal in three.

As usual, Albion were performing with much success in cup games. However, they continued to struggle in the League, as the second half of the season proved, which commenced with a 2–1 reverse against Accrington. Though followed by a 4–1 victory against Everton, with Billy Bassett scoring a brace, a 2–1 defeat against Wolverhampton Wanderers continued their indifferent League form.

Late in December, Albion secured a 2–1 home success against Blackburn Rovers to avenge the earlier humiliating defeat, with Bassett and Pearson scoring the all-important goals, which preceded a 5–0 defeat at Preston, while Wilson and Bassett were on target in a narrow victory against the struggling Stoke side. However, successive defeats against Notts County, Aston Villa and Wolverhampton Wanderers saw Albion move into the bottom half of the League table with just a couple of games remaining.

Albion's form improved during the final week of the season as Tom Pearson scored twice in a three-all home draw with Aston Villa, while Crabtree scored the only goal of the game in a 1–0 victory against Everton in his only League appearance of the season. Albion ended the campaign in sixth place, with ten victories, ten defeats and two draws, while scoring forty goals and conceding forty-six.

Tom Pearson, who finished as leading scorer in each of Albion's first five seasons in the League, had ended the campaign as joint leading goal scorer with Billy Bassett with eleven goals apiece. However, a serious leg injury sustained in 1894 resulted in Pearson retiring from the game at twenty-eight years of age.

Despite many indifferent League performances during the season, Albion had once again enjoyed success in the FA Cup, which had ended in a 1–0 defeat against Preston North End in the semi-final stage of the competition. However, consolation was achieved by winning both the West Bromwich Charity Cup and the Staffordshire Cup. There were few doubts that Albion's strength lay in the sudden death situation of cup games rather than in the need to secure results on a regular basis to earn success in the League.

ACCRINGTON

Accrington's invitation to join the newly formed Football League had not been too popular with the *Athletic News*, which reported that the club were 'not particular whether they win or lose matches with the clubs admittedly inferior to them'. However, admitted to the League they were, as holders of the Lancashire Cup.

Many of the players who had served the club in previous seasons were retained for Accrington's first League campaign, while efforts were made to sign Herbert Arthur, the Blackburn Rovers' goalkeeper. However, Arthur changed his mind, which resulted in John Horne returning from Burslem Port Vale to solve the goalkeeping problem.

Scotsmen John Stevenson and John McLellan, as well as England international George Haworth, formed a capable defence, together with recent signing Luther Pemberton. New forwards John Kirkham, Robert Brand and Alex Barbour were introduced to play alongside the experienced Jim Bonar.

On 8 September 1888, the Accrington team arrived twenty minutes late for their opening League game at Everton. In the match, goalkeeper John Horne suffered a fractured rib and Accrington lost by two goals to one. The season continued to be one of struggle as the Lancashire side fought to maintain a mid-table position. Creditable draws against Blackburn Rovers, Aston Villa, West Bromwich Albion, Wolverhampton Wanderers and Preston North End eventually saw Accrington end the campaign in seventh position, with six victories, eight draws and eight defeats in their twenty-two League games.

Accrington had shown that they were more than capable of holding their own in the newly formed Football League, while a third victory in the final of the Lancashire Cup completed an excellent season for the underdogs from Accrington.

EVERTON

Prior to their opening season in the Football League, the Everton club had signed future England internationals John Holt from Bootle and Edgar Chadwick, who had appeared for both Blackburn Rovers and Blackburn Olympic. Holt, a stocky centre half, made in excess of 200 League appearances in his ten seasons with the club and represented England on ten occasions, while Chadwick scored more than 100 goals in close on 300 games for Everton, as well as gaining seven caps for the English national team. Alfred Milward, a third future England player, who joined Everton from Great Marlow midway through the season, remained with the Merseysiders for nine seasons, in which he made in excess of 200 League appearances and played four games for England, prior to moving south towards the end of the century where he joined the Southampton club.

Everton secured a 2–1 home success against Accrington in their opening League game, with outside right Fleming scoring both goals. However, while Fleming had been a prolific scorer for the club prior to the formation of the League, he, like many players in their late twenties, missed out on the great surge of the Association game during the late 1880s and early 1890s. A week later, Everton recorded a further home win against Notts County (2–1), with Nick Ross and Edgar Chadwick on target, while successive away defeats at

Aston Villa (2–1) and Bolton Wanderers (6–2) ended their fine start to the campaign. Then followed a 2–0 home victory against Aston Villa, with Farmer and Waugh scoring rare goals for the home side. Their indifferent form continued with a 3–1 reverse at Notts County, but Everton soon returned to winning ways with a 4–2 win at Derby County, where Costley (2), Chadwick and McKinnon found the net for the visitors. A 6–2 success in the return game with Derby saw McKinnon, a recent signing from Hibernian, score the first hat-trick in the League by an Everton player, while their winning run continued with a 2–1 home victory against Bolton Wanderers, with Brown and Ross on target, which meant that Everton had won six of their opening nine League games. However, a sudden loss of form saw the Lancashire side win only three of their remaining thirteen League fixtures.

Everton's indifferent run of results began with a 3–0 defeat at Blackburn, followed by a two-all draw at Burnley, while a 3–2 victory in the return game with Burnley saw a rare success. However, a 4–1 defeat at West Bromwich Albion returned them to the doldrums, though Edgar Chadwick scored for the third game running.

Following a goalless draw at Stoke, Everton ended the year with successive away defeats at Preston (3–0) and Accrington (3–1), while the new year began with a 2–1 home success against Stoke, with Davies and Milward on target. However, defeats at Wolverhampton Wanderers (4–0), as well as at home to Preston (2–0), Wolverhampton Wanderers (2–1) and West Bromwich Albion (1–0) saw the Lancashire side struggling near the foot of the League table. The season ended with a 3–1 home win against Blackburn Rovers, with goals from Davies, Milward and Waugh securing two welcome points for the Merseysiders.

Everton had won nine, drawn two and lost eleven of their twenty-two League games while using thirty-five players, with Edgar Chadwick the only ever-present player in the side as well as the leader in the scoring with six League goals as Everton finished the campaign in a disappointing eighth place. Having managed to avoid the re-election positions, Everton soon enjoyed a reputation as one of the most consistent teams in the League, which saw them finish in a top four position on seven occasions during the Victorian period.

BURNLEY

Similar to the majority of teams in Lancashire, the Burnley side tended to be a mixture of youth and experience with a strong Scottish influence. Their regular line-up during the inaugural League season tended to be Kay, Bury, Lang, Abrahams, Friel, Keenan, Hibbert, Brady, Poland, Gallacher and Yates.

Sandy Lang, Daniel Friel and Jack Keenan had been regular members of the first team for a couple of seasons, while Jack Yates had arrived from Accrington. Yates, who scored a number of important goals during the season, became the first Burnley player to gain an England cap when selected to play against Ireland in March 1889. Despite scoring a hat-trick on his international debut, Yates was never again called upon to represent his country.

Burnley opened the season with a 5–2 defeat against Preston North End, which was followed by a 4–3 victory against Bolton Wanderers, having recovered from a three-goal deficit. A second League victory was achieved in their fifth game of the season with a further success against Bolton Wanderers (4–1), their only 'double' of the campaign.

Defeats were regular throughout the season, including a seven-goal home defeat against Blackburn Rovers, which preceded an excellent 2–0 victory against FA Cup holders West Bromwich Albion. However, on the same day as the Albion game, Burnley were able to field only their reserve team in a Lancashire Cup tie against Halliwell, resulting in a 9–4 defeat for the depleted Burnley side.

As the end of the year approached, Burnley registered their fourth victory in their fourteenth League game of the season with a 2–1 success against the struggling Stoke side, while the new year began with a creditable two-all draw against the unbeaten Preston team. However, following a 4–3 win against Old Westminsters in the first round of the FA Cup competition, Burnley suffered a second round defeat away at West Bromwich Albion by five goals to one.

On their return to League action, the Burnley side secured victories against Derby County and Notts County, who were both below them in the League, as well as a 4–0 home success against Aston Villa, who had arrived with a couple of players short, owing to the appalling weather conditions in Lancashire. Burnley eventually ended their opening League campaign in ninth place, with seven victories, three draws and twelve defeats, which had been quite a feat, considering that they had been playing the Association game for little more than six seasons. However, despite many excellent performances during the season, the Burnley club would have to apply for re-election to the League, as one of the teams finishing in the last four positions.

DERBY COUNTY

Derby County opened their League campaign with a 6–3 victory against Bolton Wanderers at Pikes Lane, having recovered from a three-goal deficit, with George Bakewell, Lawrence Plackett and Lewis Cooper all scoring twice. However, a poor run of results saw the Derby side win just one of their following thirteen League games to end the year at the foot of the League table.

County's regular team during the season saw Joseph Marshall in goal, together with Arthur Latham, Archie Ferguson, Albert Williamson, John Smith and Walter Roulstone in defence, while George Bakewell, Lewis Cooper, Alexander (Sandy) Higgins, Henry Plackett and his brother, Lawrence, formed the attack. Goalkeeper Marshall soon moved to Derby Junction, after conceding fifty goals in fourteen League appearances. Latham eventually trained the Derby side, while Ferguson, Williamson and Smith remained with Derby for their first couple of seasons in the Football League.

Walter Roulstone made in excess of one hundred League appearances for the club. George Bakewell, who had arrived from the Derby Midlands club in 1884, played close on fifty League games prior to joining Notts County; Lewis Cooper scored twenty-three goals in fifty League appearances; Sandy Higgins, a recent signing from Kilmarnock, found the net on twenty-five occasions in forty-two League games; while Lawrence and Henry Plackett joined Nottingham Forest at the season's end.

Derby's second League game ended in a 2–1 home defeat against West Bromwich Albion, which was followed by a Sandy Higgins goal in a one-all home draw with Accrington. Their indifferent form continued with heavy away defeats at West Bromwich Albion (5–0), Accrington (6–2), Everton (6–2), Wolverhampton Wanderers (4–1) and Preston North End (5–0), as well as at home to Everton (4–2). Derby had slumped to the foot of the League table at the halfway stage of the campaign.

Late December saw a return to winning ways with a 3–2 home success against Notts County, but was followed by a Boxing Day home defeat against Bolton Wanderers (3–2), with Sandy Higgins scoring both Derby goals. The year ended with a 4–2 reverse at Aston Villa, with Benjamin Spilsbury on target for County in his only League appearance for the club.

New Year saw a 3–0 home victory against Wolverhampton Wanderers, with Higgins, Cooper and Lawrence Plackett scoring the Derby goals, which preceded a 1–0 defeat at Burnley. The month ended with a 2–1 home win against Stoke, with goals from Cooper and Lawrence Plackett, securing the points for the East Midlands side.

Away from the struggles of the League, a Sandy Higgins goal earned a first round FA Cup victory against Derby Junction to secure a second round tie at Aston Villa, where they suffered a 5–3 defeat. However, their greatly improved League form continued with a 1–0 home win against Burnley, with Lewis Cooper scoring the only goal of the game, while Sandy Higgins netted four goals in an excellent 5–2 home success against Aston Villa. Lewis Cooper then scored his seventh and eighth League goals of the season in a 5–2 victory at Notts County, which was followed by a one-all draw at Stoke. The season ended with a 3–0 reverse at Blackburn and Derby ended the campaign in tenth place, having won seven, drawn two and lost thirteen of their twenty-two League fixtures, scoring forty-one goals and conceding sixty-one.

George Bakewell ended the season with six League goals; Lawrence Plackett found the net on seven occasions; Lewis Cooper scored eight goals in fifteen League appearances; and Sandy Higgins led the scoring with eleven League goals, in a season in which Derby were required to apply for re-election to the League. However, they received more than the sufficient number of votes required to maintain their League status.

NOTTS COUNTY

Notts County had been playing competitive football for twenty-six seasons prior to receiving an invitation to join the newly formed Football League.

However, their great days had been during the late 1870s and early 1880s when the Nottingham side could boast a team of England international players who had twice suffered odd goal defeats in the semi-finals of the English FA Cup.

Seven of the County team who had appeared in their semi-final sides had appeared in the English national team, however, for County's opening League fixture, the likes of Harry and Arthur Cursham, Ernest Greenhalgh, Stuart Macrae and William Gunn had either retired or left the club.

County received a visit from Everton for their opening League game, with J Holland in goal. F H Gutteridge, Tom McLean, G H Brown, B F Warburton and Alf Shelton covered the defensive positions, while W Hodder, E Harker, Robert Jardine, Albert Moore and E S Wardle formed the attack. However, the game ended in a 2–1 defeat for the Nottingham side. Albert Moore scored County's consolation goal, but these were to be few as the season was one of continual struggle.

Notts won five and lost fifteen of their twenty-two League games, which included a 9–1 defeat at Aston Villa in their third League game of the season. They also suffered seven-goal defeats against both Bolton Wanderers and Preston North End. Welcome victories were notched up against Wolverhampton Wanderers, Everton and West Bromwich Albion. A 6–1 home success against Burnley was their highest win of the campaign, with Robert Jardine scoring five of the County goals.

Following a 3–2 defeat at the Wednesday in the early rounds of the FA Cup competition, the Nottingham side ended a dismal season by finishing in eleventh place in the League. The main highlight of the season was the inclusion of Alf Shelton and Harry Daft in the England team against Ireland towards the end of the campaign. However, their poor League position resulted in them applying for re-election, which they narrowly managed upon receiving two votes more than Birmingham St George's.

STOKE

Following Stoke's invitation to join the newly formed Football League, club secretary Harry Lockett was immediately appointed as secretary of the League. The Potteries' side's usual line-up during the season saw William Rowley in goal, together with Tom Clare, Alf Underwood, Ramsey, Shutt and Smith in defence, while Sayer, McSkimming, Staton, Edge and Tunnicliffe formed a capable attack.

William Rowley had begun his career with the Stoke Club as a forward, prior to joining Burslem Port Vale. However, upon returning to Stoke, Rowley made nearly 150 appearances in goal, as well as appearing for the English national team, while fullbacks Tom Clare and Alf Underwood, having joined Stoke from local amateur teams, spent many seasons with the north Staffordshire club with whom they gained England caps.

Stoke's opening League game resulted in a 2–0 home defeat against West Bromwich Albion in front of 4,000 spectators. Their form improved as the year progressed with excellent victories against Notts County (3–0), Burnley (4–3) and Blackburn Rovers (2–1), prior to suffering a poor run of results, which included a 7–0 defeat at Preston, with the Potteries' side arriving with nine players. Preston kindly allowed Smalley and Dempsey from their reserve team to make up the Stoke numbers, which made little difference to the outcome.

Stoke eventually ended the campaign in twelfth and last place, following just four victories in the League, while scoring twenty-six goals and conceding fifty-one, with McSkimming leading the scoring with six League goals.

McSkimming and Alf Underwood had appeared in all twenty-two League games for Stoke, while William Rowley had missed just one, due to an international trial. Despite a poor season, which included a 2–1 defeat against Warwick County in the first round of the FA Cup, the Stoke ground had been chosen as the venue for the England international game against Wales, while both Tom Clare and William Rowley made their international debuts against the Welsh during the latter part of the campaign.

Re-election to the League created few problems for the popular Stoke side, who received ten votes, more than enough for them to retain their League status for the following season.

Wolves Secure Their First FA Cup Final Appearance

At the second round stage of the 1888–89 FA Cup competition, eight of the twelve members of the Football League remained in the draw, together with Grimsby, Halliwell and the Wednesday from the north of England, while Swifts, Chatham, Birmingham St George's, Nottingham Forest and Walsall Town Swifts represented the south and Midlands. Preston North End progressed to the quarter-finals with a 2–0 victory at Grimsby, Blackburn Rovers received a walkover against the Swifts, while Birmingham St George's secured a 3–2 success against Halliwell to appear in their only quarter-final. FA Cup holders West Bromwich Albion defeated Burnley by five goals to one, with Jem Bayliss scoring a brace of goals; Aston Villa secured a 5–3 victory against Derby County, with two goals apiece from Archie Hunter and Dennis Hodgetts; and Wolverhampton Wanderers enjoyed a 6–1 success against Walsall Town Swifts. Nottingham Forest suffered a 3–2 defeat against Chatham, following two drawn ties, while the Wednesday completed the quarter-final line-up with a 3–2 win against Notts County, with Winterbottom, Ingram and Cawley on target for the Sheffield side.

The quarter-final ties tended to be one-sided affairs, with Wolverhampton Wanderers defeating the Wednesday by five goals to nil, Blackburn Rovers inflicting an 8–1 defeat on Aston Villa, with Haresnape and John Southworth sharing seven of the goals, and Birmingham St George's being a little unfortunate to suffer a 2–0 reverse at Preston North End. West Bromwich Albion once again reached the semi-final stage of the competition with a 10–1 victory at Chatham, with Bassett and Bayliss both scoring twice, together with a hat-trick from Joe Wilson, and thereby teaching the army side a footballing lesson. Albion's reward for reaching the last four was a semi-final tie against Preston at Bramall Lane, Sheffield, while Wolverhampton Wanderers and Blackburn Rovers were due to meet at the Crewe Alexandra ground.

Preston had lost to Albion in the previous season's final, while the West Bromwich side were aiming for a fourth successive final appearance. However, it was not to be, as the Lancashire team held on to a 1–0 success, while the Blackburn and Wolves tie ended in a one-all draw, with Wolves securing a 3–1 victory in the replay to earn their first FA Cup Final appearance.

England Are Too Strong for the Welsh

England's opening international game of the 1888–89 season took place at the Victoria Ground, Stoke, on 23 February against the Welsh national team. It saw the recall of William Moon in goal, together with A M and P M Walters at fullback.

All three half backs were making their England debuts, with Alfred Fletcher (Wolverhampton Wanderers) making the first of two international appearances. Arthur Lowder, his Wolves team-mate, played his one England game, as did William Betts of the Wednesday. Billy Bassett (West Bromwich Albion) and John Goodall (Preston North End) once again formed the right wing partnership. Fred Dewhurst (Preston North End) made his final England appearance at inside right, while John Southworth and William Townley of Blackburn Rovers, who had both scored regularly throughout the season, gained their first international caps. Southworth scored in all three of his England appearances, while Townley scored twice in two.

As expected, the England side won with ease as Bassett, Goodall, Southworth and Dewhurst found the net in a 4–1 success.

Jack Yates Scores a Hat-trick Against Ireland

The following week saw England entertain Ireland at the Everton ground, with the selectors making eleven changes in the side after the victory against Wales, including nine new caps. William Rowley (Stoke) made the first of two appearances in goal, while his team-mate Tom Clare was included at right fullback for the first of four England games, none on the losing side.

Alfred Aldridge, who had made his England debut as a West Bromwich Albion player, gained his second cap as a member of the Walsall Town Swifts team; Frank Burton (Nottingham Forest) made his only England appearance at inside right; while Charles Wreford-Brown (Corinthians) made the first of four international appearances during a ten-year period. Wreford-Brown, a solicitor by profession, had been the gentleman reputed to have given Association Football the alternative name of 'soccer'.

Davie Weir (Bolton Wanderers) played the first of two England games and scored in both; Alfred Shelton (Notts County) followed his brother Charles into the England team for the first of six caps; while his Notts County team-mate, Harry Daft, an accomplished county cricketer with Nottinghamshire, played for his country on five occasions. John Brodie (Wolverhampton Wanderers) played the first of three England games, prior to becoming a referee; Jack Yates (Burnley) played his one England game at outside left; while Joseph Lofthouse (Blackburn Rovers) was the only England forward with previous international experience.

England won quite comfortably by six goals to one with Jack Yates scoring a hat-trick in his only international appearance, together with further goals from Lofthouse, Weir and Brodie, which meant that the England side had suffered just one defeat in fifteen games, leaving them well prepared for the game against Scotland at the Oval on 13 April.

Preston Win the 'Double'

The 1889 FA Cup Final took place at the Oval on 30 March between Preston North End, the newly acclaimed champions of the Football League, and Wolverhampton Wanderers, who had finished in third place. Preston selected the following eleven:

Dr Mills-Roberts

Howarth   Holmes

Drummond   Russell   Graham

Gordon   Jimmy Ross   John Goodall   Dewhurst   Thomson

The Wanderers selected the following team:

Baynton

Baugh   Mason

Fletcher   Allen   Lowder

Hunter   Wykes   Brodie   Wood   Knight

Major Francis Marindin once again refereed the final.

Ten of the Lancashire side had appeared in the 1888 final. Sam Thomson replaced Nick Ross, who had moved to Everton, and was the only change in the Preston team, while Wanderers included seven current or future England internationals in their side. John Baynton replaced W C Rose in goal, as the latter had appeared for Warwick County in an earlier round of the cup. Dr Mills-Roberts, who practised medicine in the Birmingham area, tended to play only in cup ties for Preston, while James Trainer, their regular goalkeeper, who had signed from Bolton Wanderers during the Christmas period of 1886, became the first goalkeeper to make 250 League appearances.

A crowd in excess of 22,000 arrived at the Oval to watch the final. The kick-off once again was delayed until 4 p.m., thus allowing the spectators the opportunity to watch the University boat race.

Team captains Fred Dewhurst (Preston) and John Brodie (Wolves) tossed up for the choice of ends, which resulted in the Lancashire side kicking with the wind against a Wanderers team wearing black armbands out of respect for their captain, who had recently suffered the loss of his father.

Wolves dominated the early play, with Brodie shooting wide, while Knight brushed the Preston goalposts with a speculative shot from the edge of the area. However, as the Preston forwards came more into the game, Gordon and Dewhurst began to dominate the proceedings, which inevitably led to the opening goal when Gordon rounded two Wolves' defenders and crossed to Jimmy Ross. He shot against the Wanderers' crossbar, while Fred Dewhurst slotted the rebound between the posts to secure a one-goal lead for the Lancashire side.

Preston continued to exert further pressure on the Wolves' defence during the first period of play with Ross and Goodall on top of their form, which eventually led to a second Preston goal, following a speculative shot from Jimmy Ross. Goalkeeper Baynton seemed to have had the shot covered. However, the ball slipped through the keeper's legs, much to the joy of the Preston supporters, whose team ended the half two goals to the good.

Wolves enjoyed the advantage of a stiff breeze during the second half, which encouraged them to play with more confidence, as Hunter and Fletcher forced excellent saves out of Mills-Roberts in the Preston goal. But their dominance soon came to an end as Ross and Gordon took on the Wanderers' defenders, which led to a fine save by Baynton from a Jimmy Ross volley. Following the clearance by Baynton, Gordon crossed to Dewhurst, who forced a further excellent save from the overworked Wolves' keeper. However, he was unable to save a Sam Thomson shot from two yards out, as Preston secured a three-goal lead, with the Wanderers' appeals for off-side rejected by Major Marindin.

Preston spent the remainder of the game in the Wanderers' half, without adding to their score. The final whistle sounded with the Lancashire side the victors by three goals to nil, and Major Marindin, in his capacity as president of the Football Association, presented the FA Cup to Fred Dewhurst, the Preston captain, who had recently collected the Football League trophy as well.

Following their success in the newly formed Football League, as well as in the FA Cup competition, the Preston team deservedly earned the appropriate nickname of the 'Invincibles', while the *Daily News* reported a little unfairly that, 'judged by their play on Saturday, the Wolverhampton Wanderers have still a good deal to learn before they can expect to cope successfully with Preston North End'. Charles Crump, in reply, said that Wolves were essentially a local team, while Preston comprised players from all corners of the United Kingdom. However, it was certainly true that the majority of teams had a fair amount of catching up to do if they were to match the excellent skills of William Sudell's Preston team.

Victory for Scotland at the Oval

The final international game of the season took place at the Oval on 13 April against Scotland, with John Brodie (Wolverhampton Wanderers) and Davie Weir (Bolton Wanderers) retaining their places from the victory against Ireland, while William Moon returned in goal, together with A M and P M Walters at fullback. Harry Allen (Wolverhampton Wanderers) and James Forrest (Blackburn Rovers) made their first England appearances for more than a year, while Henry Hammond (Corinthians), an accomplished county cricketer with Somerset, appeared in his only England game prior to pursuing a career as Director-General of Education in Rhodesia. Billy Bassett and John Goodall were recalled to the attack, together with Tinsley Lindley, who had scored in all nine of his previous appearances for his country.

In an exciting encounter at the Oval, the Scots avenged the previous season's defeat in Glasgow by winning by the odd goal in five, with Weir and Bassett on target for England.

The Football League Proves a Success

Much to the joy of William McGregor, the inaugural League season had proved a great success, with Preston North End the worthy winners of the championship as well as of the FA Cup, thus completing an excellent 'double'. There remained one outstanding issue at the close of the season that concerned Stoke, Notts County, Derby County and Burnley applying for re-election to the League, following their poor end-of-season League placings.

Stoke received ten votes, Burnley nine, Derby County eight and Notts County seven, to all retain their League status for the 1889–90 campaign, while Birmingham St George's with five votes and the Wednesday with four were the unfortunate teams to miss out. The final League table for the 1888–89 season is as listed in Table I.

Table I: *Football League results for the first season – 1888–89*

	P	W	D	L	F	A	PTS
1. Preston North End	22	18	4	0	74	15	40
2. Aston Villa	22	12	5	5	61	43	29
3. Wolverhampton Wanderers	22	12	4	6	50	37	28
4. Blackburn Rovers	22	10	6	6	66	45	26
5. Bolton Wanderers	22	10	2	10	63	59	22
6. West Bromwich Albion	22	10	2	10	40	46	22

	P	W	D	L	F	A	PTS
7. Accrington	22	6	8	8	48	48	20
8. Everton	22	9	2	11	35	46	20
9. Burnley	22	7	3	12	42	62	17
10. Derby County	22	7	2	13	41	61	16
11. Notts County	22	5	2	15	39	73	12
12. Stoke	22	4	4	14	26	51	12

Chapter XV

PRESTON RETAIN THE LEAGUE CHAMPIONSHIP – 1889–90

PRESTON NORTH END RETAIN THE LEAGUE CHAMPIONSHIP
BILLY TOWNLEY SCORES A HAT-TRICK AS BLACKBURN ROVERS WIN THE FA CUP
ENGLAND REMAIN UNBEATEN
FRED GEARY NETS THREE AGAINST IRELAND
A M AND P M WALTERS BOW OUT OF INTERNATIONAL FOOTBALL
SUNDERLAND REPLACE STOKE IN THE FOOTBALL LEAGUE

There were few surprises in the Football League during the opening weeks of the 1889–90 season as all four of the re-elected teams continued their struggle for survival.

STOKE

Stoke, who had registered just four victories during the previous campaign suffered further humiliation during the 1889–90 season with just three wins in twenty-two League games, which included a 10–1 reverse at Preston in their second fixture of the season.

Following a 2–1 home success against Wolverhampton Wanderers during the opening month of the campaign, the Potteries' side suffered a disastrous run of results, including home defeats against Bolton Wanderers, Everton, West Bromwich Albion, Blackburn Rovers and Preston North End, as well as away defeats at Notts County, Derby County, Accrington, Aston Villa, Everton and Blackburn Rovers, with the latter two by eight goals. Their only away win of the season was against fellow strugglers, Burnley. New Year saw a 5–0 defeat at Bolton, which, curiously, preceded an excellent FA Cup run, with a first round victory against Old Westminsters, as well as 4–2 home success against Everton in the second round. However, Stoke were a little unfortunate to suffer a 3–2 defeat at Wolves in the quarter-finals in the first of three successive FA Cup quarter-final appearances by the Potteries' side.

On their return to League action, the Stoke team secured a 7–1 victory against Accrington, followed by successive defeats at home to Burnley (4–3) and away at West Bromwich Albion (2–1), while the season ended with one-all home draws against Aston Villa and Notts County. This left Stoke once again at the foot of the League table, with ten points from twenty-two games. Stoke had won three, drawn four and lost fifteen of their League fixtures, while scoring twenty-seven goals and conceding sixty-nine, with Gee and Ramsey leading the scoring with four goals apiece. Ramsey and Underwood appeared in all twenty-two League games, in a season when the Potteries' side were once again required to apply for re-election to the League.

NOTTS COUNTY

Notts County were determined to improve upon their indifferent results of the 1888–89 season, which led them to journey north of the border in the hope of signing Scottish players, who had certainly improved the performances of the likes of Aston Villa and Preston North End. County eventually signed Sandy Ferguson, David Calderhead, Tom McInnes, James Oswald and James MacMillan to play alongside England internationals Harry Daft and Alfred Shelton, while goalkeeper George Toone arrived from Notts Rangers.

Notts opened the season with away defeats at Wolverhampton Wanderers and Derby County on either side of a one-all draw at Aston Villa. However, a six-game unbeaten run, which included home wins against Stoke (3–1) and Everton (4–3) as well as away victories at Accrington (8–1) and Bolton Wanderers (4–0) saw the Nottingham side move into the top half of the League table. Their unbeaten run continued with successive home draws against Burnley and Aston Villa. Then, a 9–1 reverse at Blackburn Rovers, together with further defeats at Everton and at home to Wolverhampton Wanderers, ended their excellent run of results, though the year came to an end with a 3–1 home success against Derby County. The new year showed that little had really changed. It began with defeats at West Bromwich Albion and at home to Bolton Wanderers, as well as a one-all home draw with Blackburn Rovers. Despite their indifferent League form, the Nottingham side enjoyed an excellent FA Cup run, including a 4–1 success against Aston Villa in the second round to secure a quarter-final tie at the Wednesday.

On a quagmire of a pitch at the Olive Grove ground, the Sheffield side won by five goals to one. Notts protested to the Football Association that the game should never have taken place in such appalling weather conditions, which resulted in a replay, with County winning by the odd goal in five. Wednesday then protested to the FA that County had fielded three players who had played in unauthorised games in Scotland prior to the start of the 1889–90 season. This resulted in a further replay, with Wednesday winning by two goals to one.

As the season reached its end, County's indifferent form continued with a 4–3 defeat at Preston followed by a 3–1 home success against Accrington, while further defeats at Burnley and at home to Preston, as well as a one-all draw at Stoke, saw County end the campaign in tenth place, with six wins, five draws and eleven defeats in their twenty-two League fixtures, while scoring forty-three goals and conceding fifty-one. James Oswald proved an excellent signing from Third Lanark, with fifteen goals in nineteen League appearances. However, despite an improved season, the Nottingham side was again amongst the applicants for re-election to the League.

DERBY COUNTY

Of the four teams re-elected to the Football League Derby County showed the greatest improvement during the 1889–90 campaign, which coincided with the arrival of the Goodall brothers, Archie and John. Archie had appeared for both Aston Villa and Preston during the inaugural League season, while John, an England international player, had been the star of the Preston side that had won both the League and FA Cup. John had scored five goals for Great Lever against Derby during the 1884 season. Despite the attempts of the Midlands side to sign him, Goodall was persuaded by William Sudell to join Preston, where he enjoyed great success.

In ten seasons with Derby, John Goodall made in excess of 200 League appearances, in which he scored more than eighty goals and taught the great Steve Bloomer much about the Association game. Archie, one of the great characters of Victorian football, enjoyed an even longer career with Derby, for whom he made nearly 400 League appearances and gained a number of caps for the Irish national team.

Derby opened the season with a one-all draw at Stoke, with Cooper on target, which was followed by a 3–1 home success against West Bromwich Albion, with Cooper, Higgins and John Goodall scoring for Derby, while John Goodall scored twice in a 4–2 defeat at Blackburn Rovers. John Goodall repeated his goal-scoring feat the following week in a 2–0 home win against Notts County, which preceded a two-all home draw with Everton, while a 7–1 defeat at Aston Villa taught the Derby side a footballing lesson.

County then secured successive home wins against Preston North End (2–1) and Stoke (2–0), with Cooper scoring in both victories, while Higgins, Needham and Milarvie found the net in a 3–2 success at West Bromwich Albion. This was followed by a 6–1 defeat at Accrington. The halfway stage of the campaign arrived with a three-all home draw with Wolverhampton Wanderers, with Higgins (2) and Cooper on target for the home side. Their indifferent away record continued with defeats at Bolton Wanderers (7–1) and Notts County (3–1), which preceded a 3–2 home win against Bolton Wanderers, with Holmes, Milarvie and Archie Goodall on target. The year ended with a 5–0 home success against Aston Villa, with Sandy Higgins scoring all five of the Derby goals. Higgins was again on target in the opening game of the new year in a 4–1 success against Burnley, which was followed by a 5–0 reverse at Preston in a game in which Sandy Higgins and both Goodall brothers were unavailable for selection. The following week saw an embarrassing 11–2 defeat against Everton in the first round of the FA Cup, with John Goodall scoring both Derby goals.

On their return to League action, the East Midlands side suffered a 2–1 defeat at Wolverhampton Wanderers, while Roulstone, Higgins, Milarvie and Holmes found the net in a 4–0 home success against Blackburn Rovers. Defeats against Accrington (3–2), Burnley (2–0) and Everton (3–0) saw Derby end the season in seventh place, with nine wins, three draws and ten defeats in their twenty-two League games, while scoring forty-three goals and conceding fifty-five. Walter Roulstone appeared in all twenty-two League games for Derby, while Latham, Ferguson, Williamson, Higgins and Archie Goodall missed only one in a season in which Derby had avoided the re-election positions, owing mainly to the goal-scoring exploits of Sandy Higgins who had found the net on fourteen occasions.

BURNLEY

Burnley opened the 1889–90 League campaign with draws against Aston Villa and Accrington, either side of a 2–1 reverse at Everton, which was followed by the inevitable defeat against Preston prior to entertaining Aston Villa in the return game at Turf Moor.

Admission charges were increased from four pence to six pence for the Villa visit, much to the annoyance of the Burnley supporters, especially as the likes of Everton and Preston charged just three pence. Despite the increased charges, a crowd in excess of 6,000 arrived at Turf Moor to see the visitors win by six goals to two, with Albert Allen netting a hat-trick.

A further home defeat against West Bromwich Albion then saw the Burnley side secure a rare away point in a two-all draw at Accrington, but this preceded a 7–1 defeat at Blackburn Rovers during the final week of October. The struggle continued throughout the remaining weeks of the year and included six-goal defeats against West Bromwich Albion and Preston North End, as well as a 9–1 reverse at Wolverhampton Wanderers.

Then followed a decision by the Football Association to abolish the strict residential qualifications, thus allowing Burnley the opportunity of signing Lambie, Stewart, Hill, McColl and McLardie from north of the border. This produced a slight improvement on the field of play. However, the Lancashire side continued to struggle during the new year with defeats at Derby County, as well as at home to Stoke, Everton and Blackburn Rovers.

Burnley then had a little good fortune. After a 6–3 defeat against Bolton Wanderers on a frozen pitch, Burnley lodged a complaint with the Football League committee that the game should never have taken place in such harsh conditions, which resulted in a replayed game on the opening day of March. Burnley won by seven goals to one to register their first League success of the season, with Claude Lambie scoring three of the goals.

Following their victory against Bolton, Burnley's confidence grew and there were further wins against Derby County, Stoke and Notts County, while the season ended with a two-all draw at Bolton. However, their late flourish had been to no avail, as Burnley finished the season in eleventh place, with four wins, five draws and thirteen defeats, which resulted in a further application to retain their League status.

While the Burnley side struggled in the League, they enjoyed an excellent run of results in the Lancashire Cup competition. Following a first round victory against Rossendale, centre forward Murray scored five of the goals in a 15–0 success against Haydock in the second round to secure a semi-final tie against Higher Walton, which resulted in a further victory for Burnley by seven goals to nil.

Burnley were then due to meet Blackburn Rovers in the final, who had made six previous final appearances. However, against all the odds, the Burnley team secured a 2–0 victory, with Stewart scoring both of their goals.

Rovers protested that the final should have been replayed following an encroachment by the spectators onto the field of play, but their appeals were dismissed and Burnley were awarded the trophy.

EVERTON

Everton, who had ended the 1888–89 League campaign just one place above the re-election positions, were determined to improve upon their indifferent League performances of the previous season. Their resolution saw the arrival of Alex Latta, Charles Parry and Fred Geary, while future England internationals, Alf Milward, Edgar Chadwick and John Holt remained with the club. Latta, a future Scottish cap, who had arrived from Dumbarton Athletic during the close season, made nearly 150 League appearances for Everton, prior to joining Liverpool in 1896. Welsh international, Parry, spent seven seasons with the club, while Geary, who had previously played for Grimsby Town and Notts County, scored seventy-eight goals in ninety-one League appearances for the Merseysiders, as well as scoring a hat-trick on his England debut.

Everton opened the season with a 3–2 home win against Blackburn Rovers, with Geary (2) and Parry on target, which was followed by a further home success against Burnley (2–1), with both players once again finding the net. Parry scored for the third successive game in a 2–1 reverse at Wolverhampton Wanderers. Fred Geary then scored twice in successive home and away victories against Bolton Wanderers (4–3 and 3–0), while Edgar Chadwick netted in drawn games at Derby County (2–2) and at home to Wolverhampton Wanderers (1–1) as Everton continued their excellent start to the season. However, a 4–3 reverse at Notts County ended their fine run of results, with Alf Milward scoring a brace of goals for the visitors.

Following a two-all home draw with Accrington, Fred Geary scored a hat-trick in an 8–0 home win against Stoke, while Geary scored the winning goal in a 2–1 success in the return game at Stoke. However, a 5–1 defeat against Preston saw a rare home defeat for Everton. A 2–1 victory at Aston Villa saw a return to winning ways, with Geary again scoring a brace of goals.

An Alex Latta hat-trick then secured a 5–3 home win against Notts County, which was followed by a splendid victory at Preston, where Geary and Milward found the net, and the year ended with a 4–2 success at Blackburn Rovers, with Milward (2), Brady and Latta netting for the Everton side.

Everton's winning run continued into the new year with a 7–0 home win against Aston Villa, with Brady (2), Chadwick (2), Geary (2) and Latta on target, which preceded an 11–2 success against Derby County in the first round of the FA Cup, with Brady, Geary and Milward all scoring hat-tricks. However, the Merseysiders were brought down to earth in the second round, as they suffered a 4–2 reverse at Stoke.

On their return to League action, the Everton side secured a 1–0 victory at Burnley, with Edgar Chadwick scoring the only goal of the game, which preceded a rare defeat at Accrington (5–3), with Brady (2) and Geary on target for Everton, while Alf Milward netted a brace of goals in a 5–1 home win against West Bromwich Albion.

Milward was again on target in a 3–0 home win against Derby County, while the campaign ended with a 4–1 reverse at West Bromwich Albion, as Everton finished the season as League runners-up, following just five defeats in twenty-two League games. Chadwick, Doyle, Milward, Hannah and Parry had appeared in all twenty-two League games, while John Holt had missed only one, in Everton's most successful season to date. Latta and Chadwick scored nine League goals apiece, Alf Milward found the net on ten occasions, while Fred Geary led the scoring with twenty-one goals in eighteen League appearances.

ACCRINGTON

Accrington opened the 1889–90 League campaign with a 4–2 victory at Bolton Wanderers, followed by successive draws at Burley and at home to Blackburn Rovers. Defeats at Wolverhampton Wanderers, as well as a humiliating 8–1 home defeat against Notts County, ended their fine start to the season.

Then followed further drawn games at Everton and at home to Burnley, prior to suffering the expected defeat at Preston, while a 6–1 home success against Derby County saw the Lancashire side in a mid-table position by the middle of November.

Accrington then suffered a 3–2 reverse at Blackburn Rovers. The halfway stage of the season arrived with a 4–2 home win against Aston Villa, which was followed by a further away defeat at West Bromwich Albion (4–1). However, the end of the year saw the Lancashire side return to form with successive victories at Aston Villa (2–1) and at home to Stoke (2–1).

New Year's Day saw Accrington secure their third win in a row in a 6–3 home success against Wolverhampton Wanderers, which preceded a further home victory against Bolton Wanderers (3–1) prior to playing a goalless home draw with West Bromwich Albion. Further victories at Derby County (3–2) and at home to Everton (5–3) saw Accrington climb to fifth place in the League table, but successive defeats at Stoke (7–1) and Notts County (3–1), together with a two-all home draw with Preston, saw the Lancashire side end the campaign in sixth position with nine wins, six draws and seven defeats in their twenty-two League games, while scoring fifty-three goals and conceding fifty-six. John Kirkham had ended the season as leading goal scorer, while George

Haworth had performed splendidly at the heart of the defence. Accrington had enjoyed their finest season to date, which had included a couple of excellent performances in the FA Cup competition.

Accrington were drawn at home to West Bromwich Albion in the first round, which resulted in a 3–1 victory for the Lancashire team in appalling weather conditions. However, Albion protested that the game should have been abandoned, which led to a replayed tie resulting in a further victory for the home side by three goals to nil to secure a second round tie at the Wednesday. While Accrington enjoyed the bulk of the play in Sheffield, the Wednesday were a little fortunate to win the game by the odd goal in three. However, little could be taken away from the Accrington team, who had once again proved that they were as capable as any team in England.

WEST BROMWICH ALBION

West Bromwich Albion opened the 1889–90 League campaign with a 3–1 reverse at Derby County, followed by successive wins at Notts County (2–1) and at home to Aston Villa (3–0), with Jem Bayliss on target in both victories, while a 5–0 defeat at Preston continued Albion's indifferent run of results. Pittaway and Wilson then found the net in a 2–1 success at Burnley, while defeats at home to Wolverhampton Wanderers (4–1) and away at Aston Villa (1–0) saw the West Bromwich side move into the bottom half of the League table. However, Albion soon returned to winning ways with a 6–3 home win against Bolton Wanderers, with Tom Pearson scoring four goals for the home side.

Following a 3–2 home defeat against Derby County, Albion secured a 3–1 victory at Stoke, with Perry, Pearson and Evans scoring for the visitors. The halfway stage of the season arrived with a 6–1 home success against Burnley, with Jem Bayliss scoring twice, leaving Albion with six wins and five defeats in their opening eleven League fixtures. Albion then suffered defeats at Blackburn Rovers (5–0) and Bolton Wanderers (7–0), prior to securing a 4–1 home win against Accrington, with Tom Pearson netting a hat-trick. The year ended with successive draws at Wolverhampton Wanderers (1–1) and at home to Preston North End (2–2). However, 'Darkie' Timmins sustained a broken leg during the game at Wolverhampton, which all but ended his career, following many years of excellent service with Albion.

New Year saw Tom Pearson score his third hat-trick of the season in a 4–2 home success against Notts County, which was followed by a further home win against Blackburn Rovers (3–2), with Evans scoring twice. A goalless draw at Accrington secured a welcome away point, but their indifferent away form continued with a 5–1 reverse at Everton. Albion then secured a 2–1 home win against Stoke, with Woodhall and Bayliss on target, while the season ended with a 4–1 home success against Everton, with Evans scoring a brace of goals to end the Lancashire side's hopes of the League Championship. The West Bromwich team finished in fifth position, following eleven victories, three draws and eight defeats in twenty-two League games, while scoring forty-seven goals and conceding fifty.

Ezra Horton and Tom Pearson were ever present in the Albion side, while Charlie Perry missed just one game in a season when Evans scored eight goals in thirteen League appearances, Jem Bayliss found the net on nine occasions, while Tom Pearson led the scoring with seventeen League goals.

Despite a 23–0 victory against Burton Wanderers in a local cup competition, the Black Country side struggled to find success in any cup competition during the season. There was a first round FA Cup defeat at Accrington, as well as defeats against Aston Villa and Walsall Town Swifts in local cups. However, Albion enjoyed better success in cup games throughout the remaining years of the Victorian period.

BOLTON WANDERERS

Bolton Wanderers had scouted Scotland prior to the 1889–90 League campaign, which resulted in the arrival of James Cassidy from Glasgow Hibernians and John McNee from the Renton club to bolster their attack. Cassidy eventually scored in excess of one hundred goals in nine seasons with the club, while McNee remained for four seasons, prior to joining Newcastle. Wanderers were initially fined for playing McNee without the necessary qualifying period. However, with the arrival of Cassidy and McNee, as well as the inclusion of Davie Weir, Kenny Davenport and David Jones, the Lancashire side were hopeful of improving upon the fifth place finish of the previous season.

The season opened with successive home defeats against Accrington (4–2) and Everton (4–3), followed by a 3–0 reverse in the return game at Everton, while a 6–2 home defeat against Preston North End continued their dismal start to the season.

Then followed Bolton's first victory of the campaign in a 1–0 success at Stoke, with Barbour scoring the only goal of the game. However, further defeats at home to Notts County (4–0) and away at West Bromwich Albion (6–3) saw the Lancashire side slide to the foot of the League table. Brogan, Milne and Kenny Davenport then found the net in a 3–2 home win against Blackburn Rovers, while Kenny Davenport netted a brace of goals in a 2–0 home victory against Aston Villa, Though followed by a 3–1 reverse at Preston, Bolton's much improved home form continued with a 7–1 win against Derby County, with James Cassidy scoring four of the Wanderers' goals.

Bolton secured a further seven-goal success the following week in a 7–0 home win against West Bromwich Albion, with Weir and Davenport both scoring twice. However, successive away defeats at Blackburn Rovers (7–1), Derby County (3–2) and Accrington (3–1) saw a disappointing end to the year.

Davie Weir then scored a brace of goals in a 5–3 victory at Notts County during the opening week of the new year, with Cassidy, Brogan and McNee completing the scoring. This preceded a 10–2 win against Belfast in the first round of the FA Cup competition, with Davie Weir on target on four occasions. A 2–1 League win at Aston Villa continued their excellent run of results, with Cassidy and Weir, once more on target. Bolton were then drawn at home to Sheffield United in the second round of the cup, which resulted in a 13–0 victory for the Wanderers, with goals by Cassidy (5), Weir (4), Brogan (3) and Robinson, securing a third round tie at Preston, who had twice defeated Bolton in League games during the season.

Prior to the FA Cup tie, Wanderers enjoyed a 5–0 home win against Stoke, with James Cassidy scoring a hat-trick, while Weir (2) and Brogan found the net in an excellent 3–2 victory against Preston as Bolton progressed to the semi-finals.

On their return to League action, the Lancashire side recorded their seventh successive FA Cup and League victory in a 4–1 home win against Wolverhampton Wanderers, with McNee (2), Turner and Weir finding the net. A 7–0 reverse at Burnley ended their excellent run of results, while their disappointment continued the following week in a 2–1 defeat against the Wednesday in a close semi-final tie at Perry Barr, Birmingham. Bolton then suffered a further away defeat at Wolverhampton Wanderers (5–1), and the season ended with a 2–2 home draw with Burnley, with Milne and Jones on target for Bolton.

They finished the campaign in ninth position, with nine victories, one draw and twelve defeats, while scoring fifty-four goals and conceding sixty-five. James Brogan, Kenny Davenport, David Jones and Davie Weir played in all but one of Bolton's League games, while Brogan and Davenport scored eight League goals apiece. Davie Weir found the net on eleven occasions, while James Cassidy led the scoring with thirteen goals in fifteen League appearances in a season in which Bolton would have to apply for re-election to the League.

BLACKBURN ROVERS

Blackburn Rovers had enjoyed an excellent 1888–89 season, which had included a fourth place finish in the League, as well as an appearance in the semi-finals of the FA Cup.

Joe Beverley, Fergie Suter and Jimmy Brown had decided to retire from the game, while Harry Campbell, George Dewar and Tom Brandon had arrived from north of the border to strengthen the Rovers' line-up, with Campbell making in excess of 100 appearances in five seasons with the club. Dewar played nearly 200 League games in eight seasons, while Tom Brandon enjoyed two spells with Blackburn in which he made 216 League appearances, as well as gaining a Scottish international cap towards the end of the century.

Rovers opened the 1889–90 League campaign with a 3–2 reverse at Everton, where Harry Campbell netted a brace of goals. This was followed by a 4–3 home success against Wolverhampton Wanderers, with Campbell once again on target. Campbell scored for the third game running in a 4–2 home win against Derby County, with John Southworth scoring twice and Joseph

Lofthouse, who had recently returned from Accrington, completing the scoring.

Following a two-all draw at Accrington, Rovers secured two excellent home wins against Aston Villa (7–0) and Burnley (7–1), with Southworth, Campbell and Walton finding the net in both victories. They were followed by successive defeats at home to Preston North End (4–3) and at Bolton Wanderers (3–2). However, Rovers then began a run of seven games without defeat, which would take them to second place in the League table.

Rovers' unbeaten run began with a 9–1 home success against Notts County, with Nat Walton and John Southworth both scoring hat-tricks, which preceded a further home win against Accrington (3–2), with Lofthouse, Forbes and Campbell on target. John Southworth then netted four of the Blackburn goals in a 5–0 victory against West Bromwich Albion, at Ewood Park.

Harry Campbell then scored his eleventh League goal of the season in a one-all draw at Preston, which was followed by a 7–1 home success against Bolton Wanderers, with Walton (4), Southworth (2) and Lofthouse netting the Blackburn goals. Lofthouse, Campbell and Southworth shared the goals in successive away victories at Stoke (3–0) and Wolverhampton Wanderers (4–2), as Rovers' excellent run continued. However, the tired Rovers side ended the year with a 4–2 home defeat against Everton, following their fourth League game in eight days. New Year saw Blackburn return to winning ways as John Southworth scored four of the goals in an 8–0 home win against the struggling Stoke side, which preceded a 3–2 reverse at West Bromwich Albion, while goals by Townley (2), Campbell and Barton secured a 4–2 success against Sunderland in the first round of the FA Cup to earn a second round home tie against Grimsby.

Blackburn had little difficulty in accounting for Grimsby by three goals to nil, with John Southworth once again amongst the scorers. This was followed by a 4–0 defeat at Derby County, while a 7–0 victory at Bootle saw Rovers continue their FA Cup run, with Walton (3), Southworth (2), Townley and Forbes on target to secure a semi-final tie against Wolverhampton Wanderers.

Mid-February saw a Joseph Lofthouse goal earn a one-all draw at Notts County, which preceded a 2–1 success at Burnley, with Walton and Townley on target. A John Southworth goal secured a 1–0 victory against Wolves in the semi-final of the FA Cup as Blackburn progressed to their fifth final appearance in nine seasons.

Rovers ended the season with a 3–0 defeat at Aston Villa on the final day of March, which had little bearing on the League Championship as Blackburn finished in third place, with twelve wins, three draws and seven defeats in twenty-two League games, while scoring seventy-eight goals and conceding forty-one, John Southworth, Harry Campbell, John Forbes and Tom Brandon were ever present in the Blackburn side, while James Forrest and Nat Walton missed only one game.

Joseph Lofthouse ended the campaign with eleven goals in eighteen League appearances; Nat Walton found the net on fourteen occasions; Harry Campbell netted fifteen goals; while John Southworth led the scoring with twenty-two League goals in an excellent season for the Rovers, who were looking forward to their FA Cup Final appearance against the Wednesday at the Oval on 29 March.

WOLVERHAMPTON WANDERERS

Wolverhampton Wanderers had surprised many during the 1888–89 season, with a third place League finish, as well as an appearance in the final of the FA Cup.

Wanderers continued their policy of fielding English-born players for the 1889–90 League campaign. Fletcher, Brodie, Baugh, Wood, Mason, Wykes and Allen remained in the side, while W C Rose had arrived from Preston North End to replace Baynton in goal.

The season opened with successive home wins against Notts County (2–0) and Everton (2–1) on either side of a 4–3 reverse at Blackburn Rovers, while their indifferent start to the season continued with a 2–1 defeat at Stoke. Following draws at Everton and at home to Stoke, as well as victories at West Bromwich Albion (4–1) and at home to Accrington (2–1), the Wolverhampton side moved into the top half of the League table. Further success arrived the following week when Wolves became the first team to secure a League win at Preston, as they scored twice without reply against the reigning League champions. This preceded a 2–1 reverse at Aston Villa, while a 2–1 victory at Burnley saw the Black Country side move into third place in the League at the halfway stage of the season.

Following a three-all draw at Derby County, Wolves secured a 9–0 home success against Burnley, as well as a 2–0 victory at Notts County, while a one-all home draw with Aston Villa began a run of five League games without a win. A Boxing Day home defeat against Blackburn Rovers (4–2) then saw the Molineux side end the year with a one-all home draw against neighbours West Bromwich Albion. Their indifferent form continued into the new year with a 6–3 reverse at Accrington, as well as a 1–0 home defeat against Preston North End. However, a narrow 2–1 home win against Derby County saw a return to winning ways.

Wanderers then suffered a 4–1 reverse at Bolton in the penultimate League game of the season, prior to defeating the Bolton side by five goals to one in the return game at Wolverhampton to end the campaign in fourth place following ten victories, five draws and seven defeats in their twenty-two League games, while scoring fifty-one goals and conceding thirty-eight. John Brodie scored eight goals; Worrall found the net on nine occasions; Harry Wood netted thirteen goals; while David Wykes led the scoring with fifteen League goals. While the Wolverhampton side had enjoyed a most productive season in the League, they had also performed admirably in the FA Cup, which began with a 2–0 home win against the Old Carthusians in the first round. This was an excellent result as the Old Boys had included A M and P M Walters, as well as Charles Wreford-Brown in their line-up.

Following a 2–1 home win against Small Heath in the second round, Wanderers secured a further odd-goal success in a home tie against Stoke (3–2) in the quarter-finals to reach the last four for the second year running. However, their luck ran out in the semi-finals as John Southworth scored the only goal of the game for Blackburn Rovers to deny the Wolverhampton side the opportunity of a second successive FA Cup Final appearance. Wolves' team of Englishmen had once again proved that they were more than a match for the teams who tended to rely upon the importation of players from north of the border.

ASTON VILLA

Aston Villa made few changes in their line-up for the 1889–90 League campaign following their second place finish during the previous season. Warner continued in goal, together with Cox, Burton, Coulton and Harry Devey in defence, while Albert Allen, Albert Brown, Archie Hunter and Dennis Hodgetts remained up front. Tom Green and Archie Goodall had left the club, while Scotsmen James Cowan and Billy Dickson were the most notable new arrivals to the Villa team, with Dickson destined to scored thirty-three goals in fifty-eight League appearances, while Cowan made in excess of 300 League appearances in thirteen seasons with the club. Dickson had originally played for Dundee Strathmere, with whom he had gained a Scottish international cap in a 10–2 victory against Ireland, with Dickson scoring four of the Scottish goals. This eventually resulted in a transfer to Sunderland prior to joining Villa. Cowan had arrived in Birmingham during August 1889, following an offer of a trial with Warwickshire County Cricket Club. However, he decided to sign for the Villa club with whom he won five League Championship medals and two FA Cup winners' medals, as well as representing the Scottish national side on three occasions.

Villa opened the season with Dennis Hodgetts scoring a brace of goals in a two-all home draw with Burnley, which was followed by a further home draw against Notts County (1–1), with Billy Dickson on target. Their third successive home game produced a 5–3 victory against Preston North End in the Lancashire side's first defeat in the Football League, with Cowan (2), Dickson, Brown and Albert Allen scoring for the Midlanders. However, a 3–0 reverse at West Bromwich Albion saw Villa's first defeat of the season.

A 6–2 victory at Burnley saw Villa return to winning ways, with Allen (3), Hunter (2) and Hodgetts on target, which preceded a 7–1 home success against Derby County, with Brown, Dickson and Allen all scoring twice. Then a humiliating 7–0 defeat at Blackburn Rovers soon brought the Villa team down to earth.

Following narrow home wins against West Bromwich Albion (1–0) and

Wolverhampton Wanderers (2–1), Billy Dickson scored his fifth League goal of the campaign in a one-all draw at Notts County, while late November saw successive away defeats at Bolton (2–0) and Accrington (4–2), as well as at home to Everton (2–1), and Villa moved into the bottom half of the League table.

Early December saw Villa return to form with a 6–1 home success against Stoke, with Garvey (3), Dickson (2) and Allen on target, while Hodgetts netted his seventh League goal of the season in a one-all draw at Wolverhampton Wanderers. However, the Villa side suffered a loss of form during the final week of the year with successive away defeats at Preston North End (3–2) and Derby County (5–0), as well as at home to Accrington (2–1). Villa's situation went from bad to worse during the opening week of the new year when they suffered a 7–0 defeat at Everton in a game that was marred by serious tragedy when Archie Hunter collapsed following a heart attack.

Archie Hunter, who had been the great inspiration of the Villa team for a number of years, never fully recovered, and the episode eventually resulted in his untimely death at thirty-five years of age.

Away from the pressures of the League, the Villa team managed a 4–2 victory at South Shore in the first round of the FA Cup, with goals by Hodgetts (2), Dickson and Allen securing a second round tie at Notts County. Their poor League form continued with a 2–1 home defeat against Bolton Wanderers, which preceded a further defeat at Notts County (4–1) in the second round of the FA Cup.

Albert Allen then scored a rare away goal in a one-all draw at Stoke, while the season ended with a 3–0 home win against Blackburn Rovers, with Campbell, Hodgetts and Brown on target for Villa. They ended the season in eighth position, following seven victories, five draws and ten defeats in their twenty-two League games, while scoring forty-three goals and conceding fifty-one. However, the Villa team had finished level on points with Bolton Wanderers, which meant that they suffered the indignation of having to apply for re-election to the League.

James Cowan and Albert Brown were the only ever-presents in the Villa team during the season, while Billy Dickson, Albert Allen and Dennis Hodgetts led the scoring with eight League goals apiece in a most disappointing campaign, though Villa had managed to win both the Birmingham Cup and Lord Mayor's Charity Cup.

PRESTON NORTH END

As reigning League champions, Preston North End, as expected, made few changes in their team for the 1889–90 season. The main transfer activity involved John Goodall signing for Derby County, while Nick Ross, the former club captain, returned from the Everton club, together with Bob Kelso, a Scottish international player. Kelso, who had appeared in only one game during Everton's inaugural League season following a period with Newcastle

West End, remained with Preston for two seasons prior to returning to the Everton club.

Preston opened the season with a 10–0 home victory against Stoke, with both Ross brothers and Sam Thomson amongst the goal scorers. This was followed by their first ever League defeat in a 5–3 reverse at Aston Villa. However, the Lancashire side soon returned to form with successive away wins at Burnley (3–0) and Bolton Wanderers (6–2) on either side of a 5–0 home victory against West Bromwich Albion. Then followed defeats at Derby County (2–1) and at home to Wolverhampton Wanderers (2–0), while November saw a return to winning ways as the Preston side won six games in a row to return to the top of the League table.

Preston's winning run began with a 4–3 success at Blackburn Rovers, followed by a comfortable home win against Accrington, while away wins at Stoke (2–1) and Everton (5–1), as well as home victories against Bolton Wanderers (3–1) and Burnley (6–0) continued their excellent run of results. However, following a one-all home draw against Blackburn Rovers, Preston suffered a 2–1 home defeat against the high-riding Everton team.

Christmas Day saw Preston secure a 3–2 home success against Aston Villa, while Boxing Day saw a two-all draw at West Bromwich Albion, which left the race for the League championship wide open at the turn of the year, with Preston, Everton and Blackburn Rovers all in contention to win the League title, as the League table (Table II) confirmed.

Table II: *The position at the top of the table at the end of 1889*

	Played	Won	Lost	Drawn	Points
Preston North End	17	11	4	2	24
Everton	16	10	3	3	23
Blackburn Rovers	16	10	4	2	22

Preston began the New Year with a narrow victory at Wolverhampton Wanderers (1–0) followed by successive home wins against Derby County (5–0) and Notts County (4–3), while a two-all draw at Accrington in the penultimate game of the season left Preston and Everton level on points, with one League game remaining.

Table III: *All square at the top of the League with one game to go, 1889–90*

	Played	Won	Lost	Drawn	Points
Preston North End	21	14	4	3	31
Everton	21	14	4	3	31

While Preston's goal difference was superior to the Everton team's, they were due to visit Notts County in their final League game, while Everton were at West Bromwich Albion, whom they had beaten by five goals to one just two weeks earlier. However, Albion inflicted a 4–1 defeat on the Merseysiders, while Preston secured a 1–0 victory at Nottingham five days later to retain the League Championship with fifteen wins, three draws and four defeats in their twenty-two League games, while scoring seventy-one goals and conceding thirty.

Jimmy Trainer, Jack Gordon and David Russell appeared in all twenty-two League games for the League champions, with Jimmy Ross and Bob Howarth missing only one. Geordie Drummond ended the campaign with nine League goals; Sam Thomson found the net on ten occasions; Nick Ross scored sixteen goals in nineteen League appearances; while his brother Jimmy led the scoring with twenty-four League goals. However, while Preston were worthy League champions, they had tended to struggle in the FA Cup competition, which saw them suffer a 3–2 home defeat against Bolton Wanderers in the quarter-finals.

Aston Villa Apply for Re-Election to the League

Following their last place League finish, the Stoke team once again had to apply for re-election to the League, together with Notts County and Burnley, while Bolton Wanderers and Aston Villa, who had both finished in the top five during the previous campaign, joined the three last placed teams in suffering the indignation of the re-election process.

At the close of the 1889–90 season, the League results were as in Table IV.

Table IV: *Football League results for the 1889–90 season*

	P	W	D	L	F	A	PTS
1. Preston North End	22	15	3	4	71	30	33
2. Everton	22	14	3	5	65	40	31
3. Blackburn Rovers	22	12	3	7	78	41	27
4. Wolverhampton Wndrs	22	10	5	7	51	38	25
5. West Bromwich Albion	22	11	3	8	47	50	25
6. Accrington	22	9	6	7	53	56	24
7. Derby County	22	9	3	10	43	55	21
8. Aston Villa	22	7	5	10	43	51	19
9. Bolton Wanderers	22	9	1	12	54	65	19
10. Notts County	22	6	5	11	43	51	17
11. Burnley	22	4	5	13	36	65	13
12. Stoke	22	3	4	15	27	69	10

A Lancashire–Yorkshire FA Cup Final

Nine of the twelve Football League teams remained in the 1889–90 FA Cup competition at the second round stage, with Derby County, who had suffered an 11–2 defeat at Everton, and West Bromwich Albion, who had been surprisingly beaten at Accrington, the most notable exceptions. Grimsby Town, Small Heath, Wednesday and Bootle from the recently formed Football Alliance, had reached the final sixteen, with Bootle and Wednesday progressing to the quarter-finals at the expense of Derby Midlands and Accrington.

The Football Alliance had been formed by clubs who had failed to receive invitations to join the Football League. However, with such fine sides as Birmingham St George's, Walsall Town Swifts, Nottingham Forest and Darwen, the Alliance teams were as capable as the majority of Football League teams.

Grimsby Town suffered a 3–0 defeat at Blackburn Rovers in the second round, with John Southworth amongst the Rovers' goal scorers. Wolverhampton Wanderers accounted for Small Heath by the odd goal in three, while Preston North End inflicted a 4–0 defeat on Lincoln City. Notts County defeated the out-of-form Villa side by four goals to one, Stoke secured an excellent 4–2 victory against Everton, and Bolton Wanderers scored thirteen goals without reply against Sheffield United to complete the quarter-final line-up, with James Cassidy scoring five of the Bolton goals and Davie Weir four.

Bolton then received a difficult away tie against FA Cup holders Preston North End in the quarter-finals, where goals by Davie Weir (2) and James Brogan secured a 3–2 win for the visitors, while Bootle were no match for Blackburn Rovers, as a Nat Walton hat-trick, together with a brace of goals from John Southworth, earned a 7–0 victory for Blackburn.

Wolverhampton Wanderers, who had made an appearance in the previous season's final, managed to overcome the resilient Stoke side by the odd goal in five to take their place in the semi-finals, while the Wednesday completed the semi-final line-up following a long drawn-out affair against Notts County.

Wednesday had inflicted a 5–0 defeat on the Nottingham side in the first quarter-final tie, with Tom Cawley scoring a brace of goals to bring his FA Cup goal scoring tally for the season to five. Cawley, who had been a little unfortunate to miss out on an England cap following an excellent performance in a trial game, had been a member of the Wednesday side that had appeared in the semi-finals eight years earlier, while he would score twenty-five goals in thirty-seven FA Cup appearances for the Sheffield side.

Meanwhile, Notts County had protested to the Football Association Committee that the tie should never have taken place on a quagmire of a pitch at the Olive Grove Ground, which resulted in a replayed tie. County won by the odd goal in five. However, Wednesday then complained that County had fielded three ineligible players.

Following Wednesday's protests, the FA ordered a third game, which the

Sheffield side won by two goals to one, with Tom Cawley netting both goals to secure a semi-final tie against Bolton Wanderers at Perry Barr, Birmingham. Blackburn Rovers were drawn to play Wolverhampton Wanderers at the Racecourse Ground, Wrexham.

Both semi-final ties were evenly contested, with John Southworth scoring the only goal of the game for Blackburn in a 1–0 victory against Wolves, while Albert Mumford was twice on target for Wednesday in a 2–1 success against Bolton to ensure a Lancashire–Yorkshire FA Cup Final to take place at the Oval on 29 March.

England Win Twice in One Day

England opened the 1890 international season on 15 March by fielding two teams on the same day. A slightly weaker team played against the Irish national side in Belfast, while the stronger team travelled to Wrexham to play the Welsh. William Moon wore the goalkeeper's jersey against Wales, with A M and P M Walters at fullback, while Alfred Fletcher (Wolverhampton Wanderers) and Alfred Shelton (Notts County) made their second England appearances at half back, where John Holt (Everton) made his international debut. Holt, who stood just five feet four inches tall and weighed ten stone, played the first of ten England games at centre half. His size hardly affected his footballing ability as he enjoyed a reputation as a solid tackler as well as an excellent passer of the ball. Tinsley Lindley and Billy Bassett were once again included in the England attack, together with Harry Daft (Notts County), while debuts were given to Edward Currey (Corinthians) and Harry Wood (Wolverhampton Wanderers). Currey, an Oxford Blue at Association Football, appeared twice for England prior to pursuing a career as a solicitor, while Harry Wood represented his country on three occasions during a six-year period.

As expected, England managed a 3–1 victory against the Welsh, with Edward Currey scoring two on his debut, together with a further goal from Tinsley Lindley, his thirteenth for the country of his birth.

A Nine-Goal Victory in Belfast

England included goalkeeper Bob Roberts (West Bromwich Albion) for the visit to Belfast, with Richard Baugh and Charlie Mason of Wolverhampton Wanderers at fullback, while Charles Perry (West Bromwich Albion) played the first of his three international games at centre half. Kenny Davenport (Bolton Wanderers) made his second and final appearance at inside right, while Fred Geary (Everton) played the first of two England games at centre forward in an England team that included James Forrest, Billy Townley, Joseph Lofthouse, John Barton and Nat Walton, from the successful Blackburn Rovers team. England had little difficulty in defeating the Irish, as goals by

Geary (3), Davenport (2), Townley (2), Barton and Lofthouse secured a 9–1 victory. This set up an exciting finale to the international season, when England visited Glasgow to play against Scotland. However, a week prior to the international game, Blackburn Rovers were due to play against the Wednesday in the 1890 FA Cup Final.

A High-Scoring FA Cup Final

A crowd in excess of 20,000 arrived at the Oval to see if the Wednesday could upset Blackburn Rovers, who were odds-on favourites to win the FA Cup, with Blackburn selecting the following players:

Horne

Forbes   James Southworth

Barton   Dewar   Forrest

Lofthouse   Campbell   John Southworth   Walton   Townley

Wednesday selected the following eleven:

Smith

Morley   Brayshaw

Dungworth   Betts   Waller

Ingram   Woolhouse   Bennett   Mumford   Cawley

Major Francis Marindin was again the appointed match referee.

Rovers were a team of international players with an excellent FA Cup pedigree, while Wednesday had made one previous semi-final appearance. However, the Sheffield side, who had recently won the Football Alliance Championship, could boast England internationals Edward Brayshaw and Billy Betts in their defence, who together with Albert Mumford, were products of Lockwood Brothers, the successful Sheffield works team.

John Southworth kicked off for the Rovers who attacked from the start, with Nat Walton and Billy Townley causing problems for the Wednesday defence, while the constant pressure led Dungworth to handle the ball on the edge of the Wednesday goal area.

Following the free kick from James Forrest, Townley shot at the Wednesday goal, which seemed to take a deflection off a defender, to secure an early lead for Blackburn. Wednesday came more into the game as Mumford and Cawley attacked the Rovers' defence, with little joy, as Barton and Dewar performed admirably at the back. Rovers then began to dominate the play, and Campbell saw a shot rebound from a post, which preceded a second Blackburn goal when Nat Walton converted a cross from Billy Townley. However, the Sheffield side remained patient as they sought to reduce the arrears, with Mumford, Bennett and Cawley seeking to probe the solid Blackburn defence.

A further attack by the Rovers saw Lofthouse dribble round two Wednesday defenders, prior to passing to John Southworth, whose shot went surprisingly wide. Southworth soon made amends by scoring a third goal for the Lancashire side, following excellent play from the ever busy Billy Townley.

With the half-time whistle approaching, Blackburn once again broke through a tiring Wednesday defence, with John Southworth passing to Townley, who had the simple task of scoring his second goal, and Rovers ended the half with a 4–0 advantage.

Blackburn continued to dominate proceedings during the early stages of the second half, which saw Townley given off-side on three occasions in as many minutes. However, the never-say-die attitude of the Wednesday finally bore fruit when Ingram crossed the ball to Bennett, who headed past the advancing Horne, much to the delight of the spectators on all sides of the ground. Stimulated by their success, Wednesday began to dominate the game, with Bennett and Mumford exerting pressure on the Rovers' fullbacks. However, their domination was short-lived as the Lancashire side regained their momentum, which resulted in Townley trying a speculative shot from twenty-five yards. Smith, in the Wednesday goal, managed to clear the ball to the feet of Joseph Lofthouse, who returned it into the Wednesday goalmouth, where the ever alert Billy Townley was waiting to convert the cross to register the first hat-trick scored by a player in an FA Cup Final.

As the game entered its final quarter, Haydn Morley and Edward Brayshaw continued to offer stubborn resistance in the Wednesday defence, but they were unable to prevent Joseph Lofthouse from scoring a sixth goal for Blackburn, following excellent work by James Forrest. Prior to the final whistle, hundreds of spectators swarmed towards the pavilion, which led Major Marindin to hold up play for four minutes. Soon, the Major sounded the final whistle. Blackburn had won the cup by six goals to one to register their fourth FA Cup Final success in seven seasons.

It was generally agreed that Blackburn had a little too much FA Cup experience for Wednesday, for whom Morley, Brayshaw, Mumford and Bennett performed splendidly. However, the Blackburn side had given one of the finest exhibitions of attacking football in an FA Cup Final, with England internationals Walton, Townley, Lofthouse and John Southworth at the peak of their form.

Arthur Kinnaird Replaces Francis Marindin

Following his last appearance as match referee in an FA Cup Final, Major Marindin announced his retirement as president of the Football Association, a position that he had held since 1874. He was now succeeded by Lord Kinnaird, who served the FA well into the following century, as well as serving as president of the YMCA in England and Lord High Commissioner to the Church of Scotland.

England Draw in Glasgow

England's final international game of the season took place in Glasgow against the Scots with the England selectors retaining nine of the team that had won in Wrexham, with George Haworth (Accrington) and Harry Allen (Wolverhampton Wanderers) replacing Alfred Fletcher (Wolverhampton Wanderers) and John Holt (Everton) in the half-back line.

In a close game, the visitors managed to secure a one-all draw, with Harry Wood on target for England.

A M and P M Walters Bow Out of International Football

In adhering to their father's wishes, A M and P M Walters decided to retire from international football at the close of the 1889–90 season, following the death of their younger brother during an Association game.

Sunderland Replace Stoke in the League

There remained one outstanding issue at the close of the 1889–90 season, which involved Aston Villa, Bolton Wanderers, Notts County, Burnley and Stoke applying for re-election to the Football League. Applicants to join the League included Grimsby Town, Bootle, Sunderland Albion, Newton Heath and Sunderland. The majority of teams failed in their efforts to join when it was decided that Aston Villa and Bolton Wanderers would remain in the League, while Burnley and Notts County received sufficient votes to retain their League status.

Stoke, on the other hand, were voted out of the League into the Football Alliance, with the Sunderland club replacing them. However, Harry Lockett, the Stoke secretary, would retain his position as secretary of the Football League.

Top left: Charles (E C) Bambridge, Corinthians and England. One of three brothers to represent England prior to the founding of the Football League. Bambridge would score on a dozen occasions for his country.

Top right: William (W N) Cobbold , Corinthians and England. Acknowledged as the finest dribbler of the ball during the early 1880s, the old Carthusian would score seven goals for England.

Bottom left: Charlie Athersmith, Aston Villa and England. The free-scoring winger would win many league and FA Cup honours with Villa as well as a dozen England caps.

Bottom right: Jimmy Ross, Preston North End. Preston's most prolific goal scorer as they dominated the English game, following the formation of the league.

Blackburn Rovers – FA Cup winners in 1884, 1885 and 1886.

William McGregor – founder of the Football League – felt that the Association game would become bankrupt without the discipline of regular competition.

Top: The Royal Engineers team, who were FA Cup finalists on four occasions during the 1870s (winning the trophy in 1875), with the influential Major Francis Marindin, centre in stripes.

Bottom left: Billy Bassett (left) and Steve Bloomer, the finest right wing partnership to represent England during the 1890s.

Bottom right: Ted Doig, Sunderland and Scotland. A Scottish International at the age of 20, goalkeeper Doig would miss only 13 games in fourteen seasons with the north-east side, whilst winning three league championship medals.

Chapter XVI

BLACKBURN ROVERS' FIFTH FA CUP SUCCESS – 1890–91

EVERTON WIN THE LEAGUE CHAMPIONSHIP
BLACKBURN ROVERS WIN THE FA CUP FOR THE FIFTH TIME TO EQUAL THE
RECORD OF THE WANDERERS
SUNDERLAND PROVE THEIR WORTH
ENGLAND WIN ALL THREE INTERNATIONALS
TINSLEY LINDLEY BOWS OUT OF INTERNATIONAL FOOTBALL
STOKE RETURN AS THE FOOTBALL LEAGUE IS EXTENDED

The Scots Follow Suit

Prior to the start of the 1890–91 season, the Football League Committee introduced further rules in the hope of controlling what they saw as a lack of discipline in the way that the majority of clubs operated. This meant that teams could now be fined £25 for fielding an ineligible player, £50 for fielding a weakened team, as well as face the possibility of expulsion from the League for poaching players from other League clubs.

In 1890, the Scottish Football Association decided to form its own League to stem the flow of players to the English professional clubs. However, the Scots remained strictly amateur, and the Queens Park Club refused to join the League. Queens Park eventually joined the Scottish League at the turn of the century when their great days were over, while the drift of Scottish players continued until 1893 when a motion was passed by the Scottish Football Association to legalise professionalism.

Sunderland Take Their Place in the League

The new season saw newcomers Sunderland out to prove their worth as a member of the Football League, while Notts County and Burnley were well aware of the fate of Stoke, which made them more determined to avoid the re-election places for a third successive season.

BURNLEY

Burnley enjoyed an excellent start to the 1890–91 League campaign with a one-all draw at Accrington, followed by odd-goal wins at Sunderland (3–2) and at home to Aston Villa (2–1). The month ended with a 3–3 home draw in the return game with Sunderland. Early October saw a loss of form with away defeats at Wolverhampton Wanderers and West Bromwich Albion, as well as at home to Bolton Wanderers and Blackburn Rovers, with John Southworth running the Burnley defence ragged in a 6–2 victory. Claude Lambie continued to lead the Burnley attack, while new signings included Walter Place and goalkeeper Jack Hillman in the hope of stemming the flow of goals conceded by the Burnley defence.

Burnley returned to winning ways during November with home wins against Wolverhampton Wanderers (4–0), Accrington (2–0) and Derby County (6–1), as well as a four-all draw at Aston Villa, prior to suffering a 5–2 reverse at Blackburn. December began with a 5–4 home success against West Bromwich Albion and the Lancashire side moved into the top half of the League table.

Following a 1–0 home defeat against Notts County, Burnley registered a 12–2 victory in a Christmas Day friendly game against Wrexham, while the year ended with a 7–3 defeat at Everton, with Edgar Chadwick scoring a hat-trick for the home team. However, the new year saw Burnley record their second away win of the season in a 4–2 success at Derby County.

Further away defeats at Preston (7–0) and Notts County (4–0), who had recently defeated Burnley in a second round FA Cup tie, saw the Lancashire side once again involved in the struggle to avoid re-election to the League with just three games remaining, of which two were at home to Preston and Everton, who were contesting the League Championship.

Burnley performed splendidly against Preston, as Tom Nichol scored four goals on his debut in a 6–2 victory against the title holders, which was followed by a 3–2 win against Everton. Though the season ended with a 1–0 reverse at Bolton Wanderers, Burnley ended the campaign in eighth place, with nine wins, three draws and ten defeats, thus avoiding the re-election positions.

NOTTS COUNTY

There was little doubt of Notts County's pedigree, with a team consisting of a number of players of international quality. However, they had great difficulty in adjusting to the rigours of the professional game, as they were used to the friendlier games of days gone by. Hence their indifferent League performances of the two previous seasons.

A number of players remained with the club from the previous campaign, which included David Calderhead and Alfred Shelton in defence, as well as Jimmy Oswald and Harry Daft in the attack. Jack Hendry, a Scottish fullback with a reputation for rough play, was the most notable newcomer in the Notts team for the 1890–91 League campaign. County opened the season with successive away defeats at Bolton Wanderers (4–2) and Aston Villa (3–2), which was followed by a 5–0 home success against Accrington, with Jimmy Oswald scoring a hat-trick, while a five-game unbeaten run, including away draws at West Bromwich Albion and Wolverhampton Wanderers, as well as home victories against Derby County, West Bromwich Albion and Bolton

Wanderers, saw the Nottingham side move up to fourth place in the League table.

October's end saw County lose by the odd goal in five at Accrington, followed by a 3–1 home win against Everton, as well as a creditable draw at Preston, prior to suffering their first home defeat of the season in a 2–1 reverse against Blackburn Rovers, while their indifferent form continued with a one-all home draw against Wolverhampton Wanderers.

Then followed a 7–1 home win against Aston Villa, with both Jimmy Oswald and Billy Locker scoring hat-tricks, as well as odd-goal victories against Sunderland, Preston North End and Burnley, which left the Nottingham side in an excellent position to challenge for the League title. However, successive away defeats at Derby County (3–1), Everton (4–2) and Sunderland (4–0) saw Notts' hopes of the League Championship fade, while goalkeeper George Toone sustained a broken leg in the game at Sunderland to make matters worse.

Prior to the Sunderland game, County had secured a 9–1 victory against Sheffield United in the first round of the FA Cup, with Andrew McGregor (4) and Jimmy Oswald (2) scoring the majority of the goals to earn a home tie with Burnley in the second round.

Jimmy Thraves replaced the injured George Toone for the cup game with Burnley, while former England international, William Gunn, now a club director, replaced the unavailable Tom McLean. However, the changes made little difference to County, who registered a 2–1 victory, with Harry Daft netting both goals.

Following a 4–0 League victory against Burnley, the Nottingham side secured a 1–0 home win against Stoke in the quarter-finals of the FA Cup, with Billy Locker scoring the only goal of the game. However, an incident occurred during the tie, which would eventually lead to the introduction of the penalty kick.

Jimmy Thraves in the County goal was well beaten by a goal-bound shot from a Stoke forward when Jack Hendry fisted the ball away from the goal line. However, following the free kick, the ball was cleared by a County defender, thus denying Stoke a deserved goal.

Notts were then drawn against the ever improving Sunderland side in the semi-finals, which ended in a 3–3 draw, with McInnes, McGregor and Oswald on target for County. The Nottingham side made few mistakes in the replay, as Jimmy Oswald netted a brace of goals in a 2–0 victory to secure their first FA Cup Final appearance against the holders, Blackburn Rovers.

Prior to the FA Cup Final, County visited Blackburn for their final League game of the season, which resulted in a 7–1 victory for the East Midlands side, with McGregor, Daft, Locker and Oswald sharing the goals to end the campaign in a creditable third position, with eleven wins, four draws and seven defeats in their twenty-two League games, while scoring fifty-two goals and conceding thirty-five. Jack Hendry, Archie Osborne, Tom McInnes, Andrew McGregor and Jimmy Oswald were ever present in the Nottingham side, while David Calderhead, Billy Locker, Alfred Shelton and Harry Daft missed only one game in County's finest season to date. McInnes scored seven League goals, McGregor finished the campaign with eight goals, Billy Locker found the net on a dozen occasions, while Jimmy Oswald led the scoring with fourteen League goals.

ASTON VILLA

Aston Villa had tended to struggle during the 1889–90 League campaign. However, the club kept faith with the majority of their players for the new season. Jimmy Warner continued in goal, together with Gersham Cox, James Cowan and Harry Devey in defence, while Albert Brown, Dennis Hodgetts and Billy Dickson remained in the attack. Archie Hunter, who had suffered a heart attack in a League game at Everton during the previous season, had been unable to continue his football career, while Albert Allen, who had scored a hat-trick in his one England appearance, made just four League appearances during the season prior to retiring from the game due to ill-health at the age of twenty-four.

Villa opened the season with a 2–1 defeat at Wolverhampton Wanderers, which was followed by a 3–2 home win against Notts County, with Brown, Dickson and Graham on target, while a run of defeats at Burnley (2–1), Bolton Wanderers (4–0) and at home to West Bromwich Albion (4–0) saw Villa slump to the foot of the League table.

James Cowan then found the net in a two-all home draw with Everton, which preceded a 5–4 reverse at Derby County, with Cowan twice more on target. Cowan scored for the third game running in a 4–0 home success in the return game with Derby County, with Hodgetts (2) and Albert Brown completing the scoring. Villa's improved form continued with a 3–0 victory at West Bromwich Albion, with Brown (2) and Dickson on target, which was followed by a 4–4 home draw with Burnley, with both players once more amongst the goal scorers. Further home wins against Accrington (3–1) and Bolton Wanderers (5–0) saw Albert Brown score in both games, and Villa moved into the top half of the League table. However, successive away defeats at Notts County (7–1) and Blackburn Rovers (5–1), as well as home draws against Blackburn Rovers (2–2) and Sunderland (0–0), saw the Midlands side struggling to avoid the re-election positions at the turn of the year. New Year's Day saw Villa suffer a 5–0 reverse at Everton, followed by a further five-goal defeat at Sunderland (5–1). A 13–1 home win against the Casuals in the first round of the FA Cup brought a welcome victory, with Hodgetts (4), Campbell (3), McKnight (2), Brown (2) and Graham (2) on target to secure a second round tie at Stoke.

Prior to the FA Cup game, Villa suffered a further away defeat at Preston (4–1), while a 3–0 reverse at Stoke ended their progress in the FA Cup;

however, a 1–0 home defeat in the return game with Preston saw a marked improvement in Villa's form, which coincided with the debut of eighteen-year-old Charles Athersmith, a recent signing from the Unity Gas Depot team.

Athersmith scored nearly 100 goals in more than 300 appearances for Villa during a ten-year period, in which he won numerous League Championship and FA Cup winners' medals, as well as appearing in the English national side on a dozen occasions. Sadly, like many of his contemporaries of the Victorian era, Athersmith died a comparatively young man.

In their final home game of the season, Villa secured their first League win for nearly three months with a 6–2 victory against Wolverhampton Wanderers. Athersmith scored a hat-trick together with further goals by Dickson (2) and McKnight. Dickson was twice more on target the following week in a 3–1 success at Accrington, as Villa ended the campaign in ninth position, with seven wins, four draws and eleven defeats, while scoring forty-five goals and conceding fifty-eight.

Jimmy Warner had been ever present during the season, while Cowan, Cox, Devey and Evans had missed very few games in a disappointing League campaign, in which Billy Dickson scored ten goals in eighteen League appearances, with Albert Brown leading the scoring with eleven goals in sixteen League games. However, despite winning the Birmingham, Staffordshire and Lord Mayor's Charity Cups, Villa now had to apply for re-election to the League.

BOLTON WANDERERS

Following their ninth place League finish at the close of the 1889–90 season, Bolton Wanderers travelled north of the border to recruit new players, which resulted in the arrival of defenders John Somerville, Alex Paton and Harry Gardiner, as well as outside left James Munro.

John Somerville had played for Ayr Parkhouse prior to joining Bolton, with whom he made in excess of 300 appearances in eleven seasons, while Alex Paton had appeared in a Scottish FA Cup Final with Vale of Leven prior to signing for the West Manchester Club. After Paton joined Bolton, he appeared in 215 League games in nine seasons. James Munro, who had joined Bolton from Dundee Strathmere upon reaching his twentieth birthday, scored twenty goals in fifty League appearances, including two on his League debut, while Harry Gardiner, who had begun his career with Renton, had originally signed for Sunderland. However, a change of mind saw him move to the Bolton club, for whom he made eighty League appearances, as well as appearing for the Football League Eleven against the Scottish League in 1892.

Bolton opened the season with a 4–2 home win against Notts County, with Munro (2), Davenport and Roberts on target, which was followed by a further home success against Derby County (3–1), with Davenport (2) and Barbour scoring the Wanderers' goals. However, successive away defeats at Preston North End (1–0) and Notts County (3–1), as well as at home to Everton (5–0), ended the Lancashire side's fine start to the season.

Early October saw a return to winning ways as Brogan, Bullough, Turner and McNee found the net in a 4–0 home win against Aston Villa, while McNee and Barbour were on target the following week in a 2–1 victory at Burnley. However, further defeats at Everton (2–0) and at home to Sunderland (5–2) saw Bolton in the bottom half of the League table at the month's end. Then followed a 4–2 success at West Bromwich Albion, with McNee (2), Barbour and Munro scoring for the visitors. This preceded a 1–0 reverse at Wolverhampton Wanderers, while Kenny Davenport scored the only goal of the game in a 1–0 home win against Preston North End. However, a 5–0 defeat at Aston Villa added to their indifferent run of results.

Wanderers enjoyed a return to form during the final month of the year, which began with a 6–0 home win against Accrington, with Barbour (3), Cassidy (2) and Munro on target, and this was followed by a John McNee goal in a one-all draw at Derby County. The year ended with a 6–0 home victory against Wolverhampton Wanderers, with a hat-trick by John McNee, together with further goals by Turner, Gardiner and Cassidy.

Bolton then suffered a 2–1 defeat at Accrington in the opening game of the new year, which was followed by a further defeat at Accrington (5–1) in the first round of the FA Cup. Their only League game during February saw a 2–0 reverse at Sunderland. March saw a return to form for the Lancashire side, who won all four of their remaining League games. Kenny Davenport's fifth goal in twelve League games arrived in a 2–0 victory at Blackburn Rovers, with Turner completing the scoring, which was followed by a 7–1 home win against West Bromwich Albion, with Munro (2), Cassidy (2), Brogan, McNee and Turner on target. The season ended with successive home wins against Burnley (1–0) and Blackburn Rovers (2–0), with Cassidy and Munro (2) scoring the all-important goals to secure a fifth place finish for the Wanderers, due mainly to the goalkeeping skills of John Sutcliffe. Sutcliffe, who had previously represented England at Rugby Union, made more than 300 League appearances for Bolton, as well as playing for England on five occasions, thus becoming one of only three players to represent England at both codes.

Wanderers had won twelve, drawn one and lost nine of their twenty-two League games, while scoring forty-seven goals and conceding thirty-four. Alex Paton and John McNee were ever present in the team, while James Cassidy and James Munro ended the campaign with eight League goals apiece, with McNee leading the scoring with nine.

DERBY COUNTY

Derby County retained the majority of the players that had secured a mid-table League finish during the 1889–90 season for the new campaign, as Latham, Ferguson, Archie Goodall and Walter Roulstone continued in defence, while Bakewell, Cooper, Holmes and John Goodall remained in the attack.

Sandy Higgins, who had been Derby's leading goal scorer in each of the two previous seasons, had decided to join Nottingham Forest in the Football Alliance, which resulted in the arrival of McLachlan up front. Derby began the season with a new goalkeeper for the third year running, as Haddon replaced Bromage, who had previously succeeded Marshall.

Derby opened the 1890–91 League campaign with an exciting 8–5 home win against Blackburn Rovers, with John Goodall (3), Nelson (2), Chalmers, McLachlan and Archie Goodall on target for the home side. Successive away defeats at Bolton Wanderers (3–1), Notts County (2–1), Everton (7–0) and Wolverhampton Wanderers (5–1), as well as at home to Preston North End (3–1), saw Derby struggling at the foot of the League table. However, a 5–4 home success against Aston Villa saw a return to winning ways, with John Goodall scoring his second hat-trick of the season.

Then followed further away defeats at Aston Villa (4–0), Accrington (4–0) and Burnley (6–1) before Cooper and John Goodall found the net in successive home and away victories against West Bromwich Albion (3–1 and 4–3). A further run of defeats at home to Accrington (2–1) and Everton (6–2), as well as away at Preston (6–0), meant that Derby had conceded in excess of sixty goals in fifteen League games, which resulted in Charles Bunyan replacing the overworked Haddon between the posts. Bunyan had been the unfortunate custodian to have conceded twenty-six goals when keeping goal for Hyde in a first round FA Cup tie against Preston North End, but his inclusion saw an immediate improvement in Derby's fortunes. As the year ended, there was a one-all home draw against Bolton Wanderers, followed by a 3–1 home win against Notts County, with Cooper on target in both games.

New Year saw the return of Haddon in the Derby goal for a League game at Blackburn Rovers, who inflicted an 8–0 defeat on the East Midlands side in Haddon's final appearance for the club. However, the following week saw Derby secure a 9–0 home win against Wolverhampton Wanderers, with McMillan (5), Holmes (2), Roulstone and John Goodall on target. John McMillan, who had signed from the St Bernard's Club in Edinburgh during November, remained with Derby for six seasons, in which he would score forty-five goals in 116 League appearances, prior to moving to the Leicester Fosse club.

Mid-January saw the Derby side visit Royal Arsenal in the first round of the FA Cup, where Cooper and McMillan found the net in a 2–1 victory. However, County's indifferent League form continued the following week in a 4–2 home defeat against Burnley, while a 3–2 home reverse against Wednesday on the final day of March ended their FA Cup hopes.

John Goodall then scored his thirteenth League goal of the season in a 3–1 home win against Sunderland, with McLachlan and McMillan completing the scoring, while the campaign ended with a 5–1 defeat in the return game at Sunderland. Derby finished the season in eleventh position, with seven victories, one draw and fourteen defeats in their twenty-two League games, while scoring forty-seven goals and conceding eighty-one.

McLachlan, McMillan and Archie Goodall had been ever present in the Derby team, while John Goodall had led the scoring with thirteen League goals in twenty appearances. The East Midlands side were once again required to apply for re-election to the League.

ACCRINGTON

Accrington had ended the 1889–90 League campaign in sixth position, much to the delight of their supporters, who were well aware that new signings were required if they were to maintain their excellent start in the Football League.

England international George Haworth remained at the heart of the defence for the 1890–91 season, with McKay, Faulds and John Kirkham up front, while Bob Macbeth had returned to the club. However, he played just one League game prior to joining Burton Swifts as their player–coach.

Accrington opened the new season with a 1–0 home win against West Bromwich Albion, followed by successive draws at home to Burnley (1–1) and away at Blackburn Rovers (0–0). Home defeats against Everton (2–1) and Preston North End (3–1), as well as away at Notts County (5–0) and Wolverhampton Wanderers (3–0), then saw the Lancashire side struggling near the foot of the League table, having scored four goals in their opening seven League games. Accrington's form greatly improved towards the end of October with a 2–2 draw at Sunderland, followed by a 3–2 home success against Notts County. Early November saw a one-all draw at Preston, as well as a 4–0 home win against Derby County, which saw Accrington move to a respectable mid-table position at the halfway stage of the campaign.

Then followed a 3–1 reverse at Aston Villa, which preceded a 4–1 home victory in the return game with Sunderland. Away defeats at Burnley (2–0), Bolton Wanderers (6–0) and Everton (3–2) saw Accrington end the year struggling to avoid the re-election positions, with a 2–1 victory at Derby County their only success during December.

New Year's Day saw a 2–1 home defeat against Wolverhampton Wanderers, followed by a 2–1 home success against Bolton Wanderers, thus avenging the 6–0 humiliation of the previous month. However, further home defeats against Blackburn Rovers (4–0) and Aston Villa (3–1), as well as a 5–1 reverse at West Bromwich Albion, saw Accrington end the campaign in tenth position, having won just six of their twenty-two League games, while scoring twenty-eight goals, the lowest total in the League.

With McKay and Kirkham scoring a little more than a dozen League goals between them, the need for a goal-scoring forward had become the main priority of the Accrington side. However, the more skilful players tended to sign for the wealthier Lancashire clubs such as Blackburn Rovers and Preston North End rather than the low profile clubs like Accrington and Burnley.

On the FA Cup front, Accrington had suffered a 3–2 home defeat against Wolverhampton Wanderers in the second round to complete a most disappointing season, ending in the Lancashire side having to apply for re-election to the League.

BLACKBURN ROVERS

Blackburn Rovers had enjoyed an excellent 1889–90 season, which had resulted in them winning the FA Cup as well as finishing in third position in the League.

Few changes were made by Rovers for the 1890–91 League campaign as the ever reliable Brandon, Forbes, Barton, Dewar and James Forrest remained in defence, together with Lofthouse, Campbell, John Southworth, Walton and Townley in the attack. Newcomers Pennington and Gow shared the goal-keeping duties.

Rovers opened the season with an exciting 8–5 defeat at Derby County, with John Southworth scoring a hat-trick, which preceded a goalless home draw with Accrington. The month ended with a further home defeat against Wolverhampton Wanderers (3–2). However, Rovers soon returned to form by winning all four of their League games during October, which began with a 2–1 victory at Preston, where Southworth and Walton found the net, while Southworth scored a brace of goals in a 3–2 home success against Sunderland.

Then followed a 6–1 victory at Burnley, with Southworth (2), Walton (2), Barton and Lofthouse on target, while Southworth scored his ninth goal of the campaign, in a 1–0 home win against Preston. However, a 3–1 reverse at Sunderland ended their winning run.

Blackburn's excellent form continued with successive home wins against Everton (2–1) and Burnley (5–2), as well as a 2–1 victory at Notts County, with John Southworth scoring in all three games to move the Lancashire side to fourth place in the League table at the halfway stage of the campaign. November's end saw Rovers suffer a 3–1 defeat at Everton, which was followed by a John Southworth hat-trick in a 5–1 home win against Aston Villa. Southworth netted two further goals in a two-all draw in the return game with Villa. Billy Townley then scored a rare goal in a 2–1 home win against West Bromwich Albion, while the year ended with a 2–0 defeat at Wolverhampton Wanderers. However, Rovers recorded their highest League win of the season during the opening week of the new year as Hall (4), Southworth (3) and Townley found the net in an 8–0 home success against Derby County in Hall's only goal-scoring appearance in the League during the season despite playing fourteen games.

Mid-January saw Blackburn drawn away at Middlesbrough Ironopolis in the first round of the FA Cup, where goals by Hall and Southworth earned a 2–1 victory. However, a replay was ordered following a complaint by the north-eastern side, which Rovers won even more convincingly by three goals to nil, with Hall scoring twice, to secure a second round home tie against Chester. As expected, the Chester side had few answers to the Rovers' attack as John Southworth netted his fourth hat-trick of the season in a 7–0 victory to secure a home tie against Wolverhampton Wanderers in the quarter-finals, which they managed to win by two goals to nil, owing to own goals by Baugh and Fletcher in the Wanderers' defence.

Blackburn were then drawn against West Bromwich Albion in the semi-finals at the Victoria Ground, Stoke, which they narrowly won by the odd goal in five, with Hall and Southworth on target to secure Rovers' sixth FA Cup Final appearance in ten seasons. On their return to League action, Rovers secured a 4–0 success at Accrington, with John Southworth scoring his fifth hat-trick of the campaign, while successive defeats at home to Bolton Wanderers (2–0) and away at West Bromwich Albion (1–0) all but ended their hopes of the League Championship. They were further dented following a 7–1 home defeat against Notts County, their FA Cup Final opponents, however, while Blackburn fielded a reasonably strong line-up, many believed that they were saving themselves for the final.

Rovers eventually ended the campaign in sixth position, following a 2–0 defeat at Bolton, with eleven wins, two draws and nine defeats in their twenty-two League games, while scoring fifty-two goals and conceding forty-three. John Southworth scored twenty-six of the goals in eighteen League appearances. Forbes and Dewar had been ever present during the season, while the defensive line-up of Brandon, Forbes, Barton, Dewar and Forrest had missed only ten games between them. However, Rovers' priority was success in the FA Cup, which had seemed to have become a regular habit.

WEST BROMWICH ALBION

West Bromwich Albion made a number of changes in their line-up for the 1890–91 League campaign. England international goalkeeper, Bob Roberts, moved to Sunderland Albion, while many of the players who had been part of their successful cup-fighting sides of the 1880s were now nearing the end of their careers.

Fullback Harry Green made only six League appearances during the season, prior to being replaced by John Horton, the brother of Ezra, who played in excess of 250 games for Albion, while Jem Bayliss, who had been Albion's most prolific goal scorer during the previous decade, played eight League games. However, Bayliss gained a well-deserved England cap at the season's end.

Joe Reader replaced Bob Roberts in the Albion goal, where he made in excess of 300 League appearances, as well as representing the English national side, while Sam Nicholls and William Groves became regular members of the Albion team as the season progressed. Groves, who arrived from Glasgow Celtic towards the end of 1890 following a successful career in Scotland, had won a Scottish FA Cup winners' medal with Hibernian, as well as winning three Scottish caps. He had scored a hat-trick against Ireland in his second international appearance. Despite the number of changes in the Albion line-up, the West Bromwich side managed to retain England internationals Charlie

Perry and Billy Bassett, as well as prolific goal scorer Tom Pearson.

Albion opened the season with successive home defeats against Everton (4–1) and Sunderland (4–0), as well as a 3–0 reverse at Preston. Their first victory of the campaign arrived with a 4–0 success at Aston Villa, with Dyer, Pearson, Bayliss and Burns on target for Albion. Then followed a 3–1 home win against Burnley, with Burns (2) and Pearson netting the Albion goals, which preceded a 3–2 defeat at Notts County, where Tom Perry, soon to follow his brother, Charlie, into the England team, scored his first goal for the West Bromwich side. Tom Pearson found the net a week later in a one-all draw in the return game with Notts County. Albion returned to winning ways with a 3–2 victory at Everton, with Burns, Dyer and Nicholls on target. However, successive home defeats against Aston Villa (3–0) and Bolton Wanderers (4–2), as well as a one-all draw at Sunderland, saw Albion near the foot of the League table at the halfway stage of the season.

Derby County then inflicted successive home and away defeats on Albion (3–1 and 4–3), while early December saw the West Bromwich side race into a 4–1 lead in a League game at Burnley, with Pearson (2), Riley and Charlie Perry scoring for the visitors. However, the Burnley team rallied to score four late goals to run out winners by five goals to four.

Albion's losing run continued to the end of the year, with defeats at home to Wolverhampton Wanderers (1–0) and away at Blackburn Rovers (2–1), while the new year began with a 4–0 reverse in the return game at Wolverhampton Wanderers which left them at the foot of the League table. Following a 3–1 home defeat against Preston North End, the West Bromwich team secured two home wins in three days, as Pearson (2), Nicholls (2) and Groves netted in a 5–1 win against Accrington, while Roddy McLeod scored the only goal of the game in a 1–0 victory against Blackburn Rovers.

McLeod, who had recently arrived from Partick Thistle, scored in excess of fifty goals in nearly 150 appearances for Albion, while McCulloch, who had signed from a Glasgow Junior club at the same time as McLeod, played close on sixty League games for the club. However, their arrival was a little too late for Albion as the campaign ended with a defeat at Accrington, as well as an embarrassing 7–1 reverse at Bolton Wanderers, leaving the West Bromwich side in last place in the League table with just five wins in twenty-two League games, while scoring thirty-four goals and conceding fifty-four. Tom Pearson once again led the scoring with thirteen League goals.

Pearson, along with Dyer and Joe Reader, were ever present in a disappointing League campaign that ended with Albion applying for re-election. However, with their splendid FA Cup record of previous seasons, it was felt that Albion would have little difficulty in obtaining sufficient votes to retain their League status. As usual, Albion had performed magnificently on the FA Cup front when, following a first round bye, Nicholls, Dyer and Charlie Perry found the net in a 3–0 victory at Mitchell's St George's in the second round to secure a third round tie at the Wednesday, who had been beaten finalists during the previous season.

Wednesday were expected to win the quarter-final tie in Sheffield. However, Albion fought heroically to earn a 2–0 victory, with Willie Groves and Tom Pearson on target to secure a semi-final tie against Blackburn Rovers at the Victoria Ground, Stoke. Albion's semi-final performance once again belied their League position as a Willie Groves goal secured an early lead for the Black Country side, only for John Southworth to equalise on the stroke of half-time, while Rovers raced into a 3–1 lead early in the second half.

Tom Pearson then reduced the arrears for Albion, while Willie Groves twice saw shots rebound from a post, as the West Bromwich team pursued an equalising goal. However, the Lancashire side managed to hold on to a 3–2 victory to secure their sixth FA Cup Final appearance.

WOLVERHAMPTON WANDERERS

Wolverhampton Wanderers had been one of the most consistent teams in the Football League during the first two seasons of its formation, with a side consisting of English-born players.

Few changes were made in their line-up for the 1890–91 League campaign, as England internationals W C Rose, Richard Baugh, Charlie Mason, Alf Fletcher, Harry Allen, John Brodie and Harry Wood continued to serve the club, while Sam Thomson, who had arrived from Preston North End, was the most notable new signing.

Wolves opened the season with a 2–1 home success against Aston Villa, followed by a 5–0 defeat at Everton, while a five-game unbeaten run, which included narrow away wins at Sunderland (4–3) and Blackburn Rovers (3–2), as well as home wins against Accrington and Derby County, saw the Molineux side near the top of the League table. However, a 5–1 reverse at Preston ended their excellent run of results. Then followed further home wins against Burnley and Bolton Wanderers, on either side of a defeat in the return game at Burnley, while a one-all draw at Notts County, as well as a 2–0 home victory against reigning League champions Preston, maintained their challenge for the League Championship. However, Wolves were soon disappointed following a 1–0 reverse against fellow title challengers, Everton, to suffer their first home defeat of the season.

Mid-December saw Wolves secure a narrow 1–0 victory against West Bromwich Albion, prior to playing five League games in as many days during the Christmas and New Year period. They began with a 2–0 home win against Blackburn Rovers on Boxing Day, while the year ended with successive defeats at home to Sunderland (3–0) and away at Bolton Wanderers (6–0). New Year's Day saw Wolves return to winning ways with a 2–1 victory at Accrington, which preceded a 4–0 success against West Bromwich Albion. Then the tired Wolverhampton side suffered a humiliating 9–0 defeat at Derby County during the following week, with John McMillan netting five goals for the home side. Wanderers then secured a 2–1 victory at Long Eaton Rangers in the first round of the FA Cup to earn a second round tie at Accrington, which they won by the odd goal in five, while a 2–0 defeat at Blackburn Rovers in the quarter-finals ended their interest in the competition.

Wolves suffered a 6–2 reverse at Aston Villa in the final game of the season and they ended the campaign in fourth place with twelve wins, two draws and eight defeats, while scoring thirty-nine goals and conceding fifty, of which fifteen were conceded in their final two League fixtures. Harry Allen had appeared in all twenty-two League games, while Booth, Fletcher, Rose and Wykes had missed only one in a further successful season for the Wolverhampton side. Sam Thomson and Harry Wood led the scoring with ten League goals apiece. Having finished the season three points adrift from the eventual League champions, Wolves realised that they might never have a greater opportunity of securing the Football League Championship.

Sunderland's Progress to Football League Status

Like many teams in the north of England, Sunderland's early origins owed much to a Scottish influence when, during 1877, James Allan arrived in the area from Glasgow University to take up a teaching position. He introduced the Association game to his school colleagues, which eventually led to the formation of the Sunderland and District Teachers Association with their home ground based at Blue House Field, Hendon.

Following a struggle to field a full team, the players decided to admit members from outside the teaching profession, as well as changing their name to Sunderland Association Football Club, which led them to become founder members of the Northumberland and Durham Football Association, with schoolmasters John Graystone, Robert Singleton, Walter Chappell and James Allan the mainstays of the team.

The 1880–81 season saw the Sunderland team reach the semi-final of the Northumberland and Durham Challenge Cup, where they lost 5–0 to the Rangers side from Newcastle. The following season saw a move to a new ground at Groves Field, which coincided with a great improvement in Sunderland's fortunes.

Sunderland won all four of their home games during the 1882–83 season, including a 12–1 victory against Stanley Star in the Northumberland and Durham Challenge Cup as they reached the semi-final stage for the second time in three seasons. Their winning cup run continued in the semi-final with McDonald scoring the only goal of the game in a 1–0 victory against Derwent Rovers. However, the Sunderland team suffered a 2–0 defeat against Tyne in the final.

The 1883–84 season saw Sunderland move to a ground at Roker Avenue, where they secured an 8–1 victory against Castle Eden in their opening game. This was followed by success in the newly named Durham Challenge Cup with wins against Miltswell Burn (7–0), Jarrow (5–2) and Hamsterley Rangers (3–1), securing a semi-final tie against Hobson Wanderers, with the semi-final ending in a goalless draw, however, Sunderland had little difficulty in the replay, as they registered a 6–0 success to take their place in the final against Darlington at the Old Cricket Ground, Newcastle Road.

In a most exciting final, goals by Allan, McDonald, Murdoch and Graystone earned Sunderland a 4–3 victory. However, officials from the Darlington club had complained that their players had suffered constant intimidation from the Sunderland supporters, which resulted in a replay. Sunderland again won by two goals to nil, with McDonald and Joyce scoring the all-important goals to secure the north-eastern side's first trophy.

For the following season, Sunderland moved to an enclosed ground at Fulwell, where they were able to charge admission, which coincided with them entering the English FA Cup competition. However, despite an excellent start to the season, the north-eastern side suffered a 3–1 defeat at Redcar in the early rounds of the FA Cup.

Sunderland again performed with distinction in the Durham Cup, as James Allan scored a dozen goals in a 23–0 first round victory against Castletown, who had arrived with only eight players. Further wins against Wearmouth and Birtley saw the north-eastern side secure a second successive final appearance against Darlington.

Darlington totally dominated the final to secure a 3–0 victory, while Sunderland's protests of crowd intimidation fell on deaf ears. However, the north-eastern side had enjoyed an excellent season, with an 11–1 home defeat against Port Glasgow their only disappointment during the campaign.

The 1885–86 season began with successive home wins against North Eastern (4–0) and Cathedral (9–0), with Hunter and McDonald scoring hat-tricks, which were followed by a 3–0 defeat against Redcar in the qualifying rounds of the FA Cup. Following a return visit by the Port Glasgow Club on New Year's Day, the Scottish side struggled to secure a 2–1 victory, which showed the level of progress made by Sunderland during the season.

Prior to the 1886–87 season, Sunderland moved to a ground at Newcastle Road, with success in both the FA Cup and Durham Challenge Cup their main priority. In the first qualifying round of the FA Cup, the Sunderland team secured a 7–2 victory against Morpeth Harriers, with Smith (3), Lord (2), Erskine and Davison on target to secure a second round tie against West End. Sunderland won by two goals to one, in near darkness. However, following a complaint from the West End club, a replay was ordered, which West End won by one goal to nil to end Sunderland's interest in the competition.

Then followed an excellent run of results in the Durham Challenge Cup, with victories against Birtley, Gateshead and Whitburn on their way to the final, which was won when Davison scored the only goal of the game in a 1–0 success against old rivals Darlington.

Sunderland signed a number of players from north of the border in time for the 1887–88 season, which began with a run of excellent results, followed by a 4–2 success against Morpeth Harriers in the first qualifying round of the FA Cup, with Monaghan (3) and Smith on target. Morpeth then lodged a complaint that fullback Ford had failed to register within the required period. The Football Association ordered a replay, which Sunderland won by three goals to two, with Monaghan scoring a brace of goals to secure a home tie against the West End club in the second round.

Following a 3–1 victory against West End, the north-eastern side were drawn against Middlesbrough in round three, which resulted in a two-all draw. However, Sunderland secured a 4–2 win in the replay, with Stewart, Monaghan, Davison and Halliday scoring the all-important goals.

Middlesbrough then complained that Hastings, Richardson and Monaghan had received payments for playing, which resulted in an enquiry by the Football Association. While the local FA found Sunderland innocent of all charges, the FA in London found irregularities in their financial accounts, resulting in the suspension of three players for a period of three months, as well as disqualifying the club from the season's FA Cup competition.

Despite a humiliating 11–1 defeat against Cambuslang during the opening week of the new year, the north-eastern side again performed magnificently in the Durham Challenge Cup with victories against Whitburn, Southwick, Darlington and Bishop Auckland to win the trophy for a third time.

The 1888–89 season saw the arrival of Rennie from Dumfries, Mackie and Gibson from Cambuslang, as well as Dickson, Brady and Peacock from Glasgow Rangers, who all made winning debuts in a 4–3 success against Blackburn Rovers, which was followed by further victories against Bolton Wanderers, Accrington, Everton, Derby County and Preston North End from the newly formed Football League. However, a humiliating ten-goal defeat at Bolton ended Sunderland's fine run of results.

Sunderland were then drawn against local rivals Sunderland Albion in both the FA Cup and Durham Challenge Cup, which led them to withdraw from both competitions, however, in a friendly game against Albion, Sunderland ran out winners by two goals to nil.

Prior to the 1889–90 season, the north-eastern side had failed in their application to join the Football League, which led to further signings from Scotland, including Harvie, Campbell and David Hannah from the Renton club, Porteous and Smith from Kilmarnock, Auld from Third Lanark, as well as Stevenson from Kilburnie, while Scott (Albion Rovers), Gillespie (Greenock Morton) and Spence (Airdrie) arrived at the club during the season. The season opened with a 1–0 victory against Blackburn Rovers, with Campbell scoring the only goal of the game, which was soon followed by a one-all draw with reigning League champions Preston North End. Further wins against Accrington (8–2), Aston Villa (7–2), Notts County (2–1), Everton (3–2) and

159

Bolton Wanderers (1–0) continued their success against League opposition.

The Sunderland side were a little unfortunate to suffer a 4–2 defeat against Blackburn Rovers in the first round of the FA Cup, following a period of extra time. Excellent victories against Darlington St Augustine's, Birtley and Darlington saw the north-eastern side secure the Durham Challenge Cup. Then at the Annual General Meeting of the Football League Committee on 2 May 1890, Sunderland received the long-awaited news that they had been elected as members of the Football League, at the expense of the unfortunate Stoke Club.

SUNDERLAND IN THEIR FIRST LEAGUE SEASON

Sunderland were at home to Burnley in their opening League fixture, with the north-eastern side selecting Kirtley in goal, together with Porteous, Oliver, Wilson, Auld and Gibson in defence, while Spence, Millar, Campbell, Scott and David Hannah formed the attack. However, the game ended in a 3–2 defeat for the home side, with Spence netting both Sunderland goals. Wolverhampton Wanderers visited the north-east a couple of days later, which saw the home side race into a 3–0 lead through Campbell, Scott and James Gillespie. However, the Midlands team rallied during the second half to run out 4–3 winners. Then followed a 4–0 victory at West Bromwich Albion, with Millar (2), Campbell and Scott on target for the visitors, but it was then discovered that John 'Teddy' Doig in the Sunderland goal had failed to register for the required period, which resulted in a £50 fine as well as the deduction of two points.

Doig, a recent signing from Arbroath, spent fourteen seasons as the club's first choice goalkeeper, in which he made in excess of 400 League appearances, as well as representing the Scottish national team.

September's end saw Spence, Harvie and Scott find the net in a three-all draw in the return game at Burnley, which preceded a 3–2 reverse at Blackburn, while Millar scored his fourth and fifth League goals of the campaign in a two-all home draw with Accrington. Johnny Campbell then scored four goals in a 5–2 success at Bolton Wanderers as well as a brace in a 3–1 home win in the return game with Blackburn Rovers. However, an indifferent run of results, which included a one-all home draw with West Bromwich Albion, as well as away defeats at Everton (1–0), Accrington (4–1) and Notts County (2–1), saw the north-eastern side languishing near the foot of the League table by the end of November. Sunderland had secured just three victories in their opening dozen League games. However, they would suffer one defeat in their ten remaining games, which would see them end their first League campaign in a healthy mid-table position.

Their return to form began with a 1–0 home success against Everton, with David Hannah scoring the only goal of the game, which preceded a goalless draw at Aston Villa, while the year ended with a 3–0 victory at Wolverhampton

Wanderers, where Johnny Campbell scored his tenth League goal of the campaign.

New Year saw a 5–1 home win in the return game with Aston Villa, with Campbell (3) and David Hannah (2) on target, while their winning run continued with a 1–0 home success against Everton in the first round of the FA Cup, with Campbell once more on target to secure a second round tie at Darwen.

Prior to the FA Cup tie, Jimmy Millar scored a hat-trick in a 4–0 home win against Notts County, while the final day of January saw David Hannah score a brace of goals in an excellent 2–0 victory at Darwen to earn a home tie against Nottingham Forest in the quarter-finals. On their return to League action, the north-eastern side suffered a 3–1 reverse at Derby County, followed by a 2–0 home win against Bolton Wanderers, while Campbell and Millar both scored twice in a 4–0 victory in the cup game with Nottingham Forest, thus securing their first semi-final appearance. This was to take place at Bramall Lane, Sheffield, against Notts County.

A goalless draw at Preston preceded the semi-final tie, while Johnny Campbell again found the net as the cup game ended all square (3–3). However, Notts secured a 2–0 victory in the replay to end Sunderland's hopes of an FA Cup Final appearance.

Following Sunderland's FA Cup disappointment, the north-eastern team ended the season with successive home wins against Preston North End (3–0) and Derby County (5–1), with Campbell on target in both victories. They finished the League campaign in seventh position, with ten wins, five draws and seven defeats in their twenty-two League fixtures, while scoring fifty-one goals and conceding thirty-one.

Porteous, Scott and David Hannah had been ever present in the Sunderland team during the season, with Scott scoring eight League goals. Millar had found the net on ten occasions, while Campbell led the scoring with eighteen goals in twenty-one League appearances.

PRESTON NORTH END

Preston North End retained the majority of their League Championship winning team for the 1890–91 season, as Jimmy Trainer continued in goal, together with Kelso, Howarth, Holmes and Nick Ross in defence, while Drummond, Gordon and Jimmy Ross remained in the attack.

David Russell had left the club for a short period. Fred Dewhurst made a couple of appearances during the season prior to retiring from the game, while the most notable newcomers were Stewart in the defence and Gallacher up front, who had been signed to replace Sam Thomson, following his transfer to Wolverhampton Wanderers.

Preston opened the season with successive home wins against West Bromwich Albion (3–0) and Bolton Wanderers (1–0) on either side of a 3–1 victory at Derby County. However, their winning run came to an end during the opening week of October with a 2–1 home defeat against Blackburn Rovers.

Then followed victories at Accrington and at home to Wolverhampton Wanderers, as the Lancashire side moved up to second place in the League table. Then a poor run of results, which included away defeats at Blackburn Rovers (1 0) and Bolton Wanderers (1–0), as well as home draws against Accrington and Notts County, saw the title holders in a mid-table position by mid-November.

Preston returned to winning ways with a 2–0 home win against fellow title challengers Everton, but this preceded further away defeats at Wolverhampton Wanderers and Notts County, though the year ended with a 6–0 home victory against Derby County.

New Year began with a 1–0 success at Everton, which meant that Preston had accumulated eighteen points from fifteen League games, while Everton had secured twenty-nine points with only one game remaining. However, following an FA Cup defeat at the first hurdle, the Preston team achieved an excellent run of results in their efforts to catch Everton at the top of the table. Preston's return to form saw home wins against Aston Villa (4–1) and Burnley (7–0), as well as a 3–1 success at West Bromwich Albion. A goalless home draw with Sunderland moved them within four points of the League leaders with three games remaining, but a 6–2 reverse at Burnley during the opening week of March all but put paid to their League title aspirations as Everton's goals scored total was far superior.

Following their six-goal defeat at Burnley, the Preston team secured a 1–0 victory at Aston Villa to move them within two points of Everton, with both teams playing their final games of the season on 14 March. With Everton losing 3–2 at Burnley and Preston suffering a 3–0 reverse at Sunderland, the reigning League champions had to settle for the runners-up position with twelve wins, three draws and seven defeats in their twenty-two League games, while scoring forty-four goals and conceding twenty-three.

Jimmy Trainer had appeared in all of Preston's League games, while Gallacher, Dobson and Jimmy Ross had led the scoring with six League goals apiece. However, a second place League finish was viewed as a major disappointment for the Lancashire side, when judged against their previous success.

EVERTON

Everton had finished the 1889–90 season as runners-up to Preston North End, hence their reluctance to make changes in their line-up for the 1890–91 League campaign. Hannah, Doyle, Kirkwood, Holt and Parry continued in defence, together with Latta, Brady, Geary, Chadwick and Milward in the attack, while Angus and Jardine shared the goalkeeping duties.

In an excellent start to the campaign, Everton secured a 4–1 victory at West Bromwich Albion, with Geary (2), Campbell and Brady on target, which preceded further wins at home to Wolverhampton Wanderers (5–0) and away at Bolton Wanderers (5–0), with Fred Geary and Alf Milward scoring a brace of goals in both victories, while both men were on target the following week in a 2–1 success at Accrington.

Early October saw Geary and Milward score a couple of goals apiece in a 7–0 home win against Derby County, which preceded a two-all draw at Aston Villa, where Geary scored his tenth and eleventh League goals of the season, while Brady netted a brace of goals in a 2–0 home success against Bolton Wanderers. Then followed a run of defeats at Notts County (3–1) and Blackburn Rovers (2–1), as well as at home to West Bromwich Albion (3–2). Robertson, making a rare appearance for Everton, scored the only goal of the game in a 1–0 home success against Sunderland. However, a 2–0 reverse at Preston saw the Merseysiders suffer their fourth defeat in five League games. Everton returned to winning ways with a 3–1 home win against Blackburn Rovers, with Fred Geary scoring his usual brace of goals. Geary once again found the net in a 1–0 victory at Wolverhampton Wanderers, which was followed by a 6–2 success at Derby County, where outside right Wylie, a recent signing from Glasgow Rangers, scored four of the Everton goals in only his second League appearance for the club.

Christmas week saw a 1–0 reverse at Sunderland, while the year ended with successive home wins against Accrington (3–2) and Burley (7–3), with Alf Milward and Edgar Chadwick scoring seven of the Everton goals. This was followed by a 5–0 home win against Aston Villa on New Year's Day, with Brady (2), Chadwick, Geary and Milward on target. Edgar Chadwick then scored a brace of goals in a 4–2 home success against Notts County, with Geary and Milward completing the scoring, which preceded a 1–0 home defeat against Preston North End, leaving the Everton team on twenty-nine points with one League game remaining, while Preston, who were eleven points adrift, had seven games to play.

Following a 1–0 reverse at Sunderland in the opening round of the FA Cup, Everton waited a further two months to complete their League fixtures, which eventually ended with a 3–2 defeat at Burnley, with Fred Geary scoring both of the visitors goals. However, with Preston suffering a couple of defeats towards the end of the campaign, Everton were able to win the League Championship by a margin of two points, with fourteen victories, one draw and seven defeats in their twenty-two League games, while scoring sixty-three goals and conceding twenty-nine. Alf Milward, Fred Geary and Edgar Chadwick were ever present during the season, with Brady and Holt missing just one League game. Chadwick ended the campaign with ten League goals, Milward found the net on a dozen occasions, and Fred Geary led the scoring with twenty goals, to take his total to forty-one goals in forty League appearances.

The final League placings at the close of the 1890–91 season were as in Table V.

Table V: *Football League results for the 1890–91 season*

	P	W	D	L	F	A	PTS
1. Everton	22	14	1	7	63	29	29
2. Preston North End	22	12	3	7	44	23	27
3. Notts County	22	11	4	7	52	35	26
4. Wolverhampton Wndrs	22	12	2	8	39	50	26
5. Bolton Wanderers	22	12	1	9	47	34	25
6. Blackburn Rovers	22	11	2	9	52	43	24
7. Sunderland	22	10	5	7	51	31	23*
8. Burnley	22	9	3	10	52	63	21
9. Aston Villa	22	7	4	11	45	58	18
10. Accrington	22	6	4	12	28	50	16
11. Derby County	22	7	1	14	47	81	15
12. West Bromwich Albion	22	5	2	15	34	57	12

Note: *Sunderland were penalised two points for fielding John Doig prior to the League approving his registration.

Notts County Secure a Place in the FA Cup Final

The opening round of the 1890–91 FA Cup competition produced many high-scoring ties. Woolhouse scored five of the Wednesday goals in a 12–0 home win against Halliwell, while Nottingham Forest won 14–0 at Clapton, with Sandy Higgins and Tinsley Lindley sharing nine of the Forest goals. Aston Villa secured a 13–1 victory against the Casuals, with Hodgetts (4) and Campbell (3) scoring the majority of the goals, while Darwen defeated Kidderminster by thirteen goals to nil in a replayed tie.

Nine League teams remained in the competition at the second round stage, which saw Blackburn Rovers progress to the quarter-finals following a 7–0 home win against Chester, with John Southworth scoring a hat-trick, while West Bromwich Albion won 3–0 at Mitchell's St George's, with Nicholls, Dyer and Charlie Perry on target for the visitors. Stoke scored three without reply at home to Aston Villa. David Hannah scored both Sunderland goals in a 2–0 victory at Darwen, while Harry Daft netted a brace of goals for Notts County in a 2–1 home success against Burnley. Hodder, Winterbottom and Harry Brandon scored for the Wednesday in a 3–2 victory at Derby County, with Bakewell and John Goodall replying for the home side. Wolverhampton Wanderers won at Accrington by a similar score, while Nottingham Forest completed the quarter-final line-up with a 5–0 success against Sunderland Albion following two drawn ties, with Lindley and Higgins again amongst the scorers. The quarter-final draw produced just one all League encounter with Blackburn Rovers securing a 2–0 home win against Wolverhampton Wanderers, with Wolves' defenders Fletcher and Baugh scoring through their own goal. Willie Groves and Tom Pearson were on target for West Bromwich

Albion in a 2–0 victory at the Wednesday. Billy Locker scored the only goal of the game as Notts County secured a 1–0 home success against Stoke, while Millar and Campbell both scored a brace of goals for Sunderland in a 4–0 home win against Nottingham Forest to progress to the semi-finals.

Both semi-final ties were exciting encounters with Sunderland and Notts County sharing a six-goal thriller at Bramall Lane, with McGregor, McInnes and Oswald on target for the Midlanders, while Harvie, Scott and Campbell replied for the north-eastern side. However, Sunderland were outplayed in the replay as Jimmy Oswald netted a brace of goals for County in a 2–0 victory to secure their first FA Cup Final appearance, due to take place at the Oval on 21 March.

In the second semi-final at the Victoria Ground, Stoke, a Willie Groves goal secured an early lead for West Bromwich Albion, while John Southworth equalised for Blackburn Rovers during the latter stages of the opening half. This preceded further goals from Hall and Lofthouse as the Lancashire side raced into a 3–1 lead, from which Albion failed to recover despite Tom Pearson reducing the arrears. Rovers held on for their sixth FA Cup Final appearance in ten seasons.

A Four-Goal Victory Against the Welsh

Two weeks before the FA Cup Final, the English national team played twice on the same day, with the Irish national side visiting Wolverhampton, while the Welsh fixture took place at Sunderland.

England awarded six new caps for the Welsh game, which included the Everton left wing pairing of Edgar Chadwick and Alf Milward, while Thomas Porteous (Sunderland) made his only international appearance at fullback. Leonard Wilkinson (Old Carthusians), later to win an FA Amateur Cup winners' medal with the Old Boys, played his one England game between the posts. Albert Smith, who had appeared as an amateur for both Nottingham clubs, gained the first of three England caps at right half back, while Elphinstone Jackson (Oxford University), who would assist in the formation of the India Football Association, played his one England game at left fullback. John Holt (Everton) and Alf Shelton (Notts County) were once again included in the half-back line, while there were recalls for George Brann (Corinthians), John Goodall (Derby County) and John Southworth (Blackburn Rovers) in the attack. As expected, England won with little difficulty as Chadwick, Milward, Southworth and Goodall found the net in a 4–1 victory.

Tinsley Lindley Bows Out

England selected a predominantly Midlands-based side for the visit of the Irish national team to Wolverhampton, which included two players from the home club, as well as three from neighbouring West Bromwich Albion. W C Rose returned to the England side in goal, together with his Wolves' team-mate, John Brodie, while Charlie Perry, Billy Bassett and Jem Bayliss were the Albion contingent, with Bayliss making his only England appearance. Joseph Marsden (Darwen), who soon joined the Everton club, made his England debut at fullback together with Alfred Underwood (Stoke), while Harry Daft (Notts County) played his fourth England game at outside left. Completing the England line-up were three players with Corinthian connections. George Cotterill and Arthur Henfrey, both of Cambridge University, made their international debuts in the attack, while Tinsley Lindley was included for his thirteenth and final England appearance. Cotterill, an accomplished county cricketer with Sussex, was on the winning side in all four of his England appearances, while Henfrey, a Northamptonshire county cricketer, appeared on five occasions in an England shirt.

England were once again a little too skilful for the Irish as goals by Lindley (2), Cotterill, Daft, Henfrey and Billy Bassett secured a 6–1 success to continue their winning run against the luckless visitors.

Following the victory against Ireland, Tinsley Lindley, a true Corinthian in every sense of the word, announced his retirement from international football in a career that had seen him score fifteen goals in thirteen England appearances.

Five FA Cup Final Victories for Blackburn

A crowd in excess of 23,000 arrived at the Oval to see Blackburn Rovers and Notts County contest the twentieth FA Cup Final, with Blackburn selecting the following players:

Pennington

Brandon   Forbes

Barton   Dewar   Forrest

Lofthouse   Walton   John Southworth   Hall   Townley

Notts County selected the following eleven:

Thraves

Ferguson   Hendry

Osborne   Calderhead   Shelton

McGregor   McInnes   Oswald   Locker   Daft

Eight of the Rovers' team had appeared in the previous season's final, with James Forrest playing in his fifth final, while John Southworth had recovered from the leg injury that had kept him out of the Blackburn side of late.

Blackburn dominated the early stages of the final with Southworth, Townley and Walton exerting pressure on the Notts' defence, which eventually led to the opening goal when Dewar slotted home a Billy Townley cross.

Calderhead and Shelton performed heroically in the County defence. However, they were unable to prevent John Southworth scoring a second goal for the Lancashire side, while Billy Townley netted a third within five minutes and Blackburn ended the half three goals to the good.

Rovers tended to relax during the second half, seeing the game as good as won. A late effort by Jimmy Oswald reduced the arrears for the Nottingham side, but Blackburn held on for a 3–1 success to equal the five FA Cup Final victories secured by the great Wanderers' side during the 1870s.

County had been a little overawed by the great occasion and especially by the FA Cup experience of Blackburn, for whom James Forrest had won his fifth FA Cup winners' medal, thus equalling the record of Charles Wollaston (Wanderers) and Arthur Kinnaird, who had played in three winning finals for the Wanderers, as well as two for the Old Etonians.

A Narrow Victory for England

England selected four members of Everton's successful League Championship winning team for the visit of the Scottish national side to Ewood Park, Blackburn, for the final international game of the season. The team, surprisingly, failed to include a member of Blackburn Rovers' FA Cup-winning side.

John Holt made his third England appearance at centre half, while his Everton team-mates, Alf Milward, Fred Geary and Edgar Chadwick, who had scored forty-two League goals between them during the season, all gained their second England caps in the attack, where they were joined by the ever reliable John Goodall (Derby County) and Billy Bassett (West Bromwich Albion).

William Moon played his final England game between the posts; Albert Smith and Alfred Shelton were once again included in the half-back line; while Bob Howarth and Robert Holmes of Preston North End earned recalls at fullback. In a close game, the England team managed to hold on to a 2–1 victory, with John Goodall and Edgar Chadwick scoring the all-important goals.

The Alliance Prove a Point

Two weeks after England's victory against the Scots, a game took place at the Olive Grove Ground, Sheffield, between representative sides from the Football League and Football Alliance. The Alliance selected Bob Roberts (Sunderland Albion), the former West Bromwich Albion and England goalkeeper, together with Clare (Stoke), Rae (Sunderland Albion), Harry Brandon (Wednesday), McCracken (Sunderland Albion) and Clifford (Stoke) in defence, while Davis (Birmingham St George's), Smith (Nottingham Forest),

John Devey (Birmingham St George's), Edge (Stoke) and Hannah (Sunderland Albion) formed the attack.

The Football League eleven were a mixture of players who had represented England, Scotland and Wales with Jimmy Trainer (Preston North End) in goal, together with Tom Brandon (Blackburn Rovers) and Nick Ross (Preston North End) at fullback, while Calderhead (Notts County), Dewar (Blackburn Rovers) and Wilson (Sunderland) completed the defensive line-up. Charlie Athersmith (Aston Villa) and Harry Daft (Notts County) were selected on the wings, while McInnes (Notts County), John Goodall (Derby County) and Edgar Chadwick (Everton) were the three front-line players.

With little at stake, the game ended in a one-all draw, with Davis on target for the Alliance, while Chadwick replied for the Football League. However, the Alliance players had at least confirmed that they were as capable as those playing in the Football League.

The Football League Is Extended

As the 1890–91 season came to a close, the Football League Committee held their annual general meeting to discuss, amongst other things, the issue of teams applying for re-election to the League. Owing to the increasing number of applicants, it was decided to increase the League from twelve to fourteen teams, which meant that Aston Villa, Accrington, Derby County and West Bromwich Albion retained their League status, while Darwen and Stoke, who had recently won the Championship of the Football Alliance, were voted into the League.

Stoke had suffered just two defeats on their way to the Alliance title, which coincided with an injury to their goalkeeper on both occasions. However, following the arrival of Isaac Brookes in goal, the Potteries' side were unbeaten in their final dozen Alliance games.

An unfortunate incident in an FA Cup tie against Notts County saw a goal-bound shot from a Stoke forward fisted away by County fullback Hendry. The resulting free kick was cleared by the Nottingham side, who went on to win the tie by one goal to nil, with Billy Locker scoring the only goal of the game. As a result of the incident, the penalty kick was introduced in time for the 1891–92 season. The new rule was later amended so that referees could allow time to take them, as well as for other hold-ups during a game. Further changes included the compulsory use of goal nets for the following season.

Chapter XVII

SUNDERLAND ARE CROWNED LEAGUE CHAMPIONS – 1891–92

SUNDERLAND ARE CROWNED LEAGUE CHAMPIONS
WEST BROMWICH ALBION DEFEAT ASTON VILLA IN THE FINAL OF THE FA CUP
ENGLAND REMAIN UNBEATEN
THE LEAGUE DOUBLES IN SIZE
MR MCGREGOR STEPS DOWN

With the arrival of the 1891–92 season, the inclusion of Stoke and Darwen into the Football League meant that teams would now play twenty-six League games instead of the twenty-two of previous seasons.

DARWEN

Darwen were well aware of the difficult baptism into the Football League that awaited them, as they were no longer the side that had taken the mighty Old Etonians to two replays during the 1879 FA Cup competition while financial restrictions meant that players of the calibre of Fergie Suter and Jimmy Love were never replaced.

Darwen opened the season with a 2–1 home defeat against Bolton Wanderers, followed by further defeats at Everton (5–3) and in the return game at Bolton (1–0). However, successive away draws at Wolverhampton Wanderers and Accrington, as well as excellent home wins against Accrington (5–2) and Stoke (9–3) saw the League newcomers climb to a respectable mid-table position.

Then followed five-goal defeats against Blackburn Rovers, Notts County and Aston Villa, which preceded a 3–1 home success against reigning League champions Everton, while a 7–0 reverse at Derby County continued their poor away form. Within a week, Darwen had avenged the humiliating defeat at Derby by securing a 2–0 victory in the return game in Lancashire. While Darwen had tended to struggle during the opening half of the season, they had managed to avoid the bottom two positions in the League, but the second half of the campaign saw the Lancashire side lose twelve and draw one of their remaining thirteen League games.

Darwen's poor run of results began with away defeats at Stoke (5–1) and Sunderland (7–0), followed by a 4–0 reverse at Blackburn Rovers on Christmas Day, while the year ended with a further humiliating away defeat at Aston Villa (7–0).

Little changed during the new year as Darwen continued their losing run with a 4–0 home defeat against Preston North End, which preceded an embarrassing 9–0 defeat at Burnley, while a 2–0 reverse at Aston Villa in the second round of the FA Cup ended their interest in the competition.

It had become apparent that Darwen were inadequately equipped for the rigours of League football, which was confirmed by further home defeats against Notts County, Wolverhampton Wanderers and Burnley, as well as a 12–0 thrashing at West Bromwich Albion. However, pride was restored the following week when they drew with Albion in the return game at Darwen.

Further defeats at Preston (4–0) and at home to Sunderland (7–1) saw Darwen end the season in last position in the League with only four victories in their twenty-six games, while conceding 112 goals, which left them at the mercy of the other members of the Football League to decide their future. While all seemed lost, the Lancashire side were offered a lifeline to retain their League status.

STOKE

Stoke had suffered the indignation of relegation from the Football League at the end of the 1889–90 season. However, following their success in the Football Alliance, they were soon re-elected to the League.

On their return to League action, the Potteries' side secured a 2–1 home win against Derby County, which preceded successive defeats at home to Wolverhampton Wanderers (3–1) and away at Burnley (4–1), while the month ended with a one-all draw at Notts County. Then an embarrassing 9–3 defeat at Darwen continued their poor run of results.

Following a 3–0 home success against Burnley, the Stoke team shared six goals at Derby County, while they were a little unfortunate to suffer a 3–2 home defeat against Aston Villa. Further home defeats against Preston North End, Sunderland and Blackburn Rovers, as well as a 2–1 reverse at Aston Villa, saw them return to the foot of the League table.

Stoke had secured only one point during November with a one-all home draw against Bolton Wanderers. Their poor form improved during December with home wins against Darwen (5–1) and Accrington (3–1) on either side of a 1–0 away defeat against Bolton Wanderers prior to ending the year with a narrow 3–2 defeat at Preston.

New Year saw further away defeats at Wolverhampton Wanderers and Accrington, but an excellent FA Cup run saw a 3–1 success at Burnley, as well as a two-all draw with Sunderland in the quarter-finals. However, a 4–0 reverse in the replay put paid to their hopes of a place in the semi-finals.

League victories were rare towards the latter stages of the season, which saw a 3–1 home defeat against Notts County, as well as successive 1–0 defeats at home and away to Everton. Further defeats at Blackburn Rovers and Sunderland saw the Potteries' side one place away from the foot of the League table, with two games remaining. While the threat of re-election had long been a reality, the Stoke team required a couple of points to avoid the embarrassment of a last place finish.

Stoke secured a two-all draw at West Bromwich Albion in their penultimate game of the season and the campaign ended with a 1–0 home success in the return game with Albion. They finished in thirteenth position, with just five victories in twenty-six League games.

Despite their poor season, in which Turner and Christie were ever present in the Stoke team, four members of the side were selected for the end-of-season international games, with Rowley, Clare and Underwood selected for the game against Ireland, while Joseph Schofield made a winning debut against Wales. Schofield, who had joined the club from Hanley Hope Sunday School in 1890, ended the season as leading scorer with nine League goals. There still remained the fact that the Potteries' side would have to apply for re-election to the League for a third time.

WEST BROMWICH ALBION

There was little doubt that West Bromwich Albion were one of the finest FA Cup-fighting sides in all England. However, they seemed to have great difficulty in transferring their FA Cup form to League games, as their last place finish during the 1890–91 League campaign confirmed. Few changes were made in their line-up for the 1891–92 season, as Joe Reader continued in goal, with the ever reliable Charlie Perry at the heart of the defence, while Billy Bassett, Sam Nicholls, Roddy McLeod, William Groves and Tom Pearson once again formed a capable attack.

Albion opened the season with a visit from reigning League champions Everton at Stoney Lane when the West Bromwich side performed magnificently to register a 4–0 success with McLeod (2), Groves and Nicholls on target. This was followed by a 5–1 reverse at Aston Villa, while their fine home form continued with a 4–3 victory against Wolverhampton Wanderers, with Groves (2), Nicholls and Charlie Perry netting the Albion goals. However, a run of ten games without a win, would see the West Bromwich side near the foot of the League table at the halfway stage of the campaign.

Following a two-all home draw with Blackburn Rovers, Albion suffered successive away defeats at Notts County (4–0) and Sunderland (4–0), as well as a 5–2 home defeat in the return game with Sunderland. Tom Pearson netted a brace of goals in a home draw with Notts County, but further defeats at home to Bolton Wanderers (2–0) and away at Everton (4–3), where Billy Bassett scored twice, continued Albion's poor run of results. Albion suffered further home defeats against Aston Villa and Preston North End, as well as a 3–2 reverse at Burnley before their wretched run of results came to an end, which coincided with the arrival of Jasper Geddes and John Reynolds. Geddes, who had scored in both the Burnley and Preston defeats, went on to score many important goals for Albion, while Reynolds, an Irish international, had recently signed from Distillery. However, it was soon discovered that Reynolds was in fact born in England, which eventually resulted in eight appearances for the English national side. Reynolds won many honours during his career, which included FA Cup winners' medals with Albion and Aston Villa, as well as League Championship medals with Villa and Glasgow Celtic.

Early December saw Albion return to winning ways as Woodhall, Pearson and Geddes found the net in a 3–1 home win against Accrington. All three players were on target the following week in a 4–2 home victory against Derby County, which preceded a one-all draw at Bolton, with Roddy McLeod scoring for the visitors.

Albion's return to form continued as Tom Pearson scored the only goal of the game in a 1–0 home win against Burnley, which preceded a 2–1 reverse at Wolverhampton Wanderers in the final game of the year, while the new year opened with a 1–0 defeat at Preston. John Reynolds then scored a rare goal in a 3–2 away victory against the Old Westminsters in the first round of the FA Cup, with McLeod and Pearson completing the scoring. This was followed by a 4–2 defeat at Accrington, while a 3–1 home win against FA Cup holders Blackburn Rovers saw the Black Country side secure a home tie against the Wednesday in the quarter-finals, with Pearson (2) and Geddes netting the Albion goals.

Prior to the FA Cup tie, Albion drew one-all at Derby County and their FA Cup form continued against the Wednesday as goals by Nicholls and Geddes earned a 2–1 victory, with Richardson replying for the Sheffield side. Albion proceeded to the semi-finals where they met Nottingham Forest at the Molineux Ground, Wolverhampton. Following two drawn games at Wolverhampton (1–1 and 1–1), a third tie took place at Derby in a snowstorm, which suited Albion's robust style of play as they registered a 6–2 victory, with Geddes (3), Bassett (2) and Charlie Perry on target. Forest's protests for a re-match were waved aside and Albion secured their fourth FA Cup Final appearance, scheduled for the Oval on 19 March against local rivals Aston Villa.

A week prior to the final, Albion suffered a 3–2 reverse at Blackburn Rovers on a snow-covered pitch, however, the Black Country side had other things on their minds, mainly their FA Cup Final appearance at the Oval.

DERBY COUNTY

Derby County had generally struggled since the formation of the Football League, which had disappointed their many supporters who had expected a little more success from a team that included numerous skilful players.

County made a number of changes for the 1891–92 season, with only Roulstone, McMillan, McLachlan, Archie Goodall and John Goodall retaining their places from the previous campaign. Newcomers included John Robinson in goal, together with Jonathon Staley, James Methven and John Cox in defence, while Mills and Storer made several appearances in the attack. Robinson, who had arrived from Lincoln City during the close season, remained with Derby for six seasons, in which he made nearly 200 League appearances, as well as gaining a number of England caps. Staley made in excess of 150 appearances in nine seasons with the club. John Cox, who had made his League debut in the final game of the previous season following his transfer from Long Eaton Rangers, wore Derby's colours for ten seasons, making in excess of 200 League appearances, as well as securing a place in the English national team. Mills and William Storer spent a couple of seasons with the East Midlands side, with Storer better known as the Derbyshire and England wicket-keeper. The most notable new arrival to the Derby Club was fullback James Methven from the Edinburgh St Bernard's Club. Methven, who had been signed upon the recommendation of John McMillan, played in excess of 500 games for Derby, prior to managing the club.

Derby opened the season with a 2–1 defeat at Stoke, followed by a 3–1 home win against Accrington, with McMillan (2) and John Goodall on target. Both players were again on the score sheet a week later in a 3–0 home success against Notts County.

Then followed a 3–1 victory at Wolverhampton Wanderers, with John Goodall netting a hat-trick for the visitors. This preceded a further home win against Aston Villa (4–2) with Storer (2), Mills and John Goodall scoring for County, while John Goodall scored for the sixth successive game in a three-all home draw with Stoke with McLachlan and Archie Goodall completing the scoring. Archie Goodall's first goal of the season coincided with the start of a run that saw the Irish international play 151 consecutive League games.

Late October saw Derby suffer a 3–0 home defeat against Everton, followed by a 2–1 home win against Wolverhampton Wanderers, with Storer and Hardy on target, while John Goodall scored Derby's only goal in an embarrassing 7–1 defeat at Sunderland. However, the East Midlands side soon returned to winning ways with a 7–0 home success against Darwen, with McMillan and McLachlan both scoring a brace of goals.

Following a 2–0 defeat in the return game at Darwen, Derby suffered home defeats against Preston North End (2–1) and Burnley (1–0), as well as a 4–2 reverse at West Bromwich Albion. The year ended with a 3–2 home success against Bolton Wanderers, with Storer (2) and McLachlan on target for County.

New Year's Day saw Archie Goodall score a rare goal in a 3–1 defeat in the return game at Bolton, which was followed by a 2–0 victory at Blackburn Rovers, where Ekins and Storer found the net. A 6–0 reverse at Aston Villa, as well as a 4–1 defeat at Blackburn Rovers in the first round of the FA Cup, continued their indifferent run of results.

John Goodall then scored his eleventh League goal of the campaign in a one-all home draw with West Bromwich Albion, which preceded away defeats against Notts County (2–1) and Preston North End (3–0), as well as at home to Sunderland (1–0). A one-all home draw with Blackburn Rovers ended their losing run, with John McMillan netting the Derby goal.

Derby then secured a further one-all draw at Accrington, with Mills on target, to earn a welcome point, while the season ended with successive away wins at Everton (2–1) and Burnley (4–2), with John Goodall scoring a brace of goals in both games. The East Midlands side ended the campaign in tenth place, with ten victories, four draws and twelve defeats in their twenty-six League games, while scoring forty-six goals and conceding fifty-two. James Methven had appeared in all twenty-six of Derby's League games, in a season when nine of the team had missed no more than a handful of games. John Goodall had once again led the scoring with fifteen League goals.

ACCRINGTON

Accrington had managed to retain their Football League status for the 1891–92 season. However, their efforts to sign quality players for the new campaign had been to no avail, which left George Haworth once again at the heart of the defence, together with McKay, Faulds and Kirkham up front.

The season opened with a 1–0 home success against Burnley at Thorneyholme Road, which preceded successive away defeats at Derby County, Wolverhampton Wanderers and Darwen, with the latter two by five goals. However, an excellent run of results followed, which included home draws against Everton and Darwen, as well as odd-goal victories at home to Wolverhampton Wanderers and away at Bolton Wanderers that saw the Accrington side climb to a respectable mid-table position.

Then followed further defeats at Sunderland (4–1) and Burnley (2–1), as well as at home to Bolton Wanderers (2–0), while a 2–0 home success against Notts County seemed to end their disappointing run of results, however, the Nottingham side avenged the defeat the following week by scoring nine goals without reply against Accrington.

Accrington ended the year with away defeats at West Bromwich Albion (3–1) and Stoke (3–1), followed by a one-all draw at Blackburn Rovers on Boxing Day, while the new year began with a further home defeat against Preston North End (3–1). However, successive home wins against Aston Villa, Stoke and West Bromwich Albion greatly improved their chances of avoiding the re-election positions.

January's end saw Accrington suffer a 3–1 home defeat against Sunderland in the second round of the FA Cup, while their winning League run continued with a 1–0 home win against Blackburn Rovers. Accrington then suffered a loss of form, which saw them lose four and draw one of their remaining five League games.

Accrington's loss of form began with a 5–2 home defeat against Sunderland, followed by an embarrassing 12–2 reverse at Aston Villa. Away defeats at Everton (3–0) and Preston North End (4–1), as well as a one-all home draw with Derby County, saw the Lancashire side end the League campaign in eleventh place, following eight wins, four draws and fourteen defeats in their twenty-six League games. This meant that Accrington had to apply for re-election to the League.

BLACKBURN ROVERS

Blackburn Rovers had finished in a top six position in all three of their League campaigns. However, while the Lancashire side were capable of defeating any team in England, their priorities lay in FA Cup success, as their excellent cup record confirmed.

Few changes were made by the FA Cup holders for the 1891–92 League campaign, as John Forbes, George Dewar and James Forrest continued in defence, while Lofthouse, Hall, Walton, Campbell, Townley and John Southworth remained in the attack.

John Barton and Jimmy Douglas made the occasional appearance during the season, while Tom Brandon had signed for the Wednesday. However, he soon returned to Blackburn, where he remained well into the following century.

Herbie Arthur, who had recovered from a serious leg injury, was first choice goalkeeper for the bulk of the season, while Harry Chippendale, a future England international winger, was the most notable newcomer in the Rovers' side following his arrival from Nelson.

Blackburn opened the season with a 5–1 reverse at Aston Villa, followed by a 5–4 home success against Notts County, with Townley (2), Lofthouse, Dewar and John Southworth on target, while their poor away form continued with a 3–1 defeat at Everton. John Southworth then netted a brace of goals in a 3–3 home draw with Burnley, which preceded a further draw at West Bromwich Albion (2–2), with Harry Chippendale scoring both goals in only his second appearance for the club, while Hall and Southworth found the net in a 2–0 home win against Wolverhampton Wanderers.

Rovers' first away win of the season occurred with a 5–3 success at Darwen, with Southworth (2), Hall (2) and Lofthouse scoring for the visitors, while the prolific John Southworth was again on target in successive defeats, at home to Preston North End (4–2) and away at Bolton (4–2). However, the Lancashire side soon returned to winning ways with a 3–1 home victory against Sunderland, with Southworth scoring twice.

Following a 1–0 win at Stoke, where Hall scored the only goal of the game, Blackburn suffered a 3–2 defeat at Preston, while John Southworth netted a hat-trick in a 4–0 home success against Bolton Wanderers. Successive away defeats at Wolverhampton Wanderers (6–1) and Burnley (3–0) on either side of a two-all home draw with Everton saw Rovers struggling to maintain their mid-table position.

A further brace of goals by John Southworth then secured a two-all draw at Notts County, which preceded a 4–0 home win against Darwen on Christmas Day, with Southworth (2), Townley and Almond on target for Blackburn. The year ended with a two-all home draw with Accrington, leaving the Lancashire side in the top half of the League table with seven games remaining.

New Year saw Blackburn suffer a 2–0 home defeat against Derby County, who were coincidently their opponents in the first round of the FA Cup, which resulted in a 4–1 victory for the Rovers with John Southworth scoring all four goals to secure a second round tie at West Bromwich Albion.

Prior to the cup game at West Bromwich, Blackburn suffered a 1–0 reverse at Accrington, which was followed by a 3–1 defeat at Albion in Rovers' first FA Cup defeat for three seasons. However, following a five-week rest from League football, the Lancashire side registered three successive home victories, thus avoiding the re-election positions.

Their winning home run began with a 4–3 success against Aston Villa, with Billy Townley scoring twice, which was followed by further victories against West Bromwich Albion (3–2) and Stoke (5–3), with Harry Chippendale netting a brace of goals in both games, while a John Southworth goal earned a one-all draw at Derby County in the penultimate game of the season. Then a 6–1 reverse at Sunderland in the final game of the campaign ended their unbeaten run. They finished the season in ninth position, following ten wins, six draws and ten defeats in their twenty-six League games, while scoring fifty-eight goals and conceding sixty-five, with only Accrington and Darwen conceding more.

Seven members of the Blackburn team had appeared in at least twenty-one League games during the season, with Forbes, Campbell and Southworth missing no more than a couple. Walton, Chippendale and Hall ended the campaign with six League goals apiece, Billy Townley found the net on ten occasions, while John Southworth led the scoring with twenty-two League goals to bring his total to eighty-seven goals in eighty-five League appearances.

Blackburn continued to enjoy a certain amount of success during the 1890s, but their FA Cup-winning exploits during the Victorian period had now come to an end.

NOTTS COUNTY

Notts County were hopeful of further success during the 1891–92 season following their third place League finish, as well as an appearance in the FA Cup Final during the previous campaign. This resulted in few changes in their line-up for the new season as George Toone continued in goal, together with David Calderhead and Alf Shelton at the heart of the defence, while Tom McInnes, Jimmy Oswald and the ever reliable Harry Daft remained in the attack.

County opened the season with a 2–0 home win against Preston North End, which preceded successive away defeats at Blackburn Rovers (5–4) and Derby County (3–0). A home draw with Stoke, as well as home victories against Bolton Wanderers (2–0) and West Bromwich Albion (4–0), saw the Nottingham side move into the top half of the League table.

A further away defeat at Wolverhampton Wanderers preceded a 5–0 home success against Darwen, while a two-all draw at West Bromwich Albion secured their first away point of the season. However, a 5–1 reverse at Aston Villa continued County's poor away form.

Mid-November saw a 2–2 home draw with Wolverhampton Wanderers, followed by a 2–0 defeat at Accrington. Notts soon avenged the defeat by scoring nine goals without reply against the Accrington side, which left them in a mid-table position at the halfway stage of the campaign.

Notts' poor away form continued during December, with successive away defeats at Sunderland (4–0) and Preston North End (6–0). The Football League Committee ordered the game against Preston to be replayed following a complaint from the Nottingham side regarding the appalling weather conditions, which Preston again won by six goals to two. The year ended with a 2–2 home draw against FA Cup holders, Blackburn Rovers.

New Year saw County secure a 5–2 home success against Aston Villa, which preceded a 3–1 home defeat against Everton, while a 3–0 reverse at Sunderland in the first round of the FA Cup ended their interest in the competition. County complained that the poor playing conditions had given the home side an unfair advantage, which resulted in a replay, again won by the north-eastern side by four goals to nil.

On their return to League action, the Nottingham side enjoyed an excellent run of results, which included away victories at Stoke and Darwen, as well as home wins against Burnley and Derby County, moving them into the top half of the League table. However, three defeats in their final four League games would see County end the season in a mid-table position.

Their disappointing run of results saw away defeats at Bolton Wanderers (2–0), Burnley (1–0) and Everton (4–0), with a 1–0 home win against Sunderland their only success during the latter stages of the season. The Nottingham team ended the campaign in eighth place, with eleven victories and eleven defeats in their twenty-six League games.

Notts had suffered only one home defeat during the season, while securing just two victories on their travels. Despite an indifferent League campaign this time, the Nottingham side would secure a major trophy within a couple of seasons.

BURNLEY

Burnley had tended to struggle during their first three seasons in the Football League and they had twice had to apply for re-election. However, their progress had been steady, in spite of their difficulty in attracting the more skilful players to the club.

Their reputation for signing more Scottish players than other members of the Football League continued prior to the 1891–92 League campaign. They had nearly fifty Scotsmen on their books. However, the majority of their players were unable to command first team places, which usually resulted in them appearing for Burnley's reserve side in the North East Lancashire

League. Many changes were made in the Burnley line-up for the 1891–92 season, which saw Lang retain the club captaincy, and James Crabtree and Claude Lambie remaining in the attack, while Jack Hillman retained the goalkeeping position.

Burnley opened the season with a 1–0 defeat at Accrington. It was followed by successive home wins against Preston North End and Stoke, but Preston and Stoke soon avenged the defeats by winning the return games, which preceded Burnley's first away point of the campaign in a three-all draw at Blackburn Rovers. Then followed a further home success against Aston Villa (4–1), while a 2–0 reverse at Bolton Wanderers, as well as a goalless draw at Wolverhampton Wanderers, continued their indifferent away form, though home victories against Accrington and West Bromwich Albion saw the Lancashire side maintain their mid-table position.

Burnley continued to struggle on their travels, with defeats at Sunderland (2–1) and Aston Villa (6–1). A 3–0 home win against Blackburn Rovers saw a return to form in a game in which Stewart (Burnley) and Joseph Lofthouse (Blackburn) were dismissed from the field of play following a sequence of heavy tackles. Blackburn's players were a little incensed, which led them to retire to the dressing room, leaving the referee with little alternative but to award the game to Burnley.

Late December saw the Burnley side secure a rare away success at Derby County (1–0), but the year ended with a Boxing Day defeat at West Bromwich Albion (1–0). However, an excellent start to the new year saw a one-all draw at Everton, followed by a 9–0 home victory against the struggling Darwen team.

Burnley were in a rich vein of form during this period, which saw wins in friendly games against Sunderland Albion (6–1), Brierfield (6–2) and Belfast Distillery (8–3), while they recorded their eighth successive home win in the League against Everton (1–0). However, their joy was short-lived as they suffered a 3–1 home defeat against Stoke in the second round of the FA Cup.

A loss of form followed their FA Cup disappointment with successive defeats at Notts County (5–1) and at home to Bolton Wanderers (2–1). However, a one-all home draw with Wolverhampton Wanderers, together with a 6–2 victory at Darwen, saw the Burnley side in with a chance for a top four League finish, with three games remaining.

Early April saw the Lancashire side secure a home win in the return game with Notts County, while the campaign ended with home defeats against Derby County (4–2) and Sunderland (2–1). Burnley were left in seventh position, with eleven wins, four draws and eleven defeats in their twenty-six League games, while scoring forty-nine goals and conceding forty-five in their finest League campaign to date.

WOLVERHAMPTON WANDERERS

Wolverhampton Wanderers had finished in a top four position in all three seasons since the formation of the Football League. This resulted in few changes in their line-up for the 1891–92 League campaign as W C Rose continued in goal, together with Richard Baugh, Charlie Mason and Harry Allen in defence, while Harry Wood and David Wykes remained in the attack. Future England international, George Kinsey, and Will Devey, who had scored thirty-five goals in forty Football Alliance appearances for the Small Heath club were the most notable new arrivals in the Wanderers side as they sought to emulate their previous League success.

Wolves opened the season with a 5–2 reverse at Sunderland, followed by successive victories at Stoke (3–1) and at home to Accrington (5–0), in which John Heath of the Wanderers had the distinction of scoring the first penalty goal in a Football League fixture.

Then followed a poor run of results, which included away defeats at West Bromwich Albion (4–3), Preston North End (2–0) and Blackburn Rovers (2–0), as well as a 3–1 home reverse against Derby County. A 2–2 home draw with Darwen was their only success during this period. Wanderers then secured a 2–1 home win against Notts County, which preceded further away defeats at Accrington and Derby County, while the Black Country side reached the halfway stage of the season with successive draws against Burnley and Notts County, leaving them perilously close to the foot of the League table.

However, the Wanderers rallied during the second half of the season to end the campaign in a respectable mid-table position. Their improvement began with successive home wins against Everton (5–1) and Blackburn Rovers (6–1). Though followed by defeats at Bolton Wanderers (3–0) and Everton (2–1), a 2–0 home victory against Aston Villa saw a return to winning ways. Their indifferent home form continued with a 3–1 defeat against Sunderland, prior to ending the year with a 2–1 home success against West Bromwich Albion.

Wolves began the new year with a 4–1 home win against Stoke, followed by a further 4–1 success against Crewe in a first round FA Cup tie replay to secure a second round home tie against Sheffield United. This ended in a 3–1 victory for the Midlands side. However, Wolves met their match in the quarter-finals, as they suffered a 3–1 home defeat against Aston Villa.

On their return to League action, Wolves secured a 4–1 victory at Darwen, followed by a one-all draw at Burnley, while their fine form continued with a 3–0 home success against Preston North End. Their unbeaten League run came to an end with a 2–1 reverse against Bolton Wanderers in their final home game of the season. They ended the campaign with a 6–3 win at Aston Villa, leaving the Wolverhampton side in sixth position following eleven wins and eleven defeats, while scoring fifty-nine goals and conceding forty-six. Baker, Mason, Wykes, Baugh, Allen, Kinsey, Rose and Wood had played in the majority of the Wanderers' League games. Wood, Booth and Baker had netted six League goals apiece, David Wykes had found the net on nine occasions, while Will Devey had led the scoring with eighteen League goals in a further excellent season for the Wanderers.

EVERTON

Reigning League Champions Everton retained the majority of their players for the 1891–92 season, which included England international forwards Fred Geary, Edgar Chadwick and Alf Milward, together with skilful outside right Alex Latta. England centre half John Holt remained at the heart of the defence, which was strengthened by the arrival of Bob Howarth from Preston North End. Robertson, McLean and Maxwell secured regular first team places during the season, which also saw the return of Scottish international half back Bob Kelso from Preston, while Williams and Jardine shared the goalkeeping duties.

Everton opened the 1891–92 League campaign with a 4–0 defeat at West Bromwich Albion, followed by successive home wins against Darwen (5–3) and Blackburn Rovers (3–1), with Fred Geary and Alex Latta on target in both victories, while Gordon, making a rare appearance up front, scored the equalising goal in a one-all draw at Accrington.

Then followed an indifferent run of results during October, which included away defeats at Sunderland (2–1), Bolton Wanderers (1–0) and Preston North End (4–0), as well as a one-all draw in the home game with Preston. A 3–0 victory at Derby County saw their one success of the month, with Latta (2) and Chadwick on target for the Merseysiders.

Early November saw Alex Latta score a hat-trick in a 4–3 home success against West Bromwich Albion, which preceded away defeats at Darwen (3–1) and Wolverhampton Wanderers (5–1). Their unbeaten home record continued with a 5–1 victory against Aston Villa, with Chadwick (2), Latta, Maxwell and Wylie finding the net to secure a mid-table position at the halfway stage of the season.

Alex Latta was again on target in a two-all draw at Blackburn Rovers, which was followed by a 2–1 home win against Wolverhampton Wanderers, with Latta scoring for the sixth successive League game. A 4–0 defeat against Sunderland on Christmas Day saw their first home reverse of the season, however, a 4–3 victory at Aston Villa in the final game of the year saw a return to winning ways, with Maxwell and Chadwick netting a couple of goals apiece.

New Year began with a one-all draw at Burnley, with Alf Milward scoring for the visitors, which preceded a 3–1 success at Notts County, where Latta, Maxwell and Milward found the net. However, their fine start to the year ended with a 4–2 home defeat against Burnley in the first round of the FA Cup.

On their return to League action, the Everton side suffered a further defeat at Burnley (1–0), while successive home wins against Stoke (1–0) and Accrington (3–0), as well as a 1–0 victory in the return game at Stoke, saw the Merseysiders move into the top half of the League table, with Edgar Chadwick on target in all three victories. However, a 2–1 home defeat against Derby County ended their excellent run of results.

Everton then secured a 4–0 home win against Notts County, with Alex Latta scoring his second hat-trick of the season. The campaign ended with a 5–2 home defeat against Bolton Wanderers, leaving the Merseysiders in fifth position following twelve victories, four draws and ten defeats in their twenty-six League games, while scoring forty-nine goals and conceding forty-nine.

Alf Milward had appeared in all twenty-six League games for Everton, with Edgar Chadwick and Alex Latta missing only one in a season which saw the Lancashire side use twenty-six players in League games.

Fred Geary had scored six goals in ten League appearances, Edgar Chadwick had found the net on ten occasions, while Alex Latta had led the scoring with seventeen League goals, in a rather indifferent League campaign for the Merseysiders.

ASTON VILLA

Aston Villa had achieved little success during the two previous seasons, which had seen them finish in the re-election positions in both campaigns. They had also suffered FA Cup defeats at the second round stage of the competition. In spite of their indifferent run of results, the Midlands side retained the majority of their players for the 1891–92 season. Gersham Cox, William Evans, Harry Devey and James Cowan continued in the defence, together with Louis Campbell, Billy Dickson and Dennis Hodgetts up front, while Hinchley and James Warner shared the goalkeeping position.

Charlie Athersmith, who had made a couple of appearances during the previous campaign, became a regular member of the Villa team well into the following century, winning many FA Cup and League Championship Winners' medals, as well as gaining numerous international caps for England. The most notable newcomer to the Villa club was inside forward John Devey, who had played his early football with Birmingham Excelsior, Mitchell's St George's and Aston Manor prior to joining Villa. Devey, born a couple of miles away from the Villa ground, like Athersmith remained with the club until the turn of the century, winning five League Championship medals, two FA Cup winners' medals, as well as a couple of England appearances.

In a little over 300 appearances for Villa, Devey scored nearly 200 goals, while further success lay ahead on the cricket field, which saw the accomplished all-rounder score in excess of 7,000 runs for Warwickshire.

Villa enjoyed an excellent start to the season with successive home wins against Blackburn Rovers (5–1) and West Bromwich Albion (5–1), with Hislop, Devey, Dickson and Athersmith on target in both games. John Devey scored his fifth League goal of the campaign in a 1–0 success at Preston, which preceded a further home victory against Sunderland (5–3), with Devey (2), Hodgetts, Athersmith and Dickson scoring, thus continuing Villa's winning run. However, away defeats at Derby County (4–2) and Burnley (4–1), as well as at home to Bolton Wanderers (2–1), saw the Midlands side in a mid-table position by the middle of October.

Then followed a run of five successive victories, which began with away wins at Stoke (3–2) and Darwen (5–1), with Louis Campbell and John Devey scoring in both games. Their excellent form continued with a 5–1 home success against Notts County, with Hodgetts (2), Devey, Hare and Athersmith netting the Villa goals.

John Devey then scored his eleventh League goal of the season in a 3–0 victory at West Bromwich Albion, where Campbell and Hare completed the scoring, while Campbell again found the net in a 2–1 home victory against Stoke. However, a 5–1 reverse at Everton during the final week of November ended Villa's winning run.

Early December saw John Devey score a hat-trick in a 6–1 home win against Burnley, which preceded a 2–0 defeat at Wolverhampton Wanderers. Villa soon returned to form with a 7–0 home win against Darwen on Boxing Day, with Hodgetts (2), Campbell (2), Athersmith (2) and Devey on target, while the year ended with a 4–3 home defeat against Everton, with John Devey scoring a brace of goals for the home side.

Villa then suffered successive away defeats at Notts County (5–2) and Accrington (3–2) during the opening week of the new year, which preceded a 6–0 home win against Derby County, with Devey (2), Dickson, Hodgetts, Campbell and Athersmith on target. Hodgetts netted a hat-trick in a 4–1 home success against Heanor Town in the first round of the FA Cup to secure a home tie against Darwen in the second round, which the Midlanders won by two goals to nil with goals by Devey and Hodgetts earning an away tie at Wolverhampton Wanderers in the quarter-finals.

A crowd in excess of 20,000 arrived at the Molineux to witness a 3–1 victory by Villa, with Campbell, Devey and Athersmith on target for the visitors to secure a semi-final tie against League leaders Sunderland, who were favourites to win both the League Championship and the FA Cup. However, the Midlands side outplayed the men from the north-east to secure a 4–1 victory, with goals by Devey (2) and Hodgetts (2) earning Villa a second FA Cup Final appearance. This would take place at the Oval on 19 March against their old rivals, West Bromwich Albion.

Prior to the FA Cup Final, Louis Campbell scored a hat-trick in a 4–3 reverse at Blackburn Rovers, which was followed by a 12–2 home win against Accrington, with Devey (4), Campbell (4), Dickson (2), Hodgetts and Athersmith on target, leaving Villa in excellent spirits for their forthcoming FA Cup Final appearance.

BOLTON WANDERERS

Bolton Wanderers had finished in fifth position in two of the three previous League campaigns, which resulted in few changes in their team throughout the final decade of the Victorian era.

Goalkeeper John Sutcliffe made in excess of 300 League appearances for the club, as well as winning a place in the England national team, while fullbacks John Somerville and David Jones both appeared in more than 200 League games for the Lancashire side. Alex Paton retired at the turn of the century following 215 League appearances. Harry Gardiner left the Wanderers in 1894, while left half Roberts, who had played for the club since the early 1880s, retired at the end of the 1891–92 season. James Munro, James Turner, James Brogan, James Cassidy and John McNee retained their places in the attack for the 1891–92 League campaign, while outside left McFettridge replaced the injured Kenny Davenport.

Wanderers opened the League campaign with a 2–1 victory at Darwen, with McNee and Cassidy on target, which preceded a 1–0 home success in the return game with Darwen, with James Brogan scoring the only goal of the game. McNee, Cassidy and McFettridge found the net in successive home wins against Sunderland (4–3) and Preston North End (3–0). However, defeats at Notts County (2–0) and at home to Accrington (4–3) ended Bolton's fine start to the season.

Bolton soon returned to form with six wins and one draw, which saw them at the top of the League table at the halfway stage of the campaign with a realistic chance of securing their first League Championship. Wanderers' excellent run of results began with a 2–1 victory at Aston Villa, where James Munro netted both goals, which preceded three successive home wins against Everton (1–0), Burnley (2–0) and Blackburn Rovers (4–2), with James Cassidy on target in all three victories, while James Munro found the net in away wins at West Bromwich Albion (2–0) and Accrington (3–0).

David Jones then scored his only League goal of the season in a one-all home draw with Stoke, which was followed by away defeats at Blackburn Rovers (4–0) and Preston North End (4–0), while Cassidy (2) and Munro were on target in a 3–0 home success against Wolverhampton Wanderers.

Mid-December saw McFettridge score the only goal of the game in a 1–0 success at Stoke, followed by a one-all home draw with West Bromwich Albion, with James Munro scoring his ninth League goal of the campaign. The year ended with a 3–2 reverse at Derby County. However, Bolton soon avenged the defeat at Derby with a 3–1 home win against the East Midlanders on New Year's Day, with Munro, Cassidy and McFettridge scoring the all-important goals.

Bolton were then drawn away at the Wednesday in the first round of the FA Cup, which resulted in a 2–1 defeat, but, following a complaint from the Wanderers that the game should have been abandoned, a replay was ordered, with the Sheffield side winning even more convincingly by four goals to one to end Bolton's interest in the competition for a further season.

On their return to League action, Bolton suffered a 4–1 defeat at Sunderland, which preceded successive victories at Burnley (2–1) and at home to Notts County (2–0) with James Cassidy on target in both games, while outside left Bentley, making a rare appearance in the first team, scored a consolation goal in a 2–1 reverse at Aston Villa. Bentley again found the net in a 2–1 success at Wolverhampton Wanderers, with James Cassidy completing the scoring. The season ended with a 5–2 victory at Everton, with Cassidy (3), Gardiner and Bentley on target to secure a third place finish for Bolton following seventeen victories, two draws and seven defeats in their twenty-six League games, while scoring fifty-one goals and conceding thirty-seven.

Sutcliffe, Somerville, Paton, McNee, Jones, Cassidy and Gardiner were ever present in Bolton's finest season to date, with James Munro scoring a dozen League goals in twenty-five appearances, while James Cassidy led the scoring with eighteen League goals.

PRESTON NORTH END

Preston North End were a little disappointed to have finished as runners-up to Everton during the 1890–91 season. However, few changes were made by the Lancashire side for the 1891–92 League campaign as Jimmy Trainer continued in goal, together with Stewart, Gallacher, Holmes and Nick Ross in defence, while Jack Gordon, Geordie Drummond and Jimmy Ross remained in the attack. Bob Kelso had signed for Everton, soon to be joined by his Preston team-mate Bob Howarth, while the most notable newcomers were Sanders and Sharp in defence, together with forwards Becton and Towie. Towie remained for a little more than a season. Sanders and Sharp served the club for a number of seasons, while Francis Becton scored in excess of forty goals in eighty-seven League appearances, as well as securing a place in the English national side.

Preston made an indifferent start to the season with successive away defeats at Notts County (2–0) and Burnley (2–0), followed by a 3–1 home success against Sunderland. A 1–0 home defeat against Aston Villa continued their poor start to the campaign, though a 5–1 home win in the return game with Burnley saw two welcome points. Following a 3–0 reverse at Bolton Wanderers, the Preston side began a run of fifteen games without defeat, which saw them challenging for the League Championship at the turn of the year.

Preston's unbeaten run began with a 2–0 home success against Wolverhampton Wanderers, followed by a one-all draw at Everton, while a 4–2 victory at Blackburn Rovers, as well as a 4–0 home win in the return game with Everton, continued their excellent form.

Further victories at Stoke and West Bromwich Albion, together with a 3–2 home win against Blackburn Rovers, saw Preston in a top three position at the halfway stage of the campaign, while home wins against Bolton Wanderers (4–0) ands Notts County (6–0), as well as a 2–1 success at Derby County, saw the Lancashire side retain their hopes of a third League title.

As the year came to an end, Preston secured a 3–2 home victory against

Stoke, followed by a 4–0 success against Darwen on New Year's Day. Further wins at Accrington (3–1) and at home to West Bromwich Albion (1–0) maintained the high standards expected by William Sudell. Late January saw Preston secure a 2–1 victory at Middlesbrough in the second round of the FA Cup to earn an away tie at Nottingham Forest in the quarter-finals. Forest were members of the Football Alliance. While Preston were favourites to progress to the semi-finals, they were well beaten at Nottingham by two goals to nil.

On their return to League action, the Lancashire side secured a 3–0 home win against Derby County, followed by successive away defeats at Sunderland and Wolverhampton Wanderers. The campaign ended with four-goal victories against Accrington and Darwen on either side of a 3–1 reverse at Aston Villa. This left the Preston team in the runners-up position, five points adrift from the eventual League champions. Sanders, Gallacher, Jimmy Ross and Jimmy Trainer had appeared in all twenty-six League games for Preston, of which eighteen had ended in victory, while Stewart, Gordon and Robert Holmes had missed only one. Francis Becton ended the campaign with seven goals in ten League appearances, Geordie Drummond had found the net on fourteen occasions, while Jimmy Ross had led the scoring for the third successive season with sixteen League goals in a further excellent season for the 'Invincibles'.

SUNDERLAND

Sunderland had enjoyed an excellent first season in the Football League, which had resulted in a respectable mid-table finish with a team consisting mainly of Scottish-born players. Few changes were made in their line-up for the 1891–92 League campaign, as John Doig continued in goal, together with Oliver, Porteous, Gibson, Murray, Hugh Wilson and John Auld in defence, while Scott, Millar, Campbell and David Hannah remained in the attack.

Scottish internationals Donald Gow and James Hannah were the most notable newcomers to the Sunderland club, with Hannah, who had recently arrived from Sunderland Albion, making 156 League appearances in six seasons with the north-eastern side, while fullback Gow, who signed from Glasgow Rangers during the opening week of the season, made in excess of 100 League appearances in two spells with the club.

Sunderland opened the season with a 5–2 home win against Wolverhampton Wanderers, with Millar (3) and Campbell (2) on target, which preceded successive away defeats at Preston North End (3–1), Bolton Wanderers (4–3) and Aston Villa (5–3), leaving the north-eastern side near the foot of the League table by the end of September. However, early October saw Sunderland return to winning ways with Scott and Campbell finding the net in a 2–1 home success against Everton, while Scott (2), Campbell (2) and Millar were on target in a 5–2 away win at West Bromwich Albion.

Johnny Campbell then scored a hat-trick in a 4–0 victory in the return game with Albion, while James Hannah (2), Campbell and Scott netted in a further home win against Accrington (4–1). However, a 3–1 reverse at Blackburn Rovers ended their excellent run of results. Then followed a 7–1 home win against Derby County, with Jimmy Millar scoring four of the Sunderland goals, which preceded further victories at Stoke (3–1) and at home to Burnley (2–1). The halfway stage of the season arrived with a 4–0 home success against Notts County, with goals by James Hannah (2), Wilson and Campbell moving the north-eastern side into a top three League position.

Sunderland's winning run continued with a 7–0 home success against Darwen, with Millar (2), Campbell (2), David Hannah (2) and Wilson on target, and the year ended with successive away wins at Everton (4–0) and Wolverhampton Wanderers (3–1), with James Hannah scoring in both victories. These were followed by a 4–0 home win against Notts County in the first round of the FA Cup, with goals by Campbell (2), Smith and James Hannah securing an away tie at Accrington in the second round.

Accrington had few answers to the Sunderland attack as Johnny Campbell netted a hat-trick in a 3–1 victory to secure a quarter-final tie against Stoke. This ended in a two-all draw, with Campbell and Millar scoring. However, Sunderland had little difficulty in the replay, as James Hannah (2), Scott and David Hannah found the net in a 4–0 success, to secure a semi-final tie against Aston Villa at Bramall Lane.

Villa had enjoyed a reasonably successful season, but Sunderland were favourites to proceed to the FA Cup Final. Surprisingly, the League leaders were totally outplayed by the Midlands side, who registered a 4–1 victory to end Sunderland's dreams of the League and FA Cup double.

On their return to League action, the north-eastern side inflicted a 4–1 defeat on Bolton Wanderers, with James Hannah (2), Millar and Scott on target, which preceded a 5–3 success at Accrington, where Scott netted a brace of goals. Their excellent form continued with a 4–1 home win against Preston North End, with John Auld scoring a couple of goals.

Auld was again on target the following week in a 1–0 victory at Derby County, while James Hannah scored in successive home wins against Aston Villa (2–1) and Stoke (4–1), Sunderland thereby registering their thirteenth victory in a row. However, a 1–0 reverse at Notts County ended their long winning run.

Sunderland soon returned to form with a 6–1 home win against Blackburn Rovers, with Johnny Campbell finding the net on four occasions, while the campaign ended with successive away wins at Darwen (7–1) and Burnley (2–1), with Campbell scoring in both games. Hence the north-eastern side won the League Championship with twenty-one victories in twenty-six League games, while scoring ninety-three goals and conceding thirty-six. James Hannah and Jimmy Millar had ended the League campaign with seventeen goals apiece, while Johnny Campbell had once again led the scoring, with twenty-eight goals in twenty-four League appearances in a season when

Sunderland had proved worthy champions. This had posed an important question for the gentlemen on the Football League Committee. How many other English teams outside of the Football League were as capable as the north-eastern side? It would be a question on which the League Committee would ponder, prior to extending the Football League to two divisions.

The final League placings at the close of the 1891–92 season are listed in Table VI.

Table VI: *Football League results for the 1891–92 season*

	P	W	D	L	F	A	PTS
1. Sunderland	26	21	0	5	93	36	42
2. Preston North End	26	18	1	7	61	31	37
3. Bolton Wanderers	26	17	2	7	51	37	36
4. Aston Villa	26	15	0	11	89	56	30
5. Everton	26	12	4	10	49	49	28
6. Wolverhampton Wndrs	26	11	4	11	59	46	26
7. Burnley	26	11	4	11	49	45	26
8. Notts County	26	11	4	11	55	51	26
9. Blackburn Rovers	26	10	6	10	58	65	26
10. Derby County	26	10	4	12	46	52	24
11. Accrington	26	8	4	14	40	78	20
12. West Bromwich Albion	26	6	6	14	51	58	18
13. Stoke	26	5	4	17	38	61	14
14. Darwen	26	4	3	19	38	112	11

An All Midlands FA Cup Final

Of the sixteen teams remaining at the second round stage of the 1891–92 FA Cup competition, ten were members of the Football League, of which eight were drawn against each other for a place in the quarter-finals.

West Bromwich Albion and Blackburn Rovers, without doubt the finest FA Cup-fighting sides in England, fought an exciting tie, which Albion won by three goals to one, with Tom Pearson (2) and Jasper Geddes on target for the West Bromwich team, while Stoke won at Burnley by a similar score.

A Johnny Campbell hat-trick saw Sunderland secure a 3–1 victory at Accrington, John Devey and Dennis Hodgetts were on target for Aston Villa in a 2–0 home success against the struggling Darwen team, while Wolverhampton Wanderers inflicted a 3–1 defeat on Sheffield United. Preston North End won by the odd goal in three at Middlesbrough, Sandy Higgins scored the only goal of the game for Nottingham Forest in a 1–0 victory at Sunderland Albion, while the Wednesday completed the quarter-final line-up in a 2–0 home success against Small Heath, with Richardson and Thompson scoring for the Sheffield side.

Wednesday were then drawn away at West Bromwich Albion in the quarter-finals, where they narrowly lost by the odd goal in three with Nicholls and Geddes on target for the home side. Aston Villa proceeded to the semi-finals following a 3–1 away victory at Wolverhampton Wanderers, with Athersmith, Devey and Campbell netting the Villa goals. Nottingham Forest shocked the football world by inflicting a 2–0 defeat on Preston North End, with goals by Smith and Higgins earning Forest a place in the last four. Sunderland were a little fortunate to secure a two-all home draw with Stoke, prior to winning the replay by four goals to nil, with James Hannah (2), Scott and David Hannah on target to secure a second successive semi-final appearance for the north-eastern side.

Sunderland were drawn to play against Aston Villa at Bramall Lane in the semi-finals, where they suffered a 4–1 defeat, with John Devey (2) and Dennis Hodgetts (2) netting for the Midlands side, while the tie between Nottingham Forest and West Bromwich Albion took place at the Molineux Ground, Wolverhampton, which resulted in a one-all draw.

Following a further draw at Wolverhampton (1–1), Albion and Forest moved on to Derby for a second replay, where the West Bromwich side won by six goals to two, with goals by Geddes (3), Bassett (2) and Charlie Perry securing a final appearance against Aston Villa at the Oval on 19 March.

England's Unconvincing Victory in Belfast

England opened the 1892 international season by fielding two teams on the same day, with a professional side travelling to Belfast for a game against the Irish national team, while a side consisting mainly of players with Corinthian connections visited Wrexham for the fixture against Wales.

Stoke provided goalkeeper William Rowley for the Irish game, as well as his club team-mates Alf Underwood and Thomas Clare at fullback, while John Cox (Derby County) and Michael Whitham (Sheffield United) made their only England appearances at half-back. John Holt (Everton) gained his fourth international cap at centre half.

Charlie Athersmith (Aston Villa) played the first of a dozen England games at outside right, his Villa team-mate John Devey gained the first of two caps at centre forward, while John Pearson (Crewe) played his one England game at inside right, prior to enjoying a successful career as a Football League referee, which included an appearance in an FA Cup Final during the early years of the following century.

Harry Daft (Notts County) played his fifth and final England game at inside left, while Dennis Hodgetts (Aston Villa) completed the England side for his first international appearance since 1888. Despite the strong English line-up, they could only manage a 2–0 victory, with Harry Daft twice on target for the visitors.

A Little Too Skilful for the Welsh

England included eight new caps for the game against Wales, with a team consisting mainly of players with Corinthian connections. George Toone (Notts County) made the first of two appearances in goal, Harry Lilley (Sheffield United) gained his only England cap at left fullback, while Arthur Dunn received a recall for his third England game since his debut in 1883.

Anthony Hossack, William Winckworth and George Kinsey formed the half-back line, with Hossack, a solicitor by profession, making the first of two international appearances, as did fellow Corinthian Winckworth, who usually played for the Old Westminsters at club level. Kinsey, who had spent most of the season with Wolverhampton Wanderers, gained the first of four England caps.

Robert Gosling (Old Etonians), a county cricketer with Essex, and Rupert Sandilands (Old Westminsters) played the first of their five England games on the wings; Joseph Schofield (Stoke), a Staffordshire schoolmaster, gained the first of three caps at inside left; while Corinthians George Cotterill and Arthur Henfrey were recalled for their second England caps. England were a little too skilful for the Welsh, as Henfrey and Sandilands found the net in a 2–0 success.

Albion's FA Cup Experience Tells

A crowd in excess of 25,000 arrived from the Midlands to watch the 1892 FA Cup Final between Aston Villa and West Bromwich Albion, in what would be the last final at the Kennington Oval, with Albion selecting the following players:

Reader

Nicholson McCulloch

Reynolds Charles Perry (captain) Groves

Bassett McLeod Nicholls Pearson Geddes

Villa selected the following eleven:

Warner

Evans Cox

Harry Devey James Cowan Baird

Athersmith John Devey Dickson (captain) Campbell Hodgetts

Villa dominated the early proceedings, with Athersmith and John Devey exerting pressure on the Albion fullbacks. However, the West Bromwich side soon responded as Billy Bassett passed to Roddy McLeod, who crossed the ball to the waiting Geddes. He shot towards the Villa goal and Warner failed to collect the ball clearly. It rolled between the Villa goalposts to secure a surprising one-goal lead for the Albion team.

Following a period of further pressure by the Villa forwards, the ever alert Bassett won the ball on the halfway line, crossed to Jasper Geddes, who shot weakly at Warner. However, the Villa custodian once again half saved the shot, which rebounded to Nicholls, who had the simple task of deflecting the ball over the Villa goal line. Albion ended the half two goals to the good.

Albion continued to defend during the second period of play as Villa sought to reduce the arrears, which inevitably led to a further goal by the Black Country side when a twenty-five yard speculative shot by John Reynolds sailed between the Villa posts to secure an unassailable three-goal lead for Albion.

As the final whistle sounded, the score remained unchanged, with Albion the victors by three goals to nil, in spite of Villa's domination of the final. While Athersmith, Devey and Dickson had performed magnificently in the Villa attack, they had been ably dealt with by Perry, Reynolds and Nicholson in the Albion defence, and their greater FA Cup experience told.

Albion Struggle in the League

During the week following their FA Cup Final victory, Albion secured a 4–1 victory against Small Heath in the quarter-final of the Birmingham FA Cup, while their excellent form continued with a 12–0 home win in a League encounter against the struggling Darwen team, with Pearson (4), Bassett (3), Reynolds (2), Nicholls, Geddes and an own goal on target for Albion. This preceded a further success against Aston Villa in the semi-finals of the Birmingham Cup, as McLeod and Geddes found the net in a 2–0 win, with Villa missing a penalty.

On their return to League action, Albion played successive draws against Stoke (2–2) and Darwen (1–1), while the season ended with a 1–0 reverse in the return game at Stoke, which left the West Bromwich side in twelfth position, with just six victories in their twenty-six League games, while scoring fifty-one goals and conceding fifty-eight.

Billy Bassett had ended the campaign with seven League goals, Nicholls had found the net on eight occasions, while Tom Pearson had once again led the scoring with a dozen League goals. Albion were required to apply for re-election to the League.

Albion's indifferent season finally came to an end during the final week of April with successive defeats against Wolverhampton Wanderers in both the semi-final of the Birmingham Charity Cup (3–0) and the final of the Birmingham FA Cup (5–2). However, it had been a season to remember for the newly acclaimed FA Cup winners.

Aston Villa's Fourth Place League Finish

Aston Villa returned to League action a week after their FA Cup disappointment with a 2–1 reverse at Sunderland, while John Devey netted a brace of goals in a 2–1 victory at Bolton Wanderers. However, a 2–0 defeat against West Bromwich Albion in the semi-final of the Birmingham FA Cup saw their hopes of retaining the trophy disappear.

Harry Devey then scored his only League goal of the season in a 3–1 home success against Preston North End, with Billy Dickson scoring twice. The campaign ended with a 6–3 home defeat against Wolverhampton Wanderers, with Hodgetts, Dickson and John Devey on target for Villa. They ended the season in fourth position, following fifteen victories and eleven defeats in their twenty-six League games, while scoring eighty-nine goals and conceding fifty-six.

Charlie Athersmith, James Cowan, John Devey and Dennis Hodgetts missed no more than a couple of League games during the season. Hodgetts ended the campaign with nine League goals; Athersmith scored ten goals; Billy Dickson netted fourteen goals in the League; Louis Campbell found the net on sixteen occasions in nineteen League games; while John Devey led the scoring with twenty-nine goals in twenty-five League appearances.

Villa's fourth place League finish, together with their FA Cup Final appearance, had been their finest season to date. However, even greater success lay ahead during the final decade of the century.

A Four-Goal Victory in Glasgow

The English national team travelled north of the border for the final international game of the season against a Scottish side seeking their first success for three seasons against England. George Toone retained his place in goal following the victory against Wales, together with fullback Arthur Dunn, while Robert Holmes (Preston North End), John Holt (Everton) and Alfred Shelton (Notts County) were recalled to add experience to the defence.

Billy Bassett (West Bromwich Albion), John Goodall (Derby County), Edgar Chadwick (Everton), Dennis Hodgetts (Aston Villa) and John Southworth (Blackburn Rovers) formed a free-scoring attack, while John Reynolds, the West Bromwich Albion half back, who had previously played five international games for Ireland, completed the England line-up. It had been assumed that Reynolds had been born in Ireland. However, his birth certificate had proved that Reynolds was in fact English-born, which resulted in him making eight appearances in an England shirt.

England continued their excellent run of results against the Scots to secure a 4–1 victory, with John Goodall (2), Edgar Chadwick and John Southworth on target for the visitors.

All Square at Pikes Lane

A couple of weeks after England's victory in Glasgow, the Scottish Football League sent a team of players south to fulfil a fixture against a Football League Eleven at Pikes Lane, Bolton. The English League selected Joe Reader, John Reynolds, William Groves and Billy Bassett from West Bromwich Albion's FA Cup-winning team, while the League side was further strengthened by the inclusion of John Goodall (Derby County), Harry Daft (Notts County) and Edgar Chadwick (Everton) in the attack.

A splendid game produced a two-all draw, with Bassett and McInnes (Notts County) scoring for the home side, while McMahon and Taylor replied for the Scots in a fixture that would continue for more than seventy years.

The League Is Extended to Two Divisions

Late April saw a meeting of the Football League Committee to discuss a previous suggestion that a Second Division be formed to include the growing number of applicants regularly denied League status.

A decision was eventually made to increase the League from fourteen to sixteen teams, as well as to form a Second Division consisting mainly of teams in the Football Alliance, who had often proved that they were the equal of teams in the Football League.

Following a further meeting at the Queens Hotel, Sunderland, the League Committee decided to exclude West Bromwich Albion from applying for re-election in view of their FA Cup success, which left Accrington, Stoke and Darwen from the Football League, competing against Newton Heath, Nottingham Forest and Wednesday from the Alliance for five League places.

Newcastle East End, Liverpool and Middlesbrough failed in their applications to join the League, as Wednesday received ten votes, Nottingham Forest (nine), and Newton Heath (six), to attain places in the First Division, while Accrington with seven votes and Stoke with six secured sufficient votes to retain their First Division status. However, Darwen, who had received four votes, were elected to the newly formed Second Division, together with Ardwick, Bootle, Crewe, Burton Swifts, Grimsby, Lincoln, Small Heath, Walsall Town Swifts, Sheffield United, Burslem Port Vale and Northwich Victoria.

William McGregor Steps Down

William McGregor, who had recently suffered a bout of ill-health, decided to step down from his position as chairman of the Football League. However, he continued to serve the League as president for many years to come.

John Bentley of Bolton Wanderers was the natural successor to Mr McGregor, while Harry Lockett continued as secretary with an increased salary, due to his extended workload. However, William Sudell announced his resignation as treasurer of the League, owing to the current financial irregularities at Preston North End.

On 1 July 1892, a meeting of Football League members took place at the Royal Hotel, Manchester, which saw representatives of twenty-eight clubs present, double the number of the previous season's meeting.

Chapter XVIII

SUNDERLAND RETAIN THE LEAGUE CHAMPIONSHIP – 1892–93

SUNDERLAND RETAIN THE LEAGUE CHAMPIONSHIP
WOLVERHAMPTON WANDERERS WIN THE FA CUP
STEVE BLOOMER MAKES HIS LEAGUE DEBUT FOR DERBY COUNTY
A DEBUT HAT-TRICK FOR WALTER GILLIATT AGAINST IRELAND
FRED SPIKSLEY NETS A BRACE OF GOALS AGAINST WALES AND SCOTLAND AS
ENGLAND REMAIN UNBEATEN
G O SMITH'S FIRST ENGLAND APPEARANCE
THE END-OF-SEASON TEST MATCH GAMES PROVE A SUCCESS

Of the three newcomers to the First Division, Newton Heath had tended to play their football in and around the Lancashire area, while Nottingham Forest and the Wednesday had long been the equal of teams in the Football League.

WEDNESDAY

Wednesday had been formed in 1867 as the football section of the Wednesday Cricket Club, who tended to play the majority of their games during the week.

Prior to joining the Football League, the Sheffield side had won the Sheffield Challenge Cup on six occasions and had reached the final of the 1890 FA Cup competition. England internationals Billy Betts, Edward Brayshaw, Charles Clegg, William Clegg and William Mosforth had all worn the Wednesday shirt at some stage of their careers. However, with the exception of Billy Betts, all of Wednesday's international players had retired from the Association game.

Wednesday's opening League game took place at the Castle Ground, Nottingham, where a Tom Brandon goal secured a 1–0 victory against Notts County, with the Sheffield side fielding William Allan in goal, together with Tom Brandon, Albert Mumford, Hall, Billy Betts and Harry Brandon in defence, while Spiksley, Brady, Davis, Brown and Dunlop formed the attack.

Scottish-born goalkeeper William Allan made in excess of 100 League appearances in six seasons with the club. Tom Brandon, who had previously served Blackburn Rovers, returned to Blackburn at the season's end, while Albert Mumford, one of the two remaining members of the 1890 FA Cup Final side, was nearing the end of his playing career.

Billy Betts, now in his seventh season with the club, played regular first team football until 1895, replacing Tom Brandon as club captain, while Harry

Brandon, Tom's cousin, made nearly 200 appearances for the Wednesday. However, right half back Hall made only the occasional appearance for the Sheffield side. Outside left Dunlop soon moved to Darwen following a single League appearance for the club, which saw the arrival of Rowan, who missed only two League games during the season, while Brown, a recent signing from Cambuslang, remained with Wednesday for four seasons, prior to signing for Bolton Wanderers.

Alec Brady, who had arrived from Glasgow Rangers, following a spell with Everton, made in excess of 150 League appearances in seven seasons with Wednesday. Harry Davis a recent signing from Birmingham St George's, played nearly 200 games for the Sheffield team, while Fred Spiksley, who had signed from Gainsborough in 1891, was a regular member of the side well into the following century.

Spiksley scored exactly one hundred goals in 293 League appearances, as well as gaining seven England caps, while he enjoyed an excellent reputation as a football coach upon his retirement, which saw him travel to Sweden, Germany, Mexico and Spain.

Following their victory at Nottingham in their opening League fixture, Wednesday secured a 5–2 home win against Accrington, with Brown (2), Spiksley, Rowan and Davis on target, while successive away defeats at Preston North End (4–1), Bolton Wanderers (1–0) and Accrington (4–2) ended their excellent start to the season. A 2–0 home success against Burnley saw a return to winning ways, with Brown and Spiksley scoring the Wednesday goals.

Harry Davis then scored a brace of goals in a 2–2 home draw with Nottingham Forest, which preceded a 2–0 victory at Blackburn Rovers, with Rowan scoring twice, while Fred Spiksley netted the only goal of the game in a 1–0 home win against Newton Heath.

Further home wins against Sunderland (3–2) and Bolton Wanderers (4–2), saw Alec Brady and Fred Spiksley score a couple of goals apiece, while mid-November saw their winning home run end with a 3–0 defeat against Blackburn Rovers. This was followed by a 5–3 victory at Everton, with Brady, Davis and Brown once again amongst the scorers.

Wednesday's indifferent away form continued with a 2–0 defeat at Nottingham Forest, followed by a 5–3 home win against Aston Villa, with Spiksley and Rowan on target. Both players again found the net in a three-all home draw with Derby County, but a 2–0 reverse at Stoke saw the Sheffield side continue to struggle on their travels.

Fred Spiksley and Rowan then scored two goals apiece in a 5–1 success at Newton Heath in the final game of the year, while the new year began with a 6–0 home success against West Bromwich Albion with Spiksley (2), Rowan, Brady, Brown and Harry Brandon on target. However, just one victory in their eleven remaining League games saw the Sheffield side struggling to avoid the re-election positions at the season's end. Their loss of form began with successive defeats at Aston Villa (5–1) and at home to Preston North End (5–0), which were followed by a 3–2 home win against Derby County in the first round of the FA Cup, with Fred Spiksley netting all three Wednesday goals. However, following a protest by Derby, a replay was ordered, which Derby won by one goal to nil. Wednesday then registered a further protest, which resulted in a second replay, with the Sheffield side winning by four goals to two, with Betts, Spiksley, Woolhouse and Chalmers on target to secure a home tie against Burnley in the second round.

Prior to the FA Cup tie, Wednesday suffered a 4–2 defeat in a League encounter at Sunderland, while their FA Cup success continued against Burnley as Fred Spiksley scored the only goal of the game in a 1–0 victory to earn a quarter-final tie at Everton. Then, League defeats at Wolverhampton Wanderers (2–0) and at home to Everton (2–0), as well as a 3–0 reverse in the quarter-final tie at Everton, continued their indifferent run of results.

Following their disappointing FA Cup result, Wednesday suffered successive defeats at home to Wolverhampton Wanderers (1–0) and away at West Bromwich Albion (3–0), while a two-all draw at Derby County secured a rare away point. Further defeats at Burnley (4–0) and at home to Stoke (1–0) saw the Sheffield side in the re-election positions, with one League game remaining.

Wednesday managed a 3–2 home victory against Notts County in their final League game of the campaign, with Tom Brandon, Harry Brandon and Brown scoring the all-important goals, as the Yorkshire team finished the season in twelfth place, thus avoiding the re-election positions on goal difference.

William Allan and Tom Brandon had appeared in all thirty League games during the season, while Harry Brandon and Harry Davis had missed only one, with Brown and Davis netting seven League goals apiece. Rowan found the net on a dozen occasions, while Fred Spiksley led the scoring with thirteen goals in twenty-six League appearances, as well as five in the FA Cup competition.

While the Wednesday should have finished in a top five League position, all in all it had been quite a satisfactory first League campaign, while further success was expected during the final years of the century.

NOTTINGHAM FOREST

Nottingham Forest had attained Football League status as reigning champions of the Football Alliance, from which the Second Division had been formed. However, it had been felt that the Nottingham side were more than capable of coping with life in the First Division.

Forest retained the majority of their Alliance Championship-winning side for their opening League campaign as William Brown continued in goal, albeit for only half a season, prior to being replaced by Dennis Allsopp, a recent signing from Derby Junction, who would make in excess of 200 League appearances for the East Midlands side. Fullbacks Adam Scott and Archie

Ritchie, like Allsopp, continued to serve the Nottingham side until the turn of the century.

Ritchie, who had previously played for East Stirling, with whom he had gained a Scottish international cap, made in excess of 150 League appearances in his eight seasons with the club, while Adam Scott, who had arrived from Coatbridge Albion in 1890, played well over 200 games for Forest.

Scottish international John MacPherson, who had signed from Heart of Midlothian following their 1891 Scottish FA Cup Final victory, remained at centre half, where he played 225 League games. Horace Pike, a first team regular since 1888, continued to play until 1895, while Sandy Higgins, who had scored twenty-six goals in twenty Alliance appearances during the previous campaign, remained with the club until 1894, following an excellent career as one of the finest goal scorers of the Victorian era. Prior to signing for Forest, Higgins had scored four goals on his Scottish international debut, as well as twice leading the scoring for Derby County.

Tom McInnes from Clyde, who made 167 League appearances in seven seasons with the club, was the most notable newcomer in the Forest side, while Tinsley Lindley, a true Corinthian in every sense of the word, had decided to leave the Nottingham club upon their elevation to the Football League.

Forest opened the season with a two-all draw against Everton at their recently opened Goodison Park ground, with Sandy Higgins twice on target for the visitors, which was followed by home defeats against Stoke (4–3) and Preston North End (2–1), as well as a 1–0 reverse in the away game at Preston Forest recorded their first win in the League during October, as McInnes (2) and Higgins found the net in a 3–2 victory at Derby County.

Then followed a two-all draw at the Wednesday, with Pike and McInnes netting the Forest goals, while successive away defeats at Notts County (3–0) and Aston Villa (1–0) saw the League newcomers continue their struggle. However, a 2–0 home success against Bolton Wanderers saw a return to winning ways, with Sandy Higgins scoring his fifth League goal of the campaign. Forest then suffered further away defeats at Stoke (3–0) and Sunderland (1–0), as well as at home to Aston Villa (5–4), with McCallum scoring a hat-trick for the Nottingham side. Successive away draws at Wolverhampton Wanderers (2–2) and Burnley (1–1), together with a one-all home draw against Newton Heath, saw the Nottingham side end the first half of the season at the foot of the League table.

Early December saw Higgins and MacPherson find the net in a 2–0 home win against the Wednesday, which preceded a 5–0 home defeat against League leaders Sunderland. However, following a home draw with Burnley (2–2), the Forest side registered seven successive League victories to move into the top half of the League table.

Their winning run began with a 3–1 home success against Wolverhampton

Wanderers, with Smith, Higgins and MacPherson on target, which was followed by a 1–0 victory at Blackburn Rovers in the final game of the year, with inside forward Shaw scoring the only goal of the game. Then Sandy Higgins scored twice in a New Year home win against Accrington (3–0).

Tom McInnes and Horace Pike then scored in successive victories at home to Everton (2–1) and away at Newton Heath (3–1), while their winning run continued in the FA Cup with a first round home success against the Casuals, with McInnes, Shaw, Pike and Higgins on target in a 4–0 win to secure a second round tie at Everton.

Prior to the FA Cup tie, Sandy Higgins scored the only goal of the game in a 1–0 home win against Derby County, which preceded a 4–2 defeat in the cup game at Everton, while their splendid League form continued with a 3–1 home success against neighbours Notts County, with McInnes (2) and Pike on target. However, an indifferent run of results during the final month of the campaign saw the Nottingham side struggling in the bottom half of the League table at the season's end.

Early March saw Forest suffer successive home defeats against West Bromwich Albion (4–3) and Blackburn Rovers (1–0), followed by a one-all draw at Accrington, where Sandy Higgins found the net. A 3–1 reverse at Bolton Wanderers, together with a two-all draw in the return game at West Bromwich Albion, saw the Nottingham side complete their first League campaign in tenth position, with ten victories, eight draws and twelve defeats in their thirty League games, while scoring forty-eight goals and conceding fifty-two.

Tom McInnes appeared in all thirty League games for Forest, with Scott, McCracken, Higgins, Pike and William Smith missing no more than a handful. McInnes ended the campaign with ten League goals, with Sandy Higgins leading the scoring with a dozen goals in twenty-five appearances in an excellent first League campaign for Forest.

NEWTON HEATH

Newton Heath had been formed in 1878 by a group of railway workers employed by the Lancashire and Yorkshire Railway Company. They played their early fixtures against other railway teams at North Road, Monsall, but, in their pursuit of tougher opposition, the Newton Heath side organised games against the reserve teams of the likes of Bootle and Bolton Wanderers.

Sam Black had been the early inspiration in making Newton Heath one of the strongest teams in the Manchester area, while his own career culminated in an appearance for the Manchester district representative side against the Liverpool district in 1884. Following the legalisation of professionalism in 1885, the Newton Heath club were well aware of the need to strengthen their team if they were to compete on level terms with other professional clubs in the city. While the majority of local teams were signing players from north of the border, Newton Heath tended to sign players from the North Wales area where they had little competition from the wealthier clubs for their signatures.

Jack Powell, who had arrived from Bolton Wanderers in 1886 following a number of seasons with the Druids, proved an excellent signing for the Manchester club, with whom he gained Welsh international caps, while Jack and Roger Doughty, who, like Powell, had appeared in Welsh FA Cup Finals with the Druids, enjoyed much success with the Newton Heath club prior to them attaining League status.

In 1888, Jack Doughty scored four goals in an 11–0 victory against Ireland, with his brother Roger scoring twice. Both brothers, Powell, Burke and Davies from the Newton Heath club were included in the Welsh line-up against Scotland during the same season.

Following their failure to receive an invitation to join the newly formed Football League, Newton Heath were elected to the Football Alliance for the 1889–90 season, with the usual line-up of Tom Hay in goal, together with Mitchell, Jack Powell, Roger Doughty, J Owen and Joe Davies in defence, while Farman, Jack Doughty, Stewart, G Owen and Wilson formed the attack. However, with the exception of Mitchell, Farman and Stewart, who all made in excess of fifty League appearances, the remaining members of the side left the club prior to them joining the Football League.

Newton Heath's opening game in the Alliance resulted in a 4–1 home success against Sunderland Albion, with Wilson (2), Stewart and Jack Doughty on target. A poor away record that included defeats at Bootle (4–1), Walsall Town Swifts (4–0), Darwen (4–1), Grimsby Town (7–0) and Birmingham St George's (5–1) saw the Manchester side end the campaign in eighth position. There were a few highlights during the season, including a 9–1 home win against Small Heath, with inside forward Stewart scoring a hat-trick.

Jack Doughty had been ever present during the season, in which he had scored on nine occasions, while Stewart had led the scoring with ten goals in nineteen appearances. The 1890–91 season saw a number of changes in the Newton Heath line-up, with Slater replacing Hay in goal and Clements replacing Jack Powell at left fullback, while Evans, Craig, Sharpe and Milarvie secured regular first team places in the attack.

Ramsey had been signed to steady a suspect defence, while Mitchell, Farman, J Owen, Stewart, Jack Doughty and Roger Doughty were retained from the previous campaign.

The season began with a 4–2 home success against Darwen, with J Owen, Farman, Evans and Jack Doughty on target. However, their usual indifferent away form, which included defeats at Bootle (5–0), Nottingham Forest (8–2) and Birmingham St George's (6–1), saw Newton Heath in ninth position at the season's end, with only seven victories in twenty-two Alliance games. Slater, Ramsey, Farman and Milarvie appeared in all twenty-two Alliance fixtures, while Roger Doughty and Stewart missed only one, in a further disappointing season for the Manchester side, which had seen Sharpe lead the scoring with half a dozen goals.

Few changes were made in the Newton Heath defence prior to the 1891–92 season as Slater, Clements, J Owen, Stewart and Roger Doughty retained their positions. However, outside right Farman was the only remaining member of the attack from the previous campaign, which saw the arrival of Edge, Donaldson, Henrys, Hood and Sneddon at the club, albeit, with the exception of Robert Donaldson, for a little more than a season.

Donaldson, who had arrived at the club from the Scottish Borders, had the distinction of scoring Newton Heath's first goal and first hat-trick in the Football League, prior to joining Luton Town towards the end of the century following 131 League appearances for the Manchester club.

The 1891–92 season opened with a 3–2 defeat at Burton Swifts, which preceded a 4–0 home win against Bootle, with Edge netting a hat-trick, while Robert Donaldson scored hat-tricks in victories against Lincoln City (10–1), Crewe (5–3) and Walsall Town Swifts (4–1). The Lancashire side ended the campaign as runners-up to Nottingham Forest, with only three defeats in twenty-two Alliance games.

Robert Donaldson and Stewart had appeared in all twenty-two Alliance games in Newton Heath's most successful season to date. Farman ended the campaign with sixteen goals in twenty-one appearances, while Donaldson had led the scoring with twenty goals.

Newton Heath's excellent season had coincided with the decision by the Football League Committee to extend the League to sixteen teams, as well as to form a Second Division consisting mainly of teams from the Alliance. Much to the surprise of many, the Newton Heath club received sufficient votes to gain selection to the First Division, which coincided with a move to a new ground at Bank Street, Clayton, with a stand erected to seat 1,000 spectators.

Few changes were made in Newton Heath's line-up for their first season in the League. Mitchell returned to the club to partner Clements at fullback, Stewart remained at the heart of the defence, while Farman, Hood and Robert Donaldson continued in the attack.

New signings included Warner in goal to replace Slater, while defenders Perrins and Fred Erentz were the most notable newcomers in the team, with Perrins making nearly 100 League appearances in four seasons with the club. Erentz, a recent arrival from Dundee Old Boys, made in excess of 300 appearances for the League newcomers.

Newton Heath suffered a narrow 4–3 defeat at Blackburn Rovers in their opening League game, with Cooper, Donaldson and Farman on target, which preceded a one-all home draw with Burnley, with Donaldson scoring for the Manchester side. Donaldson scored for the third successive game in a 4–1 reverse in the return game at Burnley.

Then followed further defeats at Everton (6–0) and at home to West

Bromwich Albion (4–2), as well as a goalless away draw at Albion, while mid-October saw the Newton Heath team register their first victory of the season, with a 10–1 home win against Wolverhampton Wanderers, with Donaldson and Stewart scoring hat-tricks. Donaldson then scored his eighth League goal in as many games in a 4–3 home defeat against Everton, which preceded a 1–0 reverse at the Wednesday, while successive draws at Nottingham Forest (1–1) and at home to Blackburn Rovers (4–4) saw Farman on target in both games.

Mid-November saw a 3–1 home defeat against Notts County, followed by a 2–0 home win against Aston Villa, with Coupar and Fitzsimmons scoring for the Manchester side, while a 4–1 reverse at Bolton Wanderers continued their poor away form. This left the Lancashire team at the foot of the League table at the halfway stage of the season.

A further Robert Donaldson goal then secured a 1–0 victory in the return game with Bolton, which preceded successive away defeats at Wolverhampton Wanderers (2–0) and Preston North End (2–1), as well as at home to the Wednesday (5–1). The year ended with a 7–1 home success against Derby County, with Farman and Donaldson scoring three goals apiece.

Little changed in the new year as Newton Heath suffered successive League defeats at Stoke (7–1), Notts County (4–0), Derby County (5–1) and Aston Villa (2–0), as well as at home to Nottingham Forest (3–1) and Sunderland (5–0), while a 4–0 defeat at Blackburn Rovers in the first round of the FA Cup ended their interest in that competition. However, the Manchester side eventually returned to winning ways with a 1–0 home win against Stoke on the final day of March, with Farman scoring the only goal of the game. Then followed a further home success against Preston North End (2–1), with Donaldson scoring a brace of goals, which preceded a 6–0 defeat at League leaders Sunderland. The campaign ended with a three-all home draw against Accrington, with Donaldson, Stewart and Fitzsimmons on target for the home side. They finished the season five points adrift at the foot of the table, with only six victories in thirty League games, while scoring fifty goals and conceding eighty-five.

Mitchell, Erentz and Stewart had appeared in all but one of Newton Heath's League games, with Farman finding the net on ten occasions in twenty-eight appearances, while Donaldson once again led the scoring with sixteen goals in twenty-six League games.

It had been a season of struggle for the Newton Heath team, as their results had confirmed. However, the end-of-season test match games would be their saviour.

ACCRINGTON

Accrington had managed to avoid the embarrassment of applying for re-election to the Football League at the end of the 1891–92 season, owing to the decision to extend the League as well as to form a Second Division. However, the Lancashire side continued to have great difficulty in signing quality players, with goalkeeper Mason the most notable newcomer. George Haworth continued at the heart of the defence, together with John Kirkham up front, in what became the most important season in Accrington's fifteen-year history.

Accrington opened the 1892–93 League campaign with a 6–0 home defeat against reigning champions Sunderland, followed by a 5–2 reverse at the Wednesday. Accrington then enjoyed an excellent run of results, which saw them lose just one League game in seven.

Their fine run included draws at Stoke (2–2), Blackburn Rovers (3–3), Everton (1–1) and at home to Bolton Wanderers (1–1), as well as victories at Burnley (3–1) and at home to the Wednesday (4–2), while a 4–2 defeat at Sunderland saw their one disappointment during this period.

Early November saw Accrington suffer a 2–1 home defeat against Preston North End, followed by successive away defeats at West Bromwich Albion (4–0) and Wolverhampton Wanderers (5–3) as the Lancashire side moved towards the foot of the League table. However, a six-game unbeaten run saw Accrington in the top half of the table by the end of the year. Accrington's excellent run of results saw home victories against Notts County (4–2), West Bromwich Albion (5–4), Stoke (5–2) and Wolverhampton Wanderers (4–0), as well as draws at Derby County (3–3) and at home to Newton Heath (2–2). This saw the Lancashire side with eighteen points from as many League games. However, they failed to secure a victory in any of their twelve remaining games, leaving them once again in trouble near the foot of the League table.

New Year began with a one-all home draw against Blackburn Rovers, followed by successive defeats at Nottingham Forest (3–0), Notts County (2–0) and Bolton Wanderers (5–2), as well as at home to Burnley (4–0) and Everton (3–0), while a one-all home draw with Nottingham Forest continued their indifferent run of results. Further defeats at Aston Villa (6–4) and at home to Derby County (3–0) preceded away draws at Preston North End (0–0) and Newton Heath (3–3), while the season ended with their eleventh draw of the campaign at home to Aston Villa (1–1). Accrington finished the season in fifteenth position, with half a dozen victories in thirty League games, which meant that they had to compete in the end-of-season test matches to decide their League status for the following campaign.

While the season had been a little disappointing on the field of play, Accrington had managed to make a healthy financial profit, which was used to pay outstanding debts. However, it had now become imperative that they retain their First Division status to maintain their healthy bank balance.

NOTTS COUNTY

Notts County made few changes in their line-up for the 1892–93 League campaign as George Toone continued in goal, with Jack Hendry, David Calderhead and Alf Shelton in defence, while Harry Walkerdine, Jimmy Oswald and Harry Daft remained in the attack, together with Dan Bruce, a Scottish international recently signed from Glasgow Rangers.

Trent Bridge continued to be used by the Nottinghamshire Cricket Club well into September, which resulted in County using the Old Castle ground for their early season home fixtures. County opened the season with a 1–0 home defeat against the Wednesday, followed by successive draws at Sunderland (2–2) and at home to Derby County (1–1), while the month ended with a 3–0 reverse at Wolverhampton Wanderers. However, early October saw the Nottingham side register their first victory of the campaign in a 3–1 home success against Preston North End.

Then followed a further home draw against Bolton Wanderers (2–2), which preceded a 3–0 victory in their first League encounter with Nottingham Forest, with Harry Walkerdine, Dan Bruce and Harry Daft scoring the all-important goals. A 5–4 success at Derby County continued their greatly improved form, but successive defeats at Burnley (3–0) and West Bromwich Albion (4–2), as well as at home to Stoke (1–0), ended their excellent run of results. Mid-November saw County register a 3–1 victory at Newton Heath, followed by an 8–1 success against West Bromwich Albion, with Jimmy Oswald (3), Harry Daft (3) and Dan Bruce (2) on target, while further home wins against Sunderland (3–1) and Burnley (3–1) saw the Nottingham side in a healthy League position. However, successive defeats at Accrington (4–2) and Blackburn Rovers (1–0), as well as at home to Everton (2–1) and Aston Villa (4–1), saw County struggling near the foot of the League table at the end of the year.

County suffered a 6–0 reverse at Everton during the opening week of the new year, followed by a goalless home draw with Blackburn Rovers, while home victories against Newton Heath (4–0) and Accrington (2–0) saw a return to winning ways for the East Midlands side. This preceded a 3–2 success against Shankhouse in the first round of the FA Cup.

Notts then suffered a 3–2 defeat at Middlesbrough Ironopolis in the second round of the competition, which was followed by a run of away defeats at Nottingham Forest (3–1), Stoke (1–0), Aston Villa (3–1), Bolton Wanderers (4–1), Preston North End (4–1) and the Wednesday (3–2). County played one player short at Preston, owing to the non-arrival of goalkeeper George Toone who had missed his train to the Lancashire town. However, a 3–0 home win against Wolverhampton Wanderers saw the Nottingham side end the campaign with a victory. County had finished the season in fourteenth position, with ten wins, four draws and sixteen defeats in their thirty League games, while scoring fifty-three goals and conceding sixty-one, with Jimmy Oswald and Harry Daft sharing the majority of the goals. This meant that Notts would have to take part in the end-of-season test match games to decide their future.

DERBY COUNTY

Derby County had regularly been involved in the struggle to avoid re-election, owing mainly to their cavalier approach to League games. However, they had tended to avoid serious trouble because of the goal-scoring exploits of Sandy Higgins and John Goodall.

Few changes were made in the Derby line-up for the 1892–93 League campaign, as John Robinson continued in goal, together with Jimmy Methven, John Cox, Archie Goodall and Walter Roulstone in defence, while Mills, McMillan, McLachlan and John Goodall remained in the attack. Joseph Leiper arrived from the Partick Thistle club to replace Jonathon Staley at fullback, where he made in excess of 150 League appearances prior to joining Grimsby Town at the turn of the century. The most notable new signing by Derby saw the arrival of eighteen-year-old Stephen Bloomer, who had played his early football with Derby Swifts.

Cradley Heath-born Bloomer, who had scored four goals on his Derby debut against Darley Dale, spent eighteen years of his career with the East Midlands side, in which he scored in excess of 300 goals in a little over 500 appearances, while his goal-scoring exploits continued in his many appearances for the English national team, making him the finest goal scorer of the Victorian era.

Derby opened the season with a 3–1 victory at Stoke, with McMillan (2) and John Goodall on target, which preceded a 2–1 home defeat against Preston North End, while the month ended with successive one-all draws at Notts County and at home to West Bromwich Albion, with Steve Bloomer scoring his first League goal from the penalty spot.

Bloomer again found the net the following week in a 3–2 home defeat against Nottingham Forest, which preceded further defeats at Burnley (2–1) and at home to Notts County (5–4), with John Goodall on target in both games. Mills, McMillan and Archie Goodall netted in a 3–0 home success against Blackburn Rovers. However, embarrassing defeats at Aston Villa (6–1) and at home to Everton (6–1) saw Derby near the foot of the League table.

Archie Goodall then scored his third goal of the campaign in a 1–0 home win against Burnley, which was followed by a 2–2 home draw with Wolverhampton Wanderers, with Steve Bloomer scoring both goals. Their improved form continued with draws at home to Accrington (3–3) and away at the Wednesday (3–3), with John and Archie Goodall amongst the scorers.

Further home wins against Aston Villa (2–1) and Stoke (1–0) saw Derby in a mid-table position at the halfway stage of the season, while John Goodall scored his ninth League goal of the campaign in a Boxing Day home draw with Bolton Wanderers (1–1). However, a surprising 7–1 defeat at Newton Heath on the final day of the year saw Derby's seven-game unbeaten run come to an end.

New Year began with a 3–0 victory in the return game at Bolton Wanderers, with John Goodall scoring a hat-trick, which preceded a two-all draw at Blackburn Rovers, with Steve Bloomer netting a brace of goals, while a first round FA Cup tie at the Wednesday ended in a 3–2 defeat; however, following a protest by the East Midlands side, the Football Association ordered the tie to be replayed.

Prior to the replayed FA Cup tie, Derby suffered a 1–0 defeat in a League encounter at Nottingham Forest, and John Goodall scored the only goal of the game in a 1–0 cup success against Wednesday. However, the Sheffield side then protested that Derby had fielded an unregistered player, which resulted in a second replay, with the Wednesday securing a 4–2 victory to end Derby's interest in the competition.

On their return to League action, County recorded a 5–1 home success against Newton Heath, with Bloomer, Little, McMillan and both Goodall brothers on target. This was followed by successive away defeats at Wolverhampton Wanderers (2–1) and Sunderland (3–1), while Bloomer and Fred Forman found the net in a two-all home draw with the Wednesday.

Forman, who had recently arrived at the club from Beeston Town, scored three goals in four appearances for Derby, prior to signing for Nottingham Forest, with whom he would gain England caps. Late March saw Forman score a brace of goals in a 3–0 victory at Accrington, which preceded a 3–1 reverse at West Bromwich Albion, while Steve Bloomer scored his eleventh goal of the campaign in a one-all home draw with Sunderland in Derby's final home game of the season.

Derby then suffered a 5–0 defeat at Everton, and the season ended with a 1–0 victory at Preston, with McMillan netting the only goal of the game to secure a thirteenth place League finish for the East Midlands side. There were thus nine wins, nine draws and twelve defeats in their thirty League games, while scoring fifty-two goals and conceding sixty-four.

Goalkeeper John Robinson had appeared in all thirty League games for Derby, with Methven and McMillan missing only one. McMillan and Archie Goodall ended the campaign with six League goals apiece, Steve Bloomer found the net on eleven occasions. However, for the third season running, the ever reliable John Goodall led the scoring with thirteen goals in twenty-five League appearances, and Derby once again avoided the re-election positions.

WOLVERHAMPTON WANDERERS

Wolverhampton Wanderers had been amongst the front runners in all four of their previous League campaigns, which had been due mainly to the Black Country side fielding a settled team of locally born players.

England internationals John Brodie and Charlie Mason had decided to retire from the game prior to the 1892–93 season. However, with the likes of W C Rose, Kinsey, Baugh, Allen, Wood and Wykes in their line-up, the Wanderers were once again expected to mount a challenge for the League Championship.

Newcomers in the side for the 1892–93 season included fullback George Swift, who had arrived from St George's FC to replace Charlie Mason, as well as Billy Malpass from Wednesbury Old Athletic. Wingers Alf Griffin and

Richard Topham, together with eighteen-year-old centre forward Joe Butcher, were recruited from local amateur teams to bolster the attack.

Wanderers opened the season with successive home wins against Burnley (1–0) and Blackburn Rovers (4–2), followed by a 2–1 reverse at West Bromwich Albion, while their excellent home record continued with further victories against Notts County (3–0) and Aston Villa (2–1) on either side of a 3–1 defeat at Bolton Wanderers.

While the Wolverhampton side had enjoyed a fine start to the season, the players had become increasingly unhappy with the club's policies, which resulted in the threatened resignation of the committee following an embarrassing 10–1 defeat at Newton Heath, who were languishing at the foot of the League table. Their indifferent form continued with a 2–1 home defeat against Bolton Wanderers, as well as a 2–1 reverse at Stoke. Wolves then began a run of five unbeaten games, which included draws at Blackburn Rovers (3–3) and Derby County (2–2), as well as at home to Nottingham Forest (2–2), while home wins against Accrington (5–3) and Stoke (1–0) saw the Wanderers climb to a mid-table position. However, a 3–2 defeat at Everton ended their excellent run of results.

Then followed a 2–0 home win against Newton Heath, which preceded a 3–1 defeat at Nottingham Forest, while a 2–0 home victory against League leaders Sunderland saw a return to winning ways. Following a one-all home draw against West Bromwich Albion, the Black Country side ended the year with a 4–0 defeat at Accrington.

New Year saw the Wanderers suffer a 5–2 defeat at Sunderland, which preceded a one-all draw at Bolton Wanderers in the first round of the FA Cup, with Wolves winning the replay by the odd goal in three to secure a home tie against Middlesbrough in the second round. Wanderers managed a narrow 2–1 victory against Middlesbrough to earn a home tie against Darwen in the quarter-finals. This they won by five goals to nil to secure a semi-final tie against Blackburn Rovers, who had defeated them in two of the previous three FA Cup competitions. Prior to the semi-final tie, Wolves enjoyed successive home wins against Wednesday (2–0) and Derby County (2–1), while their excellent FA Cup form continued with a 2–1 victory against Blackburn to earn a second FA Cup Final appearance, scheduled for the Fallowfield Ground, Manchester, against Everton.

Wolves then secured their first away win of the season with a 1–0 victory at the Wednesday, which preceded a 4–2 home defeat against FA Cup Final opponents Everton. However, it was felt that the Wanderers' thoughts were on the FA Cup Final, rather than a meaningless League encounter.

BLACKBURN ROVERS

Blackburn Rovers had struggled throughout the 1891–92 season, which had seen them finish in ninth position in the League, as well as suffering a second round defeat in the FA Cup competition. However, the Lancashire side retained the majority of their players for the 1892–93 League campaign, as Forbes, Dewar and James Forrest continued in defence, while Chippendale, Hall, Campbell and John Southworth remained in the attack.

Herbie Arthur, who soon announced his retirement from the game, was replaced by inside forward Nat Walton between the posts, while Jimmy Douglas, Joseph Lofthouse and Billy Townley failed to make a first team appearance during the season. Newcomers included Sawers and Bowdler up front, as well as Murray, Marshall and Anderson in the defence. Murray, Marshall and Anderson served the Lancashire side for a number of seasons, while Sawers and Bowdler remained for a little more than a season.

Rovers opened the campaign with a 4–3 home win against Newton Heath, with Hall (2), Chippendale and Southworth on target, which preceded a 4–2 defeat at Wolverhampton Wanderers, with Chippendale netting a brace for the visitors. Almond and Southworth found the net in a two-all home draw with Everton, but a 5–0 reverse at Sunderland continued their indifferent start to the season. Then followed a three-all home draw with Accrington, with Bowdler, Chippendale and Southworth scoring for Blackburn, while successive defeats at Preston North End (2–1), Derby County (3–0) and at home to the Wednesday (2–0) saw Rovers struggling near the foot of the League table by the end of October. However, further home draws against Preston North End (0–0) and Wolverhampton Wanderers (3–3), as well as a four-all draw at Newton Heath, saw Blackburn move a couple of places up the League table.

John Southworth then netted a brace of goals in successive victories at the Wednesday (3–0) and at home to Bolton Wanderers (3–0), which preceded a goalless draw at Burnley, while the halfway stage of the campaign arrived with a 4–1 reverse at Aston Villa. However, a 2–0 home success in the return game with Burnley saw a return to winning ways, with Bowdler and Southworth scoring the all-important goals.

Further wins at home to Notts County (1–0) and away at West Bromwich Albion (2–1) saw inside left Sawers on target in both games as Rovers climbed to a respectable mid-table position. The year ended with 1–0 home defeat against Nottingham Forest.

New Year began with successive draws at Accrington (1–1) and Notts County (0–0), as well as at home to Derby County (2–2), which were followed by a 4–0 home success against Newton Heath in the first round of the FA Cup, with Campbell and Sawers scoring a couple of goals apiece. Their excellent League form continued with a 2–1 home win against West Bromwich Albion, with Sawers again amongst the scorers.

Blackburn then secured a 4–1 home win against Northwich Victoria in the second round of the FA Cup, with Sawers, Southworth, Bowdler and Campbell finding the net to earn a further home tie against League leaders, Sunderland, in the quarter-finals.

Prior to the quarter-final tie, Sawers netted a brace of goals in a two-all home draw with Aston Villa, while John Southworth scored twice as Blackburn inflicted a 3–0 defeat on Sunderland to secure a semi-final tie against Wolverhampton Wanderers. However, following a further home draw against Stoke (3–3), Rovers suffered a 2–1 reverse against the Wolverhampton side to end their hopes of a seventh FA Cup Final appearance.

On their return to League action, Rovers secured a 1–0 victory at Nottingham Forest, with Harry Chippendale scoring the only goal of the game. This preceded a 2–1 reverse at Bolton Wanderers, while Bowdler and Campbell found the net in a two-all home draw with Sunderland on the final day of March.

Rovers then suffered a 4–0 defeat at Everton in the penultimate game of the season and the campaign ended with a two-all draw at Stoke. The Lancashire side finished in ninth position in the League, with eight wins, thirteen draws and nine defeats in their thirty League games, while scoring forty-seven goals and conceding fifty-six. Murray and Dewar had appeared in all thirty League games for Blackburn, while John Southworth had scored ten goals in twenty-three appearances, with Sawers leading the scoring with eleven goals in twenty-four League games. While Rovers had once again enjoyed an excellent FA Cup run, their League form had left a little to be desired, which ultimately led to a number of changes in their line-up for the 1893–94 campaign.

WEST BROMWICH ALBION

West Bromwich Albion retained the majority of their FA Cup-winning side for the 1892–93 League campaign, as Joe Reader continued in goal, together with Nicholson, Reynolds and Charlie Perry in defence, while Geddes, Pearson, Groves, McLeod and Billy Bassett remained in the attack. They were joined by inside forward Bostock, who had been signed from a local amateur side.

Albion opened the season with a 3–1 defeat at Bolton Wanderers, which preceded a 2–0 home success against Wolverhampton Wanderers, with Bassett and Bostock on target, while Pearson (2) and McLeod found the net in a 3–2 home win against Aston Villa.

Then followed successive draws at Derby County (1–1) and at home to Newton Heath (0–0), while Bostock, Bassett, McLeod, Pearson and Wood were amongst the scorers in further victories at Newton Heath (4–2) and at home to Everton (3–0). A humiliating 8–1 defeat at Sunderland ended Albion's excellent start to the season. Albion soon returned to winning ways as Geddes, Pearson, Bassett and Bostock found the net in a 4–2 home success against Notts County, which preceded a 5–2 reverse at Aston Villa, with Geddes scoring both Albion goals, while Geddes was again on target in a 1–0 home win against Bolton Wanderers.

A further home win against Accrington (4–0) saw Groves (2), McLeod and Bostock score for the Black Country side, but successive defeats at Notts County (8–1), as well as at home to Stoke (2–1) and Preston North End (1–0) saw Albion in a mid-table position at the halfway stage of the season.

Bostock then netted a brace of goals in an exciting 5–4 defeat at Accrington, which was followed by home defeats against Sunderland (3–1) and Blackburn Rovers (2–1), while a Roddy McLeod goal earned a one-all draw at Wolverhampton Wanderers, but a 5–0 reverse at Burnley on the final day of the year continued their poor run of results.

Little changed in the new year as the West Bromwich side suffered a 6–0 reverse at the Wednesday, while a 7–1 home win against Burnley saw their first victory in two months. Further away defeats at Everton (1–0) and Blackburn Rovers (2–1) on either side of a 4–1 defeat at Everton in the first round of the FA Cup saw Albion continue their struggle.

With six League games remaining, the end-of-season play-off games seemed imminent for Albion. However, an excellent run of results during the final weeks of the season, saw the Black Country side end the campaign in a respectable mid-table position. Albion's improved form began with a 2–1 victory at Stoke, where Billy Bassett scored twice, which was followed by a 4–3 away win at Nottingham Forest, with Bassett netting a further brace of goals. Then McLeod, Boyd and Pearson found the net in a 3–0 home win against the Wednesday.

Charlie Perry scored a couple of goals in a 3–1 home victory against Derby County, while the season ended with successive draws at home to Nottingham Forest (2–2) and at Preston North End (1–1), with Charlie Perry on target in both games. Thus the team secured an eighth place League finish for Albion, who had won twelve, drawn five and lost thirteen of their thirty League games, while scoring fifty-eight goals and conceding sixty-nine. Joe Reader, Charlie Perry, Willie Groves and Roddy McLeod had been ever present during the season, while Bassett, Pearson and Geddes had missed only the occasional game.

Bostock had ended his first season with the West Bromwich side with seven League goals; Jasper Geddes had found the net on nine occasions; Roddy McLeod had finished the campaign with ten goals; while Pearson and Bassett were joint leading scorers with eleven League goals apiece.

STOKE

Stoke had constantly struggled in the Football League. However, the 1892–93 season saw the Potteries' side field a settled team, which was reflected on their greatly improved performances.

Few changes were made in the Stoke line-up for the new campaign, as England internationals Rowley, Clare and Underwood continued in defence, together with Christie, Proctor and Brodie, while Naughton, Dickson, Robertson and Evans joined Joseph Schofield in the attack.

David Christie had joined the Stoke Club from Forfar Athletic; David Brodie had arrived from Paisley Abercorn; William Naughton had previously played for Carfin Shamrock; while Billy Dickson had enjoyed Football League experience with Aston Villa.

Stoke opened the season with a 3–1 home defeat against Derby County, followed by a 4–3 victory at Nottingham Forest, while a 1–0 home reverse against Aston Villa continued their indifferent start to the campaign. Then followed a two-all home draw with Accrington, while successive away defeats at Burnley (3–2), Sunderland (3–1) and Aston Villa (3–2) saw the Potteries' side near the foot of the League table. However, an excellent run of results saw Stoke move into the top half of the League by the middle of December. Stoke's return to form began with a four-all draw at Bolton Wanderers, followed by home wins against Nottingham Forest (3–0) and Wolverhampton Wanderers (2–1), as well as away at Notts County (1–0). A two-all draw at Everton saw inside forward Evans dismissed from the field of play for ungentlemanly conduct.

Further home wins against Preston North End (2–1) and Burnley (4–1), together with a 2–1 success at West Bromwich Albion, saw Stoke continue their climb up the League table, while a 1–0 reverse at Wolverhampton Wanderers was a rare defeat; however, a 2–0 home win against the Wednesday saw the Potteries' side return to winning ways.

Christmas Eve saw Stoke suffer a 1–0 defeat at Derby County, followed by a 5–2 defeat at Accrington on Boxing Day, and the year ended with a further reverse at Preston North End (2–1). However, new year home wins against Newton Heath (7–1) and Bolton Wanderers (6–0) saw Stoke maintain their position in the top half of the League table.

Following an early exit from the FA Cup competition, the Potteries' side suffered successive home defeats against Everton (1–0) and West Bromwich Albion (2–1), followed by a three-all draw at Blackburn Rovers. A 1–0 home win against Notts County ended their indifferent run of results, but their joy was short-lived as further defeats at home to League leaders Sunderland (1–0) and away at Newton Heath (1–0) on the final day of March saw them move down to tenth place in the table, with two games remaining.

Stoke then secured a 1–0 victory at the Wednesday, and the season ended with a two-all home draw with Blackburn Rovers, leaving the Potteries' side in seventh position, with twenty-nine points from thirty League games, in which twelve games were won, five drawn and thirteen lost, while scoring fifty-eight goals and conceding forty-eight.

Rowley, Clare, Proctor, Brodie and Dickson were ever present during the season, while Joseph Schofield had once again led the scoring with thirteen League goals in Stoke's most successful League campaign to date.

BURNLEY

Burnley had made excellent progress during the 1891–92 League campaign, which had seen them finish in a creditable seventh position, resulting in few changes in their line-up for the 1892–93 season. Jack Hillman continued in goal, together with Nicholl, Lang, King, Mathew and Bowes in defence, while Crabtree, Chambers, Hill, Place and Claude Lambie remained up front.

Burnley opened the season with successive defeats at Wolverhampton Wanderers (1–0) and at home to Aston Villa (2–0), followed by a one-all draw at Newton Heath. Their first victory of the campaign arrived with a 4–1 success in the return game with Newton Heath, which preceded a further home win against Stoke (3–2). Then followed away defeats at the Wednesday (2–0) and Preston North End (2–0), as well as at home to Accrington (3–1). Home wins against Derby County (2–1) and Notts County (3–0) saw Burnley maintain their mid-table position. However, a loss of form during November, which included away defeats at Sunderland (2–0), Derby County (1–0) and Stoke (4–1), together with a one-all home draw with Nottingham Forest, saw the Lancashire side struggling near the foot of the League table.

Early December saw a goalless home draw with Blackburn Rovers, followed by a 3–1 reverse at Notts County. A two-all draw at Nottingham Forest continued their poor run of results, which went from bad to worse when team captain Lang was dismissed from the field of play in a 2–0 defeat at Blackburn Rovers for a series of fouls on John Southworth. However, successive victories at Everton (1–0) and at home to West Bromwich Albion (5–0) saw the year end on a high note.

New Year saw Burnley suffer a 7–1 defeat in the return game at West Bromwich Albion, which preceded a 4–0 success at Accrington, while a 1–0 defeat at the Wednesday in the second round of the FA Cup saw their usual early elimination from the competition.

With eight League games remaining, of which six were at home, the Lancashire side were in need of three or four victories if they were to avoid the relegation positions. Successive home wins against Bolton Wanderers (3–0), Preston North End (4–2), Wednesday (4–0), Wolverhampton Wanderers (2–0) and Everton (3–0), as well as an excellent 4–1 victory at Aston Villa, saw Burnley end the campaign in sixth place, with only defeats at Bolton Wanderers (1–0) and at home to Sunderland (3–2) spoiling an otherwise excellent finish to the season.

Burnley had secured thirty points in as many League games in their highest League placing to date, while scoring fifty-one goals and conceding forty-four, with only the League champions and runners-up conceding fewer.

BOLTON WANDERERS

Following their third place League finish of the previous season, Bolton Wanderers made few changes in their defence for the 1892–93 League campaign, as John Sutcliffe continued in goal, together with John Somerville and David Jones at fullback, while Alex Paton, Harry Gardiner and James Turner once again formed the half-back line.

John McNee and James Cassidy retained their places in the attack, which saw the arrival of Dickenson, Wilson, Bentley and Willocks, who had all left the club within a couple of seasons.

James Brogan had retired from the game, while Davenport, McFettridge, Munro and Davie Weir made few appearances during the season, once again leaving the responsibility for the goal scoring upon the shoulders of James Cassidy.

Bolton opened the season with a 2–1 defeat at Preston North End, with Harry Gardiner scoring a rare goal for the visitors, which preceded successive home wins against West Bromwich Albion (3–1) and Wednesday (1–0), with outside left Dickenson on target in both victories, while James Cassidy scored an excellent hat-trick in a 5–0 home success against Aston Villa.

Cassidy netted a further brace of goals the following week in a 3–1 home win against Wolverhampton Wanderers, while his sixth goal of the campaign arrived in a two-all draw at Notts County. This preceded further draws at Accrington (1–1) and at home to Stoke (4–4), with Dickenson netting a hat-trick against the Potteries' side.

Then followed a 2–0 reverse at Nottingham Forest, while further victories at Wolverhampton Wanderers (2–1) and at home to Everton (4–1) saw Willocks find the net in both games. However, a poor run of results during November saw the Lancashire side suffer defeats at the Wednesday (4–2), West Bromwich Albion (1–0) and Blackburn Rovers (3–0), as well as at home to Preston North End (4–2), which saw them in a mid-table position at the halfway stage of the campaign. Wanderers returned to winning ways during the opening week of December, with Bentley (2), Wilson and Cassidy on target in a 4–1 home success against Newton Heath. This was followed by a 1–0 reverse in the return game at Newton Heath, and the year ended with away draws at Aston Villa (1–1) and Derby County (1–1), with McNee and Willocks netting the Bolton goals.

Bolton's indifferent form continued into the new year with a 3–0 home defeat in the return game with Derby County, as well as a 6–0 reverse at Stoke, while a 2–1 defeat in a first round FA Cup replay at Wolverhampton Wanderers saw an early exit from the competition for the Lancashire side. However, following a 3–0 defeat at Burnley, the Bolton team enjoyed an excellent run of results, which saw them in a top five position at the season's end.

Wanderers' return to form coincided with the introduction of Davie Weir at centre forward, as the England international scored twice in a three-all draw at Sunderland, which preceded a narrow 1–0 home success in the return game with Burnley, while Weir netted a hat-trick in a 5–2 home victory against Accrington.

Weir's sixth League goal in five appearances arrived in a 2–1 home victory against Blackburn Rovers, with Dickenson completing the scoring, while inside forward Bentley scored a brace in a further home win against Notts

County (4–1). This was followed by a fifth successive home win against Nottingham Forest (3–1) with Dickenson, Wilson and Paton on target.

Bolton's final home game of the season resulted in a 2–1 victory against League champions Sunderland, with Bentley and Weir netting the Wanderers' goals. The campaign ended with a 3–0 reverse at Everton, leaving Bolton in fifth position, with thirteen victories, six draws and eleven defeats in their thirty League games, while scoring fifty-six goals and conceding fifty-five. John Sutcliffe, David Jones and Alex Paton had appeared in all thirty League games for the Lancashire side, while Cassidy, Dickenson, Turner, Wilson and Somerville had missed less than a handful in a further successful season for the Wanderers. Davie Weir had scored seven goals in eight League appearances, Willocks had found the net on eight occasions, while Dickenson and Cassidy had ended the season as joint leading scorers with nine League goals apiece.

ASTON VILLA

Following a couple of seasons of indifferent form, Aston Villa had enjoyed an excellent 1891–92 campaign, which had seen them finish in fourth position in the League as well as appearing in the final of the FA Cup.

Few changes were made in the Villa line-up for the 1892–93 season as John Baird, Gersham Cox, William Evans, James Cowan, James Brown and occasionally Harry Devey continued in defence, while Charlie Athersmith, Dennis Hodgetts, Louis Campbell and John Devey remained in the attack, where Albert Brown, Hare, Logan, Fleming, Woolley and Will Devey also made the occasional appearance. Billy Dickson had decided to join the Stoke club, while goalkeeper James Warner had been replaced by Bill Dunning, who had previously played for St Johnstone, Glasgow Celtic and Bootle.

Villa enjoyed an excellent start to the season with a 2–0 win at Burnley, with Campbell and Hodgetts on target, which preceded a 4–1 home success against Everton, with Fleming (2), Hodgetts and John Devey netting the Villa goals. Their winning run continued with a 1–0 victory at Stoke, where Louis Campbell scored the only goal of the game. However, five successive defeats at West Bromwich Albion (3–2), Bolton Wanderers (5–0), Everton (1–0) and Wolverhampton Wanderers (2–1), as well as at home to Sunderland (6–1), saw the Midlands side in the bottom half of the League table by the middle of October.

Then followed successive home wins against Stoke (3–2) and Nottingham Forest (1–0), with Albert Brown on target in both games, which preceded a 4–1 reverse at Preston North End, while Charlie Athersmith and John Devey netted a brace of goals apiece in a 6–1 home victory against Derby County.

A further home success against West Bromwich Albion (5–2) saw Brown (2), Hare, Burton and John Devey score the Villa goals, while Charlie Athersmith secured a hat-trick in a 5–4 victory at Nottingham Forest. However, a surprising 2–0 defeat at Newton Heath ended Villa's excellent run of results.

Dennis Hodgetts then scored his fifth League goal of the campaign in a 3–1 home win against Preston North End, with Brown and Dowds completing the scoring. This preceded a 5–3 defeat at the Wednesday, with John Devey scoring twice, while Devey netted a further brace of goals the following week in a 4–1 home success against Blackburn Rovers. Villa's indifferent run of results on their travels continued at Derby, where Logan netted his first goal of the campaign in a 2–1 defeat. This was followed by a one-all home draw with Bolton Wanderers, with Logan again on target, while the year ended with a 4–1 victory at Notts County with Athersmith, Logan, John Devey and Skea, in his only appearance for Villa, scoring for the visitors.

New Year opened with a further home win against the Wednesday (5–1) with goals by Logan (2), Hodgetts (2) and Will Devey securing a top five position for Villa. However, successive defeats at Sunderland (6–0), as well as at Darwen (5–4) in the first round of the FA Cup, ended their fine run of results.

On their return to League action, Charlie Athersmith netted a brace of goals in a two-all draw at Blackburn Rovers, which preceded a 2–0 home success against Newton Heath, with Logan scoring both Villa goals. John and Will Devey were on target in a 3–1 home success against Notts County as the Midlands side moved up to fourth position in the League table.

Late March saw Albert Woolley score twice on his Villa debut in a 6–4 home win against Accrington, with John Devey netting a further brace of goals. Woolley was twice more on target the following week in a 5–0 home victory against Wolverhampton Wanderers. However, following thirteen goals in twenty League appearances for Villa, Woolley signed for Derby County, where he suffered a premature death within a year of leaving the Villa club.

Villa then suffered a surprising 3–1 defeat against Burnley in their final home game of the season, while the campaign ended with a one-all draw at Accrington, with John Devey on target to secure a fourth place League finish for Villa with sixteen victories, three draws and eleven defeats in their thirty League games, while scoring seventy-three goals and conceding sixty-two. John Devey had appeared in all thirty League games, while Charlie Athersmith, James Cowan, Dennis Hodgetts and Bill Dunning had missed very few in an excellent League campaign for the Villa side. Woolley had scored four goals in as many League appearances; Logan had netted seven goals in ten League games; Hodgetts had found the net on eight occasions; Brown ended the campaign with nine goals; Charlie Athersmith scored ten; while John Devey once again led the scoring with nineteen League goals.

EVERTON

Prior to the 1892–93 season, the Everton club had moved to a new ground at Goodison Park, which had been jointly opened by Frederick Wall and Lord Kinnaird.

Everton made few changes in their line-up for the new season, as Williams and Jardine once again shared the goalkeeping duties, with Robertson, Collins, Kelso, Howarth and John Holt in defence, while Milward, Geary, Chadwick, Maxwell and Alex Latta again formed one of the most skilful forward lines in the land as the Everton side sought to regain the League Championship from Sunderland. Fullback McLean and inside forward Wylie had decided to join the newly formed Liverpool club, while the most notable new signing was defender Richard Boyle from Dumbarton, who made in excess of 200 League appearances for Everton.

Everton opened the season with a two-all home draw with Nottingham Forest with Geary and Milward on target, which preceded a 4–1 reverse at Aston Villa, while Latta and Maxwell found the net in a further draw at Blackburn Rovers (2–2).

Then followed a 6–0 home win against Newton Heath, with Chadwick (2), Geary (2), Maxwell and Milward scoring for Everton, while Maxwell netted his third goal of the season in a 1–0 home success against Aston Villa. However, successive defeats at home to Sunderland (4–1) and away at West Bromwich Albion (3–0) ended the Lancashire side's fine run of results.

Alex Latta then scored all four Everton goals in a 4–3 victory at Newton Heath, which preceded a one-all home draw with Accrington with Alf Milward on target, while Latta netted his seventh League goal of the campaign in a 4–1 defeat at Bolton Wanderers. A 6–1 away win at Derby County saw a return to winning ways, with both Latta and Geary scoring hat-tricks.

Mid-November saw Geary and Milward on target in a two-all home draw with Stoke, followed by defeats at home to the Wednesday (5–3) and at Preston North End (5–0), though successive victories at home to Wolverhampton Wanderers (3–2) and away at Notts County (2–1) saw Everton maintain their mid-table position, with Fred Geary finding the net in both wins.

Following defeats at home to Burnley (1–0) and away at Sunderland (4–3), Everton secured a 6–0 home victory against Notts County, with Geary (2), Chadwick, Latta, Maxwell and Milward on target, while their indifferent start to the new year continued with a 2–1 reverse at Nottingham Forest, but nine victories in their final ten League games, as well as an excellent run in the FA Cup competition, saw the Lancashire side mount a serious challenge for the FA Cup and League double.

Everton's winning run began with a 1–0 home success against West Bromwich Albion, with Fred Geary scoring the only goal of the game, which preceded a 4–1 home win against West Bromwich Albion in the first round of the FA Cup, with Geary (2), Latta and Maxwell on target to secure a home tie against Nottingham Forest in the second round.

Prior to the FA Cup tie, an Alf Milward goal earned a 1–0 victory at Stoke, while Milward (2), Chadwick and Geary found the net in a 4–2 FA Cup win against Forest. This was followed by a further League win at home to Preston

North End (6–0), with Maxwell (2), Gordon, Chadwick, Latta and Milward netting the Everton goals.

Edgar Chadwick then scored in successive victories against the Wednesday in the League (2–0) and FA Cup (3–0) as Everton progressed to the semi-finals, which preceded a 3–0 win at Accrington, with Chadwick netting a brace of goals. Chadwick scored for the sixth game in a row in a two-all draw against Preston North End in the FA Cup semi-final at Bramall Lane.

In the replay at Ewood Park, the game finished goalless and preceded a 4–2 League success at Wolverhampton Wanderers, where Fred Geary scored twice. Their winning run continued in the semi-final replay at Trent Bridge as goals by Gordon and Maxwell earned a 2–1 victory against Preston to secure Everton's first FA Cup Final appearance. This was to take place at the Fallowfield Ground, Manchester, against Wolverhampton Wanderers.

PRESTON NORTH END

Preston North End had finished the four previous League campaigns as winners or runners-up, which led to few changes in their line-up for the 1892–93 season. Jimmy Trainer continued in goal, together with Sanders, Stewart, Robert Holmes and Nick Ross in defence, while Gallacher, Francis Becton, Geordie Drummond, Jack Gordon and Jimmy Ross remained in the attack, which was strengthened by the return of David Russell.

Cowan and Grier were the most notable new arrivals, adding stability to the defence, with Cowan appearing in fifty-five League games in his two seasons with the club, while Grier, who had played one League game during the previous campaign, made in excess of 100 League appearances during his five seasons with Preston.

Preston enjoyed an excellent start to the season with home wins against Bolton Wanderers (2–1) and the Wednesday (4–1), as well as a 2–1 success at Derby County, while home and away victories against Nottingham Forest (1–0 and 2–1) continued their winning run. This ended when the Lancashire side suffered a 3–1 defeat at Notts County. However, further home wins against Blackburn Rovers (2–1), Burnley (2–0) and Aston Villa (4–1) saw Preston on top of the League table, with sixteen points from their opening nine League games.

Then followed a goalless draw at Blackburn Rovers where goalkeeper Jimmy Trainer made his hundredth League appearance, while their fine form continued with away victories at Bolton Wanderers (4–2) and Accrington (2–1), but away defeats at Stoke (2–1) and Aston Villa (3–1) saw Preston move down to second place in the League table.

Early December saw a return to winning ways, with home victories against Everton (5–0), Newton Heath (2–1) and Stoke (2–1), as well as a 1–0 success at West Bromwich Albion, while a 2–0 reverse at Sunderland saw their one disappointment during the final month of the year.

New Year saw a 2–1 defeat in the return game with Sunderland, which preceded a 5–0 away victory at the Wednesday, while FA Cup wins against Accrington and Middlesbrough Ironopolis saw Preston secure a semi-final tie against Everton.

Following a two-all draw in the semi-final at Bramall Lane, the replay finished goalless, which preceded a 4–2 reverse in a League encounter at Burnley. Preston's indifferent run of results continued in the replayed FA Cup tie as they suffered a 2–1 defeat at Trent Bridge to end their hopes of the League and FA Cup 'double'.

On their return to League action, the Preston team secured a 4–0 home success against Notts County, which was followed by a loss of form, resulting in the Lancashire side securing just one victory in their remaining half a dozen League games.

Preston's loss of form began with a 2–1 reverse at Newton Heath, which preceded further defeats against Derby County (1–0) and Wolverhampton Wanderers (2–1), as well as home draws against Accrington (0–0) and West Bromwich Albion (1–1). A 4–0 home win against Wolverhampton Wanderers saw the 'Invincibles' end the campaign in second position for the third season running, following seventeen victories, three draws and ten defeats in their thirty League games, while scoring fifty-seven goals and conceding thirty-nine.

Jimmy Trainer had been ever present during the season, while Becton, Cowan, Grier, Holmes, Sanders, Stewart and the Ross brothers had missed only the occasional game in an excellent League campaign for Preston. Jimmy Ross had netted ten League goals, David Russell had found the net on eleven occasions, with Francis Becton leading the scoring with seventeen goals in the League.

SUNDERLAND

Sunderland had become the most feared team in England within two seasons of attaining League status, with a side consisting mainly of Scotsmen.

Few changes were made by the reigning League champions for the 1892–93 League campaign. John Doig continued in goal, with Gibson, Auld, Porteous and Hugh Wilson in defence, while Scott, David Hannah, Jimmy Millar, Johnny Campbell and James Hannah remained in the attack.

Scottish international defender Donald Gow had returned to Glasgow Rangers, while fullback Murray had signed for Blackburn Rovers, which resulted in the arrival of Harvey, Dunlop and Gillespie, who all gave excellent service to the north-eastern side in a season when only fifteen players were used in League games.

James Gillespie, who had previously made a couple of appearances for Sunderland, scored fifty goals in a little over 130 League games for the club. Billy Dunlop, who arrived from the Annbank club at the turn of the year, made 134 League appearances prior to joining Liverpool in 1899. Harvey was unable to secure a first team place during his four seasons with the north-eastern side. However, he scored a number of important goals for the Sunderland team.

Sunderland opened the season with a 6–0 win at Accrington, with Campbell (3), Millar, Scott and David Hannah on target, which preceded a two-all home draw with Notts County, with Campbell and Wilson scoring for the home side, while Johnny Campbell and James Hannah netted a brace of goals apiece in a 6–1 away success at Aston Villa.

Campbell then netted a further brace of goals in a 5–0 home victory against Blackburn Rovers, which was followed by a 3–1 home win against Stoke, with James Hannah scoring twice, while James Gillespie scored a couple of goals in a 4–1 success at Everton.

A further home win against Accrington (4–2) saw Johnny Campbell score his second hat-trick of the season, while his third arrived the following week in an 8–1 home success against West Bromwich Albion, with Millar (2), Scott, Wilson and Gibson completing the scoring. Campbell netted his sixteenth League goal of the season in a 3–2 reverse at the Wednesday.

Sunderland soon returned to winning ways with successive home wins against Burnley (2–0) and Nottingham Forest (1–0), with Campbell scoring in both games, which were followed by a 3–1 reverse at Notts County, while the free-scoring Johnny Campbell netted a couple of goals in a 5–0 success at Nottingham Forest, with Gibson, Gillespie and David Hannah also on target.

Then followed home wins against Preston North End (2–0) and West Bromwich Albion (3–1), with David Hannah and James Hannah netting in both victories. The year ended with a 2–0 defeat at Wolverhampton Wanderers, though the north-eastern side avenged the defeat at Wolverhampton in the opening game of the new year as James Hannah (3), Jimmy Millar and David Hannah found the net in a 5–2 success.

James Hannah was again on target the following day in a 4–2 home win against Everton, which preceded a 2–1 success at Preston North End with James Gillespie netting a brace of goals, while Gillespie scored a further brace in a 6–0 home victory against Aston Villa, with Johnny Campbell and both Hannahs amongst the Sunderland scorers.

Sunderland's excellent League form continued in the FA Cup as Jimmy Millar scored a hat-trick in a 6–0 home win against Royal Woolwich Arsenal, which was followed by a 4–2 League win against the Wednesday with James Hannah scoring a couple of goals, while Jimmy Millar scored twice in a 3–1 victory at Sheffield United in the second round of the FA Cup to secure an away tie at Blackburn Rovers in the quarter-finals.

Prior to the FA Cup tie, the north-eastern side shared six goals at home to Bolton Wanderers, which was followed by a 3–0 reverse in the FA Cup tie at Blackburn. However, their fine League form continued at Newton Heath where Johnny Campbell scored a hat-trick in a 5–0 victory, while Campbell netted two further goals in a 3–1 home success against Derby County.

Hugh Wilson then netted a rare goal in a 1–0 victory at Stoke, which preceded a two-all draw at Blackburn Rovers, while a 2–1 reverse at Bolton Wanderers saw a rare defeat. However, the title holders soon returned to form with a 6–0 home win against Newton Heath, with Millar and Campbell scoring a couple of goals apiece. Following a one-all draw at Derby County, Sunderland ended the season with a 3–2 success at Burnley, with Harvey (2) and Wilson on target. The north-eastern side retained the League Championship by a margin of eleven points from Preston North End, with twenty-two victories, four draws and four defeats in their thirty League games, while scoring one hundred goals and conceding thirty-six.

Porteous, Gibson and Doig had appeared in all thirty League games for the north-eastern side. Jimmy Millar had ended the campaign with eleven League goals; James Gillespie had scored on a dozen occasions; James Hannah had netted nineteen League goals; while Johnny Campbell had led the scoring with twenty-eight goals in a season when Sunderland had so dominated the League competition that it seemed difficult to see them losing their hold on the League Championship for many years to come.

Promotion and the Test Match Games

Following a meeting of the Football League Committee, a decision was made to hold test match games between the three last placed teams in the First Division and the top three sides in the Second. However, those unfortunate enough to suffer the indignity of relegation would further suffer financially when playing in front of the smaller crowds in the Second Division.

Small Heath and Sheffield United had tended to dominate proceedings in the Second Division during the 1892–93 season, with the Small Heath side narrowly winning the Championship by a single point. Darwen qualified for the test match games following their third place finish in the Second Division. However, while Darwen had enjoyed an excellent League campaign, it was generally felt that they were not as well equipped as Small Heath and Sheffield United to cope with the rigours of First Division football.

The Growth of Sheffield United

Sheffield United had originally been formed as a cricket club, playing their games at the Bramall Lane Sports Ground, which had been built with the intention of developing cricket in the Sheffield area. However, following the decision of the Wednesday Football Club to move to the Olive Grove Ground, cricket enthusiasts Michael Ellison and John Wostinholm decided to form a football team to fill the gap left by Wednesday's departure.

Charles Stokes, who had previously assisted the Wednesday, added his name to those interested in forming a team. In spite of the lack of support from other clubs in the area, Sheffield United were formed in 1889 in time for the new season. United's advertisements for professional players were met with protests from a number of local teams, who felt that the area was adequately served by the Wednesday club, insisting that two clubs within a couple of miles of each other would mean financial ruin. However, the United Committee argued that if the Birmingham area could support Aston Villa, West Bromwich Albion and Small Heath within a few miles of each other, then surely the Sheffield area could. New signings included goalkeeper Charlie Howlett from Gainsborough Trinity, who usually played in spectacles, Edward Stringer from Lockwood Brothers, as well as Jack Hudson, who had made an appearance in the English national side while with the Wednesday, while centre half Walter Hobson had arrived from the Owlerton club.

Further new signings included Robertson, Galbraith and James Duncan, who had all previously played for Dundee, with Robertson obtaining the distinction of scoring United's first goal as a professional club as well as the first hat-trick by a United player. A further claim to fame would see him become the first player wearing a United shirt to be sent off the field for foul play. Billy Madin (Staveley), Mack (Notts County) and Donald Fraser from north of the border had been signed to strengthen the team. The most notable newcomer to the club was William Mosforth, the former Wednesday and England winger, who, while nearing the end of his career, continued to create excitement amongst the spectators.

United's opening game resulted in a 4–1 away defeat at Notts Rangers, which preceded successive away victories at Heeley and Lincoln City. Their first game at Bramall Lane ended in a 4–0 reverse against Birmingham St George's, who included John Devey in their line-up.

While the Sheffield side suffered a number of heavy defeats during the season, which included a 10–1 defeat against Everton as well as a 13–0 reverse against Bolton Wanderers in the FA Cup competition, they were successful in their application to join the Midlands Counties League for the 1890–91 campaign.

Further signings were made for the new season, which saw the arrival of Michael Whitham, Rab Howell and Arthur Watson from Rotherham Swifts, who all played a significant part in the club's progress. Whitham and Howell eventually represented the English national team, while Watson scored many important goals for the Yorkshire side.

Early season saw Watson and Bridgewater score hat-tricks in a 9–0 home success against the Sheffield Club, which was followed by excellent victories against Derby County (4–2) and Bolton Wanderers (2–1). A 9–1 reverse against Notts County in the first round of the FA Cup ended their interest in the competition. However, United had few problems up front during the season as Bridgewater, Robertson and Watson scored in excess of seventy goals between them.

The 1891–92 season saw many changes in the United line-up as they joined the Northern League, which included the likes of Sunderland Albion and Middlesbrough Ironopolis. Robertson, Bairstow, Bridgewater, Calder and William Mosforth had left the club, while newcomers included Harry Lilley from Staveley, Bob Cain from Bootle, Harry Hammond from Everton, as well as outside right Ernest Needham, who developed into one of the finest half-backs in England.

Charles Stokes, always seeking to strengthen the playing staff, had heard rumours that Preston North End were releasing a number of players involved in their successful teams of the late 1880s, which resulted in the arrival of Sammy Dobson, Jack Drummond and Billy Hendry. Dobson, a skilful inside forward, had been a little unfortunate to miss out on an international trial owing to an injury; Drummond scored many goals from the left wing position; while Hendry was responsible for adding the professional touch to the Sheffield side, which resulted in a rapid rise in their fortunes.

United scored nearly 200 goals in seventy-five games during the 1891–92 season, with Dobson, Watson and Hammond all scoring in excess of thirty goals. Excellent results were recorded against Bolton Wanderers (4–3), Derby County (4–1), Burnley (8–1) and Everton (5–0) as the Sheffield side went from strength to strength.

Prior to the 1892–93 season, United received an invitation to join the newly formed Second Division, which resulted in fewer changes in their line-up from previous seasons. Charlie Howlett continued in goal, with Whitham, Lilley, Hendry, Cain, Howell and Needham in defence, while Drummond, Watson, Hammond, Dobson and Scott once again formed a free-scoring attack.

United's opening League game resulted in a 4–2 home win against Lincoln City with Harry Hammond scoring a hat-trick, which preceded a run of three victories and three defeats, leaving the Sheffield side in a mid-table position. However, a run of fifteen games unbeaten saw United challenging for the Second Division title at the season's end.

An excellent 8–3 home win against Bootle saw Harry Hammond score five of the goals. This was followed by a one-all draw at League leaders Small Heath, while Hammond netted four further goals as United registered a 10–0 away victory at Burslem Port Vale. Their indifferent start to the season eventually cost them the Second Division title as they ended the campaign as runners-up to Small Heath by a single point.

As members of the Football League, United were no longer required to qualify for the FA Cup competition as they secured a 3–1 victory against Blackpool in the first round. This was followed by a 3–1 home defeat against Sunderland in the second round, however, more importantly, the Sheffield side had earned a place in the end-of-season test match games, owing mainly to the goal-scoring exploits of Harry Hammond who ended the campaign with eighteen League goals.

Small Heath Come of Age

The Small Heath club were founded in 1875, within months of their neigh-bours Aston Villa. While they enjoyed a great deal of success at a local level, the Birmingham club were without characters of the likes of George Ramsay and Archie Hunter to achieve success on a national scale, hence their lack of progress in obtaining Football League status.

Following a third place finish in the Football Alliance at the end of the 1891–92 season, Small Heath were duly elected to the newly formed Second Division for the 1892–93 campaign, which resulted in few changes in their line-up. Chris Charsley continued in goal, with Ted Devey, Billy Ollis and Caesar Jenkyns in defence, while Tommy Hands, Billy Walton, Frank Mobley, Fred Wheldon and Jack Hallam formed a free-scoring attack.

Goalkeeper Chris Charsley, a full-time police officer, gained an England cap towards the end of the season, prior to retiring from the Association game to pursue his career with the police, which eventually led to the position of Chief Constable of Coventry. Ted Devey, the brother of Will, remained with the club for a couple of seasons.

Billy Ollis made ninety-nine League appearances, prior to joining Hereford Thistle. Frank Mobley, who had signed from Singers of Coventry prior to the new season, scored sixty-two goals in ninety-two League appearances, while the hard-tackling Caesar Jenkyns, who had arrived at the club in 1888, eventually served the Woolwich Arsenal, Newton Heath, Walsall and Coventry clubs, as well as representing the Welsh national team. Billy Walton, who as a youngster had helped clear the snow from the Aston Lower Grounds prior to watching the Small Heath side lose to West Bromwich Albion in the 1886 FA Cup semi-final, remained with the club well into the following century, while wingers Jack Hallam and Tommy Hands left during the mid-1890s. However, Fred Wheldon had become the jewel in the crown for the Small Heath side, following his arrival from local amateur football in 1890. Wheldon, who had scored twice on his debut for the club, scored sixty-five goals in 109 League games for Small Heath, prior to joining Aston Villa in 1896, with whom he won League Championship and FA Cup winners' medals, as well as four England caps.

Small Heath opened the season with a 5–1 home win against Burslem Port Vale, with Wheldon (2), Short, Hallam and Edwards on target, which preceded a 3–1 victory at Walsall Town Swifts, with Wheldon again amongst the scorers. A 2–0 reverse at Sheffield United ended their fine start to the season, though a 4–1 home success against Lincoln City saw a return to winning ways, with Wheldon (2), Jenkyns and Mobley scoring for the home side.

Fred Wheldon then netted a further brace of goals in a 3–2 defeat at Grimsby, which preceded a seven-game unbeaten run, including victories against Crewe (6–0), Bootle (4–1), Darwen (3–2) and Burton Swifts (3–2 home and away), as well as draws against Ardwick (2–2) and Sheffield United

(1–1), with Wheldon, Walton, Hallam, Hands and Mobley sharing the goals.

Following a 4–3 defeat at Darwen, the Small Heath side won all nine of their remaining League games, which began with a 12–0 home success against Walsall Town Swifts, with Walton (3), Mobley (3), Hands (2), Hallam (2) and Wheldon (2) on target, while the year ended with successive away victories at Northwich Victoria (6–0) and Crewe (3–1).

New Year saw Fred Wheldon score hat-tricks in further wins at Lincoln City (4–3) and at home to Northwich Victoria (6–2), which were followed by a 2–0 reverse at Burnley in the first round of the FA Cup. Their excellent League form continued with a 6–2 home win against Bootle, with Hallam (3), Mobley (2) and Wheldon netting the Small Heath goals.

Towards the end of the season, the Birmingham side avenged the earlier defeat at Grimsby, by securing an 8–3 home success against the north-eastern side, with Walton (3), Hands (2), Hallam (2) and Wheldon on target. This preceded a 3–0 victory at Burslem Port Vale, where Walton scored a couple of goals, while the campaign ended with a 3–2 home win against Ardwick, with Hallam (2) and Walton finding the net to secure the Second Division Championship for Small Heath by a margin of one point from Sheffield United.

All five of the Small Heath attack had scored regularly throughout the season, with Tommy Hands ending the campaign with eleven League goals; Frank Mobley and Billy Walton had netted fourteen goals apiece; Jack Hallam had scored seventeen goals in twenty-one League appearances; while Fred Wheldon once again led the scoring with twenty-five League goals, and the Midlands side proceeded to the end of the season test match games.

The League tables at the close of the 1892–93 season are listed in Table VII and Table VIII, with the same top five as in the previous campaign, though Everton and Bolton Wanderers changed positions.

Table VII: *First Division Football League results for the 1892–93 season*

	P	W	D	L	F	A	PTS
1. Sunderland	30	22	4	4	100	36	48
2. Preston North End	30	17	3	10	57	39	37
3. Everton	30	16	4	10	74	51	36
4. Aston Villa	30	16	3	11	73	62	35
5. Bolton Wanderers	30	13	6	11	56	55	32
6. Burnley	30	13	4	13	51	44	30
7. Stoke	30	12	5	13	58	48	29
8. West Bromwich Albion	30	12	5	13	58	69	29
9. Blackburn Rovers	30	8	13	9	47	56	29
10. Nottingham Forest	30	10	8	12	48	52	28
11. Wolverhampton Wndrs	30	12	4	14	47	68	28
12. Wednesday	30	12	3	15	55	65	27

	P	W	D	L	F	A	PTS
13. Derby County	30	9	9	12	52	64	27
14. Notts County	30	10	4	16	53	61	24
15. Accrington	30	6	11	13	57	81	23
16. Newton Heath	30	6	6	18	50	85	18

Table VIII: *Second Division Football League results for the 1892–93 season*

	P	W	D	L	F	A	PTS
1. Small Heath	22	17	2	3	90	35	36
2. Sheffield United	22	16	3	3	62	19	35
3. Darwen	22	14	2	6	60	36	30
4. Grimsby	22	11	1	10	42	41	23
5. Ardwick	22	9	3	10	45	40	21
6. Burton Swifts	22	9	2	11	47	47	20
7. Northwich Vic.	22	9	2	11	42	58	20
8. Bootle	22	8	3	11	49	63	19
9. Lincoln	22	7	3	12	45	51	17
10. Crewe	22	6	3	13	42	69	15
11. Burslem Port Vale	22	6	3	13	30	57	15
12. Walsall Town Swifts	22	5	3	14	37	75	13

Everton's First FA Cup Final Appearance

Ten First Division teams remained in the 1892–93 FA Cup at the second round stage of the competition, together with four Second Division sides, as well as Middlesbrough and Middlesbrough Ironopolis from the north-east of England. Aston Villa and West Bromwich Albion, who had contested the previous season's final, were surprisingly eliminated in the first round.

Wednesday progressed to the quarter-finals with a 1–0 home win against Burnley, with Fred Spiksley scoring the only goal of the game. Middlesbrough were a little unfortunate to lose at Wolverhampton Wanderers by the odd goal in three, while their neighbours Ironopolis secured a 3–2 home success against Notts County.

Darwen reached the last eight following a 2–0 home victory against Grimsby Town. Preston North End secured a 4–1 win at Accrington, while Milward (2), Chadwick and Geary were on target for Everton in a 4–2 home win against Nottingham Forest, with Pike and Shaw replying for Forest.

Blackburn Rovers enjoyed a 4–1 home victory against Northwich Victoria with Bowdler, Campbell, Sawers and John Southworth finding the net, while Sunderland completed the quarter-final line-up with a 3–1 win at Sheffield United, with Millar (2) and Campbell scoring for the north-eastern side. All four quarter-final ties tended to be one-sided affairs, with Wolverhampton Wanderers inflicting a 5–0 defeat on Darwen, Preston North End scoring seven without reply against Middlesbrough Ironopolis following a two-all draw, while Chadwick, Maxwell and Geary were on target for Everton in a 3–0 home win against the Wednesday.

Blackburn Rovers once again proceeded to the semi-finals with a 3–0 home victory against Sunderland with John Southworth (2) and Bowdler netting for the Lancashire side, who were then drawn against Wolverhampton Wanderers in a tie to be played at the Town ground, Nottingham. Everton were drawn against Preston North End at Bramall Lane.

Wolves' team of Englishmen caused an upset in the semi-final by defeating Blackburn by the odd goal in three, while the Everton–Preston tie resulted in two drawn games (2–2 and 0–0). However, the Merseysiders secured a 2–1 victory at the third attempt, with goals by Maxwell and Gordon earning their first FA Cup Final appearance, which was to take place at the Fallowfield Ground, Manchester.

Walter Gilliatt Scores a Debut Hat-trick

England's opening international game of the season took place in Birmingham on 25 February against the Irish national side with the selectors choosing a team consisting mainly of players with Corinthian connections, of which seven were making their England debuts.

Chris Charsley (Small Heath), later the Chief Constable of Coventry as well as the deputy Lord Mayor of Weston-super-Mare, made a single England appearance in goal, while Alban Harrison (Old Westminsters) played the first of two England games at right fullback, with his fellow Corinthian Frederick Pelly at left back for the first of three appearances. Albert Smith and William Winckworth were recalled to the half-back line, where they were joined by Corinthian Norman Cooper for his only England cap, while George Cotterill played his third international game at centre forward, with Rupert Sandilands playing his second at outside left.

Robert Topham, an amateur player with Wolverhampton Wanderers, who had refused to play for the Welsh national team following his selection in 1885, made the first of two appearances at outside right, while Old Carthusian Walter Gilliatt made his one international appearance at inside right. He would certainly have played more, had it not been for his religious beliefs. Gilliatt, an excellent dribbler of the ball, eventually became the vicar of Iver, as well as the rector of Sevenoaks. Gilbert Oswald Smith (Old Carthusians and Oxford University), who went on to represent his country on twenty occasions in a career lasting into the following century, completed the English line-up. Smith, a true Corinthian in every sense, had once hit a century at Lords against the Cambridge University bowling attack, while his latter years were devoted to writing and teaching.

As expected, England won the game with ease as goals by Gilliatt (3), Winckworth, Sandilands and G O Smith secured a 6–1 victory. Gilliatt joined the select band of players to score hat-tricks in their only appearance in an England shirt.

Fred Spiksley Scores a Brace Against the Welsh

England's fixture against the Welsh national side took place at the Victoria Ground, Stoke, with a team consisting entirely of professional players. John Sutcliffe (Bolton Wanderers) made the first of five appearances in goal, following a previous appearance for the English Rugby Union side, while Thomas Clare (Stoke) and Robert Holmes (Preston North End) were recalled at fullback, together with Charles Perry and John Reynolds, the West Bromwich Albion half backs.

James Turner (Bolton Wanderers) played the first of three England games at left half back; James Whitehead (Blackburn Rovers) made the first of two appearances at inside right; while John Goodall (Derby County), Billy Bassett (West Bromwich Albion) and Joseph Schofield (Stoke) were once again included in the attack.

Fred Spiksley, the Wednesday outside left, completed the England line-up for the first of seven appearances in which he scored on five occasions, including two on his debut. England won by six goals to nil, with Reynolds, Goodall, Bassett and Schofield completing the English scoring.

A Narrow FA Cup Final Victory for Wolves

Everton and Wolverhampton Wanderers contested the 1893 FA Cup Final at the Fallowfield Ground in Manchester, with the Wolverhampton side selecting the following team:

Rose

Baugh   Swift

Malpass   Allen   Kinsey

Topham   Wykes   Butcher   Griffin   Wood

Everton selected the following eleven:

Williams

Kelso   Howarth

Boyle   Holt   Stewart

Latta   Gordon   Maxwell   Chadwick   Milward

With the exception of Rose and Kinsey, the Wanderers' team consisted of locally born players, while Baugh, Allen, Wykes and Wood had appeared in the 1889 FA Cup Final when the Wolverhampton team had suffered a 3–0 defeat against Preston North End.

Everton included six Scotsmen in their line-up, while the free-scoring Fred

Geary was missing from the team, owing to a leg injury, which made Wolves the slight favourites to win the much coveted trophy.

An enthusiastic crowd in excess of 40,000 arrived at the Fallowfield Ground to watch the final, which created a number of problems for the local constabulary, as skirmishes broke out as angry spectators sought to gain an advantageous view of the proceedings. The final eventually began with Everton dominating the early play as Chadwick, Maxwell and Milward exerted pressure on the Wanderers' defence.

Excellent defending by Baugh, Allen and Kinsey, together with steady goal-keeping from Rose, kept the Everton forwards at bay as the first half finished goalless. However, Wolves came more into the game during the second half, which saw them secure a one-goal lead when a speculative shot by Harry Allen slipped through the arms of Williams in the Everton goal.

Williams had performed admirably up to that point, while his defence had hardly been tested by the Wanderers' forwards. The Lancashire side's missed chances eventually cost them dearly as Wolves held on to their narrow lead to secure their first FA Cup Final victory.

On their return to Wolverhampton, the Wanderers were given a tremendous reception by their supporters, while a speculative builder in the town erected several rows of houses near their Dudley Road ground, naming the group of houses Fallowfield Terrace with a replica of the cup, made in stone, at the front of the terrace.

While Wolves and Everton soon made further appearances in the FA Cup Final, the Football Association Committee had decided that the Fallowfield Ground was totally unsuitable for large crowds, which resulted in a search for a more permanent venue with adequate facilities.

Wolves and Everton Complete Their League Fixtures

Following their FA Cup success, the Wanderers returned to League action with successive away defeats at Burnley (2–0), Aston Villa (5–0), Notts County (3–0) and Preston North End (4–0), while the season ended with a 2–1 home success in the return game with Preston. Wolves ended the campaign in eleventh position, with twelve wins, four draws and fourteen defeats in their thirty League games, while scoring forty-seven goals and conceding sixty-eight.

Richard Baugh and George Swift had appeared in all thirty League games for the Wanderers, with Harry Wood scoring thirteen League goals during the season, while teenage centre forward Joe Butcher had led the scoring with fifteen goals in twenty-one League appearances.

Everton's Fine End to the Season

Everton's excellent League form continued within days of their FA Cup Final defeat with a 4–0 home win against Blackburn Rovers, with Geary, Jones,

227

McMillan and Maxwell on target, which preceded a further home win against Bolton Wanderers (3–0), with Latta (2) and Geary netting the Everton goals. A 3–0 reverse at Burnley saw a rare defeat. However, the Merseysiders returned to winning ways in the final game of the season with a 5–0 home success against Derby County, with Geary (2), Latta (2) and Milward finding the net to secure a third place League finish with sixteen victories, four draws and ten defeats, while scoring seventy-four goals and conceding fifty-one.

Boyle, Chadwick, Holt, Howarth, Latta and Milward had missed no more than a handful of games during the season. Chadwick had ended the campaign with ten League goals; Milward had found the net on eleven occasions; Alex Latta had netted eighteen goals in twenty-eight League games; while Fred Geary had led the scoring with nineteen goals in twenty-four League appearances in Everton's most successful season to date.

England Prove Too Strong for the Scots

England's final international game of the season took place at Richmond on All Fools' Day against the Scottish national side, who were hoping to avenge the defeats of the two previous seasons.

England fielded an experienced team with Alban Harrison (Corinthians), Robert Holmes (Preston North End), John Reynolds (West Bromwich Albion), John Holt (Everton) and George Kinsey (Wolverhampton Wanderers) in defence, while Billy Bassett (West Bromwich Albion), Robert Gosling (Corinthians), George Cotterill (Corinthians), Edgar Chadwick (Everton) and Fred Spiksley (Wednesday) formed the attack.

Leslie Gay (Old Brightonians) completed the England line-up for the first of three appearances in goal. His all-round sporting ability saw him secure a place in the England cricket side, as well as representing Devon at golf.

England enjoyed an excellent performance against the Scots, with Spiksley (2), Gosling, Cotterill and Reynolds on target in a 5–2 victory to continue their fine run of results against the men from north of the border.

A Narrow Victory for the League Eleven

A week after England's victory over Scotland, the Football League sent a team to Celtic Park, Glasgow, to fulfil an inter-League fixture against the Scots with a team of international players, of which eight were from three clubs. Rowley, Clare and Schofield were selected from Stoke, John Reynolds, Charlie Perry and Billy Bassett were representatives of West Bromwich Albion, while Fred Geary and Bob Howarth were included from Everton. Completing the visitors' line-up were Ernest Needham (Sheffield United), Harry Wood (Wolverhampton Wanderers) and John Southworth (Blackburn Rovers), who all performed admirably in a 4–3 victory, with Wood, Geary, Bassett and an own goal scoring for the English.

The End-of-Season Test Match Games

The test match games had been designed to determine the relegation and promotion issues in the First and Second Divisions, as well as to act as an incentive to clubs seeking to play at a higher level.

The 1892–93 season had ended with Notts County, Accrington and Newton Heath occupying the final three positions in the First Division, while Small Heath, Sheffield United and Darwen were the top three teams in the Second.

Notts County, who had finished in fourteenth place in the First Division, managed a narrow victory against Darwen at Hyde Road, Manchester, while Jack Drummond scored the only goal of the game as Sheffield United defeated Accrington at Trent Bridge. The most surprising result of the test match games saw Newton Heath secure a 5–2 victory against Small Heath at Bramall Lane, following a one-all draw at Stoke, with Farman, Cassidy and Coupar amongst the scorers for the First Division strugglers.

As a result of the test match games, Sheffield United and Darwen were promoted to the First Division at the expense of Notts County and Accrington, while Newton Heath, who had finished the season five points adrift at the foot of the First Division, retained their place in the top Division, with Small Heath remaining in the Second.

Lincoln, Crewe, Burslem Port Vale and Walsall Town Swifts, who had occupied the final four positions in the Second Division, were re-elected for the 1893–94 League campaign. This saw the Division increased from twelve to fifteen teams.

Chapter XIX

JIMMY LOGAN SCORES A HAT-TRICK AS NOTTS COUNTY WIN THE FA CUP – 1893–94

ACCRINGTON RESIGN FROM THE LEAGUE
NOTTS COUNTY WIN THE FA CUP AS JIMMY LOGAN SCORES A HAT-TRICK
PRESTON NORTH END STRUGGLE IN THE LEAGUE
ASTON VILLA ARE CROWNED CHAMPIONS
THE STRUGGLE CONTINUES FOR DARWEN AND NEWTON HEATH
LIVERPOOL REMAIN UNBEATEN IN THE SECOND DIVISION
ENGLAND REMAIN UNBEATEN
JOHN VEITCH SCORES A HAT-TRICK IN HIS ONLY ENGLAND APPEARANCE

Accrington Resign from the League

Prior to the 1893–94 season, Accrington, who had recently suffered the indignation of relegation to the Second Division, had decided that travelling as far away as Woolwich Arsenal and Newcastle would incur further pressure on their already stretched finances. This led them to offer their resignation from the League as they wished to join the Lancashire League. However, the Football League Committee were a little annoyed that Accrington had left it so late to announce their intentions, which resulted in the League Committee instructing all members of the Football League to cease playing against Accrington, at least until their problems were resolved. Middlesbrough Ironopolis eventually replaced Accrington in the Second Division.

The following week saw further problems when Bootle tendered their resignation to the Football League Committee. However, the situation was easily resolved when their neighbours, Liverpool, replaced them in the League.

Newcomers to the First Division were Darwen, who had previously spent one season in the top Division, as well as Sheffield United, who had been formed just four years earlier.

SHEFFIELD UNITED

Sheffield United made few changes in their line-up following their promotion from the Second Division. Charlie Howlett continued in goal, with Mick Whitham, Bob Cain, Billy Hendry, Ernest Needham and Rabbie Howell in defence, while Drummond, Gallacher, Watson, Robert Hill and Harry Hammond formed a capable attack.

United's most notable new signings for the 1893–94 season included inside forward Fleming from the Darlington club, while fullback Harry Thickett, who had previously assisted the Sheffield side as an amateur, became a regular member of the team.

The season opened with a 3–2 victory at Everton, where Gallacher (2) and Fleming found the net, which preceded a 2–1 home defeat against Derby County. A run of six successive wins then saw the Sheffield side challenging for the League leadership by the middle of October. United's excellent run of results began with home wins against Darwen (2–1) and Bolton Wanderers (4–2), with Fleming and Robert Hill on target in both games, which were followed by a 4–3 away success at Wolverhampton Wanderers, with Hill (2), Needham and Fleming netting for the visitors. A 3–0 home win against Aston Villa continued their fine run of form, with Drummond, Hammond and Fleming scoring for the Yorkshire side.

Then followed single-goal victories at home to Sunderland (1–0) and away at Bolton Wanderers (1–0), with Davies and Harry Hammond scoring the all-important goals, while Robert Hill netted his sixth League goal of the campaign in a one-all home draw with neighbours Wednesday. However, successive away defeats at Aston Villa (4–0) and Derby County (2–1), as well as at home to West Bromwich Albion (2–0), ended United's excellent start to the season.

United soon returned to winning ways with a 2–1 victory against the Wednesday at the Olive Grove Ground, with Hammond and Drummond on target in a game in which Charlie Howlett saved a penalty. Successive draws at Nottingham Forest (1–1) and at home to Preston North End (1–1), as well as a 3–1 home win against Newton Heath, saw the Sheffield side in the top half of the League table, with Hammond and Fleming again amongst the scorers; however a loss of form during the final month of the year saw United suffer four defeats, leaving them in a mid-table position at the turn of the year.

Their run of defeats began with a 3–0 home reverse against Everton, with Harry Thickett making his League debut, while Hugh Morris, a recent signing from Ardwick, made his first League appearance in a 5–0 defeat at Stoke, which preceded further defeats at Burnley (4–1) and West Bromwich Albion (3–1) as the year ended in disappointment.

United's poor run of results continued throughout January with defeats against Nottingham Forest (2–0), Blackburn Rovers (4–1) and Sunderland (4–1), as well as a three-all draw at Darwen. A 3–2 home success against Wolverhampton Wanderers saw their only victory during the month, with Hammond, Morris and Howell on target for the struggling Sheffielders.

Following a 2–0 reverse at Newcastle in the first round of the FA Cup, United found themselves 3–0 ahead in a League encounter with Stoke, with Morris, Hammond and Yates finding the net. However, the Potteries' side fought their way back into the game to secure a three-all draw, and United settled for a point.

With four League games remaining, the Sheffield side had managed to maintain their mid-table position, which was strengthened by a 3–2 home win against Blackburn Rovers, with Hammond, Howell and Needham (penalty) on target, while Gallacher and Morris netted in a 2–0 victory at Newton Heath.

Harry Hammond then scored the only goal of the game in a 1–0 home success against Burnley, while the campaign ended with a 3–0 reverse at Preston North End. United finished the season in tenth place, following thirteen victories, five draws and twelve defeats in their thirty League games, while scoring forty seven goals and conceding sixty-one. Fleming had ended the campaign with eight League goals, Harry Hammond had found the net on nine occasions, while Robert Hill had led the scoring with ten League goals in an excellent season for the Sheffield side.

DARWEN

Darwen had surprised many at the end of the 1892–93 League campaign by securing a place in the First Division via the test match games, while Small Heath, who had finished six points above them in the Second Division, had failed to gain a place in the top Division.

Darwen opened the season with a 3–2 home defeat against Blackburn Rovers, followed by successive away defeats at Burnley (5–1) and Sheffield United (2–1). Their first win of the campaign arrived with a 3–1 home success against Stoke. However, further away defeats at Wolverhampton Wanderers (2–1) and Preston North End (4–1) saw the Lancashire side continue their poor start to the season.

Late September saw Darwen secure a 1–0 home victory against Newton Heath, while October saw little improvement in their results, with away defeats at Bolton Wanderers (1–0) and Everton (8–0), as well as at home in the return game with Bolton Wanderers (3–1). A one-all home draw with Aston Villa saw their only success of the month. Their situation improved during November with victories at Newton Heath (1–0) and at home to West Bromwich Albion (2–1), followed by the usual away defeats at Derby County (2–1) and Stoke (3–1).

Darwen enjoyed an excellent start to December, with a 2–1 home success against the Wednesday, followed by a two-all home draw with West Bromwich Albion, but their indifferent form returned with defeats at West Bromwich Albion (4–1) and at home to Nottingham Forest (4–0), prior to ending the year with a humiliating 9–1 defeat at Aston Villa.

New Year began with successive home draws against Everton (3–3) and Sheffield United (3–3), followed by a 5–0 reverse at the Wednesday, as well as their usual defeat in the first round of the FA Cup. However, home victories against Preston North End (2–1) and Wolverhampton Wanderers (3–1) on either side of a goalless home draw with Burnley saw Darwen in with a chance of avoiding the test match places with four League games remaining.

The Lancashire side's hopes of First Division safety were short-lived as defeats at Nottingham Forest (4–1) and at home to Derby County (3–2), as well as home and away defeats against Sunderland (4–0 and 3–0), saw Darwen end the League campaign in fifteenth position, with just seven victories in their thirty League games. Darwen's ongoing financial problems tended to reflect their indifferent results on the field of play as they continued to be dominated by the larger clubs in highly populated areas.

NEWTON HEATH

Newton Heath had struggled throughout the 1892–93 League campaign, which had resulted in a last place finish in the First Division. However, following their victory over Small Heath in the end of the season test match games, the Manchester side were able to retain their First Division status.

Despite conceding eighty-five goals during the previous campaign, Newton Heath retained the majority of their players for the 1893–94 season as Mitchell, Clements, Perrins, Stewart and Fred Erentz continued in defence, while Farman, Hood, Fitzimmons and Robert Donaldson retained their places in the attack. Newcomers included goalkeeper Fall, who remained with the club for a little more than a season, as well as left half back Davidson, who appeared in forty League games in two seasons, while Clarkin scored twenty-three goals in sixty-seven games during his three-year stay with the Manchester side. However, the most notable new signings were James McNaught and John Peden from the Linfield Club in Ireland. McNaught, later to become involved in the Players Union, appeared in excess of 150 games for the club prior to joining Tottenham Hotspur, while Irish international Peden signed for Sheffield United at the season's end.

Newton Heath opened the season with a 3–2 home win against Burnley, with Farman scoring a hat-trick, which preceded a 3–1 reverse at West Bromwich Albion, while Farman was again on target in a 1–0 victory at the Wednesday. However, following a one-all home draw with Nottingham Forest, the Lancashire side suffered successive away defeats at Darwen (1–0) and Derby County (2–0). John Peden then netted a brace of goals in a 4–1 home victory against West Bromwich Albion, which was followed by further defeats at Burnley (4–0) and Wolverhampton Wanderers (2–0), as well as at home to Darwen (1–0). A 1–0 home success in the return game with Wolverhampton Wanderers saw a return to winning ways, with Davidson scoring the only goal of the game.

Newton Heath's indifferent form worsened during the final week of November as they began a run of eleven defeats, which saw them plunge to the foot of the League table.

Following a 3–1 reverse at Sheffield United, the Manchester side suffered a 3–0 home defeat against Everton, while the year ended with further away defeats at Sunderland (4–1), Bolton Wanderers (2–0) and Preston North End (2–0), as well as at home to Aston Villa (3–1). Following new year defeats at Everton (2–0) and at home to the Wednesday (2–1), the Newton Heath side registered a 4–0 home success against Middlesbrough in the first round of the FA Cup, with Donaldson (2), Farman and Peden on target to secure a home tie with Blackburn Rovers in the second round.

Prior to the FA Cup tie, the Manchester side suffered a 5–1 League defeat at Aston Villa, while the cup game ended goalless, following a period of extra time. However, Blackburn won the replay by five goals to one to end Newton Heath's interest in the competition.

Early March saw home defeats against Sunderland (4–2) and Sheffield United (?–0), which preceded a surprising 5–1 home win against Blackburn Rovers, with Robert Donaldson scoring a hat-trick. Outside right Clarkin then netted a brace of goals in a 6–2 home defeat against Derby County.

Then followed a 6–2 home success against Stoke, with Farman (2), Peden (2), Clarkin and Erentz on target, while Donaldson and Farman found the net in a two-all home draw with Bolton Wanderers. However, their joy was short-lived as the campaign ended with away defeats at Blackburn Rovers (4–0), Stoke (3–1) and Nottingham Forest (2–0), as well as at home to Preston North End (3–1). This left Newton Heath once more at the foot of the League table with six wins, two draws and twenty-two defeats in their thirty League games, while scoring thirty-six goals and conceding seventy-two. Mitchell, Perrins, Stewart, Davidson, McNaught and Peden had missed no more than a handful of games during the season, while Peden and Donaldson had ended the campaign with seven League goals apiece, with Farman leading the scoring with eight. The test match games loomed for a second successive season.

PRESTON NORTH END

Preston North End had enjoyed success in each of the five previous seasons, which led them to retain the majority of their players for the 1893–94 League campaign. Jimmy Trainer continued in goal, together with Sanders, Grier, Holmes, Sharp and Nick Ross in defence, while Drummond, Gordon, Cowan, Becton and Jimmy Ross remained up front. David Russell and Stewart had left the club, while Nick Ross and Jack Gordon made few appearances during a season of struggle for the Lancashire side.

Preston opened the season with a 1–0 home success against Derby County, followed by successive defeats at Burnley (4–1) and at home to Sunderland (2–1), while the month ended with victories at Bolton Wanderers (3–0) and at home to Darwen (4–1). However, further defeats at Blackburn Rovers (1–0) and at home to Burnley (2–1) saw Preston in the unfamiliar position of struggling near the foot of the League table.

Late October saw victories at Everton (3–2) and at home to Bolton Wanderers (1–0), which preceded a run of eight games without a win, including away defeats at Stoke (2–1), Aston Villa (2–0) and West Bromwich Albion (2–0), as well as at home to Blackburn Rovers (1–0), Nottingham Forest (2–0) and Wolverhampton Wanderers (3–1). Drawn games at Sheffield

United (1–1) and Wolverhampton Wanderers (0–0) saw their only successes during this period of indifferent form.

Then followed a 2–0 home win against Newton Heath, while the year ended with the Lancashire side sharing six goals in a home draw with Stoke (3–3). However, new year defeats at Sunderland (6–3), Derby County (2–1), Darwen (2–1) and Wednesday (3–0), as well as at home to Everton (4–2) and Aston Villa (5–2), gave the Preston side cause for concern as they moved into the test match positions. A further embarrassment for Preston was a 3–2 defeat at Liverpool in the second round of the FA Cup, though their hopes of avoiding the end-of-season test matches were raised following a 3–1 home win against West Bromwich Albion, but a 4–2 reverse at Nottingham Forest all but condemned them to the play-off games.

Preston returned to winning ways during the final days of the season with home wins against Wednesday (1–0) and Sheffield United (3–0), as well as a 3–1 victory at Newton Heath. However, their late run of excellent results had been in vain as they ended the season in fourteenth position, following ten wins, three draws and seventeen defeats in their thirty League games, while scoring forty-four goals and conceding fifty-six.

Jimmy Trainer had once again been ever present in the Preston side, together with defender Grier. Francis Becton ended the season with six League goals; Cowan found the net on seven occasions; and Jimmy Ross led the scoring with seventeen goals in twenty-four League appearances. Preston now awaited the outcome of the end-of-season test match games to decide their future.

BOLTON WANDERERS

Bolton Wanderers had finished in a top five position in four of the previous five seasons, which resulted in few changes in their side for the 1893–94 League campaign. John Sutcliffe continued in goal, with Somerville, Jones, Paton, Gardiner and Turner in defence, while Dickenson, Wilson, Willocks, Cassidy, Bentley and Davie Weir competed for the forward positions.

John McNee had signed for the Newcastle club and James Munro had moved to Burton Swifts, while the most notable newcomer was Robert Tannahill from Kilmarnock, who remained with Bolton until 1896.

Bolton opened the season with a 4–1 home win against Stoke, with Bentley (2), McArthur and Cassidy on target, which preceded a 2–1 reverse at Wolverhampton Wanderers. A 2–1 home success against Blackburn Rovers saw a return to winning ways, with Cassidy and Hughes netting the Bolton goals. However, successive away defeats at Sheffield United (4–2) and Nottingham Forest (1–0), as well as at home to Preston North End (3–0), ended Bolton's fine start to the season.

Davie Weir then scored his first League goal of the season in a 1–0 home success against Darwen, which was followed by a 1–0 home defeat against Sheffield United, while October came to an end with victories at Darwen

(3–1) and at home to Wolverhampton Wanderers (2–0), with Cassidy, McArthur, Dickenson, Weir and Gardiner sharing the Wanderers' goals. However, a loss of form during November saw defeats at Preston North End (1–0), West Bromwich Albion (5–2) and at home to Aston Villa (1–0), leaving Bolton struggling near the foot of the League table.

Following a rare away victory at Blackburn Rovers (1–0), where McArthur scored the only goal of the game, Bolton registered a 2–0 home success against Newton Heath, with Paton and Cassidy on target. This preceded a 2–1 reverse at the Wednesday, with James Cassidy scoring for the visitors, while Cassidy scored for the third game running in a one-all home draw in the return game with the Wednesday in his hundredth League appearance for the club.

Bolton then suffered their heaviest defeat of the season in a 6–1 reverse at Derby County, while the year ended with a further defeat at Sunderland (2–1). However, their indifferent run of results improved during the opening week of the new year with a one-all home draw with Derby County, as well as a 2–0 home win against Burnley, with Ferguson on target for the third successive League game. Wanderers then suffered a 5–0 reverse at Stoke, which was followed by a 4–3 victory at Small Heath in the first round of the FA Cup, with Wilson and Cassidy netting a brace of goals apiece to secure a second round tie at Newcastle.

Prior to the FA Cup tie, Robert Tannahill scored his second League goal of the campaign in a 2–1 defeat at Burnley, while their cup run continued with a 2–1 victory at Newcastle, with Hughes and Turner on target to earn a quarter-final home tie against Liverpool, who were well ahead in the race for the Second Division Championship. Liverpool were favourites to win the tie against the struggling Bolton side. However, an excellent display by the Wanderers resulted in a 3–0 win, with Dickenson (2) and Cassidy finding the net to secure a semi-final tie against Wednesday at the Fallowfield Ground, Manchester.

Bolton were in excellent spirits for the semi-final tie, following a 3–2 victory at Aston Villa, while their FA Cup run continued with a 2–1 success against Wednesday, with Bentley scoring both goals to secure the Wanderers their first FA Cup Final appearance. This was to take place at Goodison Park on the final day of March against Notts County from the Second Division.

A week prior to the final, Bolton were expected to fulfil three League fixtures in four days, which resulted in drawn games at home to Nottingham Forest (1–1) and at Newton Heath (2–2), in John Sutcliffe's hundredth League appearance for the club, while Bentley and Wilson were on target in a 3–2 reverse at Everton. However, Bolton were obviously saving themselves for their FA Cup Final appearance.

WEDNESDAY

Wednesday had ended the 1892–93 League campaign in twelfth position, which was due mainly to their poor form during the final weeks of the season.

Nevertheless, the Sheffield side retained the majority of their players for the 1893–94 season as Allan continued in goal, with Harry Brandon and Billy Betts in defence, while R N Brown, Alec Brady, Harry Davis and Fred Spiksley remained in the attack, where Rowan and Woolhouse made the occasional appearance. Tom Brandon had returned to Blackburn Rovers, while his fullback partner Albert Mumford played only the odd game during the season. Their replacements, Jack Earp and Ambrose Langley, served the Sheffield side for a number of years, with Earp, a recent signing from Everton, playing in excess of 150 League games for the club as well as making an appearance for the Football League Eleven against the Irish League. Langley, who had arrived from Middlesbrough Ironopolis, made more than 300 appearances in eleven seasons with the Wednesday, many as team captain, prior to managing Hull and Huddersfield.

Further new signings included Jamieson from Everton, who played 125 League games in seven seasons, while Webster, Smith and Miller all played regularly in the attack. Wednesday opened the season with Miller scoring a brace of goals in a two-all home draw with Sunderland, which preceded defeats at Wolverhampton Wanderers (3–1) and Blackburn Rovers (5–1), as well as at home to Newton Heath (1–0), while Billy Betts found the net in a one-all draw in the return game at Sunderland.

Betts was again on target the following week in a 4–2 home reverse against West Bromwich Albion, which was followed by a 4–2 home success against Blackburn Rovers, with Davis, Webster, Miller and Spiksley scoring for the Yorkshire side, while a 4–1 defeat at Stoke continued their indifferent run of results.

Alec Brady then scored an excellent hat-trick in a 4–0 home win against Derby County, while Fred Spiksley found the net in successive away draws at Sheffield United (1–1) and Derby County (3–3). A further loss of form saw the Wednesday suffer home defeats against Sheffield United (2–1) and Wolverhampton Wanderers (4–1), as well as a 1–0 reverse at Nottingham Forest, while draws at home to Everton (1–1) and away at West Bromwich Albion (2–2) secured a couple of welcome points for the Sheffield side.

Early December saw Fred Spiksley score a brace of goals in a 4–1 home victory against Stoke, which preceded away defeats at Aston Villa (3–0) and Darwen (2–1), while Webster and Spiksley were on target in a 2–1 home win against Bolton Wanderers. However, an 8–1 reverse at Everton continued their poor away form.

Following a one-all draw at Bolton on Christmas Day, the year ended with a 1–0 home defeat against Burnley, which meant that the Sheffield side had won only four of their twenty-three League games, and they moved into the test match places. The new year coincided with a return to form for the Wednesday as they sought to avoid the end-of-season play-off games.

Wednesday's improvement began during the opening week of January as

Fred Spiksley scored twice in a two-all home draw with Aston Villa, which preceded a 2–1 victory at Newton Heath, where Woolhouse netted a brace of goals in his second League appearance of the season. Webster (2), Miller, Woolhouse and Spiksley were then on target in a 5–0 home success against Darwen.

Fred Spiksley then scored a further double in a 2–1 victory at Woolwich Arsenal in the first round of the FA Cup. He was again on target the following week in a 3–0 home win against Preston North End, which preceded a 1–0 home success against Stoke in the second round of the FA Cup, with Woolhouse scoring the only goal of the game to secure a home tie against Aston Villa in the quarter-finals.

Woolhouse and Spiksley were again amongst the scorers as Wednesday narrowly defeated Villa by the odd goal in five to earn a semi-final tie against Bolton Wanderers, while their winning run continued with a 1–0 home win against Nottingham Forest, with Harry Davis on target. Their splendid run came to an end at the Fallowfield Ground, where they suffered a 2–1 reverse against Bolton in the semi-final tie, with Woolhouse scoring his fourth FA Cup goal in as many games.

On their return to League action, Fred Spiksley found the net in a 1–0 victory at Burnley, while the season ended with a 1–0 defeat at Preston North End. Wednesday finished the campaign in twelfth position, following nine victories, eight draws and thirteen defeats in their thirty League games, while scoring forty-eight goals and conceding fifty-seven.

Goalkeeper Allan had appeared in all thirty League games, while Harry Davis, Alec Brady and Fred Spiksley had missed less than a handful in an excellent season for the Sheffield side. Fred Spiksley had led the scoring with thirteen League goals.

STOKE

Stoke had ended the 1892–93 League campaign in a creditable seventh position, which resulted in few changes in their side for the 1893–94 season, as Rowley continued in goal, with Clare, Brodie and Christie in defence, while Naughton, Billy Dickson and Joseph Schofield remained in the attack.

Evans, Proctor and Alf Underwood made very few appearances during the season, while McReddie and Eccles were the most notable newcomers in the team.

Stoke opened the campaign with a 4–1 reverse at Bolton Wanderers, followed by a 2–1 home win against Nottingham Forest. Away defeats at Aston Villa (5–1) and Darwen (3–1) continued their indifferent start to the season. However, a 3–1 home success against Derby County saw a return to winning ways for the Potteries' side.

Following a 4–0 defeat at Burnley, the Stoke team secured a 4–1 home win against the Wednesday, which preceded a 4–0 reverse at Sunderland. A three-all home draw with Aston Villa saw Joseph Schofield amongst the scorers, but further away defeats at Nottingham Forest (2–0) and West Bromwich Albion (4–2) on either side of a 3–1 home success against Blackburn Rovers saw Stoke near the foot of the League table by early November.

Stoke's excellent home record continued with victories against Burnley (4–2) and Preston North End (2–1), followed by the inevitable away defeat at Wolverhampton Wanderers (4–2), while further home wins against Darwen (3–1) and Sheffield United (5–0) saw the Potteries' side climb to a mid-table position.

Late December saw successive away defeats at the Wednesday (4–1) and Derby County (5–2), followed by a three-all draw at Preston North End on Christmas Day, while the year ended with a 3–0 home defeat against Wolverhampton Wanderers.

New Year saw the Potteries' side return to winning ways with home victories against Bolton Wanderers (5–0) and West Bromwich Albion (3–1). This was followed by a 1–0 home success against Everton in the first round of the FA Cup with Joseph Schofield scoring the only goal of the game two minutes from time to secure a second round tie at the Wednesday, which they unfortunately lost by one goal to nil.

Prior to the FA Cup tie, Stoke had earned their second away point of the season in a three-all draw at Sheffield United, which preceded a 3–1 home success against Everton, while a visit to strugglers Newton Heath ended in an embarrassing 6–2 defeat. Further home victories against Sunderland (2–0) and Newton Heath (3–1) saw the Potteries' side with sufficient points to retain their First Division status for a further season.

With their First Division future assured, Stoke ended the campaign with away defeats at Everton (6–2) and Blackburn Rovers (5–0), which left them in eleventh position following thirteen victories, three draws and fourteen defeats in their thirty League games, while scoring sixty-five goals and conceding seventy-nine.

McReddie and Brodie had appeared in all thirty League games for the Potteries' side, while Joseph Schofield had led the scoring for the third successive season with fifteen League goals. In reality, Stoke should have been challenging for the League title, if only their away form had matched their splendid performances at home, as shown in Table IX.

Table IX: *Comparison of home and away results for Stoke in the 1893–94 season*

	Played	Won	Lost	Drawn	For	Against	Points
Stoke – at home	15	13	1	1	45	17	27
Stoke – away	15	0	13	2	20	62	2

WOLVERHAMPTON WANDERERS

Wolverhampton Wanderers had tended to struggle in the League during the

1892–93 season. However, following their FA Cup success, the Wanderers made few changes in their team for the 1893–94 League campaign. William Rose continued in goal, with Richard Baugh, Billy Malpass, Harry Allen, George Kinsey and George Swift in defence, while David Wykes, Harry Wood, Joe Butcher and Alf Griffin remained up front.

Richard Topham had returned to college, while the most notable newcomers were Griffiths, Edge and Black, who all made regular appearances during the season, with Griffiths and Black remaining with the Wolverhampton side until the end of the century.

Wanderers opened the season with a humiliating 7–1 defeat at Nottingham Forest, followed by successive home wins against Wednesday (3–1), Bolton Wanderers (2–1) and Darwen (2–1), which saw them amongst the front runners during the early stages of the campaign. However, their joy was short-lived as they suffered defeats at Blackburn Rovers (3–0) and at home to Sheffield United (4–3).

Then followed a goalless draw at West Bromwich Albion, which preceded a 3–1 home success against Nottingham Forest, while their indifferent away form continued with a 2–0 reverse at Bolton Wanderers. They soon returned to winning ways, though, with a 2–0 home victory against the struggling Newton Heath team.

Early November saw further defeats at Sunderland (6–0) and Newton Heath (1–0), which were followed by a seven-game unbeaten run, including away wins at the Wednesday (4–1) and Preston North End (3–1), as well as home victories against Stoke (4–2), Everton (2–0), Blackburn Rovers (5–1) and Aston Villa (3–0). A goalless home draw with Preston North End saw the only point dropped by the Wolverhampton side during their excellent run of results.

Wanderers then suffered an embarrassing 8–0 home defeat against West Bromwich Albion, prior to ending the year with a 3–0 victory at Stoke. The new year began with a 2–1 home success against Sunderland, but successive defeats at Sheffield United (3–2) and Derby County (4–1), as well as at home in the return game with Derby (4–2), saw Wolves move down to a mid-table position with five League games remaining.

Following a 4–2 reverse at Aston Villa in the first round of the FA Cup, Wanderers secured a 1–0 home win against Burnley, which preceded away defeats at Darwen (3–1), Everton (3–0) and Burnley (4–2), as well as a one-all draw at Aston Villa. They ended the campaign in ninth position, with fourteen victories, three draws and thirteen defeats in their thirty League games, while scoring fifty-two goals and conceding sixty-three.

Harry Wood had appeared in all thirty League games for Wolves, while Wykes, Swift, Rose, Kinsey and Butcher had missed only a few in a most disappointing season. Harry Wood had netted eleven League goals, with Joe Butcher leading the scoring with sixteen, but the Wanderers Committee were extremely unhappy with the players' performances during the season. This led to a number of changes in the team for the 1894–95 League campaign.

WEST BROMWICH ALBION

West Bromwich Albion had achieved little success during the 1892–93 season, yet the Black Country side made few changes in their line-up for the 1893–94 League campaign. Joe Reader continued in goal, with Tom Perry, Charlie Perry and Nicholson in defence, while Nicholls, Bostock, Tom Pearson, Jasper Geddes, Billy Bassett and Roddy McLeod competed for the forward positions.

John Reynolds and Willie Groves had decided to join Aston Villa, while the most notable newcomers were Crone and Taggart in defence, as well as centre forward Williams, who scored seven goals in ten League appearances during the season.

Albion opened the season with a 3–2 reverse at Aston Villa, which preceded successive victories at home to Newton Heath (3–1) and at Derby County (3–2), with Nicholls and McLeod on target in both wins, while McLeod scored for the third game running in a one-all home draw with Burnley. Billy Bassett and Jasper Geddes then scored a couple of goals apiece in a 4–2 victory at the Wednesday, while McLeod (2) and Bassett found the net in a further away success at Nottingham Forest (3–2). Following a goalless home draw with Wolverhampton Wanderers, the West Bromwich side suffered successive defeats at Newton Heath (4–1) and at home to Aston Villa (6–3), which saw them move down to a mid-table position.

Late October saw Albion return to winning ways, as Neale and Bassett scored in a 2–0 victory at Sheffield United, which was followed by a 4–2 home win against Stoke, with Charlie Perry (2), Nicholls and McLeod on target. Tom Pearson then netted four goals in a 5–2 home success against Bolton Wanderers, but away defeats at Darwen (2–1) and Sunderland (2–1), as well as a two-all home draw with the Wednesday, halted Albion's climb up the League table.

Inside forward Norman, making a rare appearance in the Albion team, then scored a brace of goals in a 2–0 home success against Preston North End, which preceded a 3–0 defeat at Burnley, while a two-all home draw with Darwen, as well as a 3–2 home defeat against Sunderland, saw Albion continue their indifferent run of results.

Boxing Day saw the West Bromwich side secure a 3–1 home win against Sheffield United, with Bassett, Pearson and Norman on target, while an 8–0 victory at Wolverhampton Wanderers saw their finest away win of the campaign with Billy Bassett and Roddy McLeod scoring hat-tricks. However, a 7–1 reverse at Everton in the final game of the year ended their hopes of a top three League finish.

Albion soon returned to form with a 2–1 home success against Blackburn Rovers, with Williams and Hadley finding the net, which was followed by successive away defeats in the return game at Blackburn (3–0) and at Stoke (3–1). The Black Country side suffered a 3–2 reverse against Blackburn in the first round of the FA Cup in their third meeting in as many weeks against the Lancashire side, with Roddy McLeod scoring both Albion goals.

On their return to League action, Williams (2) and Pearson were on target in a 3–1 home win against Everton, which preceded successive defeats at Preston North End (3–1) and at home to Derby County (1–0), while Williams (2) and Bostock found the net in a 3–0 home win against Nottingham Forest.

Albion then ended the campaign with a 3–0 victory at Bolton Wanderers, with goals by Bostock (2) and Geddes securing an eighth place League finish for the West Bromwich side, following fourteen victories, four draws and twelve defeats in their thirty League games, while scoring sixty-six goals and conceding fifty-nine.

Joe Reader, Charlie Perry and Roddy McLeod had appeared in all but one League game during the season. Pearson, Geddes and Williams ended the campaign with seven League goals apiece; Billy Bassett had found the net on eleven occasions; while Roddy McLeod had led the scoring with fourteen League goals in a further disappointing season for Albion.

NOTTINGHAM FOREST

Nottingham Forest had ended the 1892–93 League campaign in a respectable mid-table position, which resulted in few changes in their side for the 1893–94 season. Dennis Allsopp continued in goal, with Archie Ritchie, Adam Scott, McCracken and John MacPherson in defence, while McCallum, Shaw, Pike, Sandy Higgins and Tom McInnes, remained in the attack. Newcomers included inside forward James Collins and defender Alexander Stewart, who both gave excellent service to the Nottingham club, with Collins scoring fifteen goals in forty appearances, which included a hat-trick on his League debut, while Stewart would play in excess of one hundred games in his four seasons with the club.

Forest opened the season with a 7–1 home win against Wolverhampton Wanderers, with James Collins scoring the aforementioned hat-trick. This was followed by successive away defeats at Everton (4–0) and Stoke (2–1), while McCallum (2), McInnes, Scott and Collins found the net in a 5–0 home success against Burnley.

Sandy Higgins then scored his opening League goal of the season in a one-all draw at Newton Heath, which preceded a 3–2 home defeat against West Bromwich Albion, while Tom McInnes scored the only goal of the game in a 1–0 home win against Bolton Wanderers. However, successive defeats at Wolverhampton Wanderers (3–1) and at home to Aston Villa (3–1) saw the Nottingham side move into the bottom half of the League table.

Then followed a brace of goals by James Collins in a 2–0 home success against Stoke, which preceded a further home win against the Wednesday

(1–0), with McInnes scoring the only goal of the game. A 3–1 reverse at Burnley, as well as successive home draws against Sheffield United (1–1) and Blackburn Rovers (0–0), continued Forest's indifferent run of results.

Forest returned to winning ways on the second day of December with a 2–0 victory at Preston North End, where Collins and 'Tich' Smith found the net, which preceded a further away success at Derby County (4–3), with McInnes (2), Higgins and Pike on target, while Sandy Higgins netted a brace of goals in a third successive away win at Darwen (4–0).

James Collins then scored his ninth and tenth League goals of the season in a 4–2 victory in the return game with Derby County, while MacPherson and Pike found the net in a 2–0 success at Sheffield United on New Year's day. However, a 2–1 home defeat against Sunderland ended their seven-game unbeaten run.

Following a 3–2 home win against Everton in which McInnes, Brodie and Pike were on target, centre forward Brodie netted the only goal of the game in a 1–0 home success against Heanor Town in the first round of the FA Cup. Horace Pike then scored a consolation goal in a 6–1 reverse at Blackburn Rovers. However, Forest's FA Cup run continued with a 2–0 home victory against Middlesbrough Ironopolis with goals by Brodie and Higgins securing a home tie against neighbours Notts County in the third round.

Forest were a little fortunate to hold County to a one-all draw, prior to suffering a 4–1 defeat in the replay, to end their interest in the competition. A 1–0 reverse at the Wednesday continued their indifferent form, but a 4–1 home victory against the struggling Darwen side saw a return to winning ways with Collins, Brodie, McInnes and Higgins on target for the Nottingham side.

Mid-March saw Forest suffer a 2–0 defeat at Sunderland, which preceded a one-all away draw at Bolton Wanderers, while centre half John MacPherson scored an excellent hat-trick in a 4–2 home win against Preston North End as Forest moved up to fifth place in the League table. However, successive away defeats at West Bromwich Albion (3–0) and Aston Villa (3–1) on either side of a 2–0 home success against Newton Heath saw the Nottingham side end the campaign in seventh position, with Brodie scoring both goals in the victory against the Manchester side.

Forest had won fourteen, drawn four and lost twelve of their thirty League games, while scoring fifty-seven goals and conceding forty-eight. James Collins found the net on eleven occasions, while Tom McInnes had led the scoring with a dozen League goals.

Archie Ritchie had appeared in all thirty League games, while Adam Scott, John MacPherson, James Collins and Alexander Stewart had missed only one in a season when the Nottingham team had proved that they were as capable as any other side in the First Division.

EVERTON

Following their third place League finish, as well as an appearance in the 1893

FA Cup Final, Everton made few changes in their line-up for the 1893–94 season. Williams continued in goal, with Bob Kelso, Bob Howarth, Richard Boyle and John Holt in defence, while Alex Latta, Alf Milward, Edgar Chadwick and Fred Geary remained in the attack.

Newcomers in the Everton side included Scottish defender Billy Stewart from Preston North End, as well as inside forward John Bell, who had been a member of Dumbarton's Scottish Championship winning side of 1892. The most notable new signing was John Southworth from Blackburn Rovers for a fee of £400.

Stewart, who had previously won an Irish FA Cup winners' medal with Belfast Distillery, made nearly 150 appearances for Everton, prior to joining Bristol City towards the turn of the century, while John Bell would play 199 games in an Everton shirt in two spells with the club, as well as appearing for the Scottish national side on ten occasions.

John Southworth had been a major capture by the Everton club. However, while he would continue to score on a regular basis, a serious leg injury led to his premature retirement from the game, following just thirty-one League appearances in which he would score on thirty-six occasions.

Everton opened the season with a 3–2 home defeat against Sheffield United, with Latta and Milward on target, while McMillan (2), Boyle and Milward found the net in a 4–0 home success against Nottingham Forest. A 7–3 reverse at Derby County continued their indifferent start to the campaign with John Southworth scoring a debut goal for the well-beaten Lancashire side.

Then followed a 4–2 home win against Aston Villa with Bell, Kelso, McMillan and Walker on target, while Villa reversed the result the following week with a 3–1 victory at Perry Barr. This preceded a magnificent 7–1 home success against Sunderland, with Chadwick (3), Latta (2), Milward and Southworth netting the Everton goals, but a 2–1 defeat at Burnley soon ended their celebrations.

Alf Milward then scored his fifth League goal of the campaign in a two-all home draw with Blackburn Rovers, with Southworth completing the scoring. This was followed by an 8–1 home win against the struggling Darwen team, with Latta (2), Maxwell (2), Southworth (2), Bell and Chadwick on target, while John Southworth scored a further brace of goals in a 3–2 home defeat against Preston North End.

Early November saw a further Alf Milward goal secure a one-all draw at the Wednesday, which preceded a 2–1 home reverse against Derby County, while Bell, Chadwick and Geary then shared the goals in successive victories at home to Burnley (4–3) and at Newton Heath (3–0).

Everton then reached the halfway stage of the season with a 2–0 defeat at Wolverhampton Wanderers, which was followed by a 3–0 victory at Sheffield United with Southworth netting a brace of goals, while Bell, Chadwick and

Southworth found the net in a 4–3 reverse at Blackburn Rovers. However, an excellent end to the year saw Everton register successive home victories against Wednesday (8–1) and West Bromwich Albion (7–1), with John Southworth scoring ten of the Everton goals.

New Year's Day saw Everton secure a three-all draw at Darwen, which preceded victories at home to Newton Heath (2–0) and at Preston North End (4–2), with Chadwick and Southworth on target in all three games. Successive away defeats at Nottingham Forest (3–2), West Bromwich Albion (3–1), Sunderland (1–0) and Stoke (3–1), as well as a first round FA Cup defeat at Stoke (1–0), saw Everton in the bottom half of the League table with four games remaining.

Late March saw Everton return to winning ways with a 3–0 home win against Wolverhampton Wanderers, with Geary (2) and Southworth finding the net, which preceded a further home victory against Bolton Wanderers (3–2), with Chadwick, Hartley and Southworth on target. Geary (2), Latta (2), McMillan and Hartley then scored in a third successive home win against Stoke (6–2).

Everton then ended the season with a 1–0 victory at Bolton Wanderers, with outside right Reay, making his only League appearance for the club and scoring the only goal of the game. The Liverpool side ended in sixth position, following fifteen wins, three draws and twelve defeats in their thirty League games, while scoring ninety goals and conceding fifty-seven. Alf Milward and Fred Geary ended the campaign with eight League goals apiece; John Bell and Alex Latta both scored on nine occasions; Edgar Chadwick finished the season with thirteen goals; while the ever reliable John Southworth led the scoring with twenty-seven goals in twenty-two League appearances in a further entertaining season for the Everton supporters.

BURNLEY

Burnley had ended the 1892–93 League campaign in a creditable sixth position, which resulted in few changes in their team for the 1893–94 season. Jack Hillman continued in goal, with Lang, Mathew and Bowes in defence, while Lambie, Place and Crabtree were once again the mainstays of the attack.

The season opened with a 3–2 reverse at Newton Heath, followed by successive home wins against Darwen (5–1) and Preston North End (4–1), while a 5–0 defeat at Nottingham Forest continued their indifferent start to the campaign. However, following a one-all draw at West Bromwich Albion, the Lancashire side returned to winning ways with home victories against Stoke (4–0) and Everton (2–1).

Burnley's first away success of the season was a 2–1 victory at Preston North End, which preceded a further home win against Newton Heath (4–1), while a 4–0 reverse at Aston Villa confirmed Burnley's reputation as poor travellers.

Then followed a 3–1 home victory against Nottingham Forest, while successive away defeats at Stoke (4–2), Blackburn Rovers (3–2) and Everton (4–3) saw them struggling to maintain their mid-table League position. Then, a six-game unbeaten run during December enabled the Lancashire side to begin the new year in a top six position.

Burnley's excellent run of results saw home wins against Sunderland (1–0), West Bromwich Albion (3–0), Blackburn Rovers (1–0) and Sheffield United (4–1), as well as a two-all draw in the return game at Sunderland. The year ended with a 1–0 success at the Wednesday. However, their poor away form continued into the new year with a 2–0 defeat at Bolton Wanderers.

Following their usual defeat in the first round of the FA Cup, Burnley secured a 2–1 victory in the return game with Bolton Wanderers, which preceded a goalless draw at Darwen. March began with a 1–0 reverse at Wolverhampton Wanderers, but a 3–1 home win against Derby County continued their excellent home form.

Late March saw the Lancashire side suffer successive defeats at home to the Wednesday (1–0) and away at Sheffield United (1–0), which preceded a three-all draw at Derby County. A 6–3 reverse against Aston Villa saw a rare home defeat, and a 4–2 home win against Wolverhampton Wanderers in the final game of the campaign saw Burnley finish the season in fifth place, with fifteen victories, four draws and eleven defeats in their thirty League games, while scoring sixty-one goals and conceding fifty-one.

While Burnley had enjoyed an excellent League campaign, their indifferent away form had cost them the opportunity of challenging for the League Championship, as their home and away record shows in Table X.

Table X: *Burnley's home and away performance in the 1893–94 season*

	Played	Won	Lost	Drawn	For	Against	Points
Home	15	13	2	0	43	17	26
Away	15	2	9	4	18	34	8

BLACKBURN ROVERS

Blackburn Rovers' indifferent League performances had long mystified their supporters, who had been used to regular success in the FA Cup competition. However, Rovers' team of international players had usually entertained the spectators, even if it meant conceding as many goals as they scored.

Rovers' line-up for the 1893–94 League campaign saw few changes, but the new season heralded a new era, as four stalwarts of the club either left or retired from the Association game. Goalkeeper Herbie Arthur had decided to retire owing to a number of injuries, while Nat Walton, who had replaced Arthur between the posts during the 1892–93 season, had joined Darwen following a disagreement over wages.

John Forbes made two appearances during the season, prior to retiring owing to ill-health, while the free-scoring John Southworth had moved to Everton for a fee of £400. However, the Lancashire side retained Murray, Dewar, Anderson, Marshall and James Forrest in defence, while Campbell, Hall and Chippendale continued up front.

Watts began the campaign in goal, soon to be replaced by Ogilvie, who made in excess of one hundred appearances in five seasons with the club, while outside right Whitehead, who had played one League game during the previous campaign, became a regular member of the attack.

Billy Townley had returned to the side following his unavailability during the previous season, while Tom Brandon, the former captain, rejoined the Blackburn club towards the end of the year following a spell with the Wednesday.

Rovers began the campaign with successive victories at Darwen (3–2) and at home to the Wednesday (5–1), with Campbell and Chippendale on target in both games. This preceded a 2–1 defeat at Bolton Wanderers, while Whitehead (2) and Chippendale found the net in a further home success against Wolverhampton Wanderers (3–0).

Josh Hargreaves then netted a brace of goals in a 4–2 defeat at the Wednesday, which was followed by a 1–0 home win against Preston North End, with Whitehead scoring the only goal of the game. Hargreaves scored two further goals in a two-all draw at Everton.

October's end saw Billy Townley score a couple of goals in a 4–3 home success against Sunderland, which preceded a 3–1 reverse at Stoke. Successive home wins against Aston Villa (2–0) and Burnley (3–2), as well as a 1–0 victory at Preston North End, saw Blackburn in third place in the League table by the end of November with Whitehead, Hall, Townley and Chippendale sharing the Blackburn goals.

Following a goalless draw at Nottingham Forest, Rovers suffered a 1–0 home defeat against Bolton Wanderers, while Chippendale, Sorley and Townley all netted a couple of goals apiece as Blackburn secured victories at Sunderland (3–2) and at home to Everton (4–3).

Blackburn then suffered a 1–0 reverse at Burnley, prior to enjoying a 4–1 home victory against Darwen on Christmas Day, with Sorley (2), Whitehead and Hall on target, while the year ended with a 5–1 defeat at Wolverhampton Wanderers as Rovers struggled to maintain their challenge for League honours.

New Year began with a 2–1 reverse at West Bromwich Albion, which was avenged the following week as Blackburn inflicted a 3–0 defeat on the West Bromwich side, with Hall, Chippendale and Anderson on target. A 4–1 home success against Sheffield United continued their excellent home form, with inside forward Haydock, making a rare appearance in the first team and scoring a brace of goals.

Rovers were then drawn away at West Bromwich Albion in the first round of the FA Cup where Calvey, Forrest and Chippendale found the net in a 3–0 victory to secure a second round tie at Newton Heath.

Prior to the FA Cup tie, Harry Chippendale netted a hat-trick in a 6–1 home win against Nottingham Forest, while the cup game ended goalless following a period of extra time. However, Blackburn had few difficulties in the replay as Whitehead (2), Chippendale, Haydock and Calvey were on target in a 5–1 success to earn a difficult tie at Derby County in the quarter-finals.

Blackburn enjoyed a relatively easy victory at Derby where Hayock (3) and Townley scored in a 4–1 win to secure a second successive semi-final appearance. However, a poor run of results saw the Lancashire side suffer five defeats in a row, which included the semi-final tie that they were odds-on favourites to win.

Rovers' loss of form began with a 3–2 reverse at Sheffield United, followed by a surprising 1–0 defeat against Notts County in the semi-final of the FA Cup. Further defeats at Newton Heath (5–1), as well as at home to Derby County (2–0) and Aston Villa (2–1), saw them move down to sixth place in the League table. However, Blackburn eventually returned to winning ways during the final week of March with a 4–0 home victory against Newton Heath with Hargreaves (2), Haydock and Chippendale on target.

Following a 5–2 defeat at Derby County, the Lancashire side ended the season with a 5–0 home success against Stoke. These goals by Whitehead (2), Sorley (2) and Marshall secured a fourth place League finish for Blackburn, following sixteen victories, two draws and twelve defeats in their thirty League games, while scoring sixty-nine goals and conceding fifty-three.

Josh Hargreaves had ended the campaign with nine goals in seventeen League appearances, Billy Townley had found the net on ten occasions, while Harry Chippendale had led the scoring with fourteen League goals in an excellent season. Murrey, Forrest, Anderson, Marshall, Chippendale and Hall had missed no more than a handful of games. However, Blackburn may well have achieved the FA Cup and League double if only they had retained the services of John Southworth.

DERBY COUNTY

Derby County had been involved in a struggle to avoid relegation in each of the five previous seasons, which greatly disappointed their supporters, who expected a little more success from a team who could boast half a dozen international players in their line-up.

Few changes were made by the East Midlands side for the 1893–94 season. John Robinson continued in goal, with Jimmy Methven, Joseph Leiper, John Cox and Archie Goodall in defence, while Steve Bloomer, John Goodall and John McMillan remained in the attack. Outside right Mills had left the Derby club, while Hickinbottom and Walter Roulstone made very few appearances during the season, but they were adequately replaced by Allan, Docherty and Keay, albeit for a little more than the season.

Derby opened the season with a 1–0 reverse at Preston North End, which preceded a 2–1 success at Sheffield United where Bloomer and McMillan found the net, while both players netted a brace of goals apiece in a 7–3 home win against Everton with Keay, Allan and Archie Goodall completing the scoring.

Then followed successive defeats at home to West Bromwich Albion (3–2) and away at Stoke (3–1), which preceded a one-all draw at Aston Villa, where John Goodall scored for the visitors. John McMillan secured his fourth League goal of the season in a 2–0 home win against Newton Heath, but a 4–0 reverse at the Wednesday continued their indifferent run of results.

Steve Bloomer then scored a brace of goals in a three-all draw in the return game with Wednesday, which was followed by a 5–0 reverse at Sunderland. However, a return to form during November saw Derby register successive home wins against Sheffield United (2–1) and Darwen (2–1), as well as at Everton (2–1), with Steve Bloomer on target in all three victories.

Early December saw the Derby side suffer home defeats against Aston Villa (3–0) and Nottingham Forest (4–3), which were followed by a 5–2 home success against Stoke with Bloomer (2), Allan, John Goodall and Archie Goodall scoring for County. Both Goodall brothers found the net in a 6–1 home win against Bolton Wanderers with John McMillan scoring a hat-trick.

Derby ended the year with a 4–2 reverse at Nottingham Forest, while Archie Goodall netted his fifth League goal of the campaign in a one-all draw at Bolton Wanderers, which preceded victories at home to Preston North End (2–1) and at Wolverhampton Wanderers (4–2) with McMillan and Bloomer again on target in both wins.

Following their fine start to the new year, Derby's excellent run of results continued in the FA Cup, with a 2–0 home win against Darwen in the first round with McMillan and John Goodall on target, while Allan (2), Bloomer and McMillan found the net in a 4–1 League success in the return game with Wolverhampton Wanderers.

County were then drawn against Leicester Fosse in the second round of the FA Cup, with the game ending in a goalless draw. However, Derby won the replay with ease as Allan, Francis and McMillan scored in a 3–0 victory to secure a home tie against Blackburn Rovers in the quarter-finals. This resulted in a 4–1 defeat for Derby, to end their interest in the competition.

On their return to League action, Derby suffered successive defeats at home to Sunderland (4–1) and away at Burnley (3–1), which left them in a mid-table position. Yet an excellent run of results during the final weeks of the campaign saw County challenging for the runners-up position at the season's end.

Following a 6–2 away win at Newton Heath, in which John McMillan netted his second hat-trick of the season, the East Midlands side secured further away victories at Blackburn Rovers (2–0) and West Bromwich Albion (1–0), with Francis on target in both games. Bloomer (2), Cox, Francis and

John Goodall found the net in a 5–2 success in the return game with Blackburn Rovers.

County then shared six goals with Burnley in the final home game of the season, with McMillan, Allan and John Goodall on target. The campaign ended with a 3–2 win at Darwen with goals by McMillan (2) and John Goodall. This secured a third place League finish for Derby following sixteen victories, four draws and ten defeats in their thirty League games, while scoring seventy-three goals and conceding sixty-two.

Inside forward Francis had found the net on five occasions in eight League appearances; John Goodall had ended the campaign with a dozen League goals; John McMillan had netted eighteen goals; while Steve Bloomer had led the scoring with nineteen goals in twenty-five League games in Derby's finest season to date, in which Methven, Allan, McMillan and Archie Goodall had appeared in all thirty League games.

SUNDERLAND

Sunderland had won the League Championship in each of the two previous seasons, which resulted in few changes in their team for the 1893–94 League campaign. John Doig continued in goal, with Gibson, Wilson and John Auld in defence, while Harvey, Millar, Gillespie, Campbell, Scott, James Hannah and David Hannah once again competed for the forward positions. Donald Gow had returned to the club following a spell with Glasgow Rangers, while Billy Dunlop, who remained with the north-eastern side for seven seasons, had arrived from the Annbank club. Fullback Smellie had moved to pastures new, while his fullback partner Tom Porteous made just two League appearances during the season, prior to being replaced by Meehan, a Scottish international defender from Glasgow Celtic.

Sunderland opened the season with a two-all draw at the Wednesday with James Hannah scoring both goals for the visitors, which preceded a one-all home draw with Aston Villa with Millar on target for the north-eastern side. Then James Hannah and James Gillespie found the net in a 2–1 success at Preston North End.

Then followed Sunderland's third draw in four starts in a one-all draw in the return game with Wednesday, with Millar on target, which preceded successive away defeats at Everton (7–1) and Sheffield United (1–0). A 4–0 home success against Stoke saw a return to winning ways with Millar (2), Campbell and David Hannah scoring for the home side. However, a 4–3 reverse at Blackburn Rovers continued their indifferent run of results.

Late October saw an excellent 5–0 home win against Derby County with Gibson, Auld, Gillespie, Millar and David Hannah on target. Millar (3), David Hannah (2) and Scott netted the following week in a 6–0 home victory against Wolverhampton Wanderers, but a 2–1 defeat at Aston Villa continued their poor away form.

Johnny Campbell then scored twice in a 2–1 home success against West

Bromwich Albion, which preceded a further away defeat at Burnley (1–0), while Millar and Campbell netted a brace of goals apiece in a 4–1 home win against the struggling Newton Heath side. This was followed by a 3–2 home defeat against Blackburn Rovers.

Following a two-all home draw with Burnley, the north-eastern side secured a rare away win at West Bromwich Albion (3–2) with Campbell, Millar and James Hannah scoring for the title holders, while the year ended with a 2–1 home victory against Bolton Wanderers, with Gillespie and Harvey on target for Sunderland.

New Year's Day saw a 6–3 home success against Preston North End, with Johnny Campbell and James Hannah scoring a couple of goals apiece. This was followed by a 2–1 reverse at Wolverhampton Wanderers, while a 2–1 win at Nottingham Forest commenced a run of six wins in a row as the north-eastern side mounted a late challenge to retain the League Championship. Sunderland's splendid home form continued with a 4–1 victory against Sheffield United with Campbell (2), Millar and Gow on target, which preceded a 3–0 home win against Accrington in the first round of the FA Cup, with goals by Wilson, Gillespie and James Hannah securing a second round home tie with Aston Villa. Their excellent League form continued with a 1–0 home success against Everton, with James Gillespie scoring the only goal of the game.

Villa performed magnificently at Sunderland to secure a two-all draw with Wilson and Harvey netting for the north-eastern side, while the Midlanders won the replay by three goals to one. However, Sunderland soon returned to form with a 4–2 victory at Newton Heath, with James Hannah (2), Millar and Campbell scoring for the visitors. Jimmy Millar then scored a couple of goals in a 4–1 victory at Derby County, which preceded a 2–0 home success against Nottingham Forest, with Millar and Hyslop on target, while a 2–0 reverse at Stoke ended their winning run.

Following home and away victories against Darwen (3–0 and 3–0) in which James Gillespie netted in both games, Sunderland ended the season with a 2–0 reverse at Bolton Wanderers. Hence they finished as League runners-up, with seventeen wins, four draws and nine defeats in their thirty League games, while scoring seventy-two goals and conceding forty-four.

James Hannah and James Gillespie had ended the season with eight League goals apiece, Johnny Campbell had found the net on seventeen occasions, while Jimmy Millar had led the scoring with twenty League goals. While second place would have been quite acceptable to the majority of teams in the First Division, for Sunderland it meant disappointment following their previous success.

ASTON VILLA

Aston Villa had hardly mounted a serious challenge for the League title during the previous five seasons, which resulted in a number of changes in their line-up for the 1893–94 League campaign. Billy Evans left the club, while Gersham Cox had signed for Willenhall Pickwick, thus enabling John Baird to command a regular place in the first team to partner James Welford, a recent signing from Mitchell's St George's.

Welford made seventy-nine League appearances for Villa prior to joining Glasgow Celtic, with whom he gained a Scottish FA Cup winners' medal to add to his Irish and English FA Cup winners' medals.

Albert Woolley, who had made the occasional appearance during the previous campaign, and Steve Smith, who had arrived from the Cannock area, shared the left wing position, with Smith winning many League and FA Cup honours with the club as well as appearing in the English national side.

Further signings included Bob Chatt from Middlesbrough Ironopolis, who enjoyed five successful years with the Midlands side prior to joining Stockton as an amateur player, while the most notable newcomers were John Reynolds and Willie Groves from West Bromwich Albion, for a combined fee of fifty pounds. Groves remained with Villa for a little more than a season, while Reynolds made in excess of one hundred appearances for the club, in which he won many honours, as well as further England caps. Despite the numerous changes in the Villa side, Bill Dunning retained his place in goal, with James Cowan at the heart of the defence, while England internationals Charlie Athersmith, John Devey and Dennis Hodgetts remained in the attack.

Villa opened the campaign with a 3–2 home win against West Bromwich Albion with Woolley, Reynolds (penalty) and John Devey on target, which preceded a one-all draw at Sunderland, with Dennis Hodgetts scoring for the visitors. Their excellent start continued with a 5–1 home success against Stoke, with Hodgetts (2), Woolley (2) and Logan finding the net. However, a 4–2 reverse at Everton ended their unbeaten run.

Then followed a 3–1 victory in the return game with Everton with Woolley (2) and Athersmith netting the Villa goals, while a John Reynolds goal secured a one-all home draw with Derby County. A 3–0 defeat at Sheffield United then continued their indifferent away form.

John Devey found the net in a 2–1 success at Nottingham Forest, with Willie Groves completing the scoring, while Devey was again on target in successive away draws at Darwen (1–1) and Stoke (3–3). This preceded a further away victory at West Bromwich Albion (6–3), with Devey (2), Cowan, Hare, Athersmith and Woolley scoring for the visitors.

Following a run of five successive away games, the Villa team returned to Perry Barr where they secured a 4–0 win against Burnley, with Smith, Devey, Hare and Woolley on target, while Hare netted a hat-trick a couple of days later in a 4–0 home success against Sheffield United. While Hare had proved a capable goal scorer, he struggled to command a regular first team place, as twenty-six League appearances in four seasons confirmed.

Villa's unbeaten run came to an end with a 2–0 defeat at Blackburn Rovers, which preceded a 2–1 home success against Sunderland with Devey and Reynolds (penalty) on target. Hare then scored the only goal of the game in a 1–0 victory at Bolton Wanderers.

Hare and Devey once again found the net in a 2–0 home win against Preston North End, while Dennis Hodgetts and Charlie Athersmith scored in successive victories at Derby County (3–0) and at home to the Wednesday (3–0).

Mitchell, the Newton Heath defender, then netted a couple of own goals as Villa secured a 3–1 win in Manchester, which preceded a 3–0 reverse at Wolverhampton Wanderers. The year ended with a 9–0 home win against the struggling Darwen team with goals by Devey (2), Brown (2), Hodgetts (2), Athersmith, Smith and Reynolds maintaining Villa's position at the top of the League table.

New Year saw the Midlands side secure a two-all draw at the Wednesday, with Reynolds and Woolley on target, which was followed by a 5–2 success at Preston North End with Devey (2), Cowan (2) and Hodgetts scoring for Villa. Their excellent run of results continued in the FA Cup with a 4–2 home win against Wolverhampton Wanderers in the opening round, with goals by Devey (2), Chatt and Cowan earning a second round tie at Sunderland.

Prior to the FA Cup tie, John Devey netted a hat-trick in a 5–1 home victory against Newton Heath, while the cup game ended in a two-all draw, with Cowan and Hodgetts finding the net. However, the Midlanders had few difficulties in the replay in a 3–1 success, with Athersmith, Hodgetts and Chatt on target to secure a quarter-final tie at the Wednesday.

Villa then suffered a 3–2 defeat at the Wednesday on a quagmire of a pitch, with Bob Chatt netting both goals. Chatt scored a further brace of goals in a 3–2 home defeat against Bolton Wanderers, but a 2–1 home success against Blackburn Rovers saw a return to winning ways with Bob Chatt scoring twice for the third game in a row.

Charlie Athersmith then netted his ninth League goal of the campaign in a one-all home draw with Wolverhampton Wanderers, which preceded a 6–3 win at Burnley with Groves, Hodgetts and Devey scoring a brace of goals apiece. The campaign ended with a 3–1 home success against Nottingham Forest, with Athersmith, Chatt and Devey on target to secure Villa's first League Championship title by a margin of six points from Sunderland.

Villa had suffered only five defeats in thirty League games, while scoring eighty-four goals and conceding forty-two, with Hare and Reynolds ending the campaign with seven League goals apiece; Woolley had found the net on eight occasions in fourteen appearances; Charlie Athersmith had netted ten goals; Dennis Hodgetts had scored a dozen goals; while John Devey had once again led the scoring with twenty League goals. James Cowan had been the only ever present in the Villa side, while John Baird, Dennis Hodgetts and John Devey had missed only one game in the Midlanders' finest season to date. The efforts of George Ramsay, Archie Hunter, William McGregor and Frederick Rinder had at last been rewarded.

The Race for the Second Division League Title

The race for the 1893–94 Second Division League title tended to be dominated by the newly elected Liverpool team, while reigning champions Small Heath, together with Notts County, who had lost their First Division status during the previous campaign, were amongst the Second Division front runners.

Burton Swifts' excellent home form saw victories against Woolwich Arsenal (6–2), Crewe (6–1), Ardwick (5–0), Walsall Town Swifts (8–5), Middlesbrough Ironopolis (7–0), Burslem Port Vale (5–3) and Northwich Victoria (6–2). However, an indifferent away record saw a sixth place League finish for the Staffordshire side.

Grimsby were another team to perform splendidly at home, which resulted in only two defeats, as well as seven-goal victories against Rotherham Town and Northwich Victoria. However, poor results on their travels saw the north-eastern side end the campaign in fifth position.

Notts County's Excellent FA Cup Run

Notts County made a number of changes in their line-up for the 1893–94 season, which saw Jimmy Oswald leave the club following a dispute over wages, while Arthur Watson arrived from Mansfield Town together with Sam Donnelly and George Kerr from north of the border.

Theophilus Harper became a regular member of the first team following a spell in the reserves, while England international Harry Daft, who had settled his differences with the club, returned to the side.

County opened the season with four successive victories, due mainly to the goal-scoring exploits of Jimmy Logan, a recent signing from Aston Villa, who scored twice on his debut in a 3–0 success at Grimsby, as well as a hat-trick in a 6–1 victory against Burslem Port Vale.

While County suffered occasional defeats during the season, which included a surprise home reverse against Lincoln, the Nottingham side enjoyed many excellent performances in the FA Cup, with a Jimmy Logan goal securing a 1–0 home win against Burnley in the first round, while Donnelly and Logan found the net in a second round victory against Burton Wanderers (2–0) to earn a quarter-final tie at neighbours Nottingham Forest. Following a one-all draw at Forest, County had few difficulties in the replay as goals by Bruce (2), Logan and Donnelly secured a 4–1 victory to earn a semi-final tie against Blackburn Rovers at Bramall Lane. Rovers were odds-on favourites to win the semi-final. However, County managed a 1–0 win, with Harry Daft scoring the only goal of the game to secure a second FA Cup Final appearance for the Nottingham side. This was scheduled to take place at Goodison Park on the final day of March against Bolton Wanderers.

Further Success for Small Heath

Small Heath had been surprisingly beaten by Newton Heath in the 1892–93 test match games. However, the club committee decided to keep faith with the players who had secured the Second Division title, as Billy Ollis, Caesar Jenkyns and Ted Devey continued in defence, while Jack Hallam, Billy Walton, Fred Wheldon, Frank Mobley and Tommy Hands once again formed the attack. England international goalkeeper Chris Charsley made only four League appearances during the season prior to announcing his retirement from the game, with Hollis replacing him between the posts.

Small Heath's season opened with successive victories at home to Rotherham Town (4–3), Burton Swifts (6–1) and Walsall Town Swifts (4–0), as well as away in the return game at Walsall Town Swifts (3–1). This was followed by away defeats at Liverpool (3–1) and Burslem Port Vale (5–0). However, the Birmingham side secured twenty-one victories in their twenty-eight League games, which included wins against Grimsby Town (5–2), Burton Swifts (6–1), Burslem Port Vale (6–0), Ardwick (10–2), Crewe (6–1 and 5–3), Lincoln (5–2 and 6–0) and Northwich Victoria (8–0 and 7–0), to finish the campaign in second position, thus earning a place in the end-of-season test match games.

Small Heath's free-scoring attack put away in excess of one hundred League goals during the season. Hallam scored nine League goals; Hands had found the net on fourteen occasions; Walton had netted sixteen goals in twenty League appearances; Fred Wheldon had ended the campaign with twenty-two goals; while Frank Mobley had led the scoring with twenty-four goals in twenty-one League games. The Birmingham side thus secured a further opportunity to achieve their ambition of promotion to the First Division.

Liverpool's Swift Progress

Liverpool had been formed in 1892, following Everton's move to the Goodison Park ground. However, their application to become members of the Football League had been rejected, which led them to join the Lancashire League.

Following a successful season in the Lancashire League, in which Liverpool registered seventeen victories in twenty-two games, the Lancashire side added the local cup trophy to their League title. Sadly, both trophies were stolen from the club house, which cost Liverpool in excess of one hundred pounds to replace.

With the charismatic John McKenna at the helm of the club, Liverpool began recruiting players from north of the border, which resulted in the arrival of Tom Wylie from Glasgow Rangers, following a spell with Everton, while Andrew Hannah, Duncan McLean and John McBride were signed from the Renton club.

John Millar had moved from Dumbarton, while Malcolm McVean had previously played for Third Lanark. However, the most notable new signing was the skilful Jimmy Ross from Preston North End.

Liverpool opened the 1893–94 season with a 2–0 victory at Middlesbrough Ironopolis, with Malcolm McVean having the distinction of scoring the Lancashire side's first goal in the League. Their excellent form continued throughout the season, with comprehensive home wins against Rotherham Town (5–1), Newcastle (5–1) and Middlesbrough Ironopolis (6–0), as well as away victories at Woolwich Arsenal (5–0) and Crewe (5–0).

All fourteen home games were won, as Liverpool remained unbeaten throughout the season to capture the Second Division Championship by a margin of eight points from Small Heath, who now joined them in the end-of-season test match games, together with Notts County, who had finished the campaign in third place.

The final League placings at the close of the 1893–94 season are shown in Table XI and Table XII.

Table XI: *First Division Football League results for the 1893–94 season*

	P	W	D	L	F	A	PTS
1. Aston Villa	30	19	6	5	84	42	44
2. Sunderland	30	17	4	9	72	44	38
3. Derby County	30	16	4	10	73	62	36
4. Blackburn Rovers	30	16	2	12	69	53	34
5. Burnley	30	15	4	11	61	51	34
6. Everton	30	15	3	12	90	57	33
7. Nottingham Forest	30	14	4	12	57	48	32
8. West Bromwich Albion	30	14	4	12	66	59	32
9. Wolverhampton Wndrs	30	14	3	13	52	63	31
10. Sheffield United	30	13	5	12	47	61	31
11. Stoke	30	13	3	14	65	79	29
12. Wednesday	30	9	8	13	48	57	26
13. Bolton Wanderers	30	10	4	16	38	52	24
14. Preston North End	30	10	3	17	44	56	23
15. Darwen	30	7	5	18	37	83	19
16. Newton Heath	30	6	2	22	36	72	14

Table XII: *Second Division Football League results for the 1893–94 season*

	P	W	D	L	F	A	PTS
1. Liverpool	28	22	6	0	77	18	50
2. Small Heath	28	21	0	7	103	44	42
3. Notts County	28	18	3	7	70	31	39
4. Newcastle	28	15	6	7	66	39	36
5. Grimsby	28	15	2	11	71	58	32
6. Burton Swifts	28	14	3	11	79	61	31
7. Burslem Port Vale	28	13	4	11	66	64	30
8. Lincoln	28	11	6	11	59	58	28
9. Woolwich Arsenal	28	12	4	12	52	55	28
10. Walsall Town Swifts	28	10	3	15	51	61	23
11. Md. Ironopolis	28	8	4	16	37	72	20
12. Crewe	28	6	7	15	42	73	19
13. Ardwick	28	8	2	18	47	71	18
14. Rotherham Town	28	6	3	19	44	91	15
15. Northwich Vic.	28	3	3	22	30	98	9

Bolton Wanderers' First FA Cup Final Appearance

There were few surprises in the opening round of the 1894 FA Cup competition with Preston North End's 18–0 victory against Reading the highlight of the round that saw ten First Division teams remaining in the competition at the second round stage.

Blackburn Rovers secured a place in the quarter-finals with a 5–1 victory against Newton Heath following a goalless draw, with Whitehead (2), Chippendale, Calvey and Haydock on target, while Aston Villa inflicted a 3–1 defeat on Sunderland in a replayed tie, with Athersmith, Hodgetts and Chatt scoring for the Midlanders.

Stoke suffered a 1–0 defeat at the Wednesday, with Woolhouse scoring the only goal of the game for the Sheffield side. Both Nottingham clubs progressed to the quarter-finals with Forest winning by two goals to nil at Middlesbrough Ironopolis, while County defeated Burton Wanderers by a similar score.

Liverpool secured an excellent home win against Preston North End by the odd goal in five, Bolton Wanderers managed a 2–1 victory at Newcastle, with Hughes and Turner on target, while Allan, Francis and McMillan found the net for Derby County in a 3–0 success against Leicester Fosse following a goalless draw.

Nottingham Forest and Notts County were then drawn against each other in the quarter-finals, which resulted in a one-all draw. However, County had little difficulty in winning the replay as goals by Bruce (2), Donnelly and Logan secured a 4–1 success, with McInnes replying for Forest. Haydock netted a hat-trick for Blackburn Rovers in a 4–1 victory at Derby County.

On a quagmire of a pitch at the Olive Grove Ground, Wednesday secured a 3–2 win against Aston Villa, with Spiksley, Betts and Woolhouse scoring for the Yorkshire side, while Bolton Wanderers enjoyed a 3–0 home success against Liverpool, with goals by Dickenson (2) and Cassidy earning a semi-final appearance for the Wanderers.

Bolton were then drawn against the Wednesday in the semi-finals at the Fallowfield Ground, Manchester, while Notts County were due to play against Blackburn Rovers at Bramall Lane, with the odds on a Wednesday–Blackburn final. However, there were shocks in store for the cup favourites, as a Harry Daft goal earned Notts County a 1–0 victory against Blackburn, while a brace of goals by Bentley secured a 2–1 win for Bolton, who now made their first FA Cup Final appearance.

A Narrow Victory for the English League Eleven

Prior to the 1894 FA Cup Final, the English national team travelled to Belfast and Wrexham to fulfil international fixtures against Ireland and Wales, as well as an inter-League game against the Irish League in Belfast.

The Football League fielded an attacking side for the visit to Belfast that included Joe Reader (West Bromwich Albion) in goal, with Howarth (Everton), Thickett (Sheffield United), Perry (West Bromwich Albion), Holt (Everton) and Crabtree (Burnley) in defence, while Wykes (Wolverhampton Wanderers), Hammond (Sheffield United), Geary (Everton), Wheldon (Small Heath) and Wood (Wolverhampton Wanderers) formed a formidable attack.

While the English Eleven secured a 4–2 victory, with Wheldon (2), Geary and Wykes on target, it had become apparent that the gap between the Irish and English players had certainly narrowed.

Further Success for the Irish

A couple of weeks after the inter-League encounter in Belfast, the English national team returned to Ireland for the opening international game of the season with a side that included four members of the successful League team.

Joe Reader (West Bromwich Albion) and James Crabtree (Burnley) made their England debuts, with the Everton pair of Bob Howarth and John Holt in defence, while the Aston Villa trio of John Reynolds, John Devey and Dennis

Hodgetts were selected in recognition of their team's excellent performances in the League.

Robert Holmes (Preston North End) gained the sixth of his seven England caps at left fullback, Harry Chippendale made his only England appearance at outside right, while James Whitehead, his Blackburn Rovers' team-mate, played his second and final England game at inside right. Fred Spiksley (Wednesday) completed the English line-up for a game which the visitors were expected to win with ease. However, the expected victory failed to materialise as England returned home with a two-all draw, with John Devey and Fred Spiksley scoring the English goals.

England Field a Team of Corinthians Against the Welsh

Mid-March saw the England team visit Wrexham for the international fixture against Wales with a side consisting entirely of players with Corinthian connections. Leslie Gay (Old Brightonians) made his second appearance in goal with Frederick Pelly and Anthony Hossack in defence, while Charles Wreford-Brown played the third of his four England games at centre half. Arthur Topham (Casuals), a schoolmaster, who had gained an Oxford Blue, made his one England appearance at left half back, while his brother, Robert, who had appeared in Wolverhampton Wanderers' 1893 FA Cup-winning side, made his second appearance at outside right. Robert Gosling, G O Smith and Rupert Sandilands were recalled to the attack, Lewis Lodge (Casuals), an accomplished county cricketer with Hampshire and Durham, made the first of five appearances at right fullback, while John Veitch (Old Westminsters) made his single England appearance at centre forward.

England performed splendidly against the Welsh, with John Veitch joining a select band of players to score a hat-trick on his debut. The visitors won by five goals to one, with Gosling and an own goal completing the scoring.

Notts County Dominate the FA Cup Final

Owing to the lack of terracing at the Fallowfield Ground, a decision was made to play the 1894 FA Cup Final at Goodison Park with Bolton Wanderers, who had spent most of the season struggling near the foot of the First Division, playing against Notts County, who were near the top of the Second Division.

England winger, Davie Weir, had been left out of the Bolton line-up following a disagreement with the club directors, while James Turner and David Willocks were unfit to play. However, Gardiner, Paton and Bentley all passed fitness tests to take their places in the Bolton team.

Notts were at full strength when, on the morning of the final, a message arrived of the sudden death of Sandy Ferguson, who had appeared for County in the FA Cup Final just three years earlier.

Bolton selected the following players for their first FA Cup Final appearance:

Sutcliffe

Somerville   Jones (captain)

Gardiner   Paton   Hughes

Tannahill   Wilson   Cassidy   Bentley   Dickenson

Notts County selected the following eleven:

Toone

Harper   Hendry

Bramley   Calderhead (captain)   Shelton

Watson   Donnelly   Logan   Bruce   Daft

A crowd in excess of 30,000 saw David Calderhead win the toss for County, who made all the early running with Logan and Watson exerting pressure on the Bolton defence. County's constant pressure eventually told when, following a cross by Logan, Donnelly hit the upright, which rebounded to Watson, who had the simple task of steering the ball past the advancing John Sutcliffe to secure a one-goal lead for the East Midlands side.

Bolton resumed with vigour, as shots by Tannahill, Dickenson and Bentley went close. However, County secured a further goal on the half-hour when Jimmy Logan found the net following some excellent wing play from Harry Daft. Thus half-time arrived with County two goals to the good.

Wanderers came more into the game during the early stages of the second half with Bentley, Dickenson and Cassidy forcing saves from Toone in the County goal. However, an excellent spell of play by Jimmy Logan saw him score twice in three minutes to complete a memorable hat-trick, as well as secure a four-goal lead for the Nottingham side.

James Cassidy netted a late consolation goal for Bolton to reduce the arrears, but the final whistle sounded with Notts the worthy winners by four goals to one, with Lord Kinnaird presenting the trophy to David Calderhead, the proud captain of Notts County.

Notts County and Bolton Complete Their League Fixtures

Crucial League games remained for both Notts County and Bolton Wanderers during the final month of the season, which determined their status for the following League campaign.

Bolton's three remaining League games were all on home soil, which resulted in defeats against West Bromwich Albion (3–0) and Everton (1–0), while the campaign ended with a 2–0 victory against Sunderland, with Bentley and Hughes on target. Bolton was thus in thirteenth place League and so avoided the test match placings by a single point.

James Cassidy and John Sutcliffe had appeared in all but one League game for the Wanderers, while Cassidy had led the scoring with eleven League goals in a season of disappointment for the Lancashire side.

Notts County had an easier run in than Bolton to retain their third position in the Second Division and secure a place in the end-of-season test match games.

Two Drawn Games Against the Scots

A week after the FA Cup Final, the English national team travelled to Glasgow for the fixture against Scotland with Leslie Gay, Frederick Pelly and G O Smith retaining their places from the victory against the Welsh, while John Holt, John Reynolds and Fred Spiksley were recalled from the two-all draw in Belfast earlier in the season. Billy Bassett (West Bromwich Albion), Edgar Chadwick (Everton) and John Goodall (Derby County) were included in the attack, with Thomas Clare (Stoke) at right fullback, while Ernest Needham, the hard-tackling Sheffield United half back, made the first of sixteen appearances in an England shirt.

England had defeated the Scots in each of the three previous seasons. However, they were a little fortunate to hold on to a two-all draw in Glasgow, with Reynolds and Goodall on target for the visitors.

All Square at Goodison Park

Late April saw a Scottish League Eleven arrive at Goodison Park for the annual fixture against the English League Eleven, which included Reynolds, Holt, Needham, Goodall and Spiksley from the draw in Glasgow, while Charlie Athersmith (Aston Villa), John Devey (Aston Villa) and Fred Wheldon (Small Heath) were selected in the attack. John Sutcliffe (Bolton Wanderers) appeared in goal, while James Crabtree (Burnley) and Robert Holmes (Preston North End) completed the English line-up. The game ended in a one-all draw, with John Goodall scoring for the home side.

The 1893–94 Test Match Games

The 1893–94 test match games saw Second Division Champions Liverpool play against Newton Heath at Ewood Park, Blackburn. Small Heath, the Second Division runners-up, were due to play against Darwen at the Victoria Ground, Stoke, while Notts County, the recent FA Cup winners, were down to play against the once mighty Preston North End at Bramall Lane, Sheffield.

Small Heath, who had suffered a surprising defeat against Newton Heath during the previous season's test match games, made few mistakes against Darwen as goals by Wheldon, Walton and Hallam secured a 3–1 victory, while

Notts County had few answers to the Preston attack as the Lancashire side registered a 4–0 success.

Liverpool, who had remained unbeaten in the League throughout the 1893–94 season, continued their excellent run of results with a 2–0 victory against Newton Heath to secure a place in the First Division. They were joined by Small Heath at the expense of Darwen while Preston North End and Notts County remained in their respective divisions.

Old Carthusians Win the FA Amateur Cup

Towards the end of the 1893–94 season, the first Amateur FA Cup Final took place between the Old Carthusians and the Casuals with the Old Charterhouse Boys winning by the odd goal in three. They became the first team to win both the Amateur and FA Cups. However, while the Old Carthusians appeared in two further Amateur Finals during the last decade of the century, the gap between amateur and professional players had widened to such an extent that, with the exception of the Corinthians, few northern clubs would entertain amateur sides in friendly games, as spectators preferred the competition offered by the League system.

The Second Division Is Extended

Following the close of the 1893–94 League campaign, the Football League Committee decided to extend the Second Division from fifteen to sixteen teams for the 1894–95 season, which meant that all teams in the League would now play thirty League games.

Chapter XX

SUNDERLAND'S THIRD LEAGUE TITLE IN FOUR SEASONS – 1894–95

SUNDERLAND SECURE THEIR THIRD LEAGUE TITLE IN FOUR SEASONS
ASTON VILLA DEFEAT WEST BROMWICH ALBION IN THE FINAL OF THE FA CUP
STEVE BLOOMER SCORES A BRACE OF GOALS ON HIS ENGLAND DEBUT IN A 9–0
VICTORY AGAINST IRELAND
ENGLAND REMAIN UNBEATEN TO WIN THE INTERNATIONAL CHAMPIONSHIP
ALBION'S AMAZING ESCAPE FROM THE TEST MATCH POSITIONS
BURY'S SUCCESS CONTINUES
MUCH SORROW AT THE MOLINEUX

SMALL HEATH

Following many successful seasons at a local level, the Small Heath club had at last realised their ambition of playing their football in the First Division for the 1894–95 League campaign, which was a just reward for their exciting style of play.

Few changes were made in their line-up for the new season, which saw the arrival of Partridge to replace Charsley and Hollis between the posts, together with a new fullback pairing of Purves and Oliver. However, Billy Ollis, Caesar Jenkyns and Ted Devey remained at half back, while Jack Hallam, Billy Walton, Frank Mobley, Fred Wheldon and Tommy Hands continued up front.

Small Heath opened the campaign with successive away defeats at Aston Villa (2–1) and Everton (5–0), which preceded a 2–0 home win against Bolton Wanderers, with Fred Wheldon scoring a brace of goals, while Wheldon was again on target the following week in a 2–1 reverse at Wolverhampton Wanderers.

Tommy Hands then scored the only goal of the game in a 1–0 victory at Preston North End, while the return game with Preston finished in a four-all draw, with Mobley (2), Wheldon and Hands scoring for the home side. This was followed by a 4–3 home success against Wolverhampton Wanderers, with Walton (2), Wheldon and Mobley on target for Small Heath.

Mid-October saw a 3–1 defeat at Burnley, which preceded successive draws at home to Aston Villa (2–2) and Everton (4–4), as well as at Stoke (2–2), while a 4–1 reverse at West Bromwich Albion continued their indifferent run of results. However, a 4–2 home success against Stoke saw a return to winning ways for the Birmingham side, with Walton, Hallam, Mobley and Wheldon scoring the all-important goals.

Further victories at Bolton Wanderers (2–1) and at home to Sheffield United (4–2) saw Fred Wheldon on target in both games, with Leatherbarrow netting a hat-trick against the Sheffield side. Successive away defeats at Sunderland (7–1), Liverpool (3–1) and Wednesday (2–0), as well as at home to Nottingham Forest (2–1), saw the Birmingham side move into the bottom half of the League table, while the year ended with a 3–0 home win against Sunderland, with Mobley, Walton and Lewis scoring the Small Heath goals.

New Year began with an embarrassing 9–1 defeat at Blackburn Rovers, which preceded a further away defeat at Nottingham Forest (2–0), while a 2–1 reverse against West Bromwich Albion in the first round of the FA Cup continued their poor start to the new year.

Then followed six successive home games, which resulted in draws against Sunderland (1–1), Blackburn Rovers (1–1) and Wednesday (0–0), as well as defeats against West Bromwich Albion (2–1) and Derby County (5–3), while a 1–0 success against Burnley saw two welcome points, with Fred Wheldon scoring the only goal of the game.

Following a 4–1 reverse at Derby County in their penultimate League game of the season, the Small Heath side managed a 2–0 victory at Sheffield United in the final game of the campaign, with goals by Frank Mobley and a United defender securing a twelfth place League finish for the Midlanders, one point away from the test match positions.

Small Heath had won nine, drawn seven and lost fourteen of their thirty League games, while scoring fifty goals and conceding seventy-four. Jack Hallam, Tommy Hands and Billy Walton ended the campaign with half a dozen League goals apiece, Fred Wheldon had found the net on ten occasions, while Frank Mobley once again led the scoring with fourteen League goals. More importantly, the Small Heath side had retained their First Division status for the 1895–96 season.

LIVERPOOL

Liverpool had totally dominated the Second Division during the 1893–94 League campaign, which resulted in few changes in their line-up for the 1894–95 season. McQueen, Hannah, McOwen, McLean, Dick, Henderson, Gordon, McVean, McBride, McQue and Jimmy Ross remained with the club, while Harry Bradshaw had arrived from Northwich Victoria.

Liverpool opened the season with successive away draws at Blackburn Rovers (1–1) and Burnley (3–3), with Harry Bradshaw on target in both games, while Bradshaw netted his third goal of the campaign in a 2–1 home defeat against Aston Villa. This preceded further defeats at West Bromwich Albion (5–0) and at home to Bolton Wanderers (2–1). Then followed home draws against Blackburn Rovers (2–2) and Sheffield United (2–2), as well as away defeats at Wolverhampton Wanderers (3–1) and Everton (3–0). Their first victory of the season arrived with a 2–0 home success against Stoke, with Jimmy Ross scoring both Liverpool goals.

Further away defeats at Aston Villa (5–0), Stoke (3–1) and at home to Burnley (3–0), preceded a two-all draw in the return game with Everton, while the first half of the season ended with a 3–2 reverse at Sunderland, which left Liverpool at the foot of the League table with one victory in fifteen League games.

Early December saw successive draws at home to Wolverhampton Wanderers (3–3) and away at Sheffield United (2–2), followed by a 3–1 home victory against Small Heath, while the year ended with away defeats at Bolton Wanderers (1–0) and Small Heath (3–0). However, the Merseysiders returned to winning ways on New Year's Day as Harry Bradshaw netted a brace of goals in a 4–0 home win against West Bromwich Albion.

Liverpool's poor away form continued with a 5–0 defeat at the Wednesday, which preceded home wins against Nottingham Forest (5–0) and Derby County (5–1), as well as a 1–0 success in the return game at Derby. A 3–2 home defeat against Sunderland ended their excellent run of results.

Following a 4–2 home win against the Wednesday, the Liverpool side suffered a 3–0 reverse at Nottingham Forest, which preceded a creditable two-all draw at Preston. The season ended with a 5–2 defeat in the return game with Preston, which condemned Liverpool to last place in the League with seven victories, eight draws and fifteen defeats in their thirty League games, while scoring fifty-one goals and conceding seventy.

Harry Bradshaw had led the scoring with seventeen League goals in a season that had included a first round FA Cup defeat against Nottingham Forest, as well as a defeat against Everton in the final of the Liverpool Cup. The end-of-season test match games would decide which division they would be playing in during the 1895–96 League campaign.

DERBY COUNTY

Following their third place finish at the end of the 1893–94 League campaign, Derby County kept faith with the majority of their players for the 1894–95 season. John Robinson continued in goal, with Jimmy Methven, Joseph Leiper, John Cox, Archie Goodall and Docherty in defence, while John McMillan, John Goodall and Steve Bloomer remained up front, where Keay, Hamilton, Paul, McLachlan and Albert Woolley made occasional appearances.

Derby opened the season with an away fixture at Sunderland where, owing to the late arrival of the match referee, a local official was used, which hardly helped the Midlands side as they soon found themselves three goals down. However, following the arrival of the official referee, Derby elected to restart the match, a decision they soon regretted as they suffered an 8–0 defeat.

Then followed a 4–2 home win against Nottingham Forest, with McMillan (2), Raybould and Bloomer on target, which preceded successive home defeats against the Wednesday (2–1), Aston Villa (2–0) and Sunderland (2–1), as well as a 2–0 reverse at Burnley. Home and away draws against West

Bromwich Albion (1–1 and 2–2) continued their poor start to the season, with Keay scoring in both drawn games.

Further defeats at Nottingham Forest (2–1) and Preston North End (3–2) saw Archie Goodall find the net in both games, which were followed by a 2–1 victory in the return game with Preston, with McLachlan and John Cox on target, while Keay netted his fourth goal in five League appearances in a two-all draw at Wolverhampton Wanderers, where Archie Goodall completed the scoring.

Walter Roulstone then made his final League appearance for the club in a 2–0 home defeat against Burnley, which preceded a 4–1 home success against Sheffield United, with Paul (2), Bloomer and Archie Goodall on target, while Hamilton (2), McLachlan and Bloomer found the net in a further 4–1 success against the Sheffield club on Christmas Day.

Derby then ended the year with drawn games at the Wednesday (1–1) and at home to Bolton Wanderers (2–2), with Steve Bloomer scoring all three goals. New Year's Day saw a 6–0 defeat in the return game at Bolton, which preceded further defeats at Aston Villa (4–0) and at home to Liverpool (1–0) as the East Midlands side moved down to the foot of the League table.

Mid-January saw Derby secure successive home draws against Everton (2–2) and Stoke (1–1), which preceded a 3–1 home reverse against Wolverhampton Wanderers, while a 2–1 defeat at Aston Villa in the first round of the FA Cup ended their interest in the competition.

County's poor away form continued with a 5–1 defeat at Liverpool, which preceded a 5–3 away success at Small Heath, with John Goodall (2), McMillan, Woolley and Bloomer on target for the visitors, while Steve Bloomer netted his eighth League goal of the campaign in a 4–1 reverse at Stoke.

Derby returned to form during the final weeks of the campaign, which began with a 4–1 home win in the return game with Small Heath, with Paul (2), McMillan and Woolley netting the County goals. This preceded goalless draws in the home and away fixtures against Blackburn Rovers, while the season ended with a 3–2 victory at Everton with Bloomer (2) and John Goodall scoring for Derby.

They secured a fifteenth place League finish, with seven wins, nine draws and fourteen defeats in their thirty League games, while scoring forty-five goals and conceding sixty-eight.

Jimmy Methven and Archie Goodall had appeared in all thirty League games for Derby, with John Cox and Steve Bloomer missing only one game, in a season when Archie Goodall (six) had led his brother John (four) in the goal-scoring stakes. Steve Bloomer had led the scoring with ten. However, the important test match games awaited the Derby side to decide their future in the Football League.

STOKE

Stoke had managed to avoid the test match positions in each of the two previous seasons, which was mainly because of their excellent home record, hence the reluctance of the Club committee to make changes in the side for the 1894–95 League campaign. William Rowley continued in goal, with Eccles, Brodie and Tommy Clare in defence, while Joseph Schofield and Billy Dickson were once again the mainstays of the attack.

The most notable newcomer in the Potteries' side was England international defender James Turner from Bolton Wanderers, while centre forward Tom Hyslop signed from Sunderland during the latter stages of the season to score seven goals in as many League appearances, including a hat-trick on his debut.

Stoke opened the season with a two-all draw at Bolton Wanderers, which preceded successive defeats at home to Everton (3–1) and Sheffield United (3–1), as well as at Blackburn Rovers (6–0), prior to securing a 4–1 home success against Aston Villa. Further away defeats at Sunderland (3–1) and Liverpool (2–0), together with a 3–0 home reverse against Nottingham Forest, continued the Stoke team's poor start to the season.

Then followed a two-all home draw with Small Heath, while home victories against Liverpool (3–1) and Preston North End (2–1) saw Stoke climb away from the test match places. However, a further poor run of results, which included away defeats at Small Heath (4–2), West Bromwich Albion (3–2), Preston North End (3–0) and Aston Villa (6–0), as well as at home to the Wednesday (2–0), saw Stoke near the foot of the League table at the turn of the year.

New Year began with a 3–0 reverse at Everton, followed by a 5–0 home victory against Bolton Wanderers, as well as a one-all draw at Derby County, while a 5–2 home defeat against Sunderland dashed their hopes of climbing the League table.

Following a second goalless draw against Wolverhampton Wanderers, the Potteries' side suffered successive away defeats at Sheffield United (3–0) and Nottingham Forest (3–1), however, a return to form during the final weeks of the campaign saw Stoke enjoy a six-game unbeaten run, which coincided with the arrival of Tom Hyslop from Sunderland.

The free-scoring Hyslop skilfully led the attack in home victories against Derby County (4–1), Burnley (5–1) and Blackburn Rovers (5–1), as well as away wins at the Wednesday (4–2) and Burnley (2–1). A one-all home draw with West Bromwich Albion saw the only point conceded during their excellent run of results. The Potteries' side had left their revival a little too late, though, as they ended the campaign in fourteenth position, which meant that they now had to take part in the end-of-season test match games to decide their First Division future.

Stoke had won nine, drawn six and lost fifteen of their thirty League games, while scoring fifty goals and conceding sixty-seven. Meanwhile, a 2–0 reverse at Wolverhampton Wanderers in the second round of the FA Cup had ended their interest in the competition.

Eccles and David Brodie had appeared in all thirty League games for the Potteries' side, while Billy Dickson and Joseph Schofield had ended the campaign with thirteen League goals apiece. However, it was imperative that the Stoke team continue their fine run of results in the test match games.

WEST BROMWICH ALBION

West Bromwich Albion had tended to settle for mid-table stability rather than pursue success in the Football League. However, they had regularly enjoyed FA Cup success, which had seen four appearances in the final, of which two had resulted in victory.

Albion made a number of changes in their team for the 1894–95 League campaign. Joe Reader continued in goal, with John Horton, Taggart, Tom Perry and Charlie Perry in defence, while Billy Bassett and Roddy McLeod remained up front. Tom Pearson and Sam Nicholls had retired from the game, Jasper Geddes had signed for Millwall Athletic, while defender Mark Nicholson had joined Luton Town. This resulted in a number of new arrivals as the West Bromwich side sought to retain their First Division status.

Billy Williams had arrived from Old Hill Wanderers to replace Nicholson at fullback where he made in excess of 200 appearances, as well as appearing in the English national team. Hutchinson and William Richards replaced Pearson and Geddes up front, with newcomers Newhall and Banks sharing the left wing position.

Albion opened the League campaign with a 2–1 reverse at Sheffield United, followed by successive home wins against Wolverhampton Wanderers (5–1) and Liverpool (5–0), with McLeod, Richards, Bassett and Hutchinson on target in both victories. Albion's fine start to the season came to an end with away defeats at Sunderland (3–0), Everton (4–1) and Aston Villa (3–1), as well as home and away draws against Derby County (2–2 and 1–1).

Early November saw Albion return to winning ways as Hutchinson scored the only goal of the game in a 1–0 home success against Sheffield United, which preceded a one-all home draw with Bolton Wanderers, with Hutchinson again on target. Further home wins against Small Heath (4–1) and Aston Villa (3–2) saw the West Bromwich side climb to a mid-table position, with Hutchinson and Richards once again amongst the goal scorers. Unfortunately, nine defeats in their following ten League games would see Albion move swiftly down the League table.

Albion's disastrous run of results began with a 2–0 reverse at Burnley, followed by further defeats at home to Everton (4–1) and away at Nottingham Forest (5–3), while two welcome points arrived with a 3–2 home success against Stoke, with Hutchinson (2) and Taggart scoring the all-important Albion goals. Albion's joy was short-lived as the year ended with defeats at

Blackburn Rovers (3–0) and Wolverhampton Wanderers (3–1), as well as at home to Sunderland (2–0) and Burnley (1–0).

New Year's Day saw a 4–0 reverse at Liverpool, followed by a 5–4 home defeat against Preston North End, with Hutchinson (2), Bassett and Richards on target for the Black Country side, while Banks and Hutchinson found the net in a 2–0 home success against Blackburn Rovers during the final week of January.

Away from the pressures of the League, Albion managed a 2–1 victory at Small Heath in the first round of the FA Cup, with goals by Banks and Roddy McLeod securing a second round tie against Sheffield United at Bramall Lane. There a Billy Bassett goal earned Albion a one-all draw. Their luck held in the replay as Hutchinson and a Willie Foulke own goal helped Albion to a 2–1 success to secure a home tie against Wolverhampton Wanderers in the quarter-finals.

Prior to the quarter-final tie, Taggart netted a brace of goals in a 2–1 victory at Small Heath, which preceded a 5–0 reverse at Preston North End, while a Roddy McLeod goal earned Albion a 1–0 victory in the cup tie with Wolves to secure a semi-final tie against the Wednesday at the County Ground, Derby.

Albion dominated the early stages of the semi-final, which resulted in them taking the lead when Hutchinson converted a William Richards pass. Albion went further ahead minutes later when Billy Williams scored from the penalty spot following a foul on Billy Bassett.

While Wednesday made every effort to reduce the arrears, Albion held on to a 2–0 victory to secure their fifth FA Cup Final appearance, due to take place at Crystal Palace on 20 April against Aston Villa. However, prior to the final, Albion had a number of important League games to play if they were to avoid the end-of-season test match games.

During the final week of March, Roddy McLeod found the net in a one-all draw at Stoke, which preceded a 3–2 defeat at the Wednesday, where McLeod netted both Albion goals. Their indifferent League form continued with a 5–0 reverse at Bolton Wanderers, where goalkeeper Joe Reader received his marching orders for ungentlemanly behaviour. However, Albion managed a 1–0 home success against Nottingham Forest a couple of days prior to the final, with Jasper Geddes, recently re-signed from Millwall Athletic, scoring the only goal of the game.

WOLVERHAMPTON WANDERERS

Wolverhampton Wanderers had finished the two previous League campaigns in a mid-table position, which resulted in a number of changes in their side for the 1894–95 season. William Rose, George Kinsey and George Swift had left the club, while ill-health had forced Harry Allen into retirement, however, there remained a measure of stability within the team as Richard Baugh, Joe Butcher, Dunn, Haynes, Black, Alf Griffin, Griffiths, Billy Malpass, Harry

Wood and David Wykes continued to serve the club, while Joshua Hassall replaced William Rose between the posts.

Wolves opened the season with successive home defeats against Preston North End (3–1) and Sheffield United (3–0), followed by a 5–1 reverse at West Bromwich Albion. A 2–1 home victory against Newton Heath saw their first win of the campaign.

Then followed a run of away defeats at Burnley (2–1), Small Heath (4–3), Preston North End (2–0) and Sunderland (2–0), while their home form greatly improved with victories against Liverpool (3–1), Wednesday (2–0) and Bolton Wanderers (4–2), which saw the Wolverhampton side in the bottom half of the League table by early November.

Wanderers' indifferent form continued with home draws against Nottingham Forest (1–1), Stoke (0–0), Derby County (2–2) and at Liverpool (3–3), as well as away defeats at the Wednesday (3–1) and Bolton Wanderers (6–1). Then, following a 4–0 home defeat against Aston Villa, the Black Country side returned to form during the final week of the year with successive home wins against Burnley (1–0) and West Bromwich Albion (3–1).

New Year saw the Wanderers secure a third successive home victory against Everton (1–0), followed by defeats at home to Sunderland (4–1) and at Sheffield United (1–0), while a 3–1 victory at Derby County saw a rare away success.

Wolves then secured a further away point in a goalless draw at Stoke. This was followed by a 2–0 victory against Darwen in the first round of the FA Cup in a replayed tie to earn a home tie with Stoke in the second round. That resulted in a 2–0 success, but a 1–0 reverse at West Bromwich Albion in the quarter-finals ended their interest in the competition.

February's end saw Wolves share six goals with Blackburn Rovers at the Molineux, while Blackburn won the return game by five goals to one. The Wanderers were left near the foot of the League table, desperately in need of points to avoid the end-of-season test match games, with only three away fixtures remaining.

A 2–1 reverse at Everton saw the Wolverhampton side in further trouble, however, a 2–0 victory at Nottingham Forest, as well as a two-all draw at Aston Villa, saw the Wanderers end the campaign in eleventh position, just one point away from the test match places.

Wanderers' poorest season to date had seen nine victories in thirty League games, while scoring forty-three goals, the lowest in the division. Harry Wood found the net on ten occasions, while Alf Griffin had ended the campaign with eleven League goals.

Joshua Hassall had appeared in all thirty League games for the Wolverhampton side, in a season that was marred by the sudden deaths of three fine players, including Hassall himself, who passed away during the close season following a bout of pneumonia. David Wykes succumbed to typhoid, while Harry Allen passed away at the age of twenty-nine.

Association Football seemed totally unimportant when compared with the sadness and grief caused by the sudden deaths of three excellent players. However, the Wanderers were aware that, if only in their memory, the great game must continue.

BOLTON WANDERERS

Bolton Wanderers had narrowly avoided the test match positions during the 1893–94 League campaign, but the Lancashire side retained the majority of their players for the 1894–95 season. John Sutcliffe continued in goal, with John Somerville, David Jones and Alex Paton in defence, while Bentley, Tannahill, Cassidy and Davie Weir remained up front.

Harry Gardiner had returned north of the border to Glasgow Rangers, while England international defender James Turner had signed for Stoke. However, they were adequately replaced by McGeachan and Archie Freebairn, who both gave excellent service to Wanderers, with McGeachan making close on seventy League appearances, while Freebairn, who had played much of his early football with Wheatburn and Partick Thistle, played in excess of 300 games in his thirteen seasons with Bolton.

Newcomers in the attack included McGinn, Andrews, Henderson and Jimmy Settle, but all four players had left the club by the season's end.

Bolton opened the season with a two-all home draw with Stoke, with Bentley and David Jones on target, which preceded a 2–0 reverse at Small Heath. Their first victory of the campaign was a 2–1 success at Liverpool, with Robert Tannahill and James Cassidy scoring for the visitors. However, successive defeats at home to Preston North End (2–1) and away at the Wednesday (2–1) continued their indifferent start to the season.

Then followed a 4–1 home success against Sunderland, with Paton, Henderson, Cassidy and Settle finding the net, which preceded a run of ten games without a win, including away defeats at Blackburn Rovers (2–1), Wolverhampton Wanderers (4–2), Sunderland (4–0) and Everton (3–1), as well as at home to Blackburn Rovers (3–1), Everton (3–1) and Small Heath (2–1). Drawn games at Preston North End (2–2), West Bromwich Albion (1–1) and at home to Burnley (1–1) saw Bolton's only successes during this period of poor form.

Mid-December saw a return to winning ways for the Lancashire side as Henderson (3), Somerville, Settle and McGinn were on target in a 6–1 home win against Wolverhampton Wanderers, which preceded a further home success on Christmas Day as Jimmy Settle found the net in a 1–0 victory against Liverpool. The year ended with a two-all draw at Derby County, with Paton and McGinn netting for the visitors.

New Year's Day saw Bolton score six goals without reply in the return game with Derby, with Henderson (4), McGinn and Cassidy, scoring the

Wanderers' goals, which was followed by a 1–0 defeat at Burnley. Alex Paton netted a brace of goals in a two-all home draw with the Wednesday, but a 5–0 reverse at Stoke continued their indifferent away form.

Bolton then scored six goals for the third time in five home games in a 6–2 win against Sheffield United, with Cassidy (2), Spence (2), Paton and Tannahill on target, which preceded a 2–1 reverse at Aston Villa, while David Jones scored the only goal of the game in a 1–0 home success against Woolwich Arsenal in the first round of the FA Cup to secure a home tie with Bury in the second round.

James Cassidy then scored the only goal of the game in a 1–0 victory against Bury, to earn a visit to Sunderland in the quarter-finals. However, Bolton's luck ran out in the north-east as they suffered a 2–1 defeat to end their hopes of a second successive final appearance.

On their return to League action, Wanderers secured a three-all draw at Nottingham Forest, with James Cassidy netting a brace of goals, which was followed by a 4–3 home success against Aston Villa with Henderson (2), Turnbull and Bentley on target. Their excellent form continued with a 4–1 home win in the return game with Nottingham Forest, with Joyce (2), Cassidy and Turnbull scoring for the Lancashire side.

Turnbull then netted a hat-trick in a 5–0 home win against West Bromwich Albion, with Freebairn and Joyce completing the scoring. The season ended with a 5–0 reverse at Sheffield United, leaving Bolton in tenth position, with nine victories, seven draws and fourteen defeats in their thirty League games, while scoring sixty-one goals and conceding sixty-two.

Alex Paton had appeared in all thirty League games for the Wanderers, while John Sutcliffe, John Somerville and Archie Freebairn had missed only one in a most disappointing League campaign. Charlie Henderson had led the scoring with fourteen goals in twenty-eight League appearances.

BURNLEY

Burnley had finished the 1893–94 League campaign in a creditable fifth position, which resulted in few changes in their line-up for the 1894–95 season. Jack Hillman remained in goal, while Taylor, Bowes, Walter Place and James Crabtree continued to be the mainstays of the team.

Burnley opened the season with away defeats at Nottingham Forest (2–1) and Sunderland (3–0) on either side of a three-all home draw with Liverpool. However, following a further draw at Sheffield United (2–2), the Lancashire side moved to a mid-table position with successive home victories against Wolverhampton Wanderers (2–1) and Derby County (2–0).

Then followed a 4–3 reverse at the Wednesday, while a 3–1 success against Small Heath continued their excellent home form, however, following a one-all draw at Bolton Wanderers, the Burnley side suffered their first home defeat of the season against Nottingham Forest (1–0).

Early November saw a 3–0 victory at Liverpool, which preceded a 3–0 home success against the Wednesday, while a 1–0 defeat at Blackburn Rovers ended their excellent start to the month. However, the Lancashire side soon returned to winning ways with successive home wins against West Bromwich Albion (2–0) and Preston North End (2–1), as well as a 2–0 success at Derby County.

Burnley then suffered defeats at home to Sheffield United (4–2) and at Wolverhampton Wanderers (1–0), prior to ending the year with a 1–0 victory at West Bromwich Albion. The new year began with home wins against Bolton Wanderers (1–0) and Blackburn Rovers (2–1) as the Lancashire side sought their highest League finish to date, but their hopes of success soon faded, following one draw and eight defeats in their remaining nine League games.

Burnley's loss of form began with a 4–0 reverse at Preston North End, which preceded a three-all home draw with Aston Villa. Further defeats at home to Everton (4–2), as well as at Everton (3–2), Small Heath (1–0), Stoke (5–1) and Aston Villa (5–0), continued their poor run of results. Matters worsened during the final week of the campaign with home defeats against Sunderland (3–0) and Stoke (2–1) as Burnley finished the season in ninth position with eleven victories, four draws and fifteen defeats in their thirty League games, two points away from the test match places.

If the Lancashire side had continued their early season form, they may well have been challenging for the League title at the season's end rather than struggling to avoid the test match positions, as the League table confirmed.

Table XIII: *Burnley's astonishing run of poor form in the second half of the 1894–95 season*

	Played	Won	Lost	Drawn	For	Against	Points
12 January	21	11	7	3	35	26	25
20 April	30	11	15	4	44	56	26

WEDNESDAY

Wednesday had finished the two previous League campaigns in twelfth position. However, their excellent reputation had been built on their fine FA Cup performances, prior to attaining League status in 1892.

Few changes were made in the Wednesday line-up for the 1894–95 season, as William Allan continued in goal, with Jack Earp, Ambrose Langley, Jamieson and Harry Brandon in defence, while Harry Davis, Alec Brady, Woolhouse and Fred Spiksley remained in the attack.

Wednesday's most significant new signings for the 1894–95 League campaign were Tom Crawshaw from Heywood Central to replace Billy Betts at centre half, while Petrie, Bob Ferrier and Archie Brash had all arrived from north of the border.

Crawshaw made nearly 500 appearances in fourteen seasons with the

Sheffield side, as well as appearing for the English national team on ten occasions. Petrie, a former Dundee player, played 52 League games prior to joining Southampton; Ferrier, a product of the successful Dumbarton club, made in excess of 300 League appearances in eleven seasons; while Archie Brash, a recent arrival from St Mirren, played 119 League games in six seasons.

Wednesday opened the season with a 3–1 reverse at Everton, which preceded successive home wins against Preston North End (3–1) and Blackburn Rovers (4–1) with Davis and Earp on target in both victories. Davis found the net for the third game running in a 2–1 success at Derby County, where Archie Brash completed the scoring.

Fred Spiksley then netted his first goal of the campaign in a 2–1 home win against Bolton Wanderers, which was followed by a 3–1 defeat at Blackburn Rovers. A 4–3 home success against Burnley saw a return to winning ways with Brash, Brady, Crawshaw and Ferrier scoring the Wednesday goals. However, successive defeats at Wolverhampton Wanderers (2–0) and at home to Sheffield United (3–2) saw the Yorkshire side move down to a mid-table position.

Early November saw Alec Brady score a rare goal in a 1–0 home success against Aston Villa, which preceded a 3–0 defeat at Burnley. Brady again found the net in a 3–1 home win against Wolverhampton Wanderers, with Harry Davis and Harry Brandon completing the scoring. However, a 3–1 reverse at Aston Villa continued their indifferent away form.

Then followed a 2–0 victory at Stoke with Davis and Spiksley on target for the visitors, which preceded a goalless home draw with Nottingham Forest, before Crawshaw and Ferrier found the net in a 2–0 home win against Small Heath.

Tom Crawshaw then netted a further goal in a one-all home draw with Derby County in the final game of the year, and the new year began with home victories against Everton (3–0) and Liverpool (5–0), with Davis, Woolhouse, Spiksley and Harry Brandon sharing the goals as Wednesday moved towards the top of the League table. A loss of form during the final weeks of the season saw the Yorkshire side win only one of their remaining eleven League fixtures to settle for a mid-table position at the season's end.

Wednesday's poor run of results began with a two-all draw at Bolton Wanderers, where Woolhouse and Spiksley were on target, while successive away defeats at Sheffield United (1–0) and Nottingham Forest (2–1) continued their loss of form. While the Sheffield side had struggled in the League, they enjoyed an excellent FA Cup run, which saw a 5–1 home success against Notts County in the first round, with Brash (2), Davis, Spiksley and Ferrier scoring to secure a second round home tie with Middlesbrough.

Middlesbrough posed few problems for Wednesday, as Davis (3), Spiksley (2) and Brady found the net in a 6–1 victory to earn a further home tie against Everton in the quarter-finals. Their indifferent League form continued with a 3–1 reverse at Sunderland, but an excellent display against Everton resulted in a 2–0 success with Brady and Ferrier on target to secure a semi-final tie against West Bromwich Albion at the County Ground, Derby.

Albion had long enjoyed the reputation as one of the finest FA Cup-fighting sides in England, hence the lack of surprise when Wednesday suffered a 2–0 defeat. A return to League action saw a 2–1 home defeat against League leaders Sunderland.

Following a goalless draw at Small Heath, the Sheffield side suffered a 4–2 reverse at Liverpool, prior to securing a rare home win against West Bromwich Albion (3–2), with Brady, Jamieson and Brash netting the all-important goals. Away defeats at Preston North End (3–1) and West Bromwich Albion (6–0) on either side of a 4–2 home reverse against Stoke saw Wednesday finish the League campaign in eighth position, following twelve victories, four draws and fourteen defeats in their thirty League games, while scoring fifty goals and conceding fifty-five.

Allan, Brady, Brandon, Brash, Crawshaw, Jamieson, Langley and Spiksley had missed no more than a handful of games during the season, while Woolhouse had scored six goals in as many League appearances.

Fred Spiksley had ended the campaign with seven League goals, while Harry Davis had led the scoring with eight goals in twenty-three League games in an excellent season for the Wednesday, who had once again confirmed that they were capable of greater success.

NOTTINGHAM FOREST

Nottingham Forest had finished the 1893–94 League campaign in seventh position, due mainly to many excellent defensive performances, which resulted in few changes in their team for the 1894–95 season. Dennis Allsopp continued in goal, with Archie Ritchie, Adam Scott, Alexander Stewart, John MacPherson and Peter McCracken in defence, while Horace Pike, Arthur Shaw, Tom McInnes and James Collins remained in the attack.

Sandy Higgins had announced his retirement from the game, which saw the arrival of Tom Rose and Albert Carnelly up front. However, while Carnelly scored twenty-four goals in fifty-two League appearances, neither player remained with the club for more than a couple of seasons. The most notable newcomer to the Nottingham club was Fred Forman from Derby County during the latter stages of the previous campaign, while his brother Frank followed at the turn of the year. Fred and Frank both represented the English national side during their long careers with Forest, for whom Fred made nearly 200 appearances, while Frank made in excess of 250 in eleven seasons with the club.

Forest opened the season with a 2–1 home success against Burnley with Tom Rose netting a brace of goals, which preceded a run of defeats at Derby County (4–2), Everton (6–1) and Sheffield United (3–2), as well as at home to Everton (3–2) and Preston North End (2–0). A 2–1 home victory against Aston

Villa saw two welcome points, with Rose and MacPherson on target for the Nottingham side. Then followed a 3–0 victory at Stoke, where McInnes (2) and Carnelly found the net, while Horace Pike scored in successive wins at Burnley (1–0) and at home to Derby County (2–1). This preceded a one-all draw at Wolverhampton Wanderers with Tom Rose scoring for the visitors.

Forest's excellent run of results continued with a 3–0 home success against Sheffield United with Carnelly (2) and Pike on target, while a 4–1 reverse at Aston Villa ended their splendid run. A 5–3 home win against West Bromwich Albion saw a return to form, with Collins (2), MacPherson, Rose and Carnelly scoring for the East Midlands side.

Mid-December saw a goalless draw at the Wednesday, which preceded successive victories at Small Heath (2–1) and at home to Sunderland (2–1), with Carnelly, Pike, Rose and Fred Forman sharing the Forest goals. The year ended with a 3–2 home defeat against Blackburn Rovers, with Fred Forman twice more on target.

New Year's Day saw Forest secure a goalless draw in the return game at Blackburn, while Geary and Pike found the net in a two-all draw at Sunderland. However, following a 5–0 reverse at Liverpool, Forest secured successive home wins against Wednesday (2–1) and Small Heath (2–0) to move up to sixth place in the League table, with Collins (2), MacPherson and Pike again amongst the goal scorers.

Away from the rigours of the League, the Nottingham side secured a 4–1 home success against Southampton St Mary's in the first round of the FA Cup, with Rose (2), Pike and Carnelly on target, while Stewart and McInnes found the net in a 2–0 victory at Liverpool in the second round to earn a quarter-final tie at Aston Villa.

Prior to the FA Cup tie, Forest registered a 3–1 home win against Stoke, with Carnelly (2) and McInnes on target, while the quarter-final tie at Aston Villa ended in a 6–2 defeat. This was followed by a three-all home draw with Bolton Wanderers with Pike, McInnes and Scott netting the Forest goals.

Forest then suffered a 3–1 reverse at Preston North End, followed by a 3–0 home success against Liverpool, with Carnelly (2) and McInnes scoring for the Nottingham side. The season ended with successive defeats at Bolton Wanderers (4–1) and West Bromwich Albion (1–0), as well as at home to Wolverhampton Wanderers (2–0).

Forest finished the campaign in seventh position, with thirteen victories, five draws and twelve defeats in thirty League games, while scoring fifty goals and conceding fifty-six. Archie Ritchie and Adam Scott had appeared in all thirty League games in an excellent season. Horace Pike had netted nine League goals, while Albert Carnelly had led the scoring with sixteen.

SHEFFIELD UNITED

Sheffield United had finished their first campaign in the top division in tenth place, which resulted in few changes in their team for the 1894–95 season. Bob

Cain, Harry Thickett, Michael Whitham, Rab Howell, Billy Hendry and Ernest Needham continued in defence, while Jimmy Yates, Robert Hill, Harry Hammond, Arthur Watson and Hugh Morris remained in the attack. New arrivals included outside right Peden from the north of Ireland, as well as Welsh internationals Joe Davies and Jack Jones, while centre forward Docherty arrived later in the season, along with Arthur Wharton, the Rotherham Town goalkeeper.

Trinidad-born Wharton had been the Amateur Athletic Association's hundred yards champion in both 1886 and 1887, as well as one of the first black professional footballers in England. However, his first team appearances were limited owing to the arrival of Willie Foulke from the Blackwell club in Derbyshire.

Foulke, who stood six feet and two inches tall, with a natural weight of thirteen stone, dominated the United goal area well into the following century, when his weight exceeded twenty stone. He played a leading part in United's success of the late 1890s as well as appearing in the English national side.

United opened the season with a 2–1 home success against West Bromwich Albion, with Hugh Morris and Jack Jones on target in a game in which Peden, Jones and Foulke made their first team debuts, with the latter saving a penalty. Morris and Jones were again amongst the goals in a 3–0 victory at Wolverhampton Wanderers, but a 2–1 reverse at Preston ended their fine start to the campaign. Then followed a two-all home draw with Burnley, with Hammond and Morris finding the net, while Hammond was again on target in a 3–1 victory at Stoke. This preceded a 3–2 home success against Nottingham Forest with Harry Hammond scoring for the third game in a row.

Early October saw Yates and Morris on target in a two-all draw at Liverpool, which was followed by a 3–0 home success against Blackburn Rovers with Hammond, Watson and Morris netting the United goals. A 1–0 reverse against Preston North End saw their first home defeat of the season, but the Sheffield side soon returned to winning ways with a 2–1 home success against Aston Villa, as well as a 3–2 victory at the Wednesday with Hill, Yates, Watson, Hammond and Howell sharing the United goals.

United then suffered successive away defeats at West Bromwich Albion (1–0), Aston Villa (5–0), Nottingham Forest (3–0) and Small Heath (4–2), while their excellent home record continued with a two-all draw with Liverpool, with Hammond and Hill on target. A 4–1 reverse at Derby County, though, saw a further defeat on their travels.

Docherty then netted a brace of goals in a rare away success at Burnley (4–2), which was followed by successive defeats at home to Derby County (4–1) and at Blackburn Rovers (3–2). The year ended with a 7–3 reverse against the great Corinthian team at Bramall Lane, thus confirming the belief that the amateur players were more than capable of competing against the finest professional players in the land.

New Year saw the Sheffield side embark on a three-day tour of Scotland where victories were secured against Leith Athletic (2–1), Dundee (2–0) and Raith Rovers (4–2). Their winning ways continued in the League as Robert Hill scored the only goal of the game in a 1–0 home success against the Wednesday, but a 6–2 reverse at Bolton Wanderers ended their excellent start to the year.

Jimmy Yates then netted his fourth League goal of the campaign in a 1–0 home win against Wolverhampton Wanderers, which preceded a one-all draw at Everton where Joe Davies found the net, while Hammond, Hill and Davies were on target in a 3–1 home success against Millwall Athletic in the first round of the FA Cup to secure a home tie against West Bromwich Albion in the second round.

Prior to the FA Cup tie, Hammond (2) and Davies scored in a 3–0 home win against Stoke, while Davies again found the net as the Cup game with Albion ended in a one-all draw. However, a 2–1 defeat in the replay ended United's hopes of a successful FA Cup run.

On their return to League action, the Sheffield side suffered a 2–0 reverse at Sunderland, which preceded a 4–2 home success against Everton, with Harry Hammond netting a hat-trick. A 4–0 victory in the return game with Sunderland continued their excellent home form, with Watson (2), Docherty and Davies on target for the Yorkshire team.

United then suffered a 2–0 home defeat against Small Heath, while the season ended with a 5–0 home win against Bolton Wanderers with goals by Hill, Whitham, Docherty, Yates and Howell securing a sixth place League finish for the Sheffield side following fourteen victories, four draws and twelve defeats in their thirty League games, while scoring fifty-seven goals and conceding fifty-five.

Robert Hill had scored six League goals during the season, Docherty had found the net on eight occasions, while Harry Hammond had led the scoring with a dozen League goals in a most successful League campaign. It would lead to further success for United towards the end of the century.

BLACKBURN ROVERS

Blackburn Rovers had enjoyed an excellent 1893–94 season, which had resulted in a fourth place League finish as well as in reaching the semi-final stages of the FA Cup, where they suffered a surprising 1–0 defeat against Notts County.

Few changes were made in the Rovers' line-up for the 1894–95 League campaign. Ogilvie continued in goal, with Murray, Anderson, Dewar, Tom Brandon and James Forrest in defence, while Whitehead, Sorley, Hall, Harry Chippendale and, occasionally, Josh Hargreaves, remained in the attack.

John Forbes had retired from the game, while Harry Campbell and Billy Townley had left the club. Killean arrived, however, who played in excess of one hundred games for the Rovers, and so did Cleghorn, who made forty-five

League appearances in two seasons, while outside right Haydock, a scorer of five goals in seven appearances during the previous campaign, made the right wing position his own.

Blackburn opened the season with a one-all home draw against Liverpool with Hall on target, which preceded a 4–1 reverse at the Wednesday. Their first success of the campaign was a 6–0 home win against Stoke with Hall (3), Whitehead (2) and Stuart finding the net.

Whitehead and Stuart were again on target the following week in a two-all draw at Liverpool, while outside right Wade, making his only League appearance for the club, netted a brace of goals in a 3–1 home success against the Wednesday. This preceded a further draw at Preston North End (1–1) where Whitehead scored for the visitors.

Following a 3–0 reverse at Sheffield United, Whitehead and Haydock found the net in a 2–1 home win against Bolton Wanderers, while both players were on the score sheet a week later in a 4–3 home victory against Everton. Then there was a one-all home draw with Preston North End, with Haydock on target for the third successive game.

Rovers secured their first away success of the season in a 3–1 victory at Bolton Wanderers with Stuart, Anderson and Chippendale scoring for the visitors, which was followed by a one-all home draw with Sunderland with Hall netting the Blackburn goal. Harry Chippendale scored the only goal of the game in a 1–0 home win against Burnley as the Lancashire side continued their excellent start to the season. However, successive away defeats at Everton (2–1), Aston Villa (3–0) and Sunderland (3–2), as well as at home in the return game with Aston Villa (3–1), saw Rovers move down to a mid-table position.

Blackburn soon returned to winning ways with a 3–0 home success against West Bromwich Albion with Cleghorn (2) and Anderson on target, which preceded a further home win against Sheffield United (3–2) with Whitehead (2) and Walton scoring the Rovers' goals. The year ended with a 3–2 victory at Nottingham Forest with Chippendale (2) and Sorley netting for the Lancashire side.

New Year began with a goalless home draw in the return game with Nottingham Forest, which preceded a 9–1 home success against Small Heath with Chippendale (3), Killean (3), Anderson, Gordon and Sorley on target, while successive away defeats at Burnley (2–1) and West Bromwich Albion (2–0) ended their fine start to the year.

Blackburn then managed a narrow 2–1 victory at Burton Wanderers in the first round of the FA Cup, with a brace of goals from Haydock securing a second round tie at Everton. This ended in a one-all draw with James Forrest netting his only goal of the season. However, Rovers were a little unfortunate to lose the replay by the odd goal in five to end their interest in the competition.

On their return to League action, Rovers secured a three-all draw at

Wolverhampton Wanderers, with Josh Hargreaves netting a brace of goals, which preceded a further draw at Small Heath (1–1) with Harry Chippendale scoring for the visitors. Chippendale (2), Anderson, Killean and Gordon were on target in a 5–1 home success against Wolverhampton Wanderers as the Lancashire side moved up to fourth place in the League table. Unfortunately, goalless home and away draws against Derby County, as well as a 5–1 defeat at Stoke, saw Blackburn end the campaign in fifth position, with eleven victories, ten draws and nine defeats in their thirty League games, while scoring fifty-nine goals and conceding forty-nine.

Harry Chippendale and goalkeeper Ogilvie had appeared in all thirty League games for Rovers, while Chippendale had led the scoring with a dozen League goals.

PRESTON NORTH END

Preston North End had managed to retain their First Division status for the 1894–95 season via the test match games. Their sudden and dramatic loss of form may well have been attributed to the death of Nick Ross from tuberculosis, as well as the resignation of William Sudell, who was now awaiting the outcome of an embezzlement charge.

Geordie Drummond, Jack Gordon, Robert Holmes and James Trainer were the only remaining members of the great Preston team of the late 1880s, as Jimmy Ross had left the club. However, Sharp, Dunn, E D Smith, Sanders, Henderson, Grier and Francis Becton were retained from the previous campaign, while inside forward Barr was the most notable new arrival, albeit for a little more than a season.

Preston opened the campaign with a 3–1 victory at Wolverhampton Wanderers, which preceded a 3–1 reverse at the Wednesday, while successive wins at home to Sheffield United (2–1) and at Bolton Wanderers (2–1) saw the Lancashire side move to third place in the League table. A 1–0 home defeat against Small Heath, as well as a four-all draw in the return game with the Birmingham side, ended their fine start to the season.

Early October saw a return to form with away victories at Sheffield United (1–0) and Nottingham Forest (2–0), followed by a one-all home draw with Blackburn Rovers. Their excellent run of results continued with a 2–0 home success against Wolverhampton Wanderers, but a one-all draw at Blackburn Rovers, together with away defeats at Aston Villa (4–1) and Stoke (2–1), saw the Preston side move down to a mid-table position.

Then followed a 3–2 home win against Derby County, which preceded a 2–1 reverse in the return game at Derby, while their fifth draw of the campaign was a 2–2 home affair with Bolton Wanderers. Further defeats at Burnley (2–1) and at home to Everton (2–1) continued to frustrate their loyal supporters.

Preston soon returned to winning ways with a 3–0 home success against the struggling Stoke side, while the year ended with a further home victory against League leaders Sunderland (1–0). However, the north-eastern side soon avenged the defeat in a 2–0 victory against the Preston team on New Year's Day.

Following a 5–4 victory at West Bromwich Albion, the Lancashire side suffered a 1–0 home defeat against Aston Villa, while a 4–0 success against Burnley secured a further home win. Then a 2–0 defeat at Sunderland in the second round of the FA Cup ended their interest in the competition.

On their return to League action, Preston suffered a 4–2 defeat at Everton, followed by successive home victories against West Bromwich Albion (5–0) and Nottingham Forest (3–1), as well as a two-all home draw with Liverpool. The campaign ended with further wins at home to the Wednesday (3–1) and away at Liverpool (5–2). These saw Preston in fourth place in the League with fifteen victories, five draws and ten defeats in their thirty League games, while scoring sixty-two goals and conceding forty-six.

James Trainer, who had missed only two League games in seven seasons, had been the only man ever present in the Preston side, while Robert Holmes, who had missed eleven games since the formation of the Football League, played in all but one in an excellent League campaign. Henderson and Barr had netted ten League goals apiece; Francis Becton had found the net on eleven occasions; while E D Smith had led the scoring with a dozen League goals.

William Sudell eventually received a three-year prison sentence following his embezzlement trial. However, the well-meaning Sudell, who had used his ill-gotten gains for his beloved Preston North End, resurrected his career as a sports reporter in South Africa upon his release from prison. The Preston supporters received a further shock at the season's end when the death was announced of England international Fred Dewhurst, a member of the original 'Invincible' side.

ASTON VILLA

As reigning League Champions, Aston Villa made few changes in their line-up for the 1894–95 season. Bill Dunning continued in goal, with John Baird, James Welford, John Reynolds and James Cowan in defence, while Charlie Athersmith, Bob Chatt, John Devey, Dennis Hodgetts and Steve Smith remained in the attack. However, Dunning and Baird made few appearances during the season as Tom Wilkes took over the goalkeeping duties while Howard Spencer replaced Baird at fullback.

Wilkes made in excess of seventy League appearances in five seasons with the club, while Birmingham-born Spencer, a recent signing from Birchfield Trinity, made nearly 300 appearances in fourteen seasons as well as appearing in the English national team.

Spencer, who would remain with Villa as a player and a director for forty-two years, was generally regarded as one of the most gentlemanly of players to have played the Association game, while his reputation as a scrupulously fair player became legendary.

Willie Groves had decided to return to Scotland. However, he was adequately replaced by George Russell, who had made five appearances during the previous campaign.

Villa opened the season with successive victories at home to Small Heath (2–1) and away at Liverpool (2–1), with Steve Smith on target in both games, while Smith scored for the third game running in a 2–1 home defeat against Sunderland. Villa soon returned to winning ways with a 2–0 success at Derby County, with Bob Chatt and John Devey scoring for the visitors. Then followed away defeats at Stoke (4–1) and Nottingham Forest (2–1), while Dennis Hodgetts netted a brace of goals in a 3–1 home win against West Bromwich Albion, with Albert Woolley completing the scoring in his penultimate appearance for the club.

Dennis Hodgetts again found the net in a two-all draw at Small Heath, which preceded a 2–1 reverse at Sheffield United, while Reynolds (2), Cowan, Dorrell and Hodgetts were on target in a 5–1 home success against Liverpool. A 1–0 defeat at the Wednesday then continued their indifferent away form.

Villa soon returned to form with excellent home wins against Preston North End (4–1) and Wednesday (5–0), with John Devey and Bob Chatt scoring three goals apiece in the two victories, which were preceded by a 3–2 defeat at West Bromwich Albion. Villa reached the halfway stage of the season with a 4–1 home win against Nottingham Forest with goals by Devey (2), Cowan and Hodgetts maintaining Villa's mid-table position. The victory was marred by the announcement of the death of Archie Hunter at the age of thirty-five. The inspirational Hunter, who had done much to guide Villa through their early years, had suffered a heart attack during a League game against Everton in 1890, from which he had never really recovered. However, he was long be remembered as one of the giants of the Association game.

Early December saw Steve Smith score a hat-trick in a 3–1 victory at Blackburn Rovers, which preceded a 3–1 home success against the Wednesday, with Russell, Devey and Reynolds on target. Devey scored a further brace of goals in a 3–0 home win in the return game with Blackburn.

Villa's excellent run of results continued with a 4–0 away win at Wolverhampton Wanderers where Hodgetts (2), Devey and Athersmith were on target, while the year ended with a 6–0 home victory against Stoke, with Athersmith (3), Reynolds, Devey and Chatt scoring, to maintain Villa's hopes of retaining the League Championship. These were improved during the opening week of the new year as the Midlands side secured a four-all draw at Sunderland with Smith (2), Reynolds and Devey netting the visitors' goals.

Steve Smith and Dennis Hodgetts then scored their tenth League goals of the season in a 4–0 home success against Derby County, which preceded a 1–0 victory at Preston North End with John Devey scoring the only goal of the game. Villa's unbeaten run came to an end with a 4–2 reverse at Everton. However, a 2–1 home win against Bolton Wanderers saw a return to winning ways with John Devey scoring his fifteenth League goal of the campaign.

Away from the rigours of the League, Villa managed a 2–1 home success against Derby County in the first round of the FA Cup with goals by Smith and Devey earning a home tie against Newcastle in the second round. In this match Villa raced into a 6–1 half-time lead, while they managed to score one further goal in the second half to register a 7–1 victory with Dorrell (2), Athersmith (2), Devey (2) and Russell on target to secure a third successive home tie against Nottingham Forest in the quarter-finals.

Prior to the quarter-final tie, Villa earned a point in a three-all draw at Burnley with Chatt, Athersmith and a James Crabtree own goal scoring for the visitors. Their FA Cup success continued at Perry Barr where goals by Chatt (2), Smith (2), Russell and James Cowan earned a 6–1 victory against the Nottingham side to secure a semi-final appearance against League leaders Sunderland at Ewood Park, Blackburn.

Sunderland, who had inflicted upon Villa their only home defeat of the season, were expected to win the tie, which seemed a formality when a James Hannah goal secured a 1–0 half-time lead for the north-eastern side. However, Villa rallied during the second half, as a brace of goals by Steve Smith earned the Midlanders a 2–1 victory to secure a third FA Cup Final appearance. This was to be against local rivals West Bromwich Albion, their opponents in both of their previous finals.

On their return to League action, Villa suffered a 4–3 reverse at Bolton Wanderers, with Smith, Athersmith and Devey on target, which preceded a 5–0 home success against Burnley, with Dorrell (2), Athersmith, Chatt and Hodgetts finding the net. Howard Spencer and James Cowan netted rare goals in a two-all home draw with Wolverhampton Wanderers. However, Villa had other things on their minds, mainly their appearance in the FA Cup Final.

EVERTON

Following their sixth place League finish during the previous campaign, Everton made few changes for the 1894–95 season. Williams continued in goal, with Bob Kelso, Richard Boyle, John Holt and Billy Stewart in defence, while Alex Latta, Fred Geary, John Bell, John Southworth, Edgar Chadwick and Alf Milward once again formed the free-scoring attack. However, John Southworth appeared in nine League games during the season prior to sustaining a serious leg injury, which resulted in his premature retirement from the game, while Fred Geary, who had scored seventy-four goals in eighty-three League appearances for Everton, played eight League games during the season, prior to joining the Liverpool club.

Bob Howarth shortly returned to Preston North End, which saw Welsh international Parry make the left back position his own. The most notable new signings were Adams, a defender from Heart of Midlothian, as well as inside forward McInnes from the Third Lanark club.

Everton used four goalkeepers during the season prior to the arrival of Jack Hillman from Burnley during the latter stages of the campaign. However,

Williams retained the goalkeeper's jersey during the opening weeks of the season as the Everton side secured eight successive League wins.

The season opened with a 3–1 home success against Wednesday with Bell, McInnes and Chadwick on target, which preceded a further home win against Small Heath (5–0) with Southworth (3) and Bell (2) netting the Everton goals, while Chadwick, Latta and McInnes found the net in a 3–1 victory at Stoke.

John Southworth scored his second hat-trick of the campaign in a 6–1 home win against Nottingham Forest, which was followed by a further victory in the return game at Forest (3–2), where Bell, Chadwick and Southworth were on target. Their winning run continued with a 4–1 home success against West Bromwich Albion, with Bell, Chadwick and Southworth once again amongst the scorers.

Early October saw Bell, Latta and McInnes find the net in a 3–1 success at Bolton Wanderers, while all three players netted the following week in a 3–0 home win against Liverpool. This preceded a 4–3 defeat at Blackburn Rovers. However, successive draws at Small Heath (4–4) and Liverpool (2–2), as well as at home to Sunderland (2–2), saw the Everton side maintain their position at the head of the League table, with Alex Latta scoring a hat-trick in the game at Small Heath.

Everton then secured a 2–1 home success against Blackburn Rovers with Bell and Milward on target, which was followed by a 4–1 victory at West Bromwich Albion with Latta, Chadwick, Milward and Stewart scoring for the visitors. Chadwick, Latta and McInnes then netted in a 3–1 home win against Bolton Wanderers. Alf Milward, who had missed eleven of the opening dozen League games, scored his third goal of the campaign as Everton ended the year with a 2–1 victory at Preston North End to maintain the leadership of the League. Then new year defeats at the Wednesday (3–0) and Wolverhampton Wanderers (1–0) saw the Lancashire side move down to second place in the League table.

Mid-January saw Everton return to winning ways with home victories against Stoke (3–0) and Aston Villa (4–2) on either side of a two-all draw at Derby County, with Fred Geary on target in all three games, while McInnes subsequently found the net in a one-all home draw with Sheffield United.

Following a John Bell hat-trick in a 3–0 victory at Southport in the first round of the FA Cup, Everton received a home tie against Blackburn Rovers in the second round, which ended in a one-all draw with Edgar Chadwick scoring for the home side. Surprisingly, Everton won the replay by the odd goal in five with Chadwick scoring a brace of goals to secure a third round tie at the Wednesday.

Prior to the FA Cup tie, Bell, Chadwick, Hartley and Milward found the net in a 4–2 home victory against Preston North End, which preceded a 4–2 defeat at Sheffield United. Further disappointment arrived in the cup game with a 2–0 reverse at the Wednesday. However, the Lancashire side soon returned to form with successive home and away victories against Burnley (3–2 and 4–2) with Alf Milward and John Bell on target in both games.

Bell and Milward then scored for the third League game in succession in a 2–1 home victory against Wolverhampton Wanderers, which left Everton two points adrift from Sunderland, with a game in hand. However, their hopes of winning the Championship ended with successive defeats at home to Derby County (3–2) and away at Sunderland (2–1), while the season came to a close with a two-all draw at Aston Villa, and Everton finished the campaign as League runners-up.

Everton had won eighteen, drawn six and lost six of their thirty League games, while scoring eighty-two goals and conceding fifty. John Southworth scored nine goals in as many League appearances; Milward and McInnes had found the net on ten occasions; Latta and Chadwick had scored eleven League goals apiece; while John Bell had led the scoring with fifteen League goals in an excellent season for the Lancashire side, for whom Richard Boyle had been ever present. The loss of John Southworth had arguably cost Everton the opportunity of a second League Championship.

SUNDERLAND

Sunderland had been thwarted by Aston Villa in their quest for a third successive League title during the 1893–94 season. However, their team had a familiar look to it for the 1894–95 League campaign as John Doig continued in goal, with Meehan, Hugh Wilson, Billy Dunlop and Donald Gow in defence, while Millar, Scott, James Gillespie, John Campbell and James Hannah remained in the attack.

Tom Porteous had joined Rotherham Town; Gibson had returned to Glasgow Rangers; John Auld would shortly sign for the Newcastle club; while David Hannah moved to the Liverpool club during the early stages of the season.

Inside forward, Tom Hyslop, a future Scottish international who had joined Sunderland from the army in the January of 1894, scored seven goals in thirteen League appearances prior to signing for Stoke, while McReadie, McNeill and Johnston had arrived from north of the border.

McReadie, a Scottish international, had signed from Glasgow Rangers, where he would return within a couple of seasons, while McNeill and Johnston had arrived from Clyde, with McNeill eventually making in excess of 150 appearances for the north-eastern side, while Johnston played sixty League games prior to moving to Aston Villa.

Sunderland opened the season with an 8–0 home success against Derby County with Gillespie (2), Millar (2), Hyslop (2), Campbell and James Hannah on target, which preceded a further home win against Burnley (3–0) with Tom Hyslop netting all three goals. Their fine start to the season continued with victories at Aston Villa (2–1) and at home to West Bromwich Albion (3–0) with Johnny Campbell scoring in both games. However, a 4–1 reverse at Bolton Wanderers ended their winning run.

Then followed victories at home to Stoke (3–1) and away at Derby County (2–1) with Millar, Hyslop and Campbell once again amongst the goals, which preceded a two-all draw at Everton where Millar netted a brace of goals. Millar scored his sixth League goal of the season and Johnny Campbell his fifth in a 2–0 home success against Wolverhampton Wanderers.

Early November saw McReadie on target in a one-all draw at Blackburn Rovers, followed by a 4–0 home win against Bolton Wanderers with James Hannah (2), Campbell and Gillespie netting the Sunderland goals. The same players scored the following week in a 3–2 home success against Liverpool.

Sunderland then secured a 7–1 home win against Small Heath with McReadie, Wilson and Gillespie netting a brace of goals apiece, while Gillespie scored for the fourth successive game in a 3–2 home victory against Blackburn Rovers. However, following a 2–0 success at West Bromwich Albion, the north-eastern side ended the year with successive away defeats at Nottingham Forest (2–1) and Preston North End (1–0).

New Year's Day saw Sunderland secure a 2–0 victory in the return game with Preston with Hannah and Millar on target, which preceded a four-all home draw with Aston Villa with Hannah scoring a hat-trick. Their third home game in five days ended in a two-all draw against Nottingham Forest with Millar and Campbell finding the net.

Late January saw the north-eastern side secure successive away victories at Wolverhampton Wanderers (4–1) and Stoke (5–2) with Johnny Campbell netting a brace of goals in both games. They were followed by an 11–1 home success against Fairfield in the first round of the FA Cup with Jimmy Millar (5), James Hannah (3), Scott, McReadie and Gillespie on target to earn a home tie against Preston North End in the second round.

Prior to the FA Cup tie, the north-eastern side managed a one-all draw in a League encounter at Small Heath, which preceded a 2–0 victory against Preston in the FA Cup, with Johnny Campbell scoring twice, while Campbell again found the net in successive home wins against Sheffield United (2–0) and the Wednesday (3–1).

Sunderland were then drawn at home to Bolton Wanderers in the quarter-final of the FA Cup, which resulted in a 2–1 victory with Hugh Wilson scoring a brace of goals to secure a semi-final tie against Aston Villa. However, prior to the FA Cup game, the north-eastern side suffered a 4–0 defeat at Sheffield United, while their hopes of winning the cup ended at Ewood Park where Villa won by the odd goal in three.

On their return to League action, the Sunderland team secured successive away victories at Wednesday (2–1), Liverpool (3–2) and Burnley (3–0), with Dunlop, Campbell, Wilson, Millar, McReadie and Gillespie sharing the visitors' goals. The campaign ended with a 2–1 home success against second-placed Everton, which saw Sunderland secure their third League title by a five-point margin, following twenty-one wins, five draws and four defeats in their thirty League games, while scoring eighty goals and conceding thirty-seven.

Johnny Campbell and John Doig had appeared in all thirty League games for the newly crowned champions. James Hannah had ended the campaign with eleven League goals, James Gillespie and Jimmy Millar had netted a dozen goals apiece, while Johnny Campbell had once again headed the goal scoring list with nineteen League goals.

Bury Secure the Second Division Championship

Eight teams were involved in the race for the Second Division test match places during the 1894–95 League campaign, which saw Woolwich Arsenal register 7–0 home victories against Crewe and Burslem Port Vale, while Burton Wanderers inflicted comprehensive defeats on Walsall Town Swifts (7–0), Manchester City (formerly Ardwick) (8–0) and Newcastle (9–0).

Grimsby Town scored seven goals against both Burton United and Burton Swifts, while Darwen secured an 8–2 home success against Leicester Fosse. However, the Leicester side enjoyed an excellent season, which included a 9–1 home win against Walsall Town Swifts. Manchester City recorded relatively easy home wins against Notts County (7–1) and Lincoln (11–3), but their indifferent away form saw them finish in a mid-table position. Newcastle, whose fine home form included victories against Burton United (6–3), Crewe (6–0) and Walsall Town Swifts (7–2), recorded only one win on their travels.

NEWTON HEATH

Newton Heath had finished in last place in the First Division in each of the two previous seasons, which had resulted in relegation to the Second Division for the 1894–95 League campaign. However, the Manchester side retained the majority of their players for the new season as Erentz, Stewart, McNaught and Perrins continued in defence, while Douglas replaced Fall between the posts. McArtney replaced Mitchell at right fullback, while Peters and Smith formed a new left wing partnership.

Newton Heath opened the season with a 1–0 away defeat at Burton Wanderers, which preceded an eight-game unbeaten run, including a 5–2 victory against Manchester City in which Smith found the net on four occasions.

Defeats were few for the Newton Heath side, who lost only seven of their thirty League games. They remained unbeaten at home, with a 9–0 success against Walsall Town Swifts their highest win of the campaign with Cassidy, Donaldson, Peters and Smith netting a brace of goals apiece.

FA Cup success had once again eluded the Manchester side, who suffered a 3–2 home defeat against Stoke in the opening round. However, they had managed to achieve a third place League finish, due mainly to the goal-scoring exploits of Smith who had ended the campaign with nineteen goals in twenty-nine League appearances. This enabled the Newton Heath team to take part in the end-of-season test match games.

NOTTS COUNTY

Notts County had tended to struggle during their time in the First Division, but as reigning FA Cup holders, they were expected to be amongst the Second Division front runners at the season's end.

County made few changes in their line-up for the 1894–95 League campaign. George Toone continued in goal, with Bramley, Harper, Hendry, Calderhead and Alf Shelton in defence, while Arthur Watson, Sam Donnelly, Jimmy Logan, Dan Bruce and Harry Daft remained in the attack.

Walter Bull, a free-scoring outside left, had been the most notable new arrival to the Nottingham club. He soon reverted to the centre half position, from where he gave many excellent displays prior to joining Tottenham Hotspur.

County opened the season with a six-game unbeaten run, which included home wins against Darwen (2–1), Lincoln (3–0), Grimsby (3–2) and Leicester Fosse (3–0). A loss of form during October saw the Nottingham side win three of their following ten League games, leaving them in a mid-table position at the turn of the year.

Following a 2–1 reverse at Bury on New Year's Day, the Nottingham side secured successive home wins against Burton Wanderers (2–0) and Burton Swifts (5–1), as well as away victories at Crewe (3–0) and Grimsby (1–0), while Dan Bruce netted five goals in a 10–0 home win against Burslem Port Vale. However, a 7–1 defeat at Manchester City ended their excellent run of results. County eventually ended the campaign as League runners-up, with only eight defeats in their thirty League games, which meant a place in the end-of-season test match games. A major disappointment during the season saw County suffer a 5–1 defeat at the Wednesday in the first round of the FA Cup.

BURY

Bury, a small town on the outskirts of Manchester, were elected to the Second Division of the Football League prior to the 1894–95 season. With few expectations, they surprised many during their first League campaign as they totally dominated the race for the Second Division title.

Bury opened the season with twelve victories and one defeat, which included four-goal home wins against Manchester City, Newcastle, Burslem Port Vale and Crewe, as well as five-goal victories in the return game at Crewe and at home to Grimsby.

Further four-goal wins were registered against Burton Wanderers, Lincoln, Walsall Town Swifts and Leicester Fosse, while a 1–0 reverse at Bolton Wanderers in the second round of the FA Cup saw a rare disappointment for the Bury side. However, following their excellent League campaign, in which all fifteen home games were won, the Lancashire team were crowned

Champions of the Second Division by a margin of nine points over Notts County.

Walsall Town Swifts Suffer an Injustice

At the close of the 1894–95 League campaign, the last three teams in the Second Division were required to apply for re-election to the League for the following season. Crewe, who had lost all fifteen of their away fixtures, were rooted at the foot of the table with ten points, while Burslem Port Vale finished one place above them on eighteen points.

Lincoln and Walsall Town Swifts, who had secured twenty points apiece during the season, were both required to apply for re-election, which resulted in Lincoln, Crewe and Burslem Port Vale retaining their Football League status, while Loughborough Town received sufficient votes to gain a place in the Second Division at the expense of Walsall Town Swifts.

As a result of the injustice to the Walsall side, it was decided in future to determine a team's League standing on goal average rather than a voting system.

A Third FA Cup Final Meeting Between Villa and Albion

At the second round stage of the 1894–95 FA Cup, thirteen of the sixteen teams remaining in the competition were from the First Division, together with Bury, Newcastle and Middlesbrough. All three teams from outside the top Division failed to progress to the quarter-finals. Bury suffered a 1–0 defeat at Bolton, with James Cassidy on target for the Wanderers; Middlesbrough were well beaten at the Wednesday by six goals to one, with Davis (3), Spiksley (2) and Brady scoring for the home side; while Newcastle suffered a 7–1 reverse at Aston Villa, with Athersmith (2), Dorrell (2), Devey (2) and Russell netting for the Midlands team.

Wolverhampton Wanderers secured a 2–0 home success against the struggling Stoke side. Johnny Campbell scored a brace of goals for Sunderland in a 2–0 home victory against Preston North End, while Stewart and McInnes found the net for Nottingham Forest in a 2–0 win at Liverpool.

Everton narrowly won at Blackburn Rovers by the odd goal in five, following a one-all draw, with Chadwick (2) and Hartley on target for the Liverpudlians. West Bromwich Albion completed the quarter-final line-up with a 2–1 victory against Sheffield United in a replayed tie, with Hutchinson and a Willie Foulke own goal scoring for the West Bromwich side.

Albion were then drawn at home to Wolverhampton Wanderers in the quarter-finals, which resulted in a 1–0 win with Roddy McLeod scoring the only goal of the game. Sunderland proceeded to the semi-finals with a 2–1 home success against Bolton Wanderers, with Hugh Wilson netting a brace of goals for the League leaders.

Aston Villa enjoyed a relatively easy passage into the semi-finals with a 6–2 home victory against Nottingham Forest with Chatt (2), Smith (2), Russell and Cowan on target, while Brady and Ferrier found the net for the Wednesday in a 2–0 home win against Everton.

Both semi-finals proved exciting affairs, with Steve Smith scoring twice for Aston Villa in a 2–1 victory against Sunderland at Ewood Park, while goals by Hutchinson and a Billy Williams penalty earned Albion a 2–0 success against the Wednesday at the Derby Ground to secure a fifth FA Cup Final appearance. This was to take place at Crystal Palace on 20 April in the third FA Cup Final meeting with Villa.

England Prove Too Strong for Ireland

England's opening international game of the season took place at the County Ground, Derby, on 9 March against Ireland, with England selecting an attacking side, which included four new caps.

Francis Becton (Preston North End) and Robert 'Rabbi' Howell (Sheffield United) made the first of two appearances for their country. Thomas Crawshaw (Wednesday) played the first of ten England games at the heart of the defence, while the most notable newcomer in the England side was Steve Bloomer (Derby County), who gained the first of his twenty-three England caps.

John Sutcliffe (Bolton Wanderers) made his second international appearance in goal, while there were recalls for James Crabtree (Burnley) and Robert Holmes (Preston North End) in defence, together with Billy Bassett (West Bromwich Albion) and John Goodall (Derby County) in the attack.

James Turner (Stoke), who had previously represented England while a Bolton Wanderers' player, played his second international game at half back, while Joseph Schofield, his Stoke team-mate, made his final appearance at outside left.

Following many hours of torrential rain in the Derby area, the crowd was disappointingly low, however, the absent spectators missed a treat as goals by Bloomer (2), Goodall (2), Becton (2), Howell, Bassett and an Irish own goal secured a 9–0 victory for the English.

Wales Hold England to a Draw

A week after the victory against Ireland, the Welsh national side arrived at the Queens Club, Kensington, to play against an England team that consisted entirely of players with Corinthian connections, including five members making their international debuts.

George Raikes, who played county cricket for both Norfolk and Hampshire, made the first of four appearances in goal, prior to being ordained, while William Oakley, a former long jump champion of England, gained the first of his sixteen caps at left fullback. Richard Barker, who had played for the Casuals in the 1894 FA Amateur Cup final, played his one England game at left half back, while there were single England appearances for Gerald Dewhurst and Morris Stanbrough, a schoolmaster who had won an Amateur Cup winners' medal with the Old Carthusians.

Lewis Lodge, Arthur Henfrey and Charles Wreford-Brown completed the defensive line-up, while there were further appearances for Rupert Sandilands, Robert Gosling and Gilbert O Smith in the attack. However, the expected English victory did not materialise as they were held to a one-all draw by the visitors, with G O Smith scoring for the home side.

England Remain Unbeaten

Two weeks prior to the FA Cup Final, the Scottish national team visited Goodison Park, hoping for a victory to secure the 1895 international Championship.

Lewis Lodge and Robert Gosling were retained following the one-all draw with Wales, while John Sutcliffe (Bolton Wanderers), James Crabtree (Burnley), Billy Bassett (West Bromwich Albion), John Goodall (Derby County) and Steve Bloomer (Derby County) were recalled from the 9–0 victory against Ireland. Ernest Needham (Sheffield United), John Holt (Everton) and John Reynolds (Aston Villa) made their first England appearances of the season, while Steve Smith (Aston Villa) gained his only England cap in the attack.

A crowd in excess of 30,000 arrived at Goodison Park to witness an excellent display by the English forward line, which resulted in Steve Bloomer securing an early lead, while further goals by Steve Smith and a Gibson own goal saw the home side three goals to the good at the halfway stage of the game. However, despite constant pressure during the second half, the England team failed to add to their score and their unbeaten run stretched to eighteen games.

A Hat-trick for Francis Becton

Following the victory against the Scots, a Football League eleven travelled to Celtic Park, Glasgow to play the annual inter-League game against the Scots with the English including John Reynolds, Charlie Athersmith, John Devey, Dennis Hodgetts and Steve Smith from the successful Aston Villa team, together with Storer (Woolwich Arsenal) in goal.

Robert Holmes (Preston North End), James Crabtree (Burnley), Tom Crawshaw (Wednesday) and Ernest Needham (Sheffield United) completed the defensive line-up, while Francis Becton, who had recently moved from Preston North End to Liverpool, led the attack.

Becton's recent transfer had certainly revitalised his game as he netted a hat-trick in a 4–1 victory, with John Devey completing the English scoring.

A Single Goal Wins the Cup for Aston Villa

The 1895 FA Cup Final took place at Crystal Palace on 20 April with West Bromwich Albion meeting their local rivals Aston Villa, with Albion selecting the following eleven:

Reader

Williams   Horton

Tom Perry   Higgins   Taggart

Bassett   McLeod   Richards   Hutchinson   Banks

Villa selected the following players:

Wilkes

Spencer   Welford

Reynolds   James Cowan   Russell

Athersmith   Chatt   John Devey   Hodgetts   Smith

John Lewis of Blackburn was appointed as match referee.

Joe Reader, Billy Bassett and Roddy McLeod had appeared in Albion's FA Cup-winning side against Villa three years earlier, together with John Reynolds, who had since joined Villa, while James Cowan, Charlie Athersmith, John Devey and Dennis Hodgetts had been members of the losing Villa team.

Following the winning of the toss, Albion elected to kick with the wind with the sun on their backs. However, Villa dominated the early proceedings as Charlie Athersmith rounded Albion defender John Horton, prior to passing to Bob Chatt, who shot towards the West Bromwich goal. Joe Reader managed to half-save the goal attempt, but John Devey scrambled the loose ball over the Albion goal line to secure a one-goal lead for Villa.

Villa continued to dominate the first half as Athersmith, Hodgetts and Devey repeatedly had the Albion defence in trouble, with only late clearances by Williams and Higgins keeping the score down to a single goal. As the first half progressed, Albion came more into the game and Billy Bassett made many excellent runs down the wing, which resulted in three successive corners, ably dealt with by the Villa defence.

As the half-time whistle approached, Devey and Higgins clashed heads during a tussle for the ball, which resulted in the latter leaving the field of play to receive medical treatment. However, Higgins soon returned to see the inspirational Billy Bassett create a couple of goal-scoring chances for centre forward Richards, unfortunately both missed.

Albion made few goal scoring attempts during the second half, while Devey and Chatt forced excellent saves out of Joe Reader in the West Bromwich goal. Neither side found the net during the remainder of the game and Villa held on to win the FA Cup for a second time. Albion goalkeeper Reader had constantly been called into action, while his opposite number Wilkes had hardly had a shot to save. There was little argument that Billy Bassett had been the finest player on view, in spite of the meagre help from his team-mates, who mostly had been subdued by the Villa defence.

Albion Struggle to Avoid the Test Match Positions

Following their FA Cup disappointment, the Albion team had one League game remaining in which a victory was required if they were to avoid the end-of-season test match games. Liverpool, Stoke and Derby County were the teams immediately above the West Bromwich side, who needed to win their final game against the Wednesday by five clear goals, as the League table in Table XIV confirms.

Table XIV: *First Division League positions before West Bromwich Albion's last game of the 1894–95 season*

Position	Team	Played	Won	Lost	Drawn	For	Against	Points
13th	Stoke	30	9	15	6	50	67	24
14th	Derby County	30	7	14	9	45	68	23
15th	Liverpool	30	7	15	8	51	70	22
16th	West Brom Albion	29	9	16	4	45	66	22

With the exception of Richards and Banks, who were replaced by Tom Green and Jasper Geddes, Albion fielded their FA Cup Final side in the hope of retaining their First Division status for a further season.

Albion had few problems against the Wednesday as goals by Geddes (2), Green and Hutchinson saw them race into a 4–0 lead, while second half goals by Roddy McLeod and Tom Perry secured a 6–0 victory for the Black Country side, who thereby avoided the test match places by the narrowest of margins.

Hutchinson, Reader and Tom Perry had appeared in all thirty League games during Albion's eventful season. Billy Bassett ended the campaign with seven League goals, McLeod had found the net on nine occasions, while Hutchinson had led the scoring with fifteen League goals. However, the West Bromwich side gained a little consolation at the season's end with a 1–0 victory against Aston Villa in the final of the Birmingham Cup, with Hutchinson scoring the only goal of the game in a replayed tie.

ASTON VILLA

Aston Villa completed their League fixtures with a two-all home draw with Everton, with Smith and Athersmith on target, which made little difference to their League placing as they ended the campaign in third position following seventeen victories, eight defeats and five draws in their thirty League games, while scoring eighty-two goals and conceding forty-three.

James Cowan and Charlie Athersmith had been ever present in the Villa side, with Chatt, Devey, Hodgetts, Russell, Smith and Welford missing no more than a handful of games. Dennis Hodgetts had ended the campaign with eleven League goals, Steve Smith had found the net on thirteen occasions, with John Devey leading the scoring with sixteen League goals.

The final League placings at the close of the 1894–95 season are in Table XV and Table XVI.

Table XV: *First Division Football League placings at the end of the 1894–95 season*

	P	W	D	L	F	A	PTS
1. Sunderland	30	21	5	4	80	37	47
2. Everton	30	18	6	6	82	50	42
3. Aston Villa	30	17	5	8	82	43	39
4. Preston North End	30	15	5	10	62	46	35
5. Blackburn Rovers	30	11	10	9	59	49	32
6. Sheffield United	30	14	4	12	57	55	32
7. Nottingham Forest	30	13	5	12	50	56	31
8. Wednesday	30	12	4	14	50	55	28
9. Burnley	30	11	4	15	44	56	26
10. Bolton Wanderers	30	9	7	14	61	62	25
11. Wolverhampton Wndrs	30	9	7	14	43	63	25
12. Small Heath	30	9	7	14	50	74	25
13. West Bromwich Albion	30	10	4	16	51	66	24
14. Stoke	30	9	6	15	50	67	24
15. Derby County	30	7	9	14	45	68	23
16. Liverpool	30	7	8	15	51	70	22

Table XVI: *Second Division Football League placings at the end of the 1894–95 season*

	P	W	D	L	F	A	PTS
1. Bury	30	23	2	5	78	33	48
2. Notts County	30	17	5	8	75	45	39
3. Newton Heath	30	15	8	7	78	44	38
4. Leicester Fosse	30	15	8	7	72	53	38
5. Grimsby	30	18	1	11	79	52	37

	P	W	D	L	F	A	PTS
6. Darwen	30	16	4	10	74	43	36
7. Burton Wanderers	30	14	7	9	67	39	35
8. Woolwich Arsenal	30	14	6	10	75	58	34
9. Manchester City	30	14	3	13	82	72	31
10. Newcastle	30	12	3	15	72	84	27
11. Burton Swifts	30	11	3	16	52	74	25
12. Rotherham Town	30	11	2	17	55	62	24
13. Lincoln	30	10	0	20	52	92	20
14. Walsall TS	30	10	0	20	47	92	20
15. Burslem Port Vale	30	7	4	19	39	77	18
16. Crewe	30	3	4	23	26	103	10

Bury's Swift Progress Continues

As the 1894–95 season came to a close, there remained one important issue that concerned the test match games between the last placed three teams in the First Division and the top three teams in the Second.

Liverpool, who had finished in last place in the First Division, were due to play Bury, the Second Division Champions, at Ewood Park; Derby County would meet Notts County at the Leicester Fosse ground, while Stoke would play Newton Heath at the Burslem Port Vale ground.

Stoke had little difficulty in retaining their First Division status following a 3–0 victory against Newton Heath, with Joseph Schofield scoring a brace of goals. Bury secured a 1–0 success against Liverpool to gain promotion to the top Division at the first attempt.

Derby County were a little unfortunate during the early stages of their game with Notts County as Steve Bloomer and John McMillan saw goalbound shots hit the Notts goalposts. In spite of Derby dominating the game, the Nottingham side ended the first half one goal to the good when John Robinson failed to hold a half-hit shot from outside right Fletcher.

Little changed during the second half as Derby pursued the equalising goal with Paul rattling the Notts goalposts with an excellent volley. With seven minutes remaining, Jimmy Methven tried a speculative shot from twenty-five yards, which rebounded to the waiting Steve Bloomer, who levelled the scores. Further pressure from the Derby side saw John McMillan score what turned out to be the winning goal, following excellent play by John Cox.

As a result of the test match games, Stoke and Derby County retained their First Division status, while Bury were promoted from the Second Division.

Chapter XXI

ASTON VILLA REGAIN THE LEAGUE TITLE – 1895–96

ASTON VILLA WIN THE LEAGUE CHAMPIONSHIP
WOODEN SPOONISTS WEST BROMWICH ALBION AVOID RELEGATION
STOKE'S TOP SIX FINISH
A SWIFT RETURN FOR LIVERPOOL
AN ALL-TIME LOW FOR NOTTS COUNTY
WEDNESDAY WIN THE FA CUP
ENGLAND'S UNBEATEN RUN ENDS IN GLASGOW
STEVE BLOOMER SCORES FIVE AGAINST WALES

BURY

Bury's domination of the Second Division during the 1894–95 campaign had resulted in their promotion to the top Division within a year of joining the Football League. However, the ambitious Lancashire side were well aware of the difficult task that lay ahead as members of the First Division.

Bury had been formed during April 1885 following a meeting at the White Horse Hotel, which resulted in the election of Colonel John Hall as club president, who made arrangements for a field in Gigg Lane to be used for home fixtures.

Their opening game took place at Little Lever where they secured a two-all draw, while their first game at Gigg Lane resulted in a 4–3 victory against Wigan with a team consisting mainly of local players of which Ghent, Lee, Douglas, Ward, Pollock, Clark, J Wright, F Wright, Malpass and J A Ross were regular members.

Early 1887 saw the arrival of George Ross from Bury Wesleyans, who served the club in various capacities for twenty years, which coincided with the erection of a covered stand. However, the Lancashire side were hardly ready to play at the top level, as a 10–0 FA Cup defeat against Blackburn Rovers confirmed.

The 1888–89 season saw excellent victories against Belfast Athletic (7–0), Brierfield (13–0) and Darwen Old Wanderers (9–0), as well as a 3–2 success against Kilmarnock, who had been the first Scottish team to visit Gigg Lane, while a 5–0 win against Accrington showed the measure of their improvement.

Following the success of the newly formed Football League, Bury were invited to become one of the founder members of the Lancashire League, which saw them finish the 1889–90 season as runners-up to Higher Walton by a single point. However, a 2–1 victory against Blackpool in the final of the Lancashire Junior Cup more than made up for their disappointment.

Prior to the 1890–91 campaign, Bury acquired the services of Jack Plant, an outside left from Bollington, who, like George Ross, served the club for a number of years. The season ended with Bury winning the Lancashire League Championship following fifteen victories in twenty League fixtures.

Further success was attained during the following season as Bury retained the Lancashire League title, while victories against Newton Heath (2–0), Everton (2–0) and Accrington (4–0) saw them reach the final of the Lancashire Senior Cup at their first attempt, where they met Blackburn Rovers, the finest cup-fighting side in all England.

Rovers were expected to win the final at the Preston ground by a considerable margin. However, Bury managed to secure a 2–0 victory, with the following players doing them proud:

Lowe

Cooper   Warburton

Pemberton   Jobson   Ross

Wilkinson   Spence   Conroy   Bourne   Plant

The 1892–93 season saw the debut of Billy Barbour, who eventually captained Bury into the Football League, while their season ended in a third place finish. Improved performances during the 1893–94 campaign saw Bury finish as runners-up in the Lancashire League, as well as winning the Manchester Cup, which led them to receive an invitation to join the Second Division of the Football League prior to the 1894–95 season.

Bury's opening game in the Football League resulted in a 4–2 home success against Manchester City, with Billy Barbour having the distinction of scoring their first goal in the League. Success continued throughout the season, which saw the Lancashire side win twenty-three of their thirty League games, including all fifteen on home soil, as they were crowned as Second Division Champions, thus securing a place in the end-of-season test match games.

Liverpool, who had finished at the foot of the First Division, were Bury's opponents in the test match games, with Bury fielding the following eleven:

Montgomery

Davidson   Davies

McNaughton   Clegg   Ross

Wyllie   Miller   Barbour   Henderson   Plant

However, Bury were soon reduced to ten men when goalkeeper Archibald Montgomery received his 'marching orders' for ungentlemanly misconduct. Nevertheless, the ten men managed a 1–0 victory to secure a place in the First Division for the 1895–96 League campaign.

Few changes were made in the Bury line-up for their first season in the top Division, with future England international Jimmy Settle from Bolton Wanderers the most notable new arrival. A wretched start to the season saw successive away defeats at Nottingham Forest (5–0), Everton (3–2) and Burnley (3–0) as well as at home to Bolton Wanderers (3–0), leaving the First Division newcomers at the foot of the League table.

Then followed a 1–0 home success against Sheffield United, which preceded a goalless draw at Sunderland, while their excellent form continued with a 4–2 away victory at Bolton Wanderers. But odd-goal defeats at Derby County (2–1) and at home to Small Heath (5–4) saw the Lancashire side once again struggling near the foot of the table.

Bury soon returned to winning ways, with home victories against West Bromwich Albion (3–0) and the Wednesday (6–1), which were followed by narrow home defeats against Derby County (2–1), Stoke (1–0) and Preston North End (2–1), while a rare away success was obtained in a 2–0 victory at Stoke. However, a 2–0 defeat at Aston Villa in the final game of the year continued Bury's indifferent run of results.

New Year's Day saw Bury suffer a further home defeat against Burnley (4–3), which left them with eleven points from their opening seventeen League games; however, an excellent run of results during the latter stages of the season saw the Lancashire club climb to a mid-table position.

Their return to form began with a 2–0 victory at Blackburn Rovers, followed by a one-all home draw with Everton, while FA Cup wins against Stockton and Newcastle saw them progress to the quarter-final stages of the competition. This preceded further home wins against Wolverhampton Wanderers (3–0) and the Wednesday (3–1), but a 2–0 reverse at Bolton Wanderers in the quarter-finals of the FA Cup ended their hopes of a semi-final appearance.

Following a 1–0 reverse at Small Heath, Bury secured successive home wins against Aston Villa (5–3) and Nottingham Forest (1–0) as well as a 3–1 victory at West Bromwich Albion. Their winning run ended with a 2–1 home defeat against Sunderland.

Early April saw the Bury team secure a point in a one-all draw at Preston North End, which preceded away defeats at Sheffield United (8–0) and Wolverhampton Wanderers (1–0). The season ended with a 2–0 home success against Blackburn Rovers, leaving Bury in eleventh position in the League following twelve victories, three draws and fifteen defeats in their thirty League games, while scoring fifty goals and conceding fifty-four.

WEST BROMWICH ALBION

West Bromwich Albion had enjoyed a mixed 1894–95 season, which had seen them narrowly avoid the play-off positions in the final game of the campaign, as well as reaching the final of the FA Cup.

Few changes were made in the Albion line-up for the 1895–96 League campaign. Joe Reader continued in goal, with Williams, Horton, Higgins, Taggart and Tom Perry in defence, while Bassett, McLeod, Hutchinson, Banks and William Richards remained in the attack.

Jasper Geddes, who had scored three goals in as many games during the previous season, had returned to Millwall Athletic, while the most notable newcomer was Jack Paddock from local amateur football, as well as Flewitt from Everton, who scored eighteen goals in sixty-five League appearances for the West Bromwich side.

Albion opened the season with a 1–0 reverse at Aston Villa, followed by successive home defeats against Burnley (2–0) and Preston North End (2–1). A 3–1 defeat at Stoke continued their poor start to the season, but late September saw their first victory of the campaign as Paddock (2) and Billy Bassett found the net in a 3–1 home success against Nottingham Forest. Then followed a 5–3 defeat at the Wednesday, with Hutchinson (2) and William Richards on target for the visitors, while Jack Paddock and Roddy McLeod netted the Albion goals in successive draws at Everton (1–1) and at home to Aston Villa (1–1). Further home defeats against the Wednesday (3–2) and Bolton Wanderers (3–2), as well as a 3–0 reverse at Bury, saw Albion languishing at the foot of the League table following one victory in their opening eleven League games.

Roddy McLeod then scored the only goal of the game in a 1–0 home win against Stoke, which preceded defeats at Nottingham Forest (2–0) and at home to Everton (3–0). Richards and McLeod were again on target in a 2–1 home success against Wolverhampton Wanderers, but a 4–1 reverse at Derby County continued their poor away form.

Albion then secured a two-all draw at Small Heath where Banks and McLeod found the net, while Billy Bassett scored a rare goal in a one-all home draw with Sunderland in the final game of the year. The new year saw further disappointment for the Black Country side with away defeats at Sheffield United (2–0), Burnley (3–0) and Sunderland (7–1), with a goalless home draw against Derby County their only consolation during a dismal month.

Away from the pressures of the League, Albion began their FA Cup campaign with a 2–1 victory at Blackburn Rovers, with William Richards scoring the winning goal to secure a second round tie at Grimsby. This ended in a one-all draw, with Roddy McLeod on target for the visitors. Prior to the FA Cup replay, Albion suffered a 1–0 reverse in a League encounter at Blackburn Rovers. However, their excellent FA Cup form continued with a 3–0 success against Grimsby with William Richards (2) and Roddy McLeod on target, while Richards again found the net in a much needed home win against Sheffield United (1–0).

February's end saw the West Bromwich side suffer a 1–0 defeat at Derby County in the quarter-final of the FA Cup, while their improved League form saw a 2–1 away success at Wolverhampton Wanderers with Richards and Flewitt scoring the all-important Albion goals. Successive defeats at home to

Bury (3–1) and away at Bolton Wanderers (2–1), as well as goalless draws at Preston North End and at home to Small Heath, saw Albion return to the foot of the League table with the end-of-season play-off games imminent.

Albion managed a 3–2 home success against Blackburn Rovers in their final game of the campaign, with Richards, Taggart and Hutchinson on target, but it had been a little too late for the West Bromwich team. They had finished in sixteenth position in the League with six wins, seven draws and seventeen defeats in their thirty League games, while scoring thirty goals and conceding fifty-nine. McLeod, Williams, Higgins and Tom Perry had been ever-presents in Albion's most disappointing season to date. William Richards and Roddy McLeod had led the scoring with six League goals apiece. However, it was apparent that Albion required a little more effort if they were to retain their First Division status.

SMALL HEATH

Small Heath had managed to avoid the test match positions at the end of the 1894–95 League campaign, despite conceding more goals than any other First Division side. This resulted in a number of changes in their defensive line-up for the 1895–96 season. Goalkeeper Charles Partridge had joined Willenhall Town, leaving William Meates and James Roach to share the goalkeeping duties, while William Purves and Ted Devey left the club during the early weeks of the season, together with Caesar Jenkyns, who had signed for Woolwich Arsenal. Jack Hallam, Billy Walton, Frank Mobley, Fred Wheldon and Tommy Hands retained their places in the attack, while newcomers included defender Frank Lester from Walsall Unity, who made seventy-one League appearances in five seasons with the club, as well as Adam Fraser, who remained for one season following his transfer from Glasgow Nomads.

Alec Leake, who had arrived from Old Hill Wanderers to replace Caesar Jenkyns at centre half, made in excess of 200 appearances for the Birmingham side, as well as appearing in the English national team, while inside forward, John Jones, who had made one appearance during the previous campaign, scored fifteen goals in thirty-five League games for the club.

Small Heath opened the season with successive away defeats at Sheffield United (2–0), Aston Villa (7–3), Nottingham Forest (3–0) and Preston North End (3–2), as well as at home to Stoke (2–1) and Bolton Wanderers (2–1). Their first victory of the campaign was during the second week of October with a 5–4 success at Bury where Wheldon (2), Jones (2) and Mobley found the net. Further defeats at Stoke (6–1) and at home to Aston Villa (4–1) saw the Birmingham side in serious trouble at the foot of the League table.

Frank Mobley then netted his sixth League goal of the campaign in a 1–0 home victory against Nottingham Forest, which preceded a 5–2 home win against Preston North End with Wheldon (2), Jones (2) and Mobley on target. However, their improved form soon came to an end with successive defeats at

Derby County (8–0) and Sunderland (2–1), as well as at home to Everton (3–0).

Then followed a two-all home draw with West Bromwich Albion with Adlington and Bruce on target for the home side, which preceded a 1–0 home success against Burnley in the final game of the year with Adlington scoring the only goal of the game. The new year began with a 3–1 home defeat against Derby County with Adlington finding the net for the third successive game.

Small Heath then secured their fifth League win of the campaign in a 3–2 home success against Wolverhampton Wanderers with Adlington, Bruce and Ollis on target, which preceded away defeats in the return games at Wolverhampton Wanderers (7–2) and Everton (3–0) on either side of a 4–1 home defeat against Bury in the first round of the FA Cup.

Early February saw Alec Leake score his only League goal of the season in a one-all home draw with the Wednesday, which was followed by successive home wins against Blackburn Rovers (2–1) and Bury (1–0) with Robertson, Wheldon and Haddon scoring the Small Heath goals. A 2–1 reverse at Blackburn Rovers, though, saw the Birmingham side desperately in need of points with five League games remaining, of which three were away from home.

Small Heath's situation hardly improved during the final month of the campaign with away draws at Burnley (1–1) and West Bromwich Albion (0–0) on either side of a 3–0 reverse at the Wednesday, while Frank Mobley netted a brace of goals in a 2–1 home victory against Sheffield United. However, a 1–0 home defeat against Sunderland in the final game of the season saw Small Heath end the campaign in fifteenth position with eight wins, four draws and eighteen defeats in their thirty League games, while scoring thirty-nine goals and conceding seventy-nine.

Fred Wheldon had appeared in all thirty League games for the Small Heath side in which he had scored on seven occasions, while Frank Mobley had led the scoring with eleven goals in twenty-eight League appearances. It had been a further season of struggle for Small Heath.

WOLVERHAMPTON WANDERERS

Wolverhampton Wanderers had been one of a number of teams involved in the struggle to avoid the test match positions during the 1894–95 League campaign, which had hardly been a surprise judging by the turmoil within the club. The sudden deaths of Harry Allen, Joshua Hassall and David Wykes had added to their problems. However, few changes were made in the Wanderers' line-up for the 1895–96 season as Richard Baugh, Tommy Dunn, Billy Malpass, Hill Griffiths, David Black, Alf Griffin and Harry Wood continued to serve the club.

Tennant replaced the unfortunate Joshua Hassall between the posts prior to the return of William Rose from Loughborough Town, while the most notable newcomers included Tonks, Owen and Nurse, together with Dick Topham, who returned from Oxford University to make occasional appearances for the club.

Joe Butcher, who had scored only twice in nineteen League appearances during the previous campaign, soon moved to West Bromwich Albion, which saw Billy Beats, a recent signing from Burslem Port Vale, replace him up front. Charlie Henderson arrived from Bolton Wanderers to replace David Wykes.

Wolves opened the season with successive home wins against Burnley (5–1) and the Wednesday (4–0) on either side of a 4–3 reverse at Preston North End, while a two-all draw at Sunderland continued their excellent start to the campaign. However, a 3–2 home defeat against Everton ended a mostly productive month for the Wolverhampton side.

Early October saw the Wanderers return to winning ways with a 1–0 home success against Stoke, which preceded a 3–1 reverse at the Wednesday, while their fine home form continued with a 4–1 victory against Sheffield United. Successive away defeats at Derby County (5–2), Everton (2–0) and Blackburn Rovers (3–1) saw the Black Country side move down to the bottom half of the League table.

Wanderers soon avenged the defeat at Derby County with a 2–0 success at the Molineux, which was followed by successive defeats at Stoke (4–1) and West Bromwich Albion (2–1), as well as at home to Blackburn Rovers (2–1), leaving Wolves with eleven points from fifteen games at the halfway stage of the season. Their indifferent form continued to the end of the year when, following a 2–1 home victory against Preston North End, the Molineux side suffered home defeats against Aston Villa (2–1) and Sunderland (3–1).

Little changed during the new year as the Wanderers suffered away defeats at Bolton Wanderers (4–0) and Small Heath (3–2), though the month ended with a 7–2 victory in the return game with Small Heath. However, their joy was short-lived as away defeats at Sheffield United (2–1), Bury (3–0) and Burnley (3–1) soon followed.

Fortunately for the Wolverhampton side, they had enjoyed an excellent start in the FA Cup competition when, following a one-all draw at Notts County, they had inflicted a 4–1 defeat on the Second Division side to secure a home tie against Liverpool in the second round. Wolves' superior FA Cup experience told as a 2–0 victory earned them a further home tie against Stoke in the quarter-finals, which would be a little more difficult as the Potteries' side were enjoying their finest season to date.

Prior to the FA Cup tie, the Wanderers suffered a 2–1 home defeat against West Bromwich Albion, while a 3–0 victory against Stoke saw them drawn against Derby County in the semi-finals with the East Midlands side favourites to reach the final. However, Wolves fought magnificently to win by the odd goal in three to secure their third FA Cup Final appearance, which was to take place at Crystal Palace on 18 April against the Wednesday.

On their return to League action, the Wolverhampton team secured a 6–1 home win against Nottingham Forest, followed by successive away defeats at Aston Villa (4–1) and in the return game at Nottingham Forest (3–2). This meant that victories were required in both of their remaining League games if they were to avoid the test match places. Wolves managed home wins against Bury (1–0) and Bolton Wanderers (5–0) to end the campaign in fourteenth position, thus avoiding the end-of-season play-off games by a single point.

Wanderers had won ten, drawn one and lost nineteen of their thirty League games, while scoring sixty-one goals and conceding sixty-five. David Black ended the campaign with seven League goals; Charlie Henderson had found the net on nine occasions; Harry Wood netted a dozen goals; while Billy Beats had led the scoring with sixteen League goals in a further indifferent season for the Molineux side. Charlie Henderson, Billy Owen and Richard Baugh had appeared in all thirty League games. All would be forgiven, however, if the Wanderers were successful in the final of the FA Cup.

NOTTINGHAM FOREST

Nottingham Forest had finished the two previous League campaigns in a creditable seventh position, which resulted in few changes in their line-up for the 1895–96 season. Dennis Allsopp continued in goal, with Archie Ritchie, Adam Scott, Frank Forman, Alexander Stewart, John MacPherson and Peter McCracken in defence, while Tom Rose, Fred Forman, Horace Pike, Albert Carnelly, Arthur Shaw and Tom McInnes contested the forward positions.

David Smellie and Charles Richards were the most notable newcomers to the club with Smellie remaining for a little more than a season, while Richards scored eighteen goals in seventy-two League appearances in four seasons with the Nottingham side.

Forest opened the season with a 5–0 home success against Bury with Rose (2), McInnes, Carnelly and Shaw on target, which preceded successive away defeats at Everton (6–2) and Blackburn Rovers (2–0), while a 3–0 home win against Small Heath saw a return to winning ways with McInnes, Rose and Frank Forman netting for the home side. However, further defeats at West Bromwich Albion (3–1) and at home to Derby County (5–2) saw Forest near the foot of the League table by early October.

Tom McInnes then netted a brace of goals in a 2–1 home success against Everton, which was followed by odd-goal defeats at Bolton Wanderers (2–1) and Small Heath (1–0), as well as at home to Preston North End (1–0), while John MacPherson scored his only goal of the season in a 2–0 home win against West Bromwich Albion, with Fred Forman completing the scoring.

November's end saw Forest suffer successive away defeats at Sheffield United (2–1) and the Wednesday (3–0) on either side of a 4–0 home victory against Stoke, with McInnes (2), Pike and Smellie on target for the Nottingham side, while the halfway stage of the season arrived with a 4–0 reverse at Derby County. Forest remained near the foot of the table with ten points from fifteen games. However, an excellent run of results towards the end of the year saw Forest climb to a mid-table position by the middle of January.

Forest's excellent run of results began with a 3–1 home win against Sheffield United, with Pike, Shaw and Fred Forman on the score sheet, which preceded a goalless draw at Burnley, while Carnelly (2), McInnes and Shaw found the net in a 4–2 home success against Blackburn Rovers in the final game of the year.

New Year opened with a goalless home draw with Bolton Wanderers, followed by a 3–1 home victory against Sunderland with Shaw, Richards and McInnes on target. Their unbeaten run came to an end with a 3–1 reverse at Aston Villa, as well as a 2–0 home defeat against Everton in the first round of the FA Cup.

On their return to League action, the Nottingham side secured a one-all draw at Sunderland, with Charles Richards scoring for the visitors, while a 6–0 reverse at Preston North End continued their poor away form. However, a 2–1 home success against Burnley saw Forest maintain their mid-table position, with Richards and Carnelly scoring for the home side. Then followed successive away defeats at Stoke (1–0), Bury (1–0) and Wolverhampton Wanderers (6–1), as well as a 2–0 home reverse against Aston Villa, which saw Forest perilously close to the test match positions. Fortunately, home victories against Wolverhampton Wanderers (3–2) and the Wednesday (1–0) during the final week of the season saw Forest end the campaign in thirteenth position with eleven victories, three draws and sixteen defeats in their thirty League games, while scoring forty-two goals and conceding fifty-seven.

Archie Ritchie and Tom McInnes had appeared in all thirty League games for Forest in a mostly forgettable season, while McInnes had led the scoring with nine League goals.

SHEFFIELD UNITED

Sheffield United had finished the 1894–95 League campaign in sixth position, which resulted in few changes in their team for the 1895–96 season. Willie Foulke continued in goal, with Harry Thickett, Mick Whitham, Bob Cain, Rab Howell and Ernest Needham in defence, while Docherty, Bob Hill, Arthur Watson, Harry Hammond and Jimmy Yates remained in the attack. However, Bob Hill would shortly move to Manchester City, together with Hugh Morris and Joe Davies, while Docherty signed for the Bury club.

The most notable new signings by the Sheffield side were Walter Bennett, a speedy outside right from Mexborough, as well as centre half Tommy Morren, who had captained Middlesbrough in the 1895 FA Amateur Cup final.

United opened the season with a 2–0 home win against Small Heath, with Watson and Hammond on target, which preceded a 1–0 reverse at the Wednesday, while Hill and Morris found the net in a 2–1 home success against Aston Villa. However, a 1–0 defeat at Bury continued their indifferent away form.

Then followed successive home wins against Stoke (1–0) and Preston North End (2–1), with Docherty, Richardson and Hammond netting the United goals. Further away defeats at Everton (5–0), Wolverhampton Wanderers (4–1) and Stoke (4–0), as well as at home to Sunderland (2–1) and Everton (2–1), saw the Sheffield side struggling near the foot of the League table by the middle of November.

United's first away point of the season arrived in a two-all draw at Aston Villa, with club trainer George Waller, only playing because of injuries, scoring one of the goals, which preceded a 2–1 home success against Nottingham Forest with Draper and Hammond on target. Further defeats at Preston North End (4–3) and in the return game at Nottingham Forest (3–1) saw their struggle continue. Then a five-game unbeaten run saw the Yorkshire side climb to a respectable mid-table position during the opening weeks of the new year.

United's unbeaten run began with successive home draws against Derby County (1–1) and the Wednesday (1–1), with Arthur Watson on target in both games. A League encounter at Burnley, in which Tommy Morren made his first team debut, was abandoned owing to the atrocious weather conditions. However, the weather improved sufficiently within a couple of days for the Sheffield side to secure a 1–0 home success against Bolton Wanderers, with Ernest Needham scoring the only goal of the game. Needham was again on target in a 2–0 home win against West Bromwich Albion in the opening game of the new year, with Ross completing the scoring, which preceded a one-all draw at Sunderland, with Egan netting for the visitors. Their unbeaten run came to an end with a 1–0 reverse at Blackburn Rovers.

Early February saw United drawn away at Burton Wanderers in the first round of the FA Cup, where an Ernest Needham goal earned a one-all draw, which was followed by a 5–0 defeat in the re-arranged League game at Burnley. Needham continued his habit of scoring important goals by netting the only goal of the game in the replayed tie with Burton to secure an away tie at Everton in the second round.

Prior to the FA Cup tie, the Sheffield side gained a 2–1 home success against Wolverhampton Wanderers, with Ross and Yates on target, while their hopes of FA Cup success ended with a 3–0 reverse at Goodison Park. This was followed by a 1–0 defeat at West Bromwich Albion, where Walter Bennett made his first team debut.

Harry Hammond then found the net in a one-all home draw with Blackburn Rovers, which preceded a 2–0 victory at Derby County, with Ross and Yates scoring for the visitors. Harry Hammond was then again on target in a one-all home draw with Burnley. However, a 4–1 defeat at Bolton Wanderers continued their indifferent away form. United then secured an 8–0 home success against Bury with Hammond (4), Egan (3) and Cain scoring for the Sheffield side. The campaign ended with a 2–1 reverse at Small Heath as

United finished the season in twelfth place following ten wins, six draws and fourteen defeats in their thirty League games, while scoring forty goals and conceding fifty.

Harry Hammond had led the scoring with a dozen League goals in a season in which the Yorkshire team had twice beaten the mighty Corinthians while narrowly avoiding the end-of-season test match games. However, great success still lay ahead for United.

BURNLEY

Burnley had regularly finished previous League campaigns in the top half of the table, which had been quite a feat considering their lack of financial resources. However, their supporters were a little annoyed that two of the most popular players were allowed to leave the club prior to the 1895–96 campaign.

Goalkeeper Jack Hillman had joined Everton during the latter stages of the previous season, while James Crabtree had signed for Aston Villa for the sum of £250. Still, there remained a measure of stability within the club as Reynolds, McLintock, Beveridge, Bowes and Walter Place retained their places in the team for the new season.

Burnley opened the campaign with a 5–1 reverse at Wolverhampton Wanderers, followed by a 2–0 success at West Bromwich Albion and a goalless home draw with Sunderland. Their excellent form continued with a 3–0 home win against Bury, but a 1–0 defeat at Bolton Wanderers ended their fine run of results.

Then followed a 1–0 home victory against Preston North End as Burnley maintained their mid-table position. However, a disastrous run of twelve games without a win would see the Lancashire side struggling near the foot of the League table at the turn of the year.

Burnley's disappointing run of results began with a 1–0 reverse at Blackburn Rovers, followed by a 2–1 home defeat against Bolton Wanderers, while successive draws at Preston North End (1–1) and at home to Everton (1–1) continued their indifferent form. It further deteriorated with away defeats at Aston Villa (5–1), Derby County (5–1), Everton (2–1), Stoke (2–1) and Wednesday (1–0) as well as at home in the return game with Aston Villa (4–3).

Mid-December saw a goalless home draw with Nottingham Forest, which preceded a 1–0 reverse at Small Heath in the final game of the year. However, a 4–3 victory at Bury on New Year's Day saw a return to winning ways for the Burnley team, while further home wins against Wednesday (2–0), West Bromwich Albion (3–0) and Sheffield United (5–0) saw the Lancashire side climb to a mid-table position.

Following a one-all draw at Stoke in the second round of the FA Cup, Burnley suffered a 7–1 defeat in the replay to end their interest in the competition. It preceded a 3–1 reverse in a League encounter at Sunderland, while their excellent home form continued with a 3–1 success against Wolverhampton Wanderers.

Early March saw the Lancashire side suffer a 2–1 defeat at Nottingham Forest, followed by a 2–0 home win against Stoke. Successive draws at home to Small Heath (1–1) and Derby County (2–2), as well as at Sheffield United (1–1), continued their improved form, which was maintained to the end of the season with a 6–0 home victory against Blackburn Rovers. Burnley ended the campaign in tenth position following ten wins, seven draws and thirteen defeats in their thirty League games, while scoring forty-eight goals and conceding forty-four, an excellent achievement considering the loss of their most influential players.

PRESTON NORTH END

Preston North End had reaffirmed their reputation as one of the finest footballing sides in England during the 1894–95 League campaign. However, the number of players associated with their sides of the late 1880s further diminished during the 1895–96 season, with Robert Holmes and James Trainer the only remaining first team regulars.

Francis Becton and E D Smith, who had scored twenty-three League goals between them during the previous campaign, soon left the club, while Jack Gordon and Geordie Drummond were unable to command first team places. However, Grier, Cunningham, Dunn, Sanders, Sharp and Henderson retained their positions from the 1894–95 season, together with Blyth, Orr, Tait and Pierce, who had all made occasional first team appearances, while Stevenson and T Smith were the most notable newcomers in the attack.

Preston opened the season with a 4–1 reverse at Sunderland, followed by successive victories at home to Wolverhampton Wanderers (4–3) and away at West Bromwich Albion (2–1), while the month ended with away defeats at Burnley (1–0) and Sheffield United (2–1). Then a 3–2 home success against Small Heath saw a return to winning ways for the Lancashire side.

Following a 3–0 defeat at Blackburn Rovers, Preston enjoyed a four-game unbeaten run, which included home draws against Burnley (1–1) and Blackburn Rovers (1–1), as well as victories at Nottingham Forest (1–0) and at home to Bolton Wanderers (1–0). Successive away defeats at Stoke (4–0) and Small Heath (5–2) saw them in a mid-table position by late November, but home wins against Sheffield United (4–3) and Aston Villa (4–3), as well as a 2–1 success at Bury, saw them move up to fifth place in the League table by the middle of December.

Preston then ended the year with successive defeats at Wolverhampton Wanderers (2–1) and at home to Stoke (1–0), which were followed by a one-all draw at the Wednesday on New Year's Day. A 4–1 home success against Sunderland saw an excellent display by the Preston attack, though a 1–0 defeat at Aston Villa continued their indifferent run of results.

Late January saw a one-all home draw with Everton, which preceded a 4–1 reverse at Sunderland in the first round of the FA Cup, while a 6–0 home victory against Nottingham Forest saw the Lancashire side register their highest win of the campaign. However, their joy was short-lived as successive away defeats at Derby County (1–0), Everton (3–2) and Bolton Wanderers (1–0) saw a return to the bottom half of the League table.

With four home games remaining, Preston had already avoided the test match positions, while a 1–0 victory against Derby County, as well as drawn games with West Bromwich Albion (0–0) and Bury (1–1) saw the Lancashire side in with a chance of a top six League finish. However, a 1–0 home defeat against the Wednesday saw Preston end the campaign in ninth position following eleven wins, six draws and thirteen defeats in their thirty League games, while scoring forty-four goals and conceding forty-eight.

Blyth and Robert Holmes had appeared in all thirty League games for Preston, with Holmes reaching the milestone of 200 League appearances during the season, while Jimmy Trainer had ended the campaign on 199 in a disappointing season for the Lancashire side, for whom Pierce had led the scoring with eight goals in nineteen League games.

BLACKBURN ROVERS

Blackburn Rovers' greatly improved League performances had seemed to coincide with their indifferent FA Cup results, which was hardly a surprise, as the majority of the players involved in the FA Cup-winning teams of the mid-1880s and early 1890s had either retired or left the club.

Few changes were made in the Rovers' line-up for the 1895–96 League campaign. Ogilvie continued in goal, with Murray, Dewar, Anderson, Cleghorn, Killean and Tom Brandon in defence, while Haydock, Whitehead, Chippendale and Josh Hargreaves remained in the attack. Newcomers up front included Wilkie and Turnbull to replace Hall, Stuart and Sorley, while the most significant change within the club saw England international James Forrest sign for Darwen following twelve successful seasons with the Rovers, in which five FA Cup Finals had been won.

Rovers opened the season with a 2–1 reverse at Sunderland, followed by successive victories at home to Nottingham Forest (2–0) and away at Everton (2–0) with Haydock, Tierney, Anderson and Whitehead sharing the Blackburn goals, while Harry Chippendale found the net in a one-all home draw with Aston Villa.

Chippendale was again on target the following week in a 1–0 home success against Burnley, while Hargreaves netted a brace of goals in a 3–0 home win against Preston North End. However, successive defeats at Aston Villa (3–1) and at home to Sunderland (4–2) saw the Lancashire side in a mid-table position by late October.

Then followed a one-all draw at Preston North End, with Chippendale scoring for the visitors, which preceded a 3–1 home success against Wolverhampton Wanderers, with Turnbull (2) and Haydock on target. A further home win against the Wednesday (2–1) saw Harry Chippendale once again amongst the scorers.

Tom Brandon then netted his only League goal of the campaign in a one-all draw at Bolton Wanderers, which preceded successive victories in the return game with Bolton (3–2) and at Wolverhampton Wanderers (2–1) with Turnbull scoring in both games as Rovers climbed up to third place in the League table. However, away defeats at Nottingham Forest (4–2) and Wednesday (3–0), as well as at home to Everton (3–2) and Bury (2–0), saw Blackburn return to a mid-table position by the middle of January.

Late January saw Blackburn return to winning ways as Wilkie scored the only goal of the game in a 1–0 home success against Sheffield United, which preceded a 2–1 home defeat against West Bromwich Albion in the first round of the FA Cup. Rovers soon avenged the FA Cup defeat by securing a 1–0 victory against Albion in a League encounter at Ewood Park with Wilkie once again scoring the only goal of the game.

February's end saw Rovers suffer successive defeats at home to Derby County (2–0) and away at Small Heath (2–1), which were followed by a one-all draw at Sheffield United where Turnbull netted his seventh League goal of the campaign. Home wins against Small Heath (2–1) and Stoke (3–1) saw Haydock on target in both victories, but a poor run of results during the final month of the season saw Blackburn struggling to maintain their mid-table position.

All five of Rovers' remaining League fixtures were away from home, which resulted in defeats at Stoke (3–0), Burnley (6–0), Bury (2–0) and West Bromwich Albion (3–2), as well as a goalless draw at Derby County, leaving the Lancashire side in eighth position with twelve wins, five draws and thirteen defeats in their thirty League games, while scoring forty goals and conceding fifty.

Goalkeeper Ogilvie had been the only ever present in the Blackburn side, while Haydock, Turnbull and Harry Chippendale had led the scoring with seven League goals apiece in a most disappointing League campaign for the Rovers.

WEDNESDAY

Wednesday had made excellent progress during their three seasons in the Football League, as well as in reaching the semi-final stages of the FA Cup competition in each of the two previous seasons. This resulted in few changes in their team for the 1895–96 League campaign. William Allan continued in goal, with Jack Earp, Ambrose Langley, Harry Brandon, Tom Crawshaw, Petrie and Jamieson in defence, while Archie Brash, Harry Davis, Bob Ferrier, Alec Brady and Fred Spiksley remained in the attack.

The most notable new signings by the Sheffield side were centre forward Lawrence Bell from the Third Lanark club and Jimmy Massey, who had been signed from Doncaster Rovers to share the goalkeeping duties with William Allan.

Wednesday opened the season with a two-all draw at Everton, with Bell and Crawshaw netting for the visitors, while Bell was again on target the following week in a 1–0 home success against Sheffield United. However, successive away defeats at Wolverhampton Wanderers (4–0) and Derby County (3–1) ended the Yorkshire side's excellent start to the campaign.

Then followed a 5–3 home victory against West Bromwich Albion, with Spiksley (2), Brady, Earp and Davis finding the net, which preceded a further home win against Wolverhampton Wanderers (3–1), with Brandon, Petrie and Brady on target. Harry Davis (2) and Lawrence Bell then netted the Wednesday goals in a 3–0 home victory against Sunderland.

Davis and Bell scored their fourth League goals of the season in a 3–2 success at West Bromwich Albion, which was followed by a one-all home draw with Bolton Wanderers, while Wednesday were swiftly brought down to earth with a humiliating 6–1 defeat at Bury. Wednesday's excellent home record continued with victories against Stoke (2–1) and Nottingham Forest (3–0) on either side of a 2–1 reverse at Blackburn Rovers, with Tom Crawshaw scoring in both wins.

Following a 5–0 defeat at Stoke, Alec Brady scored the only goal of the game in a 1–0 home success against Burnley, while Bob Ferrier netted his only goal of the season in a one-all draw at Sheffield United. A 4–0 reverse against Derby County in the final game of the year saw the Sheffield side suffer their first home defeat of the campaign.

New Year's Day saw Harry Davis on target in a one-all home draw with Preston North End, which preceded a 2–0 reverse at Burnley, while Bell, Richards and Spiksley found the net in a 3–0 home win against Blackburn Rovers. However, a 3–1 reverse against League leaders Aston Villa saw a further home defeat.

Early February saw the Yorkshire side secure a 3–2 victory at Southampton St Mary's in the first round of the FA Cup, where Brady (2) and Davis found the net to earn a home tie with Sunderland in the second round.

Prior to the FA Cup tie, Wednesday drew one-all at Small Heath, while their FA Cup success continued against Sunderland, as Bell and Spiksley were on target in a 2–1 victory to secure a further home tie against Everton in the quarter-finals.

Wednesday then entertained Everton in a League encounter at the Olive Grove Ground where Bell, Spiksley and Davis scored in a 3–1 success, which preceded a 3–1 home defeat against Bury. However, a 4–0 victory against Everton saw the Yorkshire side earn a third successive semi-final appearance, with Bell and Brash scoring a brace of goals apiece.

On their return to League action, Wednesday suffered successive away defeats at Sunderland (2–1) and Aston Villa (2–1), while an Archie Brash goal secured a one-all draw with Bolton Wanderers in the semi-final tie at Goodison Park. The Sheffield side had few difficulties in the replay as Crawshaw, Davis and Spiksley found the net in a 3–1 success to secure a final appearance against Wolverhampton Wanderers at Crystal Palace on 18 April.

Early April saw Wednesday enjoy successive victories at home to Small Heath (3–0) and away at Preston North End (1–0),with Harry Davis on target in both games, which were followed by a 1–0 reverse at Nottingham Forest. With only one League game remaining, the Sheffield side had more important things on their minds, namely their forthcoming FA Cup Final appearance.

STOKE

Stoke had managed to avoid relegation to the Second Division at the end of the 1894–95 League campaign following a victory against Newton Heath in the play-off games. However, while their away form had been a little disappointing, the Potteries' side had performed splendidly on home soil, which resulted in few changes in their line-up for the 1895–96 season. George Clawley continued in goal, with Robertson, Brodie, Turner, Christie and Thomas Clare in defence, while Billy Dickson, Joseph Schofield and Tom Hyslop remained in the attack.

Prior to the new season, the Potteries' side had signed Willie (W S) Maxwell from the Dundee club, who led the goal scoring in five successive seasons for the Stoke team as well as appearing in the Scottish national side.

Stoke enjoyed an excellent start to the season, with home wins against Bolton Wanderers (2–0), Derby County (2–1) and West Bromwich Albion (3–1), as well as a 2–1 victory at Small Heath. Successive away defeats at Sheffield United (1–0), Wolverhampton Wanderers (1–0) and Derby County (2–1) ended their splendid run of results.

Stoke's excellent home form continued to the end of the year with victories against Small Heath (6–1), Sheffield United (4–0), Preston North End (4–0), Burnley (2–1), Wolverhampton Wanderers (4–1) and Wednesday (5–0), with only a 2–0 defeat against Bury spoiling their run of home wins. However, away defeats at Bolton Wanderers (3–1), West Bromwich Albion (1–0), Nottingham Forest (4–0), Everton (7–2) and Wednesday (2–1) saw the Potteries' side struggling to maintain their top six position.

Then followed a 2–1 home defeat against Aston Villa during the opening week of the new year, which preceded an excellent FA Cup run. A 7–1 victory against Burnley was the highlight of their FA Cup success, but the Potteries' side were a little unfortunate to be drawn away at Wolverhampton Wanderers in the quarter-finals, where they suffered a 3–0 defeat.

On their return to League action, the Stoke side suffered a 5–2 reverse at Aston Villa, while their excellent home form continued with victories against Sunderland (5–0), Nottingham Forest (1–0) and Blackburn Rovers (3–0). Their usual away defeats at Burnley (2–0), Sunderland (4–1) and Blackburn Rovers (3–1), as well as a 2–1 home defeat against Everton in the final game of the season, saw Stoke end the campaign in sixth position, their highest League finish to date.

Stoke had won fifteen and lost fifteen of their thirty League games, while scoring fifty-six goals and conceding forty-seven, with a dozen of their victories on home soil. Only the League Champions achieved more home wins.

Thomas Clare and Billy Dickson had appeared in all thirty League games for the Potteries' side, while Tom Hyslop had led the scoring with seventeen League goals, a club record.

SUNDERLAND

As reigning League Champions, Sunderland made few changes in their team for the 1895–96 season. The ever reliable John Doig continued in goal, with McNeill, Gow, Gibson, Wilson, McReadie, Johnston and Billy Dunlop in defence, while Scott, Harvey, Jimmy Millar, James Gillespie, James Hannah and Johnny Campbell remained up front together with Cowan, a recent signing from Motherwell, who scored eight goals in nineteen League appearances for the club.

Sunderland opened the season with a 4–1 home win against Preston North End, with Gillespie (2), Johnston and Millar on target, while Cowan and James Hannah found the net in a further home success against Blackburn Rovers (2–1). An indifferent run of results that included away defeats at Derby County (2–0) and Aston Villa (2–1), as well as draws at home to Wolverhampton Wanderers (2–2), Bury (0–0) and away at Burnley (0–0), saw the north-eastern side in a mid-table position by the middle of October.

Then followed a 2–1 success at Sheffield United, with McReadie and Wilson scoring for the visitors, which preceded a 3–0 reverse at the Wednesday, while Johnny Campbell netted his first goal of the campaign in a 4–2 victory at Blackburn Rovers, with Scott, Gillespie and Harvey completing the scoring.

Early November saw Gillespie and Campbell on target in a two-all home draw with Derby County, while Campbell scored for the third game in succession in a 2–1 home success against Aston Villa, which preceded a 1–0 defeat at Everton. However, home wins against Bolton Wanderers (1–0) and Small Heath (2–1) saw the reigning League Champions climb up to fifth place in the League table, with Gillespie and Campbell once again amongst the scorers.

Sunderland's indifferent away form continued with a 1–0 reverse at Bolton Wanderers, followed by a one-all draw at West Bromwich Albion where Jimmy Millar found the net. The year ended with a rare away win at Wolverhampton Wanderers (3–1) with Johnny Campbell netting a brace of goals; however, a 4–1 defeat at Preston North End during the opening week of the new year saw the north-eastern team's hopes of a fourth League title slowly diminishing.

Following a one-all home draw with Sheffield United, the Sunderland team suffered a 3–1 reverse at Nottingham Forest, but a 7–1 home success against West Bromwich Albion saw a return to winning ways with both Jimmy Millar and Johnny Campbell scoring hat-tricks. Millar and Campbell netted a further brace of goals apiece in a 4–1 home victory against Preston North End in the first round of the FA Cup to secure a second round tie at the Wednesday.

Prior to the FA Cup tie, Johnny Campbell found the net in a one-all home draw with Nottingham Forest, while their hopes of FA Cup success ended with a 2–1 defeat at the Wednesday. However, successive home wins against Burnley (3–1), Everton (3–0) and Wednesday (2–1) saw the north-eastern side maintain their top five position, with Cowan, Millar, Campbell, Gillespie and James Hannah sharing the Sunderland goals.

Mid-March saw the Sunderland team suffer an embarrassing 5–0 defeat at Stoke, which was soon avenged as the title holders inflicted a 4–1 defeat on the Potteries' side in the return game at Newcastle Road with Campbell (2), Millar and Cowan on target. The season ended with away victories at Bury (2–1) and Small Heath (1–0), with Johnny Campbell and Jimmy Millar scoring the goals to secure a fifth place League finish for Sunderland, who had won fifteen, drawn seven and lost eight of their thirty League games, while scoring fifty-two goals and conceding forty-one.

Sunderland had remained unbeaten at home throughout the season, while their indifferent away form had resulted in five victories, much to the disappointment of a club that had won three League Championships.

Johnny Campbell had appeared in all thirty League games for the north-eastern side, while James Hannah, James Gillespie and John Doig had missed less than a handful of games in a season in which Johnny Campbell had led the scoring with fifteen League goals.

BOLTON WANDERERS

Bolton Wanderers' slightly improved League form during the previous campaign had resulted in few changes in their line up for the 1895–96 season. John Sutcliffe continued in goal, with Somerville, Jones, Paton, McGeachan and Archie Freebairn in defence, while Robert Tannahill, James Cassidy and William Joyce remained in the attack. The latter were joined by newcomers Bob Brown, Jocky Wright, Bob Jack and inside forward Gunn, who scored five goals in six League appearances during the season. Brown, Wright and Jack, who had all played their early football north of the border, served the Lancashire side for a number of seasons, with Brown and Jack making in excess of one hundred League appearances for the club.

Wanderers opened the season with a 2–0 reverse at Stoke, which preceded a 3–0 away win at Bury, with McGeachan, Brown and Paton on target. Martin, Cassidy and Joyce found the net, in a 3–1 home success against Everton at Bolton's newly acquired Burden Park ground. Bolton then secured a further home win against Burnley (1–0), with Gunn scoring the only goal of the game, while the month ended with a 2–1 away victory at Small Heath, with Brown and Wright scoring for the visitors. However, a 4–2 home defeat against Bury saw their winning run come to an end with Joyce netting both goals for the Wanderers.

Then followed a 2–1 success at Burnley where Brown and Joyce found the net, which preceded a 2–1 home win against Nottingham Forest, with Tannahill and Wright on target, while goals by Joyce (2) and Brown secured a 3–1 home victory against Stoke as the Lancashire side moved up to second place in the League table.

Willie Joyce then scored his seventh League goal of the campaign in a one-all draw at Sheffield United, while his eighth and ninth League goals arrived a couple of days later in a 3–2 away win at West Bromwich Albion. An indifferent run of results then saw the Bolton team register just one victory in eight games to end the year in a mid-table position.

Wanderers' poor run of results began with successive away defeats at Preston North End (1–0) and Sunderland (1–0), followed by a one-all home draw with Blackburn Rovers, while further away defeats at Blackburn Rovers (3–2) and Aston Villa (2–0) continued their loss of form. It improved with a 1–0 home success against Sunderland, with Willie Joyce scoring the only goal of the game, but defeats at Derby County (2–1) and Sheffield United (1–0) saw a miserable end to the year for the Lancashire side.

New Year's Day saw a return to winning ways as Gunn netted a brace of goals in a 2–1 home success against Derby County, which preceded a 4–0 home win against Wolverhampton Wanderers, with Tannahill, Joyce, Cassidy and Paton on target, while a goalless draw at Nottingham Forest continued their excellent start to the year. Bolton then enjoyed a 4–0 victory at Crewe in the first round of the FA Cup, with Brown, Gunn, Tannahill and Wright scoring to earn a second round tie at Blackpool. This resulted in a 2–0 success for the Wanderers, with Cassidy and Wright netting the all-important goals to secure a home tie against Bury in the quarter-finals.

Prior to the FA Cup tie, inside forward Gunn scored a couple of goals in a 4–1 home victory against Small Heath, while their excellent form continued in the FA Cup competition as Wright and Gunn found the net in a 2–0 success against Bury to earn a semi-final tie against the Wednesday.

Early March saw Cassidy and Wright on target in a two-all home draw with Aston Villa, which preceded a 1–0 home victory against Preston North End, with Bob Jack scoring the only goal of the game. Robert Tannahill found the net in a one-all draw against the Wednesday in the semi-final at Goodison Park. However, Bolton suffered a 3–1 defeat in the replay at the Town Ground, Nottingham, to end their interest in the competition.

On their return to League action, the Lancashire side secured a 4–1 home success against Sheffield United, with Paton, Tannahill, Nicholl and Jack on target, while their excellent home form continued with a 2–1 victory against West Bromwich Albion with Cassidy and Jack netting for the home side. However, following a one-all draw at Everton, the Bolton team suffered a 5–0 reverse at Wolverhampton Wanderers, prior to ending the season with a 2–0 home win against Wednesday, with goals by Cassidy and Jack securing a fourth place League finish for the Wanderers, following sixteen victories, five draws and nine defeats in their thirty League games, while scoring forty-nine goals and conceding thirty-seven.

Archie Freebairn, Alex Paton and Jocky Wright had appeared in all thirty League games in Bolton's finest season to date. Gunn, Brown and Jack had ended the campaign with five League goals apiece, James Cassidy had found the net on seven occasions, while Willie Joyce had led the scoring with twelve goals in twenty League appearances.

EVERTON

Everton had ended the 1894–95 League campaign as runners-up to Sunderland, hence their reluctance to make changes in their team for the 1895–96 season. Jack Hillman continued in goal, with Adams, Kelso, Boyle, Holt and Billy Stewart in defence, while Hartley, Bell, McInnes, Chadwick, Milward and Alex Latta remained up front, where they were joined by Cameron, a recent signing from the Queens Park Club.

John Southworth had been forced to retire from the game following a serious leg injury; Fred Geary had signed for Liverpool, where he was soon joined by Alex Latta, while Bob Kelso returned north of the border. Welsh international fullback Charlie Parry moved to Manchester City during the early weeks of the season, which allowed fellow Welsh international Smart Arridge the opportunity of holding down the left back position, having made only five League appearances during the two previous seasons.

Everton opened the season with a two-all home draw with the Wednesday, with Boyle and Milward on target, which preceded a 6–2 home win against Nottingham Forest, with Milward (2), Chadwick (2), Bell and Flewitt finding the net. Alf Milward scored for the third game running in a further home success against Bury (3–2), with Bell and Chadwick completing the scoring. However, successive defeats at Bolton Wanderers (3–1) and at home to Blackburn Rovers (2–0) ended their excellent start to the season.

Late September saw a return to winning ways as McInnes (2) and Milward found the net in a 3–2 away victory at Wolverhampton Wanderers, which was followed by a 4–3 reverse at Aston Villa, with John Bell netting all three of the visitors' goals, while Edgar Chadwick scored a hat-trick the following week in a 5–0 home win against Sheffield United, with Milward and Latta completing the scoring.

Edgar Chadwick then scored his seventh League goal of the campaign in a 2–1 reverse at Nottingham Forest, while successive draws at home to West Bromwich Albion (1–1) and away at Bury (1–1) saw the Merseysiders in a mid-table position by the end of October. A run of nine successive victories then saw Everton challenging for the League title by the turn of the year.

Everton's splendid run of results began with a 2–0 home success against Wolverhampton Wanderers with Chadwick and Milward on target, which preceded a 2–1 victory at Sheffield United, where Hartley and Milward found the net. Alf Milward netted further goals in wins at home to Sunderland (1–0) and away at West Bromwich Albion (3–0).

Fullback Adams then netted his only League goal of the season in a 2–1 home success against Burnley, with Richard Boyle completing the scoring, which preceded a 3–0 victory at Small Heath with Milward scoring all three goals, while McInnes (3), Bell (2), Cameron and Milward were on target in a 7–2 home win against Stoke.

Tom McInnes and John Bell then secured their eighth League goals of the campaign in a 2–0 home victory against Aston Villa in the final game of the year, which preceded a 3–2 away win at Blackburn Rovers on New Year's Day with Bell and Chadwick once again amongst the scorers. The month ended with successive away draws at Bury (1–1) and Preston North End (1–1) as Everton maintained their challenge for the League Championship.

Early February saw Chadwick and Milward find the net in a 2–0 victory at Nottingham Forest in the first round of the FA Cup, which preceded a 3–0 home success in a League encounter with Small Heath, with Hartley netting a brace of goals. Their excellent form continued in the FA Cup with a 3–0 home win against Sheffield United, with goals by Bell, Cameron and Milward securing a quarter-final tie at the Wednesday.

Prior to the quarter-final tie, Everton suffered successive away defeats at the Wednesday (3–1) and Sunderland (3–0), which were followed by a further defeat at the Wednesday (4–0) in the FA Cup game. A 3–2 home win against Preston North End saw two welcome points, with Boyle, Hartley and Milward on target for Everton.

Following successive home draws against Derby County (2–2) and Bolton Wanderers (1–1), the Merseysiders suffered a 2–1 defeat in the return game at Derby County, prior to ending the season with a 2–1 victory at Stoke, with Hartley and Schofield netting the Everton goals to secure a third place League finish, with sixteen wins, seven draws and seven defeats in their thirty League games, while scoring sixty-six goals and conceding forty-three.

Richard Boyle had appeared in all thirty League games for the Lancashire side, while Adams, Hillman, Milward, Stewart and Edgar Chadwick had missed no more than a couple in an excellent League campaign. Tom McInnes had netted eight goals; John Bell had found the net on nine occasions; Edgar Chadwick had ended the campaign with eleven League goals, while Alf Milward had led the scoring with seventeen goals in the League.

DERBY COUNTY

Following their 2–1 victory against Notts County in the 1894–95 test match games, Derby County had managed to retain their First Division League status, which resulted in few changes in their line up for the 1895–96 season. John Robinson continued in goal, with Jimmy Methven, Joseph Leiper, John Cox and Archie Goodall in defence, while John McMillan, Steve Bloomer, John Goodall and, occasionally, outside right Paul remained in the attack.

George Kinsey had arrived from Wolverhampton Wanderers to replace Docherty at left half back, while Johnny Miller and Jimmy Stevenson became regular members of the attack, which was further strengthened by the signing of outside left Hugh McQueen, who had been a member of the successful Liverpool team that had won the Second Division Championship in the 1893–94 season. McQueen would make 150 League appearances in six seasons with Derby prior to joining Queens Park Rangers at the turn of the century.

Derby opened the season with a 2–1 reverse at Stoke, with Steve Bloomer scoring for the visitors, while Bloomer netted a brace of goals the following week in a 2–0 home success against Sunderland in the first League game at the Baseball Ground. However, a 4–1 defeat at Aston Villa continued their indifferent start to the campaign. Then followed a 3–1 home win against the Wednesday, with Bloomer, McMillan and Archie Goodall on target. This preceded a 5–2 victory at Nottingham Forest, with Steve Bloomer scoring a hat-trick, while Bloomer and Miller found the net in a 2–1 home success against Stoke.

Johnny Miller was again on target the following week in a 2–1 home win against Bury, while Steve Bloomer netted his second hat-trick of the season in a 5–2 home success against Wolverhampton Wanderers with a brace of goals by Jimmy Stevenson completing the scoring. A two-all draw at Sunderland ended Derby's winning run, with John Goodall scoring his only League goal of the campaign from the penalty spot.

Steve Bloomer then scored his twelfth League goal of the season in a 5–1 home victory against Burnley with McQueen (2), Miller and Archie Goodall completing the scoring, which was followed by a 2–0 reverse at Wolverhampton Wanderers. A 2–1 win at Bury saw a return to winning ways, with Bloomer and Stevenson netting for the visitors.

Late November saw the Derby side register their highest victory of the campaign in an 8–0 home win against Small Heath, with Miller (2), Paul (2), Stevenson (2), McQueen and Bloomer on target. Their splendid home form continued with victories against Nottingham Forest (4–0) and West Bromwich Albion (4–1), with Johnny Miller and Steve Bloomer scoring all eight of the Derby goals between them.

Following a one-all draw at Sheffield United, the East Midlands side ended the year with successive wins at home to Bolton Wanderers (2–1) and away at the Wednesday (4–0), with Jimmy Stevenson netting in all three games. However, a 2–1 reverse at Bolton Wanderers on New Year's Day ended a seven-game unbeaten run.

Derby soon returned to form with a 3–1 success at Small Heath, with Cox, McQueen and Archie Goodall on target, while a goalless draw at West Bromwich Albion maintained their excellent League form. This continued in the FA Cup, as Bloomer and Miller netted a brace of goals apiece in a 4–2 home win against Aston Villa in the opening round to secure a second round tie at Newton Heath.

Prior to the FA Cup game, Derby shared four goals with Aston Villa in a League encounter at the Baseball Ground, with Bloomer and Stevenson scoring for the home side, while the cup game at Newton Heath ended in a one-all draw, with Bloomer again on target. However, the Derby side had few difficulties in the replay as Miller (3), Bloomer and McQueen found the net in a 5–1 success to earn a home tie against West Bromwich Albion in the quarter-finals.

On their return to League action, the East Midlands side enjoyed a 2–0 victory at Blackburn Rovers where Bloomer scored both goals, while their FA Cup success continued with a 1–0 win against Albion, with Archie Goodall scoring the only goal of the game to secure a semi-final tie against Wolverhampton Wanderers, who were struggling near the foot of the League table.

Early March saw Johnny Miller on target in a 1–0 home win against Preston North End, which preceded a 2–0 reverse against Sheffield United in their only home defeat of the season, while a 2–1 defeat against Wolves in the semi-final at Perry Barr ended their hopes of the FA Cup and League double.

Following a further defeat in the return game at Preston (1–0), the Derby team secured successive away draws at Everton (2–2) and Burnley (2–2), which preceded a 2–1 home success against Everton with McMillan and Paul on target. The season ended with a goalless home draw against Blackburn Rovers as County settled for the runners-up position with seventeen victories, seven draws and six defeats in their thirty League games, while scoring sixty-eight goals and conceding thirty-five.

John Robinson, George Kinsey, Johnny Miller and Archie Goodall had appeared in all thirty League games in Derby's finest season to date. Miller had netted one dozen League goals, Jimmy Stevenson had found the net on fourteen occasions, while Steve Bloomer, who led the scoring on fifteen occasions during his long career with Derby, once again led the scoring with twenty-two goals in twenty-five League games, as well as scoring five in as many FA Cup appearances.

ASTON VILLA

Following their FA Cup success of the previous season, Aston Villa retained the majority of their players for the 1895–96 League campaign. Tom Wilkes continued in goal, with Howard Spencer, James Welford, John Reynolds and James Cowan in defence, while Charlie Athersmith, John Devey, Bob Chatt, Dennis Hodgetts and Steve Smith remained in the attack. England international James Crabtree had arrived from Burnley for a £250 fee to replace George Russell at left half back, while John Cowan and Johnny Campbell were signed to bolster an already outstanding forward line.

Crabtree made 200 appearances in seven seasons with the club, winning many League and FA Cup honours, as well as making a further eleven appearances for the English national side. Scottish international Campbell, who had arrived from Glasgow Celtic prior to the new season, scored thirty-nine goals in fifty-five League games for the Birmingham side, while John Cowan, the brother of James, who had previously played for Preston North End and Glasgow Rangers, remained with Villa for four seasons.

Villa opened the season with a 1–0 home success against West Bromwich Albion with John Devey scoring the only goal of the game, which was followed by a 7–3 home win against Small Heath with Johnny Campbell (4), John Devey (2) and James Cowan on target. However, within days of the victory, the FA Cup was stolen from the window of William Shillcock, a boot manufacturer of 73, Newtown Row, which resulted in a £25 fine for the cup holders, as the trophy was never recovered.

Following the loss of the FA Cup, Villa suffered a 2–1 reverse at Sheffield United, which preceded a 4–1 home win against Derby County with John Cowan, John Devey, Johnny Campbell and James Cowan netting for the home side, while Campbell scored his sixth League goal of the campaign in a one-all draw at Blackburn Rovers. Johnny Campbell again found the net in successive home wins against Everton (4–3) and Sunderland (2–1), which were followed by a one-all draw at West Bromwich Albion with Campbell scoring for the fifth game in a row. Dorrell and Crabtree netted their first goals of the season in a 3–1 home success against Blackburn Rovers with Dennis Hodgetts completing the scoring.

Late October saw John Devey score a brace of goals in a 4–1 victory at Small Heath, which preceded a 5–1 home win against Burnley with Charlie Athersmith netting a hat-trick. A 2–1 reverse at Sunderland saw a rare defeat. However, following a two-all home draw with Sheffield United, the Midlanders returned to winning ways with a 4–3 win at Burnley with Athersmith (2), Devey and Reynolds scoring for the visitors.

Villa's indifferent run of away results continued with defeats at Preston North End (4–3) and Everton (2–0) on either side of a 2–0 home success against Bolton Wanderers, with Welford and Campbell on target. These were followed by a 2–1 victory at Wolverhampton Wanderers where Spencer and Smith found the net, while the year ended with a 2–0 home win against Bury, with Campbell scoring both Villa goals as they moved up to second place in the League table. Campbell netted a further brace of goals in a 2–1 success at Stoke during the opening week of the new year, which preceded a 1–0 home win against Preston North End with John Cowan scoring the only goal of the game. Cowan again found the net in victories at the Wednesday (3–1) and at home to Nottingham Forest (3–1).

Early February saw the Villa team suffer a 4–2 defeat at Derby County in the first round of the FA Cup, which was followed by a two-all draw in a League encounter at Derby, with Devey and Athersmith scoring for the visitors, while Johnny Campbell netted a hat-trick in a 5–2 home success against Stoke, which saw Villa at the head of the League table by the end of February.

John Devey then scored a couple of goals in a two-all draw at Bolton Wanderers, which preceded a 2–1 home win against Wednesday, with Johnny Campbell and John Cowan on target. Both players found the net the following week in a 5–3 reverse at Bury, though successive victories at Nottingham Forest (2–0) and at home to Wolverhampton Wanderers (4–1) saw Villa secure the League Championship by a four-point margin from Derby County, with Campbell scoring in both wins.

John Devey had appeared in all thirty League games for the newly crowned champions, while Tom Wilkes, Howard Spencer and Charlie Athersmith had missed only one game in a most enjoyable League campaign. John Cowan had scored nine goals in twenty-two League appearances, John Devey had found the net on sixteen occasions, while Johnny Campbell had led the scoring with twenty-six goals in as many League games.

A Tight Finish to the Second Division

Four teams had been involved in the race for the Second Division championship during the 1895–96 League campaign, with Burton Wanderers, Grimsby Town, Manchester City and Liverpool ending the season within four points of each other.

Burton Wanderers had enjoyed an excellent season in which twelve of their fifteen home games had resulted in victory. However, their indifferent away form had seen the Midlands side finish in fourth position, four points adrift from the eventual winners.

Grimsby Town had finished one place above Burton Wanderers on the same number of points, following fourteen wins and one draw in their fifteen home games.

Manchester City had remained unbeaten on home soil, which included victories against Darwen (4–1), Crewe (4–0), Lincoln (4–0), Loughborough (5–1) and Newcastle (5–2), as well as away wins at Burton Swifts (4–2) and Loughborough (4–2). However, having ended the campaign with the same number of points as Liverpool, the Manchester side were forced to concede the Second Division championship to the Merseysiders, who had scored 106 League goals as against City's total of sixty-three.

Williams, Robson and Finnerhan had appeared in all thirty League games, and Billy Meredith had led the scoring with a dozen League goals. The

Manchester team thus secured a place in the end-of-season play-off games.

Liverpool had secured the Second Division championship following many high-scoring games, which included home wins against Burton Swifts (6–1), Crewe (6–1), Lincoln (6–1), Newton Heath (7–1) and Rotherham (10–1), as well as away victories at Burton Swifts (7–0) and Crewe (7–0), due mainly to the goal-scoring exploits of George Allen, a recent signing from Leith Athletic.

Allen, who had scored twenty-five of Liverpool's 106 League goals became the first Liverpool player to represent the Scottish national team, prior to suffering a sudden death at the age of twenty-four.

Crewe had ended the season at the foot of the Second Division, with twenty-two defeats in their thirty League games, which included defeats at Woolwich Arsenal (7–0), Darwen (6–1), Lincoln (6–2), Liverpool (6–1), Newcastle (6–0) and Notts County (6–0), as well as a 7–0 home reverse against Liverpool. Rotherham, who had finished four points ahead of Crewe, had suffered comprehensive defeats at Liverpool (10–1), Darwen (10–2), Leicester Fosse (8–0), Burton Wanderers (6–1) and Newcastle (6–1), conceding ninety-seven goals altogether. However, the most disappointing team in the division saw Notts County finish in tenth position, following their splendid FA Cup Final victory only two years earlier.

Liverpool and Manchester City would now join West Bromwich Albion and Small Heath in the end-of-season play-off games, while the unfortunate Crewe, Rotherham and Burslem Port Vale were relegated out of the League to be replaced by Blackpool, Walsall and Gainsborough Trinity for the 1896–97 season.

The final League placings at the close of the 1895–96 season are shown in Tables XVII and XVIII.

Table XVII: *First Division Football League results for the 1895–96 season*

	P	W	D	L	F	A	PTS
1. Aston Villa	30	20	5	5	78	45	45
2. Derby County	30	17	7	6	68	35	41
3. Everton	30	16	7	7	66	43	39
4. Bolton Wanderers	30	16	5	9	49	37	37
5. Sunderland	30	15	7	8	52	41	37
6. Stoke	30	15	0	15	56	47	30
7. Wednesday	30	12	5	13	44	53	29
8. Blackburn Rovers	30	12	5	13	40	50	29
9. Preston North End	30	11	6	13	44	48	28
10. Burnley	30	10	7	13	48	44	27
11. Bury	30	12	3	15	50	54	27
12. Sheffield United	30	10	6	14	40	50	26
13. Nottingham Forest	30	11	3	16	42	57	25

	P	W	D	L	F	A	PTS
14. Wolverhampton Wndrs	30	10	1	19	61	65	21
15. Small Heath	30	8	4	18	39	79	20
16. West Bromwich Albion	30	6	7	17	30	59	19

Table XVIII: *Second Division Football League results for the 1895–96 season*

	P	W	D	L	F	A	PTS
1. Liverpool	30	22	2	6	106	32	46
2. Manchester City	30	21	4	5	63	38	46
3. Grimsby Town	30	20	2	8	82	38	42
4. Burton Wanderers	30	19	4	7	69	40	42
5. Newcastle	30	16	2	12	73	50	34
6. Newton Heath	30	15	3	12	66	57	33
7. Woolwich Arsenal	30	14	4	12	59	42	32
8. Leicester Fosse	30	14	4	12	57	44	32
9. Darwen	30	12	6	12	72	67	30
10. Notts County	30	12	2	16	57	54	26
11. Burton Swifts	30	10	4	16	39	69	24
12. Loughborough	30	9	5	16	40	67	23
13. Lincoln	30	9	4	17	53	75	22
14. Burslem Port Vale	30	7	4	19	43	78	18
15. Rotherham Town	30	7	3	20	34	97	17
16. Crewe	30	5	3	22	30	95	13

Wednesday Secure an FA Cup Final Appearance

Blackpool were the only team from outside the Football League to reach the second round stage of the 1896 FA Cup competition. However, the Lancashire side attained League status for the following season.

Stoke progressed to the quarter-finals with a 7–1 victory against Burnley in a replayed tie; Liverpool, the Second Division leaders, suffered a 2–0 reverse at Wolverhampton Wanderers; while Milward, Cameron and John Bell were on target for Everton in a 3–0 home success against Sheffield United.

Derby County secured a 5–1 win against Newton Heath following a one-all draw, with Miller (3), Bloomer and McQueen scoring for the East Midlanders; Bolton Wanderers enjoyed a 2–0 victory at Blackpool, with James Cassidy and Jocky Wright on target for the visitors; while newly promoted Bury won by three goals to one at Newcastle.

West Bromwich Albion earned a place in the quarter-finals with a 3–0 success against Grimsby in a replay with William Richards (2) and Roddy McLeod netting the Albion goals, while Wednesday completed the quarter-final line-up as Lawrence Bell and Fred Spiksley found the net in a 2–1 home success against Sunderland, with Jimmy Millar replying for the north-eastern side.

Wednesday were then drawn at home to Everton, which resulted in a 4–0 victory for the Yorkshire side with Archie Brash and Lawrence Bell netting a brace of goals apiece, while Bolton Wanderers secured a 2–0 home success against Bury, with Gunn and Wright on target for the Wanderers.

Wolverhampton Wanderers proceeded to the semi-finals at the expense of Stoke (3–0), while Archie Goodall scored the only goal of the game for Derby County in a 1–0 home win against West Bromwich Albion to complete the semi-final line-up.

Derby were then drawn to play against Wolverhampton Wanderers in the semi-finals at Perry Barr, Birmingham, where they lost by the odd goal in three with Steve Bloomer scoring his customary goal for the losers. The Wednesday–Bolton tie at Goodison Park ended in a one-all draw. However, the Sheffield side's greater FA Cup experience told in the replay as goals by Crawshaw, Davis and Spiksley earned a 3–1 victory to secure a final appearance at Crystal Palace on 18 April.

An Unconvincing Victory in Belfast

England opened their international season with a visit to Belfast on 7 March with a mixed team of amateur and professional players, which included George Raikes, making his second appearance in goal, together with his fellow Corinthians Lewis Lodge and William Oakley at fullback.

James Crabtree, who had recently moved from Burnley to Aston Villa, gained his fourth England cap at right half back, Tom Crawshaw (Wednesday) played his second England game at centre half, while George Kinsey (Derby County) completed the defensive line-up.

Billy Bassett (West Bromwich Albion), Steve Bloomer (Derby County), G O Smith (Corinthians), Edgar Chadwick (Everton) and Fred Spiksley (Wednesday) formed an attack that was as skilful as any in the land. However, England could only manage a 2–0 victory against the Irish, with Bloomer and Smith on target for the visitors.

Five Goals for Steve Bloomer

Mid-March saw the England side visit Cardiff for the game against the Welsh national team, with the visitors including Raikes, Oakley, Crawshaw, Crabtree, Kinsey, Bassett, Bloomer and G O Smith from the victory in Belfast. John Goodall (Derby County) and Rupert Sandilands (Corinthians) replaced Edgar Chadwick (Everton) and Fred Spiksley (Wednesday) up front, while Arthur Henfrey completed the England line-up at the expense of fellow Corinthian, Lewis Lodge, for a game which England won with ease, with goals by

Bloomer (5), Smith (2), Bassett and Goodall securing a 9–1 victory to extend their unbeaten run to twenty games.

England's Unbeaten Run Ends in Glasgow

Two weeks before the FA Cup Final, the England team travelled to Glasgow to fulfil the annual fixture against the Scots, with the visitors making three changes after their excellent victory in Cardiff.

George Raikes, Arthur Henfrey and Billy Bassett were making their final appearances in an England shirt in a team that included William Oakley, James Crabtree, Tom Crawshaw, John Goodall and G O Smith. Lewis Lodge returned in defence for his fifth and final England appearance at the expense of George Kinsey.

Harry Wood (Wolverhampton Wanderers) earned a surprise recall for his third cap in six seasons to replace the unavailable Steve Bloomer, while Cuthbert Burnup, a future captain of Kent in the Cricket County Championship, replaced Rupert Sandilands for his only appearance for his country.

While England performed with their usual effort, the Scots managed to win by the odd goal in three to end the visitors' long unbeaten run. Billy Bassett scored the England goal in his sixteenth and final international appearance.

The Inter-League Game with Ireland Ends All Square

During the early stages of the 1895–96 season, a Football League Eleven entertained a team of players drawn from the Irish League, with the home side selecting Turner (Stoke), Chatt (Aston Villa), Williams (Everton), Flewitt (Everton) and Dorrell (Aston Villa) from the First Division, together with Baddeley (Burslem Port Vale), Eccles (Burslem Port Vale), Swift (Loughborough), Chapman (Manchester City), Finnerhan (Manchester City) and McCairns (Grimsby) from the Second Division. However, the expected victory did not materialise for the home side. The visitors returned home with a two-all draw, with Williams and Finnerhan having netted the English goals.

The League Eleven Score Five Against the Scots

A week after England's defeat in Glasgow, a Scottish League Eleven arrived at Goodison Park for their inter-League game against the English with the home side fielding Howard Spencer, James Crabtree, Charlie Athersmith and John Devey from the successful Aston Villa team, as well as Billy Williams, Tom Perry and Tom Higgins from West Bromwich Albion. John Sutcliffe (Bolton Wanderers) returned in goal, with John Goodall (Derby County), Francis Becton (Liverpool) and Alf Milward (Everton) up front. The English side recorded a 5–1 victory, with Becton (2), Devey, Athersmith and Goodall on target to avenge the international defeat from the previous week.

Wednesday Finally Win the FA Cup

Wolverhampton Wanderers and the Wednesday contested the twenty-fifth FA Cup Final, which took place at Crystal Palace on 18 April. The Wolverhampton side selecting the following players:

Tennant

Baugh   Dunn

Owen   Malpass   Griffiths

Tonks   Henderson   Beats   Wood   Black

The Wednesday selected the following eleven:

Massey

Earp   Langley

Brandon   Crawshaw   Petrie

Brash   Brady   Bell   Davis   Spiksley

Both teams enjoyed excellent FA Cup reputations, with Wolves having won the trophy in 1893, while Wednesday had suffered an embarrassing 6–1 defeat against Blackburn Rovers in the 1890 final. However, the Sheffield side had appeared in three successive semi-finals, which made them favourites to win the trophy, as Wolves had suffered a couple of seasons of turmoil within the club.

Wednesday were at full strength for the final, while Tennant replaced the injured William Rose in the Wolves' goal, for whom Richard Baugh and Harry Wood were making their third FA Cup Final appearance.

Wednesday dominated the early stages of the final, which resulted in the opening goal when Fred Spiksley slotted an Archie Brash throw-in past Tennant in the Wanderers' goal. The Wolverhampton side were soon on level terms, though, when David Black intercepted a Tom Crawshaw clearance to place the ball wide of goalkeeper Jimmy Massey.

The Sheffield side eventually regained the lead when Harry Davis set up a goal-scoring opportunity for Fred Spiksley, who sent a tremendous shot into the Wanderers' net for his second goal of the game, while Tom Crawshaw saw a shot hit a post as Wednesday continued to dominate the proceedings. Wanderers came more into the game during the latter stages of the final as they sought an equalising goal. However, the Yorkshire side held on to a 2–1 victory as team captain Jack Earp proudly received the new FA Cup from Lord Kinnaird.

Wednesday Complete Their League Fixtures

Wednesday suffered a 2–0 defeat at Bolton Wanderers in their final League game of the season, which resulted in a seventh place finish, following twelve wins, five draws and thirteen defeats in their thirty League fixtures, while scoring forty-four goals and conceding fifty-three, with Fred Spiksley leading the scoring with ten goals.

Lawrence Bell, Tom Crawshaw, Jack Earp, Ambrose Langley, Fred Spiksley and Alec Brady had missed no more than half a dozen games for the Sheffield side, whose name now proudly appeared on the much coveted FA Cup Trophy.

The FA Amateur Cup Remains in the North-East

Following the success of Middlesbrough in the previous season's FA Amateur Cup final, the trophy returned to the north-east at the close of the 1895–96 campaign as Bishop Auckland defeated the army team from Portsmouth by one goal to nil in a close encounter at Leicester. However, the army team were not the Royal Engineers' side that had dominated the Association game during the 1870s.

Liverpool's Swift Return to the First Division

The 1895–96 season test match games were played on a League basis, with the two last placed teams in the First Division competing against the top two teams in the Second on a home and away basis, while not playing against each other.

West Bromwich Albion had finished at the foot of the First Division with one League game remaining with Small Heath one place above them, while Liverpool and Manchester City had finished the season as winners and runners-up of the Second Division.

Liverpool were the early leaders of the play-off League following a 4–0 home success against Small Heath, with Allen and Bradshaw amongst the scorers, while a Tom Perry goal earned West Bromwich Albion a one-all draw at Manchester City, with Rowan on target for the home side. However, a couple of days later, the Manchester team suffered a 6–1 defeat in the return game at Albion with Flewitt (2), Higgins, J Richards, Williams and Johnson scoring for the Black Country side, while the Small Heath–Liverpool game ended in a goalless draw.

Manchester City then secured a 3–0 home victory against Small Heath, with Davies, Rowan and Meredith on target, while Liverpool scored twice without reply against West Bromwich Albion. This saw the play-off League table as in Table XIX, with one round of games remaining.

Table XIX: *The 1895–96 test match position with one game to go*

	Played	Won	Lost	Drawn	Points
Liverpool	3	2	0	1	5
West Bromwich Albion	3	1	1	1	3
Manchester City	3	1	1	1	3
Small Heath	3	0	2	1	1

Small Heath ended Manchester City's hopes of promotion to the First Division in the final round of games as Jones (3), Wheldon (3), Abbott and Hallam found the net in an 8–1 victory for the Birmingham side. William Richards and Billy Williams were on target for West Bromwich Albion as they defeated Liverpool by two goals to nil, which meant that Albion and Manchester City retained their places in their respective divisions, while Liverpool replaced Small Heath in the First Division.

West Bromwich Albion Complete Their Season

Following their success in the play-off games, West Bromwich Albion secured a 3–2 home win against Blackburn Rovers in their final game of the campaign, with Taggart, Hutchinson and William Richards on target. However, the West Bromwich side could consider themselves a little fortunate to have retained their First Division status for the 1896–97 season.

Chapter XXII

ASTON VILLA WIN THE FA CUP AND LEAGUE DOUBLE – 1896–97

ASTON VILLA RETAIN THE LEAGUE CHAMPIONSHIP AND WIN THE FA CUP TO
EMULATE PRESTON NORTH END
BLACKBURN ROVERS' AND SUNDERLAND'S SEASON OF STRUGGLE
BURNLEY ARE RELEGATED
NOTTS COUNTY RETURN TO THE FIRST DIVISION
SCOTLAND WIN ON ENGLISH SOIL TO RETAIN THE INTERNATIONAL
CHAMPIONSHIP
A DEBUT HAT-TRICK FOR FRED WHELDON

LIVERPOOL

Following their excellent performances in the 1895–96 play-off games, the Liverpool team were promoted to the First Division for the 1896–97 League campaign, which resulted in few changes in their line-up. Henderson, Dick, Hannah, Gordon, Cunliffe and McQueen continued in defence, while McQue, Bradshaw, Ross, Becton and George Allen remained in the attack.

Liverpool opened the season with a 2–1 victory at the Wednesday, followed by successive defeats at Blackburn Rovers (1–0) and at home to Bolton Wanderers (2–0), while the month ended with wins at Bury (2–1) and at home to Derby County (2–0), as well as a goalless home draw with West Bromwich Albion, which saw the Liverpool team in the top half of the League table.

Early October saw odd-goal defeats at Everton (2–1) and Sunderland (4–3) on either side of a 3–0 home win against Nottingham Forest, while a one-all draw at Sheffield United continued their indifferent run of results. However, home victories against Blackburn Rovers (4–0) and Sunderland (3–0), as well as a 1–0 success at West Bromwich Albion, saw the Merseysiders climb up to fourth place in the table.

Then followed successive draws at Preston North End (1–1) and at home to Everton (0–0), while their inconsistent form continued with away defeats at Nottingham Forest (2–0), Derby County (3–2) and Burnley (4–1), as well as a three-all home draw with Aston Villa. A 3–1 home success against Bury was their only success during the final weeks of the year.

New Year's Day saw Liverpool secure a 4–1 victory at Bolton Wanderers, followed by a goalless home draw with Sheffield United, while further wins at Wolverhampton Wanderers (2–1) and at home to Stoke (1–0) maintained their top five position. However, the Potteries' side soon avenged the defeat with a 6–1 victory against the Merseysiders.

Liverpool then secured a 2–1 victory at West Bromwich Albion in the second round of the FA Cup to earn a home tie against Nottingham Forest in the quarter-finals, which resulted in a one-all draw. The Lancashire side performed magnificently in the replay in a 1–0 success to secure a semi-final tie against League leaders Aston Villa.

Prior to the semi-final game, Liverpool met Villa in a League encounter at Perry Barr, which ended in a goalless draw, but in the semi-final at Bramall Lane, the Liverpool side were beaten by three goals to nil to end their hopes of playing against Everton in the final.

On their return to League action, the disappointed Liverpool team suffered a 2–1 home defeat against Burnley, who were at the foot of the table, while the season ended with home draws against Wednesday (2–2) and Preston North End (0–0) on either side of a 3–0 home win against Wolverhampton Wanderers. The Merseysiders ended the campaign in fifth position following twelve victories, nine draws and nine defeats in their thirty League games, while scoring forty-six goals and conceding thirty-eight.

Bradshaw and Allen had once again scored the majority of the goals in Liverpool's finest season to date, and their success was maintained for a number of seasons.

BURNLEY

Burnley had enjoyed many excellent team performances during the 1895–96 season, despite losing the likes of James Crabtree and Jack Hillman to the more successful clubs. However, the Lancashire side retained the majority of their players for the 1896–97 League campaign. Reynolds, McLintock, Place (Senior), Longair and Taylor continued in defence, with Beveridge, Black, Towman, Bowes and Place (Junior) in the attack, while goalkeeper Jack Hillman would soon return from Everton.

Burnley opened the season with a 1–0 reverse at Sheffield United, followed by home draws against Sunderland (1–1) and Nottingham Forest (2–2) on either side of a 1–0 home victory against Bury. Away defeats at Preston North End (5–3) and Blackburn Rovers (3–2) continued their indifferent start to the campaign. However, a 2–1 success against Everton, as well as a two-all draw with Preston North End, saw Burnley remain unbeaten on home soil.

Then followed successive away defeats at Nottingham Forest (4–1), Derby County (3–2), Wolverhampton Wanderers (2–0) and Everton (6–0), as well as a 1–0 home reverse against Blackburn Rovers. Their poor run of results improved towards the end of the year with a one-all home draw against the Wednesday, prior to ending the year with a 4–1 home success against Liverpool.

New Year's Day saw Burnley secure a point in a one-all draw at Bury, which preceded an excellent 3–0 win against Aston Villa at Perry Barr. However, a further loss of form saw the Lancashire side win only two of their remaining League fixtures, leaving them struggling near the foot of the League table.

Burnley's poor run of results began with a 3–1 home defeat against Stoke, followed by a one-all home draw with Sheffield United, while further home defeats against Bolton Wanderers (2–0) and Aston Villa (4–3), together with away defeats at Stoke (3–2), Wednesday (1–0) and Bolton Wanderers (2–1), continued their dismal form.

Early March saw Burnley share the points in a one-all draw at Sunderland, followed by a 3–0 home reverse against Wolverhampton Wanderers. A 2–1 victory at Liverpool saw a rare away win, but further defeats at West Bromwich Albion (3–0) and at home to Derby County (3–2) resulted in a last place League finish for Burnley, despite securing a 5–0 home success against West Bromwich Albion in the final game of the campaign.

Burnley had won six, drawn seven and lost seventeen of their thirty League games, while scoring forty-three goals and conceding sixty-one. Their FA Cup hopes had ended at the first hurdle, too. Despite finishing four points adrift at the foot of the table, the end-of-season play-off games offered the Lancashire side the opportunity of retaining their First Division status for the 1897–98 League campaign.

SUNDERLAND

Sunderland had finished the 1895–96 League campaign in fifth position, which was a little disappointing by their own standards after their three League Championship winning seasons.

Manager Tom Watson had decided to join Liverpool prior to the 1896–97 season, while the north-east side made a number of changes in their line-up for the new campaign. However, John Doig continued in goal, with McNeill, Gow, Dunlop and Hugh Wilson in defence, while James Gillespie, Johnny Campbell and James Hannah were once again the mainstays of the attack.

Inside forward Jimmy Millar had returned to Glasgow Rangers, centre half Gibson had joined Notts County, following more than one hundred appearances for the north-eastern side, while newcomers in defence included Irish international fullback Boyle from Albion Rovers, as well as Scottish international McAllister, who arrived from Kilmarnock towards the end of the year.

McAllister played in well over 200 games for Sunderland, as did Mathew Ferguson, who had arrived from the Mossend Brigade club prior to the new season.

Morgan and Cowan had been further signings from north of the border, with Morgan making fifty-eight League appearances in three seasons, prior to joining Bolton Wanderers, while Cowan, who had arrived from Motherwell during the previous campaign, scored eight goals in nineteen League games, prior to returning to Motherwell.

Sunderland opened the season with a 1–0 home defeat against Bury, followed by successive draws at home to Bolton Wanderers (1–1) and away at Burnley (1–1), while their indifferent start to the campaign continued with away defeats at Preston North End (5–3), Sheffield United (3–0) and Bolton Wanderers (1–0), as well as at home to Wolverhampton Wanderers (3–0).

Early October saw the north-east side secure a welcome point in a goalless draw at the Wednesday, which preceded a 4–3 home success against Liverpool, with Hannah and Hamilton netting a brace of goals apiece. Billy Dunlop scored the only goal of the game in a 1–0 victory at Wolverhampton Wanderers. However, successive away defeats at Liverpool (3–0), Nottingham Forest (2–1) and West Bromwich Albion (1–0) saw Sunderland struggling at the foot of the League table, with seven points from their opening thirteen games.

Then followed successive home draws against Wednesday (0–0) and Everton (1–1), while a 1–0 home defeat against Blackburn Rovers continued their poor run of results. Sunderland soon avenged that defeat with a 2–1 victory at Blackburn, with Gillespie and Cowan scoring for the visitors, which preceded a 5–2 reverse at Everton in the final game of the year.

James Hannah then netted his sixth League goal of the campaign in a one-all home draw with Preston North End, which was followed by a 2–1 home defeat against Derby County, while Gillespie (2), Morgan and Johnstone, found the net in a 4–2 home win against Aston Villa. However, the usual away defeats in the return games with Villa (2–1) and Derby (1–0) saw the end-of-season play-off games looming for the three times champions.

Sunderland were then drawn at Burnley in the first round of the FA Cup, where a goal by Morgan earned a 1–0 victory to secure a home tie against Nottingham Forest in the second round, which resulted in a 3–1 defeat. The north-eastern side soon returned to winning ways as Gillespie (2), Morgan and Campbell were on target in a 4–1 home success against Stoke.

Following a 1–0 home defeat against Sheffield United, Johnny Campbell netted only his third League goal of the campaign in a one-all home draw with Burnley, which preceded a 2–1 home victory against West Bromwich Albion, with Morgan and Wilson on target, while Hannah and Morgan found the net in a two-all home draw with Nottingham Forest soon after.

Cowan then netted the only goal of the game in a 1–0 success at Stoke, while the season ended with a one-all draw at Bury, which saw a fifteenth place finish for the north-eastern side following seven wins, nine draws and fourteen defeats in their thirty League games, while scoring thirty-four goals and conceding forty-seven.

Johnny Campbell had ended the campaign with a miserable four League goals, James Hannah had found the net on seven occasions, while James Gillespie had led the scoring with eight League goals in Sunderland's most disappointing season to date. Further disappointment was possible following the end-of-season play-off games.

BLACKBURN ROVERS

Blackburn Rovers' success in the FA Cup competition seemed to have drawn to a close, and they had tended to settle for a mid-table League position during previous seasons. However, few changes were made in their line-up for the 1896–97 League campaign. Ogilvie continued in goal, with Brandon, Dewar, Killean and Anderson in defence, while Chippendale, Wilkie, Haydock, Hargreaves, Tierney and Whitehead contested the forward positions.

Murray and Cleghorn had moved to pastures new, but they were adequately replaced by Booth and Albert Houlker, with Booth eventually making in excess of 120 appearances in five seasons with the club, while Houlker, who soon represented the English national side, made nearly 200 appearances for the Rovers.

Campbell, Nichol and Proudfoot were the most notable newcomers in the attack, but Campbell was the only one to command a regular first team place during the season.

Rovers opened the season with a 2–1 home defeat against West Bromwich Albion, followed by a 1–0 home success against Liverpool, with Stuart making a rare appearance in the first team and scoring the only goal of the game, while a goalless draw at Bolton Wanderers secured their first away point of the campaign.

Then followed a 4–0 home win against the Wednesday, with Tierney, Wilkie, Chippendale and Dewar on target, which preceded a one-all draw at Wolverhampton Wanderers where Tierney once again found the net. Goals by Chippendale, Dewar and an Anderson penalty secured a 3–2 home victory against Burnley, but a 3–1 reverse at Preston North End ended Blackburn's five-game unbeaten run.

Harry Chippendale then netted his third League goal of the campaign in a 1–0 home win against Bolton Wanderers, which preceded successive defeats at Liverpool (4–0) and at home to Preston North End (4–0), while Campbell's opening goal of the season secured a 1–0 success at Burnley. However, following a goalless home draw with Nottingham Forest, the Lancashire side suffered successive defeats at Derby County (6–0) and Nottingham Forest (2–1), as well as at home to Aston Villa (5–1), which saw them in the bottom half of the League table at the halfway stage of the season.

Mid-December saw Harry Chippendale score the all-important goal in a 1–0 victory at Sunderland, while the year ended with successive defeats at West Bromwich Albion (1–0) and Wednesday (6–0), as well as at home in the return game with Sunderland (2–1), as Rovers moved towards the foot of the table. A 2–0 home success against Wolverhampton Wanderers during the opening week of the new year saw a return to winning ways, with Wilkie and an Owen own goal securing both points for Blackburn.

Rovers then suffered an embarrassing 7–0 reverse at Sheffield United, which preceded a 5–2 home win against Derby County with Wilkie (2), Hargreaves, Booth and Nichol on target, while Booth and Dewar found the net in a 2–1 home success against Sheffield United in the first round of the FA Cup. However, the Sheffield side returned to Ewood Park the following week to secure a 3–1 victory in a League encounter with Blackburn.

Blackburn's FA Cup success continued in the second round with a 2–1 home win against Wolverhampton Wanderers with Wilkie and Dewar on target, which preceded a 2–1 home defeat against Bury. Their FA Cup hopes ended at Goodison Park with a 2–0 reverse against Everton, but, within a couple of weeks of the FA Cup defeat, Rovers had twice beaten Everton in the League (4–2 and 3–0), with Proudfoot netting a brace of goals in both games.

Mid-March saw Blackburn secure a third successive League win in a 2–0 home success against Stoke, with Harry Chippendale scoring his fifth goal of the campaign. The season ended with away defeats at Bury (3–0), Stoke (1–0) and Aston Villa (3–0), which saw Rovers in fourteenth position following eleven victories, three draws and sixteen defeats in their thirty League games, while scoring thirty-five goals and conceding sixty-two.

Ogilvie, Brandon, Anderson, Killean, Campbell and Wilkie had missed less than a handful of games during a most disappointing season, in which Wilkie had led the scoring with a meagre seven League goals.

STOKE

Stoke had enjoyed their most successful season to date during the 1895–96 campaign, which had seen a sixth place League finish, as well as an appearance in the quarter-finals of the FA Cup. Despite their success, the Potteries' side made a number of changes in their line-up for the 1896–97 season, due mainly to the transfer of George Clawley, Joe Turner, John Farrell, Peter Durber, as well as club trainer Billy Dawson, to the Southampton club.

Robertson, Brodie and Clare remained in the Stoke defence for the new season, while Willie Maxwell, Billy Dickson and Joseph Schofield retained their places up front in a campaign in which sixteen new arrivals would be given their Football League debuts.

Stoke opened the season with a 2–1 reverse at Aston Villa, followed by a 2–1 home success against Wolverhampton Wanderers, while successive defeats at Nottingham Forest (4–0) and Wednesday (4–3), as well as at home to Bolton Wanderers (3–2), continued their indifferent start to the campaign. However, excellent victories at Wolverhampton Wanderers (2–1) and at home to Nottingham Forest (3–0) saw the Potteries' side in a mid-table position by the middle of October.

Then followed further defeats at Bolton Wanderers (4–0) and Derby County (5–1), as well as at home to Aston Villa (2–0), while a 2–1 home win against Preston North End secured a rare victory. However, away defeats at Bury (4–2) and Preston North End (3–0), as well as home draws against West

Bromwich Albion (2–2) and Derby County (2–2), saw Stoke near the foot of the League table at the halfway stage of the campaign, with ten points from fifteen League games.

Mid-December saw Stoke register a 2–1 victory at West Bromwich Albion, which preceded a 4–2 reverse at Everton in the final League game of the year, while the struggle continued into the new year with a 3–2 home defeat in the return game with Everton. However, a 3–1 success at Burnley saw a couple of welcome points.

Following a 1–0 reverse at Liverpool, the Potteries' side played a goalless home draw with the Wednesday, while a 6–1 home win in the return game with Liverpool saw their best victory of the campaign, but a 4–1 defeat at Sunderland ended their hopes of climbing the League table.

Stoke's fine home form continued with a 3–2 success against Burnley, which preceded defeats at Blackburn Rovers (2–1) and Sheffield United (1–0), as well as at home to Sunderland (1–0). Successive home wins against Blackburn Rovers (1–0), Bury (3–0) and Sheffield United (2–0) during the final week of the campaign saw Stoke end the season in thirteenth position, following eleven victories, three draws and sixteen defeats in their thirty League games, while scoring forty-eight goals and conceding fifty-nine.

Thomas Clare had been ever present in the Stoke team for the fourth time in his career, while Willie Maxwell had led the scoring with thirteen League goals in a disappointing season. The Potteries' side had secured nineteen points on home soil, while gaining only six on their travels.

WEST BROMWICH ALBION

West Bromwich Albion had struggled to maintain their First Division status in each of the two previous League campaigns. However, the Albion directors kept faith with the majority of their players for the 1896–97 season, as Joe Reader continued in goal, with Williams, Banks, Higgins and Tom Perry in defence, while Flewitt, Richards, McLeod and Billy Bassett remained in the attack.

Tom Hutchinson and John Horton had left the club, which saw the arrival of local fullback Evans, as well as McManus from Hibernian. The most notable newcomers up front included Watson (Mansfield Town), Ford (Dundee), Cameron (Blackburn Rovers) and Ben Garfield, who had played for a number of teams in the Burton area. With the exception of Garfield, the recent signings all soon moved to pastures new.

Albion opened the season with a 2–1 success at Blackburn Rovers, with Richards and McLeod on target, which preceded a 3–1 home win against Aston Villa, with Garfield (2) and Williams netting for the Black Country side. A 3–1 reverse at the Wednesday, as well as draws at home to Preston North End (1–1) and at Liverpool (0–0), ended their fine start to the campaign.

Early October saw further defeats at home to the Wednesday (2–0) and at Aston Villa (2–0), while Roddy McLeod scored the only goal of the game in a

1–0 home victory against Wolverhampton Wanderers. However, following a goalless home draw with Bury, the West Bromwich side's indifferent form continued with a 1–0 home defeat against Liverpool.

Billy Bassett then netted his first goal of the season in a 1–0 home win against Bolton Wanderers, which preceded a 1–0 home defeat against Sheffield United, while Flewitt and Garfield found the net in a two-all draw at Stoke. Albion soon returned to winning ways with successive victories at home to Sunderland (1–0) and away at Sheffield United (1–0), leaving them in a mid-table position at the halfway stage of the campaign.

Albion continued to struggle during December with a 2–1 home defeat against Stoke, followed by a two-all draw at Bolton Wanderers, where Flewitt and Cameron found the net. An 8–1 defeat at Derby County on Christmas Day saw a really poor performance by the Albion team. However, a 1–0 home success against Blackburn Rovers on Boxing Day saw their first victory of the month, with Flewitt scoring the all-important goal.

Following a 6–1 defeat at Wolverhampton Wanderers in the final game of the year, Dean, making a rare appearance in the first team, scored the only goal of the game in a one-nil victory at Nottingham Forest. This preceded a 4–1 home defeat against Everton, while William Richards netted a hat-trick in a 4–0 home success in the return game with Nottingham Forest.

Albion were then drawn away at Luton Town in the first round of the FA Cup, where Flewitt found the net in a 1–0 victory, which was followed by a 4–1 home reverse in a League encounter with Derby County, while a 2–1 home defeat against Liverpool in the second round of the FA Cup ended their interest in the competition.

Further defeats at Sunderland (2–1) and Bury (3–0) saw Albion move towards the foot of the League table, while McLeod, Williams and Flewitt were on target in a 3–0 home win against the struggling Burnley team, though Burnley soon avenged the defeat by scoring five goals without reply against the West Bromwich side.

Then followed a goalless draw at Preston North End, while the season ended with a 6–3 reverse at Everton. Albion ended in twelfth position with ten victories, six draws and fourteen defeats in their thirty League games, while scoring thirty-three goals and conceding fifty-six.

William Richards and Ben Garfield had ended the season with five League goals apiece, while Flewitt had led the scoring with six in a further disappointing campaign for one of the finest teams in England.

NOTTINGHAM FOREST

Nottingham Forest had narrowly managed to avoid the test match positions during the 1895–96 League campaign. However, few changes were made in their line-up for the 1896–97 season. Dennis Allsopp continued in goal, with Archie Ritchie, Adam Scott, Frank Forman, John MacPherson and Alexander

Stewart in defence, while Fred Forman, Tom McInnes and Charles Richards were the mainstays of the attack.

David Smellie, Albert Carnelly and the long-serving Horace Pike had left the club, while Peter McCracken made only the occasional appearance, but they were adequately replaced by Jim Iremonger, Arthur Capes and Adrian Capes, who all became regular members of the Forest side during the season.

Iremonger, who had made a few appearances during the previous campaign, made in excess of 300 appearances for the Nottingham side, as well as winning international caps with the England team, while he would become equally famous as a county cricketer with Nottinghamshire, with whom he remained for forty seasons in various capacities.

Arthur and Adrian Capes had arrived from Burton Wanderers during the close season, following many excellent displays for the Staffordshire side. However, Adrian was soon forced into retirement due to ill-health, while Arthur made nearly 200 appearances in six seasons with Forest.

Forest opened the season with a one-all draw at Derby County, with Charles Richards on target for the visitors, which was followed by a 4–0 home success against Stoke, with MacPherson, Richards, Frank Forman and Fred Forman netting the Forest goals, while Richards scored for the third game running in a two-all draw at Burnley, where Arthur Capes scored his first goal of the campaign.

Then followed the Nottingham side's third draw in four games at home to Sheffield United (2–2) with McInnes and Fred Forman on target, which preceded successive away defeats at Liverpool (3–0) and Stoke (3–0), while Richards (2), Hollis and Arthur Capes found the net in a 4–1 home victory against Burnley.

Adrian Capes then netted a brace of goals in a two-all home draw with the Wednesday, while both Capes brothers were on target in a 3–2 reverse at Preston North End. However, following a goalless draw at Blackburn Rovers, Forest lost their unbeaten home record with a 2–1 defeat against Derby County.

November's end saw successive home wins against Sunderland (2–1) and Liverpool (2–0) with Shaw, Arthur Capes, Fred Forman and Frederick Spencer sharing the Forest goals, which preceded a 4–1 reverse at Wolverhampton Wanderers. Richards and Arthur Capes were on target in a 2–1 home win against Blackburn Rovers as the Nottingham side settled into a mid-table position at the halfway stage of the season. However, successive away defeats at Aston Villa (3–2) and Bury (2–0) continued their disappointing away form.

Forest ended the year with a 3–0 home win in the return game with Bury with McInnes, Frank Forman and Adrian Capes on target, which preceded new year defeats at home to West Bromwich Albion (1–0) and away at Everton (3–1). McInnes and Adrian Capes found the net in a 2–0 home success against Bolton Wanderers, but a 4–0 reverse at West Bromwich Albion saw the

Nottingham side's fifth successive away defeat.

Late January saw Forest secure a 1–0 victory at the Wednesday in the first round of the FA Cup, with Arthur Capes scoring the only goal of the game, while Fred Forman (2) and Tom McInnes were on target in a second round success at Sunderland (3–1) to earn an away tie against Liverpool in the quarter-finals.

Prior to the quarter-final tie, Arthur Capes, Fred Forman and John MacPherson found the net in a 3–0 victory at Sheffield United, in Forest's only away success of the season, while Richards was on target when the cup game with Liverpool ended all square (1–1). However, Forest were a little unfortunate to suffer a 1–0 defeat in the replay to end their interest in the competition for a further season.

On Forest's return to League action, Frederick Spencer netted a brace of goals in a 4–2 home defeat against Aston Villa, which preceded a 3–0 home success against Everton with Spencer, Richards and Arthur Capes on target. Successive away draws at Sunderland (2–2) and Bolton Wanderers (0–0) maintained their mid-table position with three League games remaining. Defeats at the Wednesday (3–0) and at home to Wolverhampton Wanderers (2–1), as well as a goalless home draw with Preston North End, saw the Nottingham side end the campaign in eleventh position with nine wins, eight draws and thirteen defeats in their thirty League games, while scoring forty-four goals and conceding forty-nine.

Arthur Capes had appeared in all thirty League games for Forest, with his brother Adrian missing only one in a disappointing campaign. Frederick Spencer had scored five goals in eight League appearances, Charles Richards and Adrian Capes had ended the season with seven League goals apiece, while Arthur Capes had led the scoring with eight.

WOLVERHAMPTON WANDERERS

Wolverhampton Wanderers had managed to avoid the 1895–96 test match places by a single point, but they had more than made amends by securing a place in the FA Cup Final, which resulted in few changes in their team for the 1896–97 season. Tennant continued in goal, with Dunn, Fleming, Owen and Malpass in defence, while Beats, Tonks, Miller, Griffiths and Harry Wood remained in the attack.

William Rose, Henderson, Alf Griffin and Richard Baugh had left the club, while David Black made only the occasional appearance during the season, but they were adequately replaced by Eccles, Smith and McMain.

Wanderers opened the season with a 1–0 home success against Derby County, followed by successive defeats at Stoke (2–1) and Derby County (4–3), as well as at home to Everton (1–0), while the month ended with a one-all home draw with Blackburn Rovers. However, a 3–0 victory at Sunderland saw a return to winning ways for the Black Country side.

Then followed home defeats against Stoke (2–1) and in the return game with Sunderland (1–0), as well as at West Bromwich Albion (1–0), while a goalless draw at Everton continued their indifferent run of results. Successive home wins against Burnley (2–0) and Nottingham Forest (4–1) on either side of a 3–2 reverse at Bury saw Wolves move a couple of places up the League table.

Wolves then secured draws at the Wednesday (0–0) and at home to Preston North End (1–1), which preceded a 2–1 home defeat against Aston Villa, while the year ended with an excellent 6–1 home victory against West Bromwich Albion. Their joy was short-lived as the new year began with defeats at Blackburn Rovers (2–0) and Preston North End (4–0), as well as at home to Liverpool (2–1).

January's end saw the Wanderers secure a rare away victory at Sheffield United (3–1), followed by a 2–1 success at Millwall in the first round of the FA Cup, while a 2–1 reverse at Blackburn Rovers saw them out of the competition at the second hurdle.

On their return to League action, the Wanderers played successive home draws against Bury (1–1) and Sheffield United (1–1), as well as a 3–0 reverse at Liverpool, which left them perilously close to the test match positions. However, a return to form during the final weeks of the campaign saw the Molineux side finish the season in a mid-table position.

Wanderers' improved form began with a 2–0 home win against Wednesday, followed by successive away victories at Burnley (3–0), Bolton Wanderers (2–1) and Nottingham Forest (2–1), while a 5–0 reverse at Aston Villa saw their only defeat during this period. A 4–0 home win against Bolton Wanderers in the final game of the season saw a return to winning ways that resulted in a tenth place League finish, following eleven victories, six draws and thirteen defeats in their thirty League games, while scoring forty-five goals and conceding forty-one.

Owen, Tennant and Harry Wood had appeared in all thirty League games for the Wanderers, while McMain, Miller, Smith and Tonks had ended the campaign with five League goals apiece, with Beats leading the scoring with nine.

BURY

Bury had more than held their own against other First Division opposition during the 1895–96 League campaign, which resulted in few changes in their playing staff for the 1896–97 season. Montgomery, Barbour, Davidson, Settle, Davies, Graham, Pray, Clegg, Broome, Ross, Wyllie, Barr, Miller, Henderson and Plant all remained with the club.

Bury opened the season with a 1–0 victory at Sunderland, followed by a goalless home draw with Preston North End. Successive away defeats at Burnley (1–0), Derby County (7–2) and Bolton Wanderers (2–0) as well as at home to Liverpool (2–1) saw the Lancashire side struggling near the foot of the League table by mid-October.

Then followed a run of drawn games at West Bromwich Albion (0–0) and Aston Villa (1–1), as well as at home to the Wednesday (1–1) and Bolton Wanderers (2–2), while a 4–2 home success against Stoke saw a rare victory for the Bury team.

Late November saw a further drawn game at Sheffield United (2–2), which preceded a 3–2 home win against Wolverhampton Wanderers, while a 3–1 defeat at Liverpool saw the Merseysiders complete the 'double' over Bury. However, a 2–0 home win against Nottingham Forest on Christmas Day saw the Lancashire side in a mid-table position at the halfway stage of the campaign.

Following a two-all draw at Preston North End, Bury ended the year with a 3–0 reverse at Nottingham Forest, which preceded a one-all home draw with Burnley. A 2–0 home defeat against Aston Villa continued their indifferent run of results.

Bury were then eliminated from the FA Cup competition with a 3–0 reverse at Everton in the second round. This was followed by a 2–1 victory at Blackburn Rovers, while a one-all draw at Wolverhampton Wanderers saw the Lancashire side register their ninth draw of the season.

Further success followed during March with successive home wins against Everton (3–1) and West Bromwich Albion (3–0), while a 1–0 home defeat against Sheffield United ended their splendid run of results. However, their fine home form continued with victories against Blackburn Rovers (3–0) and Derby County (1–0).

Early April saw the Lancashire side suffer successive away defeats at Stoke (3–0) and Wednesday (2–0) on either side of a one-all home draw with Sunderland. The season ended with a 2–1 victory at Everton, which resulted in a ninth place League finish for the Bury team, with ten victories, ten draws and ten defeats in their thirty League games, while scoring thirty-nine goals and conceding forty-four, with Settle and Plant scoring the majority of the goals between them.

BOLTON WANDERERS

Bolton Wanderers had finished the 1895–96 League campaign in fourth position, and had reached the semi-final stage of the FA Cup competition. This resulted in few changes in their defensive line-up for the 1896–97 season. John Sutcliffe continued in goal, with John Somerville and David Jones at fullback, while Alex Paton, James McGeachan and Archie Freebairn remained in the half-back line. However, a number of changes were made in the attack where Jocky Wright and Bob Jack were the only regular members remaining from the previous campaign.

James Cassidy, Willie Joyce and Bob Brown made few first team appearances during the season, while Robert Tannahill signed for Tottenham Hotspur following the arrival of Billy Thomson, a Scottish international winger, from the Dundee club.

Nicholl and A Gilligan replaced Brown and Cassidy up front. However, they failed to achieve the success of the latter pair who had struck up an excellent understanding of each other's play.

Bolton opened the season with a one-all draw at Sunderland where Bob Jack found the net, which preceded a 2–0 success at Liverpool with Nicholl and Jack on target, while a goalless home draw with Blackburn Rovers continued their fine start to the season.

Then followed successive victories at Stoke (3–2), as well as at home to Sunderland (1–0), Preston North End (3–1) and Bury (2–0), with Thomson, Nicholl, Jones, Wright, Jack, Gilligan and Paton sharing the Bolton goals, while a 1–0 reverse at Blackburn Rovers saw Wanderers end their seven-game unbeaten run.

Bob Jack then netted a brace of goals in a 4–0 home win against Stoke, with Thomson and Gilligan completing the scoring, while Jack was again on target the following week in a two-all draw at Bury. However, a 1–0 reverse at West Bromwich Albion continued their indifferent away form.

Mid-November saw successive away wins at Everton (3–2) and Preston North End (3–2) with Thomson, Wright and Gilligan scoring in both games, which preceded a 2–0 home win against Everton with Jack and Gilligan finding the net. Gilligan scored for the fourth game running in a two-all home draw with West Bromwich Albion as the Lancashire side reached the halfway stage of the season in the second position.

Wanderers' excellent run of results came to an end during the final week of the year with successive away defeats at Derby County (1–0) and Sheffield United (1–0), while their losing run continued into the new year with further defeats at home to Liverpool (4–1) and away at Nottingham Forest (2–0). They were followed by a goalless draw at Grimsby in the first round of the FA Cup.

Prior to the FA Cup replay, the Bolton team registered a 2–0 victory in a League encounter at Burnley where Cassidy and Jack found the net, while the cup replay with Grimsby ended in a three-all draw with Cassidy, Thomson and Jones netting for the Wanderers. However, Bolton managed to win the second replay by the odd goal in five with Joyce (2) and Jones on target to secure a second round tie at Derby County.

Bolton then suffered a 4–1 defeat in the cup game at Derby, which was hardly a surprise, as there had been a period of unrest in the Wanderers' team since the start of the new year, due mainly to the large number of people in authority within the club. As a result of the unrest, James McGeachan refused to play in a goalless draw at the Wednesday, which resulted in a period of suspension, while a 3–1 home defeat against Derby County highlighted the Lancashire side's problems.

Mid-March saw the Wanderers return to winning ways as Miller and Wright found the net in a 2–1 home success against Burnley, which preceded a goalless home draw with Nottingham Forest. Successive defeats at Aston Villa

(6–2), as well as at home to Wolverhampton Wanderers (2–1) and in the return game with Villa (2–1), saw Bolton continue their slide down the table.

Miller and Cassidy then netted Bolton's final goals of the season in a 2–1 home win against the Wednesday. The campaign ended with successive defeats at home to Sheffield United (2–0) and away at Wolverhampton Wanderers (4–0), which saw the Lancashire side in eighth position, with twelve victories, six draws and twelve defeats in their thirty League games, while scoring forty goals and conceding forty-three.

Archie Freebairn had appeared in all thirty League games for the Wanderers in a generally disappointing season, in which Bob Jack had led the scoring with eleven League goals.

EVERTON

Everton had finished the 1895–96 League campaign in third position, which resulted in few changes in their line-up for the 1896–97 season. Richard Boyle, John Holt, Billy Stewart and Smart Arridge continued in defence, while Hartley, Cameron, Chadwick, Milward and John Bell remained in the attack.

Goalkeeper Jack Hillman had returned to Burnley, which meant that local signings Menham and Briggs shared the goalkeeping duties, albeit for a little more than a season, while Kelso and Adams had returned north of the border.

Inside forward McInnes had signed for Luton Town, while Alex Latta had joined Liverpool, which saw the arrival of Storrier, a recent signing from Arbroath, into the first team, as well as outside right Jack Taylor from St Mirren, who made in excess of 400 appearances for the Merseysiders.

Everton opened the season with a 2–1 home success against the Wednesday with Cameron and Taylor on target, which preceded a 1–0 victory at Wolverhampton Wanderers, where Edgar Chadwick made his 200th League appearance for the club. A 3–2 home defeat against Aston Villa ended their fine start to the campaign.

Then followed successive victories in the return game at Aston Villa (2–1) and at home to Liverpool (2–1), with Hartley scoring in both games, while away defeats at Burnley (2–1) and Wednesday (4–1), as well as at home to Sheffield United (2–1), saw the Everton team in a mid-table position by the end of October.

Everton's indifferent run of results continued with goalless draws at home to Wolverhampton Wanderers and away at Liverpool on either side of a 3–2 home defeat against Bolton Wanderers. A 6–0 home success against Burnley saw a return to winning ways with Cameron (3), Chadwick, Bell and Milward on target, but a 2–0 reverse at Bolton Wanderers continued their poor away form.

John Holt then netted his only League goal of the season in a one-all draw at Sunderland, which preceded successive home wins against Stoke (4–2) and Sunderland (5–2) with John Bell netting a brace of goals in both games. The new year began with a 2–1 victory at Sheffield United, with Taylor scoring twice for the visitors.

Taylor again found the net the following day in a 3–2 win at Stoke, with Bell and Hartley completing the scoring, which preceded a further home success against Nottingham Forest (3–1), with Bell (2) and Taylor on target for the Lancashire side, while Taylor netted a hat-trick in a 4–1 victory at West Bromwich Albion.

Late January saw the Merseysiders secure a 5–2 home win against Burton Wanderers in the first round of the FA Cup, with Bell, Holt, Chadwick and Milward amongst the goal scorers, which was followed by a 4–3 home defeat in a League encounter with Preston North End. A 3–0 home success against Bury in the second round of the FA Cup earned a further home tie against Blackburn Rovers in the quarter-finals, with Taylor (2) and Milward netting the Everton goals.

Everton's excellent FA Cup form continued in the quarter-finals with a 2–0 victory against Blackburn, with Hartley scoring a brace of goals to secure a semi-final appearance against Derby County. This preceded successive away defeats at Bury (3–1), Blackburn Rovers (4–2) and Nottingham Forest (3–0), as well as at home in the return game with Blackburn (3–0). However, their losing run came to an end in the semi-final tie against Derby County as Chadwick, Hartley and Milward were on target in a 3–2 success to secure an FA Cup Final appearance against Aston Villa at Crystal Palace on 10 April.

On their return to League action, the Merseysiders suffered a sixth successive League defeat away at Preston North End (4–1), while their four remaining League games took place after their FA Cup Final appearance, which was probably the reason for their recent poor League performances.

WEDNESDAY

Following their splendid victory in the 1896 FA Cup Final, Wednesday retained all of their players for the 1896–97 League campaign. Jimmy Massey continued in goal, with Earp, Langley, Brandon, Petrie, Jamieson and Tom Crawshaw in defence, while Bob Ferrier, Harry Davis, Lawrence Bell, Alec Brady, Archie Brash and Fred Spiksley contested the forward positions.

Wednesday opened the season with successive defeats at home to Liverpool (2–1) and away at Everton (2–1), while James Callaghan, making his only appearance of the campaign, netted a brace of goals in a 3–1 home success against West Bromwich Albion. However, the Sheffield side's joy was short-lived as they suffered a 4–0 defeat at Blackburn Rovers.

Then followed victories at home to Stoke (4–3) and away at West Bromwich Albion (2–0), with Brady and Spiksley on target in both games, while successive draws at home to Sunderland (0–0) and at Bury (1–1) saw the Yorkshire side in a mid-table position by the middle of October.

Fred Spiksley and Alec Brady then scored their third goals of the season in a 4–1 home win against Everton, with Bell and Ferrier completing the scoring, while Spiksley netted a brace of goals the following week in a two-all draw at Nottingham Forest. Successive home and away defeats against Aston Villa (3–1 and 4–0) then ended their six-game unbeaten run.

Late November saw Fred Spiksley score two further goals in a 2–0 home win against Derby County, which preceded successive draws at Sunderland (0–0) and Burnley (1–1), as well as at home to Wolverhampton Wanderers (0–0), while a 2–0 reverse at Sheffield United continued their indifferent away form.

Wednesday returned to winning ways in the final game of the year as Bob Ferrier netted a hat-trick in a 6–0 home success against Blackburn Rovers, while the new year began with a further home win against Preston North End (1–0) with Fred Spiksley scoring the only goal of the game. However, a 2–1 reverse at Derby County, as well as a goalless draw at Stoke, saw Wednesday struggling to maintain their position in the top half of the League table.

The FA Cup holders then suffered a 1–0 home defeat against Nottingham Forest in the first round of the competition, which was followed by successive draws at Preston North End (2–2), as well as at home to Bolton Wanderers (0–0) and Sheffield United (1–1), with Harry Brandon scoring his only League goal of the season against their Yorkshire neighbours, while an Archie Brash goal secured a 1–0 home win against the struggling Burnley team.

Following a 2–0 reverse at Wolverhampton Wanderers, the Sheffield side shared four goals at Liverpool (2–2), where Davis and Brady found the net, while Harry Davis netted a further brace of goals in a 3–0 home success against Nottingham Forest. However, a 2–1 defeat at Bolton Wanderers continued their poor away form.

Wednesday eventually ended the campaign with a 2–0 home victory against Bury, with Bell and Ferrier on target for the Yorkshire side, who finished the season in sixth position, following ten wins, eleven draws and nine defeats in their thirty League games, while scoring forty-two goals and conceding thirty-seven.

Jimmy Massey and Ambrose Langley had been ever present in Wednesday's highest League finish to date, while Fred Spiksley had led the scoring with ten League goals.

PRESTON NORTH END

Preston North End had settled for a mid-table League finish at the close of the 1895–96 season, while their FA Cup hopes had ended at the first hurdle. However, the Lancashire side kept faith with the majority of their players for the 1896–97 League campaign. Jimmy Trainer continued in goal, with Dunn, Orr, Blyth, Sanders, Tait and Robert Holmes in defence, while Smith, Henderson and Stevenson retained their places up front. Cunningham, Grier, Pierce and W Eccleston made occasional appearances in the first team, while the most notable newcomers in the attack included Boyd, Brown and Pratt, who all scored regularly for the Preston side, with Pratt making in excess of 150 appearances for the club.

Preston opened the season with a 5–3 home win against Sunderland, with Jimmy Trainer making his 200th League appearance for the Lancashire side, which was followed by a further home success against Burnley (5–3). Successive away draws at Bury (0–0) and West Bromwich Albion (1–1) continued their excellent start to the campaign, though a 3–1 defeat at Bolton Wanderers ended their fine run of results.

Then followed home victories against Blackburn Rovers (3–1) and Sheffield United (1–0), as well as a 4–0 success in the return game at Blackburn, while a two-all draw at Burnley saw Preston move up to second place in the League table by late October.

Early November saw Preston secure a 3–2 home success against Nottingham Forest, which preceded an indifferent run of results that included defeats at Stoke (2–1) and at home to Bolton Wanderers (3–2) on either side of a one-all home draw with Liverpool. However, a 3–0 home victory against Stoke saw a return to winning ways, while the year ended with successive draws at Wolverhampton Wanderers (1–1) and at home to Bury (2–2).

Following a one-all draw at Sunderland on New Year's Day, the Lancashire side suffered a 1–0 reverse at the Wednesday, which preceded victories at home to Wolverhampton Wanderers (4–0) and away at Everton (4–3). A 2–1 home success against Stoke in the second round of the FA Cup resulted in a home tie against League leaders Aston Villa in the quarter-finals.

Prior to the quarter-final tie, Preston shared four goals at home to the Wednesday (2–2), which was followed by a 3–1 defeat against Aston Villa in a League encounter at Perry Barr. The Lancashire side suffered a further defeat against Villa (3–2) in a replayed FA Cup game.

On their return to League action, the Preston side secured a 2–0 victory at Sheffield United, followed by a two-all draw at Derby County, while a 4–1 home win against Everton maintained their second position in the League. However, an indifferent run of results during the final weeks of the campaign saw the Preston team end the season in fourth place, two points adrift from the runners–up spot.

Preston's poor run of results saw goalless draws at Nottingham Forest and Liverpool, as well as at home to West Bromwich Albion, while the campaign ended with successive home defeats against Derby County (2–0) and Aston Villa (1–0). The outcome was a fourth place League finish, following eleven victories, twelve draws and seven defeats in their thirty League games, while scoring fifty-five goals and conceding forty.

Jimmy Trainer and Blyth had appeared in all thirty League games for Preston, with Boyd, Henderson, Orr, Sanders, Smith and Robert Holmes missing no more than a handful. Brown had ended the campaign with nine League goals in twenty appearances, Henderson had found the net on eleven occasions, with Boyd leading the scoring with a dozen League goals in a greatly improved season for the Lancashire side.

DERBY COUNTY

Derby County had finished the 1895–96 League campaign as runners-up to Aston Villa and had reached the semi-final stages of the FA Cup competition, which resulted in only one serious change in their line-up for the 1896–97 season. John Robinson continued in goal, with Jimmy Methven, Joseph Leiper, John Cox and Archie Goodall in defence, while Johnny Miller, John Goodall, Steve Bloomer, Jimmy Stevenson and Hugh McQueen remained in the attack.

John McMillan had signed for Leicester Fosse, while George Kinsey had left the club. However, he was adequately replaced by England international defender James Turner, who had previously played for Bolton Wanderers and Stoke.

Derby opened the season with successive away defeats at Wolverhampton Wanderers (1–0) and Liverpool (2–0) on either side of a one-all home draw with Nottingham Forest, while a 4–3 home success in the return game with Wolverhampton Wanderers saw Steve Bloomer score all four of the Derby goals.

Bloomer netted a further hat-trick the following week in a 7–2 home win against Bury, with McQueen (2), Stevenson and John Goodall completing the scoring, while successive home defeats against Sheffield United (3–1) and Aston Villa (3–1), as well as in the return game at Villa (2–1), saw the East Midlands side struggling near the foot of the League table by late October.

Archie Goodall then scored his first League goal of the campaign in a two-all draw at Sheffield United, which preceded successive home wins against Stoke (5–1) and Burnley (3–2), with Miller and Stevenson on target in both games, while Stevenson scored for the fourth game running in a 2–1 victory at Nottingham Forest.

Then followed a 6–0 home success against Blackburn Rovers, with Jimmy Stevenson finding the net on four occasions, while a 2–0 reverse at the Wednesday ended their excellent run of results. However, following a two-all draw at Stoke, County returned to winning ways with a 3–2 home win against Liverpool, with Bloomer, Miller and Stevenson on target for Derby.

Christmas Day saw the Derby side register their best win of the season with an 8–1 home success against West Bromwich Albion, with Bloomer (3), Archie Goodall (2), McQueen (2) and Miller netting for the home side. The year ended with a further home victory against Bolton Wanderers (1–0) with Fisher, who scored eight goals in fifteen appearances for the club, scoring the only goal of the game.

Steve Bloomer's seventeenth League goal of the campaign arrived during the opening week of the new year in a 2–1 success at Sunderland, with Fisher completing the scoring. Fisher scored for the third game running in a 2–1 home win against the Wednesday, but a 5–2 reverse at Blackburn Rovers ended Derby's six-game unbeaten run.

January's end saw Steve Bloomer again on target in a 1–0 home victory against Sunderland, which preceded an 8–1 home success against Barnsley St Peter's in the opening round of the FA Cup, with Bloomer (3), Fisher (2), McQueen and both Goodall brothers scoring for Derby to secure a further home tie against Bolton Wanderers in the second round.

Prior to the FA Cup tie, the Derby team enjoyed a 4–1 victory at West Bromwich Albion, where Archie Goodall (2), Steve Bloomer and John Goodall found the net, while Bloomer netted his fifth hat-trick of the season in a 4–1 success in the Cup game with Bolton to earn a third successive home tie against Newton Heath in the quarter-finals. Newton Heath were enjoying an excellent season in the Second Division, but they were unable to cope with the skilful Derby attack as goals by Bloomer and McQueen secured a 2–0 victory to earn a second successive semi-final appearance, which was to take place at the Victoria Ground, Stoke, against Everton.

Early March saw Steve Bloomer score for the third successive League game in a 3–1 success at Bolton Wanderers, which preceded a 3–2 reverse in the semi-final tie with Everton, while their excellent League form continued with a two-all home draw with Preston North End, as well as in a 3–2 win at Burnley, with Steve Bloomer on target in both games.

Derby then suffered away defeats at Bury (1–0) and Everton (5–2), while Bloomer and Stevenson found the net in a 2–0 victory at Preston North End. However, a 1–0 home defeat in the return game with Everton saw County end the campaign in third position with sixteen wins, four draws and ten defeats in their thirty League games, while scoring seventy goals and conceding fifty.

Archie Goodall, Hugh McQueen and John Robinson had appeared in all thirty League games, while Jimmy Methven, Steve Bloomer and John Cox had missed only one in a most successful season. Archie Goodall had netted nine League goals, Jimmy Stevenson had found the net on fourteen occasions in twenty League appearances, while Steve Bloomer had once again led the scoring with twenty-four League goals, as well as seven in four FA Cup appearances.

SHEFFIELD UNITED

Sheffield United had ended the 1895–96 season in twelfth position, as well as suffering a 3–0 defeat at Everton in the second round of the FA Cup. However, the Sheffield side retained the majority of their players for the 1896–97 League campaign. Willie Foulke continued in goal, with Bob Cain, Mick Whitham, Tommy Morren, Ernest Needham and Rabbi Howell in defence, while Harry Thickett, who had made a speedy recovery from typhoid fever, reclaimed his fullback position.

Walter Bennett and Harry Hammond were the only forwards to retain their places from the previous campaign, as Docherty, Bob Hill, Jimmy Yates and

Arthur Watson were either unavailable or had left the club. They were adequately replaced by Fred Priest, who had arrived during the latter stages of the 1895–96 season, as well as by Charles Henderson (Wolverhampton Wanderers), George Walls (Heart of Midlothian) and John Almond (Darlington).

United opened the season with a 1–0 home success against Burnley, with Fred Priest scoring the only goal of the game, which preceded a two-all draw at Aston Villa, where Priest and Henderson were on target, while Hammond (2) and Almond found the net in a 3–0 home win against Sunderland.

Then followed successive draws at Nottingham Forest (2–2) and at home to Aston Villa (0–0), while Harry Hammond again found the net in away victories at Derby County (3–1) and Everton (2–1) as United continued their unbeaten run. However, following a one-all home draw with Liverpool, the Sheffield side suffered their first defeat of the campaign with a 1–0 reverse at Preston North End.

Ernest Needham then netted in successive home draws against Derby County (2–2) and Bury (2–2) on either side of a 1–0 success at West Bromwich Albion, where Fred Priest scored his fourth League goal of the season. The West Bromwich side soon avenged the defeat by winning the return game at Bramall Lane by one goal to nil.

Boxing Day saw United return to winning ways with a 2–0 home success against the Wednesday, with Priest and Howell on target, while the year ended with a further home win against Bolton Wanderers (1–0), with George Walls scoring the only goal of the game. However, a 2–1 home defeat against Everton on New Year's Day saw the Sheffield side suffer their second home defeat of the campaign.

Following a goalless draw at Liverpool, United registered their highest victory of the campaign in a 7–0 home success against Blackburn Rovers with Walls (3), Bennett (2), Cain and Hammond on target, which preceded a one-all draw at Burnley, where Fred Priest found the net, while a 3–1 reverse against Wolverhampton Wanderers saw a further home defeat.

United then suffered a 2–1 defeat at Blackburn Rovers in the first round of the FA Cup, which was followed by a 3–1 success against the Rovers in a League encounter at Ewood Park, with Bennett, Priest and Almond netting for the visitors. However, United's indifferent home form continued with a 3–0 defeat against Nottingham Forest.

John Almond's fifth League goal of the season arrived in a 1–0 away win at Sunderland, which preceded successive away draws at Wednesday (1–1) and Wolverhampton Wanderers (1–1), while a 2–0 home defeat against Preston North End saw the Yorkshire side struggling to maintain their top three position. Victories at Bury (1–0) and at home to Stoke (1–0) saw United challenging for second place in the League, with Bowes and Needham scoring the all-important goals.

Stoke soon avenged the defeat by inflicting a 2–0 reverse on United at the Victoria Ground, while the Sheffield team ended the campaign with a 2–0 success at Bolton Wanderers, with Priest and Needham on target to secure the runners-up position, with thirteen victories, ten draws and seven defeats in their thirty League games, while scoring forty-two goals and conceding twenty-nine, the lowest in the Football League.

George Walls and John Almond had ended the campaign with five League goals apiece; Ernest Needham had found the net on six occasions; Harry Hammond had netted seven League goals; while Fred Priest had led the scoring with ten in a most productive season for the Sheffield side.

ASTON VILLA

Aston Villa had twice won the League Championship, as well as the FA Cup, during the three previous seasons, with a team generally acknowledged as the finest in the land, which resulted in few changes in their line-up for the 1896–97 League campaign. Howard Spencer, James Welford, John Reynolds, James Cowan, James Crabtree and, occasionally, Bob Chatt continued in defence, while Charlie Athersmith, John Devey, Johnny Campbell, John Cowan and Steve Smith remained in the attack.

Tom Wilkes made eight appearances in goal during the 1896–97 season, prior to being replaced by Jimmy Whitehouse, a £200 signing from Grimsby Town, while Albert Evans, who had arrived from the North East following the recommendation of Bob Chatt, replaced James Welford at fullback during the second half of the campaign.

England international Dennis Hodgetts, who had served the Villa club for a number of years, had decided to move across the city to the Small Heath club, with Fred Wheldon moving in the opposite direction for a £100 fee, as well as the proceeds from a friendly game. Wheldon, an accomplished county cricketer with Worcestershire, scored sixty-eight goals in 124 League appearances for the club. He also appeared for the English national side on four occasions, which included a hat-trick on his international debut, thus joining Howard Vaughton, Arthur Brown and Albert Allen as one of the select band of Villa players to achieve this distinction.

Villa opened the season with a 2–1 home success against Stoke, with John Cowan and John Devey on target, which preceded a 3–1 reverse at West Bromwich Albion, while Wheldon and Burton found the net in a two-all home draw with Sheffield United. However, a 3–2 victory at Everton saw a return to winning ways, with Campbell (2) and Devey netting for the visitors.

John Devey then scored his fourth League goal of the campaign in a 2–1 home defeat against Everton in Villa's first defeat on home soil for a couple of seasons. This preceded a goalless draw at Sheffield United, while successive victories at home to West Bromwich Albion (2–0) and away at Derby County (3–1) saw Johnny Campbell and Fred Wheldon scoring in both games.

Wheldon again found the net in a 2–1 success in the return game with

Derby, with John Cowan completing the scoring, which was followed by a 2–0 win at Stoke, where Wheldon netted for the fourth game running, while Charlie Athersmith scored his opening goal of the campaign in a one-all home draw with Bury.

Mid-November saw Athersmith again on target in a 3–1 success at the Wednesday, with Campbell and Wheldon completing the scoring, which preceded a 4–0 victory in the return game with Wednesday, with Smith, Devey, Athersmith and Wheldon finding the net. The Villa team's excellent form continued with a 5–1 away win at Blackburn Rovers, where Fred Wheldon netted a hat-trick.

Then followed a 3–2 home success against Nottingham Forest, with Devey, Athersmith and Reynolds on target, while a three-all draw at Liverpool saw the Midlands side concede a rare away point, with Wheldon, Athersmith and James Cowan netting for the visitors. However, a 2–1 victory at Wolverhampton Wanderers in the final game of the year saw Villa move to the head of the League table, with Chatt and Athersmith scoring the all-important goals.

New Year began with successive defeats at home to Burnley (3–0) and away at Sunderland (4–2), which were followed by a 2–1 victory in the return game with Sunderland, with Devey and Wheldon on target. Fred Wheldon netted a brace of goals in a 5–0 home success against Newcastle United in the first round of the FA Cup to secure a home tie against Notts County in the second round.

Prior to the FA Cup tie, Johnny Campbell scored both Villa goals in a 2–0 away win at Bury, which preceded a further away success at Burnley (4–3), where John Devey netted a hat-trick. Their FA Cup success continued with a 2–1 victory against Notts County, with Wheldon and Campbell finding the net to earn a quarter-final tie at Preston North End, who were coincidentally Villa's next opponents in the League.

Villa had few difficulties in the League encounter with Preston, as Devey (2) and Athersmith were on target in a 3–1 victory, while the FA Cup tie proved a close affair, with drawn games at Preston (1–1) and at Perry Barr (0–0), with a second replay arranged for 10 March at Bramall Lane.

On their return to League action, the Villa team secured a 4–2 win at Nottingham Forest, with Devey (2), Wheldon and John Cowan finding the net, while Athersmith (2) and Campbell were on target in a 3–2 victory against Preston, as the Midlands side secured a semi-final tie against Liverpool, who were enjoying an excellent League campaign.

A week prior to the semi-final game, Villa and Liverpool played a goalless draw in a League encounter at Perry Barr. However, the Villa team totally dominated the semi-final as John Cowan (2) and Athersmith netted in a 3–0 victory to secure a fourth FA Cup Final appearance for the League leaders.

Fred Wheldon then scored a brace of goals in a 6–2 home win against

Bolton Wanderers, with Athersmith, Devey, Reynolds and Campbell completing the scoring, while Wheldon netted a further brace of goals in a 2–1 victory in the return game at Bolton. Villa had retained the League Championship with three games remaining, which left them in excellent spirits for the FA Cup Final against Everton at Crystal Palace on 10 April.

Notts County Regain Their Pride

It had become even more apparent during the 1896–97 League campaign that clubs needed to acquire First Division status if they were to make a profit, rather than visiting teams as far afield as Lincoln, Newcastle and Woolwich Arsenal in the Second Division.

Loughborough had managed to avoid the Second Division play-off positions following an excellent home record that included high-scoring victories against Woolwich Arsenal (8–0) and Burton Wanderers (6–0), while Darwen, who had finished in eleventh position, had won thirteen of their fifteen home games, including a 12–0 victory against Walsall. However, only one win on their travels had resulted in a poor League finish.

Blackpool had lost just once at home in finishing in eighth position; Newcastle's fifth place finish had been due to thirteen victories on home soil, as well as the goal-scoring exploits of Aitken, Smellie and Wardrope; while Small Heath, who had suffered the indignation of relegation during the previous campaign, could only manage a fourth place finish, despite the finest away record in the Division, as well as achieving the 'double' against the eventual champions. Their outside right Inglis had ended the campaign with sixteen League goals.

Grimsby Town, who had ended the 1895–96 League campaign in third place, once again enjoyed an excellent season. However, having lost goalkeeper Jimmy Whitehouse to Aston Villa, the north-eastern side secured only five victories on their travels to retain third position, one point adrift from the runners-up spot.

Newton Heath had lost their First Division status in both of their previous seasons in the Premier League. However, they were again amongst the early season front runners with six victories in their opening seven games, while they remained unbeaten at home throughout the campaign. They finished as runners-up, with Joe Cassidy leading the scoring with seventeen League goals.

An excellent FA Cup run had resulted in victories against West Manchester (7–0), Nelson (3–0), Blackpool (2–1, following a 2–2 draw), Kettering (5–1) and Southampton St Mary's (3–1, following a 1–1 draw), prior to suffering a 2–0 reverse at Derby County in the quarter-finals. However, the Manchester side had achieved their goal of securing a place in the end-of-season play-off games.

Following their tenth place League finish during the previous campaign, Notts County made a number of changes in their line-up for the 1896–97 season. Walter Bull, Charlie Bramley, David Calderhead, Tom Prescott, William Gibson and George Toone retained their places in the first eleven, while 'Tich' Smith had rejoined the club, following a spell with Long Eaton Rangers. Jack Hendry, Alf Shelton and Dan Bruce had left the club, while the most notable newcomers included Tom Boucher (Stourbridge), William Langham (South Shore) and John Murphy (Hucknall St John's), who were all forward players.

County enjoyed an excellent season, which included home victories against Burton Wanderers (6–1), Leicester Fosse (6–0), Woolwich Arsenal (7–4) and Lincoln City (8–0), while scoring 92 goals, by far the highest in the Football League. They secured the Second Division Championship by a margin of three points from Newton Heath. Their free-scoring attack had netted eighty goals between them, with Allan scoring nine League goals, Langham finding the net on ten occasions, Walter Bull ending the campaign with seventeen goals, and John Murphy and Tom Boucher finishing the season as joint leading goal scorers with twenty-two League goals apiece, as the Nottingham side awaited the end-of-season play-off games.

The final League tables at the close of the 1896–97 season are as listed in Tables XX and XXI.

Table XX: *First Division Football League results for the 1896–97 season*

	P	W	D	L	F	A	PTS
1. Aston Villa	30	21	5	4	73	38	47
2. Sheffield United	30	13	10	7	42	29	36
3. Derby County	30	16	4	10	70	50	36
4. Preston North End	30	11	12	7	55	40	34
5. Liverpool	30	12	9	9	46	38	33
6. Wednesday	30	10	11	9	42	37	31
7. Everton	30	14	3	13	62	57	31
8. Bolton Wanderers	30	12	6	12	40	43	30
9. Bury	30	10	10	10	39	44	30
10. Wolverhampton Wndrs	30	11	6	13	45	41	28
11. Nottingham Forest	30	9	8	13	44	49	26
12. West Bromwich Albion	30	10	6	14	33	56	26
13. Stoke	30	11	3	16	48	59	25
14. Blackburn Rovers	30	11	3	16	35	62	25
15. Sunderland	30	7	9	14	34	47	23
16. Burnley	30	6	7	17	43	61	19

Table XXI: *Second Division Football League results for the 1896–97 season*

	P	W	D	L	F	A	PTS
1. Notts County	30	19	4	7	92	43	42
2. Newton Heath	30	17	5	8	56	34	39
3. Grimsby	30	17	4	9	66	45	38
4. Small Heath	30	16	5	9	69	47	37
5. Newcastle	30	17	1	12	56	52	35
6. Manchester City	30	12	8	10	58	50	32
7. Gainsborough	30	12	7	11	50	47	31
8. Blackpool	30	13	5	12	59	56	31
9. Leicester Fosse	30	13	4	13	59	56	30
10. Woolwich Arsenal	30	13	4	13	68	70	30
11. Darwen	30	14	0	16	67	61	28
12. Walsall	30	11	4	15	53	69	26
13. Loughborough	30	12	1	17	50	64	25
14. Burton Swifts	30	9	6	15	46	61	24
15. Burton Wanderers	30	9	2	19	31	67	20
16. Lincoln	30	5	2	23	27	85	12

Aston Villa Secure a Fourth FA Cup Final Appearance

At the second round stage of the 1896–97 FA Cup competition, thirteen of the remaining sixteen teams were from the First Division, with Notts County, Newton Heath and Southampton St Mary's the exceptions.

Aston Villa proceeded to the quarter-finals with a 2–1 home success against Notts County, with Fred Wheldon and Johnny Campbell on target. Liverpool won at West Bromwich Albion by a similar score, while a Steve Bloomer hat-trick helped Derby County secure a 4–1 home win against Bolton Wanderers.

Everton inflicted a 3–0 defeat on Bury, with Jack Taylor (2) and Alf Milward scoring for the Merseysiders, Preston North End struggled to beat Stoke by the odd goal in three, while Fred Forman (2) and Tom McInnes found the net for Nottingham Forest in a 3–1 success at Sunderland.

Dewar and Wilkie netted for Blackburn Rovers in a 2–1 home win against Wolverhampton Wanderers, while the remaining tie between Newton Heath and Southampton St Mary's ended all square (1–1). However, the Manchester side had little difficulty in the replay as goals by Bryant (2) and Cassidy secured a 3–1 victory.

All four quarter-final ties proved close affairs. Centre forward Hartley scored twice for Everton in a 2–0 home success against Blackburn Rovers, Steve Bloomer and Hugh McQueen were on target for Derby County in a home win against Newton Heath by a similar score, while Liverpool progressed to the semi-finals with a 1–0 victory against Nottingham Forest in a replayed tie. Aston Villa completed the semi-final line up as Charlie Athersmith (2) and Johnny Campbell found the net in a 3–2 win against Preston North End at Bramall Lane, following drawn games at Preston (1–1) and Perry Barr (0–0).

Liverpool and Everton had managed to avoid each other in the semi-finals, with Liverpool facing Aston Villa at Bramall Lane, while Everton were drawn to play against Derby County at the Victoria Ground, Stoke. However, their hopes of an all Liverpool final ended in Sheffield as Villa inflicted a 3–0 defeat on Liverpool with John Cowan (2) and Charlie Athersmith on target, while Everton secured a 3–2 success against Derby with Chadwick, Hartley and Milward finding the net, with both Goodall brothers replying for Derby.

As a result of the semi-final ties, Aston Villa was to meet Everton at Crystal Palace on 10 April hoping to emulate Preston North End by winning both the League and FA Cup.

A Narrow Victory for the English League Eleven

The 1896–97 international season began in the opening week of November when an English League Eleven visited Belfast for the annual fixture against the Irish League. The visitors selected Joe Reader, Billy Williams, Tom Higgins and Billy Bassett from West Bromwich Albion, and Malpass, Beats and Harry Wood from Wolverhampton Wanderers. Howard Spencer (Aston Villa), W Higgins (Grimsby Town), Harry Bradshaw (Liverpool) and Steve Bloomer (Derby County) completed the English line-up.

As expected the visitors returned home with a 2–0 success. However, the Irish fought magnificently to hold the English attack for most of the game, only to concede two late goals scored by Beats and Bloomer.

Fred Wheldon's Three-Goal Debut

Late February saw the Irish national team visit Nottingham for the opening international fixture against England, with the home side fielding five new caps, with Harry Bradshaw (Liverpool) and Bernard Middleditch (Corinthians) making their only appearances for their country.

John Robinson (Derby County) made the first of eleven appearances in goal, Billy Williams (West Bromwich Albion) gained the first of six England caps at fullback, while Fred Wheldon, who had recently moved from Small Heath to Aston Villa, played the first of four England games in the attack, where he found the net on six occasions.

G O Smith (Corinthians), William Oakley (Corinthians), Tom Crawshaw (Wednesday), Ernest Needham (Sheffield United), Steve Bloomer (Derby County) and Charlie Athersmith (Aston Villa), who had made his previous appearance five years earlier, completed the English line-up.

England totally dominated the game to record a 6–0 victory. Fred Wheldon scored a hat-trick on his debut, together with further goals by Steve Bloomer (2) and Charlie Athersmith.

Alf Milward Justifies his Recall

England entertained the Welsh national team at Bramall Lane during the final week of March, with the home team retaining Oakley, Crawshaw, Needham, Athersmith, Bloomer and G O Smith from the victory over Ireland, while there were recalls for Francis Becton (Liverpool), John Reynolds (Aston Villa) and Alf Milward (Everton), who had gained his previous England cap six years earlier.

Willie Foulke (Sheffield United) made his only England appearance in goal, while Howard Spencer, the cultured Aston Villa defender, made the first of six international appearance at fullback.

England again won with ease as Alf Milward netted a brace of goals in a 4–0 success, with Ernest Needham and Steve Bloomer completing the scoring.

Scotland Retain the International Championship

A week before the 1897 FA Cup Final, the England–Scotland game took place at Crystal Palace. The English retained Oakley, Spencer, Reynolds, Crawshaw, Needham, Athersmith, Bloomer, Milward and G O Smith from the victory against Wales, while John Robinson (Derby County) replaced Willie Foulke in goal, with Edgar Chadwick (Everton) earning a recall for his seventh and final England appearance at the expense of Francis Becton.

Following a narrow defeat in Glasgow during the previous season, the English were determined to make amends. However, their worst fears were realised as Scotland won by two goals to one to retain the international Championship, with Steve Bloomer scoring England's consolation goal.

Aston Villa Win the FA Cup and League Double

With three League games remaining, Aston Villa had already been crowned as League Champions when they arrived at Crystal Palace for the 1897 FA Cup Final against the skilful Everton team.

Villa, who were favourites to win the trophy, included Charlie Athersmith, John Devey, Howard Spencer, John Reynolds and James Cowan from their 1895 FA Cup winning side, while Everton, albeit an excellent League team, had one losing FA Cup Final appearance to their credit.

Everton selected the following eleven:

Menham

Meecham   Storrier

Boyle   Holt   Stewart

Taylor   Bell   Hartley   Chadwick   Milward

Aston Villa selected the following team:

Whitehouse

Spencer   Evans

Reynolds   James Cowan   Crabtree

Athersmith   Devey   Campbell   Wheldon   John Cowan

John Lewis of Blackburn was appointed match referee.

A crowd in excess of 60,000 arrived in the capital city to witness a most exciting final in which forwards dominated the early play, as Athersmith, Wheldon and Devey attacked the Everton fullbacks while Bell and Milward tested the Villa defence.

Inevitably the opening goal was scored when Charlie Athersmith passed the ball to Johnny Campbell, who swerved a shot around the advancing Menham in the Everton goal to secure a one-goal lead for Villa. However, Everton soon equalised following a splendid shot by the ever menacing John Bell, while the Merseysiders went further ahead when Richard Boyle converted a free kick from the edge of the goal area.

Villa were stunned. However, they soon began to dominate the game in pursuit of the equalising goal, which was eventually obtained when Fred Wheldon slotted home a John Cowan cross, while Villa went ahead on the stroke of half-time when James Crabtree headed past Menham to end the half with a 3–2 advantage.

Little changed during the second half as Holt, Boyle and Storrier defended magnificently to keep the Villa forwards at bay, while the Everton forwards were equally forceful in their pursuit of an equalising goal. This failed to materialise and the Midlands side ran out winners by three goals to two, thus emulating the great Preston North End side in achieving the FA Cup and League 'double'.

Aston Villa and Everton Complete Their League Fixtures

Following the FA Cup Final, Everton had four League games remaining, while Aston Villa had three. However, the results of the games made little difference to the end-of-season League placings.

Everton returned to League action with a 5–2 home win against Derby County, with Chadwick (2), Bell, Hartley and Milward on target, while the following day saw a further home success against West Bromwich Albion (6–3), with John Bell scoring a hat-trick with further goals by Taylor, Chadwick and Milward.

Billy Stewart then netted a rare goal in a 1–0 victory at Derby County, while the season ended with a 2–1 home defeat against Bury as the Merseysiders ended the campaign in seventh position with fourteen victories, three draws and thirteen defeats in their thirty League games, while scoring sixty-two goals and conceding fifty-seven.

Jack Taylor had appeared in all thirty League games, while Billy Stewart and Richard Boyle had missed only one in an excellent campaign. Alf Milward netted nine League goals, Jack Taylor had found the net on thirteen occasions, while John Bell had led the scoring with fifteen goals in twenty-seven League appearances.

Villa Move to the Aston Lower Grounds

Aston Villa's remaining League fixtures were of little importance as they had already been crowned as League Champions. However, during the week following the FA Cup Final, the victorious Villa team had moved to a new ground at the Aston Lower Grounds, which eventually became known as Villa Park.

Blackburn Rovers were the first visitors to the new ground, which resulted in a 3–0 success for Villa, with Johnny Campbell having the distinction of scoring the opening goal at the Aston Lower Grounds. A couple of days later saw Villa register a further home win against Wolverhampton Wanderers (5–0) with John Cowan and Johnny Campbell netting a brace of goals apiece. The season ended with a 1–0 victory at Preston North End where Fred Wheldon scored the only goal of the game.

Villa had won twenty-one, drawn five and lost four of their thirty League games, while scoring seventy-three goals and conceding thirty-eight. Johnny Campbell ended the campaign with thirteen League goals, John Devey had found the net on seventeen occasions, while Fred Wheldon had led the scoring with eighteen League goals.

Fred Wheldon, James Cowan and Charlie Athersmith had appeared in all thirty League games, while Johnny Campbell and John Devey had missed only one. The 'double' winners had retained the League title by a margin of eleven points.

Notts County Return to the First Division

As the 1896–97 season approached its close, there remained a number of outstanding issues, none so important as the play-off games to decide the relegation and promotion places. This meant that Burnley and Sunderland, who had occupied the final two positions in the First Division, playing against Notts County and Newton Heath, who had finished as winners and runners-up of the Second.

The opening round of the play-off games saw Burnley secure a 2–0 home win against Newton Heath, while a late William Langham goal earned Notts County a 1–0 home success against Sunderland. However, Newton Heath reversed the scores in the second round as Boyd and Jenkyns found the net in a 2–0 victory, while Sunderland and Notts County played a goalless draw. This left Sunderland at the foot of the test match League table at the halfway stage of the competition.

Little changed following the third round games, as Notts County secured a one-all draw at Burnley, with Tom Boucher converting a penalty kick for the visitors. The Newton Heath–Sunderland game produced a similar result with goals by Boyd and Morgan cancelling each other out, which meant that any one of the four teams could finish in first or fourth position, depending on the results in the final round of games.

Notts County made sure of a return to the First Division when reserve team winger John Brearley scored the only goal of the game in a 1–0 success against Burnley, while Sunderland retained their First Division status as James Gillespie netted a brace of goals in a 2–0 home win against Newton Heath. This meant that Sunderland and Newton Heath remained in their respective Divisions, while Notts County replaced Burnley in the First Division as the final League table confirmed in Table XXII.

Table XXII: *Test Match League results at the end of the 1896–97 season*

	Played	Won	Lost	Drawn	For	Against	Points
Notts County	4	2	0	2	3	1	6
Sunderland	4	1	1	2	3	2	4
Burnley	4	1	2	1	3	4	3
Newton Heath	4	1	2	1	3	5	3

An Excellent Victory for the Scottish League

During the final week of April, a Football League Eleven travelled to Glasgow to fulfil an inter-League fixture against the Scottish League, with the visitors selecting an attacking side that included Howard Spencer, James Crabtree, Charlie Athersmith and John Devey from the successful Aston Villa team, as well as Steve Bloomer (Derby County), Harry Bradshaw (Liverpool) and Edgar Chadwick (Everton) in the attack.

John Sutcliffe (Bolton Wanderers) retained the goalkeeping position, while Billy Williams (West Bromwich Albion), Tom Crawshaw (Wednesday) and Ernest Needham (Sheffield United) completed the English line-up. However, despite their hopes of success, the Scots won by three goals to nil, with goals by McPherson (2) and Low ensuring that the visitors had a miserable journey home.

The Amateur–Professional Gap Widens

As the 1896–97 season came to an end, it had become apparent that the gap between amateur and professional teams had widened even further. While the amateur player was as capable as the professional, he tended to pursue a career outside the Association game.

The England selectors had continued to call upon the likes of Gilbert O Smith and William Oakley from the Corinthian team, while the club itself had undertaken a number of tours, in which they had competed favourably against the finest professional teams in the land. But, while the amateur played for the exercise and enjoyment of the game, for the professional it continued to offer a way out of the daily drudgery suffered by the majority of the working classes.

Top: The successful West Bromich Albion team following their 3–0 victory against Aston Villa in the 1892 FA Cup final, with England internationals Billy Bassett (extreme left) and John Reynolds (third from left) in a relaxed mood.

Bottom: The England international eleven who defeated Scotland by 5–2 at Richmond in 1893.

Back row: McGregor, Gosling, Bentley, Holt, Clegg, Kinsey, Holmes and Goodall.

Middle row: Bassett, Reynolds, Cotterill, Gay and Harrison.

Front row: Spiksley and Chadwick.

Steve Bloomer, Derby County and England. The finest goal scorer in England during the 1890s. Bloomer would eventually score in excess of 300 goals for Derby, as well as scoring 28 goals in 23 England appearances.

Bury Football Club – FA Cup winners 1900.
Back row: Darroch, Thompson and Davidson.
Third row: Fairhurst (trainer), Pray, Leeming, Ross and Wardle (chairman).
Second row: Wood, McLuckie and Sagar.
First row: Richards and Plant.

Player's cigarette cards from the period detailing the
Association Cup winners' teams

Chapter XXIII

SHEFFIELD UNITED ARE CROWNED CHAMPIONS – 1897–98

SHEFFIELD UNITED ARE CROWNED LEAGUE CHAMPIONS
FIVE TEAMS FINISH AT THE FOOT OF THE FIRST DIVISION WITH TWENTY-FOUR POINTS
BURNLEY WIN THE SECOND DIVISION TITLE
AN ALL EAST MIDLANDS FA CUP FINAL RESULTS IN A VICTORY FOR NOTTINGHAM FOREST
ENGLAND WIN ALL THREE INTERNATIONAL GAMES TO REGAIN THE INTERNATIONAL CHAMPIONSHIP
THE PLAY-OFF GAMES END IN A FARCE
THE FOOTBALL LEAGUE IS EXTENDED

NOTTS COUNTY

Following four seasons in the Second Division, Notts County had returned to the First Division by virtue of winning the Second Division title, as well as finishing at the top of the play-off League table. This resulted in few changes in their line-up for the 1897–98 campaign. George Toone continued in goal, with David Calderhead, Tom Prescott, Billy Ball and George Lewis in defence, while Tom Boucher, John Allan, John Murphy, William Langham and Walter Bull remained in the attack.

George Bramley, who had sustained a broken leg against Aston Villa during the previous campaign, played only occasionally prior to announcing his retirement from the game. The most notable new signing by the Nottingham side was outside left, John Fraser, from Motherwell, who eventually went on to win international honours for Scotland.

County opened the season with a 2–0 reverse at Stoke, followed by a one-all draw at Nottingham Forest. Their poor start to the campaign continued with defeats at home to Aston Villa (3–2) and away at Bolton Wanderers (1–0), prior to securing a point in a one-all home draw with Derby County.

Then followed further away defeats at the Wednesday (3–1) and Aston Villa (4–2), as well as at home to Nottingham Forest (3–1). A one-all home draw with Preston North End saw their third draw in nine League games, which preceded their first victory of the season, a 4–0 home win against Stoke.

Further defeats at Wolverhampton Wanderers (3–1) and at home to Bolton Wanderers (2–1) were followed by goalless draws at Bury and at home to the Wednesday, while a 1–0 reverse at Everton saw the Nottingham side at the foot of the League table at the halfway stage of the campaign, with only one victory in fifteen games.

Mid-December saw County share four goals at home to Wolverhampton Wanderers, while the year ended with a Christmas Day win at Derby County (2–1) to secure their first away victory of the campaign. However, new year defeats at home to Sheffield United (3–1) and away at Sunderland (2–0) continued their indifferent run of results.

County eventually returned to winning ways with a 3–2 home success against Everton, followed by a 1–0 home defeat in the return game with Sunderland, while successive victories at Sheffield United (1–0) and at home to Bury (2–1) saw the Nottingham side move away from the foot of the table.

The East Midlands side then secured home draws against Blackburn Rovers (0–0) and West Bromwich Albion (2–2) on either side of a 2–0 reverse at Liverpool. County soon avenged the defeat in Liverpool by inflicting a 3–2 defeat on the Merseysiders. Despite their greatly improved form, the Nottingham side remained in the play-off positions with three League games remaining, all away from home.

Following a 3–0 victory at West Bromwich Albion, County suffered a 3–1 reverse at Preston North End, while the campaign ended with a 1–0 success at Blackburn Rovers. This saw the Nottingham side in thirteenth position, with eight wins, eight draws and fourteen defeats in their thirty League games, while scoring thirty-six goals and conceding forty-six.

Notts was one of five teams to finish with twenty-four points at the foot of the League table. However, their superior goal difference resulted in their avoiding the play-off positions.

Their free-scoring attack of the previous season tended to struggle during the 1897–98 League campaign Despite their indifferent performances, as well as suffering an FA Cup defeat in the first round of the competition, County had at least retained their First Division status for a further season.

STOKE

Stoke had narrowly avoided the 1896–97 play-off positions owing mainly to their excellent home record. However, the club directors made few changes in their line-up for the 1897–98 season as Eccles, Brodie, Robertson, Murphy, Tom Clare, Joseph Schofield and Willie Maxwell remained in the side, while Tom Wilkes, the Aston Villa custodian, arrived on loan during the latter stages of the campaign. H D Austerberry had recently joined the club as manager–secretary, which saw an immediate improvement in Stoke's finances, as a local newspaper launched a 'Save the Club' fund. The most notable new signing was Alex Raisbeck from Hibernian. However, Raisbeck made only eight appearances for the Potteries' side prior to joining Liverpool, with whom he won eight Scottish caps.

Stoke opened the season with successive home wins against Notts County (2–0) and Blackburn Rovers (2–1) on either side of a two-all home draw with

Liverpool. Away defeats at Sheffield United (4–3) and West Bromwich Albion (2–0) ended their excellent start to the season, while a 2–1 home success against Derby County maintained the Potteries' side's top six position.

Then followed away defeats at Liverpool (4–0) and Notts County (4–0), as well as at home to Wolverhampton Wanderers (2–0), while a goalless home draw with West Bromwich Albion secured a much needed point. Further defeats at Derby County (4–1), Bolton Wanderers (2–1) and Sunderland (4–0), as well as at home to Preston North End (2–1) and Nottingham Forest (2–1), saw Stoke near the foot of the League table at the halfway stage of the campaign, with eight points from fifteen games.

Early December saw a 2–1 home success against League leaders Sheffield United, which preceded a goalless home draw with Aston Villa, while a 4–0 defeat at the Wednesday saw a further indifferent away performance. The Potteries' side returned to winning ways in the final game of the year with a 3–1 home win against Bury.

Stoke's improved form continued into the new year as they shared six goals in the return game at Bury, followed by a 1–0 home defeat against Sunderland. A 2–0 home victory against Bolton Wanderers saw the Staffordshire side move away from the foot of the League table, however a one-all draw at Everton, as well as a 4–2 reverse at Wolverhampton Wanderers, saw Stoke return to the bottom of the division.

Away from the pressures of the League, Stoke played a goalless home draw with Everton in the second round of the FA Cup, which was followed by a 5–1 defeat in the replay at Goodison Park. A 3–1 reverse at Nottingham Forest saw a further League defeat. However, an excellent run of results during the final weeks of the campaign saw the Potteries' side secure away draws at Preston North End (0–0), Aston Villa (1–1) and Blackburn Rovers (1–1), as well as home wins against the Wednesday (2–1) and Everton (2–0).

Despite their splendid run of form, the Stoke team had finished in last position, one of five teams with twenty-four points, with eight victories, eight draws and fourteen defeats in their thirty League games, while scoring thirty-five goals and conceding fifty-five.

While the Potteries' side had performed splendidly on home soil, they had failed to win any on their travels in a season of constant struggle. Murphy had been the only ever present, while Willie Maxwell had led the scoring with a dozen League goals.

BLACKBURN ROVERS

Blackburn Rovers had spent much of the 1896–97 League campaign struggling near the foot of the table, which resulted in a number of changes in their line-up for the 1897–98 season. Goalkeeper Ogilvie, George Dewar and Harry Chippendale had left the club, while Anderson and Hargreaves made few appearances in the first team. However, Houlker, Killean, Booth and Tom Brandon retained their places in the defence, with Proudfoot, Wilkie and

Campbell up front, while Knowles and Carter shared the goalkeeping duties.

Ball replaced Dewar in the defence, albeit for a little more than a season, while Briercliffe and Hulse formed a new right wing partnership, with Briercliffe scoring ten goals in fifty-six appearances, while Hulse found the net on twenty-two occasions in eighty-five League games.

Rovers opened the campaign with successive defeats at Derby County (3–1) and Stoke (2–1), as well as at home to Bolton Wanderers (3–1), prior to securing a 4–3 home success against Aston Villa with Campbell (2), Proudfoot and Briercliffe on target. Wilkie netted his first goal of the campaign in a one-all draw at Everton. However, a 5–2 reverse at Sheffield United continued their indifferent start to the season.

Blackburn then recorded a further home win against Preston North End (1–0) with Proudfoot scoring the only goal of the game, which preceded a 3–1 defeat at Nottingham Forest with Proudfoot again on target. Proudfoot scored for the third game running in a one-all home draw with the Wednesday.

Then followed a 4–1 victory at Preston North End with Campbell, Wilkie, Hulse and a Jimmy Trainer own goal securing the points for the visitors, which was followed by defeats at the Wednesday (4–1) and Aston Villa (5–1), as well as home draws against Sheffield United (1–1) and Derby County (1–1), leaving the Lancashire side amongst the First Division strugglers.

Mid-December saw Rovers return to winning ways with Proudfoot on target in a 1–0 success at Liverpool, which preceded a 2–1 home win against Sunderland on Christmas Day with Booth and Briercliffe scoring the all-important goals. The year ended with a one-all draw at West Bromwich Albion with Campbell netting his sixth League goal of the campaign.

Following a one-all draw at Everton on New Year's Day, where Booth converted a penalty kick, the Blackburn side secured a 2–1 home success against Liverpool, with Briercliffe and Campbell scoring for the home side. Wilkie found the net in a further home draw against Nottingham Forest (1–1), which saw Rovers in a respectable mid-table position by the middle of January.

Rovers' indifferent FA Cup form continued with a 1–0 reverse at Everton in the opening round, which was followed by a poor run of results in the League with just one victory in their ten remaining games, sending the Blackburn team plummeting down the League table. Their poor run of results saw successive home defeats against West Bromwich Albion (3–1) and Wolverhampton Wanderers (3–2), followed by a goalless draw at Notts County, while further defeats at Sunderland (2–1) and Wolverhampton Wanderers (3–2), as well as home draws against Bury (1–1) and Stoke (1–1), saw Blackburn with little chance of avoiding the end-of-season play-off games.

Blackburn's final home game of the season resulted in a 1–0 defeat against Notts County, followed by a rare away success at Bolton Wanderers (2–1), where Booth and Hargreaves found the net, and the campaign ended with a 1–0 reverse at Bury. Rovers ended in fifteenth position, one of five teams with twenty-four points, with the play-off games imminent.

In a further disappointing season, Blackburn had won only seven of their thirty League games, with Proudfoot, Wilkes, Booth and Tom Brandon playing in all but one. Wilkes and Booth had ended the campaign with six League goals apiece, Campbell had found the net on seven occasions, with Proudfoot leading the scoring with nine.

BURY

Bury had enjoyed an excellent 1896–97 League campaign, which had resulted in a mid-table finish in only their third season in the Football League, hence the reluctance of the club to make changes for the 1897–98 season. Archibald Montgomery continued in goal, with Davies, Pray, Davidson, Ross and Clegg in defence, while Miller, Barbour, Henderson, Jimmy Settle and Jack Plant remained in the attack.

Bury opened the season with successive away defeats at Wolverhampton Wanderers (3–0) and Aston Villa (3–1) on either side of a 3–1 home success against the Wednesday. A one-all draw at Sheffield United, as well as a further home win against West Bromwich Albion (3–2), continued their reasonable start to the season.

Following a two-all draw at Derby County, the Bury side suffered a 1–0 defeat against Everton, while a 2–1 home victory against Wolverhampton Wanderers saw a return to winning ways. However, their indifferent away form continued with a 3–0 reverse at the Wednesday.

Late November saw a goalless home draw with Notts County, which preceded a 2–1 home success against Bolton Wanderers, while the year ended with successive away defeats at West Bromwich Albion (1–0) and Stoke (3–1), which left the Lancashire side struggling near the foot of the League table.

Bury then began the new year with successive draws at home to Stoke (3–3) and away at Bolton Wanderers (0–0), followed by away defeats at Preston North End (2–1) and Sunderland (2–1), while a 1–0 home success in the return game with Preston saw two welcome points. Further defeats at Notts County (2–1) and Everton (4–2), as well as at home to Aston Villa (2–1) and Liverpool (2–0), saw the Bury team in last place in the table, with a one-all draw at Blackburn Rovers their only success during this period of indifferent form.

With six League games remaining, the Bury team were odds-on favourites to end the campaign in the play-off positions. However, an excellent run of results during the final weeks of the season saw the Lancashire side avoid the play-off places by the skin of their teeth.

Their fine run of form began with a 4–0 home win against Derby County, followed by successive draws at Liverpool (2–2) and at home to Nottingham Forest (2–2), while a further home victory against Sunderland (1–0) continued their excellent run of results. It came to an end with a 3–1 reverse at Nottingham Forest, but a 1–0 home success against Bolton Wanderers in the final game of the season saw Bury end the campaign in fourteenth position, one of the five teams with twenty-four points.

Bury's fine end to the season had seen their superior goal difference save them from the play-off positions, however, life would improve for the Lancashire side as the century came to an end!

PRESTON NORTH END

Preston North End had ended the 1896–97 League campaign in fourth position, with ten of their players appearing in twenty League games or more, which resulted in few changes in their line-up for the 1897–98 season. Jimmy Trainer continued in goal, with Dunn, Blyth, Sanders, Tait, Pierce, Eccleston and Robert Holmes competing for the defensive positions, while Stevenson, Brown, Pratt and Boyd were once again the mainstays of the attack, together with Halsall, who made fifty-six appearances in three seasons with the Lancashire side.

Orr had decided to leave the club, while Geordie Drummond made few appearances during a season that welcomed the return of Francis Becton, albeit only for four League appearances. Newcomers in defence included Hunter and Mathews, who remained with the club for a little more than a season. The most notable new signing was goalkeeper Peter McBride from north of the border. McBride eventually replaced Jimmy Trainer in the Preston goal, where he remained for fifteen seasons, as well as securing a place in the Scottish national team.

Preston opened the season with successive defeats at Wolverhampton Wanderers (3–0) and at home to Sheffield United (3–1), followed by a goalless draw at Liverpool. A 2–0 home success against Sunderland secured their first victory of the campaign, but away defeats at Bolton Wanderers (1–0) and Blackburn Rovers (1–0), as well as draws at home to Liverpool (1–1) and at Notts County (1–1), continued their poor start to the season.

Then followed a goalless home draw with Bolton Wanderers, which preceded further defeats at Sheffield United (2–1) and at home to Blackburn Rovers (4–1), leaving Preston at the foot of the League table with one win in eleven League games. However, successive victories at home to Aston Villa (3–1) and away at Stoke (2–1) saw the Lancashire side move up a couple of places in the table.

Mid-November saw a 4–1 reverse at Nottingham Forest, followed by a one-all home draw with Everton, while defeats at home to Wolverhampton Wanderers (2–1) and away at the Wednesday (2–1) continued their dismal run of results. The end of the year saw a return to winning ways with successive home victories in the return games with the Wednesday (2–0) and Nottingham Forest (3–0).

New Year's Day saw Preston suffer a further away defeat at Sunderland (1–0), which preceded a 2–1 home success against Bury, while away defeats at West Bromwich Albion (3–1), Aston Villa (4–0) and Bury (1–0) saw them as favourites to end the season in the play-off positions.

Following a goalless home draw with Stoke, the Lancashire side suffered a 3–1 reverse at Derby County. However, a splendid run of results during the latter stages of the campaign saw successive draws at Everton (1–1) and at home to West Bromwich Albion (1–1), as well as home wins against Notts County (3–1) and Derby County (5–0), which saw Preston end the campaign in twelfth position, one of the five teams with twenty-four points, albeit with a superior goal difference.

Their indifferent League campaign had seen Preston score only thirty-five goals in thirty League games, as well as suffering a defeat in the first round of the FA Cup competition. Stevenson had ended the campaign with eleven League goals, with Brown leading the scoring with a dozen in twenty League appearances.

BOLTON WANDERERS

Bolton Wanderers made few changes in their line-up for the 1897–98 League campaign following their eighth place finish during the previous season. John Sutcliffe continued in goal, with John Somerville, David Jones, Alex Paton, Bob Brown and Archie Freebairn in defence, while James McGeachan made only a couple of appearances during the season following a period of suspension.

Bob Jack, Jocky Wright, Billy Thomson and James Cassidy continued to be the mainstays of the attack, together with Miller, Gilligan and Nicholl.

Wanderers opened the campaign with a 2–1 reverse at Everton, followed by successive victories at Blackburn Rovers (3–1), as well as at home to Notts County (1–0) and Preston North End (1–0), with Gilligan, Nicholl, Miller, Cassidy and Bob Jack sharing the Bolton goals. Defeats at Aston Villa (3–2) and at home to the Wednesday (3–0) ended their fine start to the season.

Following a goalless draw at Preston North End, the Bolton team secured home wins against Nottingham Forest (2–0) and Sunderland (1–0) with Miller, Jack and Cassidy again on target, while early November saw a 2–0 defeat at West Bromwich Albion. However, a run of three successive victories saw the Lancashire side move up to fifth place in the League table by the end of the month.

Bolton's winning run began with a 2–1 success at Notts County, with Miller and Bob Jack on target, which preceded a 2–1 home win against Stoke, with Alex Paton scoring his only League goal of the season in his 200th League appearance for the club. John Sutcliffe played his 200th League game during the following week in a 2–0 home victory against Aston Villa, with Wright and Cassidy netting the Wanderers' goals.

The Lancashire side then suffered successive away defeats at the Wednesday (3–0), Bury (2–1) and Derby County (1–0), as well as at home to Liverpool (2–0), as they ended the year in a mid-table position. New Year home draws against Derby County (3–3) and Bury (0–0) continued their indifferent run of results, with John Somerville's 200th League appearance arriving in the Derby game.

Further away defeats at Nottingham Forest (2–0) and Stoke (2–0) were then followed by a 1–0 victory at Luton Town in the first round of the FA Cup, with James Cassidy scoring the only goal of the game. A 4–0 reverse at Sheffield United moved the Wanderers further down the League table, however, a 1–0 home success against Manchester City in the second round of the cup secured a home tie against Southampton St Mary's in the quarter-finals, with Miller netting the all-important goal.

On their return to League action, Bolton suffered a 2–0 reverse at Sunderland, while the FA Cup tie with Southampton ended in a goalless draw, but the Wanderers were well beaten in the replay as Southampton scored four goals without reply.

Early March saw the Bolton side register their first League win since the previous November with a 2–1 home success against Wolverhampton Wanderers, with James Cassidy netting a brace of goals. This preceded a one-all draw at Liverpool, while Nicholl found the net in successive home wins against Everton (1–0) and West Bromwich Albion (2–0). Their indifferent League form returned during the final week of the season with home defeats against Sheffield United (1–0) and Blackburn Rovers (2–1) on either side of a 2–0 reverse at Wolverhampton Wanderers. There resulted an eleventh place League finish, with eleven victories, four draws and fifteen defeats in their thirty League games, while scoring twenty-eight goals and conceding forty-one.

Archie Freebairn had been the only ever present in a most disappointing season. Alex Paton, John Sutcliffe and John Somerville had reached the 200 League game milestone, while James Cassidy had led the scoring with seven of Bolton's twenty-eight League goals.

DERBY COUNTY

Derby County had finished the two previous seasons in a top three position, as well as twice reaching the semi-final stages of the FA Cup competition, where they suffered odd-goal defeats. Hence there were few changes in their line-up for the 1897–98 League campaign. Jimmy Methven, Joseph Leiper, John Cox, Archie Goodall, James Turner and Jonathon Staley continued in defence, while John Goodall, Steve Bloomer, Jimmy Stevenson and Hugh McQueen remained up front, together with recent signings Maconnachie and Boag.

Maconnachie remained with the club for a little more than a season, while John Boag, who had arrived from the Ashfield Club in East Stirlingshire during the previous campaign, made in excess of one hundred League appearances in seven seasons with Derby.

Goalkeeper John Robinson had decided to join the New Brighton Tower Club following six seasons with the East Midlands side. While many felt that Robinson had been a little foolhardy in moving to a non-League team, his transfer caused him little harm as he retained his place in the English national side.

Frail initially replaced Robinson in the Derby goal. However, he failed to convince the club directors, who hastily signed John Fryer, who eventually made 173 League appearances in six seasons.

Derby opened the campaign with a 2–1 reverse at Sheffield United, which preceded successive home wins against Blackburn Rovers (3–1) and Everton (5–1), with Steve Bloomer, John Boag and John Goodall on target in both games, Bloomer (2) and Archie Goodall found the net in a further home success against West Bromwich Albion (3–2) in Archie Goodall's 150th consecutive League appearance for the club.

Then followed a one-all draw at Notts County, where Hugh McQueen netted his first goal of the season, while away defeats at Stoke (2–1), Sunderland (2–1) and Liverpool (4–2), as well as a two-all home draw with Bury, saw Derby in the bottom half of the League table by late October.

County then secured their first away victory of the campaign in a 4–3 win at Nottingham Forest with Maconnachie (2), Bloomer and Archie Goodall on target for the visitors, while John Goodall netted a hat-trick in a 4–1 home success against Stoke, with brother Archie completing the scoring. However, a further run of indifferent results, which saw defeats at West Bromwich Albion (3–1) and Wolverhampton Wanderers (2–0), as well as drawn games at Blackburn Rovers (1–1) and at home to Sheffield United (1–1), saw Derby struggling to maintain their mid-table position at the halfway stage of the campaign.

John Goodall then netted his eighth League goal of the season in a two-all home draw with Sunderland, which preceded a 2–1 home defeat against Notts County, while Steve Bloomer scored the only goal of the game in a 1–0 home success against Bolton Wanderers in the final game of the year.

New Year's Day saw Steve Bloomer score a hat-trick in a three-all draw at Bolton Wanderers, which was followed by a 3–2 home success against Wolverhampton Wanderers with Handley, Maconnachie and an Eccles own goal securing the points for Derby. A 3–1 reverse at the Wednesday ended their fine start to the year. However, County soon returned to winning ways with a 3–1 home win against Aston Villa, with Maconnachie (2) and McQueen on target against the League title holders, who were, coincidentally, Derby's opponents in the first round of the FA Cup.

Derby managed a 1–0 victory in the cup tie with Villa, with Hugh McQueen scoring the only goal of the game to secure an away tie against Wolverhampton Wanderers in the second round, which they again won by a single goal, scored by outside right Leonard to earn a quarter-final home tie against Liverpool.

Prior to the FA Cup Tie, the East Midlands side suffered a 2–1 home defeat against the Wednesday, while the cup game with Liverpool ended all square

(1–1), with Jimmy Stevenson scoring the Derby goal. County had little difficulty in winning the replay as Boag (3) and Bloomer (2) found the net in a 5–1 success to secure a third successive semi-final appearance, which was against Everton at the Molineux Ground.

Early March saw Derby suffer a 4–1 reverse at Aston Villa, which preceded a 3–1 home win against Preston North End, with Cox, Stevenson and John Goodall on target, while a 3–1 victory in the semi-final with Everton secured Derby's first FA Cup Final appearance.

With their FA Cup Final place assured, County suffered successive away defeats at Bury (4–0), Everton (3–0) and Preston North End (5–0). However, a 5–0 home success against Nottingham Forest saw a return to winning ways with Steve Bloomer netting a hat-trick. The season ended with a further home win against Liverpool (3–1), with John Boag scoring a brace of goals to secure a tenth place League finish, with eleven victories, six draws and thirteen defeats in their thirty League games, while scoring fifty-seven goals and conceding sixty-one.

Hugh McQueen had appeared in all thirty League games for Derby, with Turner, Cox, Methven and Archie Goodall missing less than a handful. Maconnachie and John Goodall had ended the campaign with nine goals apiece, with Steve Bloomer leading the scoring with fifteen goals in twenty-three League appearances. Derby's indifferent League campaign would be forgiven if they were successful in their forthcoming FA Cup Final appearance.

LIVERPOOL

Liverpool had enjoyed an excellent 1896–97 season, which had seen a fifth place League finish, as well as an appearance in the semi-finals of the FA Cup, resulting in few changes in their side for the 1897–98 League campaign. Cunliffe, Henderson, McQue, McVean, Hannah and Mathew McQueen competed for the defensive positions, while George Allen, Jimmy Ross and Harry Bradshaw remained in the attack, together with Francis Becton, who tended to move clubs on a regular basis.

Liverpool opened the season with successive draws at Stoke (2–2) and at home to Preston North End (0–0), followed by a 4–2 reverse at the Wednesday, while Cunliffe, McQue and Becton found the net in a 3–1 home success against neighbours Everton. Then followed a one-all draw at Preston North End, which preceded a 4–0 home victory against Stoke, while a 3–0 reverse at Everton ended their splendid run of results. However, the Lancashire side soon returned to winning ways with a 4–2 home win against Derby County.

The Merseysiders then suffered successive defeats at Aston Villa (3–1) and West Bromwich Albion (2–1), as well as at home to Nottingham Forest (2–1). These were followed by victories at home to Wolverhampton Wanderers (1–0) and in the return game at Nottingham Forest (3–2), while the halfway stage of the campaign arrived with further defeats at Wolverhampton Wanderers (2–1) and at home to Blackburn Rovers (1–0).

Christmas Day saw Liverpool secure a 2–0 away success at Bolton Wanderers, which preceded a loss of form that included defeats at Sheffield United (2–1), Blackburn Rovers (2–1) and Sunderland (1–0), as well as at home to Sunderland (2–0) and Sheffield United (4–0). A one-all home draw with West Bromwich Albion saw a welcome point as the Liverpool side continued their slide down the League table.

Upon reaching the final sixteen of the FA Cup competition, the Merseysiders were drawn away at Newton Heath, where they played out a goalless draw, only to win the replay by the odd goal in three to secure a quarter-final tie at Derby County, which ended all square (1–1). However, they were well beaten in the replay as Boag and Bloomer ran riot in a 5–1 success for County.

On their return to League action, Liverpool enjoyed an excellent run of results, including victories at home to Notts County (2–0) and away at Bury (2–0), as well as home draws with Bolton Wanderers (1–1) and Bury (2–2), while a 3–2 reverse at Notts County ended their unbeaten run. Then a 4–0 home success against the Wednesday saw a return to form for the Lancashire side.

Liverpool's indifferent away form continued with a 3–1 defeat at Derby County, while the campaign ended with a 4–0 home win against Aston Villa. The Merseysiders ended the season in ninth place, with eleven victories, six draws and thirteen defeats in their thirty League games, while scoring forty-eight goals and conceding forty-five.

Bradshaw and Allen had again netted the majority of the goals for the Liverpool team, for whom great success lay ahead, albeit at the turn of the century.

NOTTINGHAM FOREST

Nottingham Forest had finished the 1896–97 League campaign in a disappointing eleventh place, but the club directors kept faith with the majority of their players for the 1897–98 season. Dennis Allsopp continued in goal, with Archie Ritchie, Adam Scott, Jim Iremonger, Frank Forman and John MacPherson in defence, while Tom McInnes, Charles Richards, Arthur Capes, Fred Spencer and Fred Forman remained in the attack.

Alexander Stewart had left the club, Peter McCracken made few appearances during the season, while Adrian Capes played in the opening game prior to announcing his retirement owing to ill-health. However, he was adequately replaced by Len Benbow, who scored twenty goals in fifty-four League appearances for the Nottingham side.

William Wragg replaced Stewart at left half back, where he made forty-eight appearances in two seasons, while the most notable new signing was Alf

Spouncer from Sheffield United, who made in excess of 300 appearances for Forest, as well as appearing in the English national team.

Forest opened the season with successive home draws against Notts County (1–1) and Sheffield United (1–1) on either side of a 2–0 reverse at West Bromwich Albion, with Arthur Capes on target in both drawn games. Further draws at Wolverhampton Wanderers (0–0) and at home to Sunderland (1–1) continued their reasonable start to the season, which improved even further with victories at Notts County (3–1) and at home to Blackburn Rovers (3–1), with Len Benbow scoring in both wins.

Then followed defeats at Bolton Wanderers (2–0) and at home to Derby County (4–3). However, successive away wins at Liverpool (2–1) and Stoke (2–1), as well as at home to Preston North End (4–1), saw Forest in a top five position by late November, with Spouncer, Benbow, Richards, Spencer and McInnes sharing the Forest goals.

Len Benbow then netted his sixth League goal of the campaign in a 3–2 home defeat against Liverpool, which preceded a one-all draw at Sheffield United, where John MacPherson converted a penalty kick. The year ended with defeats at home to West Bromwich Albion (1–0) and away at Preston North End (3–0) as Forest returned to a mid-table position.

New Year's Day saw the Nottingham side register their highest victory of the campaign with a 6–3 success at the Wednesday, where Benbow (2), Richards (2), MacPherson and Frank Forman found the net. This preceded a 2–0 home win against Bolton Wanderers, with Benbow and MacPherson again on target, while Charles Richards scored his sixth League goal of the season in a one-all draw at Blackburn Rovers.

Forest's unbeaten run continued with a 1–0 home success against the Wednesday, with Tom McInnes scoring the only goal of the game. Capes (2), McInnes and Richards netted in a 4–0 home win against Grimsby Town in the first round of the FA Cup to secure a home tie against Gainsborough Trinity in the second round, which they won by a similar score, with Richards (2), McInnes and Benbow on target.

On their return to League action, the Nottingham side secured a 3–1 home victory against Stoke, with Spouncer, Capes and Frank Forman netting the Forest goals, while their excellent FA Cup form continued with a 3–2 success at West Bromwich Albion, where Richards, Spouncer and Frank Forman found the net to earn a semi-final tie against Southampton at Bramall Lane.

Prior to the semi-final game, Arthur Capes netted a brace of goals in a two-all home draw with Everton, while Len Benbow found the net as the semi-final tie with Southampton ended all square (1–1). However, Forest had few difficulties in the replay at Crystal Palace as goals by Tom McInnes and Charles Richards earned a 2–0 victory to secure their first FA Cup Final appearance, which was to take place at Crystal Palace on 16 April against Derby County.

Late March saw Forest secure a 3–1 home success against Aston Villa, with Benbow (2) and Capes on target, which preceded a 2–0 reverse at Everton. Successive draws at Bury (2–2) and at home to Wolverhampton Wanderers (1–1), as well as a 3–1 home win against Bury, saw the Nottingham side maintain their top five position, with Frank Forman netting a brace of goals in the victory against Bury.

Forest then fielded a weakened side in a 5–0 away defeat at FA Cup Final opponents Derby, but it was obvious to all that the Nottingham side were saving themselves for the forthcoming FA Cup Final rather than a meaningless League encounter.

WEST BROMWICH ALBION

West Bromwich Albion's twelfth place finish during the 1896–97 League campaign surprisingly resulted in few changes in their line-up for the 1897–98 season. Joe Reader continued in goal, with Billy Williams, George Banks, Tom Perry, John Horton and, occasionally, McManus in defence, while Bassett, Flewitt, Garfield, William Richards and Tom Higgins, who had previously appeared at the heart of the defence, competed for the forward positions.

Inside forward Roddy McLeod and fullback Evans had left the club, while the most notable newcomers included fullback George Cave, who had made five appearances during the previous campaign, as well as centre half Abe Jones.

Alex McKenzie replaced Roddy McLeod in the attack, while inside forward Reid partnered Billy Bassett on the right wing, albeit for eleven appearances.

Albion opened the season with a 4–3 reverse at Aston Villa, with Higgins, McManus and McKenzie on target for the visitors, which preceded a 2–0 home success against Nottingham Forest, with Ben Garfield netting a brace of goals. A 3–2 defeat at Derby County continued their indifferent start to the season, but a 2–0 home win against Stoke saw a return to winning ways, with Higgins and Flewitt scoring for the Black Country side.

Then followed a 3–2 defeat at Bury, with Bassett and Higgins scoring for the Midlanders, while Ben Garfield found the net in a one-all home draw with Aston Villa, as Albion moved to a mid-table position. However, a 2–0 victory at Sunderland saw a return to form, with Bassett and a McNeill own goal securing the points for Albion.

Late October saw the West Bromwich side play successive draws at home to Wolverhampton Wanderers (2–2) and away at Stoke (0–0), while their excellent League form continued as Abe Jones scored in home victories against Bolton Wanderers (2–0) and Liverpool (2–1) on either side of a two-all home draw with Everton, with Dean and Garfield netting the Albion goals. Ben Garfield then scored his sixth League goal of the season in a 3–1 home success against Derby County, with Flewitt and Reid completing the scoring. Flewitt was again on target the following week in a humiliating 6–1 defeat at Everton, but successive wins at Nottingham Forest (1–0) and at home to Bury (1–0) saw

Albion maintain their challenge for the League Championship, with Perry and Garfield scoring the all-important goals.

Albion ended the year with drawn games at home to Blackburn Rovers (1–1) and away at Wolverhampton Wanderers (1–1), with Williams (penalty) and Reid finding the net. New Year's Day saw a further one-all draw at Liverpool with Flewitt netting his fifth League goal of the campaign, which preceded a 3–1 home success against Preston North End, with Garfield (2) and Flewitt on target.

January's end saw Albion secure a 2–0 home victory against New Brighton Tower in the first round of the FA Cup, which was followed by a 3–1 win in a League encounter at Blackburn Rovers, with Reid, Flewitt and Bassett netting for the Black Country side. A 1–0 home win against the Wednesday in the second round of the Cup saw Albion progress to the quarter-finals, where they were once again drawn at home to Nottingham Forest.

Prior to the quarter-final tie, Alex McKenzie netted a brace of goals in a two-all home draw with Sunderland, which preceded a 3–2 defeat in the cup game with Forest, despite Albion taking a two-goal lead through Bassett and Williams. Their indifferent form continued in the League with a 2–0 home defeat against the Wednesday.

Albion then regained their early season form with successive away draws at Notts County (2–2) and Preston North End (1–1) on either side of a 2–0 home win against League leaders Sheffield United, with Ben Garfield on target in all three games to maintain Albion's faint hopes of the League title. However, a poor run of results during the final month of the campaign saw defeats at Bolton Wanderers (2–0), Wednesday (3–0) and Sheffield United (2–0), as well as at home to Notts County (3–0). This left the West Bromwich side in seventh place, with eleven victories, ten draws and nine defeats in their thirty League games, while scoring forty-four goals and conceding forty-five.

Albion had managed only one victory in their final nine League games, when in reality they should have been challenging for the League title. However, the 1897–98 League campaign had been their finest for a number of years. Joe Reader, George Cave and Alex McKenzie had appeared in all thirty League games, while Ben Garfield had led the scoring with a dozen League goals.

ASTON VILLA

Following their League and FA Cup double of the previous season, Aston Villa made few changes for the 1897–98 League campaign. Jimmy Whitehouse continued in goal, with Howard Spencer, Albert Evans, Bob Chatt, James Cowan and James Crabtree in defence, while Charlie Athersmith, John Devey, Steve Smith, Fred Wheldon and John Cowan remained in the attack. Prior to the new season, Johnny Campbell and John Reynolds had decided to follow James Welford in signing for the Glasgow Celtic Club.

Reynolds had served both Villa and West Bromwich Albion for a number of seasons, as well as appearing for the Irish and English national teams, while Scottish international Campbell had scored thirty-nine goals in fifty-five League appearances for Villa.

Harvey, Fisher and Jack Sharp were initially signed to solve the goal-scoring problem created by the departure of Campbell, but despite many excellent performances by all three players, Sharp was the only player to match the goal-scoring exploits of Campbell, albeit for less than a season, when he moved to Everton, with whom he gained England caps.

Villa's most notable new signing was goalkeeper Billy George, who had been persuaded to leave the army, However, upon signing for the club, the Football Association decided that Villa had infringed their rules, which resulted in twenty-eight day suspensions for Frederick Rinder, George Ramsay and Billy George, as well as a fifty pound fine.

George eventually made in excess of 400 appearances in fourteen seasons with Villa as well as gaining three England caps.

During the opening month of the campaign, Howard Spencer sustained a serious leg injury, causing him to miss the remainder of the season, which resulted in Bert Sharp replacing him at fullback, prior to the arrival of Tom Bowman from Blackpool. He went on to make in excess of one hundred League appearances for the Aston club.

Villa opened the season with a 5–2 home success against the Wednesday, with Wheldon (3), Athersmith and John Cowan on target, which preceded a further home win against West Bromwich Albion (4–3), with Fred Wheldon netting his second successive hat-trick, while John Cowan (2) and John Devey found the net in a 3–2 victory at Notts County.

Fred Wheldon then scored his seventh goal in four League games in a 3–1 home win against Bury, with Fisher scoring a brace, while Wheldon scored a further double as Villa suffered a 4–3 defeat at Blackburn Rovers. Then followed a 3–0 reverse at the Wednesday, which preceded successive home wins against Bolton Wanderers (3–2) and Notts County (4–2) on either side of a one-all draw at West Bromwich Albion, with Jack Sharp netting five of the Villa goals to maintain their top three position.

Late October saw Billy George make his second League appearance for the club in a goalless draw at Sunderland, which was followed by a 3–1 home success against Liverpool, with Devey, Wheldon and Athersmith on target. A 3–1 reverse at Preston North End ended their five-game unbeaten run, but a 3–0 home victory against Everton saw a return to winning ways with Fred Wheldon scoring his thirteenth and fourteenth League goals of the campaign.

Following a 2–0 defeat at Bolton Wanderers, Harvey and Wheldon netted a brace of goals apiece in a 4–3 home win against Sunderland, while James Cowan, Athersmith, Wheldon, Crabtree and John Cowan found the net in a 5–1 home success against Blackburn Rovers as Villa maintained their winning home record. However, a poor run of results, which included away defeats at

Everton (2–1), Sheffield United (1–0), Derby County (3–1) and at home in the return game with Sheffield United (2–1), as well as away draws at Stoke (0–0) and Wolverhampton Wanderers (1–1), saw Villa in a mid-table position by January's end.

Villa's poor League form continued in the FA Cup, with a first round defeat at Derby County (1–0), which preceded a welcome 4–0 home win against Preston North End, with Suddick, Wheldon, Athersmith and Jack Sharp on target, while Sharp (2), Fisher and Steve Smith found the net in a further home victory against Derby County (4–1).

Jack Sharp's eleventh goal in as many League appearances arrived in a 2–1 success at Bury, with Fred Wheldon completing the scoring, but their indifferent run of results continued with defeats at Nottingham Forest (3–1), Liverpool (4–0) and at home to Wolverhampton Wanderers (2–1). There was also a one-all home draw with Stoke prior to ending the season with a 2–0 home success against Nottingham Forest, with Smith and Johnson on target to secure a sixth place finish for the title holders, with fourteen wins, five draws and eleven defeats in their thirty League games, while scoring sixty-one goals and conceding fifty-one.

Albert Evans had appeared in all thirty League games, while Wheldon, Crabtree, Athersmith and James Cowan had missed less than a handful in a most disappointing season. Jack Sharp had scored eleven goals in fifteen League appearances, while Fred Wheldon had led the scoring with twenty-three goals in twenty-six League games.

WEDNESDAY

Wednesday had finished the 1896–97 League campaign in sixth position, while their supporters had been a little disappointed by an FA Cup defeat in the opening round of the competition, especially as the holders of the trophy. However, few changes were made in their line-up for the 1897–98 season. Jimmy Massey continued in goal, with Earp, Langley, Crawshaw, Jamieson and Harry Brandon in defence, while Archie Brash, Bob Ferrier, Harry Davis, Alec Brady and Fred Spiksley remained in the attack.

Centre forward Lawrence Bell had signed for Everton, while the most notable newcomers were centre forward Kaye from Chatham, as well as Dryburgh, an outside right from Cowdenbeath.

Wednesday opened the season with successive defeats at Aston Villa (5–2) and Bury (3–0), as well as at home to Sunderland (1–0), while Kaye (2), Earp and Ferrier found the net in a 4–2 home success against Liverpool. A 1–0 reverse in the return game at Sunderland continued their poor start to the campaign in Jack Earp's 100th League appearance for the club.

Then followed successive victories at home to Aston Villa (3–0) and Notts County (3–1), as well as away at Bolton Wanderers (3–0), with Fred Spiksley netting five of the Wednesday goals, while a 1–0 home defeat against Sheffield United ended their winning run. However, following a one-all draw at

Blackburn Rovers, the Sheffield side secured further home wins against Blackburn Rovers (4–1), Bury (3–0) and Bolton Wanderers (3–0), with Spiksley once again scoring five goals for the Yorkshire team.

Early December saw Wednesday play a goalless draw at Notts County, which preceded a 2–1 home win against Preston North End with Kaye and Brady on target, while a 2–0 reverse in the return game at Preston saw the Sheffield side's first defeat since October. A 4–0 home win against Stoke saw a return to winning ways with Crawshaw, Spiksley, Brandon and Kaye netting for Wednesday. Fred Spiksley then scored his thirteenth League goal of the campaign in a one-all draw at Sheffield United in their final game of the year, with Tom Crawshaw making his 100th League appearance for the club. The new year began with successive defeats at home to Nottingham Forest (6–3) and away at Everton (1–0), while a 3–1 home success against Derby County saw two welcome points, with Dryburgh, Spiksley and a Fryer own goal securing the points for the FA Cup holders.

Following a 1–0 reverse at Nottingham Forest, Wednesday secured a 1–0 victory at Sunderland in the first round of the FA Cup, with Kaye scoring the only goal of the game, while Jamieson and Langley found the net in a 2–1 home win against Everton. A 1–0 reverse at West Bromwich Albion in the second round of the cup ended their interest in the competition.

On Wednesday's return to League action, Fred Spiksley again found the net in a 2–1 success at Derby County, which preceded further victories at home to Wolverhampton Wanderers (2–0) and away at West Bromwich Albion (2–0), with Alec Brady scoring in both games. However, a 2–1 reverse at Stoke ended their splendid run of results.

Early April saw a 3–0 home win in the return game with West Bromwich Albion, with Kaye, Spiksley and Brady on target in Brady's 150th League game for the club, while the season ended with successive away defeats at Liverpool (4–0) and Wolverhampton Wanderers (5–0). Wednesday finished the campaign in fifth position, with fifteen victories, three draws and twelve defeats in their thirty League games, while scoring fifty-one goals and conceding forty-two.

Tom Crawshaw and Fred Spiksley had appeared in all thirty League games, in a season when ten players had played in at least twenty-five games. Alec Brady had ended the season with eight League goals, Kaye had found the net on nine occasions, with Fred Spiksley leading the scoring with seventeen goals.

EVERTON

Everton had enjoyed an excellent 1896–97 season, which had resulted in a seventh place League finish, as well as an appearance in the FA Cup Final. Despite their fine season, Everton made a number of changes in their line-up for the 1897–98 campaign. Storrier, Boyce, Stewart and John Holt retained their places in the defence, while Cameron, Chadwick, Taylor and John Bell remained up front.

Smart Arridge and Alf Milward had signed for the ambitious New Brighton

Tower Club, Billy Stewart soon moved to Bristol City, while centre forward Hartley, who scored three goals in as many appearances during the season, joined Liverpool.

Briggs and Menham, who had shared the goalkeeping duties during the previous campaign, had left the club, while McFarlane and Muir had arrived from north of the border to compete for the goalkeeper's jersey. However, McFarlane, who had signed from Third Lanark, soon returned to Scotland, while Muir made 127 League appearances in five seasons with the Merseysiders.

The most notable newcomers to the club were Meecham and Divers from Glasgow Celtic, together with Lawrence Bell, who had previously played for the Wednesday, while Robertson, who had made three appearances during the previous season, replaced Billy Stewart in the half-back line. Robertson signed for Southampton at the season's end, following an appearance for the Scottish national team.

Walter Balmer had been signed from a local amateur side, but he proved an excellent servant for Everton, with whom he made in excess of 300 appearances, as well as representing the English national side.

Everton opened the season with a 2–1 home success against Bolton Wanderers, with Lawrence Bell netting a brace of goals, which preceded a 5–1 reverse at Derby County. Hartley scored a hat-trick in a 3–0 home win against Wolverhampton Wanderers, but a 3–1 defeat at Liverpool continued their poor away form.

Following a one-all home draw with Blackburn Rovers, Cameron, Divers and Lawrence Bell found the net in a 3–2 away success at Wolverhampton Wanderers, while Williams, making a rare appearance in the first team, netted a brace of goals in a 3–0 home win in the return game with Liverpool.

Outside left Divers then netted his fourth League goal of the campaign in a 1–0 victory at Bury, which preceded a 4–1 home defeat against Sheffield United. Divers and Taylor were on target in a two-all draw at West Bromwich Albion, but a 3–0 defeat at Aston Villa saw the Lancashire side in a mid-table position by mid-November.

Everton then secured a one-all draw at Preston North End, where Jack Taylor found the net, which was followed by a 6–1 home success against West Bromwich Albion, with Chadwick (2), Divers (2), John Bell and Lawrence Bell on target, while Divers netted the only goal of the game in a 1–0 home win against Notts County.

Then followed a goalless draw at Sunderland, while successive home wins against Aston Villa (2–1) and Wednesday (1–0), as well as a one-all draw at Blackburn Rovers, saw Edgar Chadwick on target in all three games. However, a 3–2 reverse at Notts County ended the Merseysiders' seven-game unbeaten run.

Mid-January saw a one-all home draw with Stoke, with Cameron scoring for the home side, which preceded a 1–0 home success against Blackburn Rovers in the first round of the FA Cup, with Williams scoring the only goal of the game. A 2–1 reverse at the Wednesday continued their indifferent League form, however, following a goalless draw at Stoke in the second round of the cup, the Merseysiders had few difficulties in the replay, as goals by Lawrence Bell (2), Cameron, Chadwick and Taylor secured a 5–1 success.

On their return to League action, the Lancashire side gained an excellent point in a goalless draw at League leaders Sheffield United, while their FA Cup form continued at Burnley, where goals by Jack Taylor (2) and Lawrence Bell secured a 3–1 victory to earn a second successive semi-final appearance against Derby County at the Molineux Ground, Wolverhampton.

Prior to the semi-final tie, Chadwick, Divers, John Bell and Lawrence Bell found the net in a 4–2 home success against Bury, while Lawrence Bell netted a brace of goals in a two-all draw at Nottingham Forest. However, they were a little unfortunate to come up against an in-form Steve Bloomer in the semi-final as the England man scored twice in a 3–1 victory for the East Midlands side, with Edgar Chadwick scoring a consolation goal for Everton.

With six League games remaining, of which four were on home soil, the Merseysiders were in with a realistic chance of securing the runners-up position, which seemed to diminish following a one-all home draw with Preston North End, as well as a 1–0 reverse at Bolton Wanderers. They soon returned to winning ways with successive home wins against Nottingham Forest (2–0) and Derby County (3–0), with Divers and Lawrence Bell scoring in both games.

Everton's hopes of a second place finish ended with a 2–0 reverse at Stoke, while the campaign ended with a 2–0 home win against Sunderland with Edgar Chadwick scoring twice as the Lancashire side settled for a fourth place finish, with thirteen victories, nine draws and eight defeats in their thirty League games, while scoring forty-eight goals and conceding thirty-nine.

Jack Taylor had appeared in all thirty League games for the Merseysiders, with Divers, Holt, Storrier and Robertson missing no more than a handful. Edgar Chadwick had ended the campaign with eight League goals, Divers had found the net on eleven occasions, with Lawrence Bell leading the scoring with a dozen League goals.

WOLVERHAMPTON WANDERERS

Wolverhampton Wanderers had finished the 1896–97 League campaign in tenth place, which resulted in a number of changes in their line-up for the 1897–98 season. Richard Baugh, Alf Griffin, David Black, Charles Henderson and W C Rose had left the club, while Tommy Dunn and Dan Nurse made only the occasional appearance in the first team. However, Fleming, Miller, Eccles, Smith, Billy Malpass, Hill Griffiths, Billy Owen, Joe Tonks, Billy Beats and Harry Wood remained at the club and Wolves continued their policy of signing locally born players.

The most notable newcomers to the club were Blackett, who made ninety-six League appearances in three seasons, as well as goalkeeper Tom Baddeley from Burslem Port Vale, who remained with the Wanderers well into the following century as well as representing the English national side.

Wolves opened the season with successive home wins against Preston North End (3–0) and Bury (3–0), followed by away defeats at Sunderland (3–2) and Everton (3–0), while home draws against Nottingham Forest (0–0) and Sheffield United (1–1) continued their reasonable start to the season. A 3–2 reverse against Everton saw the Wanderers suffer their first home defeat of the campaign. Then followed victories at Stoke (2–0) and at home to Notts County (3–1) on either side of a two-all draw at West Bromwich Albion, while a 2–1 defeat at Bury saw Wolves in a mid-table position by early November. However, a 4–2 home success against Sunderland saw a return to winning ways for the Molineux side.

Wanderers' indifferent away form continued with a 1–0 reverse at Liverpool, which preceded wins at Preston North End (2–1) and at home to Derby County (2–0), leaving them in fifth place in the League table at the halfway stage of the campaign. Their unbeaten run continued to the end of the year with a 2–1 home success against Liverpool, as well as home draws against Aston Villa (1–1), West Bromwich Albion (1–1) and away at Notts County (2–2).

New Year began with defeats at Derby County (3–2) and Sheffield United (2–1), followed by a 1–0 victory at Notts County in the first round of the FA Cup. A 4–2 home win against Stoke maintained their top five position, but a 1–0 home defeat against Derby County in the second round of the FA Cup ended their interest in the competition.

Following their FA Cup defeat, the Wolverhampton side secured a 3–2 success at Blackburn Rovers, which preceded away defeats at the Wednesday (2–0) and Bolton Wanderers (2–1), while the final month of the campaign saw home wins against Blackburn Rovers (3–2), Bolton Wanderers (2–0), Wednesday (5–0) and away at Aston Villa (2–1), as well as a one-all draw at Nottingham Forest. These saw the Black Country side end the season in third position, with fourteen victories, seven draws and nine defeats in their thirty League games, while scoring fifty-seven goals and conceding forty-one.

Ten of the Wolves' players had appeared in twenty-three League games or more, with Fleming and Blackett ever present. Joe Tonks had ended the season with seven League goals, Smith had found the net on eight occasions, Harry Wood had netted eleven goals, while Billy Beats had led the scoring for the third year running with a dozen League goals.

SUNDERLAND

Sunderland had narrowly avoided relegation to the Second Division during the 1896–97 League campaign, which resulted in a number of changes for the 1897–98 season. Donald Gow had joined the New Brighton Tower Club,

Cowan had returned to Motherwell, while Johnny Campbell, who had scored 131 goals in 190 League appearances for the Sunderland team, had signed for Newcastle, together with inside forward Harvey.

Scottish internationals James Hannah and James Gillespie had returned north of the border following many years of excellent service with the club, with Hannah having scored sixty-seven goals in 156 League appearances, while Gillespie had netted fifty goals in 135 League games. Despite the number of changes made by the north-eastern side, John Doig retained the goalkeeping position, while McNeil, Boyle, Ferguson, Dunlop, Wilson and McAllister once again competed for the defensive positions.

McAllister, who had arrived from Kilmarnock during the latter stages of the previous campaign, made in excess of 200 League appearances for Sunderland, while the most notable newcomer in defence was Philip Bach from Reading, who played forty-three League games as well as gaining an England cap. Inside forward Morgan was the only forward to retain his place from the disappointing 1896–97 League campaign, which saw the arrival of Bradshaw, Leslie, Brown and Chalmers to replace the outgoing Cowan, Hannah, Gillespie and Campbell. With the exception of Leslie, who scored twenty-four goals in ninety-three League games, the recent signings spent less than a season with the side.

Sunderland opened the campaign with successive victories at the Wednesday (2–0) and at home to Wolverhampton Wanderers (3–2), with Morgan on target in both games, which preceded a 2–0 reverse at Preston North End. Mathew Ferguson scored the only goal of the game in a 1–0 success in the return game with Wednesday. Morgan then netted his third goal in five League games in a one-all draw at Nottingham Forest, while Bradshaw and Chalmers scored their opening goals of the season in a 2–1 home win against Derby County. However, an indifferent run of results, which included away defeats at Bolton Wanderers (1–0), Wolverhampton Wanderers (4–2), Aston Villa (4–3) and at home to West Bromwich Albion (2–0), as well as a goalless home draw with Aston Villa, saw the north-eastern side in a mid-table position by early December.

Sunderland eventually returned to winning ways with a 4–0 home success against Stoke, with Dunlop, Bradshaw, Leslie and Morgan on target, which preceded successive draws at Derby County (2–2) and at home to Everton (0–0). A 2–1 reverse at Blackburn Rovers continued their poor away form, though a 2–0 victory at Liverpool saw the side end the year on a winning note with Brown netting his fifth League goal of the season.

New Year's Day saw Hugh Wilson find the net in a 1–0 home win against Preston North End, which preceded a 2–0 success at Notts County, with Brown and Leslie on target. Wilson netted in further victories at Stoke (1–0) and at home to Bury (2–1). However, following a sixth successive League win at home to Liverpool (1–0), the north-eastern side suffered a 1–0 home defeat against the Wednesday in the first round of the FA Cup to end their interest in the competition.

Following the FA Cup defeat, Dodd the Sunderland trainer, resigned from the club, which saw the arrival of Billy Williams, who remained with the side for three decades.

On their return to League action, inside forward Saxon, making his first appearance of the season, scored the only goal of the game in a 1–0 victory at Notts County, which preceded a two-all draw at West Bromwich Albion where Brown and Wilson found the net. Sunderland's excellent League form continued with successive home wins against Bolton Wanderers (2–0), Sheffield United (3–1) and Blackburn Rovers (2–1), with Jim Leslie scoring in all three games to move the team to second place in the League table.

Following their long unbeaten run, the Sunderland team suffered a loss of form during April, which resulted in away defeats at Sheffield United (1–0), Bury (1–0) and Everton (2–0), prior to ending the campaign with a 4–0 home win against Nottingham Forest with Chalmers (2), Brown and Leslie on target. This secured the runners-up position for the former champions, who had won sixteen, drawn five and lost nine of their thirty League games, while scoring forty-three goals and conceding thirty.

It may well be argued that Sunderland could have won their fourth League Championship if they had maintained their excellent form during the latter stages of the campaign. However, there could be little argument that they had once again proved themselves as one of the finest teams in the land.

Goalkeeper John Doig had appeared in all thirty League games, while Morgan, Ferguson, Wilson and Jim Leslie had missed only one. Sunderland had regained their self-respect. Brown, Wilson and Leslie ended the season as joint leading scorers with eight League goals apiece.

SHEFFIELD UNITED

Sheffield United had made rapid progress during their five seasons in the Football League, which had resulted in a second place finish during the previous campaign, due mainly to their excellent defence conceding fewer goals than all other First Division teams. As a result of their success, the Sheffield side made few changes in their line-up for the 1897–98 League campaign. Willie Foulke continued in goal, with Mick Whitham, Harry Thickett, Bob Cain, Rab Howell, Tom Morren and Ernest Needham in defence, while John Almond, Fred Priest and Walter Bennett remained in the attack.

Charles Henderson, Harry Hammond and George Walls had left the club, which saw the arrival of Logan, McKay and Cunningham to replace them in the forward line.

United opened the season with a 2–1 home success against Derby County, with Bennett and Needham on target in a game that saw the debuts of Blair, Morton and Henry White, while Priest (2) and Bennett found the net in a 3–1 victory at Preston North End, with the latter missing a penalty kick.

Walter Bennett then scored for the third successive game in a 4–3 home win against Stoke with McKay (2) and Morren completing the scoring, which preceded drawn games at Nottingham Forest (1–1) and Wolverhampton Wanderers (1–1), as well as at home to Bury (1–1), while Ernest Needham netted a hat-trick in a 5–2 home success against Blackburn Rovers in Mick Whitham's final League appearance for the club.

United's excellent start to the season continued with a 5–2 victory at Bury, where Bennett, Almond, Cunningham, Morren and Needham found the net, which was followed by a 1–0 win at the Wednesday with Bennett scoring the only goal of the game, while McKay and Needham were on target in a 2–1 home success against Preston North End in Harry Johnson's first appearance for the club.

Late October saw the Sheffield side secure a 4–1 victory at Everton, with Almond (2), Cunningham and Bennett scoring for the visitors, which preceded successive draws at Derby County (1–1) and Blackburn Rovers (1–1), as well as at home to Nottingham Forest (1–1). The halfway stage of the season arrived with a 2–1 reverse at Notts County, as United maintained their position at the head of the League table.

United's indifferent form continued throughout December with a one-all home draw with Wednesday, while the year ended with a 2–1 home defeat against Liverpool. However, a 3–1 victory at Notts County saw a return to winning ways with Ralph Gaudie scoring a brace of goals on his debut, while Walter Bennett scored the only goal of the game in a 1–0 home success against Aston Villa.

John Cunningham then netted a brace of goals in a 2–1 victory in the return game at Villa, with the winning goal arriving in the final minute, while Almond and McKay found the net in a 2–1 home win against Wolverhampton Wanderers. United's splendid League form deserted them in the FA Cup when, following a one-all home draw with Burslem Port Vale, the Sheffield side suffered a 2–1 defeat in the replay to end their interest in the competition.

On their return to League action, United secured excellent victories at Liverpool (4–0) and at home to Bolton Wanderers (4–0), with Logan netting a brace of goals in both games. They were followed by an indifferent run of results, including defeats at Sunderland (3–1), West Bromwich Albion (2–0) and at home to Notts County (1–0), as well as a goalless home draw with Everton. However, a 1–0 home success against fellow championship contenders, Sunderland, saw the Yorkshire side secure their first League Championship, with Harry Johnson scoring the only goal of the game fourteen minutes from time.

In United's penultimate game of the season, Ernest Needham found the net in a 1–0 victory at Bolton Wanderers, and the campaign ended with a 2–0 home success against West Bromwich Albion, with Walter Bennett scoring both goals in Bob Cain's final appearance for the club. The Sheffield side won the title by a margin of five points, with seventeen victories, eight draws and five defeats in their thirty League games, while scoring fifty-six goals and conceding thirty-one.

John Cunningham had ended the campaign with seven League goals; Ernest Needham had found the net on eight occasions; John Almond had netted nine goals; while Walter Bennett had led the scoring with a dozen League goals in a well-deserved championship-winning season for the Yorkshire side.

Burnley Secure the Second Division Championship

Six teams were involved in the race for the 1897–98 Second Division Championship, namely Small Heath, Woolwich Arsenal, Newton Heath, Manchester City, Newcastle and Burnley.

Small Heath had enjoyed many excellent performances during the season, due mainly to the fine displays of future England internationals Walter Abbott and Alexander Leake. However, a loss of form at the turn of the year had resulted in a sixth place finish, with Walter Abbott leading the scoring with nineteen League goals.

Woolwich Arsenal had suffered only one defeat on home soil, while six of their home wins had been by four goals or more, and they ended the campaign in fifth position.

Newton Heath, who had missed out on promotion following the 1896–97 play-off games, opened the 1897–98 League campaign with successive wins against Lincoln (5–0) and Burton Swifts (4–0), with centre forward Boyd scoring hat-tricks in both victories. However, a loss of form during the latter stages of the season had resulted in a fourth place finish for the Lancashire side, with Boyd netting twenty-two League goals.

Manchester City were once again destined to miss out on promotion despite losing only one home game. An indifferent away record had seen City finish in third position, with Gillespie leading the scoring with eighteen League goals.

Newcastle, who had finished in fifth place in each of the two previous seasons, had taken a leaf out of Sunderland's book by signing a number of players from north of the border, as well as signing Campbell and Harvey from the successful Sunderland team. Newcastle's efforts were rewarded with an excellent home record, which had included fourteen victories and one defeat, and they ended the campaign as runners-up, with Peddie leading the scoring with sixteen League goals.

Following their relegation to the Second Division during the previous campaign, Burnley made a number of changes in their line-up for the 1897–98 season. However, Reynolds, McLintock and Walter Place retained their positions in defence, while Bowes, Place (Junior), Ross and Irish international

Tom Morrison remained in the attack. Newcomers in defence included Barron and Livingstone, together with Black and Wilf Toman up front, while goalkeeper Jack Hillman returned to the club during the season.

Burnley had remained unbeaten at home throughout the season, which saw fourteen victories and one draw, including wins against Woolwich Arsenal (5–1), Blackpool (5–1), Darwen (6–1), Grimsby (6–0), Newton Heath (6–3) and Loughborough (9–3), while they suffered only two defeats on their travels. They secured the Second Division Championship by a margin of three points from Newcastle. To crown an excellent season, the Lancashire side had reached the quarter-final stages of the FA Cup competition. However, their priorities lay in a return to the First Division, via the end-of-season play-off games.

The final League placings at the close of the 1897–98 season are as shown in Tables XXIII and XXIV.

Table XXIII: *First Division Football League results for the 1897–98 season*

	P	W	D	L	F	A	PTS
1. Sheffield United	30	17	8	5	56	31	42
2. Sunderland	30	16	5	9	43	30	37
3. Wolverhampton Wndrs	30	14	7	9	57	41	35
4. Everton	30	13	9	8	48	39	35
5. Wednesday	30	15	3	12	51	42	33
6. Aston Villa	30	14	5	11	61	51	33
7. West Bromwich Albion	30	11	10	9	44	45	32
8. Nottingham Forest	30	11	9	10	47	49	31
9. Liverpool	30	11	6	13	48	45	28
10. Derby County	30	11	6	13	57	61	28
11. Bolton Wanderers	30	11	4	15	28	41	26
12. Preston North End	30	8	8	14	35	43	24
13. Notts County	30	8	8	14	36	46	24
14. Bury	30	8	8	14	39	51	24
15. Blackburn Rovers	30	7	10	13	39	54	24
16. Stoke	30	8	8	14	35	55	24

Table XXIV: *Second Division Football League results for the 1897–98 season*

	P	W	D	L	F	A	PTS
1. Burnley	30	20	8	2	80	24	48
2. Newcastle	30	21	3	6	64	32	45
3. Manchester City	30	15	9	6	66	36	39
4. Newton Heath	30	16	6	8	64	35	38

	P	W	D	L	F	A	PTS
5. Woolwich Arsenal	30	16	5	9	69	49	37
6. Small Heath	30	16	4	10	58	50	36
7. Leicester Fosse	30	13	7	10	46	35	33
8. Luton	30	13	4	13	68	50	30
9. Gainsborough	30	12	6	12	50	54	30
10. Walsall	30	12	5	13	58	58	29
11. Blackpool	30	10	5	15	49	61	25
12. Grimsby	30	10	4	16	52	62	24
13. Burton Swifts	30	8	5	17	38	69	21
14. Lincoln	30	6	5	19	43	82	17
15. Darwen	30	6	2	22	31	76	14
16. Loughborough	30	6	2	22	24	87	14

A New Name on the FA Cup

There were few surprises at the second round stage of the 1897–98 FA Cup competition, as Liverpool defeated Newton Heath by two goals to one, following a goalless draw, while Miller scored the only goal of the game as Bolton Wanderers secured a 1–0 home win against Manchester City.

Burnley had little difficulty in defeating Burslem Port Vale by three goals to nil, Everton inflicted a 5–1 defeat on Stoke in a replayed tie with Lawrence Bell (2), Cameron, Chadwick and Taylor on target for the Merseysiders, while Southampton St Mary's and West Bromwich Albion proceeded to the quarter-finals following 1–0 victories against Newcastle and Wednesday.

Derby County, who had defeated FA Cup holders Aston Villa in the opening round, won by a single goal at Wolverhampton Wanderers, with Leonard scoring the all-important goal, while Nottingham Forest, who had beaten Grimsby by four goals to nil in the previous round, defeated Gainsborough Trinity by a similar score, with Charles Richards (2), Len Benbow and Tom McInnes on target for the East Midlands side.

Southampton's excellent FA Cup run continued in the quarter-finals with a 4–0 victory against Bolton Wanderers following a goalless draw, while Everton secured a 3–1 win at Burnley with Jack Taylor (2) and Lawrence Bell on target for the visitors.

Liverpool, who were in pursuit of a second successive semi-final appearance, drew one-all with Derby County. However, the Merseysiders were well beaten in the replay as John Boag (3) and Steve Bloomer (2) found the net in a 5–1 success for Derby, while Nottingham Forest recovered from a two-goal deficit against West Bromwich Albion to record a 3–2 victory, with Frank Forman, Charles Richards and Alf Spouncer netting the Forest goals.

Forest then drew one-all with Southampton in a semi-final tie at Bramall

Lane, prior to winning the replay by two goals to nil, with Tom McInnes and Charles Richards on target to secure a first final appearance for the Nottingham side. Goals by Steve Bloomer (2) and John Goodall earned Derby a 3–1 success against Everton to make the final an all East Midlands affair, which was to take place at Crystal Palace on 16 April.

An Odd-Goal Victory in Belfast

Early March saw the English national team travel to Belfast for the annual fixture against Ireland with the visitors including four new caps. Frank Forman (Nottingham Forest) made the first of nine appearances at right half back, while Charles Richards (Nottingham Forest), Tom Morren (Sheffield United) and Ben Garfield (West Bromwich Albion) made single appearances for their country.

John Robinson, who had recently moved from Derby County to the New Brighton Tower Club, retained his place in goal, while William Oakley (Corinthians), Billy Williams (West Bromwich Albion), Charlie Athersmith (Aston Villa), G O Smith (Corinthians) and Fred Wheldon (Aston Villa) were once again included in a strong England line-up.

James Turner (Derby County) completed the England team for his third and final appearance, having previously gained caps while playing for Bolton Wanderers and Stoke.

England were expected to win with ease. However, they were a little fortunate to return home with a 3–2 victory with goals by Morren, Athersmith and G O Smith saving the English blushes.

Fred Wheldon Scores a Brace in Wrexham

Following the victory in Belfast, the England selectors retained John Robinson, William Oakley, Billy Williams, Charlie Athersmith, G O Smith and Fred Wheldon for the game against Wales, while Tom Perry (West Bromwich Albion) and Thomas Booth (Blackburn Rovers) were awarded their first international caps.

Perry, who had seen his brother Charles represent England five years earlier, played only once for his country, while Booth gained a second cap as an Everton player. Ernest Needham (Sheffield United), John Goodall (Derby County) and Fred Spiksley (Wednesday) completed the visitors' line-up, who had little difficulty in securing a 3–0 victory with Fred Wheldon (2) and G O Smith netting the England goals.

A Welcome Victory Against the Scots

Eight of the England team that had won in Wrexham were retained for the game against Scotland to decide the international championship. Robinson continued in goal, together with Williams, Oakley and Needham in defence, while Athersmith, G O Smith, Wheldon and Fred Spiksley remained in the attack. It was Spiksley's seventh and final appearance for his country.

Frank Forman (Nottingham Forest) and Steve Bloomer (Derby County) returned to the side, while Charles Wreford-Brown (Corinthians), who had made his first appearance nine years earlier, earned a recall for his final England game. England were by far the more industrious side and goals by Bloomer (2) and Wheldon earned a 3–1 success to secure the 1898 international championship.

The Irish League Eleven Are Well Beaten

Early November saw the Irish League Eleven visit Hyde Road, Manchester, for the annual fixture against the English League Eleven with the home side including Williams (Manchester City), Pumphrey (Gainsborough), Holmes (Manchester City) and Bryant (Newton Heath) from the Second Division, as well as Jack Earp (Wednesday), Thomas Booth (Blackburn Rovers), Tom Morren (Sheffield United), Steve Bloomer (Derby County), Billy Beats (Wolverhampton Wanderers), Fred Wheldon (Aston Villa) and Joseph Schofield (Stoke) from the First Division.

As expected, the English won convincingly with Bloomer, Beats, Wheldon and Schofield netting two goals apiece in an 8–1 victory.

A Scottish League Eleven Avenge the Defeat in Glasgow

A week after the England team's win in Glasgow, a Scottish League Eleven journeyed south to Birmingham, with the English fielding Willie Foulke, Harry Thickett, Tom Morren and Ernest Needham from the successful Sheffield United side, as well as Fred Wheldon, Charlie Athersmith and Steve Smith from Aston Villa. Ambrose Langley (Wednesday) and Tom Perry (West Bromwich Albion) were included in the defence, together with Billy Beats and Harry Wood of Wolverhampton Wanderers up front. Despite the strong English line-up, the visitors won by two goals to one, with Hamilton scoring both Scottish goals, while Beats replied for the home side.

The FA Cup Returns to Nottingham

A crowd in excess of 60,000 arrived at Crystal Palace for the 1898 FA Cup Final between Nottingham Forest and Derby County, with Forest selecting the following team:

Allsopp

Ritchie   Scott

MacPherson   Wragg   Frank Forman

McInnes   Richards   Benbow   Arthur Capes   Spouncer

Derby County selected the following eleven:

Fryer

Methven   Leiper

Cox   Archie Goodall   Turner

McQueen   Stevenson   Boag   Bloomer   John Goodall

Derby were favourites to win the trophy following their 5–0 victory against Forest a few days earlier. John Lewis (Blackburn) was appointed match referee.

Forest made all the early running in the final as Arthur Capes, Tom McInnes and Alf Spouncer made worthy efforts on the Derby goal, which led a charmed life. However, the pressure finally told when, following a free kick by William Wragg, the ever alert Arthur Capes shot low and hard past the advancing Fryer to secure a one-goal lead for the Nottingham side.

County's forward line, which had been a little subdued during the opening quarter of the game, began to exert pressure on the Forest defence. Efforts by John Goodall and Steve Bloomer were cleared by Frank Forman, who was performing splendidly at the back. However, on the half hour, Forman conceded a foul on the edge of the penalty area, resulting in Bloomer heading the equalising goal off the crossbar.

Within ten minutes the Nottingham side had regained the lead when Fryer saved a shot from Charles Richards, which rebounded to Arthur Capes, who side-footed the ball into the net to secure a half-time lead for Forest.

Early in the second half, Forest defender William Wragg sustained a serious leg injury, which resulted in him spending the remainder of the game as a passenger on the left wing, while the Derby forwards immediately took advantage of the situation with Stevenson and Bloomer forcing excellent saves from Dennis Allsopp. The expected equalising goal failed to materialise as the game reached its final quarter, with County noticeably tiring. With the game heading towards its close, Forest mounted a rare attack, which resulted in a corner headed clear by John Boag. However, John MacPherson intercepted the clearance to steer the ball past Fryer, thus securing a 3–1 lead for Forest.

When the final whistle sounded, the dejected Derby team left the field of play disappointed by their indifferent performance. John MacPherson collected the FA Cup from Lord Rosebury. However, the Derby side would soon return to the Crystal Palace ground to contest a further FA Cup Final.

Forest Return to League Action

Following their FA Cup Final victory, the Nottingham side completed their League campaign with successive away defeats at Sunderland (4–0) and Aston Villa (2–0), which resulted in an eighth place finish, with eleven wins, nine draws and ten defeats in their thirty League games, while scoring forty-seven goals and conceding forty-nine. Ten of the Forest side had played in twenty-two League games or more. Frank Forman and Charles Richards had ended the campaign with six League goals apiece, Arthur Capes had found the net on eight occasions, and Len Benbow led the scoring with eleven goals in twenty-four League appearances.

Middlesbrough's Second FA Amateur Cup Victory

The 1898 FA Amateur Cup final was contested at the same venue as the FA Cup Final, which resulted in a 2–1 victory for Middlesbrough against Uxbridge to secure the trophy for the second occasion in four seasons.

The Play-Off Games Create a Problem

As the 1897–98 season came to a close, there remained the important issue of the play-off games, which involved Stoke, Blackburn Rovers, Burnley and Newcastle.

Burnley were at the head of the play-off League table at the halfway stage of the competition, following home and away victories against Blackburn Rovers (3–1 and 2–0), while Stoke had secured a 1–0 home success against Newcastle, prior to suffering a 2–1 defeat in the return game.

The third round stage of the competition saw Blackburn defeat Newcastle at Ewood Park by four goals to three, while Stoke, surprisingly, won 2–0 at Burnley, which left the League table as in Table XXV, with one round of games remaining.

Table XXV: *The Test Match League results for 1897–98 with one game remaining*

	Played	Won	Lost	Drawn	For	Against	Points
Stoke	3	2	1	0	4	2	4
Burnley	3	2	1	0	5	3	4
Newcastle	3	1	2	0	5	6	2
Blackburn Rovers	3	1	2	0	5	8	2

On the last day of April, the final round of play-off games took place, with Blackburn Rovers visiting Newcastle, while Burnley travelled to Stoke, well aware that a drawn game would result in both teams playing First Division football for the following season.

Newcastle avenged the defeat at Blackburn a couple of days earlier with a 4–0 success, while the Stoke–Burnley game ended in a predictable goalless draw. This meant First Division football for Stoke and Burnley, while Newcastle would spend a further season in the Second Division, together with the once mighty Blackburn Rovers. The final play-off League tables read as in Table XXVI.

Table XXVI: *The final standings after the 1897–98 Test Matches*

	Played	Won	Lost	Drawn	For	Against	Points
Stoke	4	2	1	1	4	2	5
Burnley	4	2	1	1	5	3	5
Newcastle	4	2	2	0	9	6	4
Blackburn Rovers	4	1	3	0	5	12	2

Blackburn's Blushes Are Saved

It had been apparent to all that the Stoke and Burnley teams had agreed to play a drawn game prior to the kick-off, much to the embarrassment of Charles Sutcliffe, a long-serving director of the Burnley club. This ultimately led to a meeting of the Football League Committee to resolve the problem of two teams exploiting the rules of the game to suit their own ends.

Mr Beardsley of the Woolwich Arsenal Club suggested that two Second Divisions be formed, one in the north and one in the south, while Frederick Rinder of Aston Villa proposed a First Division of eighteen teams, as well as two Second Divisions of twelve clubs, while abolishing the play-off games for straight promotion and relegation. However, a suggestion by Charles Sutcliffe to expand both divisions to eighteen teams was eventually accepted, together with automatic promotion and relegation.

As a result of the meeting, Stoke, Burley, Newcastle and Blackburn Rovers would all play First Division football during the 1898–99 season, while Barnsley, Burslem Port Vale, New Brighton Tower and Glossop North End were all elected into the Second Division.

Chapter XXIV

ASTON VILLA WIN THE LEAGUE CHAMPIONSHIP – 1898–99

ASTON VILLA WIN THE LEAGUE CHAMPIONSHIP
WEDNESDAY AND BOLTON WANDERERS ARE RELEGATED
STOKE'S EXCELLENT FA CUP RUN
DERBY COUNTY SECURE A SECOND SUCCESSIVE FA CUP FINAL APPEARANCE
SHEFFIELD UNITED WIN THE FA CUP
GLOSSOP'S SURPRISE PROMOTION
G O SMITH SCORES FOUR GOALS IN A 13–2 SUCCESS AGAINST IRELAND
ENGLAND WIN ALL THREE INTERNATIONALS

As a result of the decision to expand the First and Second Divisions from sixteen to eighteen teams for the 1898–99 season, it now meant that teams would have to fulfil thirty-four League fixtures, as well as FA Cup ties, leaving fewer dates available for friendly games.

NEWCASTLE UNITED

Newcastle United, who had secured promotion to the First Division for the 1898–99 League campaign, had origins dating back to 1877, when a game based on the Cambridge Rules took place at the Elswick Rugby Club. This led to the formation of the Tyne Association and Newcastle Rangers Clubs, followed shortly thereafter by the East End Club, due mainly to the efforts of W A Coulson and William Findlay.

Meanwhile across the city, William Tiffen and John Black, financially assisted by William Neasham, formed the West End Football Club, playing their games on a local cricket field, prior to moving to a ground at St James's Park, where the arrival of Tom Watson, later to find fame as the manager–secretary of both Sunderland and Liverpool, inspired the team to become the finest in the area. However, the East End Club eventually persuaded Mr Watson to join them, which led them to join the professional ranks in 1889.

West End began to struggle financially during this period, which led to the East End Club taking over the St James's Park ground, while officials of both clubs formed a new committee, with a number of West End players joining East End to play in the Northern League.

During the 1892–93 season, East End decided to change their name to Newcastle United, and the following season saw them elected to the Second Division of the Football League, where they opened the campaign with a two-all draw at Woolwich Arsenal, with Sorley and Crate on target for the north-eastern side. The season ended in a creditable fourth place finish, with seven defeats in twenty-eight League games, with Thompson Crate and Wallace all achieving double figures on the goal-scoring front.

The 1894–95 season saw a disappointing tenth place League finish, with twelve victories in thirty games, with Willis netting fourteen goals in eighteen appearances, while Thompson had led the scoring with seventeen goals in twenty-eight games. However, Newcastle re-established themselves during the 1895–96 season, which coincided with the appointment of Frank G Watt as club secretary, as well as new signings in the form of Andy Aitken and Willie Wardrope from north of the border.

Aitken, who had arrived from Ayr Parkhouse club prior to the new season, made in excess of 350 appearances in twelve seasons with the club, as well as gaining international caps with Scotland. Wardrope, who had signed from the Linthouse club, would score forty-four goals in 131 League appearances for Newcastle. Following the changes, Newcastle enjoyed an excellent season, with sixteen victories in their thirty League games, which included notable home wins against Notts County (5–1), Darwen (7–2), Rotherham (6–1), Crewe (6–0), Lincoln (5–0) and Burton (5–0), resulting in a fifth place finish. They had enjoyed an excellent FA Cup run in which Thompson and Wardrope had scored eleven goals between them. Aitken had ended the campaign with ten League goals, Lennox had found the net on a dozen occasions, while Wardrope had led the scoring with fourteen League goals.

United's fine home form continued during the 1896–97 season as they finished in fifth position, four points adrift from the runners-up spot. Aitken and Wardrope had ended the campaign with eleven League goals apiece, with centre forward Smellie, a recent signing from Nottingham Forest, leading the scoring with fifteen goals in twenty-six League appearances.

Newcastle made a number of changes for the 1897–98 season, which saw the arrival of Jock Peddie and Tommy Ghee from north of the border, while Aitken and Wardrope were once again the mainstays of the attack. Centre forward Peddie, who had signed from the Third Lanark club following a friendly game with United, scored seventy-three goals in 126 League appearances, prior to moving to Newton Heath, while Ghee, an excellent swimmer and water polo player, played 134 games in five seasons following his transfer from St Mirren.

The 1897–98 League campaign opened with four successive victories, with Wardrope on target in all four games, as United won fourteen of their fifteen home games to finish the season as runners-up, thus allowing them the opportunity of taking part in the-end-of season play-off games.

United secured home victories against Stoke and Blackburn Rovers in the play-off games, while suffering defeats in the return games. However, the results proved pointless when the Football League Committee decided to extend both the First and Second Divisions to eighteen teams, which meant that Newcastle would play First Division Football during the 1898–99 League campaign.

Few changes were made in the Newcastle line-up for the 1898–99 season. Lindsay, Jackson, Ostler, Stott and Tommy Ghee continued in defence, while Willie Wardrope, Andy Aitken and Jock Peddie remained up front, together with newcomers MacFarlane, Joe Rogers and Jimmy Stevenson.

MacFarlane a versatile centre forward who had arrived from the Airdrie club, made eighty-four appearances in three seasons. Rogers, a skilful outside right who had previously played for Grimsby, played fifty-four League games for United, while Stevenson, who signed from Derby County during the early weeks of the campaign, soon moved to Grimsby. However, the most notable newcomer in the Newcastle team was goalkeeper Matt Kingsley, who had learned his trade in the Lancashire League, prior to joining the Darwen Club. Kingsley made 180 League appearances for the north-eastern side during a six-year period, as well as gaining an England cap at the turn of the century, thus earning the distinction of becoming the first Newcastle player to represent the English national side.

Newcastle opened the campaign with a 4–2 home defeat against Wolverhampton Wanderers, with Jock Peddie scoring both United goals, which preceded further defeats at Everton (3–0) and at home to Notts County (2–1). Successive draws at Stoke (0–0) and Sheffield United (2–2), as well as at home to Aston Villa (1–1), continued their indifferent start to the season.

Then followed odd-goal defeats at Burnley (2–1) and at home to Sheffield United (2–1), while Joe Rogers found the net in a one-all draw at Bury. However, a 1–0 reverse at Preston North End saw the north-eastern side complete their tenth League game without a win.

Early November saw Peddie (2) and MacFarlane on target in a 3–0 home success against Liverpool, which preceded a 2–0 defeat at Nottingham Forest, while Jock Peddle netted a brace of goals in a 4–1 home win against Bolton Wanderers. However, a 3–1 defeat at Derby County continued their poor results on their travels.

Jock Peddie was again on target the following week in a 3–0 home success against West Bromwich Albion with Rogers and Aitken completing the scoring, which preceded a 4–2 reverse at Blackburn Rovers where Jimmy Stevenson netted a brace of goals. The halfway stage of the campaign arrived with a two-all home draw with the Wednesday.

Christmas Eve then saw United secure a rare away win at Sunderland (3–2), where Peddie (2) and Wardrope found the net, but a 1–0 reverse at Aston Villa as well as a goalless draw at Wolverhampton Wanderers saw the north-eastern side near the foot of the League table at the turn of the year. United's form improved during the New Year as Aitken and Stevenson were on target in a two-all home draw with Everton, which preceded a 3–1 reverse at Notts County, while Jock Peddie netted a further brace of goals in a 3–0 home win against Stoke.

January's end saw Peddie score the only goal of the game in a 1–0 victory at Glossop North End in the first round of the FA Cup, while their winning run continued with a 4–1 home success against Burnley with Rogers (2), Lindsay and Peddie on target. Then a 3–1 defeat at Liverpool in the second round of the FA Cup ended their splendid run of results.

On United's return to League action, Jock Peddie scored twice in a 2–0 home win against Bury, which preceded a further home success against Preston North End (2–1), with Peddie on target for the seventh game in a row. However, a 1–0 home defeat against Nottingham Forest saw the north-eastern side move down to thirteenth position in the League table.

Following a goalless draw at Bolton Wanderers, Reid and Stevenson found the net in a 2–0 home success against Derby County, which preceded successive away defeats at West Bromwich Albion (2–0) and Liverpool (3–2). Then centre forward MacFarlane scored the only goal of the game in a 1–0 home victory against Blackburn Rovers.

Mid-April saw Newcastle secure a 3–1 away win at the Wednesday with Stevenson (2) and Aitken on target, while the campaign ended with a 1–0 home defeat against Sunderland. United ended the season in thirteenth position, with eleven victories, eight draws and fifteen defeats in their thirty-four League games, while scoring forty-nine goals and conceding forty-eight.

Matt Kingsley had appeared in all thirty-four League games, while Ghee, Jackson, Lindsay and Peddie had missed no more than a handful in a season in which Newcastle had established themselves in the First Division. Jock Peddie had once again led the scoring with eighteen goals in twenty-nine League appearances.

WEDNESDAY

Wednesday had finished the 1897–98 League campaign in fifth position, which resulted in few changes in their line-up for the 1898–99 season. Jimmy Massey continued in goal, with Jack Earp, Ambrose Langley, Tom Crawshaw and Bob Ferrier in defence, while Dryburgh, Kaye, Spiksley and Harry Davis remained in the attack, together with newcomers Hemmingfield and John Wright.

Hemmingfield, who had arrived from Mexborough Town during the close season, scored a dozen goals in forty-three League appearances for the club, while Wright, a £200 signing from Bolton Wanderers, found the net on forty-two occasions in 103 League games prior to returning to Bolton.

Harry Brandon had decided to return to Scotland, Archie Brash spent the season on the injury list, while Jamieson and Alec Brady made only the occasional appearance in a League campaign which saw the introduction of Herrod Ruddlesdin and Willie Layton in defence.

Ruddlesdin, a hard-tackling wing half, appeared in 259 League games for the Wednesday as well as winning three England caps. Layton, who had arrived from the Chesterfield club a couple of years earlier, eventually made the left back position his own, where he made in excess of 300 League appearances, as well as appearing in the Football League representative side.

Wednesday opened the season with a 4–0 reverse at Liverpool, followed by a 2–1 home success against Nottingham Forest, with Hemmingfield and Dryburgh on target, while a goalless draw at Bolton Wanderers, as well as further home wins against Preston North End (2–1) and Derby County (3–1) continued their excellent start to the campaign with Hemmingfield netting in both victories. However, a 2–0 defeat at West Bromwich Albion ended their unbeaten run.

Hemmingfield then scored his fourth League goal of the season in a one-all home draw with Sheffield United, which preceded a 2–1 home defeat against Blackburn Rovers, while a 3–2 home win against Bury saw a return to winning ways with Hemmingfield (2) and Dryburgh on target for the Sheffield side. A 2–0 reverse at Sunderland continued their indifferent away form.

Then followed a 3–0 home win against Wolverhampton Wanderers, with centre forward Kaye netting all three goals, while successive away defeats at Everton (2–0) and Stoke (1–0), as well as a one-all home draw with Notts County, saw the Yorkshire side in a mid-table position by late November.

Wednesday's indifferent run of results seemed to have come to an end when goals by Crawshaw, Dryburgh and Hemmingfield secured a 3–1 lead in a home game with Aston Villa; however, with a little more than ten minutes remaining, the deteriorating light forced the referee to abandon the game. Their poor form remained to the end of the year with defeats at Burnley (5–0), Sheffield United (2–1) and at home to Liverpool (3–0), as well as a two-all draw at Newcastle.

New Year began with successive away draws at Bury (0–0) and Nottingham Forest (1–1), followed by a 1–0 home success against Bolton Wanderers, with Harry Davis netting his only goal of the season. An embarrassing 9–0 reverse at Derby County ended their splendid start to the year, which went from bad to worse with a 2–0 defeat at Stoke in a replayed FA Cup tie, as well as further League defeats at home to West Bromwich Albion (2–1), Sunderland (1–0) and at Blackburn Rovers (2–0).

Following a goalless away draw at Wolverhampton Wanderers, the Sheffield side suffered defeats at home to Everton (2–1) and at Notts County (1–0), while mid-March saw the visit of Aston Villa to the Olive Grove Ground to complete the remaining ten minutes of the League game abandoned during the previous November, with Wednesday leading by three goals to one.

Wednesday managed a further goal scored by Richards to secure a 4–1 success against Villa, which preceded defeats in the return game at Villa (3–1) and away at Stoke (3–1). A John Wright penalty earned a 1–0 home victory against Burnley, but a 3–1 home defeat against Newcastle, as well as a one-all draw at Preston North End, saw the Sheffield side end the campaign at the foot of the League table, with eight wins, eight draws and eighteen defeats in their thirty-four League games, while scoring thirty-two goals and conceding sixty-one.

Jimmy Massey, Bob Ferrier and Herrod Ruddlesdin had appeared in all but one League game in Wednesday's most disappointing season to date. Hemmingfield had led the scoring with eight goals in twenty-two League appearances. However, the Sheffield side's relegation would be short-lived as their return to the First Division was swift.

BOLTON WANDERERS

Bolton Wanderers had ended the 1897–98 season in turmoil following a decision by the club directors to make less money available for players' wages, which resulted in John Sutcliffe, Jocky Wright, Alex Paton, Billy Thomson, James Cassidy and David Jones being reluctant to re-sign for the club during the 1898–99 League campaign, with Cassidy and Jones eventually moving to pastures new.

Welsh international Jones had decided to join Manchester City, James Cassidy had signed for the Newton Heath club, while Thomson, Wright and Paton played only occasionally during the season. John Sutcliffe retained his place in goal, with John Somerville, Bob Brown and Archie Freebairn in defence, while Gilligan, Miller, Nicholl and Bob Jack were once again the mainstays of the attack, together with newcomers Barlow and Morgan, who became regular members of the team during the second half of the campaign.

W H Davies replaced Alex Paton at right half back, albeit for a little more than a season, while Lockhart and R H Davies shared the left back position vacated by the departure of David Jones.

Wanderers opened the season with a three-all home draw against West Bromwich Albion with Nicholl, Wright and Miller on target, which preceded a 4–1 reverse at Blackburn Rovers, while successive draws at home to the Wednesday (0–0) and away at Sunderland (0–0) continued their indifferent start to the campaign. A 2–1 home success against Wolverhampton Wanderers saw Bolton register their first victory of the season with Jocky Wright netting a brace of goals.

Then followed defeats at Everton (1–0) and at home to Notts County (1–0), while Nicholl, Miller and Freebairn found the net in a 3–2 victory at Stoke. Further defeats at Aston Villa (2–1) and Burnley (2–0) saw the Lancashire side near the foot of the League table by early November.

Bob Jack then scored his first goal of the campaign in a 3–0 home win against Sheffield United, with Gilligan netting a brace, while Bolton's indifferent form continued to the end of the year with defeats at Newcastle (4–1), Liverpool (2–0), West Bromwich Albion (1–0) and at home to Nottingham Forest (2–0) and Bury (1–0), as well as drawn games at Derby County (1–1) and at home to Preston North End (2–2).

Bolton eventually returned to winning ways during the opening week of the new year with a 2–0 home success against Burnley with Brown and Jack on target, which preceded defeats at home to Blackburn Rovers (2–0) and at the Wednesday (1–0). Gilligan (2), Brown (2), Barlow and Barnes found the net in a 6–1 home victory against Sunderland, however, following a goalless draw at Wolverhampton Wanderers in the first round of the FA Cup, the Lancashire side suffered a 1–0 defeat in the replay to end their interest in the competition.

On their return to League action, the Wanderers suffered successive home defeats against Stoke (2–0) and Everton (4–2), as well as a 3–1 reverse at Sheffield United. However, following a goalless home draw with Newcastle United, the Bolton team secured home wins against Derby County (2–1) and Liverpool (2–1), with outside right Morgan scoring in both victories.

Early April saw further away defeats at Notts County (2–1) and Wolverhampton Wanderers (1–0), while Morgan netted a brace of goals in a 2–1 success at Nottingham Forest. A 3–1 reverse at Bury, as well as a goalless home draw against Aston Villa, condemned Bolton to the Second Division for the 1899–1900 League campaign, despite securing a 1–0 win at Preston North End in their final game of the season.

Bolton had won nine, drawn seven and lost eighteen of their thirty-four League games, while scoring thirty-seven goals and conceding fifty-one. Gilligan and Morgan led the scoring with six League goals apiece. However, as with the Wednesday, the Wanderers would soon return to the First Division.

SHEFFIELD UNITED

Prior to the 1898–99 season, the Duke of Norfolk had offered the Bramall Lane ground to Sheffield United for a little more than £10,000, which was eventually accepted upon the reigning League Champions forming a limited company.

Few changes were made in the United line-up for the 1898–99 League campaign. Willie Foulke continued in goal, with Harry Thickett, Harry Johnson, Tom Morren and Ernest Needham in defence, while Walter Bennett, George Hedley, John Almond and Fred Priest remained in the attack. John Cunningham had left the club, while McKay and Bob Cain had signed for Tottenham Hotspur. However, they were adequately replaced by fullback Peter Boyle and inside forward Billy Beer.

United opened the season with a one-all home draw against Everton, with Ernest Needham on target, which preceded a two-all draw at Notts County with Charlie Field netting a brace of goals, while Harry Johnson scored the only goal of the game in a 1–0 home success against Wolverhampton Wanderers.

Then followed further drawn games at home to Stoke (1–1), Burnley (1–1) and Newcastle United (2–2), as well as away at the Wednesday (1–1) and Aston Villa (1–1), which meant that the Sheffield side had drawn seven of the eight opening League games, while remaining unbeaten.

Early October saw United secure successive away wins at Bury (3–1) and

Newcastle (2–1) with Fred Priest and Walter Bennett on target in both victories, which preceded a further home draw against Preston North End (1–1) with George Hedley scoring for the Yorkshire side following excellent play by Francis Becton, a former Preston player. Becton had signed for United amidst rumours of his liking for alcohol, which had been cured, however, following an incident at a local ale house. The England international's career in the Sheffield area did not last long.

United then suffered successive away defeats at Liverpool (2–1) and Bolton Wanderers (3–0) on either side of a two-all home draw with Nottingham Forest, while their unbeaten home record continued with a 2–0 success against Derby County with Hedley and Whelan on target. A 3–0 reverse at West Bromwich Albion saw the Sheffield side in a mid-table position by late November.

Francis Becton then netted his first goal of the campaign in a one-all home draw with Blackburn Rovers, while Becton and Needham (penalty) found the net in a 2–0 home win against Sunderland in a game which marked the debut of Peter Boyle, a recent signing from Sunderland. However, a 4–1 reverse at Wolverhampton Wanderers continued their indifferent away form.

United soon returned to winning ways with a 2–1 home success against the Wednesday with Tom Morren and Billy Beer on target, while the year ended with a 1–0 reverse at Everton. This was followed by a poor run of results during January, including home defeats against Liverpool (2–0), Aston Villa (3–1) and away at Stoke (4–1), as well as a two-all home draw against Notts County.

Late January saw Billy Beer net a brace of goals in a two-all draw at Burnley in the first round of the FA Cup, while Morren and Bennett found the net in a 2–1 victory in the replay to secure an away tie at Preston North End in the second round.

Prior to the FA Cup tie, Bennett, Almond, Hedley and Needham (penalty) were on target in a 4–1 home win against Bury, while Bennett and Hedley again found the net in a two-all draw in the cup game at Preston. However, the Yorkshire side had few difficulties in the replay as Ernest Needham netted a brace of goals, as well as missing a penalty in a 2–1 victory, to earn a quarter-final tie at Nottingham Forest.

United then suffered a 1–0 defeat in a League encounter at Preston, while their excellent FA Cup form continued at Nottingham where Fred Priest scored the only goal of the game with four minutes remaining in a bruising FA Cup tie. Both John Almond and Ernest Needham sustained leg injuries.

Within days of their FA Cup success, the Sheffield side suffered a 2–1 defeat in a League game at Forest, which preceded a 3–1 home win against Bolton Wanderers, with Hedley (2) and Needham netting the United goals. Both players were again on target the following week in a two-all draw against Liverpool in the semi-final of the FA Cup.

In the replay at Bolton, United soon found themselves two goals down, which they managed to pull back with goals by Walter Bennett and Billy Beer. Then, following a Peter Boyle own goal, as well as a converted penalty kick, the Sheffield team were two goals in arrears, with a little over ten minutes remaining.

With very little to lose, the Yorkshire side mounted a period of all-out attack, which resulted in Fred Priest reducing the arrears, while a goalkeeping error allowed Priest a further goal in the final minute. United had secured a second replay at the Fallowfield Ground by the skin of their teeth.

Prior to the FA Cup replay, United enjoyed a 5–0 home success against West Bromwich Albion with Hedley (2), Field, Beer and Priest on target, while the FA Cup replay at Fallowfield ended in a total farce. The referee abandoned the game following frequent crowd invasions with Liverpool one goal to the good. However, United managed a 1–0 victory in the third replay at Derby with Fred Priest scoring the only goal of the game to secure a first FA Cup Final appearance for the Sheffield team.

A physically demanding FA Cup run had seen the Yorkshire side play nine games, of which five were replayed ties. The League campaign ended with successive away defeats at Burnley (1–0), Blackburn Rovers (2–1), Derby County (1–0) and Sunderland (1–0). United ended the season in sixteenth position, with nine wins, eleven draws and fourteen defeats in their thirty-four League games, while scoring forty-five goals and conceding fifty-one.

Walter Bennett and Ernest Needham had ended the campaign with six League goals apiece, Charlie Field had found the net on eight occasions, while George Hedley had led the scoring with nine League goals. However, United's thoughts lay in their forthcoming FA Cup Final appearance, which was to take place at Crystal Palace on 15 April against Derby County.

PRESTON NORTH END

Preston North End had narrowly avoided the 1897–98 play-off games, owing to a superior goal difference. While the 'Old Guard' continued to leave the club, the directors kept faith with the majority of their players for the 1898–99 League campaign. Blyth, Dunn, Sanders, Eccleston, Tait and Robert Holmes continued in defence, while Pratt, Brown and Halsall remained up front, together with newcomers Chalmers, McIntyre and Murray.

Chalmers, who had arrived from Sunderland, made ten League appearances for the club, McIntyre played eighty-seven League games in three seasons, while Murray scored a dozen goals in fifty-one League appearances. Jimmy Trainer had left the club following in excess of 250 League appearances, Bob Howarth and Geordie Drummond soon moved to pastures new, while David Russell had returned to the team, albeit for a little more than a season.

Preston opened the season with successive defeats at home to Sunderland (3–2) and away at Burnley (3–1), followed by goalless draws at Wolverhampton Wanderers and at home to Everton. Further defeats at the Wednesday (2–1) and Notts County (1–0) completed a miserable September. However, early October saw an improvement in form as the Lancashire side secured a 4–2 home success against Stoke, as well as a two-all draw at Nottingham Forest.

Following a 4–2 reverse at Aston Villa, the Preston team played successive draws at Sheffield United (1–1) and at home to Burnley (1–1), prior to ending the month with a 1–0 home win against Newcastle United. Further away defeats at Bury (3–1), Liverpool (3–1) and Stoke (2–1) saw Preston move towards the foot of the League table.

Late November saw a return to winning ways with a 1–0 home success against Nottingham Forest, followed by a two-all draw at Bolton Wanderers. Their indifferent form continued throughout December with home victories against Derby County (3–1) and Bury (3–1), together with away defeats at West Bromwich Albion (2–0) and Sunderland (1–0), as well as a one-all home draw with Blackburn Rovers.

New Year began with a 2–1 home win against Wolverhampton Wanderers, followed by a 2–0 reverse at Everton, while their hopes of FA Cup success ended with a 2–1 defeat against Sheffield United in a second round replay. However, successive home victories against Aston Villa (2–0) and Sheffield United (1–0) continued their excellent run of results on home soil.

Preston then suffered a further run of indifferent results, which saw defeats at Newcastle (2–1) and Derby County (1–0), as well as at home to Liverpool (2–1), while home wins against Notts County (2–0) and West Bromwich Albion (4–0) guaranteed their place in the top division for the following season.

Successive draws at Blackburn Rovers (2–2) and at home to the Wednesday (1–1), as well as a 1–0 home defeat against Bolton Wanderers, saw the Preston side in a disappointing fifteenth position at the end of the campaign, with ten victories, nine draws and fifteen defeats in their thirty-four League games, while scoring forty-four goals and conceding forty-seven.

Goalkeeper Peter McBride had appeared in all thirty-four League games in a season in which Preston had failed to record a victory on their travels. Murray had ended the campaign with nine League goals, with Pratt leading the scoring with thirteen goals in thirty-one League appearances.

WEST BROMWICH ALBION

West Bromwich Albion had finished the 1897–98 League campaign in seventh position, which resulted in few changes in their line-up for the 1898–99 season. Joe Reader continued in goal, with George Cave, Billy Williams, Abe Jones, Tom Perry and Banks in defence, while Flewitt, McKenzie, Billy Bassett, William Richards and Ben Garfield remained up front.

Tom Higgins had announced his retirement from the game, while centre half McManus had returned to the north, which saw the arrival of Archie Dunn to replace him at the heart of the defence.

Dunn, a product of Scottish junior football, remained with the West

Bromwich side for three seasons, while the most notable newcomers in the attack were centre forward Brett, recently demobbed from Her Majesty's army, as well as Nock, a local player, who had made a couple of appearances during the previous campaign.

Albion opened the season with a three-all draw at Bolton Wanderers with Garfield (2) and Brett on target, which preceded a one-all home draw with Derby County, with Brett netting the Albion goal. Garfield and Flewitt found the net in a 2–0 home victory against Bury, but a 4–1 reverse at Blackburn Rovers ended their fine start to the season, with Ben Garfield scoring his fourth League goal in as many games.

Early October saw Perry and McKenzie score their first goals of the campaign in a 2–0 home success against Wednesday, which was followed by successive away defeats at Sunderland (2–0) and Everton (1–0), as well as at home to Wolverhampton Wanderers (2–1). The month ended with a 2–0 home win against Notts County with Richards and McKenzie on target for Albion. William Richards then scored for the second game running in a 2–1 defeat at Stoke, while Richards netted a further brace of goals in a 3–0 home victory against Everton. Then a 1–0 home reverse against Aston Villa continued Albion's indifferent run of results.

Following a one-all draw at Burnley, where Billy Williams converted a penalty, the West Bromwich side secured a 3–0 home success against Sheffield United, with Richards, Nock and a Harry Thickett own goal earning the points for Albion. A 3–0 defeat at Newcastle United continued their poor away form, though, a 2–0 home win against Preston North End, as well as a two-all draw at Liverpool, saw the Black Country side in a mid-table position at the halfway stage of the campaign.

Nock then netted a brace of goals in a 2–0 home win against Nottingham Forest, which preceded successive defeats at home to Liverpool (1–0) and at Wolverhampton Wanderers (5–1), while the year ended with a 1–0 home win against Bolton Wanderers, with Nock scoring the only goal of the game.

New Year began with a 4–1 reverse at Derby County, followed by a one-all draw at Bury, while McKenzie (2), Flewitt (2), Bassett and Garfield were on target in a 6–2 home success against Blackburn Rovers. This preceded an 8–0 home win against South Shore in the first round of the FA Cup, with Bassett (3), Jones (2), Richards, Garfield and an own goal securing a further home tie against Bury in the second round.

Prior to the FA Cup tie, William Richards netted the only goal of the game in a 1–0 home win against Sunderland, which preceded a 2–0 victory against Bury in the FA Cup game, with Richards scoring both goals. Richards secured two further goals in a 2–1 success at the Wednesday in Albion's only away win of the campaign. However, a 2–0 home defeat against Liverpool in the quarter-finals of the FA Cup ended their unbeaten run.

On their return to League action, the West Bromwich side suffered successive home defeats against Stoke (1–0) and Burnley (1–0) on either side of a goalless draw at Notts County, while the month ended with a 5–0 reverse at Sheffield United. A 2–0 home success against Newcastle United saw a return to winning ways with Bassett and Smith on target to earn two welcome points for the Albion.

With their First Division status assured, the Albion team suffered successive away defeats at Preston North End (4–0), Nottingham Forest (3–0) and Aston Villa (7–1) to finish the League campaign in fourteenth position, with twelve victories, six draws and sixteen defeats in their thirty-four League games, while scoring forty-two goals and conceding fifty-seven.

Tom Perry and George Cave had appeared in all thirty-four League games in a most disappointing League campaign, in which Nock and McKenzie had netted six League goals apiece, while William Richards had led the scoring with ten.

STOKE

Stoke's continuing financial problems had meant that few opportunities were available to strengthen the team that had finished in last place in the First Division at the close of the 1897–98 campaign. However, the increase of the division from sixteen to eighteen teams resulted in the Potteries' side retaining their First Division status for the 1898–99 season.

Prior to the new campaign, goalkeeper George Clawley had returned from Southampton to take over the club captaincy, while Robertson, Brodie, Murphy, Jack Eccles, John Kennedy, Willie Maxwell, Alf Wood and Joseph Schofield retained their places in the first eleven, with Fred Molyneux and John Farrell competing for the centre forward position. William Rowley, who had recently taken office as club secretary while continuing his playing career, had transferred himself to Leicester Fosse with the intention of saving the Stoke Club a little money. However, his registration was immediately rejected by the Football Association, who suspended him.

Stoke made their usual indifferent start to the 1898–99 season, which began with a goalless home draw against Derby County, followed by a 3–1 reverse at Aston Villa, while a 4–1 home win against Burnley secured their opening victory of the campaign. However, successive draws at Sheffield United (1–1) and at home to Newcastle United (0–0), as well as a 4–2 defeat at Preston North End, saw Stoke in a mid-table position by early October.

Following a 2–1 home success against Liverpool, the Potteries' side suffered successive defeats at Nottingham Forest (2–1) and at home to Bolton Wanderers (3–2), prior to ending the month with a one-all draw at Derby County. Their indifferent run of results continued throughout November with home wins against West Bromwich Albion (2–1), Preston North End (2–1) and Wednesday (1–0), as well as defeats at Blackburn Rovers (4–1), Sunderland (2–0), Everton (2–0) and at home to Wolverhampton Wanderers

(4–2), which saw Stoke struggling to maintain their mid-table position at the halfway stage of the campaign.

Early December saw a one-all home draw with Notts County, which preceded a 5–2 reverse at Bury. A 2–1 home success against Nottingham Forest saw a return to winning ways, while the year ended with an excellent 3–0 home win against Aston Villa, who were once again challenging for the League Championship.

Stoke continued their winning run into the new year with a 4–1 home victory against Sheffield United, followed by a 3–0 reverse at Newcastle United. A 2–0 win against the Wednesday in a first round FA Cup replay saw the Potteries' side secure a home tie against Small Heath in the second round.

Prior to the FA Cup game, Stoke suffered their ninth away defeat of the season in a 1–0 reverse at Liverpool, while the Cup tie with Small Heath ended all square (2–2), though a 2–1 success in the replay saw the North Staffordshire team earn a home tie against Tottenham Hotspur in the quarter-finals. Then followed a rare away win at Bolton Wanderers (2–0), while a crowd in excess of 20,000 gathered to witness a 4–1 success against Tottenham to secure a semi-final tie against Derby County at the Molineux Ground, Wolverhampton.

On their return to League action, Stoke gained a second successive away victory at West Bromwich Albion (1–0), followed by a 1–0 home defeat against Blackburn Rovers. They arrived at the Molineux Ground for their semi-final game with Derby County without the influential Joseph Schofield, who was unable to play owing to a serious leg injury.

Stoke's worst fears were realised in the semi-final as Steve Bloomer netted a hat-trick in a 3–1 victory for Derby. However, the Potteries' side soon put the FA Cup disappointment behind them with successive League wins at home to Sunderland (1–0) and away at the Wednesday (3–1).

Early April saw Stoke suffer a 3–2 reverse at Wolverhampton Wanderers, while a 2–1 home success against Everton saw them move to a mid-table position. A further away defeat at Notts County (2–0), as well as drawn games at Burnley (1–1) and at home to Bury (1–1), saw the Potteries' side end the campaign in twelfth position, with thirteen wins, seven draws and fourteen defeats in their thirty-four League games, while scoring forty-seven goals and conceding fifty-two. Goalkeeper George Clawley had appeared in all thirty-four League games for the Potteries' side, while Willie Maxwell had led the scoring for the third season running with sixteen League goals in a most successful campaign for the financially stretched Stoke Club.

NOTTINGHAM FOREST

As reigning FA Cup holders, Nottingham Forest retained all of their Cup-winning team for the 1898–99 League campaign. Dennis Allsopp continued in goal, with Archie Ritchie, Jim Iremonger, Adam Scott, Frank Forman, John MacPherson and William Wragg in defence, while Charles Richards, Arthur

Capes, Fred Spencer, Tom McInnes, Fred Forman, Len Benbow and Alf Spouncer once again competed for the forward positions. The most notable newcomers in the Forest side were left half back Robert Norris from a local amateur club, as well as inside forward Grenville Morris, who had been signed from Swindon Town for a fee of £200.

Norris remained with the club for six seasons, in which he made nearly 150 appearances, while Grenville Morris, who had appeared in the Welsh national side as an eighteen-year-old, scored 199 goals in 423 League games for Forest, as well as gaining a further sixteen international caps for Wales.

Forest opened the season with successive defeats at home to Blackburn Rovers (1–0) and away at the Wednesday (2–1), which preceded a one-all home draw with Sunderland, with Arthur Capes on target. A 2–0 success at Wolverhampton Wanderers saw their first win of the campaign, with Richards and MacPherson netting the all-important goals.

Then followed a run of three drawn games, at home to Everton (0–0) and Preston North End (2–2), as well as at Notts County (2–2), while McInnes and Spencer found the net in a 2–1 home victory against Stoke. However, successive defeats at Aston Villa (3–0) and at home to Burnley (1–0) ended their six-game unbeaten run.

Early November saw Suddick and Benbow on target in a two-all draw at Sheffield United, while both players netted the following week in a 2–0 home win against Newcastle United. Successive defeats at Preston North End (1–0) and Bury (2–0), as well as at home to Liverpool (3–0), saw the Nottingham side struggling near the foot of the League table.

Grenville Morris then netted his first goal of the season in a 2–0 success at Bolton Wanderers, with Suddick completing the scoring, while Morris again found the net in a three-all home draw with Derby County. However, Forest's indifferent away form continued with defeats at West Bromwich Albion (2–0) and Stoke (2–1), prior to ending the year with a three-all draw at Blackburn Rovers, with Morris (2) and Frank Forman (penalty) scoring for the visitors.

Forest enjoyed an excellent start to the new year as Len Benbow netted a hat-trick in a 3–1 victory at Everton, which preceded successive draws at home to the Wednesday (1–1) and away at Sunderland (1–1), while Arthur Capes and Fred Forman found the net in a 2–1 home success against Aston Villa in the first round of the FA Cup to secure a second round tie at Everton.

Prior to the FA Cup game, Grenville Morris netted a brace of goals in a 3–0 home win against Wolverhampton Wanderers, which was followed by a goalless home draw with Notts County, while Fred Forman scored the only goal of the game in the FA Cup tie at Goodison Park to earn a home tie against Sheffield United in the quarter-finals.

Forest's unbeaten run continued with a 1–0 home win against Aston Villa, with Grenville Morris again on target, while their interest in the FA Cup ended with a 1–0 defeat against the Sheffield side. However, the Nottingham team soon avenged the FA Cup defeat by inflicting a 2–1 defeat on United, with Fred Spencer netting a brace of goals.

Early March saw Suddick score in a one-all draw at Burnley, which preceded successive away victories at Newcastle United (1–0) and Liverpool (1–0), with Spencer and Benbow netting the Forest goals. Home defeats against Bury (2–1) and Bolton Wanderers (2–1), as well as a 2–0 reverse at Derby County, saw their hopes of finishing in the top six come to an end. The campaign ended with a 3–0 home win against West Bromwich Albion, with Fred Forman netting all three goals.

Forest had won eleven, drawn eleven and lost twelve of their thirty-four League games, while scoring forty-two goals and conceding forty-two to finish in eleventh position. Goalkeeper Dennis Allsopp had appeared in all thirty-four League games. Grenville Morris scoring seven goals in seventeen League appearances, Len Benbow had found the net on eight occasions, while Fred Spencer led the scoring with nine goals in sixteen League games.

BURY

Bury had been one of five teams to finish the 1897–98 League campaign with twenty-four points, but financial restrictions meant that few signings could be made for the 1898–99 season. Archie Montgomery continued in goal, with Clegg, Pray, Davidson and Ross in defence, while Miller, Plant, Balfour and Jimmy Settle were once again the mainstays of the attack.

Bury opened the campaign with successive victories at Derby County (2–1) and at home to Aston Villa (2–1), followed by a 2–0 reverse at West Bromwich Albion. Drawn games at home to Burnley (1–1) and away at Blackburn Rovers (0–0) continued their excellent start to the season. However, defeats at home to Sheffield United (3–1) and away at the Wednesday (3–2) ended a splendid run of results.

Following a one-all home draw with Newcastle United, the Lancashire side suffered a 3–0 reverse at Sunderland, but an excellent run of results that included home wins against Preston North End (3–1), Liverpool (3–0), Nottingham Forest (2–0) and Stoke (5–2), as well as away victories at Wolverhampton Wanderers (2–1), Everton (1–0) and Bolton Wanderers (1–0) saw the Bury team in fourth position in the League table at the halfway stage of the campaign. A 4–1 defeat at Notts County was their only disappointment during their fine run of form.

Bury then suffered a loss of form with away defeats at Preston North End (3–1), Aston Villa (3–2), Burnley (2–1) and Sheffield United (4–1), as well as home draws against Derby County (0–0), Wednesday (0–0) and West Bromwich Albion (1–1), while a 2–1 reverse at Albion in the second round of the FA Cup left them with a little more than their pride to play for during the remainder of the season.

Mid-February saw Bury return to winning ways with a 3–2 home victory against Blackburn Rovers, which preceded further defeats at Newcastle United

(2–0) and at home to Wolverhampton Wanderers (2–0), while a 3–1 home win against Everton saw two welcome points. However, a 2–1 home defeat against Sunderland continued their indifferent run of results.

As the season came to an end, Bury recorded successive home victories against Notts County (2–0) and Bolton Wanderers (3–1), as well as a 2–1 success at Nottingham Forest, which was followed by a 1–0 defeat at Liverpool.

The campaign ended with a one-all draw at Stoke, resulting in a tenth place League finish for the Bury team, with fourteen wins, seven draws and thirteen defeats in their thirty-four League games, while scoring forty-eight goals and conceding forty-nine. Bury may well have mounted a serious challenge for the League Championship if their early season form had been maintained. However, they were reasonably happy with their mid-table finish, due mainly to the goal-scoring exploits of Jimmy Settle, who had gained his first England cap during the latter stages of the season. Settle soon joined the more successful Everton club, however, his transfer hardly affected the progress of Bury, who enjoyed great FA Cup success during the following season.

DERBY COUNTY

Derby County retained the majority of their defeated FA Cup Final team for the 1898–99 League campaign. John Fryer continued in goal, with Jimmy Methven, Joseph Leiper, Jonathon Staley, John Cox and Archie Goodall in defence, while John Goodall, John Boag, Steve Bloomer, Jimmy Stevenson and Hugh McQueen remained up front.

James Turner had left the club, which saw the arrival of John May from Glasgow junior football, who made in excess of 200 appearances in six seasons with the East Midlands side, as well as appearing in the Scottish national team.

County called upon thirty-one players during the 1898–99 League campaign, of which eighteen were forward players, with Shanks, Oakden, MacDonald, Allen and Arkesden the most notable new arrivals, albeit for a little more than a season or two.

Derby opened the season with a goalless draw at Stoke, followed by a 2–1 home defeat against Bury in Jimmy Methven's 200th League appearance for the club. Steve Bloomer netted his first goal of the campaign in a one-all draw at West Bromwich Albion. However, following a goalless home draw with Blackburn Rovers, the East Midlands side continued their poor start to the season with a 3–1 reverse at the Wednesday.

Early October saw County register their first victory of the season in a 4–2 home success against Sunderland, with Shanks (2), Burton and Handley on target, which preceded a two-all draw at Wolverhampton Wanderers, with Bloomer scoring both goals. Bloomer netted a further brace of goals during the following week in a five-all home draw with Everton with Arkesden (2) and McQueen completing the scoring.

Then followed further drawn games at Notts County (2–2) and at home to

Stoke (1–1), while a 7–1 reverse at Aston Villa ended their run of drawn games in Hugh McQueen's 100th League appearance for the club. However, a 2–1 home success against Burnley saw a return to winning ways with Arkesden on target for the third successive game.

John May then netted his one League goal of the season in a 2–1 reverse at Sheffield United, while further home wins against Newcastle United (3–1) and Liverpool (1–0) on either side of a 3–1 defeat at Preston North End saw Derby in a mid-table position by the middle of December, with Steve Bloomer scoring in all three games.

Following a three-all draw at Nottingham Forest, where Bloomer, Rutherford and Cox found the net, outside right Bosworth, making a rare appearance for the club, scored the equalising goal in a one-all home draw with Bolton Wanderers. The year ended with a goalless draw at Bury as the East Midlands side maintained their mid-table position following ten draws in their opening nineteen League fixtures.

New Year began with successive away defeats at Sunderland (1–0) and Blackburn Rovers (3–0) on either side of a 4–1 home win against West Bromwich Albion, with Boag (2), Allen and MacDonald on target. This preceded an amazing display by Steve Bloomer, who netted six goals in a 9–0 home success against the Wednesday, while a 6–0 victory at Woolwich Arsenal in the first round of the FA Cup saw Derby secure a home tie against Wolverhampton Wanderers in the second round, with Bloomer (2), Boag (2), Allen and MacDonald scoring for the East Midlands side.

Prior to the FA Cup tie, County enjoyed a 6–2 home victory against Wolverhampton Wanderers, with Boag (2), Oakden, MacDonald, Bloomer and Archie Goodall finding the net, while the FA Cup game with Wolves proved a little more difficult. Derby won by the odd goal in three, with goals by Allen and MacDonald securing a quarter-final tie at Southampton.

On their return to League action, Oakden netted a brace of goals in a 4–2 home win against Notts County, while their FA Cup success continued at Southampton, where Bloomer and Macdonald were on target in a 2–1 victory to earn a fourth successive semi-final appearance. This was to be against Stoke, at the Molineux Ground, Wolverhampton.

Steve Bloomer then scored his nineteenth League goal of the campaign in a one-all home draw with Aston Villa, which preceded a 2–1 reverse at Burnley, while Bloomer netted all three goals in a 3–1 win in the semi-final against Stoke to secure a second successive FA Cup Final appearance.

With the FA Cup Final a month away, Derby suffered an indifferent run of results, which included away defeats at Newcastle United (2–0), Bolton Wanderers (2–1) and Liverpool (4–0), as well as victories at home to Preston North End (1–0) and away at Everton (2–1). However, their forthcoming FA Cup Final appearance against Sheffield United remained their priority.

WOLVERHAMPTON WANDERERS

Wolverhampton Wanderers had ended the 1897–98 League campaign in third position. Despite their excellent season, the financial burdens on the club meant that wage increases were restricted to a minimum, which created unrest amongst the players.

Few changes were made by the Wolverhampton side for the 1898–99 season. Tom Baddeley continued in goal, with Davies, Fleming, Smith, Matthais and Joseph Tonks in defence, while Hill Griffiths, Miller, McMain, Blackett and Billy Beats remained in the attack. However, Harry Wood had joined Southampton following a disagreement over wages, while Owen and Eccles had been offered improved terms by Everton.

Nurse and Malpass seldom appeared in the first team during the season. They were adequately replaced by Worton and Pheasant, who served the Black Country side for a number of seasons, with the latter making in excess of 200 appearances for the club.

Wanderers opened the season with a 4–2 success at Newcastle United, which preceded a poor run of results, including away defeats at Sheffield United (1–0), Liverpool (1–0), Bolton Wanderers (2–1) and at home to Nottingham Forest (2–0), as well as home draws against Preston North End (0–0) and Derby County (2–2). These left the Wolverhampton side near the foot of the League table by the middle of October, though successive victories at West Bromwich Albion (2–1) and at home to Blackburn Rovers (2–1) greatly improved their League placing. Then followed a 3–0 reverse at the Wednesday, which preceded a 2–0 home success against Sunderland, before their indifferent League form continued with defeats at home to Bury (2–1) and away at Everton (2–1). However, a 1–0 home win against Notts County saw a return to winning ways for the Wanderers.

Early December saw Wolves secure a 4–2 victory at Stoke, followed by a one-all draw at Aston Villa. The halfway stage of the campaign arrived with a 4–2 defeat at Burnley, but successive home wins against Sheffield United (4–1) and West Bromwich Albion (5–1), as well as a goalless home draw with Newcastle United, saw the Wanderers in a mid-table position at the turn of the year.

New Year began with away defeats at Preston North End (2–1) and Nottingham Forest (3–0) on either side of a goalless home draw with Liverpool, which preceded a 1–0 victory at Bolton Wanderers in a replayed first round FA Cup tie. Their indifferent League form continued with a 6–2 reverse at Derby County, who were Wolves' opponents in the second round of the FA Cup.

Inevitably the Wanderers tasted defeat in the Cup tie at Derby, albeit by the odd goal in three, which preceded successive draws at Blackburn Rovers (2–2) and at home to the Wednesday (0–0), as well as a 3–0 reverse at Sunderland. An excellent run of results during the final weeks of the campaign saw the

Wolverhampton side finish in a respectable mid-table position at the season's end.

Wolves' return to form began with successive away wins at Bury (2–0) and Notts County (2–0), followed by home victories against Stoke (3–2), Aston Villa (4–0), Bolton Wanderers (1–0) and Burnley (4–0). The season ended with a 2–1 home reverse against Everton, resulting in an eighth place League finish for the Wanderers, with fourteen wins, seven draws and thirteen defeats in their thirty-four League games, while scoring fifty-four and conceding forty-eight.

Fleming had appeared in all thirty-four League games, while Baddeley, Blackett, Hill Griffiths, Miller and Joseph Tonks had missed no more than a handful in an excellent season. McMain had scored seven goals in nineteen League appearances; Blackett had found the net on nine occasions; Billy Beats had ended the campaign with ten League goals; while Miller had led the scoring with eleven.

SUNDERLAND

Sunderland had finished the 1897–98 League campaign as runners-up to Sheffield United, which resulted in few changes in their line-up for the 1898–99 season. John Doig continued in goal, with McNeil, McAllister, Philip Bach, Mathew Ferguson, Billy Dunlop and Hugh Wilson in defence, while Morgan, Brown, Saxton and Jim Leslie remained in the attack, which was strengthened by the arrival of Crawford, Fulton, McLatchie and James Farquhar.

Fulton and McLatchie arrived from Preston North End during the early stages of the season, Crawford had previously assisted Reading, while Farquhar made in excess of 200 appearances following his transfer from Elgin City.

Further signings from north of the border included Raisbeck from Clyde, who spent three seasons with the north-eastern side, as well as Scottish international fullback Andrew McCombie, who played 157 League games following his arrival from Inverness Thistle. The most notable departures saw Peter Boyle join Sheffield United, with inside forward Chalmers soon moving to Preston.

Sunderland opened the season with a 3–2 victory at Preston North End, where Morgan, Chalmers and Leslie found the net, which preceded a 1–0 home success against Liverpool, with Leslie again on target in the north-eastern side's first game at Roker Park. Hugh Wilson netted in a one-all draw at Nottingham Forest. However, following a goalless home draw with Bolton Wanderers, Sunderland suffered their first defeat of the campaign in a 4–2 reverse at Derby County.

Early October saw Jim Leslie score a brace of goals in a 2–0 home success against West Bromwich Albion, while his fifth goal of the campaign arrived in a 3–2 reverse at Blackburn Rovers. A 2–0 home win against the Wednesday saw a return to winning ways with Saxton and Wilson on target, which preceded an excellent display by Hugh Wilson, who netted a hat-trick in a 3–0 home victory against Bury.

Following a 2–0 defeat at Wolverhampton Wanderers, Crawford and Morgan found the net in a 2–1 home win against Everton, which preceded a further away defeat at Notts County (5–2). Dunlop and McLatchie were on target in a 2–0 home success against Stoke, but successive home defeats against Burnley (1–0) and Newcastle United (3–2), as well as away defeats at Aston Villa (2–0) and Sheffield United (2–0), saw the north-eastern side in a mid-table position at the halfway stage of the campaign.

Sunderland returned to form on the final day of the year with a 1–0 home victory against Preston North End, while the new year began with a further home win against Derby County (1–0), with Morgan on target in both games. However, following successive draws at Liverpool (0–0) and at home to Nottingham Forest (1–1), the three times League champions suffered an embarrassing 6–1 reverse at Bolton Wanderers.

Late January saw the north-eastern side secure a 4–2 victory at Bristol City in the first round of the FA Cup, with Crawford, Leslie, Fulton and Wilson on target for the visitors, which preceded a 1–0 League defeat at West Bromwich Albion. Their interest in the FA Cup ended at Tottenham Hotspur where they suffered a 2–1 defeat. They soon returned to winning ways with successive wins at the Wednesday (1–0) and at home to Wolverhampton Wanderers (3–0), with Raisbeck, Fulton, McLatchie and Farquhar sharing the Sunderland goals.

Further drawn games at Everton (0–0) and at home to Notts County (1–1) were followed by a 1–0 reverse at Stoke, while McLatchie and Farquhar netted a couple of goals apiece in successive wins at Bury (2–1) and at home to Aston Villa (4–2). Their indifferent form continued with defeats at home to Blackburn Rovers (1–0) and away at Burnley (1–0), prior to ending the campaign with victories at Newcastle United (1–0) and at home to Sheffield United (1–0), with McLatchie and Leslie scoring the Sunderland goals. They secured a seventh place League finish, with fifteen wins, six draws and thirteen defeats in their thirty-four League games, while scoring forty-one goals and conceding forty-one.

McAllister had appeared in all thirty-four League games in a most disappointing League campaign, in which Hugh Wilson and Jim Leslie had led the scoring with seven League goals apiece.

BLACKBURN ROVERS

Blackburn Rovers had finished the 1897–98 League campaign in fifteenth position, which was hardly acceptable for a team that had won the FA Cup on five occasions. Despite their poor season, the Lancashire side retained Carter in goal for the 1898–99 season, with Anderson, Booth, Brandon and Albert Houlker in defence, while Briercliffe and Hulse remained in the attack. Campbell, Proudfoot, Wilkie and Killean had moved to pastures new, while Chambers and Crompton, who had made the occasional appearance for the club, became regular members of the defence, together with Haworth, who made 118 League appearances in six seasons with the Rovers. Crompton, a local teenager, eventually made 530 League appearances for Blackburn, as well as captaining the English national team. Newcomers in the attack included Jackson, Hurst, Moreland and Fred Blackburn, who had all played reserve team football during the previous campaign, together with Williams at outside right.

Williams, Jackson and Moreland remained with the club for a little more than a season, Hurst scored seventeen goals in 53 League games, while Fred Blackburn made in excess of 200 appearances for the Lancashire side, as well as winning three England caps.

Rovers opened the season with a 2–1 reverse at Everton, followed by a 1–0 victory at Nottingham Forest, where Jackson scored the only goal of the game. Jackson was again on target the following week in a 4–1 home win against Bolton Wanderers, with Hurst, Hulse and Anderson completing the scoring.

Blackburn then secured a 4–1 home success against West Bromwich Albion on either side of goalless draws at Derby County and at home to Bury, with Jackson (2), Hurst and Moreland on target. Victories at the Wednesday (2–1) and at home to Sunderland (3–2) saw Jackson, Hulse and Moreland once again amongst the scorers, but successive away defeats at Wolverhampton Wanderers (2–1) and Notts County (5–3), as well as at home to Everton (3–1), saw Rovers in a mid-table position by early November.

Rovers soon returned to winning ways with a 4–1 home victory against Stoke, with Moreland (2), Anderson and Hurst on target, which preceded away defeats at Aston Villa (3–1) and Burnley (2–0), while Hulse netted his fifth League goal of the campaign in a one-all draw at Sheffield United.

Early December saw Hulse and Hurst score two goals apiece in a 4–2 home win against Newcastle United, while the halfway stage of the campaign arrived with a one-all draw at Preston North End where Jackson netted his seventh League goal of the season. However, successive defeats at Liverpool (3–1) and at home to Burnley (2–0), as well as a three-all home draw with Nottingham Forest, saw the year end in disappointment.

New Year began with a 6–0 home success against Notts County, with Crompton, Houlker, Hulse, Hurst, Haworth and Anderson finding the net, while Hurst and Jackson were on target in further victories at Bolton Wanderers (2–0) and at home to Derby County (3–0). A 6–2 reverse at West Bromwich Albion ended their splendid run of results.

Then followed a 2–0 defeat at Liverpool in the first round of the FA Cup, while outside left Hurst scored for the sixth successive League game in a 2–0 home success against the Wednesday; however, a 3–2 reverse at Bury continued their indifferent run of results.

Centre half Anderson, now converted to an inside forward, then netted for the third game running in a two-all home draw with Wolverhampton

Wanderers, which preceded a 1–0 victory at Stoke, where Hulse scored the only goal of the game. A goalless home draw with Aston Villa, as well as further wins at home to Sheffield United (2–1) and away at Sunderland (1–0), saw the Lancashire side move up to third place in the League table, with Briercliffe, Blackburn and Hulse sharing the Rovers' goals. However, away defeats at Newcastle United (1–0) and Liverpool (2–0) on either side of a two-all home draw with Preston North End saw Blackburn finish the season in sixth position, with fourteen victories, eight draws and twelve defeats in their thirty-four League games, while scoring sixty goals and conceding fifty-two.

Hulse had appeared in all thirty-four League games, with Booth, Brandon and Crompton missing no more than a couple in Rovers' highest League placing for a number of seasons. Jackson had scored ten goals in twenty-five League appearances, Hulse had found the net on a dozen occasions, and Hurst led the scoring with fourteen League goals.

NOTTS COUNTY

Following four seasons in the Second Division, Notts County had secured promotion to the First Division for the 1897–98 League campaign. The club directors retained the majority of the players for the 1898–99 season, as George Toone continued in goal, with Tom Prescott, George Lewis, Billy Ball and David Calderhead in defence, while John Fraser, Tom Boucher and Walter Bull retained their positions in the attack. Recent signings included Alex Maconnachie from Derby County, as well as Ernest Suter, a local youngster who occasionally stood in for George Toone, while fullback Jack Montgomery arrived from Tottenham Hotspur during the early weeks of the season.

County enjoyed an excellent start to the campaign with an eight-game unbeaten run, which included drawn games at Burnley (1–1) and Liverpool (0–0), as well as at home to Sheffield United (2–2), Nottingham Forest (2–2) and Derby County (2–2). Victories at Newcastle United (2–1), Bolton Wanderers (1–0) and at home to Preston North End (1–0) saw the Nottingham side amongst the front runners for the League leadership. However, a 2–0 reverse at West Bromwich Albion during the final week of October ended their splendid run of results. Then followed successive home wins against Blackburn Rovers (5–3) and Sunderland (5–2) on either side of a one-all draw at the Wednesday. Narrow defeats at Wolverhampton Wanderers (1–0) and at home to Everton (1–0) failed to dent their confidence as they soon returned to winning ways with a 4–1 home success against Bury.

Mid-December saw County secure a one-all draw at Stoke, which preceded an excellent 1–0 home win against fellow championship contenders Aston Villa. The year ended with further home draws against Liverpool (1–1) and Burnley (2–2). However, a 6–0 reverse at Blackburn Rovers in the opening game of the new year saw their heaviest defeat of the season.

Notts then registered their tenth and eleventh drawn games of the campaign at Sheffield United (2–2) and Nottingham Forest (0–0) on either side of a 3–1 home success against Newcastle United. A loss of form during February saw their hopes of the League Championship fade. Following a 4–2 reverse at Derby County, the Nottingham side suffered a 1–0 home defeat against Southampton in the second round of the FA Cup, while further drawn games at home to West Bromwich Albion (0–0) and away at Sunderland (1–1), as well as a 1–0 home success against the struggling Wednesday side, continued their indifferent run of results.

Further defeats at Preston North End (2–0) and at home to Wolverhampton Wanderers (2–0) saw County move down to fourth place in the League table. Then victories at Everton (2–1) and at home to Bolton Wanderers (2–1) saw the Nottingham side in with a chance of a top three finish, but successive away defeats at Bury (2–0) and Aston Villa (6–1) on either side of a 2–0 home success against Stoke saw Notts end the campaign in fifth position, with twelve wins, thirteen draws and nine defeats in their thirty-four League games, while scoring forty-seven goals and conceding fifty-one.

County had fielded an unchanged side for the bulk of the season, hence their excellent League placing. It was due mainly to the fine defensive performances by Tom Prescott and David Calderhead, as well as the goal-scoring exploits of Tom Boucher and Walter Bull.

EVERTON

Everton had enjoyed an excellent 1897–98 season, which had resulted in a fourth place League finish as well as an appearance in the semi-finals of the FA Cup competition. However, the Merseysiders made a number of changes in their line-up for the 1898–99 League campaign as Meecham and Robertson had moved to Southampton, Billy Stewart had joined Bristol City, while Storrier and Divers would shortly sign for Glasgow Celtic.

John Bell and Cameron joined the exodus to Tottenham Hotspur, while John Holt, who had made in excess of 250 appearances for the club, had signed for Reading. Everton had managed to sign Eccles and Owen from Wolverhampton Wanderers, while Molyneux replaced Storrier at fullback. Sam Wolstenholme became a regular member of the half-back line, where he made 160 League appearances as well as gaining an England cap, while Clarke, Kirwan, Gee, Oldham and Proudfoot were recent arrivals in the attack. With the exception of Proudfoot, who had been signed from Blackburn Rovers, the remaining players soon left the Everton club.

While the Merseysiders had made wholesale changes for the new campaign, Muir retained his position in goal, Richard Boyle and Walter Balmer remained in the defence, together with Lawrence Bell and Edgar Chadwick up front, while Jack Taylor spent the season alternating between the left half back and outside right positions.

Everton opened the season with a 2–1 home success against Blackburn Rovers, with Clarke and Proudfoot on target, which preceded a one-all draw at Sheffield United, where Proudfoot again found the net. A further home win against Newcastle United (3–0) continued their excellent start to the campaign, with Clarke, Owen and an own goal securing the points for the Lancashire side. Successive away draws at Preston North End (0–0) and Nottingham Forest (0–0), as well as a 2–1 home defeat against Liverpool, saw Everton in a mid-table position by early October. Then followed an excellent run of results that began with a 1–0 home win against Bolton Wanderers, with Oldham scoring the only goal of the game. Oldham netted a further brace of goals in a five-all draw at Derby County, with Owen (2) and Bell completing the scoring.

Everton's unbeaten run continued with victories at home to West Bromwich Albion (1–0) and away at Blackburn Rovers (3–1), with Oldham on target in both games. Bell and Kirwan found the net in a 2–0 home win against the Wednesday, but successive away defeats at West Bromwich Albion (3–0) and Sunderland (2–1) ended the Merseysiders' splendid run of results.

Late November saw a return to winning ways with a 2–1 home success against Wolverhampton Wanderers, with Bell and Kirwan netting the Everton goals, which preceded a 1–0 home defeat against Bury. Proudfoot, Chadwick and Oldham were on target in victories at Notts County (1–0) and at home to Stoke (2–0) before a 3–0 reverse at Aston Villa continued their indifferent away form.

Further home wins against Burnley (4–0) and Sheffield United (1–0) saw Everton end the year in third position in the League table, with Proudfoot scoring in both victories, while the new year began with a 3–1 home defeat against Nottingham Forest, but a two-all draw at Newcastle United secured a welcome away point, with Proudfoot netting a brace of goals.

Crompton and Kirwan then found the net in a 2–0 home success against Preston North End, which preceded a 2–0 reverse at Liverpool, while Chadwick, Proudfoot and Taylor were on target in a 3–1 home win against Jarrow in the first round of the FA Cup, but a 1–0 home defeat against Nottingham Forest in the second round ended their interest in the competition.

On their return to League action, the Merseysiders secured successive away victories at Bolton Wanderers (4–2) and the Wednesday (2–1), with Oldham on target in both games. However, following a goalless home draw with Sunderland, the Lancashire side suffered away defeats at Bury (3–1) and Stoke (2–1), as well as at home to Notts County (2–1) and Derby County (2–1), to end their hopes of securing the League Championship.

Mid-April saw Everton play successive draws at home to Aston Villa (1–1) and away at Burnley (0–0), while the campaign ended with a 2–1 victory at Wolverhampton Wanderers, where Schofield and Toman found the net to secure a fourth place League finish for the second season running, with fifteen wins, eight draws and eleven defeats in their thirty-four League games, while scoring forty-eight goals and conceding forty-one.

Jack Taylor and Richard Boyle had appeared in all thirty-four League games, while Muir and Molyneux had missed only one in a further successful season for the Merseysiders. Oldham had netted eleven goals in nineteen League appearances, with Proudfoot leading the scoring with a dozen League goals.

BURNLEY

Burnley had ended the 1897–98 League campaign as Second Division Champions, thus earning the right to play First Division football during the 1898–99 season. The team showed few changes from their title winning side as Jack Hillman continued in goal, with Reynolds, McLintock, Barron, Place (Senior) and Livingstone in defence, while McInnes, Robertson, Bowes, Place (Junior), Tom Morrison, Wilf Toman and Jimmy Ross competed for the forward positions. However, Toman soon moved to Everton, while Ross joined Manchester City during the latter stages of the season.

Burnley opened the season with a one-all home draw with Notts County, followed by a 3–1 home success against Preston North End prior to suffering successive defeats at Stoke (4–1) and at home to Aston Villa (4–2). An excellent run of results that included home victories against Newcastle United (2–1), Liverpool (2–1), Bolton Wanderers (2–0) and away at Nottingham Forest (1–0), as well as away draws at Bury (1–1), Sheffield United (1–1) and Preston North End (1–1), saw the Lancashire side near the top of the League table by early November. Then followed a 2–1 reverse at Derby County, but a one-all draw at West Bromwich Albion saw a return to form, while further home victories against Blackburn Rovers (2–0), Wednesday (5–0) and Wolverhampton Wanderers (4–2), as well as a 1–0 win at Sunderland, saw Burnley move into second place in the League table at the halfway stage of the campaign.

Christmas Eve saw Burnley suffer a 4–0 defeat at Everton, which preceded a 2–0 success at Blackburn Rovers, while the year ended with a two-all draw at Notts County. However, new year defeats at Bolton Wanderers (2–0) and Aston Villa (4–0) saw the Lancashire side move a couple of places down the League table.

Following a 2–1 home win against Bury, the Burnley side suffered away defeats at Newcastle United (4–1) and Liverpool (2–0), while early March saw a return to winning ways with home victories against Derby County (2–1) and Sheffield United (1–0), as well as a 1–0 success at West Bromwich Albion. An indifferent run of results during the final weeks of the season saw Burnley's hopes of the League title fade.

Burnley's indifferent form saw away defeats at Wolverhampton Wanderers (4–0) and the Wednesday (1–0), as well as home draws against Nottingham Forest (1–1), Stoke (1–1) and Everton (0–0). The campaign ended with a 1–0 home win against Sunderland as the Lancashire side finished in third position with fifteen victories, nine draws and ten defeats in their thirty-four League games, while scoring forty-five goals and conceding forty-seven.

While Burnley had suffered an FA Cup defeat at the first hurdle, their excellent League performances had given much encouragement to their supporters. However, their success would be short-lived as the struggle to avoid relegation lay ahead.

LIVERPOOL

Liverpool had enjoyed success in both the League and FA Cup during the two previous seasons and they had established themselves as one of the leading teams in England. However, the Merseysiders were ambitious for further success during the 1898–99 campaign, which saw the arrival of Tom Watson as manager–secretary, following a successful period with Sunderland.

Liverpool made a number of changes in their line-up for the 1898–99 season. Cunliffe, Henderson, McQueen and Malcolm McVean continued in defence, with George Allen and Harry Bradshaw up front, while local signing Willie Perkins became first choice goalkeeper. A number of new arrivals to the club during the season confirmed the Merseysiders' intentions to succeed.

Rab Howell (Sheffield United) and Billy Dunlop (Sunderland) soon signed for the club, while Jack Cox, who eventually appeared for the English national team, made the outside left position his own. The most notable new signing was Alex Raisbeck from Stoke, who made 312 League appearances in ten seasons with the club, as well as winning eight caps for Scotland.

The Lancashire side opened the season with a 4–0 home win against the Wednesday, followed by a 1–0 reverse at Sunderland, while victories at home to Wolverhampton Wanderers (1–0) and away at Everton (2–1) continued their fine start to the campaign. However, a goalless home draw with Notts County, together with defeats at Stoke (2–1), Burnley (2–1) and at home to Aston Villa (3–0), saw Liverpool in the bottom half of the League table by October's end.

Liverpool's indifferent run of results continued during November with home wins against Sheffield United (2–1) and Preston North End (3–1), as well as away defeats at Newcastle United (3–0) and Bury (3–0), while a 3–0 success at Nottingham Forest saw the Merseysiders move up to seventh place in the League table.

Early December saw Liverpool maintain their excellent home record with a 2–0 victory against Bolton Wanderers, which preceded a 1–0 reverse at Derby County, as well as a two-all home draw with West Bromwich Albion, while the halfway stage of the campaign arrived with a 3–1 success at Blackburn Rovers on Christmas Eve. Then followed further away wins at West Bromwich Albion (1–0) and the Wednesday (3–0) on either side of a one-all draw at Notts County as the year ended on a high note. The new year began with a 2–0 victory at Sheffield United, who, surprisingly, were struggling near the foot of the League table.

Early January saw the Merseysiders play successive draws at home to Sunderland (0–0) and away at Wolverhampton Wanderers (0–0), while home wins against Everton (2–0), Stoke (1–0) and Burnley (2–0), as well as a 2–1 success at Preston North End, saw Liverpool amongst the favourites to secure the League Championship.

During their unbeaten run in the League, the Lancashire side had enjoyed an excellent FA Cup run, which included victories against Newcastle United (3–1) and West Bromwich Albion (2–0), leading to a semi-final appearance against Sheffield United, whom they had twice defeated in the League.

Following a two-all draw at Nottingham, Liverpool secured a two-goal lead in the replay at Bolton, only for the Sheffield side to level the scores. However, the Merseysiders soon restored their two-goal advantage when Fred Priest netted two late goals for United to earn a second replay at the Fallowfield Ground.

Prior to the semi-final replay, Liverpool suffered a rare home defeat against Nottingham Forest (1–0), while the cup game ended in a farce, due mainly to the late arrival of the referee, as well as the fading light, which led to the referee abandoning the game, with Liverpool leading through a George Allen goal. However, in the third replay at Derby, the Lancashire side suffered a 1–0 defeat with Fred Priest scoring the only goal of the game two minutes from time to end the Merseysiders' interest in the competition.

On their return to League action, the Liverpool side suffered a 2–1 reverse at Bolton Wanderers, followed by successive home wins against Newcastle United (3–2), Derby County (4–0), Bury (1–0) and Blackburn Rovers (2–0), leaving Liverpool at the head of the League table. One game remained at Aston Villa, who, like Liverpool, had secured forty-three points from thirty-three games, which meant that the League title would be decided at Villa Park.

Liverpool had few answers to the Villa attack as John Devey and Fred Wheldon netted a brace of goals apiece in a 5–0 victory for the Midlanders, who had effectively snatched the League title from the Lancashire side at the final hurdle. However, it had been an excellent season for Liverpool, who had been close to achieving the FA Cup and League double.

Bradshaw, Cox and Allen had regularly found the net during the season, while Alex Raisbeck had excelled at the heart of a defence that had conceded only thirty-three goals, the lowest in the Football League.

ASTON VILLA

Aston Villa had secured three League titles as well as twice winning the FA Cup during the five previous seasons. However, an indifferent 1897–98 season had resulted in a sixth place League finish, as well as a first round FA Cup defeat.

Few changes were made in the Villa line-up for the 1898–99 League campaign. Billy George continued in goal, with Howard Spencer, Albert Evans, Tom Bowman, James Cowan and James Crabtree in defence, while Charlie Athersmith, John Devey, Jack Sharp, Fred Wheldon, John Cowan and Steve Smith remained in the attack.

Bob Chatt had returned to the north-east, where he had been reinstated as an amateur player with Stockton, with whom he would win an FA Amateur Cup winners' medal. The most notable newcomers in the villa team were forwards George Johnson and Billy Garraty, who had made the occasional appearance during the previous campaign.

Johnson, who had arrived from the Walsall area as cover for John Devey, netted thirty-eight goals in ninety-nine League appearances, while Garraty spent ten seasons with the club, in which he scored ninety-six goals in 223 League games as well as appearing in the English national team.

Villa opened the campaign with a 3–1 home win against Stoke, with Athersmith, Devey and Gaudie on target, which preceded a 2–1 reverse at Bury, while Athersmith, Johnson, Wheldon and Smith found the net in a 4–2 victory at Burnley. John Devey then netted both Villa goals in successive draws at home to Sheffield United (1–1) and away at Newcastle United (1–1), which were followed by a 4–2 home success against Preston North End, with Devey (2), Johnson and James Cowan on target in Charlie Athersmith's 200th League appearance for the club. Further home wins against Nottingham Forest (3–0) and Bolton Wanderers (2–1), as well as a 3–0 victory at Liverpool, saw John Devey find the net in all three wins.

Devey's tenth and eleventh League goals of the season arrived in a 7–1 home win against Derby County, with Johnson (2), Wheldon (2) and John Cowan completing the scoring, which preceded a 1–0 victory at West Bromwich Albion, where George Johnson netted the only goal of the game. Wheldon (2) and Devey then found the net in a 3–1 home success against Blackburn Rovers, while November's end saw the Midlands side play a League game at the Wednesday, where they found themselves 3–1 down with ten minutes remaining. Due to the failing weather conditions, the referee was forced to abandon the game, which resulted in the Football League Committee inviting the Villa team to return to Sheffield during the following March to complete the remaining ten minutes of play.

Early December saw the Midlanders return to winning ways with a 2–0 home success against Sunderland, with Jack Sharp netting a brace of goals, which preceded James Crabtree's opening goal of the season in a one-all home draw with Wolverhampton Wanderers in John Devey's 200th League game for Villa. Wheldon, Devey and Johnson were subsequently on target in a 3–0 home victory against Everton.

Then followed an indifferent run of results during the final week of the year with successive away defeats at Notts County (1–0) and Stoke (3–0) on either side of a 1–0 home win against Newcastle United, with Athersmith scoring the only goal of the game. New year home victories against Bury (3–2) and Burnley (4–0), as well as a 3–1 success at Sheffield United, saw Villa at the head of the League table by January's end, with Wheldon, Devey and John Cowan netting a couple of goals apiece for the Midlanders.

Villa then suffered a 2–1 reverse at Nottingham Forest in the first round of the FA Cup, which preceded successive away defeats at Preston North End (2–0) and Nottingham Forest (1–0), while their indifferent form continued with a one-all draw at Derby County, with Johnson netting for the visitors.

Mid-March saw the Villa team return to Sheffield to complete the remaining ten minutes of their fixture with the Wednesday, which eventually resulted in a 4–1 defeat. However, following a goalless draw at Blackburn Rovers, Villa inflicted a 3–1 defeat on the Wednesday in the return game in Birmingham, with Wheldon, Garraty and Johnson on target.

Further defeats at Sunderland (4–2) and Wolverhampton Wanderers (4–0), as well as away draws at Everton (1–1) and Bolton Wanderers (0–0), saw Villa move down to second place in the League table, while goals by Devey (3), Garraty (2) and Wheldon secured a 6–1 home success against Notts County. The top of the League table, as the season reached its final stages, is shown in Table XXVII.

Table XXVII: *The last stages of the 1898–99 season for Aston Villa and Liverpool*

	Played	Won	Lost	Drawn	For	Against	Points
Liverpool	33	19	9	5	49	28	43
Aston Villa	32	17	8	7	64	39	41

Within forty-eight hours, the Villa side were equal on points with Liverpool, following a 7–1 home success against West Bromwich Albion, with Garraty (3), Wheldon (2), Bowman and James Cowan on target. This meant that the 1898–99 League championship would be decided when Liverpool visited Villa Park on the final day of the season.

Villa totally dominated the Merseysiders in the all important game at Villa Park as goals by Devey (2), Wheldon (2) and Crabtree secured a 5–0 half-time lead. Despite a spirited performance during the second period, Liverpool were unable to reduce the arrears, and Villa gained their fourth League championship of the 1890s, thus reaffirming their position as the finest team in England.

Tom Bowman had appeared in all thirty-four League games for Villa, while James Cowan and Fred Wheldon had missed only one in an excellent season. Jack Sharp had scored four goals in eight League appearances; Billy Garraty had netted six goals in nine games; George Johnson had found the net on nine occasions; Fred Wheldon had ended the season with sixteen League goals; while John Devey had once again led the scoring with twenty-one goals in thirty League appearances.

Glossop Are Promoted

Eight teams were involved in the race for the Second Division Championship during the 1898–99 season, which included Newton Heath and Small Heath, as well as the ambitious New Brighton Tower Club.

SMALL HEATH

Small Heath, who had previously played First Division football during the 1895–96 League campaign, were determined to join neighbours Aston Villa in the top division, which resulted in few changes in their line-up for the new season. Future England internationals Alec Leake and Walter Abbott remained in the team, together with Bob McRoberts, a recent signing from Gainsborough Trinity, who made 173 League appearances in seven seasons with the Midlands club.

Following many excellent performances during the season, which included home wins against Gainsborough (6–1), Loughborough (6–0), Luton Town (9–0) and Darwen (8–0), the Small Heath side made an early challenge for the League title. Walter Abbott accumulated thirty-four League goals, with hat-tricks against Loughborough, Woolwich Arsenal and Gainsborough, as well as five goals against Darwen. However, Small Heath's indifferent away form had resulted in only three victories in seventeen games, and they finished the campaign in eighth place.

NEWTON HEATH

Newton Heath had previously played in the First Division during the 1893–94 season. However, they had regularly been involved in the race for the end-of-season play-off positions. Cassidy and Boyd, who had netted thirty-six League goals between them during the 1897–98 campaign, were once again amongst the goals during the 1898–99 season. Cassidy scored nineteen goals, while Boyd netted five in a dozen appearances, and the Manchester side suffered only one defeat on home soil.

Excellent home wins against Burton (6–0), Grimsby (7–2) and Darwen (10–0), saw Newton Heath amongst the League leaders. However, five defeats at the turn of the year ended their hopes of promotion as they finished in fourth position, three points adrift from the runners-up spot.

WOOLWICH ARSENAL

Woolwich Arsenal had enjoyed an excellent 1898–99 League campaign, which saw only one defeat on home soil, while achieving comprehensive victories against Gainsborough (5–1), Newton Heath (5–1), Luton Town (6–2), Blackpool (6–0) and Darwen (6–0). However, their indifferent away form saw four wins in seventeen League games, resulting in a seventh place League finish.

WALSALL

Walsall ended the season in sixth position, due mainly to their fine home record, which included victories against Luton Town (6–0), Blackpool (6–0), Gainsborough (6–1), Burton Swifts (7–1), Loughborough (7–0) and Darwen

(10–0). However, only three wins on their travels had cost them the opportunity of First Division football during the following season.

NEW BRIGHTON

New Brighton had signed a number of experienced players prior to the 1898–99 season in the hope of achieving promotion to the First Division, but, while securing eighteen victories in the League, which included six home wins by four goals or more, the New Brighton side ended the season in fifth place.

LEICESTER FOSSE

Leicester Fosse had been expected to struggle during the 1898–99 season, especially with the increase of the Second Division from sixteen to eighteen teams, but the East Midlands side remained unbeaten at home during the season, which included four-goal victories against Blackpool, Darwen, Glossop North End and New Brighton, as well as away wins at Barnsley (4–3) and Luton Town (6–1), leaving the Leicester team in third position, only one point away from a promotion place.

GLOSSOP NORTH END

Glossop North End, a small town in east Lancashire, had surprisingly gained election to the Second Division in time for the 1898–99 season just to make up the numbers, or so it seemed. However, they performed magnificently throughout, losing only eight of their thirty-four League fixtures, which included home wins against Burton (5–0), Darwen (5–0), Luton Town (5–0), Gainsborough (5–1) and New Brighton (5–0), as well as a 2–0 success at Manchester City.

Glossop eventually ended the season as runners-up to Manchester City, which meant First Division football for the following season, a situation beyond their wildest dreams.

MANCHESTER CITY

Manchester City had finished the three previous seasons near the top of the Second Division, which resulted in few changes in their line-up for the 1898–99 League campaign. Charlie Williams continued in goal, with Read, Ray, Moffatt, Holmes and William Smith in defence, while Fred Williams, Dougal, Walter Smith, Gillespie and Billy Meredith remained in the attack in a season that saw the arrival of Welsh international fullback David Jones from Bolton Wanderers.

City opened the season with a 7–2 home success against Grimsby Town, followed by an indifferent run of results. However, an excellent home record, which included a 10–0 victory against Darwen, saw the Manchester side crowned as Second Division Champions by a margin of six points, following only five defeats in thirty-four League games, while scoring ninety-two goals, the highest in the Football League.

Bobby Moffatt and William Smith had appeared in all thirty-four League games, while Charlie Williams and Billy Meredith had missed only one in an excellent campaign. Billy Gillespie had netted seventeen goals in thirty League appearances, while Billy Meredith had led the scoring with twenty-nine goals, including four hat-tricks, an amazing feat for a winger.

DARWEN

Stranded at the foot of the table were the once proud Darwen team, who had suffered humiliating defeats at Woolwich Arsenal (6–0), Barnsley (6–0), Blackpool (6–0), New Brighton (7–0), Small Heath (8–0), Luton Town (8–1), Grimsby Town (9–2), Newton Heath (9–0), Walsall (10–0), Loughborough (10–0) and Manchester City (10–0). They failed to register an away victory, while conceding 109 goals on their travels.

Darwen conceded a total of 141 goals during the season, while registering only two home victories against Leicester Fosse (3–0) and Luton Town (4–1), which left them nine points adrift at the bottom of the League, resulting in their relegation from the Football League together with the unfortunate Blackpool team, who had finished in sixteenth position. As a result of the relegation of Blackpool and Darwen, Chesterfield and Middlesbrough were elected into the Second Division.

The final League tables at the close of the 1898–99 season were as in Tables XXVIII and XXIX.

Table XXVIII: *First Division Football League results for the 1898–99 season*

	P	W	D	L	F	A	PTS
1. Aston Villa	34	19	7	8	76	40	45
2. Liverpool	34	19	5	10	49	33	43
3. Burnley	34	15	9	10	45	47	39
4. Everton	34	15	8	11	48	41	38
5. Notts County	34	12	13	9	47	51	37
6. Blackburn Rovers	34	14	8	12	60	52	36
7. Sunderland	34	15	6	13	41	41	36
8. Wolverhampton Wndrs	34	14	7	13	54	48	35
9. Derby County	34	12	11	11	62	57	35
10. Bury	34	14	7	13	48	49	35
11. Nottingham Forest	34	11	11	12	42	42	33
12. Stoke	34	13	7	14	47	52	33
13. Newcastle United	34	11	8	15	49	48	30
14. West Bromwich Albion	34	12	6	16	42	57	30
15. Preston North End	34	10	9	15	44	47	29
16. Sheffield United	34	9	11	14	45	51	29
17. Bolton Wanderers	34	9	7	18	37	51	25
18. Sheffield Wednesday	34	8	8	18	32	61	24

Table XXIX: *Second Division Football League results for the 1898–99 season*

	P	W	D	L	F	A	PTS
1. Manchester City	34	23	6	5	92	35	52
2. Glossop NE	34	20	6	8	76	38	46
3. Leicester Fosse	34	18	9	7	64	42	45
4. Newton Heath	34	19	5	10	67	43	43
5. New Brighton	34	18	7	9	71	52	43
6. Walsall	34	15	12	7	79	36	42
7. Woolwich Arsenal	34	18	5	11	72	41	41
8. Small Heath	34	17	7	10	85	50	41
9. Burslem Port Vale	34	17	5	12	56	34	39
10. Grimsby	34	15	5	14	71	60	35
11. Barnsley	34	12	7	15	52	56	31
12. Lincoln	34	12	7	15	51	56	31
13. Burton Swifts	34	10	8	16	51	70	28
14. Gainsborough	34	10	5	19	56	72	25
15. Luton	34	10	3	21	51	95	23
16. Blackpool	34	8	4	22	49	90	20
17. Loughborough	34	6	6	22	38	92	18
18. Darwen	34	2	5	27	22	141	9

Derby County Secure a Fourth Successive Semi-Final Appearance

At the second round stage of the 1898–99 FA Cup competition, all remaining teams were members of the Football League, with the exception of Southampton and Tottenham Hotspur, who both progressed to the quarter-finals at the expense of First Division teams, with Southampton securing a 1–0 victory at Notts County, while Tottenham accounted for Sunderland by the odd goal in three.

William Richards netted a brace of goals for West Bromwich Albion in a 2–1 home win against Bury, Fred Forman scored the only goal of the game as Nottingham Forest won 1–0 at Everton, while Bradshaw and Allen were amongst the scorers for Liverpool in a 3–1 home victory against Newcastle United.

Stoke progressed to the quarter-finals with a 2–1 success against Small Heath following a two-all draw. Macdonald and Allen were on target for Derby County in a 2–1 home win against Wolverhampton Wanderers, while Ernest Needham netted a brace of goals as Sheffield United defeated Preston North End by two goals to one in a replayed tie.

Tottenham Hotspur and Southampton both suffered defeats in the quarter-finals, with Willie Maxwell leading Stoke to an excellent 4–1 home success against Tottenham, while Macdonald and Steve Bloomer found the net for Derby County in a 2–1 victory at Southampton.

Liverpool, who were appearing in their third successive quarter-final, secured a 2–1 win at West Bromwich Albion, while Sheffield United completed the semi-final line-up with a 1–0 victory at Nottingham Forest, with Fred Priest scoring the only goal of the game.

Stoke were then drawn against Derby County in a semi-final tie at the Molineux Ground, Wolverhampton, where they were a little unfortunate to come up against Steve Bloomer at his best, as the England forward netted all three goals in a 3–1 success as Derby secured a second successive FA Cup Final appearance. The semi-final tie in Nottingham between Sheffield United and Liverpool proved to be a long drawn-out affair, which took four games to decide a winner.

With the original tie ending in a two-all draw, the two teams travelled to Bolton for the replay, which saw Liverpool dominate the early proceedings to secure a 2–0 lead. However, with a little over twenty minutes remaining, goals by Billy Beer and Walter Bennett saw United on level terms.

Then followed a little good fortune for the Merseysiders, as a save from Willie Foulke rebounded off fullback Boyle into his own net, while they went further ahead when Jack Cox followed up a penalty saved by Foulke to restore their two-goal advantage. However, United reduced the arrears with minutes remaining as Fred Priest scored from a speculative shot from the edge of the area, while Priest scored a second goal when the Liverpool defence failed to clear the ball to secure a second replay for the following Monday at the Fallowfield Ground, Manchester.

Owing to the late arrival of the referee, the second replay was a little late commencing, which saw Liverpool secure an early lead through an opportunist goal by Allen. However, with the light worsening, as well as the crowd encroaching onto the field of play, the referee was forced to abandon the game, with the third replay ordered to take place at Derby.

As in the three previous encounters, the teams were evenly matched, but, following a period of hard tackling by the Liverpool team, Fred Priest netted a late goal for United to earn a 1–0 victory, thus securing their first FA Cup Final appearance, which was to take place at Crystal Palace on 15 April against Derby County.

A Humiliating Defeat for the Irish

The 1899 international games all took place on English soil, which began with the visit of the Irish national team to Roker Park with a side that included Archie Goodall of Derby County at the heart of their defence. The English selected an attacking side with four new caps. Jack Hillman, the Burnley goalkeeper, and Sunderland fullback, Philip Bach, made single international appearances.

Billy Williams (West Bromwich Albion), Frank Forman (Nottingham Forest), James Crabtree (Aston Villa) and Ernest Needham (Sheffield United) completed the defensive line-up, while Charlie Athersmith (Aston Villa), Steve Bloomer (Derby County) and G O Smith (Corinthians) retained their places in the attack, together with newcomers Jimmy Settle (Bury) and Fred Forman (Nottingham Forest), the brother of Frank. Settle, who soon moved to Everton, scored on six occasions in six appearances for his country, while Fred Forman scored three goals in as many games.

England totally dominated a weakened Irish team, as their forwards scored at will, with G O Smith (4), Settle (3), Bloomer (2), Fred Forman (2), Athersmith and Frank Forman on target in a 13–2 victory, thus equalling the 13–0 success against Ireland in 1882.

A Brace of Goals for Steve Bloomer

Following their excellent display against Ireland, the England selectors made two changes for the game against Wales at Bristol. John Robinson returned in goal, while Harry Thickett (Sheffield United) replaced Philip Bach at fullback.

While the Welsh defence performed magnificently, they had little answer to Steve Bloomer, who netted a brace of goals in a 4–0 victory, with Fred Forman and Ernest Needham completing the scoring for the home team.

A Fortunate Victory Against the Scots

A week before the FA Cup Final, the Scottish national team arrived in Birmingham, hoping to avenge the 3–1 defeat of the previous season, with England making one change from the win in Bristol, as Rab Howell, now of Liverpool, replaced Billy Williams in the defence.

Scotland more than held their own against the English. However, the home side managed a 2–1 success, with Jimmy Settle and G O Smith on target to secure a second successive international championship for England.

A Football League Eleven Score Five in Belfast

Early November saw a Football League Eleven visit Grosvenor Park, Belfast, to play against an Irish League Eleven, who were hoping to improve on their 8–1 defeat in Manchester during the previous campaign.

The visitors selected an experienced defensive line-up, which included John Sutcliffe (Bolton Wanderers) in goal, together with James Crabtree (Aston Villa) and Billy Williams (West Bromwich Albion) at fullback, while Thomas Booth (Blackburn Rovers), Tom Crawshaw (Wednesday) and Ernest Needham (Sheffield United) formed a splendid half-back line. Steve Bloomer (Derby County) and Joseph Turner (Stoke) were included up front, together with newcomers Williams (Blackburn Rovers), Farrell (Stoke) and Fletcher

(Notts County), for a game which the English won with ease as Farrell (2), Bloomer, Fletcher and Needham found the net in a 5–1 victory.

An All Fools' Day Victory in Glasgow

An English League Eleven travelled to Celtic Park for an All Fools' Day inter-League fixture against the Scots, with Crawshaw, Crabtree, Bloomer and Turner retained from the victory in Belfast, and Jack Hillman (Burnley) taking over the goalkeeping duties.

Prescott (Notts County) and Eccles (Stoke) were selected at fullback, while Athersmith (Aston Villa), Settle (Bury), Toman (Burnley) and Frank Forman (Nottingham Forest) completed the English line-up. They secured a 4–1 victory, with Athersmith (2), Bloomer and Settle scoring for the visitors.

Sheffield United Win the FA Cup

A crowd in excess of 70,000 passed through the turnstiles at Crystal Palace for the 1899 FA Cup Final between Derby County and Sheffield United, which guaranteed a new name on the trophy.

United, who had surprisingly struggled to maintain their First Division status during the season, had played nine FA Cup ties on their way to the final. However, they were able to field their strongest team, which saw Willie Foulke in goal, with Thickett, Boyle, Johnson, Morren and Needham in defence, while Bennett, Beer, Hedley, Almond and Priest formed the attack. Derby County, on the other hand, included five members of their 1898 Cup final side, but it had been suggested that the County Selection Committee had chosen a far too inexperienced team for such an important occasion. John Fryer took his place in goal, with Methven, Staley, Cox, Paterson and May in defence, while Arkesden, Boag, Bloomer, Macdonald and Allen were chosen up front. Surprisingly, neither John or Archie Goodall was included in the Derby line-up.

County had the better of the opening half as Boag and Macdonald tested the United fullbacks, which resulted in the latter hitting a post. Steve Bloomer missed a couple of chances when it seemed easier to score, but the East Midlands side eventually secured the lead when John Boag steered a shot past the advancing Foulke to end the half one goal to the good.

During the early stages of the second half, John May, the Derby defender, sustained a serious leg injury, which resulted in him spending the remainder of the game as a passenger on the left wing. His team attempted to hold on to their one-goal lead, but their advantage was short-lived as Walter Bennett headed home an Ernest Needham cross to level the scores.

United, magnificently led by Needham, began to exert further pressure on the Derby defence, which led to Billy Beer, John Almond and Fred Priest scoring late goals to secure a 4–1 victory for the Sheffield side, who had now joined Preston North End and Aston Villa as one of only three teams to win both the League Championship and FA Cup.

John Fryer and John Cox had been the pick of the Derby team, while Ernest Needham, who had stifled the goal-scoring chances of Steve Bloomer, had been by far the finest player on view.

United Return to League Action

A week after their FA Cup success, the Sheffield side suffered a 1–0 defeat in a League encounter at Derby, while the campaign ended with a further defeat at Sunderland (1–0). This saw United in sixteenth position, with nine victories, eleven draws and fourteen defeats in their thirty-four League games, while scoring forty-five goals and conceding fifty-one.

Needham and Bennett had ended the season with six League goals apiece, Field had found the net on seven occasions, while George Hedley had led the scoring with nine goals in a most disappointing League campaign.

Steve Bloomer Once Again Leads the Derby Scoring

On their return to League action, the disappointed Derby team put the FA Cup Final defeat behind them by ending the season with successive home wins against Nottingham Forest (2–0) and Sheffield United (1–0), with Steve Bloomer scoring all of the County goals. The East Midlands side finished the campaign in ninth position, with twelve victories, eleven draws and eleven defeats in their thirty-four League games, while scoring sixty-two goals and conceding fifty-seven.

Jimmy Methven, John Cox, John May and Jonathon Staley had missed less than a handful of games, while Steve Bloomer had easily led the scoring with twenty-four goals in twenty-eight League appearances in a disappointing League campaign.

Stockton Win the FA Amateur Cup

Stockton, who had suffered a 4–1 defeat against the Old Carthusians in the final of the FA Amateur Cup two years earlier, secured the trophy with a 1–0 victory against Harwich and Parkeston.

The Players' Needs Are Questioned

Towards the close of the 1898–99 season, a number of players convened a meeting to discuss the possibility of forming a union, with the intention of gaining a little more financial security for a profession that lasted a little more than a decade.

Charles Clegg, the chairman of the Football Association, who had opposed professionalism in 1885, felt that longer contracts should be offered to players, as well as making transfer fees a maximum of ten pounds, rather than the inflated fees paid by the wealthier clubs. The Football League Committee, on the other hand, felt that little could be achieved by stopping the wealthier clubs paying the 'going rate' for a player, while decisions to retain or release a player were entirely their own business.

Both the Football Association and Football League Committees had had many differing points of view since the formation of the League, a situation that would continue for many years to come.

Chapter XXV

ASTON VILLA RETAIN THE LEAGUE CHAMPIONSHIP – 1899–1900

ASTON VILLA RETAIN THE LEAGUE CHAMPIONSHIP
GLOSSOP STRUGGLE IN THE FIRST DIVISION
PRESTON NARROWLY AVOID RELEGATION
WEDNESDAY AND BOLTON WANDERERS MAKE A SWIFT RETURN TO THE FIRST
DIVISION
SOUTHAMPTON SECURE A PLACE IN THE FA CUP FINAL
BURY'S FA CUP TRIUMPH
ENGLAND ARE WELL BEATEN IN GLASGOW AND ARE HELD BY THE WELSH

The Century Reaches its End

As the century headed towards its close, the gap between the amateur and professional player had widened even further as the Football League continued to go from strength to strength. It was now apparent that clubs outside the League system, especially those in the Southern League, were more than capable of competing against League teams, as Southampton, Millwall Athletic and Tottenham Hotspur had proved.

ARDWICK, THE PRECURSOR OF MANCHESTER CITY

Following a number of valiant efforts to secure a place in the First Division, the Manchester City team had achieved their ambition in time for the 1899–1900 League campaign. City had begun life in 1880 as St Mark's of West Gorton, changing to West Gorton in 1881, then to Gorton in 1884 and finally to Ardwick in 1887.

Friendly games were played against local teams at various venues, which included Pink Bank Lane, Clemington Park, Kirkmanshulme Cricket Club, Reddish Lane and Clowes Street, prior to moving to a piece of waste ground adjacent to the Galloway's Engineering Works, where they remained for nearly forty years.

Jack Hodgetts became Ardwick's first professional player during the 1887 season. As the team became a force in the area, it resulted in them joining the Football Alliance in 1891, where they finished in twelfth position, with only six victories in twenty-two League games. However, excellent results in friendly games against West Bromwich Albion (4–2), Preston North End (2–2), Renton (5–1), Notts County (3–1) and Stoke (5–1) saw the Ardwick team pleased with their season's work.

A comprehensive 4–1 victory against Bolton Wanderers saw them retain the Manchester Senior Cup, which had been won during the previous season against Newton Heath, however, their Manchester neighbours soon avenged the defeat by inflicting a 5–1 defeat on Ardwick in the first qualifying round of the 1891–92 FA Cup competition.

Despite Ardwick's struggle in the Football Alliance, the Manchester side were invited to join the newly formed Second Division prior to the 1892–93 season, which led club secretary, Lawrence Furniss, who served the club in various capacities for nearly half a century, to travel many miles in an attempt to strengthen the team in time for their opening League encounter. Davie Weir, the Bolton Wanderers and England winger, was the most notable newcomer in the side.

Ardwick performed well during their first League campaign, which began with four successive victories against Bootle (7–0), Northwich Victoria (3–0), Burslem Port Vale (2–0) and Walsall Town Swifts (4–2). However, eight defeats in their final ten League games saw the Manchester team settle for a fifth place League finish, with Davie Weir leading the scoring with eight goals in fourteen League appearances.

The 1893–94 season saw Ardwick in turmoil on and off the pitch, which eventually forced the club into bankruptcy. The season saw only eight victories in twenty-eight League games, including an embarrassing 10–2 reverse at Small Heath, and Ardwick resigned from the League. Joshua Parlby, who had recently been appointed club secretary, managed to secure local financial support to form Manchester City Football Club, who were allowed by the Football League Committee to replace Ardwick in the Second Division.

Manchester City Are Formed

With Ardwick now extinct, the newly formed Manchester City club retained few of their players for the 1894–95 season. It saw a number of new arrivals, including goalkeeper Charlie Williams from Woolwich Arsenal, as well as outside right Billy Meredith, who had played for Chirk in the Welsh League prior to making his Football League debut with Northwich Victoria. Williams made 221 League appearances for City, as well as representing the English League Eleven, while Meredith scored 145 goals in 338 League games during his first period with the club. However, following a period of suspension, due to an illegal payment and bribery scandal, Meredith signed for Newton Heath (Manchester United), with whom he won both FA Cup and League Championship Winners' medals, prior to returning to City, which led to an FA Cup semi-final appearance while in his fiftieth year.

Meredith, who made forty-eight appearances for the Welsh national team, above all had the needs of his fellow professional close to his heart, which saw him as one of the leading lights in the struggle to form a players' union.

The newly formed Manchester team tended to struggle during the opening weeks of the 1894–95 season, which saw four victories in fourteen League games, including five goal defeats against Newcastle United, Grimsby Town and Newton Heath, as well as an embarrassing 8–0 reverse at Bolton Wanderers. However, an excellent second half of the campaign resulted in nine wins for City, including home victories against Newcastle United (4–0), Notts County (7–1) and Lincoln City (11–3). The Lancashire side ended the season in ninth position, with Rowan, Finnerhan, Sharples and Meredith, all reaching double figures on the goal-scoring front.

City continued to go from strength to strength during the 1895–96 League campaign, which saw them suffer only five defeats in thirty League games, while remaining unbeaten on home soil. They ended the season as runners-up to Liverpool to secure a place in the end-of-season test match games.

Finnerhan and Morris had finished the campaign with nine League goals apiece, Rowan had found the net on eleven occasions, while Meredith had led the scoring with a dozen goals in an excellent season. City had suffered a 2–1 defeat against Bury in the final of the Manchester Senior Cup, while Chapman, Davies, Morris and Meredith had been included in the Welsh national team in a 9–1 defeat against England, with Steve Bloomer netting five of the English goals.

City then suffered an indifferent run of form in the test match games, with humiliating away defeats at West Bromwich Albion (6–1) and Small Heath (8–0), which condemned them to the Second Division for a further season.

The 1896–97 season saw the Manchester side continue to build a team capable of securing a place in the First Division. It saw the arrival of Chesterfield defender William Holmes, who made 156 League appearances in nine seasons with the club, as well as centre forward Billy Gillespie from Lincoln City, who scored 126 goals in 218 League games. However, the Lancashire team failed to produce their excellent form of the previous campaign and they finished in sixth position. A 2–0 reverse against Everton in the final of the Lancashire Senior Cup, together with a 6–0 defeat at Preston North End in the opening round of the FA Cup, completed a disappointing season for City.

Goalkeeper Charlie Williams and fullback Ray had been the only ever-presents in the City team during the season, in which Sharples had netted six goals in ten League appearances, while Billy Meredith had led the scoring with ten.

Few changes were made in the City line-up for the 1897–98 League campaign. Charlie Williams continued in goal, with Holmes, Read and Ray in defence, while Fred Williams, Billy Gillespie and Billy Meredith remained in the attack.

Bobby Moffatt, who had made thirteen appearances during the two previous seasons, made the right half position his own following his transfer from St Mirren, while further signings included centre half Bill Smith from

Buxton, as well as Walter Smith, an inside forward from Stockport County.

City opened the season with eight victories and one draw, with Billy Gillespie and Fred Williams scoring seven goals apiece, while Walter Smith netted nine. However, the Manchester side were unable to sustain their form during the latter stages of the campaign, which resulted in a third place League finish.

Billy Gillespie, Billy Meredith and Bobby Moffatt had appeared in all thirty League games, with Meredith and Walter Smith ending the campaign with a dozen goals apiece, while Gillespie had led the scoring with eighteen. City had suffered a 2–1 defeat against Stockport in the final of the Manchester Senior Cup; however, City had originally won the final by four goals to nil, when it was discovered that outside left Dougal had failed to register in time, hence the replayed final.

The 1898–99 season saw the Manchester side even more determined for success with a team showing few changes from the previous campaign. The most notable newcomers included inside forward Jimmy Ross from Burnley, as well as Welsh international fullback David Jones from Bolton Wanderers.

Ross scored twenty-one goals in sixty-seven appearances for the club, while David Jones made 114 League appearances in four seasons. However, both players suffered premature deaths while still at the peak of their careers.

City made few mistakes during the season, which saw only five defeats in thirty-four League games. They were crowned as champions of the Second Division by a six-point margin, which meant automatic promotion to the First Division as the play-off games had now been dispensed with.

An excellent home record had resulted in comprehensive victories against Loughborough Town (5–0), Barnsley (5–0), Burton Swifts (6–0), Grimsby Town (7–2) and Darwen (10–0) in City's finest season to date. Jimmy Ross had scored seven goals in nine League appearances; Fred Williams had found the net on eleven occasions; Billy Gillespie had netted seventeen goals; while Billy Meredith had led the scoring with twenty-nine goals in thirty-three League games as the Lancashire side realised their ambition.

Manchester City in the First Division

City relied upon the team that had secured the Second Division Championship for the 1899–1900 League campaign. Charlie Williams continued in goal, with Read, Jones, Moffatt, Holmes and Bill Smith in defence, while Meredith, Ross, Gillespie, Dougal and Fred Williams remained in the attack.

The 1899–1900 season opened with a 4–3 defeat at Blackburn Rovers, with Meredith, Ross and Fred Williams on target for the visitors, which was followed by a 4–0 home success against Derby County, with Meredith (2), Ross and Gillespie scoring for City. Meredith and Ross netted for the third game running in a 4–1 success at Bury.

Then followed a 5–1 home victory against Notts County, with Ross (2),

Moffatt, Gillespie and Bill Smith finding the net, while Ross scored his sixth goal in five games in a one-all home draw with Wolverhampton Wanderers. However, a 3–0 reverse at Sheffield United ended their splendid run of results.

Jimmy Ross's fine goal-scoring run continued in a 1–0 home win against Newcastle United, which preceded successive defeats at Aston Villa (2–1) and Burnley (1–0), as well as at home to Liverpool (1–0). Then successive home victories against Preston North End (3–1) and Glossop (4–1) saw the Manchester side return to winning ways, with Fred Williams and Billy Meredith scoring in both games.

Early December saw a 1–0 reverse at Stoke, followed by a 2–1 home win against Sunderland, with Moffatt and Meredith on target, while a goalless draw at West Bromwich Albion, as well as home defeats against Everton (2–1) and Sheffield United (2–1), saw City in a mid-table position at the halfway stage of the campaign. However, an indifferent run of results would see the Manchester side struggling near the foot of the League table by early March.

City's indifferent run of results began with a 2–0 defeat at Nottingham Forest, followed by successive draws at Derby County (0–0) and Notts County (1–1), as well as at home to Blackburn Rovers (1–1) and Bury (2–2), while a 3–0 reverse at Aston Villa in a replayed FA Cup tie ended their interest in the competition at the first hurdle.

A fifth successive League draw arrived during the opening week of February as Billy Meredith found the net in a one-all draw at Wolverhampton Wanderers, which preceded a 5–2 reverse at Liverpool. Meredith scored for the third game in a row in a 1–0 home win against Burnley, but a 2–0 home defeat against Aston Villa continued their indifferent run of form.

Late March saw a rare away victory at Glossop (2–0), which was followed by home wins against Stoke (1–0) and Nottingham Forest (2–0), with Davidson, Harvey, Meredith and Fred Williams sharing the City goals. A goalless draw at Newcastle United saw their eighth draw of the campaign.

Following a 3–1 defeat at Sunderland, the Lancashire side secured a 2–0 success at Preston North End where Gillespie and Dougal found the net, while Ross (2), Meredith and Gillespie were on target in a 4–0 home win against West Bromwich Albion. However, a 4–0 reverse at Everton saw City end the season in seventh position, with thirteen victories, eight draws and thirteen defeats in their thirty-four League games, while scoring fifty goals and conceding forty-four.

Charlie Williams, David Jones, Bill Smith and William Holmes had appeared in all thirty-four League games, with Billy Meredith missing one in City's finest season to date. Billy Gillespie had ended the campaign with eight League goals, Jimmy Ross had found the net on ten occasions, while Billy Meredith had once again led the scoring with fourteen goals.

GLOSSOP NORTH END

Glossop North End had surprised the football world by securing promotion to the First Division for the 1899–1900 League campaign. However, many felt that they would struggle in the top division.

Glossop opened the season with home victories against Burnley (2–0) and Nottingham Forest (3–0), as well as away defeats at Aston Villa (9–0), Preston North End (1–0), Wolverhampton Wanderers (4–0) and Stoke (1–0). A 2–0 reverse against Sunderland saw their first home defeat of the season as they moved to the foot of the League table. Then followed a further run of indifferent results with home draws against Everton (1–1), Notts County (0–0), Sheffield United (2–2) and away at West Bromwich Albion (3–3), as well as away defeats at Bury (2–1) and Manchester City (4–1). A 1–0 home success against Aston Villa saw a rare victory for the Lancashire side.

Glossop's hopes of moving up the League table were short-lived as the year ended with away defeats at Liverpool (5–2), Derby County (4–1) and Burnley (3–1). Their form went from bad to worse during the new year with home defeats against Preston North End (2–0), Wolverhampton Wanderers (3–2) and Stoke (2–1), as well as a 5–0 reverse at Nottingham Forest, and they remained stranded at the foot of the table.

February's end saw Glossop play a goalless draw at Sunderland, followed by a 4–2 home win against Blackburn Rovers, while a two-all draw in the return game at Blackburn continued their greatly improved form. However, a further loss of form saw the east Lancashire side firmly entrenched at the bottom of the League table at the season's end.

Glossop's poor run of results began with a 1–0 reverse at Newcastle United, followed by successive home draws against Bury (0–0) and Notts County (0–0). Further home defeats against Manchester City (2–0) and Derby County (3–1), as well as a 4–0 reverse at Sheffield United, saw the threat of relegation draw closer.

With little to play for other than their pride during the remaining weeks of the season, the Glossop team played successive home draws against Newcastle United (0–0) and West Bromwich Albion (1–1) on either side of a 4–1 defeat at Everton, while the campaign ended with a 2–1 home reverse against Liverpool. Glossop finished in last place, nine points adrift from the team above them, with four victories, ten draws and twenty defeats in their thirty-four League games, while scoring thirty-one goals and conceding seventy-four.

While Glossop had been out of their depth in the First Division, they could be proud of becoming the smallest town in England to achieve First Division status during the Victorian period. The early years of the following century would see both John and Archie Goodall join their playing ranks.

BURNLEY

Burnley had finished the 1898–99 League campaign in third position, which resulted in few changes in their line-up for the 1899–1900 season. Jack Hillman continued in goal, with Woolfall, Taylor, McLintock, Livingstone and Fred Barron in defence, while Morrison, Bowes, Hartley, Chadwick and Miller remained in the attack.

Burnley opened the season with successive away defeats at Glossop (2–0) and Sunderland (2–1) on either side of a two-all home draw with Stoke. Their indifferent start to the campaign continued with home wins against West Bromwich Albion (2–0), Blackburn Rovers (1–0), Bury (1–0) and Manchester City (2–0), as well as away defeats at Everton (2–0), Derby County (4–1) and Notts County (6–1), which saw the Lancashire side in a mid-table position by early November.

Then followed a goalless draw at Sheffield United, while the month ended with defeats at home to Newcastle United (3–1) and away at Aston Villa (2–0). However, a 2–1 home success against Liverpool saw a return to winning ways for the Burnley side.

Further defeats at home to Wolverhampton Wanderers (1–0) and away at Stoke (3–0), as well as drawn games at Preston North End (1–1) and at home to Nottingham Forest (2–2), saw the struggle continue. The year ended with a 3–1 home win against fellow strugglers Glossop.

New Year's Day saw a 2–0 reverse at Blackburn Rovers, while their improved home form continued with successive victories against Sunderland (3–1) and Everton (3–1) on either side of a 2–0 away defeat at West Bromwich Albion. Then a 2–1 defeat against Derby County ended their run of three successive home wins.

Late February saw Burnley secure a welcome 3–0 home win against Notts County, which preceded further away defeats at Manchester City (1–0) and Newcastle United (2–0), as well as a one-all draw at Bury, while a 2–1 home reverse against Aston Villa on the final day of March saw the Lancashire side in desperate trouble near the foot of the League table.

Following a rare away victory at Liverpool (1–0), Burnley suffered defeats at Wolverhampton Wanderers (3–0) and at home to Preston North End (1–0), which meant that the Lancashire side were required to win both of their remaining League fixtures to retain their First Division status. Despite a 1–0 home success against Sheffield United, the Burnley team suffered a 4–0 reverse at Nottingham Forest in the final game of the campaign, which condemned them to the Second Division for the following season.

Burnley had won eleven, drawn five and lost eighteen of their thirty-four League games, while scoring thirty-four goals and conceding fifty-four, as well as suffering a first round defeat in the FA Cup competition. To make matters worse, a charge of bribery had been made against goalkeeper Jack Hillman following the 4–0 defeat at Nottingham Forest.

It had been alleged that Hillman had offered the Forest players between two and five pounds to lose the match, which Hillman insisted was suggested as a joke. However, the Football League Committee felt that there had been an element of truth in the allegations, as Hillman was punished with a period of suspension for the following season, while his team returned to the Second Division.

PRESTON NORTH END

Preston North End had been involved in the fight to avoid relegation in each of the two previous seasons. No longer one of the wealthier clubs in England, the Preston team were unable to make any significant new signings for the 1899–1900 League campaign. Peter McBride continued in goal, with Eccleston, Dunn, Holmes and McIntyre in defence, while Murray, Gara and Pierce remained in the attack, together with newcomers Stevenson and Henderson.

Gara, who had made seven League appearances during the previous campaign, scored twenty-five goals in sixty-six League games for the club; Elliott became a regular member of the half-back line, while Stevenson and Henderson remained for a little more than a season in which Sanders, Tait, Brown, Blyth and David Russell had been the most notable departures from the club.

Preston opened the campaign with a 3–1 reverse at Nottingham Forest, followed by a 1–0 home win against Glossop. Away defeats at Stoke (3–1) and West Bromwich Albion (1–0), as well as at home to Sunderland (1–0), continued their poor start to the season. Then followed successive home draws against Everton (1–1) and Derby County (0–0), as well as away defeats at Blackburn Rovers (3–0) and Bury (2–0), while a 4–3 home success against Notts County saw two welcome points. However, further defeats at Manchester City (3–1) and at home to Sheffield United (1–0) saw the once great Preston team struggling near the foot of the League table.

Late November saw Preston's first away point of the season in a goalless draw at Newcastle United, which preceded defeats at Liverpool (1–0) and at home to Aston Villa (5–0), which meant that the Lancashire side had accumulated only seven points from fifteen League games and had the threat of relegation hanging over their heads. However, an excellent run of results during December, including victories at Wolverhampton Wanderers (3–1) and at home to Nottingham Forest (3–0), as well as a one-all home draw with Burnley, saw Preston end the year in high spirits.

New Year's Day saw the Lancashire side suffer a 1–0 reverse at Everton, followed by successive victories at Glossop (2–0) and at home to Stoke (3–0), prior to ending the month with a narrow 1–0 defeat at Sunderland. Then a 5–2 home win against West Bromwich Albion saw Preston return to form.

Away from League action, Preston were enjoying an excellent FA Cup run with a 1–0 home success against Blackburn Rovers securing a quarter-final tie against Nottingham Forest, who were appearing in their fifth quarter-final in six seasons. While playing a goalless draw in Lancashire, the Preston team suffered a 1–0 defeat in the replay at Nottingham to end their interest in the competition.

Preston continued their excellent home form with victories against Bury (1–0) and Newcastle United (4–1) on either side of away defeats at Notts County (3–0) and Sheffield United (1–0). Further defeats at Derby County (2–0) and Aston Villa (3–1), as well as at home to Liverpool (3–1) and Manchester City (2–0), saw the Preston side near the foot of the League table, desperately in need of points, with three League games remaining.

Following a 1–0 victory at fellow strugglers Burnley in their final away game of the campaign, the Preston side secured successive home wins against Wolverhampton Wanderers (2–0) and Blackburn Rovers (2–0) to end the season in sixteenth position, with twelve victories, four draws and eighteen defeats in their thirty-four League games, while scoring thirty-eight goals and conceding forty-eight.

Goalkeeper Peter McBride and fullback Dunn had appeared in all thirty-four League games, with Elliott, McIntyre and Eccleston missing no more than a couple. Henderson had led the scoring with eleven goals in twenty-five League appearances, and the Preston team avoided relegation by a single point.

NOTTS COUNTY

Notts County had finished the 1898–99 season in fifth position, hence the reluctance of the club directors to make changes in the team for the final season of the century. Ernest Suter continued to stand in for George Toone in goal, while Tom Prescott, George Lewis, Billy Ball, Arthur Hadley, Alex Maconnachie, Joe McMain, James Chalmers, Harry Fletcher, Walter Bull, Jack Montgomery and the ever reliable David Calderhead remained as first team regulars.

County opened the season with a 1–0 victory at Derby County, followed by successive home draws against Bury (2–2) and Wolverhampton Wanderers (0–0), while defeats at Manchester City (5–1) and at home to Sheffield United (2–1) ended their fine start to the season. However, a 2–1 home success against Liverpool maintained their mid-table position.

Then followed defeats at Newcastle United (6–0) and Liverpool (3–0), as well as at home to Aston Villa (4–1), while a 6–1 home victory against Burnley saw the Nottingham side record their highest win of the season. Further home defeats against Nottingham Forest (2–1), Stoke (3–1) and West Bromwich Albion (2–1), as well as away defeats at Preston North End (4–3) and Sunderland (5–0), saw County near the foot of the League table by early December, with a goalless draw at Glossop their only consolation during this period of indifferent form.

Mid-December saw County return to winning ways with successive victories at Everton (2–0) and at home to Blackburn Rovers (5–1), which preceded a goalless home draw with Derby County in the final game of the year. Their greatly improved form continued with a 1–0 success at Bury, as well as drawn games at Wolverhampton Wanderers (2–2), Sheffield United (1–1) and at home to Manchester City (1–1), but a 6–2 reverse at Aston Villa ended their splendid run of results.

County then suffered a 2–0 defeat against Bury in a second round FA Cup replay, while a 3–0 reverse at Burnley continued their indifferent run of results. However, victories at home to Preston North End (3–0) and away at Nottingham Forest (3–0) saw a return to form for the East Midlands side.

Late March saw a goalless home draw with the struggling Glossop team, which preceded a 1–0 reverse at Stoke, while a 3–1 home success against Sunderland, as well as drawn games at home to Newcastle United (0–0), Everton (2–2) and away at West Bromwich Albion (0–0), saw County retain their First Division status for a further season, despite suffering a 2–0 defeat at Blackburn Rovers in the final game of the campaign.

Notts had won nine, drawn eleven and lost fourteen of their thirty-four League games in a most disappointing season. However, the new century would see County mount a serious challenge for the League Championship.

BLACKBURN ROVERS

Blackburn Rovers had finished the 1898–99 League campaign in sixth position, which resulted in few changes in their line-up for the 1899–1900 season. Brandon, Crompton, Booth, Haworth, Anderson and Albert Houlker continued in defence, while Briercliffe, Hulse, Hurst and Fred Blackburn remained in the attack.

Goalkeeper Carter had left the club, together with Chambers, Moreland, Jackson and Williams, while the most notable new arrivals were Somers, Dewhurst and Arnold Whittaker, who all served the Lancashire side for a number of years, with Somers making seventy-six League appearances. Dewhurst scored forty-three goals in 169 League games, while Arnold Whittaker found the net on fifty-seven occasions in 250 League appearances as well as earning selection for the Football League representative side.

Knowles, who had made one League appearance during the previous campaign, took over the goalkeeping duties from the departing Carter, however, he was replaced by William Whittaker midway through the season, following a run of indifferent results.

Rovers opened the season with a 4–3 home win against Manchester City, with Hulse, Crook, Hurst and Crompton on target, which preceded successive away defeats at Sheffield United (3–0) and Aston Villa (3–1), as well as at home to Newcastle United (3–2). Haworth and Crook found the net in a 2–0 home success against Liverpool, but a 1–0 reverse at Burnley saw Blackburn near the foot of the League table by the middle of October. Arnold Whittaker then scored a hat-trick on his League debut in a 3–0 home win against Preston North End, which was followed by away defeats at Nottingham Forest (3–2) and Stoke (2–0), as well as at home to Sunderland (2–1). A 3–1 home victory against Everton saw a return to winning ways with Hurst, Hulse and Fred Blackburn netting the Rovers' goals.

Early December saw Blackburn suffer a 4–0 defeat at Wolverhampton Wanderers, which preceded a 2–0 success at Derby County, in their only away win of the season, with Dewhurst and Blackburn on target. Fred Blackburn again found the net in a 3–2 home win against Bury with Haworth and Hulse completing the scoring. Their indifferent form returned with a 5–1 reverse at Notts County, prior to ending the year with a one-all draw at Manchester City where Tom Booth netted his only goal of the season.

New Year began with a 2–0 home win against Burnley, with Dewhurst and Briercliffe on target, which was followed by defeats at Newcastle United (4–1) and at home to Aston Villa (4–0), while a first round FA Cup tie against Portsmouth produced successive draws (0–0 and 1–1). Following a 3–1 reverse in a League encounter at Liverpool, the Blackburn team secured a 5–0 victory in the replay with Portsmouth, with Blackburn (3) and Hulse (2) netting the goals to earn a second round tie at Preston North End. There they suffered a 1–0 defeat to end their interest in the competition for a further season.

On their return to League action, Rovers suffered a 4–2 defeat at Glossop, which preceded a two-all draw in the return game with Glossop, with Arnold Whittaker netting a brace of goals. Somers, Dewhurst, Briercliffe, Blackburn and Whittaker then shared the Rovers' goals in successive home wins against Nottingham Forest (2–1), Stoke (3–0) and West Bromwich Albion (2–0).

Following a goalless draw at Everton on the final day of March, the Blackburn side were narrowly beaten in the return game at West Bromwich Albion (1–0), while further home wins against Wolverhampton Wanderers (2–1) and Derby County (2–0) on either side of a three-all home draw with Sheffield United all but secured their place in the top division, with Dewhurst, Hulse, Somers, Whittaker and Fred Blackburn again amongst the scorers. Successive away defeats at Sunderland (1–0), Bury (2–0) and Preston North End (2–0) during the final weeks of the campaign very nearly cost them their First Division status, which was secured with a 2–0 home success against Notts County, with Whittaker and Blackburn netting the all-important goals.

Rovers eventually finished the season in fourteenth position, with thirteen wins, four draws and seventeen defeats in their thirty-four League games, while scoring forty-nine goals and conceding sixty-one. However, only one victory on their travels had nearly resulted in relegation to the Second Division.

Bob Crompton had appeared in all thirty-four League games in a most disappointing season. Fred Blackburn had netted nine League goals, while Arnold Whittaker had led the scoring with eleven goals in nineteen appearances.

WEST BROMWICH ALBION

West Bromwich Albion had been involved in the fight to avoid relegation during the 1898–99 League campaign, which resulted in the announcement by Billy Bassett that he was to retire from the game. However, Albion kept faith with the majority of their players for the 1899–1900 season, as Joe Reader continued in goal, with Banks, Abe Jones, Archie Dunn and Billy Williams in defence, while William Richards, Ben Garfield and Tom Perry, now playing at inside forward, remained in the attack. Amos Adams and Harry Hadley became regular members of the Albion defence, where George Cave made only the occasional appearance, while Flewitt had signed for Bedminster and McKenzie returned north of the border to Dumbarton.

Newcomers in the Albion team included Roberts, Chadburn and Walker, while the most notable new arrivals saw Charlie Simmons sign from Worcester Rovers for a nominal fee, with John Paddock signing from a local amateur side to replace Billy Bassett on the right wing.

Paddock's older brother William had previously played for the club, while his father Jack had been first team trainer. However, the youngster remained for a little more than a season, while Simmons on the other hand enjoyed a long career with the West Bromwich side, in which he scored seventy-five goals in 178 League appearances.

Albion enjoyed an excellent start to the season, as Simmons found the net in a one-all home draw with Newcastle United, which preceded a 2–0 victory at Aston Villa, with Garfield and Simmons on target. Ben Garfield netted a brace of goals in a 2–0 home success against Liverpool, but a 2–0 reverse at Burnley ended their unbeaten run. Charlie Simmons then scored his third goal of the campaign in a 1–0 home win against Preston North End, which was followed by a humiliating 6–1 defeat at Nottingham Forest. William Richards (2) and Billy Williams scored their opening goals of the season in a three-all home draw with Glossop, but their indifferent away form continued with successive defeats at Stoke (1–0) and Wolverhampton Wanderers (2–0) on either side of a 1–0 home success against Sunderland with Ben Garfield scoring the only goal of the game.

Early November saw Albion suffer their first home defeat of the season in a 2–1 reverse against Sheffield United, which preceded a 3–1 victory at Everton, with Richards (2) and Paddock on target. Defeats at Derby County (4–1) and at home to Bury (1–0) saw the West Bromwich side move into the bottom half of the League table, however, a 2–1 success at Notts County saw a return to winning ways with Ben Garfield netting a brace of goals for the visitors.

Then followed successive draws at home to Manchester City (0–0) and Everton (0–0), as well as away at Sheffield United (1–1), while the year ended with a 4–2 reverse at Newcastle United with Simmons netting both Albion goals. It preceded new year defeats at home to Aston Villa (2–0) and away at Liverpool (2–0) as Albion continued their indifferent run of results.

Albion then secured a welcome home win against Burnley (2–0) with Hadley and Brett scoring their opening goals of the season, which was followed by an excellent FA Cup run with victories against Walsall (6–1) and Liverpool (2–1) in replayed ties. However, a 2–1 reverse at Southampton in the quarter-final stages of the competition ended their hopes of FA Cup success for a further season.

During their FA Cup run, the West Bromwich side had suffered a 5–2 defeat in a League encounter at Preston North End, which preceded a further away defeat at Sunderland (3–1), while their fine home record continued with victories against Wolverhampton Wanderers (3–2) and Stoke (4–0) with Charlie Timmins on target in both games. A 2–0 reverse at Blackburn Rovers, as well as a goalless home draw with Derby County, saw Albion perilously close to the relegation positions by the final week of March.

Early April saw the Black Country side register a 1–0 home win against Blackburn Rovers, which was followed by a 1–0 defeat at Bury, as well as a goalless home draw with Notts County. An 8–0 home success against Nottingham Forest saw their highest win of the campaign, with Walker (3), Roberts (2), Simmons (2) and Chadburn on target. However, a 4–0 reverse at Manchester City, as well as a one-all draw at Glossop, saw Albion finish the season in thirteenth position, with eleven victories, eight draws and fifteen defeats in their thirty-four League games, while scoring forty-three goals and conceding fifty-one.

Joe Reader had appeared in all thirty-four League games in a disappointing season, while Charlie Simmons had led the scoring with a dozen goals. Further disappointment lay ahead for the West Bromwich side, who would suffer the embarrassment of relegation during the opening season of the new century.

BURY

Bury had finished the 1898–99 League campaign in a creditable mid-table position, which resulted in few changes in their line-up for the 1899–1900 season. Thompson continued to replace Montgomery in goal, with Davidson, Pray, Ross, Leeming and Darroch in defence, while Richards, Wood, McLuckie, Charlie Sagar and Jack Plant formed the attack.

Bury opened the season with a 3–0 home success against Wolverhampton Wanderers, followed by a two-all draw at Notts County, while successive defeats at home to Manchester City (4–1) and away at Sheffield United (4–0) ended their fine start to the campaign.

Then followed a run of six successive home wins against Newcastle United (2–1), Liverpool (2–1), Preston North End (2–0), Glossop (2–1), Sunderland (2–0) and Everton (4–1), as well as away defeats at Aston Villa (2–1), Burnley (1–0) and Blackburn Rovers (3–2). A two-all draw at Nottingham Forest saw the Lancashire side in the top half of the League table by early December.

Bury then secured their only away win of the season in a 1–0 victory at West Bromwich Albion, which preceded a one-all home draw with Derby

County, while a 2–1 home success against Nottingham Forest continued their excellent run of results. However, a 1–0 reverse at Wolverhampton Wanderers saw the year end in disappointment.

New Year's Day saw Bury return to winning ways with a 2–0 home win against Aston Villa, which was followed by a 1–0 home defeat against Notts County, as well as a two-all draw at Manchester City. The month ended with a 2–1 home victory against Sheffield United, but Bury's League form suffered from February onwards as they became more and more involved in the FA Cup competition.

Following a 2–1 defeat in a League encounter at Newcastle United, the Lancashire side secured a 2–0 victory against Notts County in a second round FA Cup replay to earn a difficult away tie at Sheffield United in the quarter-finals. This ended in a two-all draw, but Bury won the replay by two goals to nil to secure a semi-final tie against Nottingham Forest at the Victoria Ground, Stoke.

On their return to League action, the Bury team suffered a 1–0 reverse at Preston North End, which preceded drawn games at home to Burnley (1–1) and away at Glossop (0–0), while the semi-final tie against Nottingham Forest ended in a one-all draw. In the replay at Bramall Lane, Bury managed a 3–2 victory to secure their first FA Cup Final appearance.

Prior to the FA Cup Final, the Lancashire side suffered away defeats at Sunderland (1–0), Liverpool (2–0), Everton (2–0) and Stoke (2–0), as well as at home in the return game with Stoke (1–0). A 1–0 home win against West Bromwich Albion saw their only success during this period of indifferent form. With two League games remaining, Bury's thoughts were on their FA Cup Final appearance against Southampton at Crystal Palace on 21 April.

EVERTON

Everton had performed magnificently throughout the 1898–99 League campaign, which had resulted in few changes in their line-up for the 1899–1900 season. Muir continued in goal, with Molyneux, Eccles, Balmer, Boyle and Sam Wolstenholme in defence, while Proudfoot, Gee and Jack Taylor remained in an attack that included newcomers Jack Sharp from Aston Villa, Jimmy Settle from Bury and Wilf Toman from Burnley.

Sharp scored forty-eight goals in 300 League appearances for the Merseysiders, as well as representing the English national team on a couple of occasions. He became just as successful on the cricket field where he played for Lancashire for more than a quarter of a century, as well as appearing in three test matches, thus making him a 'double' international.

Jimmy Settle, who had made one appearance during the previous campaign, like Sharp, assisted Everton for a number of seasons, which saw him score eighty-four goals in 237 League games, as well as gaining half a dozen England caps. Wilf Toman remained for a little more than a season.

Newcomers in defence included half back Blythe, who had recently arrived from Jarrow, as well as Walter Abbott from Small Heath, who made nearly 300 appearances in an Everton shirt, as well as representing the English national team. The most notable departures from the club saw Lawrence Bell join Bolton Wanderers and Edgar Chadwick signing for Burnley following 110 goals in 300 appearances for the Merseysiders.

Everton opened the season with successive home defeats against Sheffield United (2–1) and Aston Villa (2–1), as well as away at Newcastle United (2–0), which were followed by a 2–1 success at Liverpool, with Jimmy Settle and Jack Taylor on target, while Wilf Toman netted a brace of goals in a 2–0 home victory against Burnley. Jimmy Settle then scored his third goal of the campaign in a one-all draw at Preston North End, which preceded a 2–1 home win against Nottingham Forest, with Toman and Jack Sharp netting the Everton goals. Toman and Taylor found the net in away draws at Glossop (1–1) and Stoke (1–1) as the Merseysiders extended their unbeaten run to six games. However, a loss of form during November saw the Lancashire side suffer defeats at Sunderland (1–0) and Blackburn Rovers (3–1), as well as at home to West Bromwich Albion (3–1), leaving them in the bottom half of the League table by the end of the month.

Then followed a 3–0 home success against Derby County, with Settle, Taylor and Sharp on target, which preceded defeats at Bury (4–1) and at home to Notts County (2–0), while Jimmy Settle again found the net in successive victories at Manchester City (2–1) and at home to Stoke (2–0). Following a goalless draw at West Bromwich Albion, the Merseysiders ended the year with a 5–0 reverse at Sheffield United.

Everton enjoyed an excellent start to the new year as centre forward Proudfoot found the net in home victories against Preston North End (1–0) and Newcastle United (3–2), which were followed by a Jack Taylor goal in a one-all draw at Aston Villa. Jimmy Settle netted a brace of goals in a 3–1 home success against Liverpool before a 3–0 defeat at Southampton in the first round of the FA Cup ended their splendid run of results.

On their return to League action, Everton suffered away defeats at Burnley (3–1) and Nottingham Forest (4–2), prior to securing a 1–0 home success against Sunderland, with Wilf Toman scoring the only goal of the game. Further defeats at Wolverhampton Wanderers (2–1), Derby County (2–1) and at home to Wolverhampton Wanderers (1–0), as well as a goalless home draw with Blackburn Rovers, saw the Merseysiders move into the relegation positions, with only four League games remaining.

Mid-April saw the Everton team return to winning ways with successive home wins against Bury (2–0) and Glossop (4–1), with Proudfoot on target in both games, which preceded a two-all draw at Notts County where McDonald netted for the second game running. The campaign ended with a 4–1 home success against Manchester City, with Turner (2), Proudfoot and Toman scoring for the Merseysiders, to secure an eleventh place League finish, with thirteen victories, seven draws and fourteen defeats in their thirty-four League games, while scoring forty-seven goals and conceding forty-nine.

Boyle, Balmer, Muir, Sharp, Taylor and Wolstenholme had missed no more than a handful of games in Everton's most disappointing season to date. Proudfoot and Toman had netted eight League goals apiece, with Jimmy Settle leading the scoring with ten. However, the Everton team had little to worry about, as success lay ahead during the early years of the following century.

LIVERPOOL

Liverpool had finished the 1898–99 League campaign as runners-up to Aston Villa by a margin of two points, which resulted in few changes in their team for the final year of the century. Willie Perkins continued in goal, with McQueen, Cunliffe, Billy Dunlop and the inspirational Alex Raisbeck in defence, while McVean, Bradshaw, Henderson and Jack Cox remained up front.

John Walker and John Robertson, who had both previously played for Heart of Midlothian, formed a new left wing partnership, while centre forward Sam Raybould had arrived from a local amateur side. However, his successful years would be in the following century.

Liverpool opened the season with successive defeats at Stoke (3–2), West Bromwich Albion (2–0), Blackburn Rovers (2–0), Notts County (2–1) and Bury (2–1), as well as at home to Sunderland (2–0), Everton (2–1) and Derby County (2–0), which saw the Merseysiders at the foot of the League table without a point from eight games. However, late October saw their first win of the campaign in a 3–1 home success against Notts County.

Then followed a 1–0 victory at Manchester City, while their unbeaten run continued with successive home draws against Sheffield United (2–2), Aston Villa (3–3) and Wolverhampton Wanderers (1–1), as well as away at Newcastle United (1–1). Further away defeats at Burnley (2–1) and Nottingham Forest (1–0) on either side of a 1–0 home win against Preston North End saw the Liverpool side retain their relegation position at the halfway stage of the season, with only ten points from seventeen League games.

Following a 5–2 home win against Glossop, the Merseysiders suffered a 3–2 reverse at Derby County, while the year ended with a goalless home draw against Stoke. However, the new year heralded a return to form for the Liverpool side, which would result in ten victories in their remaining fourteen League games to end the season in a respectable mid-table position.

New Year opened with a 1–0 reverse at Sunderland, followed by a 2–0 home success against West Bromwich Albion. The month ended with a 3–1 defeat at Everton, but the Liverpool team soon returned to winning ways with a 3–1 home win against Blackburn Rovers.

Liverpool were then drawn against West Bromwich Albion in the second round of the FA Cup following a first round victory against Stoke, with the Merseysiders favourites to progress to the quarter-final stages of the competition. However, the Lancashire side were disappointed as Albion won by the odd goal in three in a replayed tie.

On their return to League action, Liverpool secured victories at Sheffield United (2–1) and Wolverhampton Wanderers (1–0), as well as at home to Manchester City (5–2) and Newcastle United (2–0), while a 1–0 reverse at Aston Villa saw their only defeat during this excellent run of results. A surprising 1–0 home defeat against the struggling Burnley team saw the Merseysiders once again near the foot of the League table.

Liverpool soon returned to form with successive wins at Preston North End (3–1) and Glossop (2–1), as well as at home to Bury (2–0) and Nottingham Forest (1–0), to end the campaign in tenth position, with fourteen victories, five draws and fifteen defeats in their thirty-four League games, an excellent achievement following their poor start to the season.

STOKE

Stoke's appearance in the 1898–99 FA Cup semi-finals had been the highlight of their financially troubled history, which had seen them struggle to sign or retain players other than those with a local connection. However, the Potteries' side had managed to retain the majority of the players from the FA Cup run for the 1899–1900 season. Goalkeeper Tom Wilkes had arrived from Aston Villa on a permanent basis to replace George Clawley, while Tom Holford, who eventually made in excess of 250 appearances for the club, became a regular member of the half-back line.

Joseph Schofield had decided to retire from the game to continue his school teaching career, while Fred Molyneux and John Farrell had moved to clubs in the south of England. Robertson, Kennedy, Wood, Eccles, Turner, Johnson and William Maxwell retained their places for the new season, together with newcomers Higginson and Jim Bradley.

Stoke opened the season with successive home wins against Liverpool (3–2) and Preston North End (3–1) on either side of a two-all draw at Burnley, with Willie Maxwell scoring four of the Stoke goals. These were followed by defeats at Nottingham Forest (1–0) and at home to Wolverhampton Wanderers (3–1), but further victories at home to Glossop (1–0) and in the return game at Wolverhampton Wanderers (2–0) saw the Potteries' side in the top half of the League table by mid-October.

Then followed a 3–0 reverse at Sunderland, while their excellent home record continued with wins against West Bromwich Albion (1–0) and Blackburn Rovers (2–0), as well as a one-all draw with Everton. However, defeats at Derby County (2–0) and at home to Aston Villa (2–0) saw Stoke struggling to maintain a mid-table position.

Willie Maxwell again found the net in a 3–1 success at Notts County, which preceded a further home win against Manchester City (1–0), while successive away defeats at Sheffield United (1–0), Aston Villa (4–1) and Everton (2–0), as well as a two-all home draw with Newcastle United, saw the Potteries' side suffer a loss of form. Stoke returned to winning ways with a 3–0 home success against Burnley, prior to ending the year with a goalless draw at Liverpool.

New Year began with a 3–0 reverse at Preston North End, followed by a goalless home draw with Nottingham Forest, while a 1–0 defeat at Liverpool in a replayed FA Cup tie saw the Stoke team go out of the competition at the first hurdle. However, a 2–1 victory in a League encounter at Glossop saw the North Staffordshire team secure two welcome points.

Early March saw a further run of indifferent results with defeats at Blackburn Rovers (3–0), West Bromwich Albion (4–0) and at home to Sunderland (2–1), as well as a one-all home draw with Derby County. The month ended with a 1–0 home success against the struggling Notts County side. Yet, with five League games remaining, of which three were away from home, Stoke's First Division future was more or less assured.

During the final stages of the season, the Potteries' side suffered a 1–0 reverse at Manchester City, followed by a 1–0 success at Bury, who had an FA Cup Final appearance on their minds. Draws at home to Sheffield United (1–1) and away at Newcastle United (2–2), as well as a 2–0 home win in the return game with Bury, saw Stoke end the campaign in ninth position, with ten victories, ten draws and fourteen defeats in their thirty-four League games, while scoring thirty-seven goals and conceding forty-five.

Willie Maxwell had led the scoring for the fourth season running with eleven League goals, while Robertson had appeared in all thirty-four League games. Stoke's improved form would be short-lived as the struggle continued well into the following century.

NOTTINGHAM FOREST

Nottingham Forest's eleventh place League finish during the 1898–99 season had resulted in few changes in their line-up for the final season of the century. Dennis Allsopp continued in goal, with Jim Iremonger, Frank Forman, John MacPherson and Robert Norris in defence, while Fred Forman, Arthur Capes, Alf Spouncer, Len Benbow, Fred Spencer and Grenville Morris once again competed for the forward positions.

Archie Ritchie, Adam Scott, William Wragg, Charlie Richards and Tom Melnnes were near to retirement or had moved to pastures new. This saw the arrival of Beveridge, Edward Peers and George Robinson, however, the most notable newcomer was Jack Calvey, who scored forty-eight goals in 131 League appearances for Forest.

Harry Linacre, a nephew of Frank and Fred Forman, replaced Dennis Allsopp in goal during the latter stages of the season. He eventually made in excess of 300 League appearances between the posts, as well as gaining two England caps.

Forest opened the season with a 3–1 home success against Preston North End, with Beveridge, Calvey and Robert Norris on target, which preceded a two-all draw at Wolverhampton Wanderers where Jack Calvey netted a brace of goals. A 3–0 reverse at Glossop was a surprise defeat, but a 1–0 home win against Stoke saw a return to winning ways, with Len Benbow scoring his only League goal of the campaign.

Then followed a 1–0 defeat at Sunderland, while Fred Forman (2), Morris (2), Capes and Frank Forman found the net in a 6–1 home win against West Bromwich Albion. However, a 2–1 reverse at Everton saw Forest continue to struggle on their travels.

Mid-October saw the Nottingham side register a 3–2 home success against Blackburn Rovers, with Spencer, Beveridge and Calvey on target, which preceded successive draws at Derby County (2–2) and at home to Bury (2–2), with Jack Calvey and the Forman brothers sharing the Forest goals. Capes and Fred Forman netted in a 2–1 victory at Notts County, though a 3–0 reverse at Sheffield United ended their splendid run of results.

Frank Forman then scored the only goal of the game in a 1–0 home win against Newcastle United, while his brother Fred found the net in a two-all draw at Aston Villa, which preceded a further home success against Liverpool (1–0), with Arthur Capes netting the all-important goal. Then, following a two-all draw at Burnley, Forest suffered a 2–1 defeat at Bury on Christmas Day.

Late December saw Arthur Capes and Grenville Morris on target in a 2–0 home victory against Manchester City, while the year ended with a 3–0 reverse at Preston North End. However, the new year saw a return to form. It began with a goalless home draw with Wolverhampton Wanderers, followed by a 5–0 home win against Glossop, with Calvey (2), Norris, MacPherson and Capes netting the Forest goals.

Following a further goalless draw at Stoke, Morris (2) and Calvey found the net in a 3–0 home win against Grimsby Town in the first round of the FA Cup to secure a home tie against Sunderland in the second round. This resulted in a further 3–0 success, with Morris (2) and Calvey on target to earn a quarter-final tie at Preston North End.

Prior to the FA Cup game, Jack Calvey netted a hat-trick in a 4–2 home win against Everton, while the cup tie at Preston ended in a goalless draw. However, Forest managed a 1–0 victory in the replay, with Arthur Capes scoring the only goal of the game to secure a semi-final appearance against Bury at the Victoria Ground, Stoke.

Fred Forman then netted his sixth goal of the campaign in a 4–1 home win against Derby County, with Beveridge, Morris and Norris completing the scoring, which preceded successive defeats at Blackburn Rovers (2–1) and at home to Notts County (3–0). The semi-final game with Bury ended in a one-all draw, with Arthur Capes on target for Forest. In an exciting replay at Bramall Lane, the Nottingham side were a little unfortunate to lose by the odd goal in five, with Calvey and Capes scoring consolation goals for the East Midlanders.

Forest then secured a 4–0 home win against Sheffield United on the final day of March, with Morris (2), Calvey and MacPherson finding the net, which was followed by away defeats at Newcastle United (3–1) and Manchester City (2–0), while Beveridge scored in a one-all home draw with Aston Villa. Further defeats at West Bromwich Albion (8–0) and Liverpool (1–0), as well as at home to Sunderland (3–1), saw the Nottingham side move into the bottom half of the League table. A 4–0 home success against Burnley in the final game of the season saw Forest end the campaign in eighth position, with Calvey (2), Spouncer and Morris netting the Forest goals.

Forest had won thirteen, drawn eight and lost thirteen of their thirty-four League games, while scoring fifty-six goals and conceding fifty-five. Jim Iremonger had appeared in all thirty-four League games during their finest season to date, and Jack Calvey had led the scoring with seventeen goals in thirty League appearances.

DERBY COUNTY

Following an appearance in the 1899 FA Cup Final, Derby County retained the majority of their players for the 1899–1900 season. John Fryer continued in goal, with Jimmy Methven, Joseph Leiper, Jonathon Staley, John Cox, John May and Archie Goodall in defence, while Leckie replaced John Cox during the early stages of the season following the English international's emigration to North America.

Arkesden, McQueen, Boag and Steve Bloomer retained their places in the attack, together with outside right Wombwell, while MacDonald, Allen and Paterson, who had replaced John Goodall, Archie Goodall and Hugh McQueen in the 1899 FA Cup Final side, made only one dozen League appearances between them during the final campaign of the century.

Jimmy Stevenson had left the club during the previous season, but the most notable departure from Derby was that of John Goodall who joined the New Brighton Tower Club following 211 League appearances for County in which he had scored seventy-six goals.

Derby opened the season with successive defeats at Manchester City (4–0) and Newcastle United (2–0), as well as at home to Notts County (1–0) and Sheffield United (1–0), while their poor start to the campaign came to an end with the reintroduction of Leiper, Leckie, Boag and Archie Goodall, which coincided with a seven-game unbeaten run.

County's return to form began with successive home wins against Aston Villa (2–0) and Burnley (4–1), as well as a 2–0 success at Liverpool, with Arkesden and Bloomer sharing all eight of the Derby goals. These preceded drawn games at Preston North End (0–0) and at home to Nottingham Forest (2–2), while their excellent form continued with home wins against Stoke (2–0) and West Bromwich Albion (4–1), with Shanks, Wombwell, Cooke and Bloomer amongst the Derby scorers. However, home defeats against Blackburn Rovers (2–0) and Wolverhampton Wanderers (2–0), together with a 3–0 reverse at Everton, saw the East Midlands side in the bottom half of the

League table by mid-December, with five victories in their opening fourteen League games.

Then followed a one-all draw at Bury, with Steve Bloomer scoring for the visitors, which preceded a 3–2 home victory against Liverpool on Christmas Day, with MacDonald, Bloomer and Crump on target, while Bloomer (2) and Arkesden (2) found the net in a further home success against Glossop (4–1) as County moved up to a mid-table position at the halfway stage of the campaign.

Derby then secured a point in a goalless draw at Notts County in the final game of the year, which was followed by further draws at home to Manchester City (0–0) and away at Sheffield United (1–1). Their unbeaten run continued with a 2–1 home win against Newcastle United, with Steve Bloomer and John Boag on target. However, following a two-all home draw with Sunderland in the first round of the FA Cup, the Derby team suffered a 3–0 reverse in the replay at Roker Park to end their interest in the competition.

On their return to League action, the East Midlands side suffered away defeats at Aston Villa (3–2) and Nottingham Forest (4–1) on either side of a 2–1 success at Burnley, where Bloomer and Arkesden found the net. A one-all draw at Stoke, as well as a 2–0 reverse at Sunderland, saw Derby struggling to maintain their mid-table position, with eight League games remaining.

Late March saw County return to winning ways with a 2–0 victory in the return game with Sunderland, with Wombwell netting a brace of goals, which preceded a goalless draw at West Bromwich Albion. Further home wins against Preston North End (2–0) and Everton (2–1), as well as a 3–1 success at Glossop, saw Derby move up to fifth place in the League table, with Bloomer, Shanks, Stewart, May and Wombwell sharing the County goals. Then successive away defeats at Blackburn Rovers (2–0) and Wolverhampton Wanderers (3–0) saw the East Midlands side settle for a sixth place League finish, despite securing a 3–0 home victory against Bury in the final game of the campaign, with Steve Bloomer netting a brace of goals.

Derby had won fourteen, drawn eight and lost twelve of their thirty-four League games, while scoring forty-five goals and conceding forty-three. Jimmy Methven and John May were ever present, while Steve Bloomer had once again led the scoring with nineteen goals in twenty-eight League appearances.

NEWCASTLE UNITED

Newcastle United had managed to retain their First Division status at the close of the 1898–99 season, which resulted in few changes in their line-up for the 1899–1900 League campaign. Matt Kingsley continued in goal, with Lindsay, Higgins, Aitken and Tommy Ghee in defence, while MacFarlane, Rogers, Wardrope, Stevenson and Jock Peddie remained in the attack.

Fullback Jackson had decided to sign for Woolwich Arsenal, while half backs Stott and Ostler soon moved to Middlesbrough. However, they were adequately replaced by D R Gardner from Third Lanark and Jack Carr, who had arrived from Seaton, a local amateur side. Gardner appeared in seventy-six

League games in three seasons with the club prior to joining Grimsby Town, while Carr made in excess of 250 League appearances in thirteen seasons, as well as representing the English national side.

Further new signings included outside left Fraser from Notts County, who remained with the club for a little more than a season, as well as Alec Gardner, who made in excess of 300 appearances in ten seasons with Newcastle following his arrival from Leith Athletic.

United opened the season with a one-all draw at West Bromwich Albion, with Jock Peddie scoring from the penalty spot, which was followed by successive home wins against Everton (2–0) and Derby County (2–0), as well as a 3–2 victory at Blackburn Rovers, with Peddie on target in all three wins. A 2–1 reverse at Bury ended their excellent start to the campaign, but Newcastle soon returned to winning ways with a 6–0 home success against Notts County, with Fraser (2), Peddie, Wardrope, MacFarlane and Stevenson netting for the north-eastern side to secure fourth place in the League.

Then followed a poor run of results, which saw away defeats at Manchester City (1–0) and Aston Villa (2–1), as well as at home to Wolverhampton Wanderers (1–0), while home draws against Sheffield United (0–0) and Liverpool (1–1) continued their indifferent form. However, a 3–1 success at Burnley provided two welcome points with Fraser, Rogers and Wardrope on target for the visitors.

Late November saw a goalless home draw with Preston North End, followed by a 1–0 reverse at Nottingham Forest, while Higgins and Alec Gardner netted their opening goals of the campaign in a two-all draw at Stoke. This preceded a 4–2 home success against West Bromwich Albion in the final game of the year, with Stevenson (2), Fraser and Peddie on target.

New Year's Day saw the struggling Glossop team visit St James's Park, where they found themselves 3–2 ahead with a little more than fifteen minutes remaining. However, United's blushes were spared when the referee was forced to abandon the game owing to the foggy weather conditions. This was followed by a 3–2 reverse at Everton, while Peddie (2), MacFarlane and Carr were on target in a 4–1 home success against Blackburn Rovers.

Following a further away defeat at Derby County (2–1), the Tynesiders registered a 2–1 home win against Reading in the first round of the FA Cup, with Rogers and Stevenson scoring the all-important goals to secure a second round tie at Southampton. Jimmy Stevenson netted for the third game running in a 2–1 home success against Bury, while the north-eastern side were outplayed in the FA Cup game at Southampton, where they suffered a 4–1 defeat following an abandoned goalless draw.

On their return to League action, United earned a point in a one-all draw at Wolverhampton Wanderers, with Jock Peddie on target, which preceded a 3–2 home success against Aston Villa, with Peddie netting a brace of goals. Peddie scored his thirteenth goal of the campaign in a 1–0 home win against Glossop, but a 2–0 reverse at Liverpool ended their splendid run of results.

Late March saw Fraser and Rogers find the net in a 2–0 home victory against Burnley, which preceded successive away defeats at Sheffield United (3–1) and Preston North End (4–1), while D R Gardner (penalty), MacFarlane and Peddie were on target in a 3–1 success against Nottingham Forest as the north-eastern side continued their excellent home form.

As the season reached the final stages, the Tynesiders played successive draws at Glossop (0–0) and Notts County (0–0), as well as at home to Manchester City (0–0) and Stoke (2–2). The campaign ended with a rare away win at Sunderland (2–1), with goals by Fraser and an Alec Gardner penalty securing a fifth place League finish, with thirteen victories, ten draws and eleven defeats in their thirty-four League games, while scoring fifty-three goals and conceding forty-three.

D R Gardner, Andy Aitken and Matt Kingsley had appeared in all thirty-four League games in Newcastle's finest season to date. Jock Peddie had led the scoring for the third year running, with fifteen goals in twenty-seven League appearances.

WOLVERHAMPTON WANDERERS

Wolverhampton Wanderers had finished the 1898–99 season in eighth position, which led to few changes in their team for the 1899–1900 League campaign. Tom Baddeley continued in goal, with Davies, Fleming, Pheasant, Matthias, Dan Nurse and Joe Tonks in defence, while Miller, Blackett, Worton, Hill Griffiths and Billy Beats remained in the attack, together with Harper, George Bowen and Trevor Owen. Harper had made the occasional appearance during the two previous seasons, Bowen had arrived from the Walsall area, while Trevor Owen had appeared in the Welsh national team.

Wanderers opened the season with a 3–0 defeat at Bury, followed by drawn games at home to Nottingham Forest (2–2) and away at Notts County (0–0), while successive victories at Stoke (3–1) and at home to Glossop (4–0), as well as a one-all draw at Manchester City, saw the Black Country side in the top half of the League table by the end of September. However, defeats at home to Stoke (2–0) and away at Sheffield United (5–2) ended their splendid start to the campaign.

Then followed an excellent run of results, which included away victories at Newcastle United (1–0), Burnley (1–0) and Derby County (2–0), as well as at home to West Bromwich Albion (2–0) and Blackburn Rovers (4–0). Away draws at Aston Villa (0–0) and Liverpool (1–1) saw the Wanderers move into third place in the League table, though a 3–1 home defeat against Preston North End ended their seven-game unbeaten run.

Boxing Day saw the Wolverhampton side return to winning ways with a 1–0 home success against Sunderland, which preceded a further home success against Bury (1–0) in the final game of the year. New Year's Day saw a 2–1 victory in the return game at Sunderland as Wolves maintained their challenge for the League title.

Wanderers suffered a slight drop in form during the early weeks of the new year with successive draws at Nottingham Forest (0–0) and at home to Notts County (2–2), which were followed by a 3–2 success at Glossop, while they suffered a 1–0 home defeat against Queens Park Rangers in the first round of the FA Cup in a replayed tie.

On their return to League action, the Wanderers played successive home draws against Manchester City (1–1) and Newcastle United (1–1), while a 3–2 reverse at West Bromwich Albion saw a rare defeat. However, home and away victories against Everton (2–1 and 1–0) saw Wolves maintain their top three position.

Wolves' hopes of the League title all but faded on the final day of March, with a 1–0 home defeat against Liverpool, which preceded a further defeat at Blackburn Rovers (2–1), before a 3–0 home success against Burnley secured two welcome points; however, successive home defeats against Aston Villa (1–0) and Sheffield United (2–1) continued their indifferent League form.

Late April saw the Molineux team secure a 3–0 victory against Derby County in their final home game of the season, while the campaign ended with a 2–0 reverse at Preston North End. The Wanderers finished in fourth position, with fifteen wins, nine draws and ten defeats in their thirty-four League games, while scoring forty-eight goals and conceding thirty-seven.

Fleming and Pheasant had appeared in all thirty-four League games, while Blackett, Worton and Tom Baddeley had missed only one in an excellent League campaign. George Bowen had scored six League goals, Billy Beats had found the net on nine occasions, while Harper had led the scoring with eleven goals in twenty-six League appearances.

SUNDERLAND

Sunderland's record in the Football League had been second only to Aston Villa during the 1890s, so their seventh place League finish at the close of the 1898–99 season had been a little disappointing by their own high standards. However, the club kept faith with the majority of their players for the 1899–1900 League campaign. John Doig continued in goal, with McNeil, McAllister, Raisbeck, McCombie and Mathew Ferguson in defence, while Fulton, Crawford, McLatchie, Farquhar and Jim Leslie remained in the attack.

England defender Philip Bach had signed for Middlesbrough, with Jackson moving in the opposite direction. Further departures included Morgan to Bolton Wanderers; Brown had journeyed south to Portsmouth; Billy Dunlop had decided to join Liverpool; while Hugh Wilson had signed for Bedminster, following nine seasons with the club, in which he had scored forty goals in 232 League appearances.

Newcomers in the Sunderland attack included Becton from New Brighton Tower, Robert Hogg, who would score eighteen goals in sixty-five League games, from Selbourne Rovers, and his namesake Billy Hogg, who had played his previous football with Willington. He scored eighty-three goals in 281 League appearances for the north-eastern side, as well as appearing in the English national team.

Scottish international defender Jim Watson, who arrived from Clyde at the turn of the year, proved to be one of Sunderland's finest signings. He appeared in well over 200 League games in eight seasons with the club.

Sunderland opened the season with a 1–0 home defeat against Aston Villa, which preceded a run of victories at Liverpool (2–0) and Preston North End (1–0), as well as at home to Burnley (2–1) and Nottingham Forest (1–0), with Becton, Raisbeck, Farquhar and McLatchie sharing the Sunderland goals, while Becton netted a brace of goals in a two-all draw at Sheffield United.

Then followed further victories at Glossop (2–0) and at home to Stoke (3–0), with Becton on target in both games. A 1–0 reverse at West Bromwich Albion saw a rare defeat, but successive wins at Blackburn Rovers (2–1) and at home to Everton (1–0) saw the north-eastern side near the top of the League table by the middle of November, with Becton, McLatchie and Robert Hogg netting the Sunderland goals.

Late November saw a 2–0 defeat at Bury, which preceded a 5–0 home success against Notts County, with Raisbeck, Crawford, McLatchie and both Hoggs finding the net. A 2–1 reverse at Manchester City continued their indifferent away form. However, following a one-all home draw with Sheffield United, the Sunderland team returned to winning ways with a 4–2 success at Newcastle United where Robert Hogg netted a hat-trick.

Sunderland then suffered a loss of form during the final week of the year with successive away defeats at Wolverhampton Wanderers (1–0) and Aston Villa (4–2), while the new year began with a 2–1 defeat in the return game with Wolverhampton Wanderers. A 1–0 home win against Liverpool saw two welcome points with Raisbeck scoring the only goal of the game.

Following a 3–1 reverse at Burnley, inside forward Fulton netted his opening goal of the season in a 1–0 home victory against Preston North End. Fulton was again on target in a two-all draw at Derby County in the first round of the FA Cup, with the north-eastern side winning the replay by three goals to nil, with Robert and Billy Hogg sharing the goals. However, a 3–0 defeat at Nottingham Forest in the second round ended their interest in the competition.

On their return to League action, the north-eastern side were held to a goalless home draw by the struggling Glossop team, which was followed by a 3–1 home win against West Bromwich Albion, with McLatchie (2) and Ferguson on target, while a 1–0 reverse at Everton saw them struggling to maintain their top three position.

Outside left McLatchie then netted his tenth League goal of the campaign in a 2–0 home win against Derby County, with Robert Hogg completing the scoring, while the result was reversed three days later in the return game at

Derby. However, victories at Stoke (2–1) and at home to Bury (1–0) saw a return to form for Sunderland, with Jim Leslie and Billy Hogg again on target.

Early April saw the north-eastern side suffer a 3–1 defeat at Notts County, which preceded home wins against Manchester City (3–1) and Blackburn Rovers (1–0), as well as a 3–1 success at Nottingham Forest, with Farquhar, Leslie, Robert Hogg and Billy Hogg sharing the Sunderland goals. The campaign ended with a 2–1 home defeat against Newcastle United as the Wearsiders settled for a third place League finish, with nineteen victories, three draws and twelve defeats in their thirty-four League games, while scoring fifty goals and conceding thirty-five.

McAllister, McCombie and John Doig had appeared in all thirty-four League games in an excellent League campaign. James Farquhar and Billy Hogg had netted six goals apiece; Becton had scored seven League goals; Robert Hogg had found the net on eight occasions; while McLatchie had led the scoring with ten, as Sunderland ended a most successful decade.

SHEFFIELD UNITED

Having recently won both the League Championship and FA Cup, Sheffield United had joined Preston North End and Aston Villa as one of only three teams to have won both trophies, which left their hopes for further success high as the century reached its close.

United made few changes from their FA Cup-winning side for the 1899–1900 League campaign. Willie Foulke continued in goal, with Harry Thickett, Peter Boyle, Harry Johnson, Tom Morren and Ernest Needham in defence, while Billy Beer, John Almond, Charlie Field, Walter Bennett, George Hedley and Fred Priest contested the forward positions, which were further strengthened towards the end of the season with the arrival of Bert Lipsham, a future England international winger from Crewe.

United opened the campaign with a 2–1 victory at Everton, with Billy Beer and John Almond on target, which preceded a 3–0 home success against Blackburn Rovers, with George Hedley (2) and Fred Priest finding the net, while Almond scored the only goal of the game in a 1–0 win at Derby County.

Then followed a further home win against Bury (4–0), with Hedley (2), Bennett and Almond netting for the Sheffield side, while goals from Johnson and Priest secured a 2–1 success at Notts County. However, a two-all home draw with Sunderland saw United drop their first point of the season, with Beer and Bennett again on target.

Walter Bennett then netted a hat-trick in a 3–0 home win against Manchester City, while Billy Beer scored a hat-trick the following week in a 5–2 home success against Wolverhampton Wanderers, with Field and Boyle completing the scoring; however, a goalless draw at Newcastle United saw the Yorkshire side drop a further point.

United soon returned to winning ways with victories at home to Aston Villa (2–1) and away at West Bromwich Albion (2–1) on either side of a two-all draw at Liverpool, with George Hedley on target in all three games. A goalless home draw with Burnley saw a poor performance by the United attack, but successive victories at Preston North End (1–0) and at home to Nottingham Forest (3–0) saw the FA Cup holders maintain their unbeaten record, with Almond, Beer and Bennett sharing the United goals.

Beer and Bennett again found the net in a two-all draw at Glossop, while George Hedley scored the only goal of the game in a 1–0 home success against Stoke, which saw the Sheffield side at the head of the League table at the halfway stage of the campaign, with twenty-nine points from seventeen games.

Following drawn games at Sunderland (1–1) and at home to West Bromwich Albion (1–1), Hedley and Bennett were on target in a 2–1 victory at Manchester City, while the year ended with a 5–0 home win against Everton, with Barnes scoring a brace of goals on his League debut, together with further goals by Hedley (2) and Priest.

New Year began with an abandoned draw at Blackburn Rovers (0–0), which preceded a one-all home draw against Derby County, with Fred Priest on target. A 2–1 reverse at Bury saw United suffer their first League defeat of the season. However, a 1–0 home win against Leicester Fosse in the first round of the FA Cup saw a return to form, with Walter Bennett netting the only goal of the game to secure a second round tie against the Wednesday.

Prior to the FA Cup game, Tom Morren scored a rare goal in a one-all home draw with Notts County, while the cup tie ended in a one-all draw following two abandoned games. The replay proved a game full of incidents, with Lee of the Wednesday breaking his leg following a collision with Harry Thickett, which preceded a penalty goal by Ernest Needham to secure a one-goal lead for United.

Wednesday's hopes of an equalising goal faded when Langley and Pryce were dismissed for foul play. Billy Beer netted a second goal for the FA Cup holders to secure a home tie against Bury in the quarter-finals, which resulted in a two-all draw, with Needham again scoring from the penalty spot. However, a 2–0 reverse in the replay ended their interest in the competition.

On their return to League action, Walter Bennett found the net in a one-all draw at Aston Villa, where Billy Brawn and Bert Lipsham made their United debuts, while a 2–1 defeat at Liverpool continued their indifferent away form. However, successive home wins against Preston North End (1–0) and Newcastle United (3–1) saw the Sheffield side maintain their challenge for the League title, with Hedley, Almond, Brawn and Barnes sharing the United goals.

United then suffered a 4–0 defeat at Nottingham Forest, which was followed by a 4–0 home success against Glossop, with Brawn (2), Barnes and Bennett on target, while successive away draws at Blackburn Rovers (3–3) and Stoke (1–1) saw Bennett, Priest Morren and Hedley amongst the scorers as the season reached its final stages. The Yorkshire side needed two high-scoring victories to regain the League championship, but following a 2–1 victory at Wolverhampton Wanderers, where Beer and Hedley found the net, United suffered a 1–0 reverse at Burnley, to end the campaign as runners-up to Aston Villa by a two-point margin, with eighteen wins, twelve draws and four defeats in their thirty-four League games, while scoring sixty-three goals and conceding thirty-three.

Fred Priest and John Almond had ended the season with six League goals apiece; Billy Beer had scored ten League goals; Walter Bennett had found the net on eleven occasions; while George Hedley had led the scoring with fifteen goals in a further successful season for the Yorkshire team.

ASTON VILLA

Aston Villa had won four League Championships during the previous six seasons, which resulted in few changes in their line-up for the 1899–1900 League campaign. Billy George continued in goal, with Howard Spencer, Albert Evans, Tom Bowman, James Cowan and James Crabtree in defence, while Charlie Athersmith, John Devey, Billy Garraty, Fred Wheldon and Steve Smith remained in the attack, where George Johnson made the occasional appearance at centre forward.

John Cowan had returned to Scotland, while Jack Sharp had signed for Everton, which allowed Albert Wilkes and Robert Templeton the opportunity of regular appearances in the first team. Villa opened the campaign with a 1–0 victory at Sunderland, where Billy Garraty scored the only goal of the game, which preceded a 9–0 home win against Glossop, with Garraty (4), Wheldon (2), Smith, Devey and Athersmith on target. A 2–0 home defeat against West Bromwich Albion ended their fine start to the season, but successive victories at Everton (2–1) and at home to Blackburn Rovers (3–1) saw a return to form for the reigning League champions, with Wheldon, Garraty and Devey sharing the Villa goals.

Then followed a 2–0 reverse at Derby County, while George Johnson found the net in victories at Notts County (4–1) and at home to Bury (2–1). However, Villa's joy was spoiled by the announcement of the death of Albert Allen, who had scored a hat-trick in his only England appearance a dozen years earlier.

Fred Wheldon then netted his sixth League goal of the campaign and John Devey his fifth, in a 2–1 home win against Manchester City, which preceded a 2–1 defeat at Sheffield United. Both players were on target the following week in a 2–1 home success against Newcastle United as Villa maintained their top three position.

Mid-November saw drawn games at home to Wolverhampton Wanderers (0–0) and away at Liverpool (3–3) on either side of a 2–0 victory at Stoke, where Devey and Garfield found the net. Robert Templeton netted his opening goal of the season in a 2–0 home success against Burnley, with Fred Wheldon completing the scoring.

A rare Steve Smith hat-trick then helped Villa secure a 5–0 success at Preston North End, which preceded a two-all home draw with Nottingham Forest, with Garraty and Devey on target, while a 1–0 reverse at Glossop saw a surprising away defeat. However, the year ended on a high note with successive home wins against Stoke (4–1) and Sunderland (4–2), with Billy Garraty scoring in both games, including a hat-trick against the north-eastern side.

New Year's Day saw Villa suffer a 2–0 defeat at Bury, followed by a 2–0 victory at West Bromwich Albion, where Garraty netted a brace of goals. Charlie Athersmith found the net in a one-all home draw with Everton, as well as a 4–0 success at Blackburn Rovers, with Garraty once again scoring a brace to move the Midlands side into second position in the League table.

Villa were then drawn away at Manchester City in the opening round of the FA Cup, where a John Devey goal earned a one-all draw with the Midlanders winning the replay by three goals to nil. Garraty (2) and Wheldon were on target to secure a second round tie at Bristol City, while their excellent League form continued with a 3–2 home win against Derby County, with Garraty (2) and Wheldon netting the Villa goals.

John Devey then netted four goals in a 5–1 victory in the FA Cup tie at Bristol to secure a quarter-final tie at Millwall Athletic, while Garraty scored a further hat-trick in a 6–2 home win against Notts County. However, the cup game with Millwall proved a little more difficult when, following successive draws (1–1 and 0–0), Villa suffered a 2–1 reverse in the second replay to end their hopes of the FA Cup and League 'double'.

Prior to the FA Cup defeat, Billy Garraty had found the net in a one-all home draw with Sheffield United, which preceded a 3–2 reverse at Newcastle United while Garraty scored a brace of goals in a 2–0 victory at Manchester City as Villa sought to retain the League championship.

Late March saw John Devey score his twelfth League goal of the campaign in a 1–0 home success against Liverpool, which was followed by a 2–1 victory at Burnley, with Devey once again on target. Garraty (2) and Robert Templeton found the net in a 3–1 home win against Preston North End, but the following week saw Villa draw one-all at Nottingham Forest with fellow title contenders Sheffield United securing a similar result at Stoke, which meant that Villa had to win their final game of the season at Wolverhampton Wanderers to retain the League championship.

Villa managed a single-goal victory at the Molineux, with Robert Templeton scoring for the third game running to ensure Villa their fifth League title in seven seasons, with Steve Smith, Charlie Athersmith and John Devey winning their fifth League championship medals. The Midlanders secured twenty-two victories, six draws and six defeats in their thirty-four League games, while scoring seventy-seven goals and conceding thirty-five.

Fred Wheldon and Billy George had appeared in all thirty-four League games, while Billy Garraty had missed only one in an excellent season. George Johnson had scored five goals in nine League appearances; Steve Smith had netted seven goals; Fred Wheldon had found the net on eleven occasions; John Devey had scored thirteen League goals; while Billy Garraty had led the scoring with twenty-seven goals in the League.

Wednesday and Bolton Return to the First Division

Half a dozen teams were involved in the race for promotion to the First Division during the final year of the century, including Small Heath and Newton Heath who had previously tasted life in the top division, as well as Bolton Wanderers and the Wednesday who were both relegated at the close of the previous campaign.

GRIMSBY TOWN

Grimsby Town had once again performed magnificently in their pursuit of a promotion place. There were excellent home wins against Burton Swifts (6–0), Leicester Fosse (6–1) and Barnsley (8–1), and they finished in sixth position. However, their disappointment was short-lived as promotion was secured in the opening season of the new century.

LEICESTER FOSSE

Leicester Fosse had finished the 1898–99 League campaign in third place, only one point away from promotion. Despite losing just one game at home during the 1899–1900 season, which included five-goal victories against Gainsborough and Loughborough, the Leicester side had to settle for a fifth place League finish.

NEWTON HEATH

Newton Heath mounted a serious challenge for promotion during the 1899–1900 season, in a bid to regain the First Division League status that had been relinquished in 1894. Frank Barrett continued in goal, with Stafford, Erentz, Morgan, Griffiths and Walter Cartwright in defence, while Bryant, Gillespie and James Cassidy remained in the attack, where Smith, Jackson and Parkinson were the most notable newcomers.

An excellent home record that consisted of fifteen victories and a single defeat had seen the Newton Heath side amongst the front runners for promotion for much of the season. However, their indifferent away form cost them dearly as they ended the campaign in fourth position, with James Cassidy once again leading the scoring with sixteen goals in twenty-nine League appearances.

SMALL HEATH

Small Heath had suffered the indignity of relegation to the Second Division at the close of the 1895–96 League campaign, but they had regularly been amongst the front runners in their efforts to regain their place in the First Division.

Walter Abbott, who had scored thirty-four League goals during the previous campaign, decided to sign for Everton prior to the 1899–1900 season. However, the Small Heath side had managed to retain the services of Alec Leake at the heart of the defence, while Bob McRoberts continued to lead the attack.

Small Heath suffered one defeat on home soil during the season and obtained excellent victories against Barnsley (5–0), Chesterfield (5–3), Lincoln City (5–0), Middlesbrough (5–1), Loughborough (6–0) and Gainsborough (8–1), but like Newton Heath, their away form had been inconsistent, which resulted in a third place League finish, with Bob McRoberts leading the scoring with nineteen League goals.

BOLTON WANDERERS

Bolton Wanderers were determined to return to the First Division at the first attempt, which surprisingly led to few changes in their line-up for the 1899–1900 League campaign. John Sutcliffe continued in goal, with John Somerville, Bob Brown and Archie Freebairn in defence, while Morgan, Gilligan, Barlow and Bob Jack retained their places in the attack. Alex Paton had left the club following a wage dispute, while the most notable new signing was Lawrence Bell, a free-scoring centre forward from Everton.

Bolton performed magnificently throughout the season, which saw only four defeats in thirty-four League games and included excellent victories at Burton (5–2) and Barnsley (6–1), as well as at home to Burton (5–0), Loughborough (7–0) and Burslem Port Vale (5–0). However, the Lancashire side could do little more than finish as runners-up to the Wednesday, who had won all seventeen of their home games. Lawrence Bell had been a revelation up front where he had scored twenty-three goals in thirty-two League appearances to help the Wanderers make a swift return to the First Division.

WEDNESDAY

Wednesday had ended the 1898–99 League campaign in last place in the First Division, much to the surprise of their supporters, who had celebrated an FA Cup Final success only three years earlier. However, the Sheffield side relied upon the majority of their relegated team for the 1899–1900 season. Jimmy Massey continued in goal, with Willie Layton, Ambrose Langley, Bob Ferrier, Tom Crawshaw and Herrod Ruddlesdin in defence, while Archie Brash returned at outside right, with John Wright and Fred Spiksley once again forming the left wing partnership.

Harry Davis had left the club, Jack Earp soon moved to Stockport County following 155 League appearances for the Wednesday, while newcomers up front included Pryce from Glossop and Millar from Bury, who both signed for Queens Park Rangers within eighteen months. The most notable new signing was a second Harry Davis from Barnsley, who made in excess of 200 League appearances for the club, as well as scoring on his international debut for the English national team.

Wednesday opened the season with eleven victories and three draws in fourteen League games, with Millar (seven), Spiksley (ten) and Wright (ten) in fine goal-scoring form. Their first defeat of the campaign arrived on the final day of the year with a 1–0 reverse at Chesterfield. However, the Sheffield side won all seventeen of their home games, of which nine were by four goals or more to secure the Second Division championship by a margin of two points from Bolton Wanderers.

Herrod Ruddlesdin and Tom Crawshaw had appeared in all thirty-four League games, while Willie Layton and John Wright had missed only one. Harry Davis had scored seven goals in fourteen League appearances; Fred Spiksley had netted ten goals in twenty-one games; Millar had found the net on fourteen occasions; and John Wright led the scoring with twenty-six League goals, as the Sheffield side returned to the First Division, where they would enjoy great success during the early years of the new century.

Loughborough and Luton Are Relegated Out of the League

Loughborough had struggled throughout the 1899–1900 League campaign, which had resulted in twenty-seven of their thirty-four League games ending in defeat, including embarrassing away defeats at Small Heath (6–0), Bolton Wanderers (7–0), Barnsley (7–0) and Woolwich Arsenal (12–0). A 2–1 home win against Burton saw their only victory of the season and they finished the campaign in eighteenth position with eight points.

Luton Town had performed reasonably well on home soil during the final season of the century with excellent victories against Burton (5–2), Gainsborough (4–0), Loughborough (4–0) and Walsall (4–0), but their inability to win on their travels had resulted in a seventeenth place League finish, following only five wins in thirty-four League games. As a result of their League placings, Loughborough and Luton were relegated from the Football League to be replaced by Blackpool and Stockport for the opening season of the new century.

The final League placings at the close of the 1899–1900 season were as in Tables XXX and XXXI.

Table XXX: *First Division Football League results for the 1899–1900 season*

	P	W	D	L	F	A	PTS
1. Aston Villa	34	22	6	6	77	35	50
2. Sheffield United	34	18	12	4	63	33	48
3. Sunderland	34	19	3	12	50	35	41
4. Wolverhampton Wndrs	34	15	9	10	48	37	39
5. Newcastle United	34	13	10	11	53	43	36
6. Derby County	34	14	8	12	45	43	36
7. Manchester City	34	13	8	13	50	44	34
8. Nottingham Forest	34	13	8	13	56	55	34
9. Stoke	34	10	10	14	37	45	34
10. Liverpool	34	14	5	15	49	45	33
11. Everton	34	13	7	14	47	49	33
12. Bury	34	13	6	15	40	44	32
13. West Bromwich Albion	34	11	8	15	43	51	30
14. Blackburn Rovers	34	13	4	17	49	61	30
15. Notts County	34	9	11	14	46	60	29
16. Preston North End	34	12	4	18	38	48	28
17. Burnley	34	11	5	18	34	54	27
18. Glossop North End	34	4	10	20	31	74	18

Table XXXI: *Second Division Football League results for the 1899–1900 season*

	P	W	D	L	F	A	PTS
1. Wednesday	34	25	4	5	84	22	54
2. Bolton Wanderers	34	22	8	4	79	25	52
3. Small Heath	34	20	6	8	78	38	46
4. Newton Heath	34	20	4	10	63	27	44
5. Leicester Fosse	34	17	9	8	53	36	43
6. Grimsby Town	34	17	6	11	67	46	40
7. Chesterfield	34	16	6	12	65	60	38
8. Woolwich Arsenal	34	16	4	14	61	43	36
9. Lincoln City	34	14	8	12	46	43	36
10. New Brighton	34	13	9	12	66	58	35
11. Burslem Port Vale	34	14	6	14	39	49	34
12. Walsall	34	12	8	14	50	55	32
13. Gainsborough	34	9	7	18	47	75	25
14. Middlesbrough	34	8	8	18	39	69	24
15. Burton Swifts	34	9	6	19	43	84	24
16. Barnsley	34	8	7	19	46	79	23
17. Luton Town	34	5	8	21	40	75	18
18. Loughborough	34	1	6	27	18	100	8

Two Unlikely FA Cup Finalists

The 1899–1900 FA Cup competition had seen a number of teams from the south of England reach the final sixteen, thus reaffirming the belief that teams in the Southern League were as capable as those in the Football League.

Bristol City, Queens Park Rangers, Southampton and Millwall Athletic were all involved in second round games as they sought a quarter-final place. However, two of the southern teams were drawn against each other, as Millwall defeated Queens Park Rangers by two goals to nil. Bristol City suffered a 5–1 defeat against Aston Villa, with John Devey netting four goals for the Midlanders, while Southampton secured a 4–1 home success against Newcastle United, which had been hardly a surprise as the Hampshire side had fielded England custodian John Robinson in goal, together with former internationals Harry Wood and Alf Milward in the attack, and Arthur Chadwick and Arthur Turner both appeared in the England side during the season.

Bury progressed to the quarter-finals with a 2–0 victory against Notts County, following a goalless draw; Preston North End secured a 1–0 home win against Blackburn Rovers in a closely fought tie; while Beveridge (2) and Grenville Morris were on target for Nottingham Forest in a 3–0 home success against Sunderland.

West Bromwich Albion defeated Liverpool by the odd goal in three following a one-all draw, while in a much postponed FA Cup tie the two Sheffield sides met in a bruising encounter, which ended in a one-all draw, with goals by Archie Brash (Wednesday) and John Almond (United) cancelling each other out. However, United won the replay by two goals to nil, with Billy Beer and Ernest Needham (penalty) on target. Wednesday had eventually finished the game with eight men, owing to Lee suffering a broken leg, while Pryce and Langley were dismissed from the field of play for ungentlemanly conduct.

Southampton's success continued in the quarter-finals with a 2–1 home win against West Bromwich Albion; Bury defeated Sheffield United by two goals to nil following a two-all draw; while Arthur Capes scored the only goal of the game as Nottingham Forest defeated Preston North End in a replayed tie.

The Villa–Millwall tie proved a close affair, which produced drawn games in London (1–1) and Birmingham (0–0). However, the southern team managed a 2–1 victory in the second replay at Elm Park, Reading, with Gettins scoring the all-important winning goal for Millwall.

Millwall were then drawn against Southampton in the semi-finals, with the game ending goalless, while Nottingham Forest and Bury shared the spoils in a one-all draw at the Victoria Ground, Stoke, with Arthur Capes netting the Forest goal. Southampton had few problems in their replay, with a 3–0 victory against Millwall, while Bury managed a 3–2 win against Forest at Bramall

Lane, which meant that a new name would appear on the FA Cup in the final season of the century.

England's Unconvincing Victory in Dublin

Following six successive victories, including a 13–2 win, against the luckless Irish, the England team were confident of continuing their winning run during the final season of the century, which began with a visit to Dublin on 17 March to fulfil the annual fixture against the Irish national team.

England fielded an experienced defensive line-up, which saw John Robinson, now of Southampton, in goal, with William Oakley (Corinthians) and James Crabtree (Aston Villa) at fullback, while John Holt, who had recently moved from Everton to Reading, gained his tenth and final England cap at the heart of the defence.

Ernest Needham (Sheffield United) retained his usual position at left half back, with his Sheffield team-mate Harry Johnson making the first of six England appearances at right half back. G O Smith (Corinthians) was the only forward selected with previous international experience. Fred Priest (Sheffield United) and Daniel Cunliffe (Portsmouth) made their only England appearances in the attack, together with Arthur Turner (Southampton) and Charlie Sagar (Bury), who both played for England on a couple of occasions.

England managed a 2–0 victory against the Irish, with Harry Johnson and Charlie Sagar on target. However, it had been a far more difficult game than the visitors had expected.

An Honourable Draw for the Welsh

A little more than a week after the victory in Dublin, the England team travelled to Cardiff to compete against the Welsh national team with the visitors retaining Robinson, Oakley, Johnson, Crabtree and G O Smith from the Irish game, and there were recalls for Howard Spencer and Charlie Athersmith of Aston Villa. Arthur Chadwick (Southampton) made the first of two England appearances at centre half, Alfred Spouncer (Nottingham Forest) played his one England game at outside left, while George Plumpton Wilson (Corinthians) and Reginald Erskine Foster (Corinthians) completed the English line-up. Wilson was the younger brother of Charles Plumpton Wilson, who had made a couple of England appearances sixteen years earlier, while R E Foster, who had gained Blues in cricket, rackets and golf at Oxford University, represented England on five occasions at the Association game. However, he achieved greater fame as an English Test cricketer.

While the visitors were expected to win with ease, the Welsh fought magnificently to hold the English to a one-all draw, with Wilson scoring a debut goal for England.

A Deserved Scottish Victory

England made three changes from the draw in Cardiff for the visit to Glasgow to play the Scottish national team, as Ernest Needham (Sheffield United) and Steve Bloomer (Derby County) replaced Howard Spencer and R F Foster, while John Plant (Bury) gained his only England cap at outside left at the expense of Alfred Spouncer.

Scotland were determined to succeed against the visitors, following successive defeats in Birmingham and Glasgow, while the English had remained unbeaten in their previous eight internationals. The Scottish supporters were not to be disappointed as the English were sent home with a 4–1 defeat, with Steve Bloomer scoring a consolation goal for the visitors.

Stubborn Resistance from the Irish League

The opening inter-League fixture of the season saw an Irish League Eleven visit Bolton, with the English fielding a side mixed with experienced international players, as well as newcomers. They included Birchenough (Burslem Port Vale) in goal, Fitchett (Bolton Wanderers) and Leeming (Bury) at half back, while Johnson (Stoke) and Hurst (Blackburn Rovers) played on the wings.

Howard Spencer (Aston Villa), Billy Williams (West Bromwich Albion) and Ernest Needham (Sheffield United) completed the defensive line-up, while Steve Bloomer (Derby County), Billy Beats (Wolverhampton Wanderers) and Jimmy Settle (Everton) were included in the attack.

While the Irish offered stubborn resistance, they were eventually worn down by the English attack, as Steve Bloomer (2) and Jimmy Settle found the net in a 3–1 success for the home side.

A Draw for the Scottish League

On the final day of March, the Football League Eleven entertained a Scottish League Eleven at Crystal Palace, hoping to emulate the 4–1 success of the previous season. Willie Foulke (Sheffield United) earned a recall between the posts, with Howard Spencer (Aston Villa) and James Crabtree (Aston Villa) at fullback, while Griffiths (Wolverhampton Wanderers), Wigmore (Small Heath) and Norris (Nottingham Forest) formed an inexperienced half-back line. However, an attack consisting of Athersmith (Aston Villa), Bloomer (Derby County), Hedley (Sheffield United), Settle (Everton) and Miller (Wolverhampton Wanderers) more than made up for their lack of defensive experience.

The Scots matched the home side in all positions to return home with a well-deserved two-all draw, with Bloomer and Hedley on target for the fortunate Englishmen.

Bury Dominate the 1900 FA Cup Final

The 1900 FA Cup Final took place at Crystal Palace between Southampton, who were the first team south of the Midlands to appear in an FA Cup Final since the Old Etonians in 1883, and Bury, the unfashionable team from Lancashire.

A near 70,000 crowd gathered to watch the final on an unusually sunny April afternoon, with both teams at full strength. Bury selected the following eleven:

Thompson

Darroch   Davidson

Pray   Leeming   Ross

Richards   Wood   McLuckie   Sagar   Plant

Southampton, who included five England players in their line-up, selected the following team:

Robinson

Meehan   Durber

Meston   Chadwick   Petrie

Turner   Yates   Farrell   Wood   Milward

Mr Kingscott of Derby was appointed as match referee.

Upon winning the toss, Bury decided to kick with the sun on their backs, which resulted in serious problems for the Southampton defence as the Lancashire side directed a number of high crosses into their goal area to exert pressure on goalkeeper John Robinson.

Inevitably, the opening goal arrived following ten minutes of play when centre forward McLuckie converted a cross from Plant, while a second goal was scored within minutes when Wood slotted home a loose clearance, much to the joy of the Bury supporters.

John Robinson then made a couple of excellent saves to keep Southampton in the game, but he was unable to prevent McLuckie scoring a third goal for the Lancashire side following a fine pass from Wood, and Bury ended the first half three goals to the good.

Southampton came more into the game during the early stages of the second half, with Alf Milward and Harry Wood making several attempts on the Bury goal. However, while the Hampshire side made every attempt to reduce the arrears, it was obvious to all that the game was beyond them.

As the game entered its final quarter, John Robinson made a further excellent save from Pray, which resulted in a corner, quickly taken by Richards to the waiting Jack Plant, who shot low and hard past the overworked Robinson to secure a 4–0 victory for Bury.

It had certainly been an important toss to lose for Southampton, who may well have blamed the sun in their faces for their downfall. However, their play had generally been poor, which had resulted in Bury teaching them a footballing lesson.

Bury Return to League Action

Within a week of their FA Cup Final success, Bury had secured a 2–0 home win against Blackburn Rovers, as well as suffering a 3–0 reverse at Derby County, to finish the season in twelfth position, with thirteen victories, six draws and fifteen defeats in their thirty-four League games, while scoring forty goals and conceding forty-four. However, they had been more than pleased with their FA Cup Final victory, a feat that would be repeated during the early years of the new century.

Bishop Auckland Regain the FA Amateur Cup

Following their victory in the 1896 FA Amateur Cup final, Bishop Auckland regained the trophy for the 1900 season with a 5–1 success against Lowestoft Town at Leicester.

The Rise of the Southern Professional

During the final years of the Victorian period, it had become apparent that the FA Amateur Cup had been dominated by teams from the north-east of England rather than the amateur clubs in the south, while skilful amateur players of the likes of William Oakley, G O Smith, G P Wilson and R E Foster had earned selection to the England team for the 1900 international games. While the southern amateur clubs were no longer a force in the game, or even desired to be so, the Corinthians continued to be a match for the majority of the professional teams for many years to come, albeit as a representative team rather than a club side.

As the domination of the amateur game had moved northwards, the professional teams in the south of England were now achieving excellent results against Football League teams in the north and Midlands as the 1899–1900 season's FA Cup results had confirmed. The success of southern teams would continue into the new century, with a London club winning the FA Cup within twelve months.

Appendix A

ENGLAND'S LEADING GOAL SCORERS IN INTERNATIONAL GAMES FROM 1872 TO 1900

Goals scored	Name and Club
20	Steve Bloomer (Derby County)[*]
15	Tinsley Lindley (Corinthians)
12	Charles (E C) Bambridge (Corinthians)
12	John Goodall (Preston North End and Derby County)
12	Gilbert O Smith (Corinthians)
11	Fred Dewhurst (Preston North End)
7	William (W N) Cobbold (Corinthians)
7	Billy Bassett (West Bromwich Albion)
6	Howard Vaughton (Aston Villa)
6	Fred Wheldon (Aston Villa)
5	Fred Spiksley (Wednesday)
5	Clement Mitchell (Upton Park and Corinthians)
5	Harry Cursham (Notts County)
5	Benjamin Spilsbury (Corinthians)
4	Arthur Brown (Aston Villa)
4	Jimmy Settle (Everton and Bury)[*]
3	Charlie Athersmith (Aston Villa)
3	Fred Forman (Nottingham Forest)
3	John Yates (Burnley)
3	Alf Milward (Everton)
3	Edgar Chadwick (Everton)

Goals scored	Name and Club
3	John Southworth (Blackburn Rovers)
3	Fred Geary (Everton)
3	Albert Allen (Aston Villa)
3	William Mosforth (Wednesday)
3	Harry Daft (Notts County)
3	Joseph Lofthouse (Blackburn Rovers)
3	John Veitch (Corinthians)
3	John Reynolds (West Bromwich Albion and Aston Villa)
3	Jimmy Brown (Blackburn Rovers)
3	Francis Sparkes (Clapham Rovers)
3	Walter Gilliatt (Old Carthusians)

* Steve Bloomer and Jimmy Settle scored further goals for England during the years of the following century.

Appendix B

FOOTBALL LEAGUE CHAMPIONS – 1888–89 TO 1899–1900

Season	Champions	Runners-up
1888–89	Preston North End	Aston Villa
1889–90	Preston North End	Everton
1890–91	Everton	Preston North End
1891–92	Sunderland	Preston North End
1892–93	Sunderland	Preston North End
1893–94	Aston Villa	Sunderland
1894–95	Sunderland	Everton
1895–96	Aston Villa	Derby County
1896–97	Aston Villa	Sheffield United
1897–98	Sheffield United	Sunderland
1898–99	Aston Villa	Liverpool
1899–1900	Aston Villa	Sheffield United

Appendix C

FA CUP WINNERS – 1872 TO 1900

Year	Winners	Goals	Runners-up	Goals
1872	Wanderers (Betts)	1	Royal Engineers	0
1873	Wanderers (Kinnaird, Wollaston)	2	Oxford University	0
1874	Oxford University (Mackarness, Patton)	2	Royal Engineers	0
1875	Royal Engineers (Renny-Tailyour, Stafford)	2	Old Etonians *Following a one-all draw*	0
1876	Wanderers (Hughes [2], Wollaston)	3	Old Etonians *Following a one-all draw*	0
1877	Wanderers (Lindsay, Kenrick)	2	Oxford University (Kinnaird own goal) *After extra time*	1
1878	Wanderers (Kenrick [2], Kinnaird)	3	Royal Engineers (Morris)	1
1879	Old Etonians (Clerke)	1	Clapham Rovers	0
1880	Clapham Rovers (Lloyd-Jones)	1	Oxford University	0
1881	Old Carthusians (Richards, Parry, Todd)	3	Old Etonians	0
1882	Old Etonians (Macauley)	1	Blackburn Rovers	0
1883	Blackburn Olympic (Mathews, Crossley)	2	Old Etonians (Goodhart) *After extra time*	1
1884	Blackburn Rovers (Sowerbutts, Forrest)	2	Queens Park (Glasgow) (Christie)	1
1885	Blackburn Rovers (Brown, Forrest)	2	Queens Park (Glasgow)	0
1886	Blackburn Rovers (Brown, Sowerbutts)	2	West Bromwich Albion *Following a goalless draw*	0
1887	Aston Villa (Hunter, Hodgetts)	2	West Bromwich Albion	0

Year	Winners	Goals	Runners-up	Goals
1888	West Bromwich Albion (Woodhall, Bayliss)	2	Preston North End (Dewhurst)	1
1889	Preston North End (Dewhurst, Ross, Thomson)	3	Wolverhampton Wndrs	0
1890	Blackburn Rovers (Townley [3], Lofthouse, Walton, John Southworth)	6	Sheffield Wednesday (Bennett)	1
1891	Blackburn Rovers (Southworth, Dewar, Townley)	3	Notts County (Oswald)	1
1892	West Bromwich Albion (Nicholls, Geddes, Reynolds)	3	Aston Villa	0
1893	Wolverhampton Wndrs (Allen)	1	Everton	0
1894	Notts County (Logan [3], Watson)	4	Bolton Wanderers (Cassidy)	1
1895	Aston Villa (Devey)	1	West Bromwich Albion	0
1896	Sheffield Wednesday (Spiksley [2])	2	Wolverhampton Wndrs (Black)	1
1897	Aston Villa (Wheldon, Campbell, Crabtree)	3	Everton (Bell, Boyle)	2
1898	Nottingham Forest (Capes [2], MacPherson)	3	Derby County (Bloomer)	1
1899	Sheffield United (Bennett, Almond, Beer, Priest)	4	Derby County (Boag)	1
1900	Bury (McLuckie [2], Wood, Plant)	4	Southampton	0

Appendix D

FA AMATEUR CUP WINNERS – 1894 TO 1900

Year	Winners	Goals	Runners-up	Goals
1894	Old Carthusians	2	Casuals	1
1895	Middlesbrough	2	Old Carthusians	1
1896	Bishop Auckland	1	R A (Portsmouth)	0
1897	Old Carthusians	4	Stockton *Following a one-all draw*	1
1898	Middlesbrough	2	Uxbridge	1
1899	Stockton	1	Harwich and Parkeston	0
1900	Bishop Auckland	5	Lowestoft Town	1

Selected Bibliography

Attaway, Peter, *Nottingham Forest. A Complete Record*, UK, Breedon Books, 1991

Butler, Bryon, *The Official History of the Football Association*, UK, Queen Anne Press, 1991

Clarebrough, Denis, *The Official Centenary of Sheffield United Football Club*, UK, Tempus Publishing, 1998

Farnsworth, Keith, *Sheffield Wednesday. A Complete Record*, UK, Breedon Books, 1987

Gibson, A and Pickford, W, *Football and the Men Who Made It*, London, Caxton Publishing Company, 1906

Goble, Ray with Ward, Andrew, *Manchester City. A Complete Record*, UK, Breedon Books, 1987

Harrison, Jean, *Accrington Stanley – The Story of a Lancashire Football Club*, UK, Jean Harrison, 1972

Jackman, Mike, *Blackburn Rovers. A Complete Record*, UK, Breedon Books, 1990

Joannou, Paul, *Newcastle United. A Complete Record 1881–1990*, UK, Breedon Books, 1991

Keeton, George, *The Football Revolution*, Newton Abbott, David and Charles, 1972

Lamming, Doug and Farrer, Morley, *A Century of English International Football 1872–1972*, UK, Hale Publishing, 1981

Markland, Simon, *Bolton Wanderers. A Complete Record*, UK, Breedon Books, 1989

Martin, Wade, *A Potter's Tale – The Story of Stoke City Football Club*, UK, Sporting and Leisure Press, 1988

Mathews, Tony, *Birmingham City. A Complete Record*, UK, Breedon Books, 1989

Mathews, Tony and Goodyear, David, *Aston Villa. A Complete Record 1874–1992*, UK, Breedon Books, 1993

Mathews, Tony and Mackenzie, Colin, *West Bromwich Albion. A Complete Record*, UK, Breedon Books, 1987

Morrison, Ian and Shury, Alan, *Manchester United. A Complete Record*, UK, Breedon Books, 1992

Mortimer, Gerald, *Derby County. A Complete Record*, UK, Breedon Books, 1989

Rippon, Anton, *England – The Story of the National Soccer Team*, UK, Moorland Publishing, 1981

Ross, Ian and Smailes, Gordon, *Everton. A Complete Record*, UK, Breedon Books, 1993

Simmons, Bill and Graham, Bob, *The History of Sunderland A.F.C.*, UK, R Graham, 1986

Soar, Phil, *The Hamlyn A to Z of British Football Records*, London, Hamlyn Publishing, 1981

Soar, Phil and Tyler, Martin, *The Story of Football*, London, Hamlyn Publishing, 1986

Tyler, Martin, *Cup Final Extra*, London, Hamlyn, 1981

Warsop, Keith, *The Magpies*, UK, Sporting and Leisure Press, 1984

Wiseman, David, *Up the Clarets – The Story of Burnley F.C.*, UK, Hale and Co., 1973

Young, Percy M, *The History of British Football*, UK, Paul Publishing, 1968

Young, Percy M, *The Wolves*, London, Stanley and Paul, 1959

The Birmingham Daily Post

The Blackburn Standard

The Preston Herald

The Sportsman

The Times